A QUEST FOR THE HISTORICAL CHRIST

A QUEST
FOR THE
HISTORICAL CHRIST

Scientia Christi and the Modern Study of Jesus

ANTHONY GIAMBRONE, OP

The Catholic University of America Press
Washington, D.C.
2022

Copyright © 2022
The Catholic University of America Press

All rights reserved

Library of Congress Cataloging-in-Publication Data

NAMES:
Giambrone, Anthony, 1977- author.
TITLE:
A quest for the historical Christ: *Scientia Christi* and the modern study of Jesus
Anthony Giambrone, OP.
DESCRIPTION:
Washington, DC : The Catholic University of America Press, 2022.
Includes bibliographical references and index.
IDENTIFIERS:
LCCN 2021056120
ISBN 9780813234878 (paperback) | ISBN   9780813234885 (ebook)
SUBJECTS:
LCSH: Jesus Christ—Historicity—History of doctrines.
Catholic Church—Doctrines.
CLASSIFICATION:
LCC BT303.2 .G525 2022 | DDC 232.9/08--dc23/eng/20211130
LC record available at https://lccn.loc.gov/20

Book design by Burt&Burt
Interior set with Minion Pro and Roma

TO MATTHEW LEVERING

CONTENTS

Acknowledgments // ix
List of Abbreviations // xiii

Introduction // 1

PART I. HISTORICAL FOUNDATIONS

1. *Vera et Sincera de Iesu* // 19
2. The German Roots of Historical Jesus Research // 51
3. The "Lying Historians" and Luke 1–2 // 72
4. Memorializing Miracles in the World of the Gospels // 92
5. Eyewitness Historiography and the Resurrection // 107

PART II. THEOLOGICAL PERSPECTIVES

6. Spirit and Power // 141
7. The Revenge of Alexandrian Exegesis: Toward an Ecclesial Hermeneutic // 160
8. *Interpretatio Iudaica* // 187
9. Primitive Christology as Ancient Philosophy // 210
10. Two Loci of Greco-Roman Jewish Monotheism // 245

PART III. JESUS AND THE SCRIPTURES

11 *Scientia Christi:* Three Theses // **265**

12 Another Johannine Thunderbolt? The *Legatio Baptistae* and "The Poetic Christ" // **286**

13 "Why Do the Scribes Say?" Scribal Expectations of an Eschatological High Priest and the Interpretation of Jesus' Transfiguration // **301**

14 Prosopological Exegesis and Christological *Anagnorisis* // **335**

15 Jesus' Prophetic Knowledge and the Gospels // **357**

Appendix I: Anti-Hegelian Postlude on the Religion of the Future // **379**

Appendix II: Review of Paula Fredriksen, When Christians Were Jews: The First Generation // **386**

Bibliography // **392**

Scriptural Index // **431**

Ancient Sources Index // **438**

Subject Index // **441**

Acknowledgments

The essays in this book were authored in too many different unique circumstances to name or to thank all the people involved. I nonetheless express my general gratitude to those behind the various invitations that occasioned most of these reflections. I express my gratitude as well to the following journals and publishers for the kind permission to reprint materials: *Angelicum*; *Biblical Annals*; *Communio*; *Études bibliques* (Peeters); *Journal for the Study of the Historical Jesus*; LIT; *Nova et Vetera*; *Pro Ecclesia*; *Revue biblique*; Sapientia Press; and *Teologia w Polsce*. Editing of the manuscript was completed with the kind help of my sister, Gina Loehr, as well as Katherina Hauser and Maria Hell, while enjoying the financial support of Alexander von Humboldt-Stiftung as a *Gastwissenschaftler* at the Ludwig-Maximilians-Universität in Munich. John Martino at The Catholic University of America Press was admirable in his support for the project and his help in ensuring an expeditious publication process. Fault for the content belongs to me, but fault for the idea of creating such a volume of collected studies must be reckoned with Matthew Levering, to whom I gratefully dedicate this book.

Earlier versions of the following chapters were previously presented and published in various forums. Each is reprinted here in revised form with permission.

Chapter 1 was originally presented at the conference "Dei Verbum at 50: Towards a Clarification of the Inspiration of Scripture," held at the University of Dayton, October 25–27, 2012, and subsequently published as "The Search for the *Vera et Sincera de Iesu*: *Dei Verbum* 19 and the Historicity of the Gospels," *NV* 13, no. 1 (2015): 87–123.

Chapter 2 was originally presented at the International Meeting of the Society of Biblical Literature at the Humboldt University, Berlin, August

7–11, 2017, and subsequently published as "Schweitzer, Lagrange, and the German Roots of Historical Jesus Research," *JSHJ* 17 (2019): 1–25.

Chapter 3 was originally presented at the conference "Le corpus lucannien (Luc-Actes) et l'historiographie ancienne: Quels rapports?" held at the Université de Fribourg, September 14–15, 2017, and subsequently published as "'So That You May Know the Truth' (Luke 1:4): Luke 1–2 and the Lying Historians," in *Le corpus lucannien (Luc-Actes) et l'historiographie ancienne: Quels rapports? Théologie biblique 2*, edited by Simon Butticaz, Luc Devillers, James Morgan, and Steve Walton, 135–58 (Zurich: LIT, 2020).

Chapter 4 was originally presented at the conference "Signs, Wonders, and Mighty Works," held at the John Paul II Catholic University in Lublin, October 23–24, 2019, and subsequently published as "Jesus and the Paralytics: Memorializing Miracles in the Greco-Roman World of the Gospels," *BibAn* 10 (2020): 389–404.

Chapter 5 was originally published as "'Eyewitnesses from the Beginning': Apologetic Innovation and the Resurrection in the Autopsy of Luke-Acts," *RB* 124, no. 2 (2017): 180–213.

Chapter 6 was originally presented at the annual meeting of the Polish Society of Dogmatic Theologians at John Paul II University, Krakow, September 15–17, 2018, and subsequently published version as "'Spirit and Power': Modernity on Miracles, Biblical Studies, and the Leap of Faith," *Teologia w Polsce* 12 (2018): 19–34.

Chapter 7 was originally published as "Neo-Arians, Richard Bauckham, and the Revenge of Alexandrian Christology: In Search of an Ecclesial Hermeneutic," *Angelicum* 94, no. 2 (2017): 355–86.

Chapter 8 was originally published in a special issue of the French edition of *Communio* focused on the theme of monotheism and appeared as "*Interpretatio iudaica*: Le monothéisme juif à l'époque du second Temple," *Communio: Revue Catholique Internationale* 45 (2020): 43–60.

Chapter 9 was originally presented the conference "Thomas Aquinas and the Crisis of Christology," held at Ave Maria University, February 6–8, 2020, and subsequently published as "Primitive Christology as Ancient Philosophy," in *Thomas Aquinas and the Crisis of Christology*, edited by Michael Dauphinais, Andrew Hofer, and Roger Nutt, 33–55 (Ave Maria, FL: Sapientia Press, 2021).

Chapter 10 was originally published as "Jesus and the Jerusalem Temple: Two Monotheizing Loci in Greco-Roman Judaism," in *Des polythéismes aux monothéismes: Mélanges d'assyriologie offerts à Marcel Sigrist*, edited by Uri Gabbay and Jean-Jacques Pérennès, 15–36, ÉB 82 (Leuven: Peeters, 2020).

Chapter 11 was originally presented at the conference "The Knowledge of Christ and Contemporary Exegesis" at the Dominican House of Studies, October 2–3, 2015, and subsequently published as "Scripture as *Scientia Christi*: Three Theses on Jesus' Self-Knowledge and the Future Course of New Testament Christology," *ProE* 25, no. 3 (2016): 274–90.

Chapter 12 was originally presented at the conference "Word and Wisdom," held the University of Notre Dame, April 1–3, 2019, celebrating the release of the English edition of Olivier-Thomas Venard's *Poetic Christ: Thomistic Reflections of Scripture, Language and Reality*, translated by Kenneth Oakes and Francesca Aran Murphy (London: T&T Clark, 2019).

Chapter 13 was originally published as "'Why Do the Scribes Say?' (Mark 9:11): Scribal Expectations of an Eschatological High Priest and the Interpretation of Jesus' Transfiguration," *RB* 128, no. 2 (2021): 201–35.

Chapter 14 was originally delivered at the conference "Theological Exegesis: Scriptural Theology," held at the Angelicum in Rome, February 23–24, 2019, and subsequently published as "Prosopological Exegesis and Christological *Anagnorisis* in Jesus' Reading of Psalm 110," *NV* 18, no. 4 (2020): 1267–84.

Chapter 15 was originally delivered as an invited lecture at the Angelicum in Rome on April 17, 2018, and subsequently published as "Jesus' Prophetic Knowledge and the Gospels," *NV* 17, no. 4 (2019): 1077–99.

Appendix II was originally published in *NV* 19, no. 1 (2021): 303–9.

Abbreviations

PUBLICATIONS

AAS	*Acta Apostolica Sedes*
AB	Anchor Bible
ABRL	Anchor Bible Reference Library
ADAJ	*Annual of the Department of Antiquities of Jordan*
AJEC	Ancient Judaism and Early Christianity
AnBib	Analecta Biblica
ANF	Ante-Nicene Fathers
ANRW	*Aufstieg und Niedergang der römischen Welt*
ASE	*Annali di Storia dell'Esegesi*
ASNU	Acta Seminarii Neotestamentici Upsaliensis
ASS	*Acta Sanctae Sedis*
AThANT	Abhandlungen zur Theologie des Alten und Neuen Testaments
AYBRL	Anchor Yale Bible Reference Library
BBR	Bulletin of Biblical Research
BET	Beiträge zur biblischen Exegese und Theologie
Bib	*Biblica*
BibAn	Biblical Annals
BJSUCSD	Biblical and Judaic Studies from the University of California

BSac	*Bibliotheca Sacra*
BThSt	Biblisch-theologische Studien
BWANT	Beiträge zur Wissenschaft vom Alten und Neuen Testament
BZNW	Beihefte zur Zeitschrift für die neutestamentliche Wissenschaft
CBR	Currents in Biblical Research
CBQ	*Catholic Biblical Quarterly*
CBQMS	Catholic Biblical Quarterly Monograph Series
CCC	Catechism of the Catholic Church
CCSL	Corpus Christianorum Series Latina
CIIP	Corpus Inscriptonium Iudeae et Palestinae
ConBNT	Coniectanea biblica, New Testament
CPh	*Contributions to Philosophy*
CRB	Cahiers de la Revue biblique
CSEL	Corpus scriptorum ecclesiasticorum Latinorum
DCLS	Deuterocanonical and Cognate Literature Studies
DS	Denzinger-Schönmetzer
DV	*Dei Verbum*
ÉB	Études bibliques
EKKNT	Evangelisch-Katholischer Kommentar zum Neuen Testament
EvTh	*Evangelische Theologie*
FAT	*Forschungen zum Alten Testament*
FGrHist	Fragmente
FRLANT	Forschungen zur Religion und Literatur des Alten und Neuen Testaments
HHS	Harvard Historical Studies
HTKNT	Herders Theologischer Kommentar zum Neuen Testament

HTR	*Harvard Theological Review*
HUCA	*Hebrew Union College Annual*
JAJ	*Journal of Ancient Judaism*
JAOS	*Journal of the American Oriental Society*
JBL	*Journal of Biblical Literature*
JBLMS	*Journal of Biblical Literature Monograph Series*
JBTh	*Jahrbuch für biblische Theologie*
JECS	*Journal of Early Christian Studies*
JGRChJ	*Journal of Greco-Roman Christianity and Judaism*
JJS	*Journal of Jewish Studies*
JRS	*Journal of Roman Studies*
JSHJ	*Journal for the Study of the Historical Jesus*
JSJ	*Journal for the Study of Judaism in the Persian, Hellenistic, and Roman Period*
JSJSup	*Journal for the Study of Judaism Supplements*
JSNT	*Journal for the Study of the New Testament*
JSNTSup	*Journal for the Study of the New Testament Supplements*
JSP	*Journal for the Study of the Pseudepigrapha*
LCL	Loeb Classical Library
LHBOTS	Library of Hebrew Bible/Old Testament Studies
LNTS [JSNTS]	Library of New Testament Studies [Journal for the Study of the New Testament Supplements]
LW	Luther's Works [ed. Pelikan, Lehman]
MAAR	*Memoirs of the American Academy in Rome*
NICNT	New International Commentary on the New Testament
NICOT	New International Commentary on the Old Testament

NIGTC	New International Greek Testament Commentary
NovT	*Novum Testamentum*
NovTSup	*Supplements to Novum Testamentum*
NRTh	*Nouvelle revue théologique*
NTOA	Novum Testamentum et orbis antiquus
NTS	*New Testament Studies*
NV	*Nova et Vetera*, English Edition
PG	Patrologia Graeca (Migne)
PL	Patrologia Latina (Migne)
ProE	*Pro Ecclesia*
RB	*Revue biblique*
RBL	*Review of Biblical Literature*
RdQ	*Revue de Qumrân*
RechBib	*Recherches bibliques*
RevExp	*Review & Expositor*
RNT	Regensburger Neues Testament
SBL	Society of Biblical Literature
SBLMS	Society of Biblical Literature Monograph Series
SBLSCS	Society of Biblical Literature Septuagint and Cognate Studies
SBLRBS	Society of Biblical Literature Resources for Biblical Study
SC	Sources Chrétiennes
SEG	Supplementum Epigraphicum Graecum
SJLA	Studies in Judaism in Late Antiquity
SJOT	*Scandinavian Journal of the Old Testament*
SNTSMS	Society for New Testament Studies Monograph Series
SR	*Studies in Religion / Sciences Religieuses*
TKNT	Theologischer Kommentar zum Neuen Testament

TLZ	*Theologische Literatur Zeitung*
TS	Theological Studies
TU	Texte und Untersuchungen zur Geschichte der altchristlichen Literatur
VC	*Vigiliae Christianae*
VTS	Vetus Testamentum Supplements
WA	Martin Luther: Werke, Kritische Gesamtausgabe [Weimarer Ausgabe]
WUNT	Wissenschaftliche Untersuchungen zum Neuen Testament
ZThK	*Zeitschrift für Theologie und Kirche*
ZNW	*Zeitschrift für die neutestamentliche Wissenschaft*
ZPE	*Zeitschrift für Papyrologie und Epigraphik*

ANCIENT SOURCES

A.J.	Josephus, *Antiquitates judaicae*
Ad. Aut.	Theophilus of Antioch, *Apology to Autolycus*
Ad Haer.	Irenaeus, *Adversus Haereses*
Aet.	Philo, *De aeternitate mundi*
ALD	*Aramaic Levi Document*
AP	*Aramaic Papyri of Elephantine*
Apoc. Ab.	*Apocalypse of Abraham*
1 Apol.	Justin, *First Apology*
2 Apol.	Justin, *Second Apology*
AposCon	*Apostolic Constitutions*
As. Mos.	*Assumption of Moses*
B.J.	Josephus, *Bellum judaicum*
Bib. hist.	Diodorus Siculus, *Bibliotheca historica*

C. Ap.	Josephus, *Contra Apionem*
Cels.	Origen, *Contra Celsum*
Cher.	Philo, *De cherubim*
Comm. Jo.	Origen, *Commentary on John*
Conf.	Philo, *De confusione linguarum*
Cyr.	Xenophon, *Cyropaedia*
Dec.	Philo, *De decalogo*
Decret.	Athanasius, *de Decretis Nicaenae Synodi*
Dial.	Justin, *Dialogue*
Enn.	Plotinus, *Enneads*
Ep. Serap	Athanasius, *Letter to Serapion*
Flacc.	Philo, *In Flaccum*
Fug.	Philo, *De fuga*
GEger	*Egerton Gospel* (British Library Egerton Papyrus 2)
Gen. Rab	*Genesis Rabbah*
Geo.	Strabo, *Geographica*
H. E.	Eusebius, *Historica Ecclesiastica*
Her.	Philo, *Quis rerum divinarum heres sit*
Hist.	Herodian, *History*
	Herodotus, *The Histories*
	Polybius, *The Histories*
	Tacitus, *The Histories*
	Thucydides, *History of the Peloponnesian War*
Hist. Conscr.	Lucian, *De Historia Conscribenda*
Jub.	*Jubilees*
LAB	Pseudo-Philo, *Book of Biblical Antiquities*
Leg.	Philo, *Legum allegoriae*
Legat.	Philo, *Legatio ad Gaium*

Metam	Apuleius, *Metamorphoses*
Migr.	Philo, *De migratione Abrahami*
Mos.	Philo, *De vita Mosis*
Mut.	Philo, *De mutatione nominum*
Opif.	Philo, *De opificio mundi*
Pan.	Epiphanius, *Panarion*
Parm.	Plato, *Parmenides*
Poet.	Aristotle, *Poetics*
Praem.	Philo, *De praemiis et poenis*
Praep. ev.	Eusebius, *Praeparatio evangelica*
Prot. Jas.	*Protoevangelium of James*
QE	Philo, *Quaestiones et solutiones in Exodum*
QG	Philo, *Quaestiones et solutiones in Genesin*
Rep.	Plato, *Republic*
Sel. In Ez	Origen, *In Ezekielem*
Sent.	Thomas Aquinas, *Commentary on the Sentences*
Sib. Or	*Sibylline Oracles*
Somn.	Philo, *De somniis*
Spec.	Philo, *De specialibus legibus*
ST	Thomas Aquinas, *Summa Theologiae*
Strom.	Clement of Alexandria, *Stromata*
Super Col.	Thomas Aquinas, *Commentary on Colossians*
Super ep. ad Heb.	Thomas Aquinas, *Commentary on Hebrews*
Super Eph.	Thomas Aquinas, *Commentary on Ephesians*
Sym.	Plutarch, *Symposiacs*
Test. Ben.	*Testament of Bejamin*
Test. Dan	*Testament of Dan*
Test. Gad	*Testament of Gad*
Test. Jos.	*Testament of Joseph*
Test. Jud.	*Testament of Judah*

Test. Levi	*Testament of Levi*
Test. Reub.	*Testament of Reuben*
Test. Sim.	*Testament of Simeon*
Ver. Hist.	Lucian, *Verae Historiae*

A QUEST FOR THE HISTORICAL CHRIST

Introduction

In the following pages I will reject the word "quest," which appears in the title of this collection. If this exposes some inconstancy on my part in simple deference to the exigencies of the book market, it also hints at something more substantial. Albert Schweitzer's moral monopoly on the historical Jesus paradigm (or rather the industry, one might say) has, through the use of this evocative phrase, long cloaked itself in a curious scholar's piety: *The Quest*. Yet Schweitzer's work stems from a self-consciously anti-traditional religious impulse, quite different from my own, for which reason I protest against the affinity of our two allied enterprises by cheekily refusing him the title that I here claim.

A quest in the old chivalric sense—that is, in the Arthurian acceptation of the *Queste of the Sankgreal*—is a loose compendium of freestanding, miniature adventures, all somehow ordered by strange destiny to one elusive yet driving goal: to behold fully revealed what once appeared veiled in a transient sacramental apparition. In this precise sense of a charmingly haphazard yet forcefully unified undertaking, motivated by a deep desire awakened through a mystery of communion—a sort of Emmaus experience—I seek some romantic cover for the collection of essays presented in this volume.

The independent character of the following fifteen studies will be evident on inspection. Most are responses to invitations to give papers at various conferences where my themes were assigned from on high. A certain stubborn preoccupation with Jesus—Jesus as a single divine subject, at once confessed in the Church's *Credo* and known through the study of history—nevertheless channeled these projects down a concerted path. The continuous thread weaving them together is, accordingly, very much what Benedict called in his intimate book "My personal search for the face of Jesus": in my case, a personal search taking the particular form of an exegete's reasoned leap of faith. The invitation to gather these diverse Christological essays into a single volume thus seemed warranted to me for two reasons.

First, many of the texts were published in hard-to-reach places. Two appear in Polish journals, for instance, which even I have not managed to see. One, here translated, was originally published in French; while another, in English, sits in an unfrequented French collection. Some were placed where exegetes but not dogmatic theologians would stand to see them. Some are exposed to the exact inverse fate. One (which I rather like) is a conference paper that has not yet appeared in print. The cumulative force of all these scattered essays, once gathered, while obviously not taking the strict shape of an argument—each chapter, with varied degrees of tinkering and attempted improvements, essentially retains its original form—nevertheless presents a certain broad and distinctive way of thinking, manifest in an illustrative range of applications.

That is the second and more important reason for this book. It seemed to me worthwhile to assemble this record of reflection, insofar as it marks out several steps, if modest steps, leading in what I take to be the right direction toward the right goal. That goal is in no way hidden. My quest's titular end in a brazen breaking up and blending of the sacrosanct secular distinction between the "historical Jesus" and the "Christ of faith" is an open hint at my awkwardly unkosher program—awkward, at least, if normed by long conventional conceptual canons. Namely, it is a project that seeks in its way to leap over the "broad ugly ditch" (Lessing) and overcome the cleft that separates the words *historical* and *Christ*: flatly rejecting the construction of a neo-Kantian subjectivity with its proscription of ever attaining the Christological *Ding an sich*.[1]

If my title thus signals, on the one side, a certain breach of good manners, the questioning of superannuated canons is, on the other, also a per-

---

[1] The Kantian epistemology lurking behind the "Jesus of history vs. Christ of faith" distinction is manifest upon inspection but also demonstrable. It is clear, for instance, in Strauss, *Der Christus des Glaubens*, an important text that unfortunately receives much less attention than either his first or his second *Leben Jesu*. Strauss makes his philosophical point of departure plain throughout, and in the foreword he even offers the following revealing comparison and statement of purpose in critiquing Schleiermacher's Christology: "Mit Schleiermachers Theologie steht es heute genau so, wie es vor sechzig Jahren mit der Kantischen Philosophie stand. Während die eigentliche Wissenschaft bereits in Fichte und Schelling dazu fortgeschritten war, das durch Kant aufgestellte Prinzip zu vertiefen und weiterzubilden, hatte das Kantische Philosophieren sich in die Breite ausgedehnt, war in das allgemeine Bewußtsein übergegangen, zur Durchschnittsweisheit des Zeitalters geworden. Ebenso stehen jetzt alle diejenigen Theologen, die nicht in stumpfsinniger Reaktion erstarrt, oder zum Standpunkte der freien Wissenschaft vorgedrungen sind, mithin die bei Weitem überwiegende Mehrheit der theologischen Welt, mit allerhand Abweichungen vielleicht, aber im Wesentlichen doch auf einem Standpunkte, den man nur als den Schleiermacher'schen bezeichnen kann."

fectly fashionable thing for academics these days to do. Thus, like many, I discern a (long-standing) urgency in revitalizing modern exegesis, *scienzia biblica* as the Vatican quaintly calls it, and more specifically within this exegesis making more theologically fruitful our modern take on the "science of Jesus," which Louis de Montfort called the most vital of all imaginable sciences that might be pursued. For a longer time than is now pleasant to remember, this domain of the knowledge of Jesus has become a sterile field, void of ecclesial harvest, limited today less by the mystery of Christ and our own *docta ignorantia* as believers than by a resolute academic culture of deeply ignorant learning: that is, by an academy unilluminated by faith (sadly even in certain theology and, as a matter of principle, in all religious studies departments).

The situation is not entirely desperate, of course, and I am hardly alone in sensing these problems. Still, as a practicing, professional *Neutestamentler*, I do perceive the extreme marginalization of some rather basic Catholic instincts, both in the context of these debates and within my guild at large, which has long been dominated by a different theological (deeply Protestant) agenda. The "Catholic" redirections that I urge here are not meant to be ecumenically exclusive, however, and I already have had the pleasant experience of much positive Protestant feedback. Well-minded lowercase "catholics" should not stumble here over anything too outrageously ultramontane. Indeed, the conciliar orientation will for many be perfectly welcome. It is no shame, in any case, but a sign of the honest value of ecclesial goodwill that of all theological disciplines, exegesis has made the greatest ecumenical strides—even if neutral common ground has often only been found by avoiding the problems at issue, resting safely on the unthreatening philological level: an "ecumenical" snub, in fact, of that inexorably truth-seeking, at times anathematizing, more original *oecumenical* exegesis, with its anamnestic spelling and proud conciliar ring. For the rest, the universal Catholic view that I openly own here promises at least to provide a classic but missing interlocuter in something of an exegetical monoculture (wildly diverse as it also is, in its own contracted fashion). Not that *Catholics* have had nothing to say. Harold Bloom described John Meier, for instance, the eminent historical Jesus scholar whose graduate assistant I was fortunate to be, as "the most distinguished Roman Catholic biographer of Jesus." This is not a title for which I mean here to contend—particularly as I would entrust it to the evangelists themselves. Still, I would point out that Fr. Meier's playful fantasy of an "unpapal conclave" puts his rigorously non-confessional project in a different category than this, my own, let us call it "contextualized reading." If my own experiments, as catalogued here, at once both more premodern and postmodern than those of a Fr. Meier, can thus somehow serve other theologians and students of the Scriptures with an ecclesial interest in Jesus, then perhaps the common ecclesial project that is *sacra doctrina* will profit in some small way along the adventure toward ultimate vision.

Such a hope, I expect, is sufficiently pious and vague that some fuller word on what I mean by the "right direction" toward this "right goal" is probably in order, if only to help the reader's rapid discernment of what interest or inattention this long selection of studies deserves. By a mixture of providential good fortune, a dubious gambit on the part of the *Magister Ordinis* at Santa Sabina in Rome, and some bumbling, blind obedience on my own side, I have been doubly expatriated, living with Frenchmen living abroad, grafted as an isolated American Dominican onto the luminous patrimony of the *École biblique et archéologique française de Jérusalem*: for five generations the Church's biblical think tank, esteemed in the academy and the oldest center of research in the (much older) Holy Land. The compelling ideal of Marie-Joseph Lagrange, OP, the saintly founder of this storied school—meant to be a "school" in the strong sense of a "school of thought," not an ecclesiastical diploma factory—is a vision that will appear in chapter 2 as the Catholic foil to the radical Protestant project of Schweitzer.[2] The most decisive mark of this vision, however, is simply the École's founding commitment to two simultaneous goods, often held to stand in incompatible tension (whether in principle or just in praxis): (1) the highest, modern standards of historically informed exegetical rigor and (2) a profound commitment to the truths of Catholic faith and doctrine. Another ideal is also associated with Lagrange's name, giving color to his particular historical vision: *rapprocher le document et le monument*, that is, bringing the biblical text into close interpretative contact with archeological science. Chapter 4, "Memorializing Miracles in the World of the Gospels," offers a particularly focused example of my own effort at bringing document, monument, and theology together. In every chapter, however, it is as a proud heir of this benefic program of Père Lagrange that my attempts to forge a synthesis of historical and theological reflection must be seen.

Representing a manner of handling the Holy Scriptures that both manifests a measured respect for certain Enlightenment ideals and thereby stands dangerously close to the Modernist trap, Lagrange had difficulty finding a favorable audience in the Church of his day—even earning the badge of an unjustly martyred reputation. The Modernist panic (if not the threat) has meanwhile long since blown over. Still, the risk of finding no engaged or friendly ecclesial audience (hence no audience at all) remains quite real. In chapter 6, I will relate the blockheaded resistance of Maarten van Dorp and

---

2 On Lagrange's ideal of biblical study, see also my "In der Exegese wie im Krieg."

others like him to the rise of modern methods of interpretation, and generally I simply accept the role of exegetical boogeyman as part of theological life after Erasmus. Exegetes themselves know—and better than anyone else—that reading the published results of professional biblical research is frequently the literary equivalent of chewing cardboard. Nor need we expect what is the proper burden of specialized scholars to be popular and pleasant. For this reason, the selection of studies that I make here does not include any number of more technical investigations. Herodian numismatics will remain a connoisseur's sport and a guilty pleasure that I save for other venues (even when the *dramatis personae* of the Gospels are thereby vividly revealed).[3] The need to seek a wider ecclesial influence for biblical studies nevertheless strikes me as important. This obviously concerns breaking out of an elite academic cabal; yet I do not mean writing works of popularization.

I in no way deny that popularization plays a vital role in the trickle-down economy of every field of advanced study. (Where would I be as a dilettante of evolutionary theories without popular science?) Nor do I share the common, establishment exegete's haughty disdain of apologetics. Apologetics reaches to the very origins of Christian theology and is a task that unambiguously belongs to the vocation of the Catholic interpreter of Scripture—at least if the papal documents on the matter are respected, as well as the long history of the field. Still, there is a concerning sort of breezy and narrowly troubleshooting apologetic, which seems always to have more answers than it has questions but which is, for various reasons, gaining traction. Much could be said about this largely Anglo-American trend, particularly from the perspective of an Anglophone scholar heavily exposed to the different exegetical and ecclesial cultures alive (and often quite dead) in Europe. I am content, however, simply to point to my own concrete swing at an apology in the study of the virgin birth that I offer in chapter 3.

Clearly, the objective here is trying to penetrate beyond simplistic oppositions to the deeper sources of standing disagreement. This explains the postmodern note (still in reference to chap. 3), which sounds in linking Luke's Infancy Narrative to Hayden White and the evaluative criteria of ethics and aesthetics. Any ultimate answer to Modernism seems destined to have some such inherently "postmodern" bent. Exegesis, in any case, deserves an implacable interest in the question of truth—truth as it can still resonate with its full moral force and radiant allure today—so that the Bible might be released to speak in our historical moment with the same "spirit and power" that it always possessed. In this regard, I try to show repeatedly and

---

[3] For the intrepid or distractible reader (or simply those who prefer more pictures), see my studies "Coins of Philip the Tetrarch and the Imperial Cult" and "Note on Luke's Parable."

from various angles (in a way totally opposed to and yet fundamentally reminiscent of Bultmann) that a choice for or against faith, for or against the credibility of what we read and of those who wrote it, is an inescapable hermeneutical dimension of any confrontation with the Gospels (see, e.g., chaps. 5 and 6). This represents an attempted balancing of the *an sich* and the *für mich*: a hermeneutical negotiation of the *fides quae* and *fides qua*.

For those who follow these fifteen chapters to the end, it will not be missed that a leitmotif of "direct address" is intoned here that significantly conforms the Christian's personal encounter with the Word to that of Jesus himself, who was naturally also a reader of Holy Scripture. In chapter 12, again in a mildly postmodern mood, this scriptural encounter, for all who hold the evangelical page in hand, will emerge as our hearing of the very *vox Christi*. Through the Gospels we participate *ex auditu* in the mind of Christ—and this re-echoes in the *vox ecclesiae*, as we shall see.

So, an apology of the faith, a defense of the Christ of the Church's councils, for my purposes means at base freeing the Gospels to do their perennial work. And this, today, it seems to me, requires a new manner of encountering them as historical artifacts. I mean historical artifacts that somehow live, thus rescuing the living spirit from the analytical scalpel of the "*sarkic dullards*" (as I amuse myself to call them in chap. 1). This operation can only be performed on historical terms, for however much we may mourn the displacing of timeless metaphysics from her regal throne, history is the master science of our age. It is simply how we think. Biology, cosmology, and even philosophy are now all historical disciplines as we pursue them. This is why we famously (problematically) study theologians, not theology. I do not have myself, nor do I see on the horizon any titanic genius with the force to change this civilizational circumstance in the blink of an eye. Wisdom thus warns to go with the flow: that is, to give ample space to historical thinking—for both modern and postmodern minds do this quite easily and quite well—then within this living, rational space to look for the revelation of Jesus' divine subjectivity. One will thus find here a Christology humbly patterned, at least to this degree, on the historical shape of the Incarnation.

It will be clear that, having said this, I have not simply given up on metaphysics, without which neither divine subjectivity nor Christ's humanity can be named with sufficient precision. Conciliar Christology clearly teaches this lesson. Such extra-biblical allegiance to the categories of natural reason is, of course, a decisive point where the Catholic instinct parts ways with otherwise like-minded Protestant partners. My manner of coming at this confessional differential remains concerned to stay historically and biblically engaged, however. To this extent I aim to make the synchronic Christological perspective itself emerge from within the diachronic artifact, not because of a basic confusion about the (at times confusing) relation between history and abstract reflection, but simply to anchor the rudiments of classical Christology in the New Testament, not simply in the Fathers and later reflection (e.g., chaps. 9 and 11).[4]

The longed-for grail of a reintegrated theological culture, where systematic and biblical studies stand reconciled in shared love of *sacra doctrina*, is an intellectual hunt that not infrequently wanders off in unlikely alchemical directions. This book might well be an example of such straying, but it is clear, at least, about its determined direction and its goal. We require, as far as I can see, a new theological idiom—not simply a situation (which would be happy and unlikely enough) where exegetes and systematic theologians care about and read each other's studies. What else can disciplinary reintegration mean, if not a common language? This begins, I think, as a minimal first step, with settling on some common questions. Little of the accepted currency of questions can at present be cashed in when crossing the border from exegesis to dogmatic theology and vice versa.

Not that the frontier is formally closed. The situation is more like two neighboring Alpine cantons that speak mutually unintelligible academic dialects. Bolder spirits are naturally already free to escape the parochial, disciplinary village, equip themselves, and explore the other side, but even these adventurers are usually content to speak to the natives loudly and slowly before trudging bemused back home. Since theological patois find no special protection under the otherwise broad-minded Endangered Languages Program of the United Nations Educational, Scientific and Cultural Organization (UNESCO), let me clarify that I have no wish to see either the dogmatic or the exegetical dialect as such disappear. Both preserve rich patrimonies of a common intellectual ancestor, and the formal distinction between commentaries and *quaestiones* maps the theological topography as it should. (*Quaestiones* were born of commentaries, just to be clear on the exegetical origins of the progenitor of the two clans.[5]) I do suggest and urge, however, finding between these two magnificent, but rugged, opposing ranges of specialization some form of parlance and some sort of open

---

[4] Perhaps it is self-deception, but I take a reserved openness to various provocative and unsettled questions about philosophy's relation to historical thought to be something other than "a basic confusion." A good, classical articulation of the rights of philosophy and the metaphysical foundations of Christological reflection is available in White, *Incarnate Lord*. On the suggestion that, through the Incarnation, *history* now must now somehow reconfigure our metaphysical categories (e.g., nature), see Balthasar, *Presence and Thought*. For a balanced position and survey of the *topos* history and philosophy, see Ratzinger, "Heilsgeschichte, Metaphysik und Eschatologie."

[5] In fact, "all the scholastic literary forms—*quaestio, disputatio, summa, articulus*—arose from the activity of lecturing on a text" (Holms, "Aquinas' *Lectura in Matthaeum*," 90).

valley where both sides of the scholarly divide might meet in mass and have an exchange. For the fact is, without some shared *Hochsprache*, many barbaric misconceptions will pass for Greek. And without some more open and common terrain, into which the rich rivers of recondite learning can calmly flow—*Rigans montes*—contacts with the neighbors in their elevated professional reaches must remain the reserve of the few. Faced with the vast erosion of humanistic equipment in our day—notably, facility in ancient languages and a commonly held cultural deposit—and menaced by a fiercely provincial prejudice against the generalist temperament as such, old footholds have washed away, and the few *Dolmetchers* out there only have a passable mastery at best, both of the terrain and of the theological tongues.

We seek, therefore, not *lectio divina* or an enterprise of intra-guild vulgarization, but a disciplined discourse, pitched at a level fully fit for academic discussion, in which both sides can exercise their proper dialogical part. Catholic divines of the early and mid-twentieth century (more humanistically equipped than their poor heirs) still knew their way to this common theological site, so the paths that head there are not so hopelessly or long overgrown as we might think or fear. Whether or to what extent a twenty-first-century academy that somehow manages to pitch its camp here must be specifically Christian (or Catholic) in ethos is an important question that I will not now discuss.

I do not suppose that I have yet found my way securely to this much-needed common station, even if at various moments in what follows I fancy finding a vista that looks out upon the clearing. In fusing *Scientia Christi* with the "Modern Study of Jesus," for instance, I am pursuing exactly what I mean by a reformulated common question. One can appreciate, in any case, the strategic advantage of presenting here the outlines of a Gospel Christology born in professional conferences and vetted in peer-reviewed journals (double vetted, in fact, as suits the publications of a university press). For if there is a sadness in the respectful but uncertain reception that Benedict's powerfully synthetic but perhaps too personal books on Jesus received, it is precisely the struggle to find or create the proper audience. Where does theology on one's knees, still armed for the dialectical rigors of scholastic debate, give way to kneeling works more suited in the end for private devotion? It is hard to say. We are still searching, in any case, or so it seems to me, for Catholic theology's response to Albert Schweitzer . . . and to Lessing, and Bultmann, and the entire New *religionsgeschichtliche Schule* . . . and so on: namely, an answer that goes to the heart of how Jesus is today everywhere professionally studied.

In trying to articulate the broad gestures of some organized Catholic response, I have arranged the texts presented here into three parts. Many themes and ideas will converge, but comparing these to symphonic movements would be too grand a statement on the cohesion of what is plainly an imposed, post-factum unity. Still, as in this case the redactor happens also to be the original author, there is in truth a single vision and an intended rhythm that shapes the whole. The studies mount steadily from (1) a first approach to the Gospel data, through (2) a series of interventions that reorient the scholarly discussion, to (3) a proposed meditation on the mind of Christ.

Part I thus groups together five studies under the rubric "Historical Foundations." Both historiographical and historical reflections are in fact at work in this section. It begins with an ecclesial, and more specifically a magisterial point of orientation, which plainly marks the Catholic ethos of the project and ultimately bends me away from criteriology as the governing method (chap. 1). A ressourcement perspective is openly intoned, yet the conciliar frame of the project here opens up beyond the classicism of the fifth century, to reach as far as Vatican II. Next, staying modern and turning to a different sort of classical moment, I glance at the history of research and pass a judgment on Schweitzer's "Historical Jesus," denying him the happy word "quest," which he never used (chap. 2). This serves to contest constructions of that quest as somehow being free of all religious and philosophical commitments and aspirations. (In Appendix I, I pursue this one step further.) Together these first two studies form an opening salvo that situates all of what comes in the subsequent chapters in the fluid space between academy and Church. Three discrete exegetical probes then promptly follow, tracing a biographical arc from Jesus' infancy (chap. 3), through his public ministry (chap. 4), to his resurrection (chap. 5). This means to present a kind of compact, mini-Gospel. Synoptic and Johannine elements are both intentionally in place, but at base this material has a strong Lukan orientation, for a variety of significant reasons, including the Lukan framework that I suggest is (rightly) operative in *Dei Verbum* in chapter 1. Across these three probes, I work hard to highlight what appear to me to be the indispensable key coordinates for reactivating the Gospels as a form of living historical witness: (1) ancient rhetorical conventions and the question of truth, (2) memory as memorialization, and (3) an evangelical reconfiguration of eyewitness testimony, all inviting a decision to act and assent in faith.

Part II is titled "Theological Perspectives," though I resist the silly suggestion that theology is confined to this portion. The first essay confronts the theological angst long roused by historically minded exegesis, taking Newman and Kierkegaard as guides across Lessing's greatly overrated ditch (chap. 6). The unsubtle attention paid here to Christian subjectivity and the invocation of a number of guiding lights of so-called Christian existentialist thought (including, at least in passing, Pascal, Guardini, and Theodore

Haecker) establishes some of the essential intellectual groundwork for the broad approach I propose throughout the book. Bultmann's shadow may be recognized in this as not less important than Schweitzer's for determining the shape of an appropriate contemporary theological orientation. As a quasi-philosophical discussion of miracles, this chapter also serves as a useful bridge from many of the historical discussions in Part I to the more theoretical interests that come to the fore in Part II. The next several chapters then delve into the contemporary debates over "Christological monotheism" and articulate some foundational intuitions about what is and is not working in the current shape of the discussion. It is here that a certain Catholic, theological discomfort with the prevailing model of Early High Christology will be made clear (chap. 7). The strong emphasis placed in this whole section upon metaphysical commitments represents an important part of my suggested redirection. Exposing the character of Second Temple Judaism and primitive Christianity as phenomena closely linked to Greco-Roman philosophical monotheism accordingly occupies both chapters 8 and 9, which I hold to be rather important explorations. The Dionysian grammar engaged at this stage, with its balance of Platonic and Pauline commitments, is a significant reference, in my reckoning, for recovering a successfully integrated idiom of exegetical/systematic thought. The closing exploration of Temple Christology (chap. 10), with its indirect Chalcedonian flavor, signals, finally, a revised model for approaching the critical issue of *latreia—Christolatry*, if we like. It also further forms a bridge to the "iconic turn" that is more openly explored in Part III (this turn being a *return*, in fact—another point where I find premodern and postmodern perspectives to converge). Thomas Merton quipped in a letter that he inclined more to the "Christ of the Icons" than the Jesus of History. It is not without this comment in mind that I will (in chap. 14) take the step of invoking the *Bildwissenschaft* of Gottfried Bohm.

"Jesus and the Scriptures" is the name I give to the third and final clutch of five chapters. Each in its own way meditates upon the mystery of the Word interpreting the Word: the mystery of Emmaus again. It will be plain that I find here an important key for Christological reflection and the site of some central and classic but reconfigured theological questions. After enunciating this suspicion through three suggested theses for future research (chap. 11), I offer a series of applied illustrations (chaps. 12-15). The focus here is upon what is, in effect, a return to the widely abandoned "messianic consciousness" of Jesus, which is, or at least should be to my thinking, a cornerstone for New Testament Christology. If there is a heart of the matter to strike at in Schweitzer (or in Dale Allison, if we want a more contemporary version), it is above Jesus' self-understanding (i.e., eschatological fixations). While I seek to rearticulate this question in a fully fitting and historically informed Second

Temple fashion, I ease off on the delusional-apocalyptic-fervor approach and turn instead to Jesus' own sense of the *sensus* of the Scriptures, where I find not only his own subjective (human) self-knowledge as Christ, but also the hermeneutical ground for our own ecclesial Christological reading of Israel's Scriptures. As a strategically conceived historical-critical anchor to access this aspect of the Gospels' revelation, I first present a pair of twinned reflections on Jesus and John the Baptist. The first considers Jesus' self-attesting witness before the *Legatio Baptistae* (chap. 12). Then the very graphic, or rather *iconic*, mystery of Jesus' Transfiguration stands in the center of a study of his own diarchic messianic vision, as plotted squarely in the matrix of Jewish scribal exegesis (chap. 13). A tremendous, radiant reality is presented for our contemplation in this scripturally illuminated scene, and my conclusions about the eschatological high priesthood of Christ are in a real way the dogmatic heart of this entire project; they personalize and invigorate the mediating Temple Christology already broached in the previous section, proposed as a promising line of access to a Chalcedonian rubric. A hint of the divine light/*doxa* that I discuss in chapter 9 also comes through on Mount Tabor. The priestly and temple-based imagery of Jesus' own iconic self-presentation, then, in the following study, reinforces his unique consciousness of being the Christ, glimpsed in an experience of scriptural *anagnorisis* (chap. 14). This theoretical cornerstone, as I said I like to conceive it, enjoys sufficient explanatory power to explain even what Jesus himself was actually up to in using this self-same image and icon of the "cornerstone" for his own person. The final chapter (chap. 15) is probably the most blended instance of simultaneous biblical and dogmatic reflection that I here offer. It includes one final parry and thrust at Allison/Schweitzer, through a direct inversion of the eschatological prophet motif and an open embrace of Jesus' own *nescience*. It is here, then, that messianic consciousness as a modern exegetical problematic and the scholastic *quaestio* of Jesus' knowledge finally meet head-on. The cross and Resurrection are also here at last pulled into direct focus, and the *scientia Christi* perspective is deployed for all its worth. I am particularly happy, in this precise context, to call into question the conjured up and too easy target of the theologically handicapped (or outright godless) exegete, sharing the blame more equitably between scriptural scholars and systematicians for the contemporary breakdown of an integral culture of *sacra doctrina*.

The preponderance of Synoptic studies in these fifteen reflections is not hidden. This reflects both a personal disposition and a ready consent to operate within certain prevailing assumptions of the New Testament field. While Luke for important reasons holds a central place, I have clearly not forgotten the Fourth Gospel. I approach it as a locus of both solid memory (chap. 4) and of poignant metaphor (chap. 10)—even trying, boldly enough, to forge an alignment between the *vox ipsissima* in John and Q (chap. 12), the former of which Lessing had hoped to replace with the latter. John's Prologue equally comes into view at least twice and from two different perspectives as I try to grapple in a biblical but semi-conciliar way with "the crisis of Christology" (chaps. 9 and 10).

With John, Paul too is obviously necessary to any fully formed Christological doctrine (Lagrange saw this clearly, as I note in chap. 2), but this book is what it is, and it is essentially a set of reflections on Christ in the Gospels. Even so, an important moment of engagement with Paul comes in the monster chapter on "Primitive Christology as Ancient Philosophy" (chap. 9), which from my viewpoint is perhaps as vital as any in the whole collection. If a Platonic crack in the primitive Christology door is here indeed effectively pried open, a potent theological synergy and next step stands ready and waiting. In particular, the sublime and graphic Christological vision of Hebrews, which is silently present in these studies only as a discrete point of reference on the outer margins, invites a fused picture of Jesus as that one who is ontically higher than the angels (chap. 9) but made lower awhile within his flesh, in which he is destined to suffer in order to serve as mankind's great cosmic high priest (chap. 13). I like to imagine that I have laid out across these studies a useful Gospel groundwork for robustly embracing this elaborate gem and neglected centerpiece of early Christian reflection. Movement toward some form of correctly nuanced yet unified New Testament Christology is thus an important aspiration that emerges from, without strictly driving, this aggregate collection of essays.

In the end, pretending to make no settled or integral argument but satisfied rather to present a series of interrelated and evocative trials, I am less troubled than I might otherwise have been by the various gaps presented by unanswered historical and theological questions that arise in reading these chapters. Instead, I welcome unfollowed hints and still ungrounded intuitions as so many exegetical prompts for future research. Indeed, nothing in what I offer here, notably in Part III, intends to exclude other viable avenues of approach and meditation. The person of Jesus is simply too rich. Nevertheless, as will be clear upon reading, I do have a strong conviction that conventional scholarly perceptions and constructions of the messianism of Jesus as an apocalyptic prophet/madman are overplayed and no longer helpful, and that a scribal/priestly corrective, more attuned to deliberate philosophical and theological choices, is much in order—for the sake both of better history and (hence) better theology.[6] This broad conviction moves me directly toward

---

6 In Appendix II appears a plea for the "mandatory retirement" of this outdated view, in my review of Paula Fredriksen's *When Christians Were Jews* ("the latest iteration of the 'Jesus the

the concept of the knowledge of Christ, *scientia Christi*, which figures as a titular motif, building especially upon the essays in chapters 11 and 15. These programmatic chapters establish a manifest conceptual frame and openly engage the old medieval problematic from whence the formula originally derives, albeit reconceived here around the scribal habits of ancient Jews and the abandoned crux of Jesus' consciousness of himself as messiah.

Given the medieval pedigree of the *scientia Christi* motif, I will comment here only to say that one classic question that I have deliberately left unaddressed is the controverted issue of Jesus' beatific knowledge. While this captivating Christological topic might have provided a certain symmetry and even closure absent from these meditations, ultimately, at the shrewd advice of a friend, I preferred not to make this book one concerned with that particular problem, which I would have risked had I stepped into that hornet's nest. My search for the face of Jesus finds a point of definitive interest in the saving humanity of the Lord—though few would hazard, I think, to call the vision in these pages "low Christology" in any significant sense. The Jesus found here takes himself to be God's unique high priestly agent, a cosmic mediator that Philo identified with the *Logos*. Yet this soteriological role of linking God and men is localized, at least instrumentally speaking, resolutely in Christ's earthly nature as man, and it is especially here that I have concentrated my reflections. The cry of dereliction is, of course, the ultimate revelation of a scandalously human Jesus as a reader of Scripture: my chosen heuristic. Although it is recognized on all sides that the often soaring theses of classical dogmatics suffer an extreme stress in the face of this wrenching word of the Psalmist placed in the mouth of the dying Lord, the vision of God is a major biblical (also psalmic) motif. A fruitful exegetical approach certainly exists to illuminate Jesus' beatifying experience of the vision of his Father. "Blessed are the pure of heart, for they shall see God," Christ said, offering his own compact commentary on beatific vision and the piety of the clean-hearted *zaddiq* in the psalms. "Blessed are the eyes that see what you see," the Lord also said. It is the Son's *work*, his highest job, according to John's Gospel, simply to make the Father visible to faith. It is quite enough to see the Son. More! It is positively beatifying. Some glimpse of Jesus' human gaze on the Father fires the quest to participate in his ineffable vision. Still, that participation ever takes the form of looking at him looking at God, God whose consubstantial Son he eternally is. I am thus content to end this book with a chapter that halts at Christ's prophetic knowledge, for,

---

Failed Millenarian Prophet' series—which, like *Star Wars* books, at some point all start to look the same, with some minimal rearrangement of Wookiees and Death Stars"). The latest, latest installment (at last as I am penning this note) is Wassén and Hägerland, *Jesus the Apocalyptic Prophet*, but admittedly I might already be behind.

as I perceive it, it has the profound and revealing quality of being a glimpse of Christ's own *self-knowledge*: a supernatural channel by which the divine humanity beholds itself as in a mirror.

"The foundation of the Church is the *living* Christ, the God made man, not *das Suchen*, not the search to determine who he might be."[7] Johann Adam Möhler's word serves as a perennial cry of *Achtung!* in the direction of our theological, ecclesial questing. Our search is to know, even as he knows, the one who infallibly knows himself to be the incarnate Word, without clumsily groping to search and discover what he transparently holds in the white light of his own being: that pure light that he freely communicates and shares with his Church through the gift of supernatural faith. It is not only a bad idea; it is also a fall into devilish "wisdom" to try to mount a clever argument in the place of this simple, divine assent to belief. So, in a simultaneous confession and hermeneutical disclosure of this text's operative presuppositions, let me now unambiguously say to all who might still be reading: *credo!*

The original *Queste* was a moral journey, even an enormous allegorical lesson. All but three adventurers were finally stunted by their sins. Even the famous Launcelot ended in a discovery of his need for repentance: "Now I se and undirstonde that myne olde synne hyndreth me and shamyth me, that I had no power to stirre nother speke whan the holy Sankgreal appered before me" (*Le Morte Darthur*, "Winchester Manuscript," fol. 363r). Such self-knowledge, the evangelical *gnōthi seauton*, no less than Christ's own knowledge of who he eternally is, belongs to the redeeming fruit of the search for *Scientia Christi*. The major discovery here is an essential first principle of *docta ignorantia*: a word on ignorance, on knowledge, and on love, enunciated by St. Paul. "Anyone who claims to know something does not yet have the necessary knowledge; but anyone who loves God is known by him" (1 Cor 8:2–3). Lest later Dominicans and Franciscans endlessly quibble about it, Paul deftly steps around the circular issue: *God's knowledge of us* precedes *our love of him*. We read the Gospels to participate in the mind of Christ and so to be moved in his foreknowing by the love of him. And it is this mind of Christ—his predilection for us—that, throughout and in all these studies, we wish both to know and to make known, for love of him. "For love of us," Cyril of Alexandria says, "he has not refused to descend to such a low posi-

---

[7] "Die Grundlage der Kirche ist der *lebendige* Christus, der Mensch gewordene Gott, nicht das Suchen, wer er sein möge, und die Freiheit des Christen der legendige Glaube an ihm, der gar nicht abgeändert werden kann; denn Christus ist heute und in Ewigkeit derselbe ... Stelle man das Untersuchen als Grundsatz auf, so sei keine Aussicht, jemals zum Glauben zu kommen, was doch der vorgegebene Zweck des Suchens sei und auch kein Grund vorhanden, jemals das Untersuchen aufzugeben" (Möhler, *Die Einheit in der Kirche*, 67).

tion as to bear all that belongs to our nature, included in which is ignorance." By his human share in our own human unknowing, Christ leads us on to recognize the hyper-predicating knowledge of his divine love: "To know the love of Christ that surpasses knowledge" (Eph 3:19). In the pages to follow, in following this path, I will say "Lord, Lord" often enough to be quite dangerous by the Lord's own warning. One would gladly hear *Bene scripsisti de me* and so be known by him at the end of these studies, but that is praise reserved for sainted doctors. May it suffice that the Bridegroom not respond to this work with a cold wind of unknowing—"I do not know you"—revealing my own unknowing of him. Should it happen, nevertheless, in the studies that follow that I speak from my ignorance of Christ (which is ignorance of the scriptures) and from the shadows still lingering in my mind, clouding "the surpassing worth of the knowledge of Christ Jesus my Lord" (Phil 3:8), it would have been better that (like Launcelot) I had simply kept still. With that I happily offer this work, already submitted to two blind juries of learned academical doctors, also and above all to the unerring judgment of the Church's *magistra*—she who holds in integral love and knowledge the treasure for which all men are searching.[8]

---

[8] As the reader may know, Roman exercise of papal *magisterium* (even this concept itself) was directly shaped by medieval university culture. The reader may also know (or perhaps should) that Dominicans (to which order the author of the present work belongs) have historically not been unnuanced about the limited theological reach of Christendom's most honored and authoritative doctrinal *chair*. See Horst, *The Dominicans and the Pope*.

PART I

HISTORICAL FOUNDATIONS

CHAPTER 1

Vera et Sincera de Iesu

The twenty-fifth anniversary of the opening of Vatican II prompted René Latourelle to produce a major conciliar festschrift: *Vatican II: Assessment and Perspectives*. For the first volume of this project, José Caba contributed an essay treating the "Genesis and Fruits" of *Dei Verbum* 19.[1] In Caba's view, the council's teaching on the Gospels essentially offered "a new way of formulating the historicity problem," no longer moored to "the knowledge and truthfulness of those who were eyewitnesses." Instead, in the document's "New Framework," criteriology and redaction criticism point the way forward.

Twenty-five years later, we stand in a different historiographical place, from which both our assessments and perspectives are likely changed. If there is little to dispute in Caba's straightforward account of the succession of drafts in the article's *genesis*, one may be less satisfied with his interpretation of its *fruits*. What promptly followed the council is not necessarily what the council envisioned. In any event, Gospel scholarship itself today looks considerably different than it did just twenty-five years ago, while resistance is growing to overstated notions of the council's abrupt newness.[2] It is opportune, therefore, now a half century later, to evaluate again *Dei Verbum*'s important teaching on the Gospels' historicity.

In this chapter, I offer a revised estimate and propose that the doctrine of *DV* 19 is a classic instance of conciliar *ressourcement*. Rather than elabo-

---

1 Caba, "Historicity of the Gospels."
2 For a comprehensive statement of opposition to the entrenched perspective represented by the Bologna School of council scholarship and reception, see Marchetto, *Il Concilio Ecumenico Vaticano II*.

rating a wholly "New Framework," configured by *Formgeschichte* (and its offspring, redaction criticism) and specially calibrated to a critical quest for the historical Jesus, as that has heretofore been pursued, Vatican II recovers a fresh view of the definitive paradigm of sacred Scripture. The Church's teaching on the Gospels is thus best understood as adumbrating a Lukan Framework, and *Dei Verbum* 19 represents a certain magisterial exegesis of the preface of Luke's Gospel. It is no accident (though not noted by Caba) that the council frames its doctrine in article 19 with two programmatic scriptural texts, the pair of prologues to the Lukan *Doppelwerk*: Acts 1:1–2 and Luke 1:2–4. While this appeal to inspired Scripture remains open to (and even invites) professional historical inquiry, the *asphaleia* of the Gospels is part of the preached message itself.[3]

The study will be structured around several interlocking themes. First, I will contextualize the teaching of *Dei Verbum* 19 historically and hermeneutically, supplying a broad background that indicates the unlikelihood of any substantially "New Framework." I will also provide a description of two major responses to the issue of historicity. Finally, I will consider some trends in Gospel scholarship, positioning them in relation to the council doctrine.

OPINIONES NOVAE OR THE *RENOUVEAU*?

On June 26, 1961, while the preconciliar committees were already busily meeting, Jean Steinmann's *La Vie de Jésus* became the last title ever placed on the *Index Librorum Prohibitorum*.[4] Although the Pontifical Biblical Commission was known as a vigilant watchdog and had aggressively censured several books in the past, this solemn condemnation through the Holy Office was the only such action ever initiated by the PBC.[5] The unexplained decree came just days after a *monitum* had been promulgated, the circumstances of which help explain the severe decision.[6]

---

[3] On the theme of Lukan *asphaleia*, see chap. 3 in this volume.

[4] *In generali consessu*, AAS 53 (1961): 507–8. See Steinmann, *La Vie de Jésus*.

[5] In 1912, the PBC forbade several commentaries from being used in seminaries, including "several works by P. Lagrange." At different points the PBC also aggressively censured several other publications. See AAS 26 (1934): 130 and AAS 45 (1953): 432. These condemnations were more restricted in scope, however, and were not executed through the Holy Office and its Sacred Congregation of the Index.

[6] See AAS 53 (1961): 507. Contrast Steinmann's unexplained condemnation with Cardinal Merry del Val's ample explanation of the condemnation of Vigouroux and Brassac's *Manuel biblique* (AAS 15 [1923]: 616–19) and the reasoning provided for the PBC censure of Schmidtke's *Die Einwanderung Israels in Kanaan* (AAS 26 [1934]: 130). A letter from Car-

Steinmann was incidental to a larger controversy ignited the summer before, later nicknamed the "Battle of the Biblicum." At its heart lay a suggestive exchange: a trial run, in some regards, of those perspectives we now recognize as the two great competing conciliar hermeneutics: rupture and continuity.[7] Louis Alonso Schökel, a young professor at the Biblicum, had written a progressive piece for a popular magazine arguing that Pius XII had endorsed a broadminded shift in the direction of biblical studies, a "cambiamento nell'esegesi."[8] Antonino Romeo, a well-placed curial official and Scripture scholar at the Lateranum, let loose in response an intemperate seventy-page rebuttal, insisting on the continuity of Pacelli's program with the earlier culture of Catholic exegesis and ironically accusing Alonso Schökel (and others at the Pontificio Istituto Biblico and elsewhere) of the very *opiniones novae* and "new exegesis" (*nova exegesi*) Pope Pius condemned directly in *Humani Generis* (§22–24).[9] As the debate rapidly escalated, drawing in additional voices, attention focused especially on historicity, and soon the last spasm of anti-Modernist panic was engulfing Rome. The pope him-

---

dinal Ruffini, a member of the PBC, informed Ottaviani about the problematic nature of Steinmann's book. See Stabile, "Il cardinal Ruffini e il Vaticano II." Ruffini later published a headlining article in *L'Osservatore Romano* (August 24, 1961) in which he found fault with Steinmann for omitting the infancy narratives, reducing the public ministry to a minimum, and treating the Resurrection lightly—declaring in sum: "A rationalist Protestant could not have been more rash or radical."

7 Benedict XVI's famous December 22, 2005, address to the Roman Curia technically speaks of "the hermeneutic of discontinuity and rupture" and "'the hermeneutic of reform,' of renewal in the continuity of the one subject-Church." For an important study of the issue, see Marchetto, *Il Concilio Ecumenico Vaticano II*. These two hermeneutical perspectives had long been competing for control of Catholic exegesis, and, as elsewhere, the biblical movement is here profoundly representative of the ferment that gave rise to conciliar theology. See Schelkens, "From *Providentissimus Deus* to *Dei Verbum*." The undisguised value judgment implied in Schelkens's dichotomy of "intransigence" and "renewal" (not equally kind descriptions) indicates the basic prejudice of his study. Still, the continuous interaction of two differently oriented forces is well documented in the history of the council—even if one has trouble seeing how Schelkens's proposal of a "hermeneutic of shifting balances" does more than rephrase and dialectically attenuate the "paradigm shift" model he critiques. If Schelkens's reading prefers simply to chart the ebb and flow of opposing parties (like shifting seats in Congress), theologically the proper hermeneutic must be derived from Newman's notion of *development*. Historians of the council would thus do well to attend again to the seven notes of a "true development": (1) preservation of type, (2) continuity of principles, (3) power of assimilation, (4) logical sequence, (5) anticipation of its future, (6) conservation of action upon its past, and (7) chronic vigor.

8 Schökel, "Dove va l'esegesi cattolica?" The title ironically evokes the famous essay of Reginald Garrigou-Lagrange on the *nouvelle théologie*, "La nouvelle théologie, où va-t-elle?" Garrigou-Lagrange had warned that the new trend was a repackaged revival of Modernism.

9 Romeo, "L'Enciclica *Divino afflante Spiritu* e le *opiniones novae*."

self expressed great impatience with this "nonsense," and an intervention quickly became inevitable.[10]

In this connection, the terse *monitum* had been engineered around the obstructions of those whom the architects called the "modernists" (though John XXIII remained confident about the Biblicum).[11] The text itself, however, was open to diverse interpretations, with forward looking young exegetes like Joseph Fitzmyer insisting that the warning "should not be regarded as a condemnation of the so-called 'new direction.'"[12] The document did briefly commend the fervent study of sacred Scripture (a friendly nod to scientific methods) but expressed concern over certain circulating opinions that questioned the "genuine historical and objective truth" (*germanam veritatem historicam et obiectivam*) not only of the Old Testament—an issue, it noted, already decried in *Humani Generis*—but also of the New Testament, even doubting the words and deeds (*dicta et facta*) of Jesus. It is hard to mistake the commission's concern (shared with Romeo) that the solemn corrections Pius offered in 1950 were failing to stem a mounting tide of biblical skepticism. If Steinmann's book was made an example in this context, it neatly sidestepped the whole business with the Biblicum, Steinmann being far away in Paris. The choice likewise—and more importantly—deftly averted speculation over the use of historical-critical methods per se, for the book deployed no scientific criticism. It postured, instead, as a kind of updated Renan: a peculiarly French biographical romance, popular yet pensive—and watery at best on basic articles of the faith.[13]

Of course, if the legacy of the "liberal lives of Jesus" thus lived on in Steinmann's work, the real beachhead of critical skepticism lay elsewhere—as it also had in the time of Renan's popularized *Vie de Jésus*. The more aggressive curial reaction accordingly targeted certain exegetical technicians, and two established Biblicum professors (but not Alonso Schökel)

---

10 See Hebblethwaite, *John XXIII*, 211.

11 See Schelkens, *Catholic Theology of Revelation*, 157n2.

12 Fitzmyer, "Recent Roman Scriptural Controversy," 443–44. See also the contrasting views on the *monitum* expressed by Duncker, "Biblical Criticism," 22–23, and Spadafora, "Un document notevole per l'esegesi cattolica," 969–81.

13 Steinmann evokes Renan with the title and structure of the work and engages him directly in the (kerygmatically rather anemic) conclusion: "Renan n'a pas vu que cette mort [i.e., de Jésus] était un signe ... Cette vie est-elle absurdité ou mystère? Quel est le sens de la mort? Quel est l'ultime destin de l'homme: Dieu ou le néant? Suivant leur réponse, les homes sur terre sont à jamais divisés sous le signe de la croix." The popular audience of the book, along with this less than robust conclusion, likely contributed to the condemnation. The need for writers to avoid "spreading makeshift solutions" that "upset the faith of many" is strongly insisted upon in the final section of *Sancta Mater Ecclesia*.

were soon deposed. These suspensions, leveled against Stanislaus Lyonnet and Maximilian Zerwick, were the climax of the brief intrigue. No formal explanation was ever given; it was accomplished with silent efficiency, but the suspicion was mercilessly clear. Lyonnet had treaded into the sensitive waters of Adam and original sin, while Zerwick misstepped on Gospel historicity.[14]

If the "Modernists" were thus soundly chastened, once the conciliar winds began to blow, the imposing front of hierarchical resistance collapsed in disarray, and any clear doctrinal lesson was soon subverted. Indeed, the confusing epilogue to this whole debacle was a sudden volte face that saw the new pontiff, Paul VI, on the counsel of Cardinal Bea, reinstating both disciplined Jesuits in the spring of 1964.[15]

Although this reversal has been regarded as a full vindication, such an interpretation cannot be sustained. The decision instead appears to have been a change in ecclesiastical policy—the fall from favor of a hawkish curial party—in no way implying a *nihil obstat* on the scholars' deviant exegesis. Indeed, the issuance at the same time (April 1964) of *Sancta Mater Ecclesia*, the landmark Instruction on Historical Truth of the Gospels, a document approved by Paul VI but commissioned two years earlier by Pope John, expressly bolstered the Church's firm commitment to historicity—albeit with nuance and considerable goodwill toward modern methods. This coordinated double maneuver, loosening the reins on free debate while rearticulating the Church's perennial teaching, is critical to appreciate, for the strategy of both Roncalli and Montini, even as cardinals, was always "to speak loudly and carry a small stick," ever confident in the supremacy of dialogue. John XXIII had, in line with this, never ordered the hit on Lyonnet and Zerwick (which, in fact, he resented), while Paul VI's doggedly traditional stance on historicity was repeatedly proven both during and after the council.[16] Regardless, the Church was not accustomed to this indulgent mode of governance,

---

14 Lucien Cerfaux (a member of the Theological Commission) noted in a letter to Cardinal Van Roey: "le P. Zerwick avait une phrase malheureuse: 'Il nostro scopo è di investigare, condotti dal testo sacro stesso, fin dove giunga la libertà che la tradizione e gli Evangelisti si prendono con la realità storica dei fatti e dei dotti di Gesù.'" See Schelkens, *Catholic Theology of Revelation*, 130, cf. 115, 125. Zerwick evidently undermined the historicity of Matthew 16. See the gossipy account of former *Time* magazine correspondent at the council, Kaiser, *Clerical Error*, 130.

15 Roderick MacKenzie, SJ, rector of the PIB, requested a reexamination of the case during his audience with Paul VI in March 1964. The pope agreed and charged Cardinal Bea with the investigation. The personal displeasure of Paul VI with the Lateran was evident, since he scolded the institution for "vexatious polemics" on his first visit there (October 31, 1961), shortly after removing the rector, Msgr. Piolanti. See Harrison, *Teaching of Pope Paul VI*, 60–61.

16 See Harrison, *Teaching of Pope Paul VI*, 60–61.

and at every level the conflicting signals were too disorienting. It is small wonder that a culture of exegetical impunity came to reign—so much that the disgraced Steinmann would soon be rehabilitated as Yves Congar's elect symbol of the "Renouveau."[17]

Such provocation should not be taken at face value, of course. The Church had not so utterly abandoned the seriousness of her past commitments. Thus, if for many the Instruction on Historical Truth quickly came to represent much more than a charitable change of tone, the document's positive teaching cannot be read in isolation from the *monitum*—itself a call to attend again to *Humani Generis*. At root, the events of 1961 and the redress of 1964 were two distinct magisterial efforts that addressed the same exegetical disruption. The pontificate of Paul VI signaled that a long era of iron-fisted discipline was at an end—not that the advance of Modernist skepticism posed no further danger.

Historica Veritas

It was, fatefully, within this turbulent and uncertain air that the great Dogmatic Constitution *Dei Verbum* was drafted. Among the many sensitive points debated during the work of composition—a laborious gestation that lasted the full duration of the council—the controversy just recounted confirms the peculiarly high stakes attached to the question of historicity. While the precursor text, *De fontibus revelationis*, was sufficiently unpopular that a complete redrafting was ultimately undertaken,[18] chapter IV of that schema, *De Novo Testamento*, reveals the absolute preoccupation on the eve of the council with affirming the Gospels' historical truth.[19] Despite wide concern over the adversarial tone of the draft (which cited and even sharpened the wording of the *monitum*), the main points and structure, and in several places even the wording, of this chapter survived intact—a significant point, considering the wider fate of the infamous schema. The decisive development in reformulating the material in a more positive fashion was, of course,

---

[17] No sooner had Paul VI finally abolished the index in 1966 than the catechetical conferences of Steinmann, *Une foi chretienne pour aujourd'hui*—a dubious exercise in *aggiornimento*—were promptly posthumously published. Endorsed in a preface by Yves Congar, flush with his triumph at the council, the work was (brazenly) celebrated as the exact "renouveau" required in the Church.

[18] See the nuanced reappraisal of *De fontibus* in Schelkens, *Catholic Theology of Revelation*, 265–80.

[19] For the text of schema I, chapter IV, see Hellín, *Concilii Vaticani II Synopsis*, 186–87.

the well-timed appearance of *Sancta Mater Ecclesia*. Indeed, nowhere else in the long textual history of *Dei Verbum* is there such a major moment of magisterial intervention. Whole sentences, in fact, are lifted from the Instruction, and this document supplies the essential substance of *DV* 19.

The PBC instruction was, as just related, drafted as the Church's cautious answer to a crisis of historical skepticism, brewing at least since *Humani Generis* in 1950. As an event of direct conciliar import, however, the document also served another role. More than a few churchmen at the council, bewildered by the rumored German monster, *Formgeschichte*, required real guidance in addressing the questions on the floor.[20] To this end the PBC offered the council fathers a kind of "voter's guide" on the latest trends in exegesis, refining a private manuscript prepared by Cardinal Bea and already circulating for this purpose. While the magisterial text can hardly be read as delivering marching orders from theological hardliners, the weighty criticisms leveled against form criticism made clear the Church's profound reservations.[21] Still, a tone of ready engagement is unmistakable. Overall, the PBC's succinct critique incisively sifted out the errant principles of Bultmannian exegesis (with a prescience quite remarkable in retrospect), yet it left a door open for a legitimate (if selective) Catholic appropriation (*sana elementa*).

Unsurprisingly, the gesture of openness became the takeaway teaching of the document. Many specialists in biblical studies, whose theological culture was not yet so divorced from the heritage of dogmatic theology as it is today, eagerly embraced the forward looking methodology, confident that the extremes of German Protestantism lacked viability in the Catholic context.[22] Thus in influential quarters all attention was turned to the dif-

---

20 See the account offered in the foreword to Bea, *Study of the Synoptic Gospels*, 9–12.

21 The six principles, as enumerated by Fitzmyer, "Biblical Commission's Instruction," 386–408, are (1) denial of a supernatural order, (2) denial of God's intervention in the world in strict revelation, (3) denial of the existence and possibility of miracles, (4) incompatibility of faith with historical truth, (5) an almost a priori rejection of historical nature and value of scriptural texts, and (6) diminishment of apostolic authority as witnesses to Christ and exaggeration of creative power of the community. Through such theses, the Church understood the form critics to be profoundly misled by the errors of rationalism (*praeiudicatis opinionibus rationalismi abducti*). A famous article by Pierre Benoit ("Refléxions," 481–512), which remains one of the best treatments of form criticism and well worth reading, helped shaped the magisterial view—in both openness and critique.

22 Fitzmyer ("Biblical Commission's Instruction," 390) expresses the untroubled conviction that the six errant philosophical and theological premises "are rejected by Catholic exegetes." Whether this same confidence is possible today, it is evident that a *notional* rejection of the problematic principles is insufficient to recalibrate a method that inherently presumes such things as "scientific naturalism." On the treatment of miracles in historical method, see Gregory, "No Room for God?" See also chap. 6 in this volume.

ferentiation of Gospel strata, and the instruction's fundamental concern to secure historicity was quickly obscured in its reception. The move in this direction was immediate. Fitzmyer, for instance, an eager Rome-watcher in those days, in an early, or rather immediate, review of the document just months before the promulgation of *Dei Verbum* (with an eye no doubt to helping nudge the council fathers' thinking), managed to spin the text as strangely uninterested in historical truth—an idea one might be forgiven for gathering from the official title, *De historica evangeliorum veritate*. His insistence on the point is remarkable.

> The most important word in the title is not the word *historica*—which might have been one's initial impression ... in none of the positive directives does the phrase *historica veritas* reappear. It is evident, therefore, that the Biblical Commission is far more interested in sketching with broad lines, the character of the Gospel truth, than in just reasserting that the Gospels are historical.[23]
>
> The Commission speaks [in §9] of "truth" only, and does not specify it as "historical truth." One might wonder what it would mean if the word "historical" were understood here, after such an admission of the redactional work of the evangelists. But if one were to ask, "Well, then, if it is not a question of historical truth, of what kind is it?" the answer would have to be, "of the Gospel truth."[24]
>
> Neither the Church in her official pronouncements on the nature of inspiration, nor the theologians in their speculative treatments of it, have taught that the necessary formal effect of inspiration is historicity. The consequence of inspiration is inerrancy, i.e., immunity from formal error in what is affirmed. The opposite of inerrancy is not simply historicity, but truth. But there is poetical truth as well as historical truth, rhetorical truth as well as legal truth, mythical truth as well as the Gospel truth.[25]

And "Gospel truth," Fitzmyer finally assures, "is not something which is tied up with any fundamentalistic literalness."[26]

Fitzmyer raises some genuine issues, and the animating fear of fundamentalist literalism—the modern biblical guild's familiar *tic doloureaux*—

---

23 Fitzmyer, "Biblical Commission's Instruction," 387.
24 Fitzmyer, "Biblical Commission's Instruction," 395.
25 Fitzmyer, "Biblical Commission's Instruction," 401.
26 Fitzmyer, "Biblical Commission's Instruction," 396.

must be addressed. It is nonetheless astonishing to witness this total subversion of the text's express concern. The very notion of "historical truth" is summarily displaced by a tautology entirely of Fitzmyer's making: "Gospel truth," a nebulous notion that he finds for various reasons more commodious. Whatever valid concerns merit attention in articulating the precise modality of Gospel inerrancy, when confronted with the massive solemnity of the opening sentence of *Dei Verbum* 19—unique of its kind in the whole Dogmatic Constitution—an evasion of *historica veritas* cannot be respectably maintained: "Holy Mother Church has held and still holds (*tenuit ac tenet*) firmly and with absolute constancy (*firmiter et constantissime*) that the four Gospels, whose historicity (*historicitatem*) she unhesitatingly affirms (*incunctanter affirmat*), faithfully hand on (*fideliter tradere*) those things that Jesus the Son of God, while he lived among men, truly (*reapse*) did and taught for their eternal salvation, until the day on which he was taken up (Acts 1:1–2)."[27]

The council's language here actually strengthens the earlier wording of *De fontibus*, preferring *tenuit ac tenet* for *credidit ac credit*. The official *relatio* on this change makes clear the desire to propose a mode of truth open to rational affirmation: *fide et ratione, non tantum fide*.[28] If this transposes the speculative vision of Vatican I's *Dei Filius* into a distinctively historical and scriptural idiom and deftly decouples the council's doctrine from the fideism of a Bultmannian-Barthian dialectical dogmatics, it naturally also faces the ultimate question posed by Fitzmyer: What precisely do I assent to when I affirm the historicity of the Gospels?[29]

If "fundamentalistic literalness" poses a real problem, form criticism was not the Church's introduction to literary genre, nor was the Church as critically naive as some would conveniently pretend. The Biblical Commission, in fact, had long before officially acknowledged the possibility of merely

---

[27] The phrase *quorum historicitatem incunctanter affirmat* was added between the last draft (III) and the final text (IV) with the following remark: "Necessario inducendum est vocabulum *historicum*, quod a Magistro saepius adhibitum est, ut refrenetur audacia exegetica." The proposal of 174 fathers was *iuxta veritatem fidemque historicam tradere omnia facta et dicta quae in ipsis continentur*. The editorial note on this proposal observes that *historia* is an equivocal term, ranging in meaning from *rebus supramundanis* apprehended by faith, to *Geschichte* and *Historie*. Preference was thus given to the sense *realitatem factorem seu eventum modo concreto affirmare*, and the less ambiguous language of *historicitatis* was employed. See *Relatio Ad num*. 19 c in Gil Hellín, *Concilii Vaticani II Synopsis*, 133.

[28] Gil Hellín, *Concilii Vaticani II Synopsis*, 132.

[29] The *Time* correspondent reporting on this debate at the council put his finger on the issue at the end of his article "Vatican Council: The Uses of Ambiguity," *Time* 86, no. 19 (5 November 1965): 5. "The problem: what precisely is meant by historicity?"

"apparent history" (*species historiae*) in Scripture. Indeed, even in the worst days of the Modernist crisis, Rome allowed that in well-demonstrated cases (*non facile nec temere admittendo!*) one might hold that "the sacred author did not intend to recount true history properly so called (*veram et proprie dictam historiam*), but with the outward appearance and form of history (*sub specie et forma historiae*), intended to propose a parable or allegory or some other meaning from the properly literal or historical meaning of the words."[30] Texts like Jonah and Job are obviously in view, but the measured principle has impressive scope. All in all, when viewed against this magisterial precursor, the most pertinent doctrinal antecedent, the simplest and most ready interpretation of *Dei Verbum*'s teaching (following *Sancta Mater Ecclesia*) is that the Gospels are not to be reckoned as "specious" but *vera historia*. In other words, the "properly literal or historical meaning of the words" is indeed the meaning intended by the sacred author. This seems to capture the intent of the council's phrase, *vera et sincera de Iesu*.[31]

FUNDAMENTUM INTELLIGENTIAE SPIRITALIS

Exegetes will alternately trivialize or balk at the jejune affirmation that the Gospels must be taken literally. The "literal or historical meaning" is more profound and complex than reigning exegetical methods comprehend, however, and it invites more patient consideration. Indeed, once one appreciates that the literal sense holds foundational significance for any theology of revelation and grounds the possibility of all disciplined theological argument, the importance of getting it right will be urgently clear.[32] While this applies to all the Scriptures, the status of the Gospels must be singled out, even within the New Testament, "because they are the principal testimony for the life and teaching of the Incarnate Word."[33]

---

30 *ASS* 38 (1905/6): 124–25.

31 On the contested history of this formula, see Rigaux's Commentary on Chapter V of *Dei Verbum*, 258–60. Considered too weak by many council fathers, Paul VI intervened and proposed *vera seu historica fide digna*, which, despite the advocacy of Cardinal Bea, was considered open to a new (Bultmannian) ambiguity and rejected. The Theological Commission then clarified its intention with the original formula. It means to encompass and coordinate both the objective facts (*vera*) and the subjective activity/intentionality of the evangelists (*sincera*).

32 "Nulla confusion sequitur in sacra Scriptura: cum omnes sensus fundentur super unum, scilicet litteralem: ex quo solo potest trahi argumentum" (*ST* I, q. 1, a. 10, ad 1). See Augustine, *Epist.* 93.8.24.

33 "Neminem fugit inter omnes, etiam Novi Testamenti Scripturas, Evangelia merito excellere, quippe quae praecipuum testimonium sint de Verbi Incarnati, Salvatoris nostri, vita atque doctrina" (*DV* 18).

As a question of the first principles of theology and revelation, then, it is a matter of peculiar interest in understanding the literal and historical level of the Gospels that the robust and influential Protestant theology of revelation at the time of the council was divided into two opposing camps, with the schools of Bultmann and Cullmann fiercely split over the fundamental relation of word and deed.[34] From Cullmann's *salvation history* perspective, which generally (but not in every way) had the greater affinity with and influence on the council's ultimate doctrine, the critical danger is clear: "The Bultmannites neglect events."[35] The divine Word (*dabar*), however, is indivisibly "speech" and "history."[36] In harmony with this, the classic doctrine of Catholic hermeneutics sees words and deeds to be interpretatively inseparable: *littera gesta docet*. In this paradigm, "history" is thus at once the *prima significatio*, the scriptural "letter" having its own grammatico-literary *ratio*,[37] and the locus of the mystery of our redemption—*profundissima vallis historiae*[38]—man's deep valley into which Christ has kenotically descended.[39] The historical sense is thus the rhetorical *synkatabasis* of the divine Word.[40]

---

34 For the significance of these debates on the council's doctrine, see the commentary of Joseph Ratzinger on chapters 1 and 2 of *Dei Verbum* in Vorgrimler, *Commentary on the Documents of Vatican II*, 170–98.

35 See Oscar Cullmann's essay "Foundations: The Theology of Salvation History and the Ecumenical Dialogue," delivered during the Third Session of Vatican II, in *Vatican II*, 25. Cullmann's active participation in the ecumenical aspects of the council both presupposed a certain theological propinquity with Catholic doctrine ("as soon as we began to use salvation history in our discussions . . . we were speaking the same language") and made his greater influence on the council's outcome inevitable.

36 Precisely because "the author of sacred scripture is God, in whose power it is to signify not only by words (as man can also do), but also by the things themselves (*res ipsas*)" (*ST* I, q. 1, a. 10), the coordinated disclosure of these two registers of revealed encounter—saving deeds and scriptural text—refracts the unified action of the one divine *auctor*. This entails a firm congruence between *littera* and *gesta* and calls forth a single act of assent in faith.

37 Hugh: "Historia est rerum gestarum narratio, quae in prima significatio litterare continetur" (PL 176, 185 A). Origen: "historia proprim rationem habet—*tou echein tên historian ton idion logon*" (*Sel. In Ez.*, c. xxviii; PG 821–22 C). Aquinas: "Cum in omnibus scientiis voces significant, hoc habet proprium ista scientia, quod ipsae res significatae per voces, etiam significant aliquid. Illa ergo prima signification, qua voces significant res, pertinent ad primum sensum, qui est sensus historicus vel litteralis" (*ST* I, q. 1, a. 10).

38 John Scotus, *H. in Prol. Jo.* (PL 123, 291 B). Theo-dramatically, one might speak here with Balthasar of history as the space of the "Action."

39 The *admirabile condescensio* of *DV* 12–13 belongs here. On this theme, see the excellent and suggestive study by Betz, "Glory(ing) in the Humility of the Word."

40 The rhetorical background of the Christological category of *synkatabasis* is not often recognized; cf. Philodemus, *Rhetoric* 2.25. See Duchatelez, "La 'condescendance' divine et l'histoire du salut."

In the splendid formulation of *Dei Verbum*, the two dimensions of this living speech of God are inextricably intertwined, mutually manifesting and confirming one another: *gestis verbisque intrinsece inter se connexis*.[41] From such a perspective, the Gospels' bivalent "literal or historical meaning" is the privileged *fundamentum*, the deepest stuff of divine revelation.[42] *Jesus* is the Gospel's literal sense.

Plainly something of great moment is at stake here for the full doctrine of *Dei Verbum*. To this extent, *DV* 19 is not a stray plank of anti-Modernism in a sea of *nouvelle théologie*. Rather, operating within the relational model of revelation propounded by the council,[43] the fathers were burdened to preserve the *ephapax* character of God's climatic action in Christ, while yet affirming a living *colloquium inter Deum et hominum* (*DV* 25). The Gospels exercise a unique mediation; they somehow communicate Jesus of Nazareth.[44] But as a medium of encounter, scriptural *metaxy* is stretched toward the past. Hence the happy recovery of the God *who* reveals from a shrunken focus on *what* he reveals only bears the subjective stamp of Bultmann unless some objective, referential (here historical, Christological) meaning is upheld.[45] A genuine grasp of the scriptural letter therefore *cannot* methodologically neglect the text's "centrifugal" perspective but must, as a matter of theological principle, perceive some irremediable textual resonance with the extratextual events of the Incarnation.[46] Just as Christ the Word made flesh *is* the vision of the

---

[41] On this important phrase, see Martin, "Some Aspects of Biblical Studies since Vatican II."

[42] Everywhere in the Tradition, "history" is recognized as the *fundamentum*: "Historiae veritas, fundamentum intelligentiae spiritalis" (Jerome, *Ep.* 129, n. 6); "Omnes sensus fundentur super unum, scilicet litteralem" (*ST* I, q. 1, a. 10, ad 1). See de Lubac, *Medieval Exegesis*, 47–50.

[43] On the advent of this model, see Latourelle, *Theology of Revelation*, 207–48.

[44] The fullness of this mediation vitally depends on upholding the proper hermeneutic. Albert Schweitzer memorably captured the experience of theological loss suffered by those who resurrected the historical Jesus and "loosed the bands by which for centuries he had been riveted to the stony rocks of ecclesiastic doctrine." They rejoiced to see him "advancing, as it seemed, to meet them. But he did not stay; he passed by our time and returned to his own. What surprised and dismayed the theology of the last forty years was that, despite all forced and arbitrary interpretations, it could not keep him in our time, but had to let him go" (*Quest*, 478).

[45] A plea must be made for the balanced retention of some "propositional" aspect of revelation. For Bultmann, objective content is incompatible with the idea of genuine revelation: "It turns out in the end that *Jesus as the Revealer of God reveals nothing but that he is the Revealer*" (emphasis original). Bultmann, *Theology of the New Testament II*, 66. See the insightful analysis of Waldstein, "Foundations of Bultmann's Work."

[46] On the "centrifugal" and "centripetal" dimensions of a text, see Frye, *Great Code*, 61. "The primary or literal meaning of the Bible, then, is its centripetal or poetic meaning . . . this primary meaning, which arises simply from the interconnection of the words, is the

Father (cf. Jn 14:9), so the enscriptured Word presents a verbal image of the Image. The Gospels preserve an *adequatio ad rem*: a proper analogy to Christ by the congruence, the revelatory isomorphism of *littera* and *gesta*.

The Gospels' profound identification with the mystery of the Incarnation means that Origen's language of the literal as "body" must not be laid aside.[47] Indeed, it secures a double hermeneutical point, for it invites the key Pauline distinction between *soma* and *sarx*. There is, in other words, an inadequate sense of Scripture understood *kata sarka*. This "literalist" mishearing of the Word is always naive, but simplemindedness can be cloaked in the high sophistication of science—like an endocrinologist digging for the soul in the pineal gland. To the pitied and feared fundamentalist must then be added the (more subtle) "literalist" who wields his critical scalpel on the Gospel text as though he were studying a cadaver. Both types are *sarkic* dullards. If the "flesh" of Scripture thus supplies a public corpus that doctors of philological science may inspect with simpleminded intelligence, the deepest *fundamentum* remains imperceptible apart from faith. For, in the end, it is in the Gospels that the literal and spiritual senses meet.[48] In this regard (and in distinction to other canonical *corpora*), the Gospel's *prima significatio* comprehends the *whole incarnate Christ*—body, soul, and divinity—for here we understand "body" (*soma*) in its Hebrew sense of living totality (*basar*). From this perspective, a composite body-soul (letter-spirit) dynamic also structures the Gospels' privileged first level revelation. The work of the evangelists gives worded shape to the literal *body*, while the *res tantum* of Christ infuses their words with life-giving *spirit*. The Gospels are in this way a sacrament of the sacrament of God.[49]

---

metaphorical meaning. There are various secondary meanings, derived from the centrifugal perspective, that may take the form of concepts, predications, propositions, or a sequence of historical or biographical events, and that are always subordinate the to the metaphorical meaning." One need not doubt Frye's intelligence (or rare insight into allegorical meaning) to suspect that he has not succeeded as neatly as he imagines in marginalizing the Bible's historical claims. A basic problem is his decision to make the entire Bible into poetry. This vast conflation ensures his failure to distinguish between Old Testament and New Testament modes of *kerygma* (his term).

47 *De Principiis* IV, 2.4–5. See the collection of citations in Balthasar, *Origen*, 86–88, 100–7.

48 De Lubac propounded the patristic idea that the spiritual sense of the Old Testament is the literal sense of the New. This notion has come under criticism from the perspective of Jewish-Christian dialogue. See McKim, *Dictionary of Major Biblical Interpreters*, 685.

49 See Farkasfalvy, *Inspiration and Interpretation*, 219–21.

"Big Picture" and Plenary Perspectives

If the Reformation deeply compromised the strength of a sacramental vision, a univocal "plain sense" of Scripture was the hermeneutical fallout. The mystery of the *body* was reduced to the superficial *species*, while the juncture of letter and spirit (hence the possibility of a grounded spiritual sense) was lost to view. In the increasingly secularized exegesis that followed, the surface itself soon disintegrated—the inevitable fate of a soulless body—so that naivete today means thinking, "Jesus said and did everything that the Gospels have him say and do."[50] The task of anchoring a revelation worthy of faith and recovering a viable literal sense is thus the trick of somehow putting Humpty Dumpty together again—finding some theological soul for the Gospels' dissected body. (The slippery hermeneutical task of holding on to this egg, even as a purely pre-theological project, will be well known to readers of Lewis Carroll: "When I use a word," Humpty Dumpty said in a rather scornful tone, "it means just what I choose it to mean, neither more nor less."[51])

If a fragmentation of meaning, unhinging the corelative spiritual and literal sense, is now an assumed state of affairs, form criticism, let it be said, supplied a powerful impetus toward the Gospels' analytic breakdown.[52] Already with Conzelmann, however, the need to reassemble a coherent textual whole had become clear.[53] *Redaktionsgeschichte*, nonetheless, and the narrative criticism that it has spawned struggle to treat literary unity in a *nonfiction* framework. To this extent, the history question has remained in the custody of form criticism—bound, that is, to "the wrong tool."[54]

It is tempting to make an end run around the issue. We might ask: How does the judgment that the Gospels are *vera historia* apply to individual units of tradition? Might not the Church's doctrine have only the complete genre in view—concerned at root to fend off the extreme challenge of "mythicism"?[55] *Vera historia*, after all, cannot be pushed too far. If errors of fact

---

50 Allison, *The Historical Christ and the Theological Jesus*, 1.

51 Carroll, *Through the Looking Glass*, chap. VI.

52 This notion may be most evident in the least famous of the three cofounders of form criticism, Schmidt, *Der Rahmen der Geschichte Jesu*. Schmidt argued that Mark is a collection of preexisting units held together imperfectly by a secondary structure.

53 See the introductory remarks of Conzelmann, *Theology of St. Luke*, 9–17.

54 See the landmark essay of Hooker, "On Using the Wrong Tool." N. T. Wright correctly observes, "Form-criticism, despite often being treated simply as a tool for discovering about Jesus, is designed primarily to shed light on the early church" (*New Testament and the People of God*, 418).

55 Both the extremity and persistence of the position that the Gospels are *absolute fiction* can be seen in its opposition by as strong a skeptic as Ehrman, *Did Jesus Exist?* Convention-

(e.g., the Lukan census) are alleged but elusively unverifiable,[56] some "apparent history" is surely hosted in the Gospels. The unhistorical "letter" of the parables, for instance, is perfectly uncontroversial.[57]

Such an admission offers little traction, though, since the concern is obviously with the things predicated *of Jesus* (not the characters of his preaching). In this regard, an important narrative claim clearly separates the Synoptic presentation of Jesus' parables (ἐλάλησεν αὐτοῖς πολλὰ ἐν παραβολαῖς) from the purely ahistorical *peje Iesous* found in Thomas.[58] Jesus is said to have really said things. Deeds always envelop words in the Church's Gospels. But this only makes a judgment on the literary pattern of the *chreia* (and other like forms) inescapable.

The interest to know whether such and such a deed really happened (or whether Jesus really spoke such and such a thing) leads to a variety of possibilities. The formidable approach to this question derived from form criticism is to address it at the atomic level. Each concrete pericope comes under its own unique historical judgment. The patient labor of John Meier must stand as the definitive monument to this method (which Caba finds most consonant with *DV* 19).[59]

Meier's conceit of finding consensus in an "unpapal conclave" is (for those uncharmed by subjectivist postmodern agnosticism) a refreshing

---

ally, beginning with the work of D. F. Strauss, a more euhemeristic position is taken, and the mythic texture out of which the Jesus of the Gospels has supposedly been woven is found in the OT. Michael Goulder's high estimate of the creative haggadic content of the Gospels (conceived of as midrash on the Jewish lectionary) represents a contemporary variation on the theme. See, e.g., *Midrash and Lection in Matthew*. Some (self-published) authors search for Gospel motifs well beyond the OT, e.g., D. M. Murdock, *Christ in Egypt*. The recent studies linking the Gospels to Homer represent a less eccentric (but still eccentric) literary thesis, e.g., MacDonald, *Homeric Epics and the Gospel of Mark*. The likeness of the Gospels to Greco-Roman romance has also been promoted. See Bowersock, *Fiction as History*. The Religionsgeschichtliche School, of course, located the fictive setting in the Hellenistic cult. The PBC Instruction certainly leaves this view no space: *Nec propter cultum quo discipuli exinde Iesum ut Dominum et Filium Dei venerabantur, hic in «mythicam» personam mutatus est Eiusque doctrina deformata*. Perhaps Fitzmyer has all this in view when he poses "mythic truth" as the specific opposite of his "Gospel truth."

56 The long-running dispute over Lk 2:1–4 typifies a common problem in assessing much of biblical history: lack of independent evidence, either contradictory or confirmatory. This, naturally, is not unique to events recorded in Scripture. Reason must here be content with converging probabilities. On the census, see Giambrone, "Augustus as Censor."

57 "Sub sensu litterali includitur parabolicus seu metaphoricus" (Aquinas, *Super Galatians*, ch. 4, lectio 7).

58 For a discussion of the present tense translation of *peje Iesous* ("Jesus says"), see Plisch, *Gospel of Thomas*, 24–25. "Even in dialogues, the *Gospel of Thomas* is not interested in the historical background of a reported issue; the focus is exclusively on the Lord's sayings."

59 See Meier, *Marginal Jew*.

blast of old-fashioned Enlightenment optimism—and, in truth, not so distant from the council's intention in choosing *tenere* rather than *credere*.[60] Of course, confidence in *reason* nowhere implies an equal trust in *criteriology*. Indeed, for many today (and for a long time now, in fact) such mechanistic ratiocination is the preciously dangerous shadow side of the "Enlightenment."[61] Moreover, when the exegetical machine starts to spit out returns of *non liquet* and "not historical," not everyone is always ready to swallow the tonic of Bernanos's Doctor Delbende: "Face up to it!" The objections here go deep, and it is no longer enough to deflect the protest as "uncritical."[62]

Plenty might be said about this manner of panning for historical gold, but one result is of special interest. In spite of negative judgments in individual cases, larger patterns of "historicity" have emerged. Meier, for instance, can accept the global assertion of Jesus' identity as a miracle worker—though five hundred pages of minute case studies leave one less sure.[63] If such dissonance undermines the atomistic effort, Dale Allison's decision to abandon the "criteria of authenticity" for big, broad "gist" arguments has clear appeal.[64] The result for Allison is a curious construal of the literal sense as a kind of agnostic allegory of fabricated historical abstractions. The accounts of the Temptation, for instance, present "a narrative about events that probably never happened ... [but] nonetheless rightly catches Jesus in several respects."[65]

Doctrinally, the "big picture" position taken here might be put like this. The Gospels reliably "hand on" (*fideliter tradere*) the whole living mystery of the Christ-event in the same way that Tradition communicates the full substance of the faith—but little "t" traditions, or Gospel pericopes, can come or go. Somehow the discernment of what is majuscule is made, and this

---

60 Meier, *Marginal Jew*, 1:1.

61 In application to the question at hand, see the diversified challenge of Keith and Le Donne, *Jesus and the Demise of Authenticity*.

62 If strong nominalist strains of thought lurk here, "participatory exegesis" will have a contribution to make. See Levering, *Participatory Biblical Exegesis*.

63 Meier, *Marginal Jews*, 2:617–1138. For a critique of Meier's global criterion, see Eve, "Meier, Miracle, and Multiple Attestation."

64 See Allison's (typically) autobiographical essay "It Don't Come Easy," 186–99. See also his fourth and (he says he hopes) final book on Jesus, *Constructing Jesus*: "We should trust first, if we are to trust at all, what is most likely to be trustworthy. This requires that we begin, although we need not end, by asking, 'What are our general impressions?'" (16). The "fact-based" approach of E. P. Sanders can also be mentioned here.

65 "The story ... preserves a series of likely truth about Jesus—that he was a miracle worker, that he refused to give self-authenticating signs, that he thought himself victorious over demonic forces, that he could quote the Bible, and that he had great faith in God" (Allison, "It Don't Come Easy," 191).

or that can be pared away, but the essential integrity of revelation remains unimpaired.

Is one, then, merely accepting that the Gospels are reliable *grosso modo*, affirming a creedal skeleton or historian's précis (*Testimonium Flavianum*)?[66] This flexible commitment would offer insulation against a whole series of tangled textual details. A few nonnegotiable facts can be historically affirmed, while the risk of rude fundamentalism is held at bay. Pope Benedict himself (albeit as a private theologian) seems to point in this minimalist direction, even while underscoring historicity in the second volume of *Jesus of Nazareth*: "Many details may remain open. Yet the *'factum est'* of John's Prologue (1:14) is a basic Christian category, and it applies not only to the Incarnation: it must also be invoked for the Last Supper, the Cross, and the Resurrection."[67]

Caution is necessary, though, on the "open details" Benedict has in mind.[68] His comment is made in preface to a discussion of the difficult dating of the Lord's Last Supper, and, as the PBC Instruction makes plain, *chronology* does not compromise the truth at hand. It is hardly clear, in fact—as more than a few troubled exegetes have complained—that Benedict concedes the evangelists' fabrication of *any* concrete "deeds and words" reported in the Gospels.[69] Indeed, volume 3, on the Infancy Narratives offers the strongest conceivable demonstration of the pope's critically informed yet calmly courageous "fundamentalism."[70] Truly, had the religion reporter for *Time* any

---

66 See, e.g., Tatum, "Limits of Reliability."

67 Ratzinger, *Jesus of Nazareth: Holy Week*, 105.

68 See Benedict's programmatic remarks on faith and historicity at the beginning of *Jesus of Nazareth: From the Baptism in the Jordan to the Transfiguration*, xv-xvi.

69 Maurice Casey, for instance, maintains that Benedict is trapped in circular reasoning, defending the historicity of Jn 19:35 on the presumption that John's Gospel is "literally true from beginning to end," being eyewitness testimony (*Jesus of Nazareth*, 28-29).

70 The best expression of Ratzinger's overall position is articulated in connection with Mt 1-2: "At the end of this lengthy chapter, the question arises: how are we to understand all this? Are we dealing with history that took place, or is it merely a theological meditation, presented under the guise of stories? In this regard, Jean Daniélou rightly observes: 'The adoration of the Magi, unlike the story of the annunciation [to Mary], does not touch upon any essential aspect of our faith. No foundations would be shaken if it were simply an invention of Matthew's based on a theological idea' (*The Infancy Narratives*, p. 95). Daniélou himself, though, comes to the conclusion that we are dealing here with historical events, whose theological significance was worked out by the Jewish Christian community and by Matthew. To put it simply, I share this view. In any case, it should be noted that over the last fifty years there has been an about-turn in thinking on this question of historicity, based not on new historical knowledge, but rather on a changed attitude to sacred Scripture and to the Christian message in general. While Gerhard Delling in the fourth volume of the *Theological Dictionary of*

real nose for theological scandal, the Holy Father's recalcitrant belief in "fairy tales" like the magi and the star would have certainly made the better headline—not a pseudo-story about the imprecision of the Julian calendar ("Pope Benedict Disputes Date of Jesus' Birth").[71]

Benedict, then, conjures a different vision from the "big picture" theory, a vision (unsurprisingly) of patristic pedigree. The dispensable "details" touch the placement and expression, while the *factum est* and the meaning are affirmed.[72] In this line, one could speak of a plenary view of historicity in which problems are admitted on the level of textual arrangement, with full freedom allotted for whatever ingenious solutions one might find. But no separation into piles of "authentic" and "inauthentic" (and "I give up") is ever involved. In distinction from Allison, then, this is not a surrender of concrete deeds for a reasoned belief in dynamic abstractions (e.g., "apocalyptic Judaism"). Meier is right to care about more than vague global assertions. But dared by the legacy of D. F. Strauss to demonstrate point by point that real events lie behind the Gospels, Benedict appears humbly content to dare right back the impossible task of proving a negative (*non factum est*)—reminding proud history of its limits.[73] If the pope rests here and stops short of offering an ambitious *apologia*, perhaps the doctrine of *vera historia* means inviting

---

the New Testament (1942) was still convinced of the historicity of the Magi story on the basis of historical research (cf. p. 358, n. 11), since that time, even exegetes as ecclesially minded as Ernst Nellessen and Rudolf Pesch have rejected historicity, or at least they have let the question open. An interesting comment, in the light of this situation, is the carefully argued position presented by Klaus Berger ... 'Even when there is only a single attestation ... one must suppose, until the contrary is proven, that the evangelists did not intend to deceive their readers, but rather to inform them concerning historical events ... to contest the historicity of this account on mere suspicion exceeds every imaginable competence of historians' (*Kommentar zum Neuen Testament*, p. 20). With this view I can only agree. The two chapters of Matthew's Gospel devoted to the infancy narratives are not a meditation presented under the guise of stories, but the converse: Matthew is recounting real history, theologically thought through and interpreted, and thus he helps us to understand the mystery of Jesus more deeply" (*Jesus of Nazareth: The Infancy Narratives*, 118).

71 Sorcha Pollack, "Pope Benedict Disputes Date of Jesus' Birth," *Time*, November 22, 2012, http://newsfeed.time.com/2012/11/22/pope-benedict-disputes-jesus-date-of-birth/.

72 This is the position of the PBC Instruction, which simply follows the patristic doctrine (citing Chrysostom, and Augustine) in allowing differences in placement and wording. See Origen, *Comm. Jo.*, 10.2–4: The evangelists "sometimes altered things which, from the eye of history, occurred otherwise ... [they] speak of something that happened in one place as if it happened in another, or of what happened at a certain time as if it happened at another time ... [they introduced] into what was spoken in a certain way some changes of their own."

73 Benedict is at ease with the inconclusive nature of much historical controversy, but he is not thereby afraid to make a final judgment. On the Lukan census, for instance, he says: "The discussion could continue indefinitely ... yet the essential content of Luke's narrative remains historically credible all the same" (Ratzinger, *Jesus of Nazareth: The Infancy Narratives*, 63).

an act of credible faith and retying Schweitzer's first of the Gordian knots: the silly supernaturalist versus rationalist controversy.[74]

In highlighting only the cardinal points of Christian confession, then, Benedict chastens history.[75] But this must be carefully understood. He never suggests that faith has been penned up in some creedal Alamo, ready to die in one last stand against the destructive reach of reason. Quite the contrary! The core witness of the Gospels is in a real sense the *most* verifiable material (if not thereby the most likely to sway all historians)—not only the matter dearest to faith.[76] Even so, Benedict warns, the probative power of human science must not be exaggerated: "We may not expect . . . to find absolutely certain proof of every detail."[77] If metaphysical knowledge of necessary truth is vexed by the wounds of original sin, historical reason by its own contingent formal object deals always and only in probabilities, all the more fragile for all sorts of reasons. Much of history simply lies forever beyond our science's grasp.

The pope is not, then, promoting a theory of *obiter dicta*. It is instead a matter of faith and reason mutually tempering one another. Historical criticism, to begin, cannot insist on ever playing the judge, haughtily eschewing the servant's role of illumining the background.[78] In this sense, the reach of faith is in no way limited in its positive assent to the modest "proofs" of

---

[74] Albert Schweitzer related the history of Jesus research as the negotiation of three distinct scholarly dilemmas: supernaturalist or rationalist, Synoptic or Johannine, eschatological or non-eschatological. While the latter two forks were resolved in favor of Synoptic (via Markan priority) and *konsequente Eschatologie*, Strauss exploded the first as a false dichotomy. Naturalist (rationalist) explanations of "miracles" were as dubious as supernatural claims; both falsely assumed the occurrence of a real event. See Dennis Nineham's foreword to the complete edition of Schweitzer, *Quest*, xiii-xxxii.

[75] See Ratzinger, *Jesus of Nazareth: From the Baptism in the Jordan to the Transfiguration*, xv-xvi.

[76] The Last Supper and crucifixion are naturally less controversial as historical events than is the Resurrection, which poses a unique set of problems. If Catholic thinkers like Schillebeeckx and Gerald O'Collins (and John Meier) have ruled the Resurrection to be an eschatological event and consequently out of bounds in the study of history, Benedict at least concludes otherwise (with nuance). "The Resurrection does not simply stand outside or above history. As something that breaks out of history and transcends it, the Resurrection nevertheless has its origin within history and up to a certain point still belongs there. Perhaps we could put it this way: Jesus' Resurrection points beyond history but has left a footprint within history" (Ratzinger, *Jesus of Nazareth: Holy Week*, 275). For a powerful attempt at verifying this "footprint," see Wright, *Resurrection of the Son of God*, and Licona, *Resurrection of Jesus*.

[77] Ratzinger, *Jesus of Nazareth: Holy Week*, 105.

[78] One might consider here the works of Martin Hengel, whose erudite and dignified humanism represents a different model of history in NT scholarship than the narrow "authenticity" arbitrations of so many historical Jesus scholars: an estimable model at once more and less subservient to the interests of faith.

science. The ample use of the *non liquet* card is an open invitation to faith.[79] At the same time, the serene confidence essential to faith never tempts it to act as a superhuman surrogate for plodding, mental labor, which retains its proper scope of judgment entirely unimpaired. Human *ratio* deepens (rather than "purifies") faith's delicate conviction, gives it new dimension, by drawing it ever more into the light of understanding from the dark seat of *memoria* where God touches the mind. Properly ordered theological faith, therefore, informed as it is by the *analogia fidei* and composed by the hierarchy of truths, never swells with ill-proportioned insight or dissipates itself through undue interest in things not *revelata a Deo*. It understands that the Incarnation weighs more than the visit of the magi. Yet, thus balanced in judgment, it also knows that no "jot or tittle" is incidental. God's revelation is the ultimate measure of what man must believe—must believe for his own temporal and eternal blessing. If mystical gifts would disclose the sorts of details historians might long to know—say, that the flight into Egypt "took place in February, six days after the purification"[80]—it is enough to remark that one does not find here *veritatem, quam Deus nostrae salutis causa Litteris Sacris consignari voluit*.

Memory, Faith, and Genre

If the biblical guild can detect in Benedict anything other than a fundamentalist, he will appear unsatisfying, inscrutable, or like the curious sighting of some "premodern" animal presumed to have been long extinct.[81] In any case, where the issue has any interest, the respectable "big picture" view controls the day. A trend, or rather a cluster of trends, to note in connection with this theory is the recent rise of interest in "memory."[82] Great diversity

---

79 The objection is inevitably raised that this is a feebleminded "God of the gaps" posture, but the charge here is a rhetorical show of force. The identification of historiographical "gaps" generously recognizes the expanding conquests of historical science. The issue is more fundamental, addressing both the methodological atheism presumed by modern historians and the inherent limits of the discipline. See the suggestive (but not unproblematic) essay by Ross McCullough, "God and the Gaps."
80 Mary of Agreda, *Mystical City of God*, Bk. 4, ch. 8.
81 See, e.g., the critiques and complaints in reviews of volume one of *Jesus of Nazareth* by Luke Timothy Johnson (in *Modern Theology*) and Richard Hays (in *First Things*). N. T. Wright allows that "many ... will inevitably see [Benedict's work] as a step backwards, to a premodern, pre-critical reading" (*Times Literary Supplement*).
82 See Allison, *Constructing Jesus*, 1–30, 387–462. See also, e.g., Dunn, *Jesus Remembered*, 881–94; Bauckham, *Jesus and the Eyewitnesses*, 319–57; Le Donne, *Historiographical Jesus*; Keith, "Memory and Authenticity"; and especially the significant work of McIver, *Memory, Jesus, and*

still darkens this methodological jungle, but important insights are also present. Generally accurate in the main points but fuzzy on the details, memory has accordingly emerged in Gospel studies as a great theological hope for many, an overdue correction of form criticism (which was not uninterested in memory in its own fashion) and a way, ultimately, to pull together the evangelists' scrambled witness.

In view of this, it is of interest what attention *Sancta Mater Ecclesia* gives to the notion. The key idea has unfortunately been distorted: "The life and teaching of Jesus were not simply related so as to be remembered (*eo solo fine ut memoria tenerentur*): they were 'preached' to provide the basis of faith and morals for the Church."[83] As translated here in a blurry, unhelpful way, the statement would warn against overly rigid models of mnemonic transmission and put too disjunctive a stress on kerygmatic creativity.[84] It is clear from the document, however, that "faith by no means obliterated the memory of the events which had taken place. On the contrary, it reinforced these memories, because it rested on the things which Jesus had taught and done."[85] If this is true, and if *kerygma* and recollection are not operative in inverse proportion, the move to memory must be welcomed as a real advance—or, rather, recovery. The great merit of this paradigm is that it personalizes the process of transmission.[86]

---

the Synoptic Gospels. See now also the fairly comprehensive overview of Havukainen, *Quest for the Memory of Jesus*. In the end Havukainen himself concludes: "The memory approach offers ways forward for historical Jesus research. While the memory approach displays a methodological shift in the sense that it redefines the language and categories used about the Jesus traditions, due to the methodological diversity, one ought to refrain from declaring it a new beginning for historical Jesus research (let alone 'the Fourth Quest')" (297).

83 This is the misleading translation found in Murphy's compendium, *The Church and the Bible*. The document stresses that the purpose was not only / for the sole purpose of being remembered. "Cum ex eis quae novae inquisitiones contulerunt appareat doctrinam et vitam Iesu non simpliciter relatas fuisse, eo solo fine ut memoria tenerentur, sed «praedicatas» fuisse ita ut Ecclesiae fundamentum fidei et morum praeberent."

84 The work of Birger Gerhardsson should be mentioned. See *Memory and Manuscript, Origins of the Gospel Traditions*, and *Reliability of the Gospel Tradition*. See also McIver (*Memory, Jesus, and the Synoptic Gospels*, 167, 187), who speaks of mnemotechniques and "near verbatim accuracy." The PBC leaves the disciples' memory very much intact and even suggests a pedagogy reminiscent of Gerhardsson's rabbinic model (i.e., "firmly impressed...and easily remembered"): "Dominus, cum doctrinam ore exponebat, modos ratiocinandi et exponendi tunc temporis vulgatos sequebatur, ita ad mentem auditorum Se accommodans et efficiens ut ea quae doceret firmiter menti imprimerentur et commode a discipulis memoria tenerentur."

85 *Dei Verbum* also endorsed such language, speaking plainly of evangelists working *ex sua propria memoria et recordatio* (*DV* 19).

86 Martin Hengel has vigorously critiqued the anonymous tradition model, an issue signaled out by the PBC, rightly insisting on "the personal link of the Jesus tradition with particular tradents" (*Four Gospels*, 146).

If Fitzmyer hesitates about historicity with his murky proposal of "Gospel truth," like many he hesitates precisely at this point, hardening the disjunction between memory and kerygma. As a hedge against the difficulties of positive (asseverative) inerrancy, of course, this systematic deference to the preaching of "faith and morals" cannot entail a limiting of the formal object of inerrant revelation.[87] If by "Gospel truth," then, Fitzmyer means that the four Gospels comprise a unique literary form, possessing its own hermeneutical canons, the premise is *in principle* perfectly sound. Attention to literary conventions has been the Church's preferred response in this sensitive apologetic area in every relevant document since *Providentissimus Deus*.

The difficulty is in practice, not in theory.[88] Bultmann had pushed the claim that the Gospels were not biographies but *sui generis* faith productions.[89] His folkloric contention, however, assumed an anachronistic concept of biography (among other faulty assumptions), and since the work of Richard Burridge on ancient *bioi*, Bultmann's credibility on this point has unraveled.[90] The growing edge of Gospel research now sees the Gospels as far less determined by the needs of local communities than once assumed, while the evangelists' interest in recounting real events has become increasingly hard to deny.[91] A range of mimetic modes is indeed discernible in the Gospels, yet their literary originality is bound to historical seriousness as a basic datum.[92]

The Lukan preface merits a central place in this discussion, for it has become clear that his formal style and appeal to autopsy have their cultural and literary context in Greco-Roman historiography.[93] Though Luke

---

87 On the systematic question, see Zarafa, "Limits of Biblical Inerrancy." One may legitimately wonder whether Fitzmyer's reading simply anticipates the widely received distortion of *DV* 11. On the correct interpretation of this important text, see Marchetto, *Il Concilio Ecumenico Vaticano II*, 453–58 (chap. 30); and Pitre, "Mystery of God's Word."

88 See Diehl, "What Is a Gospel?" Diehl distinguishes between an analogical and derivational approach to the question of genre, allowing analogical affinities to the canonical Gospels but upholding their derivational originality.

89 The original influence of this thesis owes much to Schmidt, "Die Stellung der Evangelien," 50–134.

90 Burridge, *What Are the Gospels?* In the foreword to the second edition, Graham Stanton remarks, "Over the last decade or so, very few books on the Gospels have been discussed more widely or have influenced scholarly opinion more strongly."

91 See Bauckham, *Gospels for All Christians*; Klink, *Audience of the Gospels*. See also Hengel, "Sources of Earliest Christianity," 33–34, an essay on some first principles of NT historiography that should be mandatory reading.

92 See the innovative study of Taylor (*Treatment of Reality in the Gospels*) that explores Auerbach's claim that the Gospels transgress the ancient "separation of styles."

93 See chaps. 3 and 5 in this volume. For a summary of research, see Rothschild, *Luke-Acts*, 32–59. See also Aune, "Luke 1:1–4." Aune wishes to indicate that Luke's preface likely resembles

alone of the evangelists postures as an historian, it is enough that he does.[94] The formal congruence of the synoptic Gospels implies a kind of transitive *asphaleia*. As a dutiful historian, Luke assures his readers of the material they might find in Matthew and Mark.[95] Luke himself plainly recognizes his special role among the "many" who have undertaken the task of telling this story, and he sees his particular purpose in drawing up a *careful ordering* (ἀκριβῶς καθεξῆς γράψαι) of the events.

The irony of this purpose is that, at ground level, Luke's order is considered primitive and unclear.[96] While grand geographic and temporal patterns do give an intelligible, architectonic shape to the Lukan message, the way smaller units are collated can seem almost haphazard. Here Bultmann's hand becomes much stronger. Plainly, the microunits of tradition were not hammered out in the same school as the learned Lukan prologue.

One thing to be said here concerns the "Eucharistic provenance" of the Gospels.[97] Even if his explanation of the title *ho erchomenos* faces certain problems, Dennis Farkafalvy's cultic plotting of a primitive stage of the Gospels' crafting is an old idea (e.g., Dibelius) that remains in its broad lines attractive and helpful: "The consistent portrayal of Jesus as the one *coming and being encountered* [in Gospel pericopes] originates in the way memories about him were recalled, told, and retold in the presence of cultic (Eucharistic) congregations, gatherings held for the purpose of reliving the past encounters."[98] Accordingly, though one does not find in Luke (or any of the Gospels) a disciplined effort to grasp the inner connections of discrete events, such chronological inattention preserves the elemental structure of

---

"the hundreds of lost mediocre histories" and that it is misleading to gauge it only against the standard of the best Hellenistic exemplars. That the preface may be a work of "mediocre" quality, though, should not obscure its classification as *haute littérature* (at least in pretension). For the classical mind, it was the theme that determined stylistic elevation, and of Luke's theme there can be little doubt. The evangelist consciously presents his work as a thing serious and significant in the manner of a history, for history alone could bear the magnitude of "the events fulfilled among us" (Lk 1:1). On the Greco-Roman background, see Nenci, "Il motivo dell'autopsia nella storagraphia greca"; and especially Schepens, *L'"autopsie."*

94 This is not to deny the important historical concerns (and methods) of the other evangelists. See, e.g., Bauckham, "Historiographical Aspects."

95 Commentators have at times detected a note of criticism in Luke's mention of his predecessors, and such judgments were a trope in Greco-Roman historiography. For other authors, however, the polemic is much more open and unmistakable, e.g., Josephus, *B.J.* 1.1. See Marincola, *Authority and Tradition in Ancient Historiography*, 218–25.

96 Lukan order is commonly accepted as more nearly approximating the order of Q than is Matthean order.

97 See Farkasfalvy, *Inspiration and Interpretation*, 65–79; also Benoit, "Réflexions," 487.

98 Farkasfalvy, *Inspiration and Interpretation*, 74 (cf. 72n21).

the Jesus tradition as sacramental *anamnesis*.⁹⁹ To this degree, the *cultivated* memory that undergirds the Gospels responds directly to the Lord's command (*hoc facite in meum commemorationem*). It is not free fabrication.¹⁰⁰ Form critical insight into anonymous communal productions here finds its genuine but circumscribed force, as well as its correct ecclesial *Sitz-im-Leben*. It is a communal reception of personal witness.¹⁰¹

If the cultic molding of the primitive tradition indeed preserved the "*hypomnemata* of the apostles,"¹⁰² other portions of the Gospels do not betray the same origin. The Infancy Narratives, in particular, stand apart. While the expressions of Christology are pronounced in these cherished episodes, the form is different, actors other than the sacramental Lord (*ho erchomenos*) enjoy prominence, and the stories are widely seen as mere "vehicles for the evangelist's theology."¹⁰³ Yet notice has long been made that "Luke indicates from time to time that Mary, the Mother of Jesus, is herself one of his sources."¹⁰⁴ This "uncritical" position has, of course, (less) long been ridiculed as a pious (Catholic) fantasy. The model of Mary's deepening memory (Lk 2:51) is viable, however—as credible, at least, as any "Baptist source"—and more than piety is at stake.¹⁰⁵ Ultimately, a decision between the "big picture" and plenary views is closely bound to one's decision about *personal* Gospel sources.

The Third Gospel sets the parameters in which *historica veritas* must be conceived, but it is the Fourth Gospel where the issue is decided. In John, the unmistakable claim to eyewitness knowledge is melded with the most robust expression of introspective memory: the "Marian" model rigorously extended.¹⁰⁶ Such a conjunction of *witness* and *interpretation* has proven too

---

99 Discrete anecdotal ordering is characteristic of much ancient biography and represents the literary crystallization of the basic impact of the documented personality. See Hengel, "Sources of Earliest Christianity," 15–18.

100 For a wide-ranging rebuttal of the form critical canard that nameless Christian prophets were a factory of dominical *logia*, see Aune, *Prophecy in Early Christianity*.

101 On the simultaneously cultic and apostolic character of the formation of Gospel traditions, see especially chap. 4 in this volume (cf. chap. 3).

102 Justin, *First Apology*, 66.3, also 33.5; cf. *Dialogue with Trypho* 100.4, 101.3, 102.5, etc. See also Papias's description of Mark's Gospel (*H.E.* 3.39.15) and the language employed by Clement of Alexandria (*H.E.* 2.15.1).

103 Brown, *Birth of the Messiah*, 37.

104 Ratzinger, *Jesus of Nazareth: The Infancy Narratives*, 16.

105 See most recently Dillon, *Hymns of Saint Luke*, 5–14, 50, who speaks of "members of the Baptist diaspora" as the source of the Baptist nativity material but never considers pre-Lukan sources that might inform the Jesus strand.

106 See the remarks of Ratzinger: "What John says in his Gospel about how remembering becomes understanding and the path 'into all truth' comes very close to what Luke recounts about remembering on the part of Jesus' mother" (*Jesus of Nazareth: From the Baptism in the Jordan to the Transfiguration*, 233–34).

hard to swallow. As its first step in the classic *Quest of the Historical Jesus*, scholarship accordingly decided not to go down the Johannine road.[107] A new generation of scholars has begun to question this fundamental axiom, however.[108]

In any case, the council's perspective is clear from the final sentence of *DV* 19. There a distinction is drawn between those evangelists "who relied on their own memory and recollection" (making room here beside John for the traditional identity of Matthew as an apostle) and those who depended on "the eyewitnesses from the beginning" (meaning Mark and Luke).[109] Evangelists without some access to direct witness are not envisioned.

"Eyewitnesses from the Beginning"

The PBC Instruction posited three stages of Gospel tradition: the preaching of Jesus, the preaching of his apostles, and the literary activity of the four evangelists. If the innovation of this arrangement was the careful (some would say "arbitrary") distinction between periods two and three,[110] this schema is not, contrary to common opinion, ever attributed to the insights of the form critical method. All three are found explicitly in the Lukan framework: (1) all that Jesus did and taught (Acts 1:1), (2) the things handed down (*paradosis*) by the *autoptai* and ministers of the word (Lk 1:2), and (3) the undertaking to draw up a *diegesis* (Lk 1:1, 3).

If all three *tempora* reappear (without special flagging) in *Dei Verbum*, in the full doctrine of the council, Stage Two (*paradosis*) attains an unmistakable prominence. This is a key point that Caba and others miss at great cost. The clear affirmation in §18 of the Gospel's "apostolic origin" (*origine apostolica*) is only part of the council's interest in this theme, which has its

---

[107] The decisive impetus again came from D. F. Strauss, who managed to overmaster the influence of Schleiermacher's predilection for John. See Schweitzer, *Quest*, 80–83.

[108] See, e.g., Blomberg, *Historical Reliability of John's Gospel*. A variety of factors have turned scholars in this direction, not least of which is the growing fund of hard-boiled, archeological evidence. See Charlesworth, "Historical Jesus in the Fourth Gospel." See also chaps. 4 and 12 in this volume.

[109] A distinction in status was implicit in this distinction of credentials: "Cur quatuor evangelistae non per quator apostolos scribuntur, nisi per duos discipulos et duos apostolos? Quia filii Jacob de duabus liberis et duabus ancillis nati sunt" (Ps. Jerome, *Expositio quattuor evangeliorum*, PL 30, 567–77). The particular popularity of the Gospels of Matthew and John in the early Church no doubt owes much to their apostolic credentials. See Massaux, *Influence de l'Évangile de Saint Matthieu*.

[110] See the analysis of Orchard, "*Dei Verbum* and the Synoptic Gospels." The conflating of these stages took hold before 1964. See the revealing piece of Stanley, "New Understanding of the Gospels."

more important exposition in chapter II, on the Transmission of Divine Revelation. Apostolic preaching thus represents the crucial point of intersection that links the dogmatic constitution's two poorly integrated blocks in *DV* 1–2 and *DV* 3–5.[111] The affirmation itself, along with the direct identification of the sacred authors as apostles and *apostolici viri* (meaning Mark and Luke as the respective associates of the apostles Peter and Paul), represents, of course, an obvious element in the claim to historical truth.[112] It is no surprise, then, that the doctrinal precursors to this article were originally forged during the heat of the (first) Modernist crisis, in the notorious PBC *responsa*.

Much might be said about this embarrassing magisterial corpus, but only one point is necessary here. The Biblical Commission—followed implicitly by the council's preparatory Theological Commission and then the full body of council fathers—reckoned the writing of the Gospels by "the authors whose names they bear" as a revealed truth to be firmly accepted de fide.[113] If de facto the question of authorship has long since fallen into the scientific jurisdiction of the *Einleitungen*, in the mind of the PBC, "the universal and unwavering agreement," indeed "the continual, universal and solemn tradition of the Church," authoritatively settles the point. It is noteworthy in judging the rare force of this language that, by way of contrast, the PBC never made such a confident, or rather *obliging, certain affirmation* (*certo affirmare cogat*) of the "clear judgment of tradition" (*luculentum traditionis suffragium*) when addressing, for instance, the issue of Mosaic authorship of the Pentateuch. (One must note here the ignorant but persistent habit of lampooning the *responsum* genre as a regressive, repressive instrument lack-

---

[111] On this tension in the document, see Farkasfalvy, *Inspiration and Interpretation*, 168–202.

[112] The wording of *DV* 18 resumes the precise formulation of the discarded schema but significantly alters the final portion.

De fontibus revelationis 19	*Dei Verbum* 18
Quattor Evangelia apostolicam originem habere Ecclesia Dei semper et ubique sine dubitatione credidit et credit, constanterque tenuit ac tenet auctores humanos habere illos quorum nomina in Sacrorum Librorum canone gerunt: Mattheaum nempe, Marcum, Lucam et Ioannem, quem diligebat Iesus.	Quattuor Evangelia originem apostolicam habere Ecclesia semper et ubique tenuit ac tenet. Quae enim Apostoli ex mandato Christi praedicaverunt, postea divino afflante Spiritu, in scriptis, ipsi et apostolici viri nobis tradiderunt, fidei fundamentum, quadriforme nempe Evangelium, secundum Matthaeum, Marcum, Lucam et Ioannem.

[113] Augustine Bea's commentary on *Dei Verbum* (*Word of God and Mankind*, 240) provides privileged insight into the council fathers' thinking. He distinguishes between the "authenticity" of the Gospels ("that is, that they were written by the authors whose names they bear") and their "apostolic origin," and, without suggesting any doubt about the former (which is clearly articulated as doctrine in *De fontibus* 19), allows that *Dei Verbum* deals only with the "essential points": apostolic origin and historical truth.

ing all nuance.) In 1962, in fact, the debate of the drafting committee made explicit that Mosaic authorship had status as *sententia communis* but was not to be regarded (like Gospel authorship) as *traditio*.[114] Accordingly, and significantly, the PBC's much more cautiously circumscribed 1906 pronouncements on the Pentateuch never surfaced in the preconciliar schema's chapter *De Vetere Testamento*—quite in contrast to the *responsa* on the Gospels.[115] Moreover, the claim about the Gospels' origin was never *probatur ex traditione* in the errant sense undermined by the council, that is, by an incidental catena of proof texts or appeal to some "secret" stream of knowledge. It is presented, rather, as a robust expression of the Church's full living commitment, integrally and implicitly transmitted by liturgy, councils, popes, canons, the fathers, ecclesiastics, and the like. Vincent of Lérins and Congar might equally agree. The Biblical Commission's vigorous avowal of the Gospels' origin, then, was not the mere bluster of reactionary "intransigence" but a forceful, self-conscious, and mature doctrinal proposition. So it was both proffered and received.[116] This, I think, helps us evaluate the variegated magisterial weight of the PBC *responsa*.[117]

The question then becomes what to make of this. Plainly, it is a teaching that the academy has not received. Indeed, after 1965, in the blink of an eye, the two-source hypothesis—which has no place for Matthean eyewitness—came to prevail in Catholic scholarship.[118] Whether or not this hasty develop-

---

114 See Schelkens, *Catholic Theology of Revelation*, 152–53.

115 A growing recognition of the limited relevance of the *responsa* began to emerge in the years prior to the council. In 1955, a quiet policy announced by the secretary of the PBC encouraged exegetes to proceed in *aller Freiheit*, treating earlier pronouncements as the quaint relics of a difficult crisis now passed. See Athanaius Miller, "Das neue biblische Handbuch." Although this perspective was never openly authorized (preserving curial *bella figura*), the Theological Commission, which drafted the preparatory chapter in 1962 (and certainly knew the mind of the Magisterium), studiously mined the PBC documents in preparing chapter IV on the New Testament yet conspicuously neglected the same corpus in preparing chapter III on the Old Testament. Such an embrace of the full discretionary liberty to disregard the *responsa* makes the free endorsement in the case of the Gospels enormously suggestive. On the status of Miller's "clarification," see the personal account of J. E. Steinmueller (*Sword of the Spirit*, 7), who reports that Miller's action was condemned by the voting cardinals of the PBC who sought to bring him before the Holy Office.

116 The language of universal Tradition in *DV* 18 is emphatic and overt: "semper et ubique tenuit ac tenet."

117 The *responsa* represent a provisional magisterial act of "pastoral prudence," but they are not set aside *tout court*. See then-Cardinal Ratzinger's authoritative explanation of *The Ecclesial Vocation of the Theologian*: "Their core remains valid, but the individual details influenced by the circumstances at the time may need further rectification."

118 The movement in this direction began before the council, of course, and the last significant Catholic defense of Matthean apostolic authorship was Bishop Butler's 1951 book *Originality*

ment was precipitous or overdue, it simply borrowed the results of Protestant scholarship. No distinct Catholic debate ever transpired. The remarkable legacy of figures like Lagrange and Vaganay was casually laid aside like some obtuse Ptolemaic astronomy, an embarrassing and overburdened exegesis contorted by extraneous ecclesial commitments.[119] (The infamous successor project of Marie-Émile Boismard and Arnaud Lamouille *is* an embarrassing and obtuse Ptolemaic undertaking, but certainly not on account of a cramped ecclesial vision—on the contrary!—but for independent and idiosyncratic reasons that never implicate the earlier efforts of the French school.) The irony, of course, is that 1964 (the year of the PBC Instruction) saw William Farmer, the great (Protestant) champion of the neo-Griesbach hypothesis, first question Holtzmann's long-held dogma of Markan priority.[120] If today the Q hypothesis is thus facing a growing wave of scrutiny and skepticism, this has not been a Catholic crusade.[121]

It is difficult to say what is emerging here. There are zealots on both sides, yet even dogmatic adherents of Q are quietly softening their positions.[122] Pierre Benoit predicted early on that form criticism would ultimately undo the two-source hypothesis.[123] The key challenge, in any event, is articulating a firm doctrine of apostolic origin that manages to avoid meddling too much in the mechanics of the synoptic problem, and at the same time addresses the synoptic problem with honest attention to the Gospels' apostolic origin.[124]

---

of St. Matthew, recently reissued. Less than five years after the council (1968), Frederick Gast's article in the original *Jerome Biblical Commentary* calmly pronounced Markan priority the uncontroversial majority view. Lagrange (*La méthod historique*, 249) had already described the two-source hypothesis as *généralement admi*se in 1903, but this estimate clearly indicates a continental, i.e., German Protestant, consensus. Streeter's important monograph would not convince the Anglophone world until 1924. On Catholic interest in Markan priority, see Verbin, *Excavating Q*, 321–25.

119 For diagrams of the complex solutions proposed by Lagrange and Vaganay, see Verbin, *Excavating Q*, 45, 318.

120 See Farmer, *Synoptic Problem*. Farmer suggests that the triumph of Holtzmann's thesis of Markan priority had much to do with the Catholic-Protestant polemics of the *Kulturkampf*. See Verbin, *Excavating Q*, 312–21.

121 See, e.g., Watson, *Gospel Writing*; Goodacre, *Case against Q*; Peabody et al., *One Gospel from Two*; Dunn, *Jesus Remembered*, 147–60; and Dunn, "Q^1 as Oral Tradition."

122 Even Koester (*Ancient Christian Gospels*, 318) is ready to concede that "the name Matthew may have been connected" with the Synoptic Sayings Source. In this line, Viviano ("Who Wrote Q?") has also proposed regarding Q as the notebook (*pinax*) of the apostle Matthew—a conservative theory startlingly close to Robert Gundry's defense of the traditional authorship of the First Gospel, a conservative tour de force that predictably found no wide reception.

123 Benoit, "Réflexions," 483.

124 The PBC's 1912 pronouncement on the synoptic problem (*AAS* 4 [1912]: 465) articulates the range of issues to be considered before exegetes "discuss freely" various possible solutions.

Standing in the dock, of course, are many highly attenuated interpretations of "apostolicity." *Sancta Mater Ecclesia* had warned of minimizing the *munus* of the apostles, and it is pure illusion to pretend this has not happened, or that this has not had a massive practical effect. The stakes are high, and it is no coincidence that Matthean scholarship specifically has gone the way of the Fourth Gospel, with the tax collector dissolving into the reconstructed fog of a community in contest with the synagogue.[125]

As an individual, Luke is much easier to spot than Matthew. Luke speaks directly in the first person. An older Fitzmyer, in his two-volume commentary, thus mounts a substantial case that the author of the Third Gospel is indeed none other than "the traditional Luke, a sometime companion of Paul."[126] Then, in the next breath, the exegete volunteers that this "makes little difference to the interpretation of the Lucan Gospel." The simple question is: *Why not*? Why do an introduction's theses on audience have such profound interpretative value, while the *veri auctores* themselves are of so emphatically little concern? It is true that the evangelists hide themselves to a considerable degree—though this posture may be deceptively unassuming.[127] Their sheer proximity to "the things fulfilled among us" (Lk 1:1), however, demands more thoughtful attention.

Richard Bauckham has amply shown how provocative serious consideration of the claim to eyewitness sources might be.[128] If Bauckham's work has met a mixed reception, with Catholics not always eager to embrace his vision, I would argue that, although there are plenty of places for legitimate disagreement, his work allows and invites us to recover the occluded teaching of Vatican II. Most importantly, perhaps, his attempt to find in *testimony* the place where history and theology meet recognizes the space defined by facticity (*factum est*) and meaning as the substantial locus of Gospel *asphaleia*. Of course, he only pursues here what the PBC claimed

---

[125] The "Johannine Question" is therefore as critical here as the synoptic problem. See Brown, *Community of the Beloved Disciple*; and especially Hengel, *Die johanneische Frage*.

[126] Fitzmyer, *Gospel According to Luke I-IX*, 35–52.

[127] The demographics of the "audience" are not announced either, but that has not deterred ingenious exegetes. On "hidden" authors, see Baum, "Anonymity of the New Testament History Books."

[128] Bauckham, *Jesus and the Eyewitnesses*. Reaction to Bauckham's controversial thesis has been predictably lively and sharp. See, e.g., Rodgers, "Review of *Jesus and the Eyewitnesses*"; Redman, "How Accurate Are Eyewitnesses?"; Bechard, "Review of *Jesus and the Eyewitnesses*"; Schröter, "Gospels as Eyewitness Testimony?"; Evans, "Implications of Eyewitness Tradition." See especially the entire volume *JSHJ* 6, no. 2 (2008), including Bauckham, "In Response to My Respondents: *Jesus and the Eyewitnesses* in Review," 225–53. Also Bauckham, "Eyewitnesses and Critical History."

belonged to be "the sound principles of the historical method." It is incidental that it conforms also to Catholic doctrine. It is no surprise for those guided by Catholic sensibilities, though, when Bauckham both rehabilitates in the testimony of Papias a once-prized resource in Catholic exegesis and erects with his body of eyewitnesses what one scholar dubs "a Protestant form of apostolic succession"—a quasi-magisterial agency that faithfully guards and transmits the deposit.[129]

The special interest this idea holds is in surmounting the paradigm of the *duplex fons* and exposing the point where the divine impulse behind Tradition and Scripture coheres. If this structure approximates the basic Catholic view and ably cuts the legs from under rationalistic *Formgeschichte*, one could lament that it took fifty years and an Anglican to evoke the Church's vision. As with the ongoing liturgical reform, however, or the still broadly untested norms of exegesis urged in *DV* 12, implementation of the council's vision requires patience.

Conclusion

The doctrine of *DV* 19 reaffirms traditional teaching. (People at times can forget that this is what ecumenical councils do.) This implies substantial continuity with the magisterial pronouncements of the PBC, a point that has not been acknowledged—understandably, perhaps, given the uneven value of this highly contextualized material. The council's vision nonetheless offers more than repetition without reform, for it also goes *ad fontes*, offering the Church the (re)sources of divine revelation to renew itself root and stock. In this way, specifically Lukan parameters are found for addressing the issue of historical truth. The three *tempora* are an important component of this, but of greatest significance is the matter of apostolic eyewitness. In this regard, it is critical not to overstate the Church's investment in form criticism (and its methodological descendants), simply because this school helped the Church recognize the special importance of the threefold layering of tradition. The magisterium made a gesture of goodwill toward German exegesis but never irrevocably linked arms. In the postconciliar experiment, however, there has been little diversity in the matter of exegetical method, and some less acceptable assumptions of the form critics have become deeply entrenched. As part of this, the issue of apostolicity was allowed to vanish from practical consideration: a circumstance that has strongly promoted a soupy view (to put it mildly) of the Gospels' historicity.

---

129 Tatum, "Limits of Reliability," 524.

The present direction of Gospel scholarship suggests the wisdom of more clearly disentangling the Church's exegesis from the rationalistic principles still inherent in redaction criticism and criteriology. *Historica veritas*, in the end, cannot be so easily siphoned off as a scientifically controllable problem. The temptation in this direction is multifaceted, and it was a fateful rendering of the Latin Gospels to intellectualize *asphaleia* (not *aleitheia*!) as *veritas*. For Luke, though, this "reliability" is first of all confirmatory and fiducial. Faith and reason must, then, collaborate here more than they have done. The council fathers envisioned a *both/and* approach to the problem (*fide et ratione*), despite the particular need to accent reason (*non tantum fide*). This means recovering a non-rationalist (pre-Enlightenment? postmodern?) historical sensibility, above all, I might suggest, by more closely studying and understanding the patristic tolerance (and limits) of Gospel *disharmony*: reverse engineering in some way projects like Augustine's *De Consensu*. Moderating the illusory claims of positivistic history (*wie es eigentlich gewesen ist*) is, of course, indispensable too.

If the "Quest for the Historical Jesus" has advanced by always "taking one or other of two alternatives,"[130] the Church, with its famous instinct for the both/and sees this protocol as a record of dangerous neglect. To reverse the course is hard, surely, but on one front there are promising signs. Perhaps the way forward will rejoin a road not taken, for some in the academy are now turning again toward John. This must challenge our whole manner of imagining history and seeking the *vera et sincera de Iesu*.[131]

The teaching of Vatican II on the historical truth of the Gospels belongs to that significant portion of *Dei Verbum* that "still awaits completion."[132] *Sancta Mater Ecclesia* spoke truly: "There will never be an end to [biblical] problems," but "the Catholic exegete should never lose heart." With this in mind, we may express a glad hope that, even after fifty years, the council's

---

130 Schweitzer, *Quest*, xvii.

131 I would like to mention here the exegetical work of Marie-Joseph Lagrange, whose prescience, piety, and erudition can still shine as a guiding star as we continue to navigate the long wake of the storm he courageously weathered. (Another anniversary was quietly marked in 2012: the centenary of what Lagrange simply called "L'année terrible.") It is unfortunate, perhaps, that Pope Benedict missed the chance to commend Lagrange's example in his *Jesus of Nazareth* series; the evocation of figures like Guardini and Daniel-Rops indicates that his ultimate inspiration lay outside professional exegesis. Conversely, Ratzinger disavows any attempt to write a "Life of Christ" and points us instead to Thomas's *Tertia Pars* (*Jesus of Nazareth: Holy Week*, xvi). In thus offering a kind of "theological treatise on the mysteries of the life of Christ," the emeritus pontiff approaches in some ways the rare vision of Lagrange, who had the profound wisdom to understand *why* "The Gospels themselves are the only lives of Jesus that can be written" (Lagrange, *L'Évangile de Jesus Christ*).

132 Farkasfalvy, *Inspiration and Interpretation*, 168.

sacred work still requires *periti*. For, in the abundance of the Holy Spirit's gift to the Church, a special joy belongs also to those who never knew the first thrill of *aggiornamento*. The call to renewal also touches our hearts, a generation grateful to be the living first fruits of the Second Vatican Council.

CHAPTER 2

The German Roots of Historical Jesus Research

Albert Schweitzer's beguiling *Forschungsbericht*, famous in English as the *Quest of the Historical Jesus*, is not simply a landmark chronicle of his predecessors' research nor an announcement of the end of a failed modern form of thought: the death of the so-called Liberal *Vermittlungstheologie*.[1] The work is also a creative theological enterprise and one enormous *apologia pro opere suo*. Indeed, it is Schweitzer's considered attempt to inscribe himself as a champion within the history of Christian thought. It was no idle ambition. The musical, ethical, and intellectual virtuoso of Alsace and the African missions animates an extraordinary cult of exegetical hero-worship: he is, as Francis Watson says, "the patron saint of twentieth century historical Jesus scholarship."[2]

The *Quest* is thus far from a religiously or rhetorically innocent review of literature. Appropriations of the text have, by contrast, been "historiographically and hermeneutically naive," as several recent authors declare.[3] In what follows, I wish to help critically distance future scholarship from the set agenda of Schweitzer's project, with the corollary aim of problematizing the widespread "Three Quests" heuristic, so dependent upon him.

---

1 Schweitzer, *Quest*, 1. Cf. idem, *Von Reimarus zu Wrede* and *Geschichte der Leben-Jesu-Forschung*.
2 Watson, "Eschatology and the Twentieth Century," 335.
3 "Most presentations of the historical Jesus remain historiographically and hermeneutically naïve." Blanton et al., *Jesus beyond Nationalism*, 2. See also Thate, *Remembrance of Things Past?*; and Gathercole, "Critical and Dogmatic Agenda." "A century after Schweitzer's survey of life-of-Jesus scholarship was transformed into a 'quest of the historical Jesus' for the benefit of English-speaking readers, there is need for critical distance from this spell-binding work" (Watson, "Eschatology and the Twentieth Century," 347).

After first probing the book's ambition, heroes, and historical frame, I will work to expose the strongly marked German Protestant social location of Schweitzer's presentation by calling to witness one of the earliest, most complete, most reactive, yet widely neglected receptions of his work: Marie-Joseph Lagrange's *Le sens du christianisme d'après l'exégèse allemande* (1918). The very different though no less contextualized socioreligious location of this French Catholic priest will help highlight some significant phenomena obscured or excluded by the standard picture of the history of research, above all its deep theoretical roots in the Radical Reformation.

Making an Epoch

The fabulous authority that Albert Schweitzer holds in shaping perceptions in the field of *Jesusforschung* is not difficult to understand.[4] He plays an indispensable archival role with incomparable eloquence and aplomb. Heavy reliance upon Schweitzer's research report is almost unavoidable, both on account of the mountain of texts he treats, often absent even from well-supplied biblical libraries, as well as the colossal verbosity (and off-putting Gothic script) that confounds these often obscure studies. Few have the courage or patience to plough through the unabridged works of a Bruno Bauer or D. F. Strauss, not to say the writings of lesser figures like Karl Hase or Bernhard Weiss. The nineteenth-century history of the field largely comes to us exclusively on Schweitzer's testimony—borne with all the contagious zeal of his deepest religious conviction.

If a slavish scholarly debt must thus be acknowledged, there is all the more reason to appreciate critically Schweitzer's far from disinterested presentation. Despite its disarming claim of merely wishing to "fill a gap in theological literature," the text is an extended plaidoyer for his own radical position.[5] As Michael Thate says in his study of Schweitzer, "He has ordered his *Geschichte* in such a way that his construction of *konsequente Eschatologie* receives the starring role in his narrative history."[6] The claim is engraved in the very chapter titles bookending the first edition: the reader is led from

---

[4] "It may be the case that no scholar accepts Schweitzer's re-construction of Christian origins and an apocalyptic Jesus *in toto*, but the underlying assumption of his presentation are almost unanimously followed ... no one else has wielded more influence in terms of the historical framing of the discussion" (Thate, *Remembrance of Things Past?*, 21).

[5] Schweitzer, *Quest*, xxxiii (preface to 1st ed.). See also the description given of the disappointment of students in Friedrich Spitta's lectures on the Life of Jesus, since he offered no history of research, in Albert Schweitzer, *Aus meinem Leben und Denken*, 59–60.

[6] Thate, *Remembrance of Things Past?*, 23. See Rafael Rodríguez's "Review of *Remembrance of Things Past?*" See also Gathercole, "Critical and Dogmatic Agenda," 278–82.

"The Problem" (*Das Problem*, chap. I) to "The Solution" (*Die Lösung*, chap. XXI). The extra chapters supplied at the end of the expanded 1913 edition cloak this unmistakable, original frame but do not undermine the book's relentless teleological drive to celebrate the author's accomplishment[7]—a scholarly "breakthrough" that had somehow gone unnoticed when first revealed with the publication of Schweitzer's dissertation in 1901.[8] The grave hesitations of two members of the Strasbourg faculty concerning his work's suitability were thus only harbingers of the "passive hostility" and "conspiracy of silence" of a wider academic establishment.[9] From this perspective, the *Quest* represents an emphatic and self-confident, reconceived republication of his *Skizze*—this time fronted with an immense *Status Quaestionis* missing from the slim 109-page dissertation. The effect of such erudition on such a scale was this time (at least with the passage of time, even much time) much nearer to the author's aspirations.[10]

There can be little doubt, structurally speaking, that Schweitzer meant to make an epoch. If other turn-of-the-century authors, like Otto Schmiedel and Hermann von Soden, were also already offering retrospective, evaluative overviews of *Leben-Jesu-Forschung*, there is a marked consciousness in these works of the still open questions facing scholars.[11] Schweitzer, by contrast, imposes closure, and in this sense his periodization stands in service of his solution. More than this, his epochal intervention is implicitly cast as the dawning of a new religious era, the climatic act in a drama having "deter-

---

[7] The 1913 edition is a different book in many ways. The appearance of a debate over the very existence of Jesus in the intervening years made the "consistent skepticism" of Wrede no longer a useful landmark in the field. Thus the name of book changed to *Geschichte der Leben-Jesu-Forschung*, as both the temporal span of the discussion and the stakes had changed.

[8] Schweitzer, *Das Messianitäts- und Leidensgeheimnis*. The early review of this work by Heinrich Weinel ("Review of *Das Messianitäts- und Leidensgeheimnis*") was severe, finding the text superficial and historically unconvincing. The first line of the review by Paul Wernle immediately seized the connection with Schweitzer's dissertation: "Dieses Buch ruft zuerst ein älteres desselben Verfassers ins Gedächtnis zurück. 1901 hatte Schweitzer unter dem Titel ‚Das Messianitäts- und Leidensgeheimnis' eine hundertseitige Skizze des Lebens Jesu veröffentlicht."

[9] The descriptions of the scholarly "oblivion" into which Schweitzer's work initially fell come from W. Lowrie's "Translator's Introduction," 17–19. See also Weaver, *Historical Jesus*, 31. For a description of the defense at Strasbourg, see Schweitzer, *Aus meinem Leben und Denken*, 59.

[10] "That Schweitzer's work inspired great controversy is well known. That eventually his work came to dominate the twentieth century view of the historical Jesus is self-evident. It is less well known that the immediate impact of his work was something short of revolutionary" (Weaver, *Historical Jesus*, 31–38).

[11] See Schmiedel, *Die Hauptprobleme der Leben-Jesu-Forschung*; and Soden, *Die wichtigsten Fragen im Leben Jesu*. Mention might also be made of non-German authors, notably Sanday, *Life of Christ in Recent Research*.

mined the course of the religious thinking of the future" through which humanity will discover "a new dogma" and "new life and new regulative principles."[12] One may indeed plausibly wonder if Schweitzer did not fancy his own work to already anticipate that "mighty deed of some tremendous original genius," which he prophesied: "a genius powerful enough to open up with authority a new way for the world."[13] Whether or to what extent this fervor for a new moment in the progress of Christian religion means that his historiography must stand or fall with his personal proposal may remain for the moment an open question. There is a relevant rule here that touches babies and bathwater. There are, nevertheless, also other ways one could tell the story, much less preoccupied with setting the stage for the religious evolution of humankind through the triumphant arrival of radical eschatology and a Jesus "who comes to us as one unknown."[14]

Heroes in His Own Image

Unstitching the fabric of Schweitzer's story might be done in any number of ways, but it is not unduly difficult. An opening challenge might be posed, for instance, to Schweitzer's intellectual honor roll of Reimarus, Strauss, and Weiss, who all seem to function as forceful ciphers of the author's own victorious view.[15] Thate has already exposed how tenuous Schweitzer's depiction of Reimarus truly is, showing that eschatology in fact enjoys almost no centrality in his thought.[16] Indeed, "in the crucial 'fragment' published by Lessing ... Reimarus actually has more in common with Wrede" than Schweitzer.[17] Schweitzer has, by all appearances, selectively recast in his own image this not-so-original skeptic, whom Watson hyperbolically calls "at

---

12 Schweitzer, *Quest*, 3. For more on the subsequent development of this "religious thinking of the future," see Appendix I in this volume.

13 Schweitzer, *Quest*, 3–4. If the principle of "Reverence before Life" (*Ehrfurcht vor dem Leben*) was not yet fully formulated in Schweitzer's thinking, by the end of the *Quest* he had nevertheless articulated an ethical "Jesus-mysticism" free of the "Jesus-cult" by which "the liberal and conservative forms of religious thinking, which at the moment exist side-by-side, will meet and achieve unity" (486).

14 Schweitzer, *Quest*, 487.

15 "There is a strategy to Schweitzer's superlatives. Reimarus is cast in the role of the precursor to Schweitzer himself ... in his presentation of Reimarus, Schweitzer is already shaping his own self-image, preparing the way for his own entry onto the scene in his book's final chapters" (Watson, *Gospel Writing*, 67).

16 Thate, *Remembrance of Things Past?*, 60. See also Gathercole, "Critical and Dogmatic Agenda," 268; and Grappin, "La theologie Naturelle de Reimarus," 178. This analysis of Reimarus was already made by Lundsteen, *Hermann Samuel Reimarus*, 10 and 135.

17 Watson, "Eschatology and the Twentieth Century," 345.

every point dependent on English deistic literature," in order to anchor the story in a celebrated controversy.[18]

Numerous voices have complained that this wider deistic program is never credited with its rightful place in Schweitzer's account, which misleadingly presents Reimarus as a thunderbolt from the blue.[19] Although the *Quest* insists that Reimarus's work cannot be classed as a piece of deistic polemics, Mauro Pesce, for instance, highlights a long list of authors whose works must qualify such a claim. Pesce also helpfully draws attention to the complex cultural ferment at work from the sixteenth century onward in which new approaches to the Gospels developed.[20]

Why, then, begin where Schweitzer does? To laud the fragment on *The Aims of Jesus and His Disciples* as "a masterpiece of world literature" is unconvincing rhetorical cover, as actual readers of Reimarus can agree.[21] One must instead recognize that what appears here is, for Schweitzer, a vital pivot in a carefully constructed argument.[22] Specifically, it is Reimarus who, with his "clear perception of the elements of the problem," bequeaths a series of needful premises that determine the ultimate "Solution": above all (1) the fatal disjunction between Jesus, who was no founder of a new religion, and his disciples, who were; (2) a two-pronged understanding of Jewish expectation, developed along diverging immanent and transcendent lines; and (3) a preference for the Synoptics, rather than John.[23] Schweitzer will soften the radical (Wredean) discontinuity by trying to reconcile the two variant expectations in Jesus' own person, but the elements of the preferred solution are already here.

If alternative starting points to Reimarus might be imagined, it becomes clear how Schweitzer is actively working to shape a forced decision upon the reader: *Von Reimarus zu Wrede* means, in fact, *Entweder Reimarus oder Wrede*, either a historical or a literary solution.[24] The historiographi-

---

18 Watson, *Gospel Writing*, 68. Watson, dependent upon August's Lundsteen's 1939 monograph, has clearly overstated the case against Reimarus. The essential charge that he is not nearly so original as Schweitzer suggests manifestly sticks, however.

19 See, e.g., Weaver, "In Quest of the Quest."

20 Pesce, "Per una ricerca storica su Gesù."

21 See, e.g., Weaver, "Quest of the Quest," 40. Baasland acknowledges that Reimarus was "not intensely groundbreaking" yet contends that he "was the very first to intensively put forth the question—what did Jesus (and the disciples) want" ("Fourth Quest?," 32).

22 Thate, *Remembrance of Things Past?*, 102.

23 Schweitzer, *Quest*, 23. "We have reason to draw an absolute distinction between the teaching of the apostles in their writings and what Jesus himself proclaimed and taught in his own lifetime" (17).

24 "Da diesen beiden Namen also die beiden Pole bezeichnen, zwischen denen sich die Leben-Jesu-Forschung bewegt, bildete ich auch aus ihnen den Titel meines Buches" (Schweit-

cal/chronological frame again reduces to a theoretical construct, and Schweitzer's apologetic agenda takes the upper hand. In the end, we might thus venture one step beyond Thate and Watson to say that Schweitzer not only channels a dubious Reimarus. In re-presenting and interpreting Reimarus to the world, Schweitzer silently transforms himself into a modern-day Lessing, once more throwing the torch into the house of the dull theologians. Precisely like the editor of the *Fragments*, Schweitzer wished theology would face squarely the "the ugly, broad ditch" of history.[25] This language of Lessing, in fact, finds a striking echo near the end of Schweitzer's *Skizze*, where we confront "a deep ... unbridgeable chasm" (*eine tiefe ... unüberbrückbare Kluft*) that separates Jesus' *Weltanschauung* from our own.[26]

Beyond Lessing, however, stands D. F. Strauss, whose biography of the secret skeptic of Hamburg was responsible for "rediscovering Reimarus for his fellow countrymen."[27] Thus Schweitzer in making Reimarus known once again also carries on his shoulders the mantle of Strauss; and, broadly speaking, the tragically prophetic career of this latter man, intoned in the text at several reprises, can be seen to serve a similar narrative function to that discharged by the freethinking Reimarus. One might observe here a significant fact. Carlyle styled the history of the world as a series of biographies of great men, and the *Quest* was written under this nineteenth-century historiographical spell.[28] In this air, Schweitzer also imbibed what Michael Root has identified as a very German and very Protestant cult of the virtuoso theologian, the "creative mind who recasts the field," a Luther *redivivus*.[29] It is in this mold that Schweitzer crafts his avatars.

---

zer, *Aus meinem Leben und Denken*, 39–40). See also Watson, "Eschatology and the Twentieth Century," 345; and idem, *Gospel Writing*, 66.

25 Lessing, "Über den Beweis des Geistes und der Kraft," 12, 14. On this theme in Lessing, see chap. 6 in this volume.

26 Schweitzer, *Das Messianitäts- und Leidensgeheimnis*, 197. "Die Religion hat also keinen Grund der Auseinandersetzung mit der historischen Wahrheit aus dem Weg gehen zu wollen" (*Aus meinem Leben und Denken*, 42; cf. also *Das Messianitäts- und Leidensgeheimnis*, 97, 251).

27 Schweitzer, *Quest*, 71. See Strauss, *Hermann Samuel Reimarus*. It seems likely that Schweitzer himself discovered his particular construction of Reimarus through Strauss's portrayal: *nicht bloß als Vorgänger in dem Kampfe ... sondern der ganze Mann*. On Strauss, see Beiser, *David Friedrich Strauss*, esp. 276–80, where Schweitzer's reception of Strauss is discussed. Schweitzer's *Doktorvater*, Theobald Ziegler, wrote what remains a definitive biography of Strauss (*David Friedrich Strauß*), and Beiser reasonably suspects Ziegler's influence on his student. While observing Schweitzer's often insightful and even "exceptional" reading, Beiser also concludes that, "apart from scholarly errors, Schweitzer was sometimes tempted to make bold and sensational judgments which turn out to be very misleading," e.g., about Strauss's views on Jesus' messianic consciousness (278).

28 Carlyle, "Hero as Divinity," 21. Carlyle's original lectures were delivered in 1840.

29 Root, "Achievement of Wolfhart Pannenberg."

D. F. Strauss *contra mundum* is thus presented as another genius greater than his time. Schweitzer's sympathy for the misunderstood man is not hidden: "To understand Strauss, one must love him."[30] As expected, this figure's voice at points blends seamlessly into the voice of the eschatological solution: "Sometimes one almost seems to be reading Johannes Weiss," Schweitzer says.[31] This is dubious as an honest judgment; the first *Life* is not so constructed. It is a coded way of saying, "One almost seems to be reading me," for Weiss serves throughout as both mask and foil—one of Schweitzer's multiple less-than-forthright strategies for pretending not to be personally involved.[32] Paul Wernle already saw this manner of subterfuge in his 1906 review: "Der Titel des Buchs ist also falsch ... er muß heißen: Von Reimarus zu Alb. Schweitzer."[33] That, of course, would also only somehow cloud the issue, for the forced choice, in fact, is between Schweitzer and Wrede, those two representatives of two opposing visions, who published their two texts on the selfsame subject on the same fateful day in 1901.[34] To this degree, the epic historical frame, supposedly arching over more than a century, boils down to a fin de siècle dispute pitting one German's late Romantic construction of first-century messianism against another's. Peering down the deep well of the champions of German Jesus research, Schweitzer evidently saw his own face dancing on the waters.

The Road Not Taken

Schweitzer's constructed opposition is more than theatrical architecture for his own private agenda. It also contours the (problematic) idea of the so-called Third Quest.[35] N. T. Wright, with no little influence, specifically depicts his simultaneously historical and historiographical proposal

30 Schweitzer, *Quest*, 67.

31 Schweitzer, *Quest*, 87.

32 See Gathercole, "Critical and Dogmatic Agenda," 274–81. See also Watson, "Eschatology and the Twentieth Century," 336–39. Watson discerns a striking oddity in the narrative: "Schweitzer's account of his relationship to Weiss conceals a real and fundamental difference between them, while inventing a non-existent one." In fact, both men plot Jesus' life and not just his ethics/teaching in an eschatological context. By contrast, Schweitzer sees the Kingdom of God as brought that human agency in Jesus' view, while for Weiss it is a purely divine event, for which humans can only passively wait.

33 Wernle, "Review of Schweitzer, *Das Messianitäts- und Leidensgeheimnis*," 502.

34 Schweitzer, *Quest*, 296.

35 The forceful and important ongoing criticism of the "Three Quests" paradigm has not yet explored the significance of this specifically Schweitzerian filiation. See Porter, *Criteria for Authenticity*, 28–62; Allison, *Resurrecting Jesus*, 1–26; Bermejo-Rubio, "Fiction of the 'Three Quests.'"

as a choice between the *Wrede-* or *Schweitzerstrasse*, depicting the "Second Quest" as a midcentury wrong turn.[36] While alternative perceptions of this supposed third great wave of scholarship do exist, it is all but impossible to disengage such periodization from the mystique, the judgments, and the self-oriented epochal thinking of Schweitzer's project. The publication of his work is retroactively registered as an epochal event (more than its actual early reception would seem to warrant), while endorsement of the evocative "Quest" moniker makes Schweitzer's own enterprise the gold standard by which to characterize all the various phases of scholarship, for example, "Pre-Quest," "Old Quest," "No Quest," "New Quest," "Post-Quest," and the like.[37] This configuration of the whole field around Schweitzer's view of the matter is, in fact, an accidental side effect; when James Robinson fatefully coined "New Quest" in his monograph of 1959, he was entirely occupied with a narrative about Bultmannian scholarship and had nearly nothing to say about Schweitzer's work, except that "the real cause behind the end of the quest" is to be found elsewhere.[38] Nevertheless, in the estimate of the recent neo-Schweitzerian fashion, Bultmann and the massive midcentury movement that followed him—ostensibly yet demonstrably more responsible for sharply defining a new period than the publication of the *Quest*—are only a curious ("theological") interlude. From Wright to Allison, and countless many others, legitimation as a participant in the project somehow entails inscribing oneself explicitly in the tradition (and indeed the camp) of Albert Schweitzer. In Wright's openly tracing all twentieth-century Jesus scholarship back to the point of decision that Schweitzer first proposed, one appreciates just how important a clear and critical view of the narrative spell of his *Quest* must be for an accurate apprehension of where the field stands—and why. If a "Three Quests" framework is no longer convincing, perhaps the time has also arrived to moderate the Schweitzer's overdrawn influence in constructing the broad field of Jesus studies.

There is also another important, much less visible fork in the road, however, one well concealed in the narrative of Schweitzer's work. One of two conflicting Strausses must also be chosen. "Who should seek to decide which was the genuine Strauss: the Strauss of the two retreats or the Strauss of the

---

36 Wright, *Jesus and the Victory of God*, 21.

37 See, e.g., the efforts at periodization of Tatum, *In Quest of Jesus*, and Thiessen and Merz, *Historical Jesus*.

38 Robinson, *New Quest of the Historical Jesus*, 32–34. The point is often granted with respect to Schweitzer, i.e., that his work did not in fact bring or intend to bring Jesus research to a standstill. On Bultmann's views, see Painter, "Bultmann, Archaeology, and the Historical Jesus."

three advances?" So another slayer of liberal mediating theology, Karl Barth, puts the question in his own historiographical masterpiece of the era.[39] In opting resoundingly for the Strauss of 1835 and not of 1864, Schweitzer has on the one hand made the obvious choice. The first *Life of Jesus* is patently the revolutionary item, through its introduction of myth as a Hegelian *Aufhebung* in the irresolvable Supernaturalist-Rationalist debate. And yet in seeking to valorize above all a bold rejection of the Fourth Gospel, Schweitzer's choice has muted a significant dynamic in the march of Jesus research: the emergence of competing *national* claims on the historical Jesus. "Whose nationality? Which rationality?" to play on Alasdair MacIntyre's quip.

For Schweitzer, there is only one "historic Jesus"—and he is *not* he who strides through the pages of John or *Das Leben Jesu für das deutsche Volk*.[40] This is not to say that the genuine *Jesus der Geschichte* is not solidly a German possession. The sentimental, French Jesus of Ernst Renan, riding on his "long-eye-lashed gentle mule" is an abomination of bad taste, feeble intellect, and poor judgment.[41] Just what one might expect from a Catholic nation.[42] "Only in the German temperament," Schweitzer insists, "can be found in the same perfection the living complex of conditions and factors—of philosophical thought, critical acumen, historical insight, and religious feeling—without which no deep theology is possible. And the greatest achievement of German theology is the critical investigation of the life of Jesus."[43] Schweitzer leaves seemingly little room for doubt about the intellectual habitat proper to Jesus research. But when he suggests that the second *Life* fell stillborn from the press, he is not playing fair.[44] As Halvor Moxnes says bluntly in his study of nineteenth-century nationalism in the field, "Schweitzer was wrong ... *The Life of Jesus for the German People* was enormously popular and went through many editions in a short time, remaining in print for many years."[45]

---

39 Barth, *Protestant Theology in the Nineteenth Century*, 551.

40 "In his *Life of Jesus for the German People* (1864) ... [Strauss] renounced his better opinions of 1835, eliminated eschatology, and, instead of the historic Jesus, portrayed the Jesus of liberal theology" (Schweitzer, *Quest*, 90). On this second *Life of Jesus*, see Beiser, *David Friedrich Strauss*, 213–51; also 279 for a critique of Schweitzer's critique of the book as a work of "liberal theology."

41 Schweitzer, *Quest*, 162.

42 A hint at Schweitzer's general view of Catholicism as an intellectual option is gained in the description of August Friedrich Gförer as one of those victims of "self-suggestion" whose "need for some fixed point" led him into the Roman Church (*Quest*, 147).

43 Schweitzer, *Quest*, 1.

44 Schweitzer, *Quest*, 168.

45 Moxnes, *Jesus and the Rise of Nationalism*, 105. See also Graf, *Kritik und Pseudo-Spekulation*, 17–18.

Measuring by reception, the historiography now starts to look different. A hungry market for the later Strauss in the German bookshops reflects a mood with nonnegligible resonance in other works on Jesus issuing from German professors' studies. Which German Jesus is then the true Jesus of history, cornerstone for what Schweitzer forecasts as "the religious thinking of the future"?[46] Or, to ask the question as Strauss might have put it: Who has the authority to pronounce on *The Old and the New Faith*?[47]

Latent in this question is a dispute over the heritage of the Reformation. "I understand the German people (*Volk*) as the people of the Reformation," Strauss declares at the outset of his second *Life*, "which, however, I take not as a completed work, but a work that desires to go further." First came the break with the Roman Church, he explains, but now must come a far more difficult break with the Bible itself—or rather a divorce from all in the Bible that is somehow unacceptable, the sifting of "the genuine truths of salvation" (*die ächten Heilswahrheiten*) from "mere time-bound opinions" (*die bloßen Zeitmeinungen*). "Undertaking this divorce is the next task of Protestantism, and insofar as the German people carries the task of advancing Protestantism, this is the task of the German people."[48]

However adaptive to enlightened religion the principle of *semper reformanda* may be, the great offense for Schweitzer here is in the sifting out of "time-bound opinions" (*Zeitmeinungen*).[49] For Schweitzer, this proto-Bultmannian work of demythologization is precisely the fatal, historical error of the establishment view, a husk-and-kernel fallacy that found perfect form in Harnack, spokesman for the liberal consensus of Schweitzer's day.[50]

The culture-pessimist Schweitzer was later an open critic of nationalistic passions, and his discomfort with this liberal resolution was prescient; he instinctively perceived the lurking danger.[51] When the sieve used to filter out authentic, acceptable, or enduringly useful elements in the Gospels itself reduces to the *Zeitgeist*, the grossest, most distressing distortions may

---

46 Schweitzer, *Quest*, 3.

47 Strauss, *Der alte und der neue Glaube*, 252–69.

48 Strauss, *Das Leben Jesu*, xix; see also xx. See note 65 below on Sebastian Franck, whose ideas of Reformation closely resembled this position of Strauss.

49 On Schweitzer's opposition to certain forms of German theology, see Watson, "Eschatology and the Twentieth Century," 339–44.

50 See Padget, "Schweitzer and Harnack." See also Gräßer, "Die ethische Denk-Religion."

51 See, e.g., the essay "Europe and Human Culture," in Schweitzer, *Treasury*. "Hegel ventures to assert that everything subserves progress. The passions of rulers and nations are servants of progress. We can only say that Hegel did not know national passions as we know them; otherwise he would not have dared to write that!"

result.⁵² "The liberal Jesus has given place to the Germanic Jesus," Schweitzer says with disgust about the novelist and future Nazi Gustav Frenssen's 1905 book *The Life of the Saviour Portrayed According to German Research as the Basis for the Spiritual Rebirth of the German Nation*.⁵³ Behind this derisible text, however, stand the same familiar theology professors: "In reading almost every paragraph," Schweitzer says, "one can tell" whether Frenssen was consulting Holtzmann, Schmidt, or von Soden.

Which German Jesus is the *true* Jesus of history? Emphatically not the Jesus of the theologians, that is, not the Jesus of Schleiermacher and Harnack, not the Jesus whose time-bound messianic consciousness could coexist with a neatly separable, universally valid religious consciousness and ethics.⁵⁴ In the construction of Schweitzer, whose enduring influence on this point can hardly be overstated, the genuine "historical Jesus" is and can only ever be a Jesus for whom *no remainder is left over for the theologians*. He is the Jesus of yesterday, not of today—for history is the history of von Ranke, not of Hegel.

THE STORY'S SOCIAL LOCATION

The tangle of personal, political, and intellectual alliances behind the Schweitzerian abstraction of the "historical Jesus" begins to emerge here with distressing complexity, for von Ranke, teacher of Schweitzer's father-in-law, Harry Breslau, was also the ideological ally of Schleiermacher in Berlin. Further, from the 1840s, von Ranke was backed by Frederick Wilhelm IV's reformation of "Christian-German" collective memory in Prussia, an anti-Hegelian cultural program that helped secure the collapse of the philosophical system Strauss had to repudiate in 1864.⁵⁵ Von Ranke accordingly endorsed the reigning magisterium, and "the Jesus of Schenkel, Keim, Hase, and Holtzmann was given a place of honor in ... [von Ranke's] *Welt-*

---

52 It is important to recognize that the widespread understanding of Schweitzer's attack on liberal theology as a claim that reconstructions of Jesus are inevitable reflections of the scholar's own image is inaccurate. In fact, the famous image of seeing the reflection of one's face at the bottom of the well comes from George Tyrrell and "this interpretation misses the point of Schweitzer's critique." Watson, "Eschatology and the Twentieth Century," 339–40.

53 Schweitzer, *Quest*, 275. See also Crystall, *Gustav Frenssen*.

54 See Watson, " Eschatology and the Twentieth Century," 340–41; and Thate, *Remembrance of Things Past?*, 119.

55 See Thate, *Remembrance of Things Past?*, 102; and Oermann, *Albert Schweitzer*. On the influential debate over the nature of history in Berlin during this period, both in the faculties and through the agency of Frederick Wilhelm IV, see Ziolkowski, *Clio*; and John Toews, *Becoming Historical*.

geschichte," to Schweitzer's dismay.⁵⁶ Even valueless positivism in political service can go astray.

Social location, or its representation in Schweitzer's work, at this point becomes an interesting index, for he writes a deeply antiestablishment story. The perfect "living complex of conditions and factors" only found in the German spirit is, in fact, found only in those whose philosophical thought and religious feeling, no less and perhaps much more than their critical acumen and historical insight, mark them out as social pariahs: unwelcome prophets, like Reimarus, who must write his true thoughts in secret; or Strauss, ostracized from the faculties of Europe on account of his views; or Schweitzer, whose doctoral thesis was rudely ignored. Schleiermacher, founder of the first modern research university, first ever also to lecture on the Life of Jesus, does not qualify to carry—much less to light—the torch. His attachment to John and search for universal truths makes him too dangerous and too much of a company man.⁵⁷

We arrive, then, at the place to introduce a view from the other side of the Rhine. For if the story requires losers who nevertheless still count as "questers" (without them where would the forced-choice drama be?), many actors are simply written out of the history altogether. The French Catholic tradition specifically represents an "other" more marginal than any outcast Strauss, all but invisible from where Schweitzer stood. Much could be said about the trade deficit in ideas between France and Germany in biblical studies. Schweitzer saw France as retrograde, hindered from any "profound religious Enlightenment" (*jeder tieferen religiösen Aufklärung*). Of Germany, Renan by contrast subserviently confessed: *Je crois que le Christ nous viendra de là*.⁵⁸ Yet not all Frenchmen shared Renan's opinion.

A French Reading of the German Story

If France was not without a critical intelligence of its own, one figure on the disadvantaged end of this cultural exchange, whose interest for this discussion lies precisely in his minority report, is the French priest Marie-Joseph Lagrange. In his early and incisive reception of Schweitzer's account, a monograph from 1917 suggestively titled *Le sens du christianisme d'après l'exégèse allemande*, Lagrange made a fundamental move worthy of reflec-

---

56 Schweitzer, *Quest*, 188–89.

57 See Moxnes, *Jesus and the Rise of Nationalism*, 67–68 ("Schleiermacher's Sources: John as a national Gospel").

58 Quoted from Renan's *Souvenirs* by Lagrange in "Melanges," 438.

tion.⁵⁹ Exiled from Ottoman Jerusalem as an enemy national during the First World War, thus writing from the heart of a besieged Paris, this patriot of the generation of 1870 gave huge attention to the openly Germanic chest pounding of Schweitzer's story. It is only possible to offer in shorthand what Lagrange's (late colonial, anti-imperialist) reading entails, but a *Skizze* can nevertheless be made.

Reimarus is not the beginning of the story in Lagrange's telling. Nor can we simply start things with the Deists, who provide a broader context for his work. How should one understand their rationalist polemics if the curtain simply rises in medias res, with no Pietists or clamoring sectarians in sight? Are not harmonizers like Osiander essential to the story, Lagrange asks, precisely on account of their novel Lutheran hermeneutics?⁶⁰ Thate has urged plotting the rise of historical Jesus studies within a larger history of secularization, and Lagrange would entirely agree. But this must mean, as Charles Taylor has shown, reaching behind the ubiquitous "coming of age" narrative embraced as its founding myth by the *Secular Age* itself.⁶¹ Why is the story such a strikingly *German* story? Lagrange laid his finger directly on the sensitive issue: emancipation from ecclesiastical influence, the "explosion of religious and social anarchy" that came in Luther's wake.⁶² The Reformation is the starting point in Lagrange's view.

The far end of the story is also not where Schweitzer placed it, at least not in the triumphant edition of 1906, which is, significantly, where so much of the reception of Schweitzer checks out of the story. Lagrange highlights instead the long debate over the very historicity of Jesus, which ends the second edition on such a peculiar denouement. This odd, three-chapter tailspin into an even more thoroughgoing (*konsequent*) skepticism than Wrede himself represented is for Lagrange not just some bizarre outlier in the discussion. It represents an integral piece, indeed the real, inner teleology of the story. The self-consuming arc stretches *Von Luther zu Drews*.

Is this not merely a Latin priest's all-too-predictable, wartime, anti-Protestant hue and cry?⁶³ It is true that Lagrange is passionately convicted

---

59 Lagrange, *Le sens du christianisme*. I am not aware that this text has been formerly discussed in historiographical studies of Jesus research, although it represents one of the most substantial early engagements with Schweitzer's work, certainly from the French and Catholic perspective.

60 Lagrange, *Le sens du christianisme*, 70–71.

61 Taylor, *Secular Age*.

62 "La révolte de Luther contre l'Église déchaina en Allemagne une explosion d'anarchie religieuse et sociale" (Lagrange, *Le sens du christianisme*, 67).

63 Apart from Renan, Schweitzer's book has little to do with French Catholicism. The one notable cameo is the histrionic Edgar Quinet, whom Schweitzer credits with first introduc-

of the errors of German exegesis globally considered. Yet it would be a great mistake to dismiss this scholar (who did not escape suspicion and silencing from Rome) as some sort of reactionary papal polemicist.[64] Indeed, his considered perspective is illuminating precisely for the critical distance he takes from the protagonists of the tale and their conclusions (in open contrast to Schweitzer).

In the first place, Lagrange leads us ask, *Which Reformation?* Though drawing inevitable attention to Luther, Lagrange ultimately gestures away from Magisterial Protestantism, which normally hogs the attention, and highlights what Roland Bainton called "The Left Wing of the Reformation."[65] This brings on the stage Socinians and figures like Hans Denck and Sebastian Franck, on the margins (or in the vanguard?) of Luther's movement, who amazingly by the 1520s were already arming future Deists with demonstrations of the contradictions in Scripture, not in order to upend religion, but to refute faith in the letter of the Bible and mystically transcend to the spirit.[66] From their de-emphasis on doctrine to their skepticism about miracles, there are rich hints in such authors of motifs that will recur from Hegel and Strauss right down to Bultmann, who was himself understandably intrigued

---

ing German theology to the Latin nations and whose exclusive contribution to the *Quest* is an uncritical alarmist cry: "A new barbarian invasion is rolling up against sacred Rome . . . As of old Leo went forth to meet Attila, so now let the papacy put on its purple and come forth" (*Quest*, 99–100).

64 "Lagrange was a superior scholar and fully conversant with the directions taken in Liberal Protestantism and historical methodology generally. Yet he was clearly constrained by the dogmas of his church" (Weaver, *Historical Jesus in the Twentieth Century*, 16). "Constrained by dogma" is certainly not the way Lagrange understood the situation; cf. *Le sens du christianisme*, 18–19. The divergent perspectives on this issue complicate a plotting of figures like Lagrange within the historiography of Jesus research, revealing the limits of present overviews of the field. Weaver ultimately stuffs Lagrange in a grab-bag chapter titled "Themes, Topics, and Smaller Matters," under the curiosity-shop heading "Roman Catholic Lives of Jesus," although the historian records accurately that Lagrange in fact insisted that no *Life of Jesus* apart from the Gospels themselves could ever be written.

65 Bainton, "Left-Wing of the Reformation." The phrase was taken up by Reformation scholars, e.g., Fast, *Der linke Flügel der Reformation*. It is more common to speak today of the "Radical Reformation." See Williams, *Radical Reformation*; and Eire, *Reformations*, 250–55. Eire suggests that another "perhaps more appropriate" name would be "*alternative* Reformation or alternative Protestantism." He goes on: "Naming this thing, this *other* kind of Reformation, has been a problem for far too long."

66 On Franck, see Graf-Reventlow, *History of Biblical Interpretation*, 165–75. D. F. Strauss's notion that the future form of the Reformation must dispense with Scripture as it earlier did with the pope is anticipated three centuries in advance by Franck: the antichrist, he says, "who is now sick and tired of the pope . . . will assume another guise and set himself down in the middle of the letter of Scripture" (*Der alte und der neue Glaube*, 170).

by Franck's *Paradoxa* (1534).[67] Lagrange is intent that we show German exegetes the good faith of understanding them not as atheistic freethinkers or Deists, but as the religious thinkers they claimed to be.[68] On this principle, it would accordingly be useful to search for their intellectual roots in the Radical Reformation, especially where it specifically crossed with humanistic learning, Pyrrhonian skepticism, and later Enlightenment currents, as among the "Evangelical Rationalists and Anti-Trinitarians."[69] This also means reading Schweitzer himself as a religious writer, standing on the radical end of the Protestant tradition, and recognizing, in this light, the importance of his wider theological oeuvre and particularly that his unorthodox theory on mysticism in Paul is not only a massive, open, and ongoing challenge to the core of Magisterial Lutheranism, but also has high relevance for his construction of Jesus.

This leads directly to the second point about Jesus' existence. Lagrange was convinced that Paul is much more central to the discussion than he at first seems.[70] For if Jesus stays historically confined, imprisoned as it were in first-century Palestine, if this Jewish messiah is no founder of a Church sent

---

[67] See Bultmann, "Review of Landräumig," 314. The appeal of these figures as visionary models for a new dogmatic at the turn of the century is evident from a text such as Haake, *Hans Denk*.

[68] "Ce serait donc une erreur de regarder ces critiques, professeurs de théologie dans les facultés protestantes, comme de simples libres penseurs à la Voltaire. L'épithète de rationaliste leur était une injure ... il n'est pas sans intérêt pour nous de savoir qu'ils ont entrepris de fonder un christianisme nouveau sur les bases de leur érudition, qu'ils ont espéré l'imposer a tout le protestantisme, en attendant mieux, comme la religion de l'avenir, une religion allemande, issue de la réforme de Luther" (Lagrange, *Le sens du christianisme*, 307–8). The echo of Schweitzer's "religion of the future" rhetoric is strong and likely to be in Lagrange's mind in this echo.

[69] On this taxonomy, see Eire, *Reformations*, 254–55. The Amsterdam Centre for the History and Heritage of Protestantism hosted a symposium on July 13, 2017, titled "Radical Reformation & Enlightenment." The following abstract was published for the event: "Sixteenth-century radical reformers undermined traditional Christianity by their groundbreaking thought on church-state relations, religious toleration, human perfectibility, miracles and biblical authority. Their focus on an inward spirituality and moral improvement offered a viable alternative to the organized churches that were so closely linked with the massive outbursts of religious violence of that century. After the sixteenth century, writings of radical reformers continued to be published and their ideas continued to be debated. Because of their pleas for religious toleration, their skepticism about miracles and their de-emphasizing of doctrine, scholars assume a profound influence of the Radical Reformation on the Enlightenment. These themes were indeed crucial to Enlightenment thought. However, these similarities between Radical Reformation and Enlightenment thinking do not prove any direct dependency. Hence the question whether a link between the Radical Reformation and the Enlightenment existed and how Enlightenment thinkers may have used Radical Reformation thought continues to be a matter of debate." See, e.g., Blough, *Jésus-Christ*.

[70] Lagrange, *Le sens du christianisme*, 274.

out to the nations—that particular honor must inevitably pass to the Apostle to the Gentiles. Many have, in fact, long accepted this conclusion. At that point, however, both history and theology must test the terrible question: "Is Jesus still necessary?" Hence the inevitability of the Christ-myth debate and experimentation in dispensing with the Jesus hypothesis altogether. Lagrange is not so far in his logic from the Modernist George Tyrrell's view of the problem.[71] One is well placed here to understand the phenomenon of Bultmann.[72]

At that early date, Lagrange was not yet hypnotized, as we are, by an institutionalized Arthurian "Quest of the Historical Jesus"—an evocative terminology that has overrun the field and is but the Romantic obfuscation of Montgomery's translation.[73] It is a catchy but unhelpful terminology, without basis anywhere in the German, and it would be better to drop it altogether. From where he stood, before the development of a vast international Jesus industry, Lagrange was poised to ask and answer with a fresh perspective: What has everyone been seeking? His answer is not "the historical Jesus." Rather, in his view, for four centuries since Luther, German exegesis has been one continuous quest to regain the origins of the Gospel, to reach back to the primal configuration, bypassing the existing social order of religion to attain to the true form and *meaning of Christianity* (*le sens du christianisme*). This is the central phenomenon that gives coherence to the nineteenth-century, characteristically German exegetical saga, variegated as it is, and the explanation why from Paulus to Jahn we find the *Quest* littered with revealing bipartite titles: *Das Leben Jesu als Grundlage einer reinen Geschichte des Frühchristentums*.[74]

---

[71] "The problem of present-day Catholicism is, not to reconcile itself with that of the earlier centuries, to find in both a common 'idea' of ecclesiasticism, but to find ecclesiasticism of any sort in Jesus Christ as He is given to us by historical criticism; to find in the earliest Catholicism a true development of the 'idea' of Christ . . . the antiquity of the leading features and principles of Catholicism has been pushed further and further back till its beginnings are found in the New Testament itself. The hierarchy is felt in the Pastoral Epistles; sacramentalism in S. Paul; theology in the Johannine writings; ecclesiasticism in S. Matthew; the Petrine ascendancy in S. Matthew and the Acts" (Tyrrell, *Christianity at the Cross-Roads*, 36).

[72] Bultmann's *religiongeschichtlich* dabbling in Mandean, Indian, and Buddhist myths and materials put him in direct contact with Drews's preferred corpora. The professor of Marburg's program of de-mythologization (*Entmythologisierung*) opted for another route than the proponent of the Christ-myth, however, and in the end Bultmann's neo-Kantian / existential notion of *sola fide*, so circumspect about the Jesus known by historical reason, meant to save the day from a more aggressive skepticism than Schweitzer's historical program could finally digest.

[73] See Watson, "Eschatology and the Twentieth Century," 331–33.

[74] Among the titles considered by Schweitzer are a large number with an expressed interest in early Christianity in their titles: e.g., Hennell, *Inquiry Concerning the Origin of Christian-*

Such projects persist to the present day.⁷⁵ At a certain point—a point closely allied with the rise and role of the modern university, as well as by simple reason of specialization and the waxing size of the undertaking—this search for a comprehensive picture of Christian origins seemingly took the distinct turn of becoming a detached search for a post-confessional Jesus, a "new Jesus" to borrow a piquant phrase from Flannery O'Connor.⁷⁶ There is an analogy here to the new renditions a man like Michaelis gave to Moses.⁷⁷ A new social order required a new secular consensus around its grounding religious figures. After the medieval perspective decomposed in a welter of Reformation disagreement, the rising liberal establishment in the West, fatigued by sectarian hyper-pluralism and interminable religious strife, decided to settle the matter peaceably with universal reason, an "unpapal conclave" if you like—leaving fanaticism safely behind in first-century texts. But again the question, "Whose rationality?"⁷⁸ *Cuius regio, eius ratio.*⁷⁹

Neutral Ground?

In the end, Lagrange refuses to accept Schweitzer's "Solution" (*Lösung*) on what he understands as historical and exegetical, not dogmatic or nationalistic, grounds. It was not the bluff of a novice. Schweitzer might have read Lagrange's own four-hundred-page monograph on messianism from 1909, which, it may be said, has weathered better than Schweitzer's own ideas on this matter.⁸⁰ Evidently, he took no note.

---

ity; Bauer, *Christus und die Cäsaren*; Brandt, *Die evangelische Geschichte*; Pfleiderer, *Das Urchristentum*; Wernle, *Die Anfänge unserer Religion*; Hartmann, *Das Christentum des Neuen Testaments*; Kautsky, *Der Ursprung des Christentums*; and Jahn, *Über die Person Jesu*. Both Strauss and Renan dropped the projected second volumes of their *Lives*, which were to handle dogmatic issues either from a systematic (Strauss) or historical (Renan) perspective.

75 James Dunn's *Christianity in the Making* and N. T. Wright's *Christian Origins and the Question of God* series both embed historical Jesus research as part of a larger project centered on early Christianity. See also, from a different perspective, Destro and Pesce, *From Jesus to His First Followers*. In the book's introduction the authors explain that the text is closely connected with their earlier study, *Encounters with Jesus*.

76 O'Connor, *Wise Blood*.

77 On the fascinating project of Johann David Michaelis at the University in Göttingen, see Legaspi, *Death of Scripture*.

78 For objections to Meier's "conclave" idea, including the elite Western bias of its form of rationality, see Simpson, "Current Trends in Third-Quest Research," 200–1.

79 The Peace of Augsburg in 1555 proclaimed the principle *cuius region, eius religion*, bringing an end to the first wave of organized military action between Catholic and Protestants.

80 Lagrange, *Le messianisme chez les Juifs*.

A meeting of minds would not have been simple, of course, and Lagrange was not slow to contrast Latin mental hygiene from Germanic intellectual vice in ways that make us squirm. If in its wartime context this impulse took the form of sharp nationalist constructs[81]—a discourse that has become newly sensitive in our present political climate—Lagrange remains generous, all things considered, and his stereotypes at least serve him to underscore the profoundly social and contingent character of human reason: a theme paradoxically present and yet suppressed in Schweitzer's telling. In articulating where the national and religious premises differed, however, Lagrange also upholds a confidence in reason's universal character. In this light, perhaps the key insight he offers at the end of our study is that the genealogy of Jesus studies (*Leben-Jesu-Forschung*) must be grounded in *hermeneutical* precision before it can be approached *historically* as a story. What is the actual project, and what premises does it require? *Sola scriptura* and metaphysical naturalism, Lagrange claimed, are the essential philosophical furniture of the *Quest*. Both are necessary for the story Schweitzer tells.

As a historical critic dangerously near to Modernist circles, on the near end of what Ulrich Lehner calls the "Catholic Enlightenment," Lagrange was optimistic about non-confessional exegesis.[82] "A perfect unbeliever might be an excellent commentator of the texts," he says.[83] Still, Lagrange, who was perfectly acquainted with the progress of modern science, wonders why it is so difficult to find dispassionate objectivity in the matter of miracles.[84] Many have been socialized in their own secular dogmatic tradition, it seems. A metaphysical decision point surrounding the possibility of supernatural reality thus hinders "objective" exegetical consensus more than any merely national factors in Lagrange's estimation.[85]

---

81 On this nationalistic feature of Lagrange's work, see my "In der Exegese wie im Krieg."

82 Lehner, *Catholic Enlightenment*. Lehner's work is a helpful resource in deconstructing a monolithic, areligious construction of the "Enlightenment."

83 Lagrange, *Le sens du christianisme*, 6.

84 Lagrange, *Le sens du christianisme*, 6, 13–14.

85 ee, e.g., Lagrange, *Le sens du christianisme*, 28. The question of miracles is debated differently today than it was a century ago, on both sides of the aisle. On the prejudice against miracles in contemporary history scholarship and its origins, see, e.g., Gregory, "No Room for God?"; and idem, *Unintended Reformation*. In Gregory's view, today's supposedly neutral critics often lack the most basic philosophical formation and unwittingly hold a late medieval nominalistic doctrine of the univocity of being, propagated half-unwittingly by the Reformers: a doctrine that binds them needlessly to a dubious, empiricist Humean historiography. For a recent rejection of the dominant naturalist worldview by a prominent atheist philosopher (who proposes no alternative and is not convinced that its rejection implies the acceptance of Theism), see Nagel, *Mind and Cosmos*. Naturalistic philosophical underpinnings can obviously affect exegetes' prejudgments, but other sorts of objections to Gospel miracle stories must nevertheless also obviously be registered and addressed, e.g., construction according to biblical patterns, internal inconsistencies, and so on.

From his vantage point, aided by the story told by Schweitzer, Lagrange described a liberal Protestantism that had forfeited the foundational philosophical and theological commitments of the Christian tradition. At the foundation of his rational disconnect with the German project (which he viewed as a whole and not with the ambiguous stance adopted by Schweitzer) thus lies the bold rejection of ecclesiastical tradition as a supposedly distorting and benighted factor in exegesis. Indeed, the open celebration of this rejection as an unproblematic and complete emancipation tightly binds *sola scriptura* with the *Aufklärung* in a supercilious "escape from nonage" attitude (*aus seiner selbst verschuldeten Unmündigkeit*), making any rapprochement with Catholic modes of rationality a challenging affair to say the least. Johann Gabler's anti-dogmatic intervention, important as it is for the discipline of biblical science in its modern academic configuration, clearly "stood on solid Protestant ground" as far as this goes.[86] Gabler simply introduced history as the rational path to the perspicuity of Scripture—displacing a simple (impractical) trust in the Spirit's guidance. In this Gabler was harbinger of an emergent historical mode of rationality that would soon profoundly reshape European culture and become a kind of common intellectual ground in the following century and beyond. Accordingly, Lagrange himself also espouses a "commonsense" view of exegesis—not as the result of a Protestant hermeneutics of biblical perspicuity, but on account of a common, late modern, European positivism and trust that historical and philological tools could serve as objective controls.[87] Here, of course, Lagrange shares an ongoing and defining presupposition with a large sector of the contemporary field, as well as with his German contemporaries and opponents. But he also obviously immediately parts ways. Neutral as the historical method was in his view, ecclesial tradition is not a threat to such objectivity as far as Lagrange was concerned. On the contrary! All thought, like religion, is social and bound up in cultural forms, he declares.[88] It is *sola scriptura* that, in his view, has for centuries enabled the illusory dream of a presuppositionless encounter with the text, holding out the Grail-like promise of access to a Gospel older than the Church and a newly defined *sens du christiansime*.

---

[86] "Gabler stood on both firm exegetical and solid Protestant ground. The meaning of Scripture must be identified without prejudice from the potentially erroneous theologizing of generation upon generation of churchmen" (Muller, *Post-Reformation Reformed Dogmatics*, 454).
[87] Lagrange, *Le sens du christianisme*, 1–30, esp. 6.
[88] On multiple occasions, Lagrange is positive toward the insights of Émile Durkheim, founder of modern social science. See, e.g., *Le sens du christianisme*, 68.

Conclusions

1. The "Three Quests" historiographical schema is intimately bound up with and oriented around the rhetorical self-promotion of Albert Schweitzer's theological project and its largely uncritical, romanticized reception. Alternative perspectives exist, however, which indulge greater freedom of thought in framing the same material and which give more open attention and space to the strongly socioreligious character of the story (while being less invested than Schweitzer in the shaping "the religious thinking of the future"). Without insisting on apodictic judgments between various competing accounts, and without discounting the considerable genuine contributions of Schweitzer, entertaining a greater diversity of voices, including characters like Marie-Joseph Lagrange, who have been largely written out of the script, will help make reformulations of the history of the field more comprehensive and supple. Additionally, a complete and careful history of the reception of Schweitzer's work (to which Lagrange emphatically belongs) would contribute much to a better presentation of the history of research, including an account of the rare authority Schweitzer presently holds among Jesus scholars.

2. As a thinker, Albert Schweitzer belongs squarely within the socioreligious heritage of the Radical Reformation, as do many, or rather most, of his story's chosen heroes. This insight of Lagrange merely echoes Schweitzer's own self-understanding. Replotting the history of research to better accommodate and emphasize this fact could present a helpful reference point and resource in isolating the roots, the premises, and the wider aims of much Jesus research. Unhelpful recourse to a vague "Enlightenment" construct, by contrast, conceived of as an essentially areligious (superior) form of rationality, should be either refined or retired as an explanatory category.

3. Acknowledgment of the deep influence of specifically Protestant forms of thought will help in better integrating the important (and importantly theological) Bultmannian phase of research into a wider view of the field. Here both radical experimentation with the irrelevance/nonexistence of Jesus and dispute about the relationship between theological and historical truths could be revealed as issues much more central to crucial dividing lines in the broad project of Jesus research than is generally accepted or understood.

4. Greater attention to the influence of the Radical Reformation tradition upon historical Jesus research invites an attempt to offer hermeneutical and typological, not only narrative, descriptions of the field. Both philosophical and theological presuppositions should accordingly be more explicitly

acknowledged and articulated in efforts at categorizing scholars and their views. Metaphysical naturalism and *sola scriptura* are two postulates to investigate in this way. A more critical appreciation for unspoken assumptions that condition the distinctly modern, largely positivistic, academic historical imagination would also contribute much to a clearer understanding of the rise of interest in studies of the "historical Jesus" during the nineteenth century and the ways in which consensus has remained difficult to achieve.[89]

---

89 See, e.g., White, *Metahistory*. Referring to the work of continental thinkers (e.g., Valéry, Heidegger, Sartre, Lévi-Strauss, Foucault) and Anglo-American philosophers alike, White contends that "the historical consciousness on which Western man has prided himself since the beginning of the nineteenth century may be little more than a theoretical basis for the ideological position from which Western civilization views its relationship not only to cultures and civilizations preceding it but also to those contemporary with it in time and contiguous in space. In short, it is possible to view historical consciousness as a specifically Western prejudice by which the presumed superiority of modern, industrial society can be retroactively substantiated" (2).

CHAPTER 3

The "Lying Historians" and Luke 1–2

Ancient readers of Luke's Gospel were unburdened by nineteenth-century historicism. When they encountered the historiographical signals sent by the author's prologue, they accordingly interpreted his product against a premodern grid. This in no way means that the text's first readers lacked the conceptual resources to distinguish trustworthy accounts from dubious reports or fabrication, yet ancient categories of evaluation were not the positivistic canons of most modern exegesis. Ethical and aesthetic judgments were instead of primary concern. Interestingly, premodern and postmodern perspectives on history writing share much in common in this regard. Better comprehension of this situation and a readiness to pose a less anachronistic set of questions to the text will advantageously position contemporary scholars in their effort to address hitherto frustrating problems about the truth of Luke's narrative.[1]

Evaluating Historiography in the Greco-Roman Context

Plutarch's petulant ad hominem attack on the *pater historiae*, the *de Malignitate Herodoti,* is an ill-tempered and parochial, yet broadly revealing, cultural artifact. While the overzealous effort to defend the reputation of his ancestral Boetians is a tedious and often futile exercise, which has embarrassed Plutarch scholars since at least the mid-nineteenth century, there is

---

[1] For a useful study with many contacts to the present treatment, see Backhaus, "Asphaleia."

a representative significance to the project.² In contrast to the high-minded and masterfully controlled criticism of a treatise like Dionysius's *Letter to Gnaeus Pompeius*, with its positive and carefully principled account of Herodotus's aesthetic execution, Plutarch's blunt charge of mendacity summarily exposes the ethical canons that govern most historiographical evaluation in the ancient world. Morality rather than style—or, better, truthfulness as communicated through style—was the ultimate criterion of judgment.

The topos of the lying historian is well known, of course, above all from the agonistic depictions of authors' predecessors and rivals.³ Josephus, for instance, makes space for his account of the war with Rome by dismissing those who "either from flattery towards the Romans or hatred for the Jews lied about the events" (καταψεύδονται τῶν πραγμάτων, *B.J.* 1.15). In fact, according to Josephus, the problem of untruthfulness is endemic to the entire project of Greek historiography, as the catalogue of confused and conflicting accounts in the opening of his *Contra Apionem* means to show. "Ephorus demonstrates Hellanicus to have told lies in the greatest part of his history; as does Timaeus in like manner to Ephorus, and the succeeding writers do to Timaeus, and all the later writers do to Herodotus ... Thucydides himself is accused by some as writing ὡς ψευδόμενος" (*C. Ap.* 1.23; cf. *B.J.* 1.16). All this mess of disharmony convicts those Greeks "who tell lies" (τοὺς ψευδομένους) and serves to elevate the alternative Near Eastern model of historiography that Josephus claims as the background for his own project.

It is important not to confine the motif of the mendacious historian too narrowly to the strategies of authorial self-assertion, however. Lucian's *How to Write History* incorporates the charge as a fundamental foil for his instructional admonition. In contrast to pretenders like a certain unnamed Corinthian historian, whose fabricated travel credentials condemn his work from the outset as a fraud, respectable writers of history should consecrate themselves to a disinterested and informed presentation of the truth, Lucian says.⁴ The outrageous *True Story*, probably a companion piece to the *Conscribenda*, is a full-scale satire on the degenerate state of historiography, notably the extravagant utopian island accounts of authors like Euhemerus and Dionysius of Skytobrachion—writers regarded as sufficiently reputable to be included in Diodorus Siculus's *Library* (§41.4, 42.4).⁵ Seneca, also the

---

2 See, e.g., Smith, *New Classical Dictionary*, 366.

3 See Wiseman, "Lying Historians."

4 This pretender remains unnamed in *Hist. Conscr.* 29. Ctesias and Iambulus are named in *Ver. Hist.* 1.3.

5 On the relationship between these two texts, see Georgiadou and Larmour, "Lucian and Historiography."

author of an absurd historiographical parody, *The Apocolocyntosis* or *Pumpkinification of Claudius*, similarly disparages the whole lying industry in his *Questiones Naturales*.

> It is not a great effort to destroy the authority of Ephorus: *historicus est*, he is an historian ... Some historians are credulous; others are negligent. On some, falsehood (*mendacium*) creeps unawares; some it pleases. The former do not avoid falsehood, the latter actively seek it. What the whole tribe has in common is this: they do not think their works can be approved and become popular unless they sprinkle them with lies (*mendacio aspersit*). (§7.16.1–2 [Corcoran, LCL])

If Seneca's round denunciation made implicit provision for grades of historiographical culpability, a further measure of nuance was possible. In one of his methodological asides, Polybius was thus able to distinguish between intentional and unintentional falsehood in history writing, mercifully observing that the latter was to some extent unavoidable and should simply be pardoned and corrected in a generous spirit. Deliberate falsehood, by contrast, poisoned an entire work and deserved only the harshest censure (Polybius, *Hist.* XII, 25c.5). Such censure was not administered sparingly, as Polybius's treatment of the unfortunate Timeaus of Tauromenium shows.

The Gospels as Lying Histories

It is of considerable interest that the evangelists were pulled directly into this antique polemic. In a fragment of pagan controversy preserved in Macarius Magnes's *Apocriticus* (§II.12), for instance, the evangelists are denounced as "fabricators not historians" (ἐφευρετὰς οὐχ ἵστορας), on exactly the same grounds that Josephus brought against the Greeks: their mutual disaccord.[6] If Celsus belabored precisely this charge of disaccord among the evangelists in his anti-Christian treatise *On True Doctrine*, as Porphyry would later also do in his turn, this must accordingly be recognized as a conventional mode of historiographical refutation, deployed in a large number of ancient works. It is not a special argument devised to undermine a set of *sui generis* Christian texts. In fact, Christian sects themselves resorted to the same line of attack in their own canonical disputes. According to Epiphanius's report, the so-called *Alogoi*, perceiving a chronological discrepancy between John and the Synoptics' alternate versions of the

---

6 For the full text, see Harnack, "Kritik des Neuen Testaments."

events following Jesus' baptism, concluded that "the Gospel in John's name is lying" (τὸ δὲ εὐαγγέλιον τὸ εἰς ὄνομα Ἰωάννου ψεύδεται, *Pan.* 51.18.1). His Gospel was accordingly deemed untrustworthy as an ecclesial text. Of course, the rejection or ridicule of a historian's competence did not always require elaborate synoptic demonstrations, for the distance from mendacity to naivete was not great. Jerome, in his *Commentary on Matthew*, accordingly reports another form of the charge: "Porphyry and the emperor Julian argue in this place [Mt 9:9] that [this shows] either the inexperience of the lying historians (*inperitiam historici mentientis*) or the stupidity of those who immediately followed the savior."[7] Epistle 57 repeats a similar accusation of deception (*arguam falsitatis*).[8]

From such charges we may deduce, significantly, that the Gospels were judged as historical works—if also, significantly, as works worthy of derision by this standard. There is, naturally, an irony in this situation. To call a work a lie was to honor it as morally measured by the truth, an aspirational metric that is often far from clear in the literature of the period. In an excellent study of the topic, T. P. Wiseman registered seven species of ancient historiographical mendacity: (1) tendentiousness, (2) myths, (3) traveler's tales, (4) rhetoric and drama, (5) *aphegesis*, or storytelling for its own sake, (6) elaboration of detail to achieve vividness, and (7) sparseness of detail, also for effect.[9] It should be obvious from the ongoing contemporary discussion of Luke-Acts and ancient fiction, now entering its second generation with scholars like Alan Bale, how pertinent these precise, ancient categories of mendacity are, for they correspond precisely to the *Schwerpunkte* of the debate.[10] It should also be evident, or at least worth considering, how this integrative trope of "lying history" might supersede an anemic Greco-Roman genre theory as the ancient matrix most supplely suited to advance the Lukan discussion. It at once accommodates the complex topical hybridity and gives a needed moral weight to the ever-nagging "truth question."

Mythography and History Writing

Simultaneously at the font of both ancient genre theory and the historiographical censure of lying literature stands the same, all-important canoni-

---

[7] CCSL 77, 55.
[8] CSEL 54, 518.
[9] Wiseman, "Lying Historians," 122–46.
[10] Bale, *Genre and Narrative Coherence*. See also, e.g., Pervo, *Profit with Delight*; MacDonald, *Does the New Testament Imitate Homer?*; Alexander, *Acts in Its Ancient Literary Context*; and Backhaus and Häffner, *Historiographie und fiktionales Erzählen*.

cal source: Plato's critique of the poets. It is not by accident that Plutarch opens his *de Malignitate* with a quotation from Book II of the *Republic*, nor that he devoted an entire treatise to the problem: *How the Young Man Should Listen to the Poets*. Plato famously first fired at Homer as a malign liar, while ambiguously also underwriting the poetic project.[11] When Aristotle later distinguished poetry from history, his characterization of the latter as speaking τὰ γενόμενα and the former as relating οἷα ἂν γένοιτο meant in fact to privilege tragic poetry for its more abstract and thus philosophical character (*Poet.* §9.1451). So, too, his aristocratic consignment of prose to the treatment of low subjects—that is, slaves and those of base character—fell on the side of drama and effectively signaled a kind of return shot in what was already underway as a contest for the philosophical high ground. The result of this sustained, cultural quarrel was a sort of double literary mitosis. First history divided off from epic mythography, then romance split from history (in order, finally, to return and consume it: the cyclic, satirical revenge of poetry on prose). The stages of these separations could obviously be multiplied: Hesiod's didactic epic was already a break with and critique of the Homeric heroic mode, just as Thucydides's work was a Hesiodic response to Herodotus's fanciful odyssey. In the course of this drawn-out process, *historia* was idealized—at least by the historians—as "true" *diegesis*, philosophical narrative, systematically detached from mythmaking, beyond the fictive shoals of lying *poesis*.

From here, we see that Wiseman's second mode of mendacity, myth, is more than simply one type of lie among others. It reaches to the very roots of the cultural struggle and history's self-perception. Strabo's stance toward myth in his *Geography* is representative and exemplifies the idealized but imperfect state of separation.[12] Frequently, myth is excluded on principle as the very antipode to history and philosophical truth. Thus in §8.3.9 he remarks that "The early historians say many things that are not true, because they were accustomed to falsehoods on account of the use of myths in their writings" (τῷ ψεύδει διὰ τὰς μυθογραφίας). Again, in chastising Ephorus for his treatment of the Delphic Oracle, Strabo wonders aloud whether the purported historian "wished to confound the two types, history and myth" (τόν τε τῆς ἱστορίας καὶ τὸν τοῦ μύθου τύπον, §9.3.12). Strabo's mission statement is clear: to keep myth and history apart (τὸ μυθῶδες καὶ τὸ ἱστορικὸν διωρισμένον), for the things that are ancient and false and monstrous are called myths, while history desires the truth (ἡ δ' ἱστορία βούλεται τἀληθές, §11.5.3).

---

[11] On Plato's complex view of poetry and poets, see Destrée and Herrmann, *Plato and the Poets*.
[12] See Paterson, "Geographers as Mythographers."

Clear as this all appears in principle, in practice, Strabo himself, like most other similarly high-minded ancient writers, generously transgresses.[13] Heroic myths and fabulous etiological legends play a major part in his account. The reason seems to be largely his perception that often such fantastic stories have something philosophical to teach and that the mythic dressing can serve as a bait to lure the masses, a perspective with a Platonic pedigree.[14] The double binary myth-history/falsehood-truth thus corresponds to a sociological dichotomy of vulgar-elite.

Ancient Strategies of Demythologization and the Virgin Birth

Now, one of the significant characteristics of the early Christian community, notably the Pauline circles connected with the Pastoral Epistles, is an articulate effort to distinguish its message clearly from mythological material: "Have nothing to do with profane myths and old wives tales" (1 Tm 4:7; e.g., 1 Tm 1:4; 2 Tm 4:4; Ti 1:14; cf. 2 Pt 1:16). In the Roman context of Justin's *Apology*, this religio-cultural bias for history is bound up with an acute recognition of the strong similarities binding the Gospel story with well-known mythic motifs.[15] At least five different times Justin returns to the subject (1 *Apol.* 21–22, 33, 54, 67; *Dial.* 67), in dialogue, interestingly, with both pagans and Jews. In Justin's view, the congruence is most striking at the narrative extremes: the virgin birth and Resurrection/Ascension. Thus the apologist constantly cycles back to the many sons of Zeus and, echoing the explicit charge of his Jewish interlocutor Trypho, Justin repeatedly compares Jesus' birth to that of Perseus from Danaë and Zeus, who came to the virgin in the form of golden rain. The point, to be clear, is not that Justin's theology in any way understood Jesus as a demigod or saw the Gospel story as a myth; this seems demonstrably out of the question. Rather, the clear fact is that pagan hearers of the Gospel, no less than Jews, certainly could and apparently did.

Against this background (and without prejudice to the hypothesis of a Proto-Luke missing the infancy narrative), it is arresting how abruptly the Third Gospel—which bears important links both to Justin and the Pasto-

---

13 Paterson, "Geographers as Mythographers," 208.
14 Paterson, "Geographers as Mythographers," 209.
15 Although Justin ultimately castigates the whole lot of myths as fables, inspired by demons in order to deceive the human race, his approach is not *purely* negative, for these deceptive tales are parodies of biblical prophecy. One might note this perspective as a less sanguine precursor to Lewis's idea of Christianity as the myth that "really happened." See Lewis, "Myth Became Fact"; also idem, "Letter to Arthur Greeves."

rals—not only transitions stylistically from its elegant periodic prologue to a paratactic, LXX-style narrative, but also moves so quickly from the promise of a reliable and well-researched *diegesis* to an infancy account that for many ancient readers evidently resonated with Greco-Roman mythography.

On the one hand, given the example of an author like Strabo, this odd conjunction of methodological statement and actual practice should occasion no surprise. That Luke could assure Theophilus of the *asphaleia* of his account, then promptly confront him with a story of divine conception, is not extraordinary in itself. What is extraordinary, rather, is how straightforwardly the evangelist presents his story. Indeed, Strabo strains to rationalize his use of mythic material in a way entirely foreign to Luke.

> Who were the Myrmidons of Aegina? Ants turned to men by a prayer of Aeacus? No, they were humans who dug into the earth like ants to produce tillable soil . . . Was the pelt of the famous Calydonian Boar responsible for the war between the Curetes and the people of Calydon . . . ? No, it was a territorial dispute . . . Was the Golden Fleece real? No, it is based on the fleecy skins that the natives of Colchis use to catch the gold that flows down from the mountains.[16]

Strabo's demythologization is a traditional historiographical technique reaching back to the earliest four fragments in Jacoby's collection—Hecataeus, Acusilaus, Pherecydes, and Hellanicus—thus marking the earliest efforts at a self-conscious separation of history from myth. Herodorus of Heracleia and Herodotus himself might be added to the list of rationalizers, though the most interesting and important representative is the paradoxographer Palaephatus, a fourth-century contemporary of Aristotle whose *Peri Apiston* was later a favorite of Byzantine Christian authors in their opposition to pagan myth.[17] In the New Testament period, both Diodorus Siculus and Plutarch still employ the method, the latter openly claiming in his *Lives* to be "purifying Fable (τὸ μυθῶδες) and making her submit to reason and take on the semblance of history" (*Life of Theseus* §1). In this spirit, significantly, Plutarch applies his method to the wondrous narratives that surround the birth of Romulus. Thus, although the mother declared Mars to be the child's father, she "was really deflowered by Amulius who came to her in armor and ravished her." Or, again, Plutarch explains, since for the Latins *lupae* means both she-wolves and whores, it may be that the wife of Faustulus, the children's foster father, was a woman of loose character and the true

---

[16] Patterson, "Geographers as Mythographers," 212.
[17] On Palaephatus, see Stern, *Palaephatus*.

nurse of the story (*Life of Romulus* iv). Celsus's story about Panthera, with its punning, etymological explanation of the supposedly virgin (*parthenos*) mother of Jesus, is enormously reminiscent here of Plutarch and belongs entirely to this tradition of irreverent historical demythologization (*Cels.* I. 28, 32–33). It is not, in fact, so very original, either as polemics or the mere cultured exposure of a lying pseudo-history.

Enlightened modern exegetes and theologians may repeat the ancient exercise and insist that Luke's essential point in recounting the virginal conception was actually an abstract Christological theologoumenon about "Gottessohnschaft" or the effort to promote a rivalry with the also supposedly miraculously conceived *divus Augustus*.[18] Both motifs (not unrelated) are admittedly present.[19] Nevertheless, the sanitized tack of demythologization was not invented with Bultmann. It was already an available historiographical technique had Luke chosen to adopt and employ it. It is, accordingly, difficult to accept that such reductive readings exhaust the literal meaning of the text *as Luke intended*.

The principal observation here is simple. Luke signals absolutely no critical distance from the ostensibly mythographic divine conception he recounts. This is one aspect—quite important—of his noticeably non-intervening authorial persona, a major divergence from the historiographical precedent and practice of the time. A negative measure of this silent Lukan posture is the absence of what I have called elsewhere *rumor rhetoric*, the characterization of dubious material as circulating hearsay.[20] In effect, such rhetoric concretizes the counsel of Lucian:

> If a myth comes along you must tell it but do not believe it entirely;
> no, make it known for your audience to make of it what they will—
> you run no risk and lean to neither side. (§60 [Kilburn, LCL])

Thus, when Dionysius of Halicarnassus recounts the story of Ocrisia, for example, the virgin inseminated by a fire demon, or perhaps by Vulcan himself, a tradition often brought into the Lukan discussion, the historian elaborately distances himself. First, he frames his myth-telling as serving the archival purpose of an antiquarian collector: "There is also current in the local records (ἐν ταῖς ἐπιχωρίοις ἀναγραφαῖς) another story relating to [Tullius's] birth which raises the circumstances attending to the realm of the fabulous, and we have found it in many Roman histories" (§4.2.1). He

---

18 "The narrator's aim is not to report a gynecological miracle. The aim is to confess Jesus as the messianic Son of God and to point at the very beginning of his life to the divine origin of his person" (Moltmann, *Way of Jesus Christ*, 83).
19 See, e.g., Blumenthal, "Augustus' Erlass und Gottes Macht."
20 See chap. 5 in this volume.

likewise adds a pious caveat, parading his rational belief that divinities are not such as popular stories suggest: "This account—if it be pleasing to the gods and the lesser divinities that it be related—is somewhat as follows." Finally, most importantly, Dionysius appends the whole fantastic tale as a curious appendix to an alternative, perfectly straightforward narrative of Tullius's nativity, with which version the author says, "I can best agree" (μάλιστ' ἔγωγε συγκατατίθεμαι). The reader is not corralled into accepting a single totalizing account but is presented with graded options. Obviously, there is a level of historiographical sophistication to such circumscribed mythography entirely missing from the Third Gospel's approach.

Luke's distance from Dionysius can be registered on several levels. First, one must concede that wild details like the phantom phallus suddenly appearing to Ocrisia out of the fire make anything more than the most abstract comparison with the structure of the Lukan story a strained exercise. In a similar way, the fact that the annunciation is not placed in a remote past—in a Thucydidean archeology—but is related rather as contemporary history (even precisely dated) likewise distinguishes it, not insignificantly, from such parallel traditions. Finally, these peculiarities of content must be factored against a major peculiarity of form. Supposing Luke indeed had some essentially historiographical intention—to write a true *diegesis*, as he seems to say—the lofty mode of universal erudition manifestly has no claims on his narrative enterprise (no more than utility for a political or military career). Luke does not tell his story with the distant reserve of other historians of the day, and his writing is not calibrated for a social elite. Some other purpose is driving Luke's project. Where, then, does this leave us? Pervo's "Profit with Delight"? Unlikely, I think, and a jump to fiction as the point of reference should be resisted.

The Historiographical Home of Nativity Tales

With respect to the mode of historiography in which Luke 1–2 moved, Dionysius's mention of "local records" offers an interesting hint. Nearly forty years ago, Emilio Gabba pointed to the importance of the local history gathered for tourists by guidebook authors such as Pausanias, depositories of material culled in large part from the popular, priestly lore that accumulated around regional sanctuaries.[21] Such literature, Gabba argued, represents an important historiographical bridge to the emerging Greco-Roman romance literature. Dionysius's witness confirms that it also served as a source for tales of miraculous births.

Interestingly enough, such divine conception stories failed to take hold in the pagan romances as did the omnipresent *Scheintod* motif. The sole miraculous birth to appear in the Greco-Roman novels can nevertheless be traced directly to a local cult setting. The case is not unknown to students of the gospels, dubious as the parallel is on nearly every level.[22] It concerns the ruse of Nektanebos, in the *Alexander Romance*, in which the magician and deposed king of Egypt sires the child Alexander with Queen Olympias of Macedon by dressing himself with the golden hair and horns of the Libyan god Ammon. Of interest here is not the farcical content but the fact that the indecorous nativity burlesque has its evident origin in the cultic proclamation of Alexander as a god and as the legitimate ruler of Egypt by the Sibyl of Zeus Ammon at the Siwa Oasis in the Libyan desert.[23]

The special case of the *Alexander Romance* indicates how specifically biographical interests might crystallize around hero cults, and ultimately the nativity fable gravitated more typically to Greco-Roman *bioi* as a host genre than to the novel.[24] It is thus significant that the nativity accounts that often preface these lives are also in open contact with such local shrine legends. This applies, once again and still more clearly, to the second nativity parallel conventionally invoked in Lukan studies: Suetonius's account of the marvelous conception of Augustus by Atia in his *Life of the Deified Augustus*. Atia, Suetonius recounts, was impregnated by a serpent as she slept in Apollo's temple, the serpent being taken by some to be the god Apollo himself. The source of the story, however, as the historian explicitly says, was a collection of priestly legends: the books of Asclepiades the Mendesian, that is, his θεολογουμενῶν, an explanation of bizarre cultic rituals by equally bizarre etiological tales.

A mixture of arcane learning and on-the-ground research (*historia*)—or at least acquaintance with provincial tales recounted in geographies and other local literature—thus gives a special flavor to this nature of nativity report. Suetonius, for instance, not only relies upon erudite collections like Asclepiades. The biographer also records the following on-the-spot information about Octavian's place of birth:

---

21 Gabba, "True History and False History."

22 See, e.g., Funk, *Acts of Jesus*. For an aggressively maximalist view of the mythical background of the Gospel story, see Rhys, *Shaken Creeds*.

23 The flowering of ruler cults in the Hellenistic age was closely tied to claims of divine descent. See Green, *Alexander to Actium*, 397.

24 The importance of *bioi* for study of the Gospels is widely accepted. See Burridge, *What Are the Gospels?*

> A small room like a pantry is shown (*ostenditur*) to this day as the emperor's nursery in his grandfather's country-house near Velitrae, and the opinion prevails in the neighborhood that he was actually born there. No one ventures to enter this room except of necessity and after purification (*huc introire nisi necessario et caste religio est*), since there is a conviction of long standing that those who approach it without ceremony are seized with shuddering and terror. (§VI [Rolfe, LCL])

The emperor's birthplace has evidently become an attraction and a shrine, and one is in close contact here with the store of traditions held and purveyed by local residents and guides. The same essential *Heimatkunde* context informs Philostratus's account of the birth of Apollonius, which is connected with the description of a fountain sacred to Zeus in the city of Tyana. While Apollonius's actual descent from Zeus is not directly endorsed, Philostratus nevertheless recounts such divine paternity as what οἱ ἐγχώριοί φασι, what "the locals say" (§I.6).

It is not without interest in view of such local lore to recall that Justin, a citizen of Nablus (biblical Shechem in Roman Palestine), within a lifetime of the writing of the Gospels, evidently knew a local tradition of Jesus' being born in cave (*Dial.* §78; cf. *Prot. Jas.* §18.1), a tradition still preserved and actively propagated during Origen's pilgrimage around AD 215:

> There is shown (δείκνυται) in Bethlehem a cave (σπήλαιον), where he was born, and in the cave the manger (ἡ ἐν τῷ σπηλαίῳ φάτνη), where he was wrapped in swaddling clothes. And this site (τὸ δεικνύμενον τοῦτο) is greatly talked of in the region (ἐν τοῖς τόποις), even among the enemies of the faith, it being said that in this cave was born that Jesus who is worshipped and reverenced by the Christians. (*Cels.* I, 51 [ANF])

Luke, who mentions neither cave nor stable but only a φάτνη (Lk 2:7), can himself in no way be the source of this detail about the σπήλαιον or its precise location. Local tradents of a story of Jesus' nativity clearly existed in Bethlehem and Judea from an impressively early date. While Luke's own infancy narrative manifestly fueled this entire business, on the basis of the parallels from the other Greco-Roman *bioi*, the evangelist himself may nevertheless be cautiously imagined to be working with similar local shrine/attraction sources—most likely oral (cf. Lk 1:2)—albeit at a more primitive stage in the shaping of information about this regional celebrity's birth. The closely related Baptist material offers witness to the inevitable dynamic of local storytelling, albeit without the historiographical distancing strategy normally seen. "All these things were talked about (διελαλεῖτο πάντα τὰ ῥήματα ταῦτα) throughout the entire hill country of Judea" (Lk 1:65)—talked about for some time, even down to Luke's day, we may well believe. Exceptionally strong reasons already exist for connecting Luke's genealogy with primitive family traditions about Jesus. I see no reason not to imagine similar circulating reports about Jesus' birth informing *both* the Gospel and later pilgrims like Justin and Origen. It is a recognizable "pre-, para-, and post-Lukan" framework of tradition and transmission.[25]

The provenance of miraculous nativity stories in the context of provincial cult legends helps to conceptualize a historiographical context for Luke 1–2. Whatever one makes of the broader thesis of Gregory Sterling—there are excellent insights but also certain problems—he makes a useful move in highlighting the national literature of priests like Berossos and Manetho.[26] When Josephus in the *Contra Apionem* thus paints the Jewish Scriptures as a specimen of just this sort of Eastern sacerdotal lore, a kind of sanctuary archive of the famous temple state in Jerusalem, a characterization found likewise in 2 Maccabees 2:13 and the *Letter to Aristeas*, we have the grounds to link Luke to the Greco-Roman idea of ἀναγραφαί ἐπιχώριαι through his link to Israel's sacral *Heimatkunde*.

LUKAN LITERATURE AND ISRAEL'S ARCHIVES

There is every reason to advance this perspective in application to the infancy narrative—and this from two directions. First, on the simple level of narrative appearance, the affinity is clear. Whatever else the pervasive Temple setting of Luke 1–2 may accomplish, it certainly establishes a forceful hieratic atmosphere. Priestly courses, incense offerings, ascetic prophets and inspired, versified oracles, pilgrimages to the national shrine, and sages discoursing in its precincts all contribute to conjure the vivid activity of a world-famous sanctuary. If romance literature took an interest in exotic locales along with their shrines, the absence in Luke of the island motif and, still more, the absence in the novels of any real interest in miraculous births inclines me to hear Luke's opening overture in a different connection. For a Greco-Roman reader, these chapters would have likely recalled those theological books and local cult histories that made up the piecemeal mesh of material from which the universal historians and biographers drew their

---

[25] See Giambrone, "Comments on a New Fragment."
[26] See Sterling, *Historiography and Self-Definition*.

reports. This gives a bit more color and purpose to Aune's description of Luke-Acts as one of "the hundreds of lost mediocre histories."[27]

My judgment that Luke's work might keep company with "mediocre" historical texts of local provenance and theological orientation should not be misunderstood or obscure the Third Gospel's broad horizon, which gains an epic scope from its grafting onto the specific national Scriptures of the Judeans, their cult, and their god. For the classical mind, it was the theme that determined stylistic elevation, and of Luke's theme there can be little doubt. The evangelist announces a thing universally serious and significant in chronicling "the events fulfilled among us" (Lk 1:1). This leads to the second point.

On the level of Luke's actual sources, there is additional cause to imagine him working in a distinctly Judean historiographical mold. I do not know if anyone has offered more than tautologies regarding the *Sitz im Leben* of Luke's putative "Baptist Source," but whether we think of Essenes in the desert, Judean hill folk, or some records of priestly descent, we will find ourselves in the same basic context. As for Jesus' own genealogical records, there are, as I've said, solid arguments to accept Luke's contact with traditions held by the so-called *desposynoi*.[28] The wider question of a possible Semitic *Vorlage* beneath Luke 1–2 remains an open question, despite Chang-Wook Jung's recent effort to resolve the matter.[29] His stress on the LXX, however, cannot fundamentally lead us astray. Everything in Luke's two annunciation scenes, from sterile women to angelic messengers and canticles of praise, points to Old Testament precedent.[30] This is what Fitzmyer presumably, hopefully means when he labels the Lukan infancy narrative "imitative historiography"—historical matter assimilated to other literary patterns.[31] If these Scriptures were approached in the archival spirit of a Josephus, Luke emerges, like him, as kind of *continuator* of Israel's national literature, in the infancy narrative even as the author of a genealogical micro-history/short story like Ruth.[32] "In the days of" was an Old Testament formula not unlike Xenophon's *meta tauta*, and one need not embrace all Conzelmann's ideas to envision the LXX as a Lukan prequel.

---

27 Aune, "Luke 1:1–4."

28 See Bauckham, *Jude and the Relatives of Jesus*; and Giambrone, "Comments on a New Fragment."

29 Jung, *Original Language of the Lukan Infancy Narrative*.

30 In Bultmann's influential view, of course, the original Semitic story "could not have contained the motif unheard of in a Jewish environment, of a virgin birth. It was first added in the transformation in Hellenism, where the idea of the generation of a king or a hero from a virgin by the godhead was widespread." Bultmann, *History of the Synoptic Tradition*, 291–92.

31 Fitzmyer, *Gospel According to Luke I-IX*, 309.

Another prequel to the Third Gospel, though written in its wake, confronts us with the risks this imitative history writing entails. At the very opening of the *Infancy Gospel of James*, Joachim, reproached for his childlessness, responds with a decision to consult the local records: "I'm going to check the book of the twelve tribes of Israel to see whether I am the only one in Israel who hasn't produced a child. And he searched (the records) and found that all the righteous people in Israel did indeed have children" (1.6).[33] The miraculous birth of Mary that soon follows, possibly a virginal conception depending on the manuscripts one follows, is thus inscribed within the ongoing history of the twelve tribes. The extension of the nation's history thereby takes its form as the flagrant fabrication of an established literary pattern.

A great many stylistic details separate Luke from this Christian infancy romance, but his one-upmanship in recounting a birth more miraculous than even Isaac's suggests a conscious engagement with a whole family of Old Testament texts.[34] While it is vital to bear in mind the crucial difference between "scripture historicized" and "history scripturalized"—biblical dressing is no litmus test for judging an event's facticity—such scriptural patterning nevertheless highlights the ever-lingering truth question.[35]

The Truth Question

Loveday Alexander remarked that lurking behind the debate about genre in Lukan studies is ever the yawning question of reliability: Is it true?[36] Raymond Brown's attempt to ponder the question betrays the confusion of contemporary efforts to render a judgment.

---

32 On this generic designation, see Hubbard, *Book of Ruth*, 48.

33 According to Ronald Hock's note on the Greek text, although the word "book" is not present, it is "widely assumed by scholars" and may imply "some sort of genealogical register" (*Infancy Gospels of James and Thomas*, 33).

34 See Hartsock, "Call-Stories in Luke."

35 On this language, see Goodacre, "Scripturalization in Mark's Crucifixion Narrative." Bart D. Ehrman (*Jesus, Interrupted*, 74) opines: "Matthew wrote that Jesus was a virgin because that's what he thought the scripture predicted." Dale Allison (*Constructing Jesus*, 389) comments: "To biblicize is not necessarily to invent. Eusebius, when recounting Constantine's victory over Maxentius at the battle of the Milvian bridge, cast the latter in the role of Pharaoh, the former in the role of Moses, which does not mean that they fought no such battle ... that a story is scripturally indebted or lays implicit or explicit claim to fulfill prophecy does not, in and of itself, tell us whether it has an anchor in history."

36 Alexander, "Fact, Fiction, and the Genre of Luke-Acts."

> I do not imply that Matthew and Luke presented the virginal conception only as a symbol and were indifferent to what really took place. I think that both of them regarded the virginal conception as historical, but the modern intensity about historicity was not theirs. For them the primary import of the virginal conception was theological.[37]

I confess a certain puzzlement at this statement. For Alexander, the truth question was not accessible on the textual order. For Brown, the author's intention is also irrelevant. But why? Is it not possible that "the modern intensity about historicity," so obviously foreign to the original authors, is thus simply an unhelpful anachronism? And, if so, must not an alternative approach be in order? The ancients were perhaps not entirely wrong to address the problem of their texts ad hominem, for the vexing question of what is properly historiography and what is fiction is drawn, at least at one level, by the ethical line between credulity and fabrication. Evidently, Luke thought he was telling the truth. In ancient terms, one might accordingly ask: Was the evangelist credulous or was he simply negligent? Or was he, by contrast, a trustworthy source?

We are living in a postmodern moment, however groggy from a prolonged positivistic hangover. Hayden White, for all the ambiguities his work entails, thus seems to point us broadly in a helpful direction.[38] In a word, we must reconceive historiography as an aesthetical and ethical enterprise. As it so happens, this is to conceive it as the premodern ancients also did. Aristotle's τὰ γενόμενα is not at all Ranke's *wie es eigentlich gewesen ist*. I can here only make a couple gestures at where this reorientation might lead us, but it seems to me worth addressing both Luke's aesthetical and ethical orientation.

---

37 Brown, *Birth of the Messiah*, 517.

38 White, *Metahistory*. White subjects what Brown calls "the modern intensity about historicity" to a powerful critique. Referring to the work of continental thinkers (e.g., Valéry, Heidegger, Sartre, Lévi-Strauss, Foucault) and Anglo-American philosophers alike, White contends that "the historical consciousness on which Western man has prided himself since the beginning of the nineteenth century may be little more than a theoretical basis for the ideological position from which Western civilization views its relationship not only to cultures and civilizations preceding it but also to those contemporary with it in time and contiguous in space. In short, it is possible to view historical consciousness as a specifically Western prejudice by which the presumed superiority of modern, industrial society can be retroactively substantiated" (2).

The Aesthetics of Luke 1–2

Luke's nativity diptych is an aesthetically complex composition. If Dionysius of Halicarnassus and Lucian can be taken as any gauge of ancient historiographical, literary taste, Luke's choice of precisely this beginning for his account would probably have won praise for the favorable way it compares with the abrupt and unexplained appearance of both John the Baptist and Jesus at the start of Mark's Gospel. On the measure of White's formalist "Poetics of History," a similar significance might be attributed to Luke's option for specific inaugural motifs, which elevates his construction to the level of a *story*, in contrast, for instance, to Matthew's *chronicle* style opening.[39] This implies, moreover, that Luke selects distinctive terminating motifs as well, avoiding again the curiously open-ended Matthean chain of prophetic fulfillments (cf. Mt 2:22–23).

In fact, Luke's infancy narrative is very much a Gospel in miniature and therefore a kind of comedy, just like the Gospel at large. What is striking in the structure of Luke 1–2 is that the essential comic motif of separation and reunion, accomplished with the loss of the Christ child and his climatic recovery and return home introduces the Father's will, the divine *dei*, as the separating obstacle. This announces a theological program and is not without precedent. Northrup Frye, for instance, observes how many of Shakespeare's comedies are structured around law as the plot complication.[40] It is nevertheless startling that there are simply no villains in Luke's infancy narrative. A glance at Matthew will indicate that this was hardly inevitable. The fact is more impressive given Luke's technique of contrasting narrative foils. Rather than a bloodthirsty anti-king Herod, Luke provides only the poor, sympathetic, unbelieving Zachariah. Such distance from Matthew's aggressive and exaggerated tactic is highly representative, I suggest, of a much milder and more nuanced Gospel-wide posture. One might think of Luke's complex portraits of Pilate or the Pharisees (cf. Mt 23).

The Augustan setting and bucolic mood, particularly in Luke 2, naturally reinforce the pacific effect of the overall composition. The work stops well short of being a pastoral idyll, however (cf. Vergil, *Eclogue* IV; *Sib. Or.* 3:372; 8:478). Ultimately, I would link this strong impression of Luke's gentle touch with the criterion of impartiality/goodwill (εὐμένεια), in the ancient sense of Plutarch, Lucian, Josephus, and others: the fair handling of friends and foes alike and the opposite of mendacious behavior. To be equally beyond both acrimony and flattery was to stand in solid service of the truth. In this

---

39 See White, *Metahistory*, 5–7.
40 Frye, *Anatomy of Criticism*, 166.

respect it is not at all incidental that exegetes cannot decide whether in the end Luke is pro- or anti-Roman—he is both and neither—he is, perhaps, fair. If the Third Evangelist thus avoids the sorts of harsh words, abusive digressions, and omission of good things noted by Plutarch and on display in the First Gospel, what analysis might be made of the ethical appeal of the author we call "Luke"?

The Author's Ethical Appeal

Ancient theorists disagreed on the precise locus of ethical persuasion. Aristotle, in his *Rhetoric*, placed the power of personal character in the speech act itself, not in previously held opinions about the speaker's person.[41] Later Roman writers, by contrast, notably Cicero in the *De Oratore*, insisted upon an author's lived moral existence. Both positions obviously comprehend significant aspects of the dynamics of persuasion, and it seems best simply to accommodate both views.

At the level of reception, it is easy to see how the extratextual persona of "Saint Luke" contributed to the perception of his text as making an honest and credible claim to be telling the truth. The so-called Anti-Marcionite Prologues and other similar, prefaced materials textualized this hagiographic persona in the manner of a "paratext," to use the language of Gerard Genette.[42] In this way, the process of textual transmission itself incorporated an appeal to trust the words of Paul's inspired companion. If weight is given to Hengel's argument about the circulation of named titles with the earliest manuscripts, it is clear that this ethical paratext in some form or another was the primitive envelope in which the Gospel *ad Theophilum* was delivered to its readers.[43]

Both the importance of such a *text-cum-auctor* transmission as a factor in assessing the text's truthfulness as well as the methodological challenges facing a reconstruction of the early forms of the Gospel's circulation are apparent in a highly significant comment by Tertullian.[44]

---

[41] See Marincola, *Authority and Tradition in Ancient Historiography*, 129.

[42] Genette, *Paratexts*.

[43] See Hengel, "Die Evangelienüberschriften." See also the comprehensive treatment of the manuscript evidence by Gathercole, "Titles of the Gospels."

[44] The debate over the relation of Marcion's version of the Third Gospel to its canonical form raises the legitimate question of whether this unnamed text was not in fact the primitive form. The issue is complicated, however, by Marcion's apparent desire to validate an original Pauline form of the Gospel, with the Apostle himself (not a putative traveling companion) as the authority, while nevertheless naming the text simply "The Gospel," thereby rejecting a

> Marcion, you must know, ascribes no author to his Gospel (*nullum adscribit auctorem*) ... here I might now make a stand, and contend that a work ought not to be recognized (*non agnoscendum*) ... which gives no promise of credibility (*nullam fidem*) from the fullness of its title and the just profession of its author. (*Adversus Marcionem* 4.2 [ANF])

The failure of the third evangelist to identify himself explicitly in the text and specifically within the prologue contrasts markedly, of course, with all historiographical convention. For this reason, Bovon confesses in his commentary on 1:4: "The absence of the author's name in the prologue remains a riddle to me."[45] From Hecateaus of Miletus to Herodotus of Halicarnauss and all the way down, the name of the historian was an essential element in the construction of a prologue, often the very first word.[46]

In the face of this firm Greco-Roman practice, Armin Baum has argued that an alternative ancient Near East historiographical convention, to which the historical books the Old Testament belong, preferred to minimize the author and elevate the subject matter through a literary convention of anonymity.[47] This is an interesting prospect, worthy of attention. Still, the messy redactional histories as well as the absence of proper prologues in this literature complicate it as an obvious paradigm for Luke. The Lukan literary *novum* is placed at the peculiar conjunction of broad Greco-Roman and native Jewish traditions, and this extends to conventions governing the frame-breaking interventions of the author.

---

pluriform, name-based paradigm ("according to"). On the broad question of Marcion's relation to Luke, Dieter Roth resists the bold claims of several recent authors (e.g., Klinghardt, Vinzent) who would give priority to Marcion, urging caution and underlining the need for a critical text. See Roth, "Link between Luke and Marcion's Gospel." See also my "Comments on a New Fragment."

45 Bovon, *Luke 1*, 18. Schurmann (*Das Lukasevangelium*, 2n8) is content to say that Luke's exclusively intra-ecclesial audience made the convention of naming himself superfluous (presumably because he was already known).

46 Both the search for fame and a statement of one's qualifications demanded the author's self-identification. Almost Arrian alone rejected the tradition, but only because he already felt he had all the fame and standing he required: "I need not write my name, for it is not at all unknown among men, nor my country, nor my family" (§1.12.5). The authors of the novels, unlike the historians but like the authors of epic poetry, remain consistently anonymous—apart from Chariton, who stands at the origin of this literature and identifies himself tersely by name, city, and occupation. Formal prologues, however, are also unconventional in this literature, even if the rhetoric of autopsy and documentation is adopted as an artifice in the works themselves.

47 Baum, "Anonymity of the New Testament History Books."

The anonymous Greek prologue of 2 Maccabees 2:19–32 perhaps brings us closest to Luke. The basic ethical appeal of this text is the claim to have sweated and labored hard in the selfless effort to produce something pleasantly beneficial for the reader. Luke develops nothing so explicit or pathetic, but behind his claim to have carefully tracked everything down from the start readers could certainly discern his implicit labors. Here the prologues part ways, however. The epitomizer ultimately betrays the anonymity of his history in order to shield himself from blame as a liar, naming Jason of Cyrene and laying the burden of historical accuracy at his door: "leaving the responsibility for exact details to the compiler" (2 Mc 2:28), as he says. The epitomizer's appeal for good will thus stops short of guaranteeing truthfulness, content to cover only the last two of Lucian's three historiographical objectives: utility and pleasure. "We have aimed to please those who wish to read, to make it easy for those who are inclined to memorize, and to profit all readers" (2 Mc 2:25). The Third Evangelist, by contrast, explicitly takes upon himself the responsibility of confirming the reliability (ἀσφάλεια) of what others had already propounded and his readers had already heard.

Conclusion

Was Luke a lying historian? In both the ancient world and still today, the answer is *yes* for some and for others, obviously, *no*. Can anything more be said? Several observations are possible at the conclusion of this study. First, it is not without genuine interest that the typically modern strategy of rationalistic demythologization was available to, but not employed by Luke's infancy narrative. Reducing his account to a *theologoumenon* accordingly appears misguided. At the same time, the evangelist's evident proximity to local birth traditions about Jesus known to have been circulating in Judea at an early date connects his work with a brand of guidebook, regional historiography seen above all in the context of other *bioi*. The identification of such a primitive source stratum is both promising and precarious for judging the value of Luke's report. If precisely such local nativity fables were generally, openly rejected by historians of the Greco-Roman age, Luke's tacit acceptance of a broad motif of divine paternity should not hide the considerable distance of his account from the parallels. His infancy story fits much more naturally as a continuation of Old Testament type scenes. Yet this scriptural affinity, too, implies that the embarrassing question should be forced: Is such a tale to be believed?[48] Or as the ancients and postmoderns might more poignantly put

---

48 One should mention here two cultural contexts, in addition to the mythological/folkloric motif, which have often been invoked to explain the origins of the doctrine of the virgin

it: Is this the work of an honest and able historian? Or is the *auctor* behind this text a "liar"?

In the end, White's subjective turn in historiography need not stand in absolute tension with a theory of truth as *adequatio ad rem*, and he is right to protest against relativism. The ethical turn to the author—the challenge posed by a *de Malignitate*—keeps in balance a kind of New Criticism aestheticism, reminiscent of the Second Sophistic concerns of the *Letter to Gnaeus*, for the author is where the text and the world outside the text converge. If from the prologue on Luke establishes himself as a much less interventionist authorial persona than other historians of the period, this forces us finally to take his measure by other means.[49] Luke's gentle and fair-handed manner (εὐμένεια), noted above, hints at an ancient construction of impartiality, for instance, that might be profitably pursued. Yet an entire world of moral exploration here opens up and obliges our attention. Luke's love for the poor and his handling of the rich, his political vision of turning the "world upside down," his doctrine of forgiveness, *aphesis,* and his vision of Israel—and not least the philosophical parameters of the possible as Luke conceives it: "Nothing will be impossible for God" (Lk 1:37)—all this, no less than the stubborn riddle of a worldwide census, is relevant to a judgment of the historical *asphaleia* of the Gospel *kata Lukan*.[50]

---

birth: ancient medicine and antique views of sexuality (i.e., idealization of virginity). See, e.g., Emmenegger, *Wie die Jungfrau zum Kind kam*. Another familiar explanation with an ancient pedigree is that the illegitimacy of Jesus' birth was apologetically transformed into a story of virginal conception. See, e.g., Lüdemann, *Virgin Birth?* Philosophically, the question of miracles is naturally a foundational issue. On the contours of this long debate, see Sweeney, "Modern and Ancient Controversies." See also the unusual position of Lincoln, *Born of a Virgin?*

49 See Sheeley, *Narrative Asides in Luke-Acts*.

50 On the Lukan census, see Giambrone, "Augustus as Censor."

CHAPTER 4

MEMORIALIZING MIRACLES IN THE WORLD OF THE GOSPELS

The recent turn to memory in historical Jesus research is a major and healthy paradigm shift. It has rebooted the methodology in foundational ways and revised the broad agenda of askable questions. In the eager mood that this new *Traditionsgeschichte* perspective has awakened, interest has been redirected frequently (and fruitfully) toward the old chestnut of oral traditions, rethinking those critical and complex dynamics. Interdisciplinary dabbling in cognitive neuroscience is also to be seen.[1] By contrast, an energetic rapprochement between memory and material culture is, on my inspection, largely missing.

This is curious, for the bridge is not difficult to build. The ancient world, as known to us both through texts and archeological discovery, abounded in physical memorials. Memory was not purely an abstract mental operation (as neuroscience confirms) but conventionally invested in concrete things and places. In the Greco-Roman context, one might reasonably speak of a near obsession with memorial statuary, monuments, and inscriptions.[2] The cultivation of these carefully engineered acts of remembering is particularly

---

1 While Birger Gerhardsson long advocated a certain variation on the memory approach to Gospel studies, a significant new wave of research has been energetically exploring new avenues for approximately the past twenty years, and the bibliography is by now too substantial to be easily cited. See, e.g., Byrskog, *Story as History*; Dunn, *Christianity in the Making*, vol. 1; Bauckham, *Jesus and the Eyewitnesses*; Le Donne, *Historiographical Jesus*; Allison, *Constructing Jesus*; Rodriguez, *Structuring Early Christian Memory*; Byrskog et al., *Social Memory and Social Identity*; Kirk, *Memory and the Jesus Tradition*. See also the overview of Havukainen, *Quest for the Memory of Jesus*.
2 See Ramsay MacMullen's classic essay, "Epigraphic Habit in the Roman Empire."

rich, for these crafted *aide-mémoires* both preserved in a kind of frozen form and worked actively to mold the living shape of public recollection. If much of this memorial lavishness derives from the honor-based ethos and considerable capital (both social and economic) of Rome's *honestiores*, memorialization through artifacts was not exclusively elite behavior. An excellent example is ex-voto culture.

The Ex-Voto Habit

Ex-votos might range from entire temples to the simplest, most homely objects. The *Templum Lares Permarini* in the southern Campus Martius in Rome, for instance, was built to fulfill a vow made by Lucius Emilius Regillus during a naval battle in 190 BC.[3] A grateful boy at a shrine in Asia Minor, by contrast, dedicated his ten dice to the resident god.[4] At the sacred wood of Persaro, stones were offered as votives and simply inscribed with the deity's name: IVNO LOVCINA, MAT[ER]-MATVTA, SALVTE, archaic Latin goddesses of childbirth and health.[5] Figurines, cups, bowls and amphorae, plaques, tripods, swords, shields, and stelae: anything one vowed to the gods in return for a favor might be accepted into the treasuries of a sanctuary. All these gifts served to augment the shrine's prestige—if not through monetary worth, at least through testamentary value to the efficacy of the local god's power. The practice accordingly cuts across class lines, as the sheer multitude of the excavated ex-votos also attests. At Ponte di Nona, a small sanctuary located nine roman miles east of the *Urbs*, eight thousand votives items were recovered.[6] So common was the offering of these devotional memorials that votive items were mass produced, and the ritual Latin formula was simply abbreviated VSLM: *votum solvit libens merito*, "freely discharges the vow, as deserved." The habit of such thank offerings was, naturally, by no means confined to the Greco-Roman context. The same phenomenon has exceptionally deep roots in the ancient Near East, from Ayssria to Uratu to Phoenicia, Egypt, and beyond.[7] The temple-based act of recording a divine favor with some inscribed object, celebrating the god's gracious intervention, was all but ubiquitous in the eastern provinces of the empire.

---

3 See Orlin, "Augustan Reconstruction and Roman Memory."
4 See LiDonnici, *Epidaurian Miracle Inscriptions*, inscription {A8}. Henceforth, alphanumeric citations in curly brackets refer to the inscriptions from this collection.
5 See Graham, "Mobility Impairment in the Sanctuaries of Early Roman Italy."
6 See Graham, "Mobility Impairment in the Sanctuaries of Early Roman Italy," 248–66.
7 See, e.g., del Olmo Lete, "Les inscriptions puniques votives."

Although the relevant epigraphical haul in southern Syria and Judea during the early Roman period is far from overwhelming, these regions should not be exempted from this wider culture. Ex-voto inscriptions naturally intensify dramatically with the arrival of legionary soldiers after 70 AD.[8] One may nevertheless presume a basic continuity of praxis in pagan centers like Caesarea, where temples to Roman gods were known from the very start. No less than soldiers, exposed to all manner of danger, sailors are high performers when it comes to offering ex-votos, and it is right to imagine many paying vows for their safe arrival in the harbor at Sebastos. The Decapolis predictably carried this culture inland. In first-century Gerasa, Demetrius, son Apollonius, a priest of the imperial cult, dedicated a statue at the temple, while a certain Artemidora offered a small limestone altar, likely to her patron, Artemis, one of the city's two main divinities.[9]

Healing Shrines

Within this obviously robust ex-voto culture, healing shrines deserve to be specially singled out. It has often been observed (normally with poorly hidden value judgments) that an unbroken line can easily be drawn between pagan popular religion and the Catholic cult of the saints.[10] Anyone who has visited Fatima and observed the piles of crutches and wax effigies of body parts will immediately recognize the perennial type of the healing shrine. Huge numbers of ancient terra cotta votives fill museum collections—heads, faces, eyes, ears, teeth, tongues, hands, fingers, feet, toes, arms, legs, genitals, breasts, babies, bladders, and other diverse manner of innards—each one the memorial of a healing. Some of these commemorations in clay of answered prayer reach back as far as four thousand years, like the Minoan members held in the British Museum (BM 1907.1–19).[11]

Regional healing shrines were dotted across the empire, and based on the preponderance of one or another body part among the votives, it is

---

8 See CIIP 1128–1138.

9 See Gatier, "Inscriptions du 1er siècle a Gérasa"; and Gatier et al., "Greek Inscriptions in the Jordan Museum."

10 See, e.g., the highly erudite and equally meandering "classical Sebastianism" of Bettini, "Looking at Ourselves Backwards," who reflects on the link between a statue of St. Giuseppe Moscati in Naples and the ancient cult of Asclepius. More sober and succinct, see the commonplace observation of Colazilli, "Reproducing Human Limbs."

11 The specific practice is again widespread. The Temple of Hathor in Deir el Bahari, for instance, abounds in phalli and seems to have specialized in cures for impotence. See Colazilli, "Reproducing Human Limbs," 160.

often possible to surmise what sort of healings this or that shrine especially promised. At the monumental Etrurian site of Ara della Regina at Tarquinia, for instance, 26 legs, 225 feet, and 233 wombs were found in a deposit of 759 votives, suggesting a concentration on mobility impairments and infertility.[12] The occasional presence of medical professionals among the priests tending such shrines helps explain this sort of specialization.

This alliance with ancient medicine brings one healing cult into view, which rises far above all the others: the cult of Asclepius, son of Apollo and patron of the Greek medical arts. Without being a franchise, the ancient world knew a massive number of centers dedicated to this demigod. Archeologists have identified more than three hundred separate shrines, from Corinth to Carthage, Rhodes, and Rome—all radiating out, beginning in the sixth century BC, from the greatest and most celebrated Asclepion in Epidaurus, his traditional birthplace.[13] Regional variation contoured these various sites, which had their own specializations and protocols as well as their unique votive traditions. In Corinth, terra cotta body parts abound; in Athens and Piraeus, it was stone reliefs. Still, the basic character of the Asclepius cult was clear.

The open cultivation of temple medicine under Asclepius's patronage is an interesting phenomenon in itself, for it evinces a view of divine healing that is different than our own. Vitruvius, for instance, in describing the proper site for building a healing shrine, hints at the uncomplicated cooperation between the god's intervention and what we might today consider entirely natural factors.

> For all temples there shall be chosen the most healthy sites (*saluberrimae*) with suitable springs in those places where shrines are to be set up; secondly and especially for Asclepius and Salus, and generally for those gods by whose medical power sick persons are manifestly healed. For when sick persons are moved from a pestilent to a healthy place, and the water supply is from wholesome fountains, they will more quickly recover. So it will happen that the divinity, from the nature of the site (*ex natura loci*) will gain a greater and higher reputation and authority. (*On Architecture* 1.2.7 [Henderson, LCL])

---

12 See Comella, *Il deposito votivo presso l'Ara della Regina*.
13 For this number, see Fant and Reddish, *Lost Treasures of the Bible*, 363. On Asclepius, see above all see Edelstein and Edelstein, *Asclepius*. For a close study of one such sanctuary, see Lang, *Cure and Cult in Ancient Corinth*.

Healing sanctuaries were thus sanatoria in the ancient mode; worshippers might stay for weeks or months, and as at Lourdes or Baden-Baden and the other nineteenth-century *Kurorte*, the importance of the springs must not be neglected. Aristides, the orator, invalid, and zealous devotee of the doctor-god, offered several full orations on the waters of Asclepius.

> The god uses this well as a kind of co-worker (συνεργῷ) ... for just as the servants of physicians (ἰατρῶν) and miracle workers (θαυματοποιῶν) are trained to ministrations, and, working with their superiors, astonish those who behold them and ask their advice, so is this well the discovery of the great miracle worker (τοῦ μεγάλου θαυματοποιοῦ) who does everything for the salvation of men. (Oratio XXXIX, 14)[14]

The surgeons who staffed an Asclepion were, of course, along with the waters, also *synergoi* of "the great miracle worker." The astonishment that the advice and ministrations of these coworkers occasioned refers, it would seem, to the wide range of flamboyantly absurd prescriptions connected with the cult: eating partridge stuffed with frankincense, for instance. Coupled with the prescribed rituals, above all the incubation and reception of a dream-message from the god,[15] the intervention of the ancient physicians—in their better moments through ointments, compounds, *pharmaka*, induced vomiting, freezing baths, fasting, incisions and the like [317; 432]—lends the whole process a note of odd credibility, which has led the Edelsteins to suspect real healings at work in this enormously (and otherwise inexplicably) successful cult.

IAMATA—Remembering Healings

However we choose to handle the data and the Edelsteins's suspicion, healings in huge numbers are recorded. Asclepius's shrines were famously full of ex-votos that memorialized cures: σφόδρα ἔνδοξον καὶ πολλῶν ἀναθημάτων μεστὸν ἱρεόν, Strabo says of the temple at Cos; it was "exceedingly famous and full of numerous votive offerings" (*Geo.* XIV, 2.19 [794]). In fact, the offering of an ex-voto was clearly expected (τὰ νομιζόμενα), even on pain of reversing a healing or having your fish stand struck by lightning, if the debt went unpaid {B2 (22); C4 (47)}. With the cock he owed, Socrates,

---

14 For Greek text and English translation, see Edelstein and Edelstein, *Asclepius*, text #804. Henceforth, numbered citations in square brackets refer to texts from this collection.

15 In the Latin West, the practice of incubation may not have been observed. See Renberg, "Public and Private Places of Worship."

Asclepius's most famous and philosophical patient, was but one of a multitude of beneficiaries and benefactors of the god.

As part of this hieratic system of payment, the narrative memory of specific healings was proactively promoted at certain Asclepian shrines by the centralized inscribing of special commemorative stelae. These so-called *Iamata* ("Healings") contained succinct but lively accounts of medical cases and cures, the stories behind various ex-votos. They are known to have been mounted not only at the mother shrine in Epidaurus, from which sixty-six inscriptions, from four of the original six stelae erected around the grounds in the fourth century, still survive in whole or in part. Similar installments were present in other locales like Cos and Tricca [735]. At Lebena, private cure inscriptions were displayed,[16] while Aelianus mentions a catalogue of votive offerings in the Asclepion of Athens [731]. Though this may be an inventory of the temple treasures, it is not unlikely that the circumstances of donation—namely, brief memos of healing—were also there recorded. It is clear enough, in any case, that the cult was linked to an important operation of collecting, recording, and broadcasting personal tales of healing, all meant for public consumption.

The following example, chosen nearly at random, helps expose the character, both of the cult and of the surviving corpus of Epidaurian inscriptions.

> {A4} Ambrosia from Athens, blind in one eye. She came as a suppliant to the god. Walking about in the sanctuary, she ridiculed some of the cures as being unlikely and impossible, the lame and blind becoming well from only seeing a dream. Sleeping here, she saw a vision. It seemed to her the god came to her and said he would make her well, but she would have to pay a fee by dedicating a silver pig in the sanctuary as a memorial of her ignorance. When he had said these things, he cut her sick eye and poured a medicine over it. When day came she left well.

The "didactic nature" of these inscriptions has rightly been observed, though the expression is perhaps a little weak.[17] Here one detects not only the financial *enjeux* at stake in ancient health care, in the form of a coerced ex-voto silver pig, along with the supportive role played by publicly posted testimonials of healing, but also the anxiety that might surround such advertising. Certain examples, like the parturition of a grown child by a certain Kleo who endured a five-year-long pregnancy {A1}, do indeed strain credulity, and one can well understand the Athenian Ambrosia's first impression.

---

16 See Edelstein and Edelstein, *Asclepius*, 239–40, 252–54.
17 See Dillon, "Didactic Nature of the Epidaurian Iamata."

Multiple inscriptions, accordingly, make a rather blunt reply to the hemorrhaging problem of disbelief.

Healing Sites in the Gospels

The corpus of these healing inscriptions is obviously of immense interest. New Testament scholars have not failed to engage the texts, though not always with the most insightful or compelling results. The structural (*formgeschichtliche*) parallels between the Epidaurian narratives and Gospel miracle accounts are not greatly illuminating in all frankness. Essentially, both recount healings and have a beginning, a middle, and an end—like aspirin commercials, as my professor in the seminary once quipped. The transfer over time of *Wunderberichte* from this medical cult onto the heroes of historical and biographical texts obviously marks an important development in preparing the literary context of the Gospels.[18] Still more interesting, I propose, is pondering these *Iamata* texts specifically in their integral linkage to concrete *Gnadenorte* that function as sacred *lieux de memoire*. For the cultivation of memory in conjunction with concrete, sacred locales open an interesting window upon a number of Gospel miracle traditions. Indeed, Gospel miracles plotted in a narrative *nowhere* are remarkably rare.

Jesus and the Paralytic in John 5

The topographically rich Fourth Gospel is a good place to begin. It happens, famously, that a shrine of Asclepius-Serapis is known to have existed in Jerusalem, in a section of the city just north of the Temple and Antonia fortress, beside two large, adjacent pools that share a common wall, today by the church of St. Anne. Serapis is a conglomerate deity of Ptolemaic Egyptian provenance, who assumed many attributes of Asclepius and was often fused with him in the Greek context. More than twenty such Asclepius-Serapis cultic sites have been located throughout Syria-Palestine, and several votive finds point clearly to this identification in Jerusalem, including a marble foot with the inscription "Pompeia Lucilia dedicated this," a miniature temple with a serpent (joint emblem of Asclepius and Serapis), and two small boats that hint at Serapis's additional role as a patron of safe sea travel.[19] Despite

---

[18] See Dormeyer, "Wundergeschichten in der hellenistischen Medizin und Geschichtsschreibung."

[19] Asclepius was also associated with rescue at sea. See Aristides, *Oratio* XLII, 1–15; and Edelstein and Edelstein, *Asclepius*, 162.

some grounds for hesitation—notably the missing remains of any columns from the supposed five-sided portico—the site of this Asclepion-Serapeum is today confidently identified as the same Pool of Bethesda where John intentionally places his account of Jesus' healing of the paralyzed man (Jn 5:1–15).[20]

The coincidence is not likely accidental. The question is what this collocation suggests exactly. The ex-voto finds date essentially from the second century AD, though several scholars have argued that the healing shrine existed already in Jesus' own day. As an openly *pagan* cult (serving the soldiers of the Antonia, for instance), this is rather difficult to concede.[21] First-century Jewish monotheism indulged more latitude than modern monistic reconstructions often allow, however, and a properly Jewish variant of the wider Mediterranean culture of cultic springs is not hard to imagine.[22] In any case, John clearly indicates that the spot was associated with healing powers prior to Jesus' encounter with the paralytic. The presence of "many invalids—blind, lame, and paralyzed," all hoping to enter the water, makes this plain (Jn 5:3, 5:7). An intriguing and difficult textual variant further preserves a tradition that an angel was the agent stirring up the waters. As popular piety, the tradition sounds plausibly compelling. Critically, the text is hard to decide. Archeologically, Shimon Gibson thinks that the effect was produced by opening a sluice gate that separated the northern and the southern basins.[23] As for the invalid crowds waiting to enter the pools, Gibson further surmises that "those precluded from admission to the Temple, owing to disabilities and bodily defects, would have sought miraculous healing at the pools."[24] We have no way to confirm or reject this speculation; still, Jesus subsequently finds the man precisely in the Temple (Jn 5:14), so his healing does appear ordered

---

20 See the discussion of Thompson, "Healing at the Pool of Bethesda." Confusion surrounds the precise name of the site, with variants appearing in the manuscripts of Jn 5:2 (Βηθζαθα, Βηθεσδα, Βηθσαιδα, Βελζαεθα), Josephus (Βεζεθα, *B.J.* 5.149–151), and the Copper Scroll from Qumran (*bbyt 'sdtyn*, 3Q15).

21 Duprez (*Jésus et les dieux guérisseurs*, 98–127), for instance, argues that the origins of the cult should be sought in old Semitic traditions of healing activated by the Jewish encounter with Hellenism. In such extreme and flagrant proximity to the Jerusalem Temple, however, this scenario remains rather difficult to accept. Additionally, it now seems clear that the pools were transformed from reservoirs into *miqvoth* under the Maccabees—so that tracing the origins of a cult back to the period of Ptolemaic influence will no longer accord with the archeological evidence.

22 On the parameters of the Jewish (and pagan) monotheism of the period, including a similar logic of the shrine/temple, see chaps. 8 and 10 in this volume.

23 Gibson, "Pool of Bethesda," 287.

24 Gibson, "Pool of Bethesda," 271. It is true that the northern pool was indeed oriented to participation in the Temple cult, being repurposed, it seems, around 150 BC from a reservoir into a ritual bath (*miqveh*).

to his entrance into that cultic space, where we might perhaps imagine some thankful offering. Whatever the precise reconstruction, the minute accuracy of John's description (not paralleled in any ancient miracle accounts that I know) makes a strong impression. One is transported by sheer literary force into some Jewish variant of just the sort of healing shrine simply presumed by the Epidaurian inscriptions. In understanding John's text, we must accordingly reckon with both a strong rhetoric of place—specifically sacred place—and a formidable verisimilitude coloring the whole picture.

Verisimilitude can mislead, of course, as the skeptics are quick to answer. Against this view of some preexisting site of healing, Jodi Magness thus thinks that John's entire depiction simply presupposes the transformation of the site into a pagan cult sometime after AD 70.[25] In this case, the Gospel's retrofitted memory is of a different Jerusalem long after Jesus' time, into which the miracle story has been inserted. Yet if not a pure narrative fabrication, a concocted event meant to profit from a real and suggestive setting, then it would seem that Jesus did indeed work some wonder at what was then simply a large *miqveh* near the Temple. Memory of this healing, moreover, would itself have helped fuel that site's subsequent transformation into a Roman shrine. For the question must inevitably be asked: If there was no preexisting cult, as Magness suggests, why the Roman shrine precisely here? A memory of Jesus' own healing would provide an obvious answer. The phenomenon in this case would then be parallel to the attempted *damnatio memoriae* that Hadrian, in re-creating Jerusalem as the pagan Aelia Capitolina, worked on the site where Jesus' resurrection was revered, strategically planting there a temple of Venus. Ironically, by this very act, he preserved an underground memory of the precise spot among believers. Conversely, this supercessionist choice of location might just be an illustration of the less sinister and widely attested rule of continuity of sacred locales. Either way, one might easily argue that, even on Magness's account, the anachronism testifies precisely to an accurate local memory preserved in the traditions informing John's Gospel.

The origin of the Asclepion and question of just who is transforming whose healing shrine leads us back to the text itself. In the Fourth Gospel, Jesus is constantly presenting himself in various ways (and among other things) as the source of living water. His ostentatious neglect of the health-bringing waters at Bethesda, Asclepius's celebrated "coworker," curing the

---

[25] See Magness, "Sweet Memory." Against the assumption that the cult arrived with Hadrian and the founding of Aelia Captiolina, Duprez (*Jésus et les dieux guérisseurs*, 106–7) points to a Latin inscription found near Zion's gate, dating from the end of Trajan's reign, between 115 and 117, erected by the Third Legion and addressed to *Jovi Op[tumo] Max[imo] Sarapido*.

man with a bare word of command, accordingly allows Jesus' own healing power to function in the waters' place, making him appear (once again) as the true life-giving spring. From the perspective of *constructing a memory*, the evocative, water-rich, shrine-like setting of the scene as described in John's text is thus a great success. Robin Thompson helpfully observes that "Regardless of where John's readers were from, surely this sort of description would bring to mind the sanctuaries of Asclepius found everywhere in the Roman empire: sanctuaries that were marked by porticoes where the sick came to be healed."[26] Taken as a story set in a place immediately reminiscent of readers' own native memories of "*salubrious places* with suitable springs," the story thus comes with its own key for interpretation. Not only was Jesus "able to provide more than the great Greco-Roman god of healing" (cf. Justin, 1; *Apol.* 22.6, 69.3);[27] he also replaces the specifically Jewish form of hope for cures. For readers, Jewish and pagan alike, the miracle story as John recounts it thus, in the first place, *triggers* memories, antecedent associations (drawn both from their "cultural encyclopedia" and earlier passages in the Gospel) through which Jesus, this truest μεγάλος θαυματοποιός, may be properly perceived and understood.

As John's story develops, it quickly becomes a sabbath controversy and not a discourse on living water, however. This prompt displacement of sacred place by sacred time seemingly short-circuits any ongoing function for the local memory of the site at Bethesda. At this point, the healing scene would by all accounts be more fittingly placed in a synagogue, where, as in the story of the man with the withered hand (Mk 3:1–6), the Jews routinely gathered on the seventh day. In contrast to this synoptic report, however, in John it is not *Jesus'* deed that is condemned as sabbath breaking. It is rather the healed man himself who is caught carrying about his mat (Jn 5:8–12). The *krabattos* thereby emerges as the vital link between the story's time and place.[28]

In the Epidaurian *Iamata* there are multiple cases where the cause or emblem of a person's malady becomes a souvenir of their healing. "Euhippos bore a spearhead in his jaw for three years," we are told, and upon being healed by the god, "he walked out well having the spear head in his hands" {A12}. Another man had a stone that he ejected during his incubation at the shrine. "Picking it up," the inscription says, "he departed with it in his hands" {A14}. Gorgias of Herekleia was healed of a barb in his lung. He too left carrying the barb in his hand {B10}. This terminal formula ἐν ταῖς χερσὶν ἔχων (or φέρων), which closes these inscriptions so effectively with such dramatic,

---

26 Thompson, "Healing at the Pool of Bethesda," 81.
27 Thompson, "Healing at the Pool of Bethesda," 81.
28 *Pace* Lohse, "Jesu Worte über den Sabbat," 79–80.

graphic force, hints at the way narrative/rhetorical art and enacted ritual were fused and bound to the cultivation of a patient's private memory, publicly memorialized. One might well imagine items like Gorgias's barb being treasured like scars—and like scars that serve as the occasion for recounting fabulous stories. But not all walked out with a medical miracle memorial in their hands. The cure of one Damosthenes, who was paralyzed in the legs and carried into the sanctuary upon a couch (ἐπὶ κλίνας), is celebrated in the following lapidary phrase: "He went into the Abaton with two crutches (μετὰ δύο βακτηριᾶν), he went out healthy (ὑγιὴς ἐξῆλθε)" {C21}. The crutches evidently stayed behind.

The similarity of Damosthenes's situation to the Gospel paralytic is fascinating. On the one hand, Jesus' calculated decision not to let the liberated man leave his mat behind, as Damosthenes left behind his canes, ensures that credit for the wonder (or blame, as it happens) is ultimately directed to Jesus himself. For were an empty mat simply to lay there where the paralyzed man used to be—an ex-voto trophy in a known site of healing—the abandoned mat would have redounded to the waters' glory. At the same time, the ostentatious portage of the *krabattos* resembles the showy healing of Gorgias and Euhippos. That the man's mattress relic successfully occasioned and triggered the recounting of his incredible story is the very premise of John's continued narrative as it develops. In this way, John's account accomplishes for Jesus something similar to what the *Iamata* accomplish for their own institutional interests, forging a memory that magnifies the *doxa* of the divine source of healing (Jn 5:23; cf. 2:11). Jesus himself has in this way rhetorically displaced the epoch's wonderworking shrines and personally become the locus of healing: beneficiary of the beneficiary's ex-voto souvenir.

Jesus and the Paralytic in Mark 2

In Mark 2:1–10, another story of a paralytic is recounted, again with strong links to Damosthenes and John 5, but where the relation to place takes a different turn. The setting in Mark has shifted to Galilee and the village of Capharnaum, where Jesus is said to be ἐν οἴκῳ (Mk 2:1). The "house" in question, to follow from the context, must be the house of Simon Peter, located somewhere near the synagogue of the village (Mk 1:29). What is especially remarkable about these two opening chapters in Mark is the way so many healings all transpire at this selfsame locale. First Peter's mother-in-law is healed (Mk 1:29–31); next, at evening, huge crowds are brought to the house where they are healed (Mk 1:32–34). Finally, with Jesus again back in the house, a paralyzed man is carried in on a mat and let down through the roof.

To judge from the similar case of a certain Diatos of Kyrna and in contrast to the man in John 5, Mark's paralyzed man may have been well-to-do, for the paralyzed Diatos was carried around on his mat by his servants (ὑπηρέτας) {B18 (38)}, implying some means. Whatever the case, after forgiving the man's sins, Jesus tells him to pick up his mat and go home (Mk 2:11). The words ἔγειρε ἆρον τὸν κράβαττον are exactly the same as in John.

More likely than two massively garbled versions of the same healing, we likely confront here the principle "same sickness, same formula."[29] However we explain the recurrence of the miracle-working logion—as Jesus' habitual speech or something shaped or duplicated in later transmission—the saying is more integral to the narrative in John 5. For although the Markan tale is, as in John, also the mixture of a miracle and controversy story, in Mark, carrying away the mat is pure dramatic effect, with no relation to the dispute about forgiveness. If the mat does play an integral role in Mark's memorable scene of opening up the roof, it is the house itself that becomes the critical prop in the Markan story. The cognitive support for a mental *schema* and *script* represented by Peter's *oikos* is recognizable by modern memory theory. One can (to this day) retell this story easily, for one remembers the odd manipulation of the props. When John Meier in reference to Mark 2 thus pronounces himself "inclined to think that some event in the public ministry stuck in the corporate memory precisely because of the strange circumstance," the strange circumstances have everything to do with this healing's location inside a crowded home.[30]

It is interesting in precisely this regard that, similar to John 5, Mark's localization of the miracle had a cultic afterlife—and possibly a cultic prior life as well. In this case, it is not an Asclepion but a first-century house shrine, later a *Domus Ecclesia* (still later an eight-sided Byzantine church), planted on the presumed site of Peter's own home. There was accordingly in Capharnaum an *aide-mémoire* built in solid black basalt, which was certainly the occasion to preserve and promote the bundle of miracle stories recorded in Mark 1–2. Whether veneration of this site predates Mark's Gospel or is instead the Gospel's fruit no one can say. Both scenarios are easily imagined—nor are they entirely exclusive options. In any case, the extremely early date of the sanctuary's first stratum should not be underestimated. We are well informed, moreover, that (as still today) locals in the Greco-Roman world guarded and gladly told tales about hometown celebrities. It may well be that, just as the house of Augustus's grandfather in Velitrae, where the future emperor was born, quickly became a draw for ancient tourists—with

---

29 So Meier, *Marginal Jew*, 2:680.
30 Meier, *Marginal Jew*, 2:680.

no help from any circulating texts—so Peter's house was promptly valorized, even without the intervention of a written Gospel. The extraordinarily early pilgrim traffic through Bethlehem, which Justin already knows, elicited traditions about the localization of Jesus' birth never recorded in the Gospels; namely, its occurrence in a cave.[31] The evidence of a primitive Galilean pendant to this Judean life of Jesus tourism, with its own store of local lore about his miracles, may thus represent a sort of archeological "multiple attestation" in favor of Mark's story. It is with good reason that we speak of the Holy Land as the "Fifth Gospel." Under whatever conditions and whenever it began, pilgrims came to Peter's house searching for help from the personal power who once passed that way and healed the paralytic. This is born out in the Christograms and prayers left in four languages of ancient graffiti.

In evoking the cultic context of Jesus traditions that circulate in ancient Capharnaum—a much thicker description than appeals to murky pre-Gospel *Sitz-im-leben* normally provide—one major fact must not be lost from sight. In Mark 1–2, we are dealing specifically with the home of one of the best-known and authoritative individuals in the first Christian generation.[32] The lack of any comparable "House of the Centurion" shrine in the same village is an interesting index of the Petrine orientation of the local tradition. Such linkage to the named person of Peter reconfigures the calculations around what students of oral transmission call a "controlled tradition." Peter is indeed the earliest identified source behind the writing of Mark's Gospel, as Papias's Presbyter already recounts, and we have more here than simply the memorably "strange circumstances" evoked by Meier. We have an unforgettable event that purportedly took place in the Gospel's *auctor*'s living room (he who had later to repair his torn-up roof).

The form of control in Mark is thus distinct from the institutional and hieratic supervision at work behind the redaction of the *Iamata*, where huge economic implications have manifestly produced and shaped the whole collection. This is personal memory to the highest degree, at least as Mark's Petrine Gospel itself was remembered. Thus, while the accounts of the miracles associated with Peter's own home are composed in the third person like the third-person stories of named individuals at Epidauris, the Gospel's rhetorical purpose is actually much nearer to Aristides's first-person act of witness: his exuberant rhetorical celebration of Διός τε Εὐαγγελίος καὶ Ἀσκληπιος

---

[31] A formal similarity can be observed here in terms of these miracle stories' tradition-transmission process and their pre-, para-, and post-Gospel relations to the canonical account. See chap. 3 in this volume.

[32] On the cultic context and apostolic authority at work in the formation of the Gospel tradition, see chap. 1 in this volume.

Σωτῆρ, "Zeus the Gospel bringer and Asclepius the Savior" [806.3]. Aristides's witness is an evangelical testimony driven by honest zeal, zeal born of personal experience and his desire to erect a fitting oratorical monument for his multiple healings (a sign, one might cynically object, that those healings had not taken root). He was determined to expend himself expressing his thanks "as long as we shall have any memory (μνήμης) and thought left" [317]. Even so, his effusive, highly personal oratory cannot escape co-option by the self-serving culture of publicity cultivated by Asclepius's cult. *Nolens volens* Aristides's orations still ultimately function like the first-person ex-voto of one Marcus Julius Apellas, who recounts his story because, as he says, ἐκέλευσεν ἀναγράψαι ταῦτα, the god commanded him to write it [432]. The cult of Asclepius was immensely jealous for good press and glory.

Conclusion

The Christ cult was not less jealous for glory than that of Asclepius the healer. Yet the publicity generated around the person of Jesus and the sort of memory associated with the healings at Peter's house and at Bethesda reveal something rather striking about the Gospel tradition. It is a form of historical memory that at once results in the creation of shrines and also actively undermines them, paradoxically. It takes shape in concretes places and leaves behind its trace yet overthrows the universalizing Asclepion branch model (where healings presuppose the shrine, rather than vice versa). John promotes a memory of Jesus as the sole true and personalized sacred locus: "The hour is coming when you will worship the Father neither on this mountain nor in Jerusalem ... but in spirit and in truth" (Jn 4:21). Peter grounds a tangible memory in the personal framework of Jesus' *bios*. There cannot be two Peter's houses, as there can be an Asclepion in every town. Together, the universal and particular dimensions bound up in this fruitful Johannine and synoptic-Petrine tension confer on the cultic memorialization of Jesus' wonder-working power in a grounded yet transcendent, incarnational, divine-human—and, let us say it, Chalcedonian—grammar.

One more difference might finally be mentioned regarding Jesus' healing power. Damosthenes's cure took four whole months, the longest convalescence recounted in the Epidaurian inscriptions. Aristides, when he was "helplessly bedridden" (κατακλίσεις ἀπόρους), was healed, he says, by a vigorous regime of long, forced marches [317.8]. Kleimenes of Argos, paralyzed in body, was healed by having a large snake wrapped around him as he drank {B17 (37)}. The wealthy Diatos, for his part, was yoked to a team of horses, circled the sanctuary three times, then ritually trampled under their hooves, which all somehow made him well {B18 (38)}—a miracle cure indeed. Jesus' healing of the paralytic in Peter's home, like his healing of another at Bethesda, was remembered, by contrast to these ridiculous spectacles of mixed medicine and superstition, for the astonishment caused by his simplest and most sovereign word of command: "Rise, pick up your mat and go."

CHAPTER 5

Eyewitness Historiography and the Resurrection

The preface to Luke's Gospel promises eyewitness testimony as an assurance of the "reliability" (ἀσφάλεια) of the following story. While this appeal is perfectly characteristic of Greco-Roman history writing, Luke's development of the idea transforms a commonplace principle of historiographical verification into one of the most prominent theological categories of the entire two-volume history. The "witnesses" of Luke-Acts are those whose access to events is not merely proximate and privileged but whose testimony is pneumatically charged to advance universal adherence to their story. "You will receive power when the Holy Spirit comes to you; and you will be my witnesses in Jerusalem, and in all Judea and Samaria, and even to the ends of the earth" (Acts 1:8).

Luke's striking fusion of his historiographical guarantors of reliability with the narrative agents of the evangelical mission raises a series of questions. Are there parallels in ancient historiography to the *divinely empowered testimony* credited to the Lukan witnesses? Is there precedent for a comparable *corporate body of witnesses* that authorize other ancient histories? Were other contemporary histories written, like Luke-Acts, purely on the autopsy of *actors other than the author*? Overall, what explains Luke's peculiar treatment of his witnesses?

In considering such questions, it is significant that New Testament scholarship has recently begun to stress the role of eyewitness testimony in the composition of the Gospels. Martin Hengel, notably, launched a forceful critique of the anonymous tradition model employed in form criticism and insisted upon "the personal link of the Jesus tradition with particular tradents."¹ Two other scholars, Samuel Byrskog and Richard Bauckham, have supplemented this with sustained research into the way participants functioned in the evangelists' compositional work. The monograph of Byrskog attempts to understand autopsy in the context of Greco-Roman historiography and then apply that perspective to the oral formulation of the Gospels.² Bauckham, who builds on Byrskog's findings, pioneers interesting new angles of approaching NT data to uncover untapped signs of eyewitness testimony, offering what is clearly the most important (and controversial) contribution on the issue of autopsy in the Gospels.³

If Bauckham takes the Lukan promise of using αὐτόπται with new seriousness, his interest is to rehabilitate the eyewitness value of the Fourth Gospel, not the Third, and Luke-Acts receives little sustained attention. In this essay, therefore, I would like to extend Bauckham's line of inquiry not with the ambitious aim of toppling form criticism or identifying the Beloved Disciple, but with the much less controversial hope of advancing an appreciation for Luke's overt historiographical rhetoric of *eyewitness*.⁴

While recognizing discordant voices like of that of Richard Pervo, my argument rests upon the broad consensus that, at least to some appreciable degree, Luke-Acts functions on the model of other Greco-Roman histories,⁵

---

1 Hengel, *Four Gospels*, 146. On the role of named "apostolic" tradents in the work of Gospel formation (including Luke as a "sometime companion of Paul"), see chaps. 1, 3, and 4 in this volume.

2 Byrskog, *Story as History*.

3 Bauckham, *Jesus and the Eyewitnesses*. Reaction to Bauckham's controversial thesis has been lively and sharp. See, e.g., Rodgers, "Review of *Jesus and the Eyewitnesses*"; Redman, "How Accurate are Eyewitnesses?"; Schröter, "Gospels as Eyewitness Testimony?"; Evans, "Implications of Eyewitness Tradition." See especially the entire volume *JSHJ* 6, no. 2 (2008), including Bauckham's response to his critics. Also Bauckham, "Eyewitnesses and Critical History."

4 Martin Hengel's substantial article "Der Lukasprolog und seine Augenzeugen" deserves mention, for Hengel draws consciously upon Bauckham's work. Of special importance in Hengel's wide-ranging essay is his stress on the centrality of Peter and the apostles as eyewitness authorities. Hengel moves in different directions than the present study but helpfully undergirds the comparative discussion here undertaken.

5 On this broad discussion, see Pervo, *Profit with Delight*; Sterling, *Historiography and Self-Definition*; and Becker, *Die antike Historiographie*, particularly the contribution of Gehrke, "Die Bedeutung der (antiken) Historiographie," 29–52. Gehrke's opposition to wide comparisons between Christian and Greco-Roman modes of historiography and call for case-by-case attention accord with the analysis adopted here. Many scholars are beginning to question strict oppositions between myth/fiction versus history/fact; see, e.g., Marguerat, *First Christian Historian* and chap. 3 in this volume. Such easing of rigid classifications accords with the kerygmatic innovations in historiographical writing traced in this essay. Marguerat's notion of Luke's "poetic" historiography (cf. Ricoeur), documenting essentially unverifiable events of divine intervention, provides a suitable context for tracking the specific features of Luke's

and my assumption is that, chronologically and by his position in the early Christian community, Luke could indeed have had genuine access to certain firsthand sources.⁶ With this in mind, I will expose Luke's rather peculiar interaction with the tradition of contemporary historiography. Specifically, I will highlight that Luke's appeal to eyewitness informants about the Resurrection left his work exposed to common critiques on two particular fronts: (1) the evangelist himself could boast no authorial autopsy, while (2) his audience could neither verify nor refute his report. In response to this and the unique historiographical difficulties of chronicling a purported event like the Resurrection, I suggest that Luke innovates within the broad Thucydidean tradition of ancient history writing and deploys several strategies of accreditation to buttress the unlikely testimony of his αὐτόπται. From this perspective it will be seen that a major burden of Luke's second volume is to substantiate the "credibility" (ἀσφάλεια) of the first. The ethical appeal that warrants a judgment of the truthfulness of Luke's story was accordingly tied to the remarkable witness of a living community of Christian believers.

Eyewitness Testimony in Greco-Roman Culture

The antiquity of common sense appears in an old maxim of Heraclitus: "Eyes are surer witnesses (ἀκριβέστεροι μάρτυρες) than ears."⁷ In the context of ancient Greek philosophy and science, this epistemic preference for eyewitness took on peculiar importance, and it was largely technicians and physicians who established autopsy as a professional methodology.⁸ In a world where learning was not sequestered into specialized disciplines, however, polymath scientists tended also to be political leaders and men of

---

"witness" rhetoric here in view. For the perspective of classics, see Pelling, *Literary Texts and the Greek Historian*; and, with reference to the Gospels' Resurrection accounts, Bowersock, *Fiction as History*. Judgments about *history* are implied in, but distinct from, questions about *historiographical* practice. Luke's credentials as a trustworthy historian are a matter of long debate; see again chap. 3 in this volume. See also Gasque, *History of the Criticism of the Acts of the Apostles*.

6 If with Fitzmyer the Gospel's author is accepted as "the traditional Luke, a sometime companion of Paul," there is no reason to reject, and every reason to entertain, the possibility of Luke's access to such sources. See the discussion in Fitzmyer, *Gospel According to Luke I-IV*, 35–52. The supposition does not require a drastic redating of the Gospel. Papias in the same period claimed to be collecting eyewitness testimony from Jesus' personal disciples. On the dating of Papias, see Bauckham, *Jesus and the Eyewitnesses*, 12–38.

7 Diels/Kranz, 22B Frag. 101a.

8 See Alexander, *Preface to Luke's Gospel*, 80–82.

letters.⁹ Crossover figures like Ctesias of Cnidus, personal physician of the Persian emperor and author of a twenty-three-volume ethnography, the *Persica*, personify the close link between autopsy in medical and historical investigations.¹⁰

The historiographical acceptance of eyewitness nonetheless remained naive and never came under real scrutiny, as it did in other connections.¹¹ This is one reason why autopsy could flourish as such a defining feature of historical writing. Indeed, the very etymology of ἱστορία came to be understood in direct connection with ἰδεῖν.¹² History was to see for oneself. Aulus Gellius, the Roman grammarian of the second century AD, explained that *history* differed from *annals* in that "history is properly of those events in which he who narrates takes part (*quibus rebus gerendis interfuereit is qui narret*) . . . since ἱστορία in Greek means a knowledge of current events (*rerum cognitionem prasentium*)."¹³ This identification of history with participatory witness owed much, naturally, to the long tradition of historical writers and especially to the influence Thucydides.

Authorial Eyewitness as the Privileged Genre of History

However much Herodotus, the *pater historiae*, embodied the method of the curious investigator, it was Thucydides who established the precedent for identifying history with personal involvement. His severe judgment that antiquarian interests were beyond the scope of sure information (σαφῶς εὑρεῖν) was his methodological warrant for focusing attention on contemporary matters and making the canon of autopsy a question of seeing not *evidence* but *events*.¹⁴ The decision to record a war in which he had been (at different times) both an active participant and a close observer thus fundamentally reshaped the possibilities of writing history. It promoted the accepted preference for autopsy as determinative of generic content. The need for direct attestation was no longer simply a critical principle applicable

---

9 See Nenci, "Il motivo dell'autopsia nella storagraphia greca."

10 The ninth-century AD epitomizer, Photius, testifies of Ctesias: "He says that having been an eyewitness himself of most of what he recounts (φησὶ δὲ αὐτὸν τῶν πλειόνων ἃ ἱστορεῖ αὐτόπτην γενόμενον), or having heard from the Persians themselves that which he could not see, he thus composed the history" (quoted in Byrskog, *Story as History*, 51).

11 See Marincola, *Authority and Tradition in Ancient Historiography*, 66.

12 Byrskog, *Story as History*, 52.

13 Byrskog, *Story as History*, 52.

14 *Hist.* 1.1, 1.3: τὰ γὰρ πρὸ αὐτῶν καὶ τὰ ἔτι παλαίτερα σαφῶς μὲν εὑρεῖν διὰ χρόνου πλῆθος ἀδύνατα ἦν, ἐκ δὲ τεκμηρίων ὧν ἐπὶ μακρότατον σκοποῦντί μοι πιστεῦσαι ξυμβαίνει οὐ μεγάλα νομίζω.

to this or that item of inquiry; it was the essential criterion by which the valid object of history itself was decided.

If the project of Thucydides aimed to reconfigure the object of historiography, it also shifted the concrete expressions of eyewitness within such literature. Autopsy was no longer a periodically interjected call for credence or ground for refutation (εἶδον δὲ καὶ αὐτός), such as one finds in Herodotus (e.g., *Hist.* 1.51, 2.5, 2.10, 2.12, 2.44, 2.75, 2.99, 2.131, 2.147, 2.156, 3.12, 4.195, 5.59, 6.47, 7.129).[15] It was instead a grand, unspoken authority: the ethical appeal underwriting the full truth of the text. Accordingly, Thucydides offers little indication within *The Peloponnesian War* of what he himself could specifically confirm, and the precise language of "autopsy" never actually appears in his work.[16]

This understated reliance on eyewitness misled Loveday Alexander into supposing that ultimately the concept was more at home in scientific literature than in history writing.[17] While this conclusion may indicate a principal literary locus of the αὐτοψία word group, Guido Schepens's definitive study secures its profound pertinence to history writing: "Chez Thucydide, l'autopsie est pour le première fois intégrée dans une déclaration théoretique décrivant la méthod historique qui trouve son application dans toute l'oeuvre."[18]

The prestige and precedent of Thucydides launched the great tradition of contemporary histories, and it was in this tradition that subsequent talents of ancient historiography such as Polybius, Josephus, and Tacitus were to prove themselves. A self-conscious methodological superiority invests these authors' efforts. In announcing his decision to write on the Jewish War, for instance, Josephus does not hesitate to vaunt over the judgment of "those erudite Greeks" (τοῖς Ἑλλήνων λογίοις) who take up antique themes rather than the great deeds transpiring around them. He even goes so far as to identify the authentic tradition of historiography exclusively with the writing of contemporary history (ignoring many inconvenient counterexamples and prejudicing his own future work):

> The ancient historians set themselves severally to write the history of their own times (τὰ ... κατ' αὐτοὺς), a task in which their presence at the events (τὸ παρατυχεῖν τοῖς πράγμασιν) added

---

15 See Schepens, *L'"autopsie."*

16 Schepens, *L'"autopsie,"* 111–86.

17 See Alexander, *Preface to Luke's Gospel,* passim. Alexander aligns Luke's preface with scientific writing in several areas (author's name, dedication, themes, sources, preface length). She further contests the literal meaning of "eyewitness" in ancient texts (120–22). These concerns are addressed by Adams, "Luke's Preface and its Relationship to Greek Historiography," 187–90.

18 Schepens, *L'"autopsie,"* 197.

lucidity to their record, while mendacity brought an author into disgrace with readers who knew the facts.[19]

Only contemporary history could be rigorously verified; therefore contemporary history was the only occupation of the genuine historian. Serious historiography, in short, was the record of actual eyewitnesses.[20]

If a lively taste was still preserved for writing on antiquities, it is fair to see this literary line as alternately a pedantic or popular indulgence that never quite escaped the shadow of Thucydides's critique.[21] In this connection it is important that, though historians' lies were denounced on all sides, we do not find anything like Josephus's polemic reversed in antiquarian writing: no one thought to argue that "true" history was concerned with forgotten deeds of the past. Isocrates's supposed claim in this direction—that ears are surer than eyes, hence ancient reports superior to contemporary—has been thoroughly misconstrued.[22] The writing of ancient history was secure as a literary occupation and perfectly able to justify itself in any number of ways.[23] It was never justified, however, as a more prestigious and sober mode of history. That high ground was conceded to records written by participants.

Luke's Double Disadvantage

The preface of Luke's Gospel belongs to the tradition of contemporary histories. This is widely recognized.[24] Aune's judgment that the preface is a

---

19 Josephus, *B.J.* 1.15. All translations of Josephus are adapted from Thackery, *Josephus*.

20 A statement of Ephorus (FGrHist 70 F 9) explains the ἀκρίβεια to be expected of various histories: "Ephorus says that when writing about our own times, we consider those speaking most accurately (ἀκριβέστατα) to be the most reliable; but concerning things long ago (τῶν παλαιῶν), those who proceed in such a way we consider most untrustworthy, since we assume that it is not probable, given the great distance in time, that all of the deeds or a majority of the speeches would be remembered." See Byrskog, *Story as History*, 219.

21 It is illuminating also to observe how literary fashions followed the imperial mood. On the penchant for antiquities during the Antonine period, e.g., see Kemezis, "Lucian, Fronto, and the Absence of Contemporary Historiography."

22 See Marincola, *Authority and Tradition in Ancient Historiography*, Appendix III, 276–79.

23 One such justification was the kind of "apologetic" intention that Sterling (*Historiography and Self-Definition*) sees in Josephus and others like Berossus and Manetho, i.e., a demonstration of the hoary antiquity of an *ethnos*. While Luke is concerned to graft the young Christian movement onto the venerable history of Israel, his historiographical register is not that of a writer of antiquities, which poses a difficulty for Sterling's proposal.

24 For a summary of research, see Rothschild, *Luke-Acts and the Rhetoric of History*, 32–59. Alexander intends only to associate the preface with technical or scientific treatises; Luke-Acts as a whole is recognized to have historiographical content.

work of "mediocre" quality should not obscure its classification as reputable history, serious and of universal import, if not *haute littérature,* at least in pretension.[25] For the classical mind, it was the theme that determined stylistic elevation, and of Luke's theme there can be little doubt.[26] The evangelist consciously presents his work as a thing momentous in the manner of a history, for history alone could bear the magnitude of "the events fulfilled among us" (Lk 1:1). Just as Thucydides undertook to chronicle "a great (μέγαν) war and more worthy of relation (ἀξιολογώτατον) than any that had preceded it" (*Hist.* 1.1) and Polybius "an event for which the past affords no precedent (ὃ πρότερον οὐχ εὑρίσκεται γεγονός)" (*Hist.* 1.1), so Luke determined to recount a historic happening, profoundly worthy of worthy record.[27] Even if certain generic conventions of history ultimately break down, to rank Luke's preface alongside professional manuals is gravely to miss the tone the evangelist set to strike.

Appreciating this position within the tradition of contemporary historiography, one finds it immediately striking that Luke grounds his account not

---

[25] Aune contests Loveday's position and claims that Luke's preface likely resembles "the hundreds of lost mediocre histories," and that it is misleading to gauge it only against the standard of the best Hellenistic exemplars. See Aune, "Luke 1:1–4."

[26] See Kennedy, *New Testament Interpretation through Rhetorical Criticism*, 98, 107–8.

[27] Morgenthaler, *Die lukanische Geschichtsscreibung als Zeugnis*, 98, captures the sentiment moving Luke's historiographical undertaking: "Dass dabei etwas anderes herauskommen wird als in des Thukydides' 'Geschichte vom grossen Krieg' oder in Plutarchs 'Vitae parallelae' oder in Caesars 'Bellum Gallicum,' ist lediglich im Objekt begründet, das zu beschreiben war. Es gab und gibt in der Weltgeschichte viele Menschenleben zu beschreiben, viele Kriegszüge, viele Schlachten, viele Feldherrenreden usw. Es gibt aber nur eine wunderbare Geburt und nur eine Auferstehung, nur ein Pfingsten usw. Die absolute Singularität dieser Ereignisse macht auch die darauf bezogene Geschichtsschreibung zu einer absoluten Singulären. Aber die Geschichtsschreibung bleibt auch der Bericht von diesen Ereignissen." Along with the rhetorical excess of Thucydides and Polybius in describing the *unprecedented* character of the events they relate, recent work on apotheosis traditions perhaps advises caution in addressing how Luke or his readers may have understood the "singularity" of Jesus' resurrection as his chosen theme. See, e.g., Cotter, "Greco-Roman Apotheosis Traditions," 127–53. Nevertheless, if Luke, with Paul as his mouthpiece, demonstrates a certain nonchalance in making his claim ("Why is it thought incredible by any of you that God raises the dead?" Acts 26:8), this can only be understood as the expected fulfillment of "the promise made by God to our fathers, to which our twelve tribes hope to attain" (Acts 26:6–7). Ultimately, within this scriptural framework, Luke's appeal to prophetic texts such as Hab 1:5 in Acts 13:41 ("I do a deed in your days, a deed you will never believe, if one declares it to you") indicates his clear sense that what he relates has an epochal and unique significance. Thus, even if, with certain present-day scholars, we granted (not at all to be assumed in my opinion) that Luke imagined other isolated wonder events similar to the rising of Jesus to have happened in the course of history, the covenantal context of *this* resurrection supplies it with distinct historical frame and a peerless importance in Luke's eyes.

on his *own* personal involvement in the events he will relate, but on the attestation of *others* who were "eyewitnesses from the beginning" (οἱ ἀπ'ἀρχῆς αὐτόπται, Lk 1:2). This authorial distance from the events represents a break with the ideal mold. Thucydides, Xenophon, Polybius, Tacitus, and Josephus were all, in one way or another, close observers and participants in the histories they record. The precedent is strong enough[28] that we are even led to ask: Did any other ancient historians record *contemporary* histories of which they themselves had no firsthand knowledge?[29]

It is surprisingly difficult to find a concrete example. When Timaeus of Tauromenium is scored as one who "does not write with the evidence of his eyes (διὰ τὴν ἀορασίαν)," it is the inexperienced bookworm's lack of judgment that Polybius impugns, not his dependence on others.[30] Verisimilitude is thus the issue and not authentication: he is unable to reconstruct ancient battles convincingly or paint a vivid *ekphrasis*.[31] More importantly, in contrast to Luke, Timaeus writes principally as an *antiquarian*.[32]

---

28 Appeal to autopsy extends to the work of many minor and lost historians. Theopompus's claim to eyewitness experience, e.g., is recorded in Dionysius of Halicarnassus's *Letter to Gnaeus Pompeius*. Many of the historians of Alexander claimed the same: e.g., Callisthenes of Olynthus, Chares of Mytilene, Onesicritus of Astypalaea, Nearchus of Crete, Aristobolus, Ptolemy. See Pearson, *Lost Histories of Alexander the Great*.

29 The possibility that the author might be signaled in the "we" passages in Acts is obviously relevant to this discussion—but not so as to negate the apparent anomaly. The Gospel prologue evidently includes Luke himself among those who are beneficiaries of the testimony of the "eyewitness" (καθὼς παρέδοσαν ἡμῖν οἱ ἀπ' ἀρχῆς αὐτόπται, Lk 1:2), and, as is clear from Acts 1:22, Luke's technical notion of "witness" is concerned with the life, death, and resurrection of Jesus. The Muratorian Canon is accordingly right to distinguish between two orders of witness: [Lukas] *Dominum tamen nec ipse vidit in carnem*, yet the events in Acts happened *sub praesentia ejus*. If Luke's own eyewitness is thus indeed incorporated into Acts, this "witness" has been subordinated to his secondhand accounts of the risen Lord—a remarkable reordering of the hierarchy of attestation. On the controversial "we" passages, see the contrasting views of Thornton, *Der Zeuge des Zeugen*, and Campbell, *"We" Passages in the Acts of the Apostles*.

30 *Hist.* 12.25g.4.

31 Polybius is ultimately more interested in αὐτοπάθεια and πολυπραγμοσύνη than αὐτοψία. "Since nothing written by students of books is either experienced [firsthand] or vivid, the matters they recount are not practical to those encountering them ... being unfamiliar on the basis of experience, by necessity it happens ... many things worthy of mention are omitted and many things not worthy of much discussion are present. Often this happens with Timaeus on account of the fact that he was not an eyewitness" (*Hist.* 12.25; cf. 12.27–28).

32 The use of autopsy in the contemporary portion of Timaeus's account is difficult to assess. He may have made a return to Sicily, or he may have "relied on eyewitnesses and participants who reported to him during his exile at Athens." Marincola, *Authority and Tradition in Ancient Historiography*, 71.

In his satirical romance *Verae Historiae*, Lucian takes occasion to lampoon several untrustworthy historians: "Ctesias of Cnidos, the son of Ctesiochus, wrote an account of India and its customs; he himself neither saw nor heard from another trustworthy source (αὐτὸς εἶδεν μήτε ἄλλου ἀληθεύοντος ἤκουσεν) the things he wrote about. Iambulus, too, wrote a long account of the wonders of the great sea; anybody can see it is fictitious, but it is still quite entertaining as a theme."[33] Lucian is obviously poking fun, however, and the very premise of his mocking is that these literary "liars" claimed eyewitness status (whether sincerely or by convention does not matter).[34] Furthermore, though their works are lost (if they in fact ever existed), it is clear they composed *periplous* literature and were not historians in the Thucydidean mold.

Another text of Lucian, his *Life of Demonax*, as a *bios* belongs to an important penumbra of historiographical literature, where at least the first half of Luke's two-volume work also belongs.[35] In this connection it is interesting that Lucian's account begins with a clear statement of the contemporary subject and a claim to firsthand knowledge:

> It was in the cards, it seems, that our modern world should not be altogether destitute of noteworthy and memorable men, but should produce enormous physical prowess and a highly philosophic mind. I speak with reference to the Boeotian Sostratus, whom the Greeks called Hercules and believed to be that hero, and especially to Demonax, the philosopher. Both these men I saw myself, and saw with wonderment (οὕς καὶ εἶδον αὐτὸς καὶ ἰδὼν ἐθαύμασα); and under one of them, Demonax, I was long a student. (§1 [Harmon, LCL])

Other contemporary *bioi* (in the generic sense) observe the same convention.[36] Xenophon's *Agesilaus* (paralleled by passages in his *Hellenica*) recounts

---

33 *Ver. Hist.* 1.3. Translation adapted from Reardon, *Collected Ancient Greek Novels*.
34 The same charge is made in Lucian's *Hist. Conscr.* 29. An unnamed historian is cited as saying, "I write what I have seen, not what I have heard (γράφω τοίνυν ἅ εἶδον, οὐχ ἅ ἤκουσα)." Lucian in reply joked that the writer had never "set foot outside Corinth." On the relationship between these two texts, see Georgiadou and Larmour, "Lucian and Historiography."
35 On the emergence of *bios* literature from within the context of ancient history writing, see Momigliano, *Development of Greek Biography*; and Burridge, *What Are the Gospels?*, 53–77.
36 A tradition of antiquarian *bioi* also exists, exemplified, e.g., by the anonymous second- or third-century *Life of Aesop*, Satyrus's *Lives of the Tragedians*, Philo's *Moses*, and Plutarch's *Parallel Lives*. The lost *Philippica* of Theopompus was "not a biography but the history of events that occurred in Greece at the time of Philip, a history that had as a unifying element the affairs of Philip and Macedon." Vattuone, "Looking for the Invisible."

the life of the great Spartan soldier under whom Xenophon himself had served in the Persian campaign.[37] The *Atticus* of Nepos relates the life of the author's patron, and though his *Cicero* is lost, we also know of Nepos's close acquaintance with that famous statesmen.[38] Nicholas of Damascus is known to have been close to the emperor Augustus, whose life he wrote.[39] In *Agricola*, Tacitus wrote the life of his father-in-law. The ideal of personal, firsthand knowledge is clear.

Like history proper, the field of *bioi* is large and diverse, however. Philostratus's *Apollonius of Tyana* provides an example *close* to the sort we are seeking, for the author ostensibly relies upon the eyewitness of another in compiling his account of the wonder-working philosopher. Philostratus's famous and problematic *bios* should probably be reckoned as some sort of ancient historical fiction, with much borrowing from the techniques of ancient romance writing,[40] but it is significant in just this respect that the marked historiographical rhetoric surrounding the work appeals to a variety of written sources, including letters and public documents, earlier lives, as well as the testimony of Damis, a former disciple of Apollonius who left behind his written memoirs (ὑπομνήματα) (1.3.1)[41]—though the "evident debt to Plato" in Damis's dialogues with the master leads one to doubt the genuineness of this source.[42] Whatever estimate one ultimately makes of the truthfulness of *Apollonius*, it was neither a full-fledged antiquarian enterprise nor precisely a contemporary history, since the protagonist (ca. 40–120) *died* a good half century before the *birth* of Philostratus (ca. 170–245). No such gap can be posited between the events of the Gospel and the lifetime of Luke.

---

37 Xenophon's *Cyropedia* confesses its secondhand character, relating "all that we learned about him from others or could infer for ourselves" (1.5). The text is widely classified as a romance rather than a bios, however. See Holzberg, *Ancient Novel*, 11–14.

38 See, e.g., Roberts, *Selected Lives from Cornelius Nepos*, ix.

39 The story of Augustus being unusually pleased by a gift of dates from Nicholas is preserved in different forms in three different sources, i.e., Plutarch, *Sym.* 8.4, Photius (Bibl. 189), and Athenaeus (14.652). According to Sophronius of Damascus, Nicholas instructed the children of Anthony and Cleopatra, who were in the custody of Octavia. This scholar's proximity to the imperial family would thus be clear.

40 See Dzielska, *Apollonius of Tyana*; also Francis, "Truthful Fiction." Similar to the trend noted in connection with Marguerat above (note 5 above), Francis questions "the old answers [that] set 'fiction' and 'history' as opposite poles." The *Cyropaedia* of Xenophon and the *Alexander Romance* should also be classed with *Apollonius* as "fictional biography"; see Holzberg, *Ancient Novel*, 11–14.

41 On this Damis of Niniveh, see Jacoby et al., *Die Fragmente der griechischen Historiker*, 162–65. "Since D.'s account is often quite fantastic and in many instances the chronological references are plainly wrong, it is clear that D.'s *Hypomnemata* had a fictional character and that D. as a companion of Apollonius is a fictitious person" (162). Debate exists, however, about whether Damis is the pseudonym of another real author or the pure invention of Philostratus.

42 Jones, *Philostratus*, 6.

Philostratus's *Apollonius* remains intriguing nonetheless. Granting the text's full and complex range of literary affinities, at least the document-based pattern of research and the recent-but-not-contemporary theme fit well with the essentially archival mode of *near* contemporary biography practiced by figures such as Suetonius (*Lives of Illustrious Men* and *Lives of the Caesars*) and Plutarch in the final few figures of his *Parallel Lives*.[43] Philostratus's own *Lives of the Sophists*, of course, also belongs here.[44] The encyclopedic and anthological character of these and similar collections of *bioi* (e.g., *Lives of the Prophets*, Satyrus's *Lives of the Tragedians*, Diogenes's *Lives of the Philosophers*) naturally allowed a greater authorial distance from the subject matter than otherwise obtained. In almost all cases this represented a temporal distance, however—at times substantial. These collections were thus not in any sense essentially the accounts of recent people or events, and the author of a genuine contemporary *bios*, devoted to the life of a single man, was still expected to be acquainted with his hero. Here, for all their points of contact, Luke and Philostratus thus stand essentially apart.

If good parallels to Luke's informant-based contemporary history/ *bios* have not survived, similar works certainly existed.[45] Fronto evidently planned an account of Lucius Verus's wars in Parthia, drawn up from the emperor's own account and those solicited from his generals (*Ad Verum Imp.* 1.2; cf. *Principiae Historiae*). If this project amounts to a courtesan fashion of ghostwriting, Josephus's *Bellum* (1:1), which also relied on imperial accounts, nevertheless opens with a thrust precisely against those historians who wrote of the war yet boasted no personal involvement:

> Some, having not been there in the action (οὐ παρατυχόντες τοῖς πράγμασιν), have collected from hearsay random and contradictory accounts (ἀκοῇ συλλέγοντες εἰκαῖα καὶ ἀσύμφωνα

---

[43] The last Romans in Plutarch's collection are Galba and Otho, who died in 69. The scope and project of Plutarch are like that of a universal history, traced from earliest times down to the present.

[44] The *Lives* extend from ancient times and the school of Gorgias down to Philostratus's own day and the reign of Alexander Severus or Caracalla.

[45] The other canonical Gospels should obviously be mentioned in this discussion. John's assertion of eyewitness testimony is plain (Jn 19:35). Mark and Matthew, however, make no such direct claim, though tradition identified Matthew as an apostle. See chap. 1 in this volume. It is significant that the apocryphal Gospels are consistently attributed to figures that could have borne eyewitness testimony (e.g., Thomas, Philip, Peter, James, Nicodemus, and the like). The failure of Mark and Luke to be associated with any similar claim, but to be bolstered instead by traditions of close association with an eyewitness (Peter and Paul respectively), is a liability and strong argument in favor of the primitive character of their authorial attributions.

διηγήματα), which they have written up in a rhetorical style (σοφιστικῶς).

Josephus's dismissal of these bunglers obviously means to delegitimize their misinformed secondhand efforts and make room for his own insider account.[46] Unfortunately, the stylized charge of dressing up "hearsay" (ἀκοή) with fancy rhetoric (σωφιστικῶς) tells us little about this brand of history and, importantly, whether it would have protested the same careful inquiry and attention to firsthand sources we find highlighted in Luke 1:1–4. Regardless, it becomes clear from this passage, as much as from Lucian and Polybius, that an author's distance from the descriptions in his account was represented as a vulnerable liability.

Of course, even for a participant, some reliance upon other witnesses was necessary, and this fact was accepted (e.g., Lucian, *Hist. Conscr.* 47). Polybius is typically to the point:

> Since many events occur simultaneously in different places, and one person cannot be in several places at once, nor is it possible for a single person to have seen with his own eyes every place in the world and all the peculiar features of different places, the only thing left for an historian is to inquire from as many people as possible, to believe those worthy of belief and to be a competent critic of the reports that come to him.[47]

If allowance was thus made, it is clear that dependence on reportage was a concession and a compensation for the limits of personal attestation. Although Thucydides puts his observations and the reports of others in parallel (οἷς [i.e., ἔργοῖς] ... αὐτὸς παρῆν and οἱ παρόντες τοῖς ἔργοις ἑκάστοις, *Hist.* 1.22.2–3), the value of *authorial* autopsy over the reports of eyewitnesses was never in doubt. A figure like Herodian was thus proud to promote (repeatedly) his own firsthand qualifications:

> I have written a history of the events following the death of Marcus which I saw and heard in my lifetime. I had a personal share in some of these events during my imperial and public service. (*Hist.* 1.2,5; cf. 2.15,7 [Whittaker, LCL])

---

[46] Josephus is even more harsh on these pretenders in *C. Ap.* 1.46 (cf. 1.54–56): "We have actually had so-called histories even of our recent war published by persons who never visited the sites nor were anywhere near the actions described, but, having put together a few hearsay reports, have, with the gross impudence of drunken revelers, miscalled their productions by the name of history" (Thackeray, LCL).

[47] *Hist.* 12.4c.4–5. Translation from Skuckburgh, *Histories*.

His dependence upon the information of others, in contrast, is presented almost as an apology, expressed as a matter needing careful control:

> My policy has been not to accept any second-hand information which has not been checked and corroborated. I have collected the evidence for my work with every attention to accuracy, limiting it to what falls within the recent memory of my readers. (*Hist.* 1.1–3 [Whittaker, LCL])

Plainly, a discriminating use was required, for this testimony was expected to be riddled with inaccuracies.

The point in all this is simply that, despite advertising his star witnesses in the preface, Luke's efforts to establish the ἀσφάλεια of his story labored under an evident historiographical handicap. Where modern sensibilities might appreciate Luke's professional distance, ancient critics would have noted his pure reliance upon reports. Contemporary historiography in its optimal form was founded on eyewitness—but that witness was the witness of *the author*.

Herodian's appeal to the "recent memory of my readers" exposes an additional difficulty confronting the Lukan project. Both author and *audience* had a key part in writing histories. The latter specifically played a recognized role in monitoring contemporary claims. This is clear from the passage earlier quoted from Josephus: "Mendacity brought an author into disgrace with readers who knew the facts" (τὸ ψεύδεσθαι παρ'εἰδόσιν αἰσχρὸν ἦν, *B.J.* 1.15).[48] Indeed, Josephus himself was a reader "who knew the facts" and intervened in writing to set the record straight, debunking many false records of the war. For an account such as the *Bellum*, dealing with "vast disturbances" (ὑπερβολὴν θορύβων) and "affairs of great moment" (ἐπὶ τηλικούτοις πράγμασι), an appropriately wide forum of reader-witnesses could be assumed. But what of events which had no such theatre? What about an account no one could confirm or refute?

Luke seems to have been aware of this issue. On the one hand, he studiously portrayed Jesus' crucifixion and death as highly public events: "Are you the only visitor to Jerusalem who does not know the things that have

---

[48] In *Vita* 361–367, Josephus takes the approbation of qualified readers as an endorsement of his full veracity: "I presented the books to the Emperors themselves, only just after the events had taken place. For myself I knew that I had preserved the true tradition ... but to many others right away I presented the history, some who had taken part in the war, such as King Agrippa and some of his relations." In the *Bellum*, Josephus directly commends his account to "those experienced with these matters and falling in the war" who can rightly judge its truthfulness (*B.J.* 1.30). See Moessner, "'Eyewitnesses.'"

happened there in these days?" (Lk 24:18). This is a strategic *amplificatio* and resembles Polybius's rhetorical questions at the end of his preface: "Who could be so absorbed in other subjects" as to have no attentive interest in the rise of Rome? Luke casts the crucifixion as an event of wide interest and wide knowledge, and he has embedded this publicity into his narrative. Romans and Jews, Pilate, Herod, "the chief priests and the leaders and the people" (Lk 23:13) all have some involvement in the episode.

The Galilean ministry is also attested by a wide network of witnesses, as Peter reveals at Pentecost (Acts 2:22), mentioning the "wonders and signs that God did through him [Jesus] *in your midst, as you yourselves know* (ἐν μέσῳ ὑμῶν, καθὼς αὐτοὶ οἴδατε)." The assumption that all the people know of the ministry of Jesus corresponds to a recurring detail in the Gospel (e.g., Lk 4:42, 5:15, 5:19, 5:29, 7:11, 8:4, 8:40, 9:37, 13:17, 19:37, 22:47, 23:1, 23:27, 23:48). Lest Jesus' public be underestimated, the regional magnitude of these myriad crowds is vividly recorded (Lk 6:17, 12:1).

All this publicity has testimonial value: Jesus' life and death are a matter of public record. Paul aptly expresses this discoursing before King Agrippa (Acts 26:26):

> The king knows about these things and I am speaking to him boldly, for I cannot believe that any of these things have escaped his notice, for this did not happen in a corner (οὐ γάρ ἐστιν ἐν γωνίᾳ πεπραγμένον τοῦτο).

"This did not happen in a corner!" Even if the king was not a witness, like Herod he must have heard the reports (Lk 23:8; cf. 4:14–15, 4:37, 5:15–16, 7:17). This is evidentiary language, and Luke like John understands the full forensic significance of Jesus' open activity: "I always taught in a synagogue and in the Temple, where all the Jews gather, and in secret I said nothing ... Ask those who heard what I said" (Jn 18:20–21; cf. Lk 22:53).

Seen in this light, the *Resurrection* posed a considerable historiographical problem. As the centerpiece of the Luke-Acts narrative, Jesus' rising was strangely, embarrassingly private—at least in Luke's presentation. While Paul is keen to note the huge number of (still living, examinable) witnesses (1 Cor 15:6), himself included, for Luke the event did not happen before the people any more than it happened before the author. Instead, a suspiciously select set of witnesses held complete custody of the evidence.

> We are witnesses to all that he did both in the country of the Jews and in Jerusalem, he whom they killed by hanging him on a tree. Yet God raised him on the third day and made him manifest—*not to all the people but to us who were chosen beforehand*

> *by God as witnesses* (μάρτυσιν τοῖς προχειροτονημένοις ὑπὸ τοῦ θεοῦ), we who ate and drank with him after he rose from the dead. And he commanded us to preach to the people, and to testify (διαμαρτύρασθαι) that he is the one ordained by God to be judge of the living and the dead. (Acts 10:39–42)

Luke's decision to draw attention to the exclusive character of the witnesses to Jesus' rising is intriguing, especially after stressing the public nature of Jesus' ministry and death.

It is impossible to decide whether or in what form Luke may or may not have known the tradition of the five hundred witnesses preserved in 1 Corinthians 15:6. Are they to be understood in "the Eleven gathered together and those who were with them" who saw they Lord after his appearance to Simon (Lk 24:33; cf. Acts 1:13–15)? It is striking, in any event, that Luke makes no appeal, implicit or overt, to the large number of witnesses. What is clear is that Paul's testimony, like Luke's account, highlights Peter in a primary position and understands the other witnesses to be a group specifically of *believers* (ἐπάνω πεντακοσίοις ἀδελφοῖς). Paul himself is the sole exception, disrupting the appearance of an "inside job," and here Luke is again essentially in accord.

Even granting the considerable strategic, apologetic significance of Paul's outsider witness, repeated three times for good measure in the course of Acts (Acts 9:1–9, 22:4–16, 26:9–17),[49] Luke's account is nevertheless left historiographically in a doubly awkward position. Not only was his own authorial qualification uncertain, but also his audience could not play its normal role. The testimony of those "chosen beforehand by God" was not subject to confirmation or refutation by another body of witnesses in the know. Thus, when it came to the central claim of the history, *simple assent or rejection were the two and only two forced options*. Corrective interventions had no place. Arbitration through a process of public scrutiny was formally excluded, for all the evidence was in the hands of the believers. Accordingly, Luke's composition acquires an entirely unusual character. By displacing the structures of authentication classically invested in author and audience, the evangelist amplifies the status of reporting and puts himself in a unique solidarity with his readers: both are at the mercy of what "the eyewitnesses from the beginning handed on *to us*" (παρέδοσαν ἡμῖν οἱ ἀπ'ἀρχῆς αὐτόπται).

---

[49] Licona has strongly underscored the apologetic significance of Paul's witness: "Paul's conversion is especially interesting because he was an enemy of the church when his experience of the risen Jesus occurred. Therefore Jesus' resurrection is reported not only by his friends but also by at least someone who was a vehement foe at the time of the experience" (*Resurrection of Jesus*, 437).

Narrating Wonders and Naming Witnesses

The peculiar circumstances of the Resurrection of Jesus imposed on Luke a need for adaptation. Accounts of revived human beings were, of course, known in the ancient world, but these reports regularly appear in a different literary key: mythography. The *Library* of Apollodorus, for instance, recounts the miraculous arts of Asclepius (who raised men to life with the blood of the Gorgon entrusted to him by Athena) alongside a report of the surgeon's birth from Apollo and instruction by the centaur Chiron (*Library*, 3.10.3; cf. Justin, *Dial.* 69.6; 1 *Apol.* 22.6, 54.10; Lucian, *Of Pantomime* 45).[50] Such mythic accounts could indeed be tolerated and hosted in the less exigent genre of antiquarian historiography (e.g., Diodorus Siculus, *Bib. hist.* 4.71.2–3). Nevertheless, it would be a great blunder to confuse Luke's aspiration of relating a recent eyewitness event with such promiscuous tale-telling.

Plutarch's *Romulus* presents a more interesting parallel. While it is obviously a case of antiquarian historiography/biography, "archeology" in the Thucydidean sense, the postmortem appearance at the end of the text of Rome's eponymous founder is supported by an account of the sworn testimony of a highly reputable, named eyewitness.

> It is said that one of the patricians, a man of noblest birth, and of the most reputable character, a trusted and intimate friend also of Romulus himself, and one of the colonists from Alba, Julius Proculus by name, went into the forum and solemnly swore by the most sacred emblems before all the people that, as he was travelling on the road, he had seen Romulus coming to meet him, fair and stately to the eye as never before, and arrayed in bright and shining armor. He himself, then, affrighted at the sight, had said: "O King, what possessed thee, or what purpose hadst thou, that thou hast left us patricians a prey to unjust and wicked accusations, and the whole city sorrowing without end at the loss of its father?" Whereupon Romulus had replied: "It was the pleasure of the gods, O Proculus, from whom I came, that I should be with mankind only a short time, and that after founding a city destined to be the greatest on earth for empire and glory, I should dwell again in heaven. So farewell, and tell the Romans that if they practice self-restraint, and add to it valor, they will reach the utmost heights of human power. And I will be your propitious deity, Quirinus." These things seemed to the Romans worthy of belief, from

---

50 On this text, see Lehtipuu, *Debates over the Resurrection of the Dead*, 28–29. On Asclepius and Jesus, see chap. 4 in this volume.

the character of the man who related them, and from the oath which he had taken; moreover, some influence from heaven also, akin to inspiration, laid hold upon their emotions, for no man contradicted Proculus, but all put aside suspicion and calumny and prayed to Quirinus, and honored him as a god. (Perrin, LCL)

Richard Miller has provocatively highlighted many contacts between the Roman apotheosis tradition and the Gospel Resurrection stories.[51] To his list may be added the overtly forensic character of Julius Proculus's testimony here, which resembles a feature of Lukan discourse discussed below. For all the ethical appeal conjured up in the citation of this patrician eyewitness's noble character, the suspicion that hung over all antiquarian historiography nevertheless inevitably tainted Plutarch's account. What confronted Luke was accordingly the task of refashioning into contemporary historiography the sort of back-from-the-dead *fabulae* conventionally marred with the dubious status of a "prehistory." In Luke's case, as mentioned, such material was also further complicated by a double distance (author/audience) from the remarkable events.

A similar set of constraints may be seen at the end of Philostratus's *Apollonius*, where in the final few paragraphs Philostratus relates a series of variants on Apollonius's end, including his apparition, perhaps in a dream, transfigured and immortal, to a young student of philosophy who doubted the immortality of the soul (8.31.3). Significantly, Damis's eyewitness reporting explicitly ends before this closing apparition, however.[52] After thus resigning his historiographical pretensions, Philostratus even intentionally conjures the mystique of rumor to help Apollonius fade away into a twilight of legend: "some say ... others say" (περὶ γὰρ τρόπου, καθ᾽ ὃν ἐτελεύτα, εἴγε ἐτελεύτα, πλείους μὲν λόγοι, Δάμιδι δὲ οὐδεὶς εἴρηται, 8.29.1; cf. 30.1–2).

Philostratus's calculated shift at the conclusion of his text to competing stories and *rumor rhetoric* echoes the language of mythography ("the story goes," "some say," etc.) and marks an intentional shift from (pretended?) historical science to a softer, more allusive ending, less stringently occupied with making a firm truth claim.[53] A similar, casual rhetoric of "some consider ... others think" (ἀλλ᾽ οἱ μὲν εἴκαζον ... ἕτεροι δ᾽ οἴονται) importantly contours Plutarch's account of Romulus's apotheosis as well (*Romulus* 27.4–6). Noth-

---

51 Miller, "Mark's Empty Tomb," 772–73.

52 Τὰ μὲν δὴ ἐς Ἀπολλώνιον τὸν Τυανέα Δάμιδι τῷ Ἀσσυρίῳ ἀναγεγραμμένα ἐς τόνδε τὸν λόγον τελευτᾷ (8.29.1).

53 For an additional consideration of "rumor rhetoric," see chap. 3 in this volume. The echo of this rhetoric, arching across the centuries and still sounding—e.g., in Jean Steinmann's open-ended conclusion to his *Vie de Jésus*—is a curious affinity and phenomenon to observe; see chap. 1 in this volume.

ing of this uncommitted tone can be found in Luke's language, however. The *believers'* account is never countered by other possibilities, from which the reader may choose according to his own discretion and personal canons of plausibility.

It would be unimaginable for Luke to trot Jesus off into a sunset of hearsay the way Philostratus does with his hero, retire his star witness before the final act, or offer the reader a choice of several possible endings. Luke's eyewitnesses are witnesses specifically to Jesus' resurrection. Their testimony does not run out just at the critical moment, like that of Philostratus's Damis. On the contrary, everything depended upon what they said they saw! Their account is the only possible reality that the Third Gospel's readers are offered. Competing rumors do not figure within the Lukan frame, even in order to be rejected (cf. διεφημίσθη ὁ λόγος οὗτος παρὰ Ἰουδαίοις μέχρι τῆς σήμερον, Mt. 28:11–15). Another manner of reporting was thus required in Luke's case, for a different, more absolute sort of claim was being made.

The rather incidental quality of Apollonius's final apparition should also be underscored. However impressive, confirmatory, and climatic, the thaumaturge's final victory over death is only an accidental episode at the end of a long biography (the longest preserved from antiquity) and only one of the possible endings of the story (as is also the case with Romulus's apotheosis). Another vitally important difference from Luke is thus clear. For the evangelist and author of Acts, the Resurrection of Jesus holds massive centrality for the entire story. The narrative shape of the whole Lukan enterprise accordingly compelled, once more, a different sort of presentation.

In response to all these various historiographical challenges posed by the Resurrection, Luke essentially reconfigured the Thucydidean model of history and infused it with an earlier Herodotean type of autopsy. The evangelist writes contemporary history, yet he organizes it around a private event. In effect, this transposes to the historiographical center a mode of witness calibrated for *isolated wonders* (θαῦμα), a marginal phenomenon that especially punctuates Herodotean outgrowths like *periegesis* literature and paradoxography but is reminiscent also of the incidental nature of Apollonius's final apparition in Philostratus. This brand of testimony narrates exceptionalities and extraordinary reports and simply demands the reader's belief or nonbelief (usually the latter) with no prospect of personal verification. Plutarch's quarrelsome *de Malignitate Herodoti*, written against Herodotus's mendacity, demonstrates to what extent assent or non-assent is the forced choice.[54]

In Herodotus, the verity of "wonder" reports is still frequently linked to the ethical appeal of authorial autopsy (used to confirm local rumor):

---

54 It is revealing that Plutarch "in challenging Herodotus ... can do little more than quote what Herodotus says and deny it ... the argument from implausibility or impropriety are

> I saw (εἶδον) a great wonder (θῶμα μέγα) on the site of the battle, about which the people of the country had told me ... the skulls of the Persians are so brittle that if you throw a tiny pebble it will pierce them, but the Egyptian skulls are so strong that the blow of a stone will hardly crack them.[55]

Direct confirmation was not always available, however, and sometimes ears had to replace eyes. A more helpful analogy to Luke's problem is thus seen in a story from the Battle of Marathon that concerns a certain Epizelus:

> The following marvel (θῶμα) happened there: an Athenian, Epizelus son of Couphagoras, was fighting in the battle like a brave man when he was deprived of his sight, though struck or hit nowhere on his body, and from that time on he spent the rest of his life in blindness. I have heard that he tells the following story about his misfortune (Λέγειν δὲ αὐτὸν περὶ τοῦ πάθεος ἤκουσα τοιόνδε τινὰ λόγον): he saw opposing him a tall armed man, whose beard overshadowed his shield, but the phantom passed him by and killed the man next to him. I learned by inquiry that Epizelus himself recounts these things (Ταῦτα μὲν δὴ Ἐπίζηλον ἐπυθόμην λέγειν).[56]

Herodotus's professional inquiry here presents a contemporary, eyewitness report about a privately attested wonder that transpired perhaps fifty years before. While the event is perfectly incidental to the Battle of Marathon and the Persian Wars more generally—thus utterly different from Luke's Resurrection accounts—the historiographical constellation of author, witness, and readers is essentially the same. The reality of the event depends upon the credibility of Epizelus.

Given this complete dependence on the veracity of the witness, it is worth noting Herodotus's special care to pin the story to a named individual. Luke displays the same historian's impulse.[57] The Emmaus tradition associ-

---

in heavy use" (Bowen, *Plutarch*, 4). The appeal to Charon of Lampsacus in §20 is the first use of an alternative authority to counter Herodotus. This type of argument is obviously confined to recorded, public events. Prehistory and wonder narratives elicit a different order of counter-assertion.

55 *Hist.* 3.12,1–4. Translations of Herodotus adapted from Godly, *Herodotus*.

56 *Hist.* 6.117.

57 Luke's impulse toward specification extends beyond a concern for concrete names. Richard Dillon (*From Eye-Witnesses to Ministers of the Word*) stresses how carefully Luke frames all his Resurrection accounts with a notation of *time, place, and persons*. On the absence of narrative nowheres in Gospel miracle accounts, see chap. 4 in this volume.

ated with Cleopas is a good example (Lk 24:12–35).⁵⁸ As seen in Mark 16:12–13, the story also circulated in a much less specified form.⁵⁹ Mark preserves a resurrection appearance to "two of them" (δυσὶν ἐξ αὐτῶν) anonymously walking somewhere "in the country" (εἰς ἀγρόν): no more satisfactory as the stuff of solid history than is a secondhand story of bizarre war lore. Luke is not as intrusive as Herodotus in disclosing his every methodological move, yet based on the Gospel's programmatic preface, we should take seriously the prospect that a Herodotean act of "inquiry" (ἐπυθόμην) lies behind Luke's account, attached as it is to a definite figure, time, and locale.

It is helpful in this connection to find the blind old soldier, Epizelus, actively rehearsing his tale as a kind of patterned performance one could go hear (or hear about).⁶⁰ The same phenomenon should be recognized as an important component in the formation of the Gospel tradition and a prime source tapped by Luke.⁶¹ Cleopas can simply be expected to have told his amazing story—frequently.⁶² Bauckham makes this point in his important study of the use of proper names in the Gospels. About the specified women witnesses at the tomb, for instance, he remarks:

> It is natural to suppose that these women were well-known not just for having once told their stories but as people who remained accessible and authoritative sources of these traditions as long as they lived.⁶³

---

58 Bauckham offers a comment worth quoting at length: "The story does not require that he [Cleopas] be named and his companion remained anonymous. There seems no plausible reason for naming him other than to indicate that he was the source of this tradition. He is very probably the same person as Clopas, whose wife Mary appears among the women at the cross in John 19:25. Clopas is a very rare Semitic form of the Greek name Cleopas, so rare that we can be certain this is the Clopas who, according to Hegisippus, was the brother of Jesus' father Joseph and the father of Simon, who succeeded his cousin James as leader of the Jerusalem church (*apud* Eusebius, *H. E.* 3.11; 4.22.4). Cleopas/Clopas was doubtless one of those relatives of Jesus who played a prominent role in the Palestinian Jewish Christian movement. The story Luke tells would have been essentially the story Cleopas himself told about his encounter with the risen Jesus. Probably it was one of many traditions of the Jerusalem church which Luke has incorporated into his work" (*Jesus and the Eyewitnesses*, 47).

59 Lukan knowledge of the longer ending of Mark's Gospel would be a fringe theory and cannot be assumed. Arguably, Mark attests an independent, pre-Lukan oral form of the tradition. See Bovon, *Das Evangelium nach Lukas III/4*, 554. It is also possible, however, that Mk 16:9–20 represents a late addition, fully dependent upon and summarizing the other canonical resurrection accounts. On the unlikelihood that Mark intended the Gospel to end at 16:8, see Stein, "Ending of Mark," 79–98.

60 It is widely recognized that Herodotus, Thucydides, Xenophon, and other classic historians were heavily reliant upon such oral sources. See Byrskog, *Story as History*, 94–99.

61 Byrskog, *Story as History*, 100–5.

62 This is especially true if we accept Hegisippus's information. See note 61 above.

Acts even gives us an example of this very thing. The experience of sudden blindness seemingly affected Paul no less forcefully than poor Epizelus, and neither man was hesitant to tell the tale. If the details of Acts' three accounts are confounding, Luke has certainly not invented Paul's penchant for repeating his remarkable story (even should we allow that Luke might have embellished the account). The letters also presume a pattern of repeated recitation: "You have heard of my former life in Judaism" (Gal 1:13–24; cf. Phil 3:4–11; 1 Tm 1:13–14).

In contrast to Paul's two rehearsals (Acts 22:1–21, 26:1–29), it is notable that Luke chooses not to present the Emmaus account in direct speech—despite a perfect opportunity when Cleopas returned and "told what had happened on the road" (Lk 24:35; cf. Acts 10–11). Quoted speeches were considered a place of compositional freedom, of course, and expressions of a historian's virtuosity (amply indulged by Luke in Acts). *Narrative* (διήγησις), in contrast, was the mode of "accurate" historical rendition. Herodotus accordingly also eschews direct speech (or *oratio obliqua*), and rather than embed a transcription of Epizelus's testimony, he offers a third-person account of the event (peppered with characteristic commentary).[64] This seems to have been the normal way eyewitness testimony (and source material in general) was incorporated into historical writing: it was simply woven into the texture of the narrative.[65] This is evident not only from the conventional suppression of an author's first person perspective (as when Thucydides or Polybius refer to their own actions in the third person with no particular attention to their privileged vantage point and with no interjected remarks of verification).[66] The same feature of folding eyewitness material into the fabric of the narrative is also found in the use of ancillary witnesses, as seen in the example of Titus's testimony in the *Bellum*. The well-connected Josephus announces that his own testimony is supplemented by *the* essential witness: μάρτυς αὐτὸς ὁ πορθήσας Καῖσαρ Τίτος (*B.J.* 1.10).[67] Yet the "testimony" of

---

63 Bauckham, *Jesus and the Eyewitnesses*, 51.

64 The avoidance of indirect speech is also interesting in the Epizelus account, since "Herodotus often uses the infinitives of indirect speech in his own narrative in order to show that he is telling a story which may be no more than a story" (Bowen, *Plutarch*, 6).

65 Schepens, *L'"autopsie*," 96–97.

66 See Marincola, *Authority and Tradition in Ancient Historiography*, 182–206. The narrator's persona is distinct from the persona of the historical actor and does intrude (particularly in Polybius), yet this distinction is rigorously maintained. Even Polybius's estimate of his own friendship with Scipio is written in the third person. An interesting example of eyewitness frame-breaking appears in Jn 19:35, curiously still phrased in the third person: ὁ ἑωρακὼς μεμαρτύρηκεν, καὶ ἀληθινὴ αὐτοῦ ἐστιν ἡ μαρτυρία.

67 On Josephus's reliance upon informants see Moessner, "'Eyewitnesses,'" 113–15.

Titus never emerges in an explicit record of his report.[68] The future Caesar simply appears a key actor, while readers must guess or recognize where he functioned as a special source.

Luke's Resurrection narratives bear no proportion to the grand *Bellum*, and unlike Josephus, Luke is not a co-witness with his αὐτόπται. An account like the Emmaus episode is scaled more nearly to Herodotus's succinct report about Epizelus, and on this metric Luke offers a much fuller measure of detail. This can be attributed to two things. (1) First, the Resurrection is *vastly* more important to Luke's project than is the blinding of Epizelus to Herodotus. Luke, to repeat, has transposed a marginal phenomenon of attestation to the center of his history. It is true the characteristic language of "wonder" (θαῦμα) has been adapted (Lk 24:12, 24:41); still, the numinous content is similar (cf. Lk 24:37), and most importantly the problem of private witness is identical. (2) Second, the greater specification in Luke's story of Cleopas suggests closer contact to the source than Herodotus enjoyed. Luke's story has seemingly been patterned by the form in which Cleopas told it, down to the ineffably deep impact the whole experience had upon him (Lk 24:32).[69] Naturally, Luke has written up the account, and there is no need to deny the presence of characteristic themes. Josephus's account of Titus also bears the historian's fingerprints. Nonetheless, real contact with the source is likely and could help explain several unique expressions in Luke 24:13–35.[70] Just as σκιαζεῖν is a *hapax* in Herodotus and the queer detail of the phantom's beard sounds like a quaint echo of Epizelus (identifying the ghost as a Persian), so

---

68 Perhaps the most critical episode in Josephus's *Bellum* is the long, suspenseful account of the burning of the ναός (*B.J.* 6.220–270). The critical feature of this event is that, although the tragedy transpired before the eyes of thousands, the ultimate cause was occult. How did the fire start, and more importantly, what was the role of Titus? The question was controversial (see *b. Gittin* 56b; Barnes, "Fragments of Tacitus' Histories"), and important because the razing of the Temple epitomizes Josephus's entire thesis in the work: the irresistible divine fate of destruction worked through recalcitrant Jews, not Roman aggressors. For the truth in this highly sensitive matter, Josephus had to rely upon Titus. At the crucial moment in the narrative, however, no special attention is drawn to Titus's role as an eyewitness. The story is simply told of how he learned about the fire and vainly tried to stop it. On the blame games and conflicting perceptions that arose around the question of the fire, see Giambrone, "Temple Arsons and Murder of the Prophets."

69 Bauckham observes that the Emmaus account is "certainly told from the perspective of the named characters" and that if the details are really recollected and not "the product of the storytelling imagination" of Luke, "they can only have been recollected by ... Cleopas (or his anonymous companion)" (*Jesus and the Eyewitnesses*, 55).

70 For a discussion of the Lukan and pre-Lukan elements see Bovon, *Das Evangelium nach Lukas III/4*, 552–54. "Das Vokabular und der Stil zeigen klar, dass die Erzählung früher zum Sondergut gehörte ... Lukas übernehme eine traditionelle Geschichte und bearbeite sie." Before a comprehensive decisions can be made concerning the sources behind Lukan Sondergut, the material deserves a thorough reassessment along the oral lines proposed by Byrskog.

we plausibly hear Cleopas's voice in unnecessary details like Jesus' pretension to be going further (Lk 24:28). If such features might always be mocked up by an author, they are also demonstrably found in true eyewitness reporting.[71]

Editorial shaping and selection are unavoidable in the narration of genuine testimony, but we should assume some minimal accuracy in reporting *what the witnesses said*. It would be gratuitous to suppose a real Epizelus did not tell (in some form) the tale we find recorded. The issue confronting readers of *The Histories* was less whether Herodotus (or his sources) invented this storytelling soldier, but whether the storyteller himself was in fact an *inventor*. Luke's readers similarly had to ask: Is Cleopas's story (or Paul's) worth believing?

Accrediting the Witnesses

Establishing the credibility of his informants was important for Luke in showing the ἀσφάλεια of their account and evoking a corresponding act of belief. Such buttressing of the "witnesses" was fundamental to Luke's initiative in writing and helps explain how his two volumes are vitally hinged at the Resurrection. Here I would like to suggest briefly that Acts augments the status of the eyewitnesses in three key ways.

Historiographic Accreditation

If eyewitnesses like Cleopas "remained accessible and authoritative sources" from whom the evangelist might have gathered his testimony, in the context of Acts, Luke intentionally narrows the circle of witnesses to a select group of authorized tradents.[72] Cleopas's account is immediately credible to those in Jerusalem because it corresponds with the experience already had by Peter (24:34). This deference to the Petrine testimony is a move that almost certainly reflects a genuine circumstance in the early Church: specifically, the testimonial stewardship of the Twelve, Birger Gerhardsson's "authoritative collegium."[73] Hengel has rightly highlighted here the intersection between preaching and witness.[74] The specifically historiographical

---

[71] See Redman, "How Accurate Are Eyewitnesses?," 3–13.
[72] On this specific group of witnesses, centered upon Peter, see Hengel, "Der Lukasprolog und seine Augenzeugen," 256–80.
[73] Gerhardsson, *Reliability of the Gospel Tradition*, 73. See also Gerhardsson, *Memory and Manuscript*, 329–30.
[74] Hengel, "Der Lukasprolog und seine Augenzeugen," 257.

dimension of this "specialization" in witness-bearing should not be missed, however.[75] Through the mouth of Peter, Luke clarifies the basic qualification of these titular μάρτυρες τῆς ἀναστάσεως: they must have accompanied the Lord "beginning (ἀρξάμενος) from the baptism of John until the day he was taken up from us" (Acts 1:22; cf. Jn 15:26–27). The formulation of this criterion clearly echoes the preface (οἱ ἀπ'ἀρχῆς αὐτόπται), and since none of the Lukan disciples (not even Peter) strictly meet the standard (having been called after Jesus' baptism), we can recognize here a historiographical desideratum. Witnesses should, like Josephus, have been "present in person at all the events" (*C. Ap.* 1.47).[76] More than anyone else, it is the person of Peter who provides the continuity of witness in Luke-Acts; his testimony is the historiographical spine of the Lukan project.

Forensic Accreditation

The displacement of the witnesses named in Luke 24 with the college of witnesses in Acts cannot be entirely explained as a historiographical exigency. Joanna and Mary Magdalen also accompanied Jesus during his period of ministry—as Luke clearly notes (Lk 8:1–3). Paul's failure in 1 Corinthians 15:4–5 to mention the women at the tomb as the first witnesses of the risen Jesus, in deference to Peter, corresponds to the narrative in Luke 24:1–10, which, in contrast to Matthew 28:1–7, shows no knowledge of the tradition preserved in Mark's longer ending of an appearance to Mary Magdalene. Luke does uphold the women as witnesses of the empty tomb, however, in contrast to Paul's summary of the events. In the view of Bauckham, this is even enshrined in a special "inclusio of eyewitness" narrative device.[77] The existence of such a device is open to question, however, and Peter/Simon's name is in any case the more obvious inclusio around the story of Jesus' public life (Lk 5:1–10, 24:34).

---

75 Hengel ("Der Lukasprolog und seine Augenzeugen," 257) rightly observes that Luke's emphasis on Peter and the Twelve is not intended to generate a false air of historical credibility, and that is not the suggestion here. It is simply pointed out that these accredited preachers/witnesses are presented in conscious conformity to a historiographical desideratum.

76 Establishing the proper "beginning" was important in ancient historiography. See, e.g., Dionysius of Halicarnassus, *De Veterum Censura* 11.

77 See Bauckham, *Jesus and the Eyewitnesses*, 129–32; and also Hengel, "Der Lukasprolog und seine Augenzeugen," 293–97. Bauckham contends that, in conformity with Acts 1:22, Lk 8:1–3 is the front end of "the inclusio of eyewitness," closed with renaming of the witnesses in the Resurrection account at 24:10. Hengel points to the two mentions of the memory of Mary the mother of Jesus (Lk 2:19, 2:51).

If the Markan status of the empty tomb is supplanted in Luke's narrative by visions of the risen Jesus himself, this can be broadly understood as a Pauline perspective. The minimization of the women witnesses should perhaps also be viewed in a forensic context, however. In the courts, a woman's formal testimony was viewed askance: "Let not the testimony of women be admitted, on account of the levity and boldness (κουφότητα καὶ θράσος) of their sex."[78] Such misogynist suspicion did not simply determine the practice of historians, however. Josephus is perfectly content to base his entire account of the mass suicide at Masada on the word of two women (*B.J.* 7.399–406). If the suggestive evidence in that case could be confirmed by a whole legion of Roman witnesses (if not by modern archeologists), Luke is also careful to add that the women's testimony was confirmed by "some of those who were with us" who went to the tomb and found all just as the woman had said (Lk 24:24). If historians could thus find a way to integrate the witness of women, it is nevertheless the *rhetoric of the courts* that distinguishes the model of witness developed in Acts from the Gospel's more conventional historiographical presentation—and here the retirement of the women (though perhaps not the empty tomb tradition; Acts 2:29–35) is complete.

In Acts, Luke repeatedly situates the testimony of the eyewitnesses in a forensic setting. The popularity of trial scenes in the Greco-Roman novels, like the solemn affidavit of Julius Proculus in Plutarch's *Romulus*, offers a cultural context for this brand of witness.[79] For Luke, these courtroom scenes do more than satisfy the tastes of a rhetorically educated readership, however; they fulfill the prophecy of Jesus that "you will be brought before kings and governors ... εἰς μαρτύριον" (Lk 21:12–13). At the same time, the interrogations introduce an official and public solemnity to the act of giving witness. The record of these depositions is not like the comparatively uncontrolled testimony of an eyewitness storyteller, an ol' Epizelus on the porch in his rocking chair.[80] By turning to the apostolic testimony, Luke attends to a kind

---

78 Josephus, *A. J.* 4.219. See *m. Yebamot* 15.1,8–10; 16.7; *m. Ketubot* 1.6–9.

79 "The inclusion of at least one trial in each of the extant Greek novels, as well as in the Latin novels of Petronius and Apulius, attests to the appeal of this type scene, and indeed its centrality to the genre. The prevalence of such scenes reflects the importance of rhetoric in the literary culture of the Roman empire. The novelists, as well as their audience, had a taste for legal complexities—a taste informed by their rhetorical education" (Schwarz, "Clitophon the *Moichos*").

80 It is important to recognize that the primacy of the apostolic witness over that of Cleopas is already expressed in Lk 24, even if the full importance of this authoritative testimony is only explored in Acts. Dillon rightly draws attention to Lk 24:34 ("The Lord is truly risen and has appeared to Simon"), which precedes the report of the pilgrims: "The fact that 'the Eleven and their company' are the speakers of the formative confession, and that they speak it *first*

of affidavit pronounced before the authorities. He thus registers in Acts a *confessional* form of witness that, significantly, now appears in the mode of *direct speech*. This innovation represents a shift from the narrative form proper to the historiographical rhetoric of the Gospel and signals at once a transition to kerygmatic testimony and a creedal streamlining of content. *That Jesus died and rose* becomes the emphatic point of witness—superseding in importance the vivid detail of the narrative tradition (and leaving forever hidden the τεκμηρίοι of the forty days). The fully corporate nature of this witness is crucial to understand. A formal *coetus testium* has suppressed the individuality of discrete resurrection appearances and distilled a common ecclesial testimony: *cruxifixus ... tertia die resurrexit ... ascendit ad caelos* (e.g., Acts 2:22–36, 3:12–16, 4:10, 5:29–32). This simple and stylized ecclesial form of witness neutralizes isolated testimony (*testimonium unius*) with the concerted force of corroboration.[81] Obviously, highlighting such collective testimony served Luke as a powerful accreditation of his witnesses' word, and this emphasis seems creative in the historiographical tradition.

One further, important element of the forensic context in which Luke situates the act of testimony is the witnesses' endurance of *torture*. When Peter and John are called before the council in Acts 5 and for the second time they refuse to halt speaking about what they have seen and heard, they are beaten and harshly threatened (Acts 5:40; cf. 4:20). The witnesses' steadfast resistance to all the repeated forms of authoritative coercion, climaxing in open persecution and imprisonment, is on the one hand an evident argument for the witnesses' reliability. Perverse as the whole institution was, torture was designed to extract truth—and resistance could also make the point, as historians like Tacitus saw.[82] At the same time, the joy of the disciples in their suffering is something extraordinary and clearly the sign that these witnesses possess a Spirit-endowed and insurmountable power. Here

---

before the travelers' report, is all true to the Lukan concept of the apostolic circle as primary μάρτυρες τῆς ἀναστάσεως αὐτοῦ ... The Petrine apparition and the testimony of the apostolic circle thus obtain logical priority in the building of the church ... the happening 'on the road' is authenticated and confirmed by being incorporated into the united Easter witness of the apostolic assembly" (*From Eye-Witnesses to Ministers of the Word*, 98).

81 Jewish law stipulated the need for two or three witnesses in capital cases (Nm 35:30; Dt 17:6). In Roman law, the testimony of a single witness was generally inadmissible, but in cases of solemn interest, seven witnesses were required. See Berger, *Encyclopedic Dictionary of Roman Law*, 734–35.

82 Tacitus recounts Poppaea's torture of Claudia Octavia's maids (*Annals* 14.60–64). This was meant to secure false confessions of Octavia's infidelity to Nero, but although a few succumbed to the pains of the torturers, "the majority unflinchingly maintained her innocence." All this is rhetorically designed by Tacitus to secure sympathy for Octavia and confirm the truth about her. See Murgatroyd, "Tacitus on the Death of Octavia."

the forensic coloring of Lukan kerygmatic witness shades into what might be called the prophetic mode, also an innovation within the tradition of history writing.

Prophetic Accreditation

If Acts' forensic context highlights the need for juridically admissible testimony (*testis idoneus*), it is all the more interesting to find the base social standing of the eyewitnesses explicitly exposed—in contrast to Plutarch's emphasis on the patrician respectability of Julius Proculus. The aristocratic chief priests marvel at the boldness (παρρησία) of Peter and John, discerning them to be ἄνθρωποι ἀγράμματοι ... καὶ ἰδιῶται (Acts 4:13). In the ancient world, of course, one's credibility in the courtroom stood in direct proportion to one's social status.[83] Luke thus explodes any merely forensic defense of his eyewitnesses. They are not ultimately worthy of attention because of any juridical status: being men (not women) or coming in sufficient number. Luke rather insists upon the complete disproportion between the witnesses themselves, whoever they may be, and the divine power of their testimony. The *Holy Spirit* speaking through them is the *witness* who merits a hearing from Luke's audience. The clearest expression of this pneumatic witness conjoined to the apostolic testimony is Acts 5:32:

> We are witnesses of these things, and *so is the Holy Spirit* whom God has given to those who obey him. (Acts 5:29–32; cf. Mk 13:11; Mt 10:20; Jn 15:26–27)

Lukan pneumatology is obviously an enormous theme, and the *prophetic* quality of the Spirit's activity is multifaceted in Luke-Acts.[84] It is enough here simply to note the connection to our subject. The "promise of the Father" is a δύναμις that empowers those who beheld the risen Lord to witness "even to the end of the earth" (Acts 1:4, 1:8). All the Spirit-led boldness, all the wonders, the inspired exegesis, the fortitude, and unlikely success of the eyewitnesses and their message contribute to an unsubtle apology for the credibility of their claim.

Mantic figures are, of course, common as characters in Greco-Roman histories, but it is vain that we search for any parallel where such a vibrantly charismatic endowment conferred upon a whole body of witnesses is claimed

---

83 See, e.g., Mirhady, "Athens' Democratic Witnesses."
84 See Menzies, *Development of Early Christian Pneumatology*. Menzies argues that Lukan pneumatology is essentially prophetic and not soteriological.

as the underwriting authentication of an entire contemporary history. Josephus, of course, makes much of his own prophetic insight (*BJ* 3.400–402). The sheer weight of his personal status, however, and his already huge credentials in writing preclude this type of inspiration from functioning as an endorsing attestation like the Holy Spirit in Acts. Rather, Josephus's self-presentation as a prophet serves to place him on the right side of history and undergird his complex thesis that the Roman victory was orchestrated by the Jewish God.[85] Luke has a different vision. His final word of confirmation for Theophilus is nicely encapsulated in a comment of Paul: "Our gospel came to you not only in word, but also in power and in the Holy Spirit and with full conviction" (1 Thes 1:5).[86]

"You Will Be a Witness"

A Pauline addendum must be added to the modes of accreditation just described. As already mentioned, the apologetic force of the outsider Saul's experience of the resurrected Jesus—the experience of one heartily disinclined to believe—invests the event with a convicting power not lost on Luke, Paul's own "sometime companion." Although Paul appears too late on the scene to fulfill Peter's (historiographical) criterion in selecting a new "witness to the resurrection" (Acts 1:22), Paul is nevertheless chosen as a witness by a violent divine intervention: "The God of our Fathers appointed you ... to see the Just One ... for you will be a witness for him to all men of what you have seen and heard" (22:14–15).

The uniquely impressive character of Paul's form of witness is underscored by his broader status as a mystic in Luke's presentation.[87] From the dream vision of the Macedonian man (Acts 16:9) to the trance-like vision of Jesus in the Temple (22:17), Paul sees a range of supernatural phenomena imperceptible to others. His luminous experience of the risen Lord, placed as it is after the time of the Lord's Ascension on high, recalls the experience of Stephen, explicitly named as a "witness/martyr" (22:20), who also saw the exalted Lord and testified to him at the moment of his death. Here the prophetic power of the chosen witnesses reaches a kind of apex. *Paul's testimony thus serves as an emphatic supernatural seal on the more historiographically conventional mode of Petrine witness.* Without being yoked to Peter's more earth-bound form of witness, however, the spiritualism of the Pauline tes-

---

85 See Kelley, "Cosmopolitan Expression of Josephus' Prophetic Perspective."
86 On this verse and motif, see chap. 6 in this volume.
87 See Jervell, *Unknown Paul*.

timony would risk veering off in all manner of ahistorical, ghost-like directions. The two protagonist pillars of Acts thus establish the space in which a uniquely Lukan construction of eyewitness and Jesus' resurrection can be developed.

Conclusion: A Ghost Story?

Historiographical reporting in Luke's testimony to the Resurrection fits within a tradition, but it is nonetheless unprecedented. At the level of attestation, it parallels the bizarre account of a bearded phantom at the Battle of Marathon, yet it has lost all proportion to such minor "wonder" tales, particularly in the thrice-repeated tale of Paul's own blinding vision, which looms large in Luke's account. It is no surprise, then, if the Resurrection looked distressingly like an overgrown ghost story (ἐδόκουν πνεῦμα θεωρεῖν; Lk 24:37).[88] This was precisely the false reception the Gospel risked (perhaps more than docetism)—particularly when viewed as one of those "fabulous and incredible stories... beginning to circulate in Palestine and the Greek East."[89] Mediterranean *fabulae* indeed share real points of contact with the Resurrection accounts as Glen Bowersock, Robert Miller, and others are keen to note.

The *Scheintod* motif of Greco-Roman romance is familiar with an astonished disbelief similar to what appears at the end of Luke's Gospel. Theagenes, for example, mistakes the supposedly dead Chariclea for a ghost (e.g., *Ethiopian Tale* 2.7). Luke's portrayal of the resurrected Jesus nevertheless stands closer in important respects to the *paradoxographers*, who were occupied with the collection and narration of wonders. The story of revenants such as Philinnion is suggestive: a fully corporeal, eating, drinking, and even copulating (!) ghost recounted in Phlegon's *Book of Marvels*.[90] If the dubious character of this literature gives it the sensationalist aspect of a freak show, its (semi-)scientific quality in the ancient context and nearness to

---

88 Ghost stories could be taken seriously even by serious persons. In Letter 7.27, Pliny the Younger asks Licinius Sura for his opinion on *phantasmata*, citing as an example the account of Curtius Rufus about a haunted house (cf. Tacitus, *Annals* 11.21), also mentioning a story found in Lucian.

89 Bowersock, *Fiction as History*, 27. Miller ("Mark's Empty Tomb," 759) is convinced that "several factors conspire... prohibiting a clear understanding of how such a text [as Mark, or by extension Luke] would have likely performed in an ancient Mediterranean world."

90 See Prince, "'Ghost of Jesus.'"

the Herodotean (θαῦμα) tradition should not be missed. Nor should appeals to *autopsy* in this peculiar form of "micro-historiography" be overlooked.[91]

The relative sobriety of Luke's Gospel in comparison to Phlegon's outrageous anthology is obvious on inspection. Luke is nevertheless sensitive to the danger, particularly after his report of Emmaus and the marvelous body of the risen Jesus, that his history will be mistaken for the story of a shade. He thus magnifies his wonder report accordingly, and this act of paradoxography exceeding Phlegon's own tall tale explains Luke's care to anchor the eyewitnesses' report in their un-lying senses:[92] "Handle me and see (ψηλαφήσατέ με καὶ ἴδετε); for a spirit (πνεῦμα) has not flesh and bones as you see (θεωρεῖτε) that I have" (Lk 24:39; cf. 24:41–43). Hard confirmation of Jesus' resurrected body was entailed in the astonishing experience of the witnesses. A more unearthly (Pauline) mode of visionary witness ("spiritual body") is thus complemented with tactile empiricism, and a report of robust sensory attestation is registered. Eyes are surer than ears, and hands are surer than both.

Luke's rhetoric of certification here makes an altogether different claim on reality than the novels, where the unlikely "postmortem" reunions remain benignly within the fictive narrative frame, for the evangelist draws his αὐτόπται out of the story world and into the prologue, where they confront *the reality of the reader's own world* and demand a decision for or against belief.[93] In this regard the evangelist's ethical appeal resembles that of a Phlegon, who even openly confronts his readers with a decision about his own credulity: "One should not disbelieve the forgoing narrative," he repeats.

---

[91] Phlegon's "source" for the story of Philinnion is supposedly the letter of an eyewitness.

[92] Prince ("Ghost of Jesus," 297–98) shows that Luke's resurrected Jesus "disorients the reader" and fits with neither ancient stories of disembodied spirits nor accounts of embodied revenants. An apology against the former is clearly at work in Lk 24:39, after Jesus' disappearance at Emmaus (before eating) seemingly aligned his state with a purely spiritual apparition. On the peculiar shape of early Christian belief in Jesus' physical resurrection, see Wright, *Resurrection of the Son of God*. Lehtipuu (*Debates over the Resurrection of the Dead*, 23–66) contests Wright's overly tidy classification of the Jewish/Christian category of "resurrection" and prefers to see a blurry picture of overlapping concepts. She is certainly correct to show the terminological imprecision of *egeiro/anastasis* language in an ancient context: "Clearly there is no terminological difference between resurrection of the dead and revival of the dead" (30). The relevant point in the present context, however, is that none of the texts that Lehtipuu highlights are contemporary historiography.

[93] Of course, "it is a common novelistic practice to pretend that the narrative is based on the report of an eyewitness" (Jacoby et al., *Fragmente der griechischen Historiker*, 163). The novels actually turn historiographical autopsy on its head, however, preferring to stoke the reader's gullibility with a preference for spoken reports—so argues Graverini, "The Ass's Ears and the Novel's Voice."

The seriousness of both authors as trustworthy researchers is on trial—as is inevitably, more profoundly, *the reader's* judgment.

It is critical to see in all this that Luke did *not* imagine such "proofs" (τεκμήριοι) as he narrated had autonomous probative power. The story challenged belief no matter what the witnesses saw (or touched) or how credible they may have been. "These words seemed to them like nonsense and they did not believe them" (Lk 24:11). The notion of λῆρος—trash, humbug, or even *delirium*—is a poignant Lukan touch, with an echo in Plutarch, who notes that many supposed the fantastic tale of Romulus's apotheosis was a "silly tale" imposed on simple-minded people (Rom 27:8). Both Mark and Matthew are content to record the disciples' disbelief, without coloring the outlandish report so unfavorably. This is interesting, for generally Luke's disciples come off much better than their synoptic counterparts at the Resurrection: they disbelieve "for joy" (ἀπὸ τῆς χαρᾶς; Lk 24:41). It is thus the astonishing message itself and not the disciples' incredulity that Luke has in view.

This frank perspective on the improbable, indeed *unbelievable* nature of the witnesses' claim is not unexpected. Luke's reflection upon the literally incredible proclamation of the Resurrection can only have been deepened through his account of the Church's mission—and its scoffing reception in places like Athens (ἀκούσαντες δὲ ἀνάστασιν νεκρῶν οἱ μὲν ἐχλεύαζον; Acts 17:32). Such rejection was prophetically foreseen, however, as a thing fated by *the singular magnitude of God's deed in Christ*:

> Behold you scoffers and wonder, and perish, for I do a deed in your days, a deed you will never believe, if one declares it to you. (Acts 13:41; cf. Hab 1:5)

Luke, in short, was alert to the prophetic drama of belief and disbelief, grounded upon God's great ἔργον revealed to chosen witnesses. This conception greatly colors Luke's idea of the progress of their testimony (Acts 28:26-27; cf. Is 6:9-10).

For Luke it is clear. Testimony to the Resurrection exposes the limits of historiography. No amount of accreditation can secure the conclusion. The evidence of history is like the empty tomb, a footprint inviting judgment. In the end, the Gospel witness cannot be accepted by any human power of assent, but only by a direct operation of God: "The Lord opened her heart (διήνοιξεν τὴν καρδίαν) to accept the things spoken by Paul" (Acts 16:14; cf. 3:37, 15:9). This is true not only for those like Lydia, who are moved to trust the words of the kerygma. Even the *eyewitnesses themselves* are "stupid and slow of heart" (Ὢ ἀνόητοι καὶ βραδεῖς τῇ καρδίᾳ; Lk 24:24) and must be touched by this divine grace of *opening* (διανοίξις). Only then can they apprehend *what their own eyes behold*: "Then their eyes were opened and they recognized him" (αὐτῶν δὲ διηνοίχθησαν οἱ οφθαλμοὶ καὶ ἀπέγνωσαν αὐτόν; Lk 24:31; cf. 24:16, 24:32, 24:45).[94]

---

[94] The vision/blindness dialectic, which captures the mysterious experience of the unseeing witnesses at Emmaus, has its most potent expression in the person of Paul. The importance of the theme as an adjunct to the *witness* motif is significant. Hamm ("Paul's Blindness and Its Healing") shows Luke's heavy reliance upon Isaiah in developing this blindness/vision motif. By tapping into Isaiah's expansive metaphor, Luke is able to amplify the import of Paul's personal experience: "Paul is pictured here living out the image of converted and saved Israel, moving from darkness to light, from blindness to sight" (70n16). Paul's paradigmatic experience finds direct expression in the final conversion account (Acts 26), when it is no longer the *persecutor's* blindness and new vision that merits mention, but the blindness of the *nation* in need of light. In the end, the task of the one who saw the light is precisely "to open *their* eyes (ἀνοῖξαι ὀφθαλμοὺς αὐτῶν) that they may turn *from darkness to light*" (26:18), to accept Jesus who came "to proclaim *the light* both to our people and to the Gentiles" (26:23).

PART II

THEOLOGICAL PERSPECTIVES

CHAPTER 6

Spirit and Power

A short history of theological angst surrounding the advent of modern biblical criticism would be a useful and perhaps surprising story to tell. In many ways, of course, it would be simply one more variation on the story of modernity itself. To that degree, the tale belongs as a chapter in Charles Taylor's magisterial *Secular Age*.[1] Indeed, those of us socialized into the exegetical guild could recite like a catechism lesson the specific "coming of age narrative" that functions as our founding myth. Emancipation from the nonage of ecclesiastical dogma is the predictable cornerstone of the project, whether the version we learned traces the birth of the field back to Luther, Lefèvre, Gabler, or some alternate exegetical hero.

Clustered around such pioneering figures is naturally a great deal of shortsighted, establishment opposition, which becomes the easy prey of retrospective satire. An early, entirely superfluous but revealing, confrontation occurs already in the year 1515. Upon publication of Erasmus's *Novum Instrumentum*, Maarten van Dorp, mouthpiece of the faculty of theology at Leuven, formally reproached the humanist's audacity in applying the same philological and text-critical methods to the sacrosanct vulgate that he had laudably used in restoring the original text of Jerome's epistles.[2] Such ignorant obstruction resembles the attitudes one still finds shaping study of the Quran. Erasmus replied to Dorp at length in a letter appended to his treatise *Praise of Folly*, pleading "what is plain even for the blind to see, that there are often passages where the Greek has been badly translated...and often a true

---

1 Taylor, *Secular Age*.
2 For a brief account of the exchange with Dorp, see Andersen, "Erasmus the Exegete." For an excellent and thorough exposition of Erasmus's biblical scholarship, see the introduction of Sider, *Collected Works of Erasmus*, 1–388.

and faithful reading has been corrupted by uneducated copyists."[3] In the end, only stultified intransigence would barricade Christian theology against the salubrious ventilation of superior learning. With the added intervention of Thomas More on Erasmus's behalf, the resistance quickly melted, and Dorp himself renounced his folly.

Not all resistance dissolves so meekly, of course, and many examples of stultified intransigence could be produced: the repeated Parisian censures and Roman investigations of Cajetan's remarkable biblical commentaries, for example.[4] Judaizing, Lutheranism, and a lack of reverence for the fathers are among the unmeasured and downright silly allegations. If the heavy machinery of dull suspicion might thus be wound up in the service of excitable and extravagant objections, even this level of institutional obstruction can often evaporate as an ephemeral thing, like the seed on rocky soil, for lack of root. Some resistance is dogged, however, lingering on perennially for generations, because some fears are more than the illusory phantoms of a decadent theological regime.

Among the most earnest and animating anxieties troubling the rise of modern biblical science is the delicate matter of miracles. Here the foundations of a whole supernatural religious system are unambiguously at stake. Already targeted by Erasmus, the rank superstition and overgrowth of so many miraculous medieval legends became an obvious item on the agenda of religious reformers. Three basic positions ultimately emerged. The "Catholic Enlightenment," to use Ulrich Lehner's phrase, sought to weed out deviant frauds and cultivate a sober, discerning, scientifically informed faith.[5] Protestant controversialists developed, by contrast, a dispensationalist doctrine of cessation. While the wonders of the biblical age were accepted in toto as part of God's plan to establish the church and convert men to the Gospel, mass rejection of all subsequent, so-called ecclesiastical miracles became a polemical bulwark against the force of Roman claims and popish abuse.[6] The third and most radical solution, of course, was the a priori rejection of all miracles whatsoever. The awkward posture of the Protestant position is obvious, and it felt philosophical pressure especially from the radical side (though Immanuel Kant found it a reasonable compromise between social

---

3 Erasmus, *Praise of Folly*, 244.

4 See O'Connor, *Cajetan's Biblical Commentaries*, 238–49.

5 Lehner, *Catholic Enlightenment*.

6 The title of Anglican Bishop John Douglas's treatise nicely captures the spirit of the teaching: *The Criterion or Rules by Which the True Miracles Recorded in the New Testament Are Distinguished from the Spurious Miracles of Pagans and Papists* (1774). "It has long been observed that Popish miracles happen in Popish countries, that they make no converts" (Paley, *On the Evidence of Christianity*, 103).

order and *Aufklärung*).[7] Thus, all through the eighteenth century, beginning with Locke's *Discourse on Miracles* in 1706 and peaking with Hume's celebrated *Essay on Miracles* in 1748, the very possibility of miracles was the occasion for much crossing of intellectual swords, as two competing theological worldviews fought for survival.[8] The liveliness of the debate might be gauged from the case of Thomas Woolston, whose grossly provocative *Six Discourses on the Miracles of Our Savior* led to his imprisonment on charge of blasphemy in 1729.

Inscribed within this context of waxing Deism is a tumultuous little drama that must count as one of the more spectacular failures of the civic guardians of orthodoxy to address the escalation of critical questioning of the Bible: the fantastically obtuse efforts of three successive German pastors to force Gotthold Ephraim Lessing to surrender during the famous *Fragmentenstreit*. The issue concerned the latter's piecemeal publication of Reimarus's skeptical thoughts about Christianity and the Bible, supposedly unearthed by Lessing in the library of Wolfenbüttel. According to Albert Schweitzer's canonical account, this marks the true beginning of historical Jesus research.[9] The inevitable hullabaloo that resulted from the publication was intended from the outset and stage-managed by the dramaturge as a kind of live theological theater. (In a letter, in fact, Lessing had promised his brother "a little comedy with the theologians").[10] The most famous act is a prolonged, eight-scene joust with Herr Hauptpastor Goeze of Hamburg, whose censorious, sermonizing exhortations to repentance spent the two combatants' energy in an irrelevant pamphlet war. Less bombastic yet equally inept was the earlier intervention of one Johann Heinrich Reß, whose chivalrous but confused essay was dispatched with disdainful irony and embarrassing ease by the able young Lessing. Most interesting of all and most decisive, however, is Lessing's brief exchange with J. D. Schumann, who was first in this triple wave of hapless *fidei defensores*.[11]

Perceiving the whole edifice of Christian religion to be under threat by the publication of Lessing's second "fragment," which had pressed in the direction of a natural, non-revealed religion, Schumann followed a well-worn apologetic course. He appealed to the fulfilled prophecies and miracles enshrined in the New Testament as universally compelling evidence for the

---

[7] Wood et al., *Kant*, 98–102.
[8] See Burns, *Great Debate on Miracles*.
[9] Schweitzer, *Quest*, 14. On Schweitzer, Reimarus, and Lessing, see chap. 2 in this volume.
[10] Letter dated November 11, 1774, in Lachmann and Muncker, *Gotthold Ephraim Lessings Sämtliche Schriften*, 117, ll. 12–15.
[11] On this exchange, see Grube, "Lessing/Schumann Controversy."

certainty of Christian truth. The work is comparable in this regard to William Paley's better-known treatise, *A View of the Evidences of Christianity* (1794), which aimed to answer the challenge posed by Deist critics, especially Hume.

In cocksure possession of his own superior powers, like Erasmus toying with the schoolmen, Lessing dazzlingly blazed forward on his determined course. In his short tract *Ueber den Beweis des Geistes und der Kraft* (1777), he answered Schumann with devastating concision. At issue in the title is a phrase of St. Paul and a passage from the opening of Origen's *Contra Celsum* (1.2), as cited by Schumann at the beginning of his own ample work, *Ueber die Evidenz der Beweise für die Wahrheit der christlichen Religion*.

> Die Lehre Jesu hat eine besondere und eigene Art des Beweises, die viel höher und edler ist, als daß sie mit der griechischen Kunst zu schließen und zu beweisen verglichen werden könnte. Der Apostel nennet diesen göttlichen Beweis den Beweis des Geistes und der Kraft. Er heißt der Beweis des Geistes, der Weißagungen halber, die so klar und deutlich sind, daß sie einen jeden überzeugen müssen. Er heißt der Beweis der Kraft, wegen der erstaunenden Wunder, die zur Bestätigung der Lehre Christi geschehen sind.[12]

This genuinely, profoundly suggestive thought of Origen leaves Lessing strangely unmoved. He is pointed and succinct in his principled opposition.

> Ein andres sind erfüllte Weissagungen, die ich selber erlebe, ein andres erfüllte Weissagungen, von denen ich nur historisch weiß, daß sie andre wollen erlebt haben. Ein anderes sind Wunder, die ich mit meinen Augen sehe und selbst zu prüfen Gelegenheit

---

[12] "The teaching of Jesus has its own special and proper type of proof, which is much higher and nobler than that it could be compared with the Greek art of concluding and proving. The Apostle names this divine proof the proof of spirit and power. It is called the proof of spirit on account of the prophecies, which are so clear and distinct that they must convince everyone. It is called the proof of power, because of the amazing miracles, which happen as a confirmation of Christ's teaching" (Schumann, *Ueber die Evidenz*, 2). "We have to say, moreover, that the Gospel has a demonstration of its own, more divine than any established by Grecian dialectics. And this diviner method is called by the apostle the manifestation of the Spirit and of power: of the Spirit, on account of the prophecies, which are sufficient to produce faith in any one who reads them, especially in those things which relate to Christ; and of power, because of the signs and wonders which we must believe to have been performed, both on many other grounds, and on this, that traces of them are still preserved among those who regulate their lives by the precepts of the Gospel" (Origen, *Cels.* 1.2, [ANF]).

habe, ein anderes sind Wunder, von denen ich nur historisch
weiß, daß sie andre wollen gesehn und geprüft haben.[13]

Origen, Lessing says, may have himself still enjoyed the possibility of beholding with his own eyes these miraculous demonstrations of divine power and accordingly rightly surrendered his intelligence in belief. "But I, who am not in the situation of Origen, who live in the 18th century, when there are no more miracles ... [for me] this demonstration of the Spirit and of power has neither Spirit nor power any longer, but is reduced to human testimony to Spirit and power."[14] With a curt wave of the hand, Lessing means to silence the whole testamentary value of the Church's Scriptures. The report of a miracle is itself no miracle, he protests; it thus commands no convicting power. We are wanting a *Beweis des Beweises*, a proof of the "proofs."

The absolute distance Lessing takes here from the existential force of the Scriptures is startlingly and elegantly aloof. Even the philosophical question has been implicitly retired. In the course of the Enlightenment miracle debate, this response represents a new moment, a kind of revolutionary disinterest, an altogether sovereign indifference that wonderfully anticipates the methodologically insulated attitude that now reigns in biblical studies. The content of the Bible no longer involves me directly; it obliges no firm metaphysical commitments; it neither forces a claim upon my religious assent nor incites my impassioned rejection. This evacuation of spirit and power from the biblical text as such has become an axiomatic protocol of professional good order for modern scholars. Confrontation with the sacred text is made religiously banal by a formal pronouncement.

In part, of course, this neutering of Scripture has been a matter of public policy, desirous like Lessing to be finally free of the whole debate. In his monograph *The Death of Scripture and Rise of Biblical Studies*, Michael Legaspi highlights the role of post-confessional politics in the German research university of the first portion of the nineteenth century as a background for scholars' philological retreat into theological irrelevance.[15] Beleaguered by incessant, irresolvable sectarian controversy, the academic establishment moved (in both conscious and unconscious ways) to defang the Bible, a book that, since the collapse of the medieval consensus into a welter of stri-

---

13 "Fulfilled prophecies that I myself have experienced are one thing; fulfilled prophecies about which I only know historically that others are supposed to have experienced them are another. Miracles that I see with my own eyes and have the opportunity to examine for myself, are one thing; miracles about which I only know historically that others are supposed to have seen and examined them are another" (Lessing, *Die Erziehung des Menschengeschlechts*, 32).
14 Lachmann and Muncker, *Gotthold Ephraim Lessings Sämtliche Schriften*, 4.
15 Legaspi, *Death of Scripture*.

dent religious dissent, was no longer serving successfully as a social glue for the Protestant world. The explosion of historical Jesus research in the same time and place should be viewed in this same light. Indeed, the new renditions of Moses constructed by scholars like J. D. Michaelis resemble the hunt for a post-confessional Jesus: "a new jesus" in the wonderful, penetratingly ungraceful phrase of Flannery O'Connor's Hazel Motes, self-proclaimed soapbox "preacher to that church where the blind don't see and the lame don't walk and what's dead stays that way."[16]

> Listen here. What you need is something to take the place of Jesus, something that would speak plain. The Church without Christ don't have a Jesus, but it needs one! It needs a new jesus! It needs one that's all man, without blood to waste, and it needs one that don't look like any other man so you'll look at him. Give me such a jesus, you people. Give me such a new jesus and you'll see how far the Church without Christ can go![17]

A new social order requires a new secular consensus around its grounding religious figures. This consensus, moreover, faces the pretty pickle of making its "new jesus" at once perfectly irrelevant ("all man") and captivatingly central ("don't look like any other man")—a thing not easily achieved except through some zealous, dialectical opposition to the rejected dogmatic/ecclesial order: by masked polemics, in other words, which defeats the whole purpose of the purportedly irenic, purely "secular" exercise.

It should be obvious that as the cultural importance of our religious pantheon continues to recede in the post-Christian West, the secularizing urgency to remove all cause for choler also fades—which is oddly encouraging for the theologically minded. Sadly, the "canonical" status of the Bible as a normative reference in intellectual and social life recedes apace. Religious irrelevance breeds academic irrelevance, to which the increasing disappearance of theology from university life attests. The rescue measures of teaching the Bible as literature or Near Eastern history or ancient Mediterranean religion are but a series of parachute jumps into the faculty of arts that only hasten the inevitable result. More and more, the last vestiges of its sacred origins in *divinity* are effaced, until the professional discipline of "biblical studies" in its modern configuration, that vast federation of microscopic specializations and fashionable methods, vanishes into the academic herd

---

16 O'Connor, *Wise Blood*, 142.
17 O'Connor, *Wise Blood*, 193–94. O'Connor's brilliant solution for Haze's a-theological need comes in the form of Gonga the gorilla.

of overgrown *humanities* departments, indentured to a mercenary publishing industry.[18]

For contemporary biblical study the report of a miracle remains precisely what Lessing called it: the *report* of a miracle and nothing more. "Miracle discourse" and *Wundererzählungen*, the Greco-Roman rhetoric of recounting supposed miraculous happenings and wonders, has today become the reconceptualized datum rendered to New Testament exegetes as the proper object of their investigation.[19] As a matter of principle, the *res* itself, the *magnalium Dei*, the living event in its demonstration of godly power, never comes into view for consideration. Here, indeed, is an odd *Church without Christ* where "the blind don't see and the lame don't walk and what's dead stays that way." One is stunted at discourse about discourse about God. Judgment here is not only suspended; it is also disabled. Contemporary exegetes in their professional capacity are trapped within a perennial, phenomenological *epoché*.

Culturally, then, but also by methodological decision, Scripture scholars find themselves squarely within what Taylor calls the "Immanent Frame"—that typically modern worldview in which the old assumption of God's agency in history has been eclipsed.[20] "We cannot use electric lights and radios and, in the event of illness, avail ourselves of modern medical and clinical means and at the same time believe in the spirit and wonder world of the New Testament."[21] So runs the infamous Bultmannian dictum. Minus the radios and electric lights, Lessing's eighteenth-century world was already sufficiently similarly disenchanted. How to respond? The architects of the *nouvelle théologie*, at precisely the same time as Bultmann, sought to elaborate the foundations of a new "Christian humanism," corresponding to an advanced new moment in the history of our secular age.[22] This effort to radically reorient the Church's theological culture in many ways simply replayed Erasmus's hand, assaulting neoscholastics with gargantuan erudition the way he had abused the late medieval schoolmen. De Lubac's *surnaturel* can be seized here as a defining doctrine, for miracles are as representative of the nature-grace debate as is the natural desire for God.[23] Is the rejection

---

18 "Brill does not sell books; they hold them hostage," John P. Meier has wittily quipped.

19 See, e.g., Watson, *Miracle Discourse in the New Testament*; Nicklas and Spittler, *Credible, Incredible*; and Kollmann and Zimmermann, *Hermeneutik der frühchristlichen Wundererzählungen*.

20 Taylor, *Secular Age*, 274.

21 Bultmann, *New Testament and Mythology*, 4.

22 See the historical discussion of Swafford, *Nature and Grace*, 25–66.

23 de Lubac, *Surnaturel*; and idem, *Le Mystère du surnaturel*, esp. 87–88, 142, 179–89. On the broader question of miracles in Aquinas's specific nature-grace framework, including the relevance of the category of "obediential potency," see Pouliot, *La doctrine du miracle*, 64n2.

of *natura pura*, then, an escape from the iron heavens of the "Immanent Frame"? Or might the exegetes of miracle stories profit from discredited but hard-won neoscholastic conceptual tools, like the *super*, *contra*, and *extra naturam* of the old manuals?

A great many issues are at play in such questions, which I hardly mean to resolve, but de Lubac's cartoon of a two-storied universe should above all be placed in its own particular historical context as an admirably vigorous effort to refresh a desiccated theological culture. That is, it should not prejudice us against the recovery of an unmistakably *vertical* biblical view of the world. When Paul says in 1 Corinthians 2:4 that his proclamation of the Gospel was not made with words of human wisdom but in a demonstration of Spirit and power, he is echoing his clean *kata sarx / kata pneuma* opposition. The display of godly *dynamis* in the community through miracles and overflowing *charismata* marks a superhuman agency for Paul, which issues from beyond the sublunary world: the *dynamis* of a divine Spirit, strong to drive away dark principalities and powers, strong to inhabit and empower the bodies of believers through ritual acts with water and through sacred meals. Naming this ancient worldview "magical," which *faute de mieux* has become standard exegetical practice, may successfully evoke a view of things not normed by disenchanted Enlightenment experience, yet it roundly fails to overcome the chauvinistic stance that this view is benighted superstition. Bultmann and his school accordingly wished to argue against magic, "against viewing the soteriological event as taking place apart from man's will."[24] The alternative was a demythologized cosmos and an existentially revised self-perception. E. P. Sanders expressed himself rightly dissatisfied with this manner of solution but also conceptually helpless before the problem: "We seem to lack a category of 'reality' . . . which lies between naive cosmological speculation and magical transference on the one hand and a revised self-understanding on the other."[25] Jettisoning as naive the notion of a hierarchical, cosmic superstructure of elemental powers may nicely accommodate de Lubac's layer-cake critique, but it will not help bridge the alienation of the modern and biblical worlds any more than Bultmann's eradication of so-called myths.

The modern flight from metaphysics—to which we owe the missing category mentioned by Sanders—has visibly reinvested its reality discourse in historical reason. But here too there are problems. Did Jesus multiply the loaves, or was it a "miracle" of sharing? Did he walk upon the waves or just well-hidden stones? What *really* happened? When D. F. Struss cut the

---

[24] So is the object of Bultmann's critique characterized by Sanders, *Paul and Palestinian Judaism*, 522.

[25] Sanders, *Paul and Palestinian Judaism*, 522.

Gordian knot of this century-old Rationalist-Supernaturalist debate, declaring both sides fundamentally misguided, he contented himself (and many others besides) that in point of fact *nothing really happened*. He thus sought a new source of meaning in mythology. Decades before, Lessing also lightly bounded over the entire problem of the event but took a different course. Did Jesus indeed raise the dead? Did he himself rise from the dead, as we hear reported? Let it be or let it not. For Lessing it does not matter: what the medieval doctors called the historical sense is void of all possible theological force.[26] The *sensus literalis* is nontheological space; the recorded *gesta* are religiously irrelevant deeds. "The Letter is not Spirit," he says in the third of his *Axiomata*, "and the Bible is not Religion. Consequently," he continues in the following axiom, "objections against the Letter and against the Bible are not objections against the Spirit and against Religion."[27] Complex and slippery as his intellectual allegiances ultimately were, Lessing is at this point waving the old banner of the left wing of the Reformation, seeking somehow to fly straight on to the spirit—ironically, through a rejection of the letter wherein the spirit is found.[28]

This is the final upshot of Lessing's momentous move in the final portion of his treatise, where he jumps suddenly from a blithe disinterest in reports of miraculous deeds to a rough dismissal of all historical truths. He sees well that miracle reports and the humanistic historiographical enterprise itself must both stand or fall together. And neither can serve as a possible basis for Christian religion, Lessing avers: *Zufällige Geschichtswahrheiten können der Beweis von notwendigen Vernuftswahrheiten nie werden*. We are gazing at Lessing's infamous, unbridgeable ditch.

> Das, das ist der garstige breite Graben, über den ich nicht kommen kann, sooft und ernstlich ich auch den Sprung versucht habe. Kann mir jemand hinüberhelfen, der tu' es; ich bitte ihn, ich beschwöre ihn. Er verdient ein Gotteslohn an mir.[29]

---

26 On the theological place of the literal/historical sense, see chap. 1 in this volume.

27 Lessing, *Gotthold Ephraim Lessings Sämtliche Schriften*, 114–15.

28 See Bainton, "Left-Wing of the Reformation." On the "Radical Reformation" and this aspiration to establish a new *sens du christianisme*, see chap. 2 in this volume. Note how Lessing's formulation of a religion somehow beyond the Bible stands in full harmony with D. F. Strauss's own expressed aspiration, building on the heritage of figures like Sebastian Franck. Lessing's personal concern in the *Fragmentenstreit* not to be mixed up with the so-called *neue Reformatoren* and their *intolerante Theologie* entails a complex commitment to tradition in the form of a perennial dialectic of faith at open enmity with reason, in opposition to any proposed rationalized pacification and reconciliation of the two. See Vollhart, *Gotthold Ephraim Lessing*, 106.

29 "Contingent historical truths can never become the proof for necessary truths of reason ... That, that is the ugly, broad ditch over which I cannot come, as often and as honestly as

There seems little doubt that Lessing entertained a repudiation of the essential *factum est* of the Christian creed, even if the virtuoso high-wire walker nimbly watched his words.³⁰ The odious shadow of this abjuration must not mask his more fundamental and more prescient repudiation, however: a rejection of historical positivism, still only dawning and poised to surge in the following years. Lessing's ditch thus serves him ultimately as an earthwork against the assault of any imaginable Reimarus, fortifying a rationally airtight *Credo* against any conceivable historical critique. There is a real parallel here to Bultmann's own effort to mount a theology stronger than the severest skepticism, by making Jesus himself an extraneous presupposition. Both men thus stand at the extreme, opposite pole from Schweitzer, who (like a great many of his heirs) meant to found what he called "the religious thinking of the future" upon the *Jesus der Geschichte*.³¹

Viewed from this more sympathetic perspective, one understands why Kierkegaard in section II of his rambling *Concluding, Unscientific Postscript* pays Lessing such fulsome (but also ironic) praise.³² Whether he has finally confessed or undermined Christianity—Kierkegaard says that Lessing has succeeded as no other in the arduous task of keeping quiet even while speaking—whether or not Lessing preserved a personal faith, he successfully recentered the whole question of the certainty of Christian truth. He has shifted the matter from an objective, historical demonstration to a seemingly impossible, subjective *Sprung*. It was not a jump the freethinking Saxon felt prepared to venture and he settled for an abstract, ethical, nonhistorical, non-biblical religion. The Danish believer, however, like Bultmann in his own turn and in his own existentialist way, cheerfully took the "qualitative leap."³³

I have attempted the leap. If anyone can help me over, let him do it; I beg of him, I adjure him. He will earn a reward from God on my account" (Lessing, *Gotthold Ephraim Lessings Sämtliche Schriften*, 34).

30 Grube ("Lessing/Schumann Controversy," 102) may be correct that Lessing intends not to exclude historical truth per se from the religious sphere, but only to object to the use of mediated historical evidence functioning as a self-sufficient epistemological foundational (*Beweis*). As a historical analysis, Grube's highly sympathetic account of Lessing's aims and beliefs through the contemporary lens of "foundationalism" and "anti-foundationalism" is open to question, however. Nevertheless, Grube's reading does correctly help emphasize the inadequacy of naked historical reasoning in dogmatic argumentation.

31 Schweitzer, *Quest*, 1. See chap. 2 in this volume.

32 Kierkegaard, *Post-Scriptum définitif*, 61–68.

33 On the distinct ways the problem of the "ditch" is articulated in Lessing and Kierkegaard, see Michalson, "Lessing, Kierkegaard, and the 'Ugly Ditch.'" Michalson holds that two distinct ditches are in view, based on differing premises about the epistemology of religion.

A strong hue of anti-intellectualism colors Kierkegaard's passage to faith, and for Lessing, history evidently does not even count as human reason, or at least not as reason adequate for religion. Does the work of historical criticism thus in the end contribute anything whatsoever to the search for Christian truth, apart from a witness to the feeble, inconclusive nature of historical claims? Does it reveal anything more than the pressing need for some surer epistemological ground—be it universal reason or a radical faith? On the one hand, one appreciates the modesty when a John Meier adds to the repertoire of historical Jesus research the honest shoulder shrug of *non liquet*.[34] At times, the historical evidence is indeed forcefully or fragilely uncertain. On the other hand, there remains at the core of the whole vast project of the so-called quest an unfashionably positivistic hope. This confidence in the ultimate power of historical reasoning to reach real and convincing conclusions remains important and deeply refreshing. It also remains painfully constrained by a criteria-driven model of ratiocination, however. Meier's playful conceit of an "un-papal conclave" is also, in its way, an inhibiting factor on account of its naive aspiration for universal consensus. The whole thing has the air of a lightly chastened *âge des Lumières* redux. The risk is accordingly clear: a methodological lobotomy of reason in protested service of "reason." For the "rationalization" inherited from Enlightenment thinkers inevitably introduces their own confused relation to historical thought into our attempts to be clear minded: it is a big black fly in the exegetical ointment (think here, with appropriate adjustments, of Benedict's Regensburg lecture).

The question thus remains: How far can history go in speaking a theological truth? Further perhaps than one imagines. A fascinating, largely unnoticed debate appeared several years ago in the journal *History and Theory*, concerning the proper methodology for handling miracle reports. Though the exchange brought no final resolution, "the metaphysical postulate of naturalism and its correlative empiricist epistemology" are now under direct fire; while the claim is made—with stupefying good sense—that "historians of religion not only need not assume that atheism is true in their research, but should not do so if they want to understand religious people on their own terms."[35] In other words, the systematic, methodological exclusion of miracles, *understood and accounted as miracles*, risks distorting the whole enterprise of historical investigation as such. From this perspective, it no longer seems that history is obliged to insulate itself from philosophical and theological learning—quite the contrary. Thus if in fact, as Dirk-Martin Grube seems to think, Lessing himself wanted to do no more than assert

---

34 Meier, *Marginal Jew*, 183.
35 Gregory, "No Room for God?"

philosophy's primordial rights in thinking dogmatically about historical truths, then perhaps the issue boils down to finding the right philosophical handmaiden for our historical work.[36] Are there not, then, perhaps, from history so conceived, objective reasons that press us toward subjective religious assent? This is certainly the view of the First Vatican Council, which found in miracles and prophecy—let us say in historical proofs—external confirmations (*auxiliis externa*) of God's revelation.[37]

A worthy interlocutor arises at this point, and it is a useful exercise to set Lessing in dialogue with John Henry Newman. Here at last is a match for the brash and brilliant gadfly, whose eating alive of Hamburgers like Goeze was always something short of fair sport. Melancholy and pensive with a tender conscience and empathetic fine-feeling, *bref*, in full contrast to Lessing, Newman in his autobiography identifies the rising tide of skepticism as the great animating theological issue of his life: "the mistake" as he calls it "of subjecting to human judgment those revealed doctrines which are in their nature beyond and independent of it."[38] In his masterful *Essay in Aid of a Grammar of Assent*, the fruit of a life's reflection, Newman offers his most mature and comprehensive response to this problem by carefully developing his doctrine of the "illative sense." This famous category—"a grand word for a common thing," as Newman privately said[39]—essentially represents an expanded vision of human rationality, enabling a standard of certainty poised somewhere between Kierkegaard's willful leap and Lessing's fastidious submission to narrow *Vernunftswahrheiten*. "Reason never bids us to be certain except on an absolute proof," Newman insists, and the illative sense is ultimately for him "the true healthy action of our ratiocinative powers, an action more subtle and more comprehensive than the mere apprehension of a syllogistic argument."[40] No deductive bridge is built to span Lessing's ditch, and the crossing proposed by the illative sense never aims to reach a

---

36 Grube, "Lessing/Schumann Controversy," 104–7.

37 *Dei Filius*: "In order that the obedience of our faith be in harmony with reason, God willed that exterior proofs (*auxiliis externa*) of his revelation, viz., divine facts, especially miracles and prophecies, should be joined to the interior helps of the Holy Spirit; as they manifestly display the omnipotence and infinite knowledge of God, they are the most certain signs of the divine revelation" (DS 3009).

38 Newman, *Apologia Pro Vita Sua*, 256. One recognizes in Newman's description the outlook intoned in Kant's *Religion within the Bounds of Bare Reason*, but also the same historical skepticism that troubled Lessing and finally moved him in Kant's direction: claiming to determine on intrinsic grounds the truth and value of propositions that rest for their reception on the external authority of the Divine Word.

39 Newman, *Letters and Diaries*, 375.

40 Newman, *Essay in Aid of a Grammar of Assent*, 271.

promised land of pure (narrowly defined) *notwendige Vernunftswahrheiten*. Newman seeks a truth larger and more elusive than geometrical proof can offer. His existential object is "real" not merely "notional" assent.

In elaborating this framework, Newman's line of argument adds something essential and new to the stalled Schumann-Lessing debate. A subjective turn is acknowledged, presciently sensed by Lessing but altogether missed by Schumann, who was preoccupied with mounting apologetic claims of objective universal validity on the basis of an almost one-dimensional historical foundation.[41] Newman's subjective turn is nevertheless more supple and broad than Lessing's.

The "real-notional" distinction is admittedly not free of difficulties. As the logician H. H. Price says, it seems that all assent has something notional about it, and Newman has perhaps "set up a hard and fast distinction of kind, where there is in fact a rather complicated distinction of degree."[42] Theodor Haecker, however, a regretfully unknown figure, a translator of both Kierkegaard and Newman and a philosopher himself, saw clearly both the correctness and the limited force of this objection, which fails to grasp the real center of Newman's project.[43] Appeal to the Pascalian *vérités de coeur* is not out of place here as an aid in rephrasing the issue.[44] Nevertheless, Newman's specific language of the real, a robust *ad rem* manner of thought, remains evocative and useful. As Haecker puts it, Newman's concern is "die reale Erfassung von einer äußeren oder inneren Realität, von einem Ding und seinen Attributen, nicht nur von dem Wesen dieses Dinges und seiner Attributen aber, sondern notwendig mit einbeschlossen auch von der Existenz dieses Dinges, nicht nur von einem Sein irgendwelcher Art oder Stufe, sondern von einem Dasein, von existierenden, in emphatischem Sinn: *existierenden* Dingen, von konkreten Dingen; dem analog ist begriffliche Erfassung die [diesmal natürlich nur intellektuelle Erfassung] von Begriffen."[45]

---

41 According to Grube, Schumann's "argument does not consist of the more moderate point that the considerations on the historical claims implied in Christianity are valid for Christian believers who have come to believe on other than historical grounds. No, his point is stronger, viz. that looking at the historical evidence (plus presupposing a certain epistemic apparatus) forces believer and unbeliever alike to acknowledge the veracity of the Christian claims" ("Lessing/Schumann Controversy," 101).

42 Price, *Belief*, Series II, Lecture 5, "Reformulation of the Real-Notional Antithesis."

43 Haecker, *Christentum und Kultur*, 140–44. See the chapter titled "Über Kardinal Newmans Grammatik der Zustimmung," 138–62, originally published in 1921, shortly after Haecker converted to Catholicism, largely from reading and translating Newman's work.

44 On this theme, see the helpful insights of Guardini, *Christliches Bewußtsein*, 127–52.

45 "The real apprehension of an external or internal reality, of a thing and its attributes, but not only of the essence of this thing and it attributes, but necessarily included therein also of

Set in contrast with a removed, theoretical ("notional") apprehension, this existentially earnest concern for the "real" resembles Meier's own somewhat perplexing distinction, at the very opening of his *Marginal Jew*, between "the real Jesus" and "the historical Jesus." In an age when history serves as the language of the real, it is revealing that even this "real Jesus" is likened to a historical reconstruction, like the "real Richard Nixon" advertised by a well-documented biography.[46] Whatever exactly Meier means to achieve with his precise pairing—which inevitably recalls (even if working to avoid) the more dubious and conceptually sharp "Christ of faith/Jesus of history" divide—it is clear that by consciously centering his project upon the latter, Meier forgoes the hope of knowing the "real Jesus" through any exercise of historical reason (since the evidence is too sparse), and he promises to deliver us only a fragmentary "modern abstraction and construct."[47] That this resulting, fragmentary abstraction should lack all the motive force of religion would be obvious to Newman and pleasing to our present (purportedly) post-confessional order (though problematic for any more thoughtful modern Hazel Motes), for Newman reserved religious power to an apprehension of the real. Meier's historical Jesus may indeed be credited with deeds anemically "claimed by some participants or observers to be a miracle."[48] In other words, something really happened—or at least *seemed* to happen, whatever it *really* was; thus "the sins of ecclesiastical recall did not thoroughly corrupt everything."[49] But in the end Meier's "historical Jesus" does not rise from dead—though we may confidently imagine that his "real Jesus" (of faith?) presumably did. In this sense, what is dead decorously stays dead, at least for the academy and trade-book market. Lessing's victory is, to this extent, already beyond complete: in Meier's view, though the miracles of the public ministry might merit five hundred pages, even to engage *the reports* of the Resurrection would be to confuse theology and history, contaminating the latter with the former. So much for N. T. Wright's ambition of "shooting at the sun."[50] Here is a *gran rifiuto* for some irascible Dante to damn. In "*Noli*

---

the existence of this thing, not only of a being of whatever sort or degree, but of a being there, of an existing entity, in the emphatic sense: *existing* things, of concrete things; analogous to which is conceptual apprehension (this time naturally only intellectual apprehension) of concepts" (Haecker, *Christentum und Kultur*, 143).

46 Meier, *Marginal Jew*, 1:21.

47 Meier, *Marginal Jew*, 1:25. One might recall here the option of *Dei Verbum* 19 for *tenuit ac tenet* rather than *credidit ac credit* in describing the Church's firm commitment to the historicity of the Gospel message. See chap. 1 in this volume.

48 Meier, *Marginal Jew*, 2:514.

49 Allison, *Constructing Jesus*, 23.

50 Wright, *Resurrection of the Son of God*, 3–31.

Me Tangere," William Lane Craig subtitles his article on the subject "Why John Meier Won't Touch the Risen the Lord."[51]

Newman, who considered himself a Church historian, understood his own historical research in a different, helpfully challenging way. To investigate sacred history was not simply some specialization within the broader historians' art—an interest in ecclesiastical themes, as one might indulge a taste for fourteenth-century English land deeds or Russian railroads after 1850. Study of the Acts of the Apostles, to take an important example, need not inevitably be rendered as pedantic and harmless as the study of Roman provincial coinage minted in Asia Minor in the mid-first century CE. Rather than being an impotent *Beweis* in unending search of its own *Beweis*, the truth or falsity of the wonders reported by Luke might be openly accepted as bearing immense existential, subjective interest: advancing a real, acceptable, or dismissible yet palpable claim upon *my world*. For Newman, Church history was in this sense a fully theological science, a study of reality and of the real world in which we live and move and have our being—not a recondite, aloof, doctrinally unconcerned, and hence socially approbated "objective" subject matter. Sacred history could call upon premises of perennial philosophy, and it assumed faith's assent; its object was the very medium of divine providence and revelation. "The author of Holy Writ is God, in whose power it is to signify his meaning, not by words only (as man can also do), but also by things themselves" (*ST* I, q. 1, a. 10). Beyond the text and beyond its discourse, even beyond the recounted deeds themselves, stands the all-important signified *res*.

In his two essays *On Biblical* and *On Ecclesiastical Miracles*, written separately while still an Anglican cleric, Newman develops certain criteria of judgment that answer Lessing's out-of-hand dismissal of miracle reports. Most significantly, eyewitness testimony holds inherent value in Newman's estimation, "the credibility ... of Testimony depending," as he says, "on the evidence of honesty and competence in those who give it."[52] This critical attention to the value of witness is a foundational mark that is dramatically missing from the criteriology of modern exegetes, although it has entered the discussion since Richard Bauckham's epochally important and thus con-

---

51 Craig, "*Noli Me Tangere*."

52 Newman, *Two Essays*, 75. Newman's acceptance is not uncritical, and he suggests a series of circumstances and dispositions that might compromise the value of a witness, e.g., desire of gain or power or other temporal advantage; party spirit or rivalry; previous character for falsehood; inconsistencies or prevarications in the testimony; deficient examination; enthusiasm, ignorance, or habitual credulity; endorsing a cause already embraced; love of the marvelous, novelty, and the like.

troversial *Jesus and the Eyewitnesses*.[53] Within a certain nuanced framework, I believe that we have here the key to embracing the strong teaching of *Dei Verbum* 19 on the historicity of the Gospels.[54]

The heritage of a radical, modern Western individualism must be flagged in Lessing's a priori rejection of witness reports. This is a major plank, as well, in Hume's position.[55] The social character of knowledge, the fundamental, interpersonal place of testimony and transmission in our basic epistemic condition, is subjected to an automatic, excessive suspicion and, in a happy illusion of autonomy, finally subordinated to the gold standard of my own private perceptions and cogitation. This heritage has clearly infected modern biblical hermeneutics in substantial ways, from the open distrust of tradition to its queer indifference to and frequent irritability concerning eyewitness claims. Newman's approach is wary of systematic doubt and much more congenial to a commonsense philosopher like Hume's contemporary Thomas Reid, who accorded an equal place in the work of reason to both the "social" and the "solitary operations of mind." It is a salutary perspective. What is above all important, however, is that, like Lessing, Newman grasps that historical knowledge as such is at stake in the miracle question: "In proof of miraculous occurrences we must have recourse to the same kind of evidences as that by which we determine the truth of historical accounts in general ... Testimony being the main assignable medium of proof for past events of any kind."[56] The decision about miracles *is* the decision about history and vice versa. The two will fall or stand together as one reckons witness. The modern historical-critical exegetical project has not yet faced this situation squarely, though it represents the proper passage into the discipline's postmodern reconfiguration.

---

53 Bauckham, *Jesus and the Eyewitnesses*.

54 See chaps. 1 and 5 in this volume.

55 While general considerations clearly play a major role—are miracles possible in the first place, for instance—abstractions emphatically cannot decide the question. In an apposite text from the *Grammar*, Newman quotes the famous argument of Hume that since we have no experience of a violation of natural laws and much experience of the violation of truth, "we may establish it as a maxim that no human testimony can have such force as to prove a miracle, and make it a just foundation for any such system of religion." It is a sentiment in full accord with Lessing. With Newman, however, we may happily accept Hume's general proposition yet resist its entire pretended force. For the question of miracles is not whether human fabrications are *in general* more common than infringements in the laws of nature. They certainly are. At issue is the specific question of whether in this case the testimony of this concrete individual in these circumstances rationally warrants assent. This is precisely what carries us from the notional to the real: Do I accept this testimony of Peter or John or Luke?

56 Newman, *Two Essays*, 13.

Lessing's ditch is real, but typically he has overdramatized the whole affair. It is nearly robbed of all force by a simple, old, manualist distinction: not *evidenter vera* but *evidenter credibilia*.

> Thus: Wenn ich ... historisch nichts darwider einzuwenden habe, daß Christus einen Toten erwekt, muß ich darum für wahr halten, daß Gott einen Sohn habe, der mit ihm gleiches Wesen sei?
> —*No, but you would have reason to do so.*
> Wenn ich historisch nichts darwider einzuwenden habe, daß dieser Christus selbst von dem Tode auferstanden, muß ich darum für wahr halten, daß ebendieser auferstandene Christus der Sohn Gottes gewesen sei?
> —*No, but the claim grows increasingly trustworthy and strong.*[57]

The ditch may be a parry, a defensive moat meant to ward off and hold back skepticism, a preemptive answer to the next, disturbing fragment Lessing meant to leak: Reimarus's aggressive thrust against the Resurrection. It would have been better, however, to hold the historical field and fight. In the end, the decision about miracles boils down to a decision about the Resurrection, and Lessing, who saw no miracles, saw no need for this historical truth.

Between Spirit and power, Newman for his part clearly preferred the former. Prophecy, he notes, "is a growing evidence, and appeals more forcibly than Miracles to those who are acquainted with the Miracles only through testimony."[58] Thus his *Grammar* ends with an eloquent, illative proof built around this biblical base. In opting for prophecy rather than signs, Newman follows the tack of a worthy teacher, who when asked for a sign gave in return only a prophecy of his death and resurrection (Mt 12:38–40) and who, on the road to Emmaus, before he opened his disciples' eyes to recognize him resurrected and standing there before them, first opened their minds to

---

[57] "If I have nothing historically to object to that Christ raised a dead person, must I therefore hold as true that God should have a Son who would be of a like nature as he? ... If I have nothing historically to object to that this Christ himself rose from the dead, must I therefore hold as true that this same resurrected Christ should be the Son of God?"

[58] Newman observes: "Miracles are but a branch of the evidences, and other branches have their respective advantages. Prophecy, as has been often observed, is a growing evidence, and appeals more forcibly than Miracles to those who are acquainted with the Miracles only through testimony ... Nor must it be forgotten than the evidences of Revelation are cumulative, that they gain strength from each other; and that, in consequence, the argument from Miracles is immensely stronger when viewed in conjunction with the rest, than when considered separately" (*Two Essays*, 8).

understand what the Scriptures foretold (Lk 24:26, 24:31).[59] There is undoubtedly something different in the act of faith in these two cases, receiving a miracle and receiving a prophecy. One sort of data is more naturally received, and the infusion of grace is different on each side. Pursuing this thought and with a brief nod to my own area of research, I shall conclude and concretize these reflections.

As it happens, a study of Greco-Roman "miracle discourse" shows an interesting resemblance between Lukan history writing and the ancient paradoxographers, those pseudoscientific authors who collected reports of freaks and wonders and urged their truth with the guarantee of eyewitness.[60] None of the standard historiographical mechanisms for audience verification are included, and one must simply trust the author's word. In this light, Luke is incredibly bold, provocative in fact, in openly coloring his tale like a ghost story: "They thought they were seeing a ghost ... a ghost does not have flesh and bones" (Lk 24:37, 24:39). His use of the Greek word λῆρος—"it seemed to them like humbug" (Lk 24:11)—suggests a story one might find in some Greco-Roman tabloid. Like the disreputable paradoxographers, Luke knows the unbelievable nature of his claim, and like a first-century *Ripley's Believe or Not*, he makes a naked appeal to faith. It is not a *credo quia absurdam* (which is a slander of Voltaire and was never Tertullian's actual phrase),[61] but one is nonetheless challenged to assent to Luke's report of Jesus as one is challenged simply to swallow or reject Phlegon of Tralles's report of a certain revenant named Philinnion, a fully corporeal, eating, drinking, and occasionally even copulating zombie. "In this regard [Luke] the evangelist's ethical appeal resembles that of ... Phlegon, who even openly confronts his readers with a decision about his own credulity. 'One should not disbelieve the foregoing narrative,' he repeats. The seriousness of both authors [Luke and Phlegon] as trustworthy researchers is on trial—as is, inevitably, more profoundly the *reader's* judgment."[62] Such *miracle discourse* itself intentionally breaks the frame of the *epoché* and grabs us. It teases our gullibility and invites our consent; it openly interacts with the reader. Whether that reader belongs to the first or the twenty-first century, to understand this *discourse*, to encounter the text, one must decide or else make the *gran rifiuto*. Is it true or is it so much λῆρος? Shall the evangelist and his witnesses be believed?

---

59 The studies offered in Part III of the present volume can be profitably viewed in dialogue with this preference for proofs from prophecy. On the interaction of miracles and prophecy, see in particular chap. 15.

60 See chap. 5 in this volume.

61 Harrison, "I Believe Because It Is Absurd."

62 See chap. 5 in this volume.

Modern historical research helps us to see that this is how the raw miracle of Jesus' resurrection confronts us: tilted to the Kierkegaardian side of the ledger. Make the jump or walk away; the text puts us to the test.

What, then, of Lessing and *notige Vernunftswahrheiten*? "Was it not *necessary* that the messiah should suffer these things and so enter into his glory"? Lessing might have fared better considering prophecy rather than signs, for as Aquinas says, even the contingent truths of history acquire an aspect of necessity when viewed from the perspective of *prophetic knowledge*. The famous Lukan *dei* thus plants us suddenly in a different realm of discourse, and I would argue that we apprehend in this "it is necessary to die and rise" a fixed idea not only of the "real" but even of the "historical Jesus"—certainly of the "Jesus of memory" to adopt the latest tag. I believe, moreover, that one might show to the satisfaction of historical reason that Jesus of Nazareth had this idea from his knowledge and interpretation of Scripture (cf. Lk 22:37, 24:25–27; Mk 8:31, 14:27, 14:49; Mt 26:31–35, 26:53–54, 26:56; Jn 1:51, 3:14–15, 13:18).[63] He was convicted and announced in advance that he must die and rise. Here again, "ecclesiastical recall did not thoroughly corrupt everything." This is no little result: "To foresee one's death is one thing; to foresee one's resurrection after three days is quite another ... Foretelling a miracle *super naturam* is itself *super naturam*."[64] That what Jesus *foretold* was also in fact *fulfilled* thus circles us back to the stumbling block of the sign of Jonah—though this time with new evidence in its favor. Such cycles can be repeated a thousand ways from a thousand angels, but the breakthrough only comes when God opens our eyes. Hence white smoke from the un-papal conclave is never assured. I wonder, however, if this merely means that when the social tables are turned, the civic guardians of the post-Christian creed can be just as worried, excitable, and embarrassing a band of intransigent, blundering boneheads as that earlier caste of ecclesiastical jackasses at times incontestably were. After all, the pull leading us from historical to theological assent can sometimes grow irresistibly strong, so that an illative instinct intervenes with the real force of religious felling, sending the signal to resist and dig in for trench warfare. This goes, importantly, for both sides. Yet for those exegetes who have the historical mind of Christ and whose eyes are opened, the ditches dug by doubters are only "difficulties," crossed lightly with a bound made easy by grace.

---

[63] Jesus read Israel's Scriptures with an eye for its prophecies and for that great, pervasive pattern of the death and resurrection of the beloved son, which the Jewish scholar Jon Levenson has found underwriting the length and breadth of the tradition. See *Death and Resurrection*.
[64] See chap. 15 in this volume.

CHAPTER 7

The Revenge of Alexandrian Exegesis
Toward an Ecclesial Hermeneutic

"The past is never dead. It is not even past," William Faulkner said in *Requiem for a Nun*. In exegesis and theology, it is useful to bear this in mind. For nearly two and a half centuries now, a low-grade iteration of the Nicene crisis has been disturbing the world of New Testament studies, as the divinity of Jesus is alternately undermined and defended. If we thus stand perennially, typologically still somewhere in the fourth century, more recent history also exerts its force upon our age. As so often the onset of Enlightenment rationality, with its dramatic reconceiving of religion, configures our situation in a powerful way.[1] Gotthold Ephraim Lessing's various writings (e.g., *Die Religion Christi* and *Die Erziehung des Menschengeschlechts*), but above all his complex patronage of Reimarus, might arbitrarily be signaled as the formal founding of the modern Arian revival.[2] Of course,

---

1 One should be critically cautious of adopting this received, anti-religious construction of the "Enlightenment." See the provocative study of Lehner, *Catholic Enlightenment*.

2 There is an irony in laying such a charge at Lessing's doorstep, for he recognized this heterodox tendency in his thought and naturally protested his orthodoxy and abhorrence for the Arian heresy (i.e., *Thoughts on the Moravian Brethren* and *Letter to Nicolai*, March 30, 1779). Lessing's sensitivity to the issue was so keen that his aggressive, rationalist critique of the "Neologists" strategically sought, in two elusive fragments (i.e., *Vom Arianismus* and *Über den Arianismus von Philalethes dem Mittlern*), to provoke an attack from these "Arians" in advance of the Christological bombshell he was preparing in the release of Reimarus's papers. This was meant to secure preemptively his own innocence from any charge of Arianism with respect to the Wolfenbüttel Fragments. See Nisbit, *Gotthold Ephraim Lessing*, 130, 516–19. On the significance of Reimarus and the *Fragmentenstreit*, see Boehart, *Politik und Religion*.

"neo-Arians" in the Lessing line are far less generous to Christ's divinity than were their confessing forebears.³ No demiurgic or angelic status comes into question for them in their own understanding of Jesus. Conversely, it is precisely some such heavenly mediator that serves them to model and interpret the beliefs of the primitive Church.⁴

The Arian impulse is not purely a secular phenomenon, it bears saying. Philip Cary has recently registered his astonishment at the warm welcome many evangelicals have shown to a functional subordination of the eternal Son to the unbegotten Father: an idea fully unthinkable for the patristic mind (though often ignorantly presented in evangelical circles as having a patristic pedigree). Such ideological hospitality to what Cary unambiguously names a "heresy" is largely and lamentably, he says, motivated in these groups "in order to ride their hobby horse about the subordination of women."⁵ Bad doctrine and bad praxis are evidently related.

The point in drawing attention to this surprising rise of subordinationist thought is first to underscore the eroding hold of classical theological categories on much present-day theological thinking—even in ecclesial communions where self-consciously orthodox inclinations might be expected. The fundamentalist tenor of the modern subordinationists also reveals something more. It indicates the essentially exegetical nature of the struggle, and how a naive adoption of biblical language can be turned to dramatically ill dogmatic effect. For indeed there are verses in Scripture where "subordination" seems manifest.⁶ But this is hardly a new or decisive observation. Just as Athanasius in *de Decretis* described how the Arian camp deployed a range of thoroughbred biblical terms to undermine the wider "sense of the scriptures," so these modern theologians fail to read Scripture rightly despite their explicit efforts to conform theology to a genuine biblical idiom. There is nothing new under the theological sun, and one must ever recall that it was the heterodox at Nicaea who protested most loudly that they were the biblical party.⁷

---

3 On the "Ebionite" Christology of Lessing in *Die Religion Christi* and *Die Erziehung des Menschengeschlechts*, see Geldhof, *Revelation, Reason and Reality*, 47–48. One observes what may similarly be labeled an "Ebionite" position in many contemporary studies of the historical Jesus, e.g., Gerd Lüdemann. Epiphanius's treatment of the "Ebionites" in *Panarion* 1.2.30 may be dubious as a historical witness to the sect, but his Nicene perspective on their position provides a valuable taxonomical label for theologians pursuing a conciliar hermeneutic. Cf. Denz. §157.

4 See, e.g., Ehrman, *How Jesus Became God*.

5 Cary, "New Evangelical Subordinationism," 2. See also Giles, *Modern Evangelicals*.

6 See, e.g., Grundem, "Biblical Evidence."

7 See Newman, "Text of Scripture Not a Sufficient Protection."

At present, the so-called Early High Christology School represents a kind of Athanasian moment in this momentous yet slowly simmering debate. The energy and confidence, not to say innovative and often brilliant scholarship of the concerted movement—which broadly links the work of exegetes like Martin Hengel, Larry Hurtado, Richard Bauckham, Simon Gathercole, and C. Kavin Rowe—merits serious attention and is applauded by many committed to traditional conciliar Christology.[8] It is no surprise that the school is now capturing the imagination of a new generation of young exegetes.

The newest wave of High Christology scholarship is built solidly upon the work of these previous scholars while pursuing a yet more ambitious and ecclesial exegesis. One of Rowe's recent doctoral students, Joshua Leim, in his book on Matthew's use of προσκυνέω, notably means to advance an "ecclesially located theological reading of Scripture" that recognizes "the hermeneutical benefits of the Church's trinitarian and christological Creeds for reading the biblical texts."[9] He thereby has the ultimate aim of exposing not merely the divinity of Christ, but also the First Gospel's robust Trinitarian grammar. (Where shall Trinitarian theology be found if not in Matthew, i.e., Mt 28:19?) Without ever highlighting the fact, Leim's argument is plainly mounted upon the two great pillars of the Early High Christology School: Hurtado's argument from worship and Richard Bauckham's plaidoyer for "divine identity" Christology.

The commanding role that the signature ideas of Hurtado and Bauckham play in this new effort at an "ecclesially located" exegesis invites reflection, for it is not evident that the "hermeneutical benefits" of classical creedal Christology are entirely compatible with the positions these scholars take. A certain theological immaturity or imprecision in the Early High Christology School must, in fact, be flagged. For, despite a great deal that is perfectly sound and helpful in the models being proposed, the discernment of theologically oriented exegetes has been a bit lax in making demands for conceptual precision. It is, in fact, conspicuously rare that an exegete is ever

---

8 The nickname "Early High Christology Club" originated in the 1990s among a theologically diverse group of scholars (including non-Christians) participating at the annual SBL meetings in the "Divine Mediators in Antiquity Group." A foundational text in the emergence of the movement was Martin Hengel's *Son of God*. It is important not to collapse the range of positions held by various scholars arguing for an early High Christology into any one single theological camp or mold. Nevertheless, strong strains of confessional and even apologetic exegesis characterize much of the work done in this area. See, e.g., Bird, *How God Became Jesus*. Along with Hengel, Bauckham and Hurtado are founding figures of this school. They continue to be productive and influential, but younger scholars are also associated. See, e.g., Gathercole, *Preexistent Son*; and Rowe, *Early Narrative Christology*.

9 Leim, *Matthew's Theological Grammar*, 244.

confronted for the technical or doctrinal soundness of his or her theological ideas, as though this order of reflection is somehow extraneous and beside the point if one's business is primarily reading the Bible. This is not to suggest that the theological rhetoric and commitments that can nevertheless be prominent (or implicit) in an exegete's work have no power to sway both book markets and academic fashions. The combined result of coupled influence and free pass, however, is a rather uncritical reception of views arguably deficient from a classical dogmatic perspective, moved often by a grateful deference to any biblical scholar publicly ready to entertain the "divinity" of Christ. In the modern embattled climate, even Christologies that incline in distinctly subordinationist or Monophysite directions appear to be helpful correctives and an improvement. Such a situation is a bit concerning (at least for the theologically concerned), but, like all theological exchange and debate, it may also be taken as the useful occasion for a necessary advance in the discussion: an opportunity to help move promising streams of New Testament Christology beyond an underdeveloped Nicene-era discourse in a more complete and properly Chalcedonian direction. This entails not simply reading current exegetical theories through the classical lens of conciliar thought, but also explicitly connecting the theories in question with contemporary (often questionable) trends in Christology and fundamental theology, for despite the elaborate *wissenschaftliche* trappings of the biblical guild, the theological impartiality of exegetes is a dangerous myth, like the political impartiality of judges.

In this chapter I will consider the theological contributions of and some associated concerns about the two exegetes most responsible for the present vigor of the High Christology viewpoint in New Testament studies, that is, Larry Hurtado and Richard Bauckham. The treatment of Hurtado serves as a kind of hermeneutical prelude and will focus upon the issue of "subordinationism" in his "chief agent" Christological model and his problematic adoption of "proto-heterodox" terms as an analytic, historical descriptor for "proto-orthodox" beliefs. This methodological/taxonomical confusion will highlight the importance of recovering confidence in the original categories of conciliar theology as a legitimate and indeed necessary heuristic device in any openly "ecclesial" exegesis. In light of this conclusion, Bauckham's "divine identity" Christology will then be examined as an effort—animated directly by the work of Jürgen Moltmann and more distantly by Karl Barth—to evade the natural theology that undergirds Chalcedon's canonized two natures language and to replace it with a kind of narrative theology. Bauckham's implicit discomfort with the metaphysical tradition is not unique, of course. It represents a familiar antipathy aimed at erecting a more "biblical" doctrine of Christ. It ultimately stalls his "divine identity" paradigm, however, at the level of a single-subject Christology and thus runs a perceptible Monophysite risk—especially when handled by overzealous, apologetical disciples wielding a conceptual/doctrinal weapon that they appear only poorly to comprehend. Deploying this novel Christological category, which is bound tightly to the commitments of neoorthodoxy and the Moltmannian project, such an exegetical program arguably fails in its ultimate confessional and doctrinal aspiration. It is implicitly hostile to analogical predication, the *sine qua non* of intelligible theological discourse, and tacitly disdainful of the ancient and universal confessional tradition of East and West: an oecumenical culture that has ever spoken its creed in an exegetical language reliant on metaphysics. As a result, it remains questionable as a base for any "ecclesially located" exegesis.

Larry Hurtado and Primitive "Proto-Orthodoxy"

The oeuvre of Larry Hurtado, above all his monumental *Lord Jesus Christ*, illustrates well the imposing solidity of the Early High Christology position.[10] It exposes at the same time one of the fundamental, hermeneutical issues at stake. How shall the beliefs of the earliest Christians about Jesus (or their "Christ devotion," as Hurtado prefers) best be modeled and described?

Hurtado's work represents a massive bulwark against the old theory of Wilhelm Bousset and the *religionsgeschichtliche Schule* that Jesus' divinity was a late creation of the Hellenistic mission, an accommodation thus in some regard to Greco-Roman polytheism, and not an original datum of the Gospels born on monotheistic Jewish soil.[11] (Lessing's old wedge between the religion of Jesus and the subsequent "Christ religion" is replayed here with the virtuosity of Bousset's imposing historical erudition—then countered by Hurtado's alternative proposal.) Hurtado's bold response is methodologically innovative in its concentration on the dynamics of primitive Christian worship rather than on confessional titles. Some explosive religious experiences must be posited, Hurtado insists, to explain what he ingeniously detects as the sudden (formerly unthinkable) insertion of Jesus into Jewish devotional patterns otherwise reserved exclusively to YHWH. This practical intrusion

---

10 See Hurtado, *Lord Jesus Christ*. See also Hurtado's important *One God, One Lord*, especially the revised 3rd ed., which contains a fifty-three-page epilogue that chronicles changes in the field since the book's first publication, as well as *How on Earth Did Jesus Become God?* and *God in New Testament Theology*.

11 In his introduction to the recent reprint of Bousset's classic text (*Kyrios Christos*), Hurtado describes the text of his "sparring partner" as "surely one of the most influential academic books in the history of scholarship on the New Testament and the origins of Christianity."

of Jesus into the One God's proper cultic domain, at the earliest stage and in the purest of Jewish air, cleverly upsets the supposition of a blundering crossbreed of Jewish monotheism and Greco-Roman idolatry.

The Christological pattern that emerges from this cultic alignment of Jesus and Israel's God Hurtado dubs to be "binitarian" in form, or more recently (and less hazardously) the expression of a "dyadic devotional pattern."[12] This dyadic model, taken as such, presents us with a doctrine plainly awaiting some Cappadocian intervention, an intonation of the *homotimia* paid also to the Spirit.[13] If this dogmatic deficit is obvious, it is important also to appreciate Hurtado's work as a theory of doctrinal development, focused narrowly on primitive Christian devotional patterns, seen as a "mutation" within Second Temple Jewish praxis.[14] The fourth-century "binitarianism" of the semi-Arian *Pneumatomachi*, in other words, represents a distinct historical and theological phenomenon from the generative Jewish context that Hurtado describes.[15]

The fourth-century debate is nevertheless instructive. The *latreia* argument was a sound strategy for Basil, and in principle there is no reason why Hurtado's application to Christ should be any less definitive or ingenious.[16] As a demonstration of Christian belief in Jesus' divinity, it wonderfully,

---

12 Hurtado explains his terminology: "Although 'di-theism' might well represent the sort of charge that at least some critics might have hurled at them [i.e., the early Christians], the term does not seem to represent their own views of the devotional pattern. I propose that in this characteristic 'two-ishness' of their devotional practice there is also a pattern of religious behavior that links Christ with God in ways that seem intended to maintain an exclusivist 'monotheistic' stance" (*At the Origins of Christian Worship*, 70). The post-2011 shift in terminology to "dyadic" represents Hurtado's unsuccessful attempts to clarify his meaning with "binitarian."

13 Denz. §150; cf. §152–80 ("Tomus Damasi"). On Basil's pneumatology, see James, "Examination of Homotimia."

14 Hurtado allows the "triadic" (or even "proto-Trinitarian") shape of "God-discourse" in the New Testament (*God in New Testament Theology*, 43–46, 73–94). It is the worship of the Spirit, rather than its divinity that he finds absent.

15 Both Athanasius and Basil reckoned the *Pneumatomachoi* as a kind of derivative species of Arian. The first line of Basil's *On the Holy Spirit* reads: "The heresy of Arius lowered the dignity of the Holy Spirit as well as that of the Son." The same basic view is taken by Epiphanius (*Pan.* 3.14; §74), who compares these "Semi-Arians" to "a sort of monstrous half-formed people" holding an orthodox view of the Son, but a blasphemous view of the Holy Spirit. Cf. Denz. §155.

16 In addition to Leim, whose *proskynesis* argument clearly functions like Hurtado's, see, e.g., Dunn, *Did the First Christians Worship Jesus?*, which is dedicated to Hurtado and Richard Bauckham, "partners in dialogue." Dunn's much more cautious approach to the issue of early Christ devotion prefers to stress that worship goes "through" Jesus to the Father—a curious clash with Basil's own prepositional theology, inasmuch as Basil stresses "that the Father does not accept 'from whom' exclusively and abandon 'through whom' to the Son" and that there is

elegantly works—*supposing* (!) the doctrine of a shared divine *ousia* is first in place. In other words, it is not simply a historical accident that Constantinople followed Nicea.[17] Unless the doctrine of God's being is first secured, patterns of devotion are susceptible to diverse interpretation—particularly in the devotionally promiscuous atmosphere of Greco-Roman antiquity. Arius agreed that it was right to worship Jesus.

Concretely, Hurtado models Jesus' heavenly status on what he calls "divine agent figures," that is, a range of Jewish intermediaries that includes everything from personifications like Wisdom to principal angels to exalted patriarchs and prophets like Moses.[18] Within this framework, Hurtado then names Jesus "God's chief agent."[19] There is a tremendously significant matrix of ideas exposed at this point. The ease by which such language moves in a subordinationist direction, however—"subordinationist" in the precise theological sense—is also evident.

---

a general sharing of prepositional predications between the three persons (*On the Holy Spirit* 1.5.7). Dunn's acute concern about a "Jesus-olatry," in which "Jesus is absorbing the worship due to God alone," exposes a curiously thin Christology, in any event. He invokes the theology of icons as an analogy of Christ, the *eikōn* of the Father (cf. Col 1:15), but he seems unaware of or unwilling to the engage the careful Studite Christology behind this ancient source of theological reflection. (Basil himself had already developed a theology of the icon, later redeployed in the iconoclast controversy. See *On the Holy Spirit* 18.44.) For Theodore, icon worship is directed to a depiction of Christ's divine person rather than his human nature. This conciliar, two-nature framework amply and easily accommodates the troubling fact Dunn highlights, that Jesus is not only the recipient of worship but also an intercessory mediator.

17 Nor is it without significance that Athanasius's (often forgotten) arguments for the divinity of the Spirit in his *Letter to Serapion* (ca. 358) are developed in strict analogy to the theology of the Son's *homoousia* articulated at Nicea, e.g., "The Spirit bears the same relation to the Son as the Son to the Father" (*Ep. Serap.* 1.21; cf. 1.14, 3.3). Basil modeled himself upon this Athanasian theology, as James shows: "Just as Athanasius first establishes homoousia for Father and Son as the basis for the equal nature of the Spirit, Basil first establishes homotimia for Father and Son (chs. 6–8) as the basis for the equal honor of the Spirit" ("Examination of Homotimia," 260–64). Moreover, this *homotimia* argument appears only as the final of the three theses Basil develops in the main body of *On the Holy Spirit*. These follow a logical order, culminating in the doxological claim but beginning with the metaphysics of the divine nature: (1) the Spirit's ontological equality with the Father and the Son, (2) the Spirit's inseparable operation with the Father and the Son in the economy, and (3) the Spirit's equal honor with the Father and the Son. In contrast to Athanasius and Gregory of Nazianzen, Basil's argument about the Holy Spirit does avoid applying the term *homoousia* to the Spirit, for reasons that are debated. The language of "nature" is nevertheless part of Basil's explicit lexicon for describing the Spirit's ontological divinity (e.g., 13.30). The *Tomos Damasi* (382) begins its confession anathematizing all who fail to acknowledge the Spirit *cum Patrie et Filio unius potestatis esse atque substantiae* (Denz. §153; cf. §168, *sicut Filium, de divina substantia et Deum verum*). Only at the very end of the list of anathemas is the issue of worship introduced (§175): *si quis non dixerit adorandum Sanctum Spiritum ab omni cratura sicut Filium et Patrem: hereticus est*.

18 Hurtado, *Lord Jesus Christ*, 52–53.

19 See especially Hurtado, *One God, One Lord*, 97–130.

This points to an unsettling aspect in Hurtado's paradigm. The distinctly subordinationist character of his description, rather than the dyadic exclusion of the Holy Spirit, is in the end the more troubling feature. Historically, and metaphysically too, it is not self-evident why worship alone is sufficient for a complete explanation of what Hurtado believes he has shown about Jesus' divine status. If we accept the post-Hengel consensus of a highly Hellenized construction of the Judaism of the era, as we undoubtedly should, is it not rather easy to imagine the possibility of some sectarian, Jewish-flavored version of proto-Arianism? Theologically, moreover, the subordinationist strain represents not an imperfect developmental stage of the full Niceno-Constantinopolitan position (like the dyadic pattern), but a doctrinal element that cannot ultimately be integrated into the orthodox view. Hurtado is fully aware, of course, of the negative baggage that besets the word "subordination." He nevertheless adopts this term to designate the shaped structure of the divine dyad he perceives, without wishing to import the whole troubled theological history connected with the word.[20] This is manifest wishful thinking and the imprudent grasping of a terminological nettle.

It is accordingly difficult to determine what exactly to say here. A loaded theological canon is rolled out into the field, while those watching with interest are conceptually disarmed by force. Even the most rudimentary creedal distinctions (i.e., the two natures) are outlawed from the analysis as inadmissible anachronisms and distorting alien modes of thought drawn in from ecclesial bias.[21] If all previous reflection about this question is thus imagined to have precisely nothing to offer, then perhaps the most to be said here is that "participatory exegesis" deserves a hearing.[22]

The heavenly agent model is, without the slightest doubt, a genuine and highly illuminating historical background. But can it be that without also simultaneously being and bearing some metaphysical or theological claim? The "Two Gods/Powers in Heaven" topos, pioneered by Alan Segal, roguishly picked up in various ways by Barker and Boyarin, and now being forcefully pushed by Peter Schäfer, is not an unimportant partner in this con-

---

20 See, e.g., Hurtado, *Lord Jesus Christ*, 52–53. On his blog (https://danutm.wordpress.com/2010/07/13/the-larry-hurtado-blog/), Hurtado remarks candidly, "There is a subordination (at least functionally) of the one (Jesus) to the other (God). (I know, I know, 'subordinationism' has a complicated theological history, but I don't want to get into that, and I don't intend any importation of that history into my use of this term.)"

21 The banning of hard-won conceptual precision from all modern exegetical accounts of subjects classically considered in theological reflection has not yielded happy results of new-found clarity. Quite the reverse. See, e.g., my "Review of John Barclay's *Paul and Gift*," where a useful discussion of grace is crippled by its inattention to a whole range of apposite analytic tools forged in the tradition. We require more, not less, distinction.

22 Levering, *Participatory Biblical Exegesis*.

versation, however unlikely an overly coherent pre-Christian "binitarian/ dyadic" paradigm may still seem in the view of most scholars.[23] In any event, without greater precision and transparency regarding the particular theological freight an openly subordinationist "chief agent" Christology ultimately carries—that is, whether it means to supply a category for understanding primitive Christology's divine claims or rather a way to speak about Jesus' instrumental soteriological mediation—talk of "subordination" must be the cause of discomfort from several perspectives. Ecclesially, in evaluating the adequacy of such a "chief agent" Christology as Hurtado proposes, it is ultimately critical to bear firmly in mind that Christ's divine status was never, at least in classic conciliar theology, located in his unique, priestly work of mediation. The slippage from a confession of *homoousios* would be logically unavoidable. The sole mediation between man and God is instead placed emphatically on the human order—as Paul said explicitly to Timothy, "There is one mediator between God and man, the *man* Christ Jesus" (1 Tm 2:5).

The supreme challenge of forging categories at once historically and exegetically accurate as conceptual models (optimally non-anachronistic) and metaphysically (thus theologically) precise becomes acute in assessing Hurtado's work. Let the point be misunderstood: historical analysis has its proper rules and objectives, and it represents a real discipline and domain. Yet historical analysis is only by a convenient methodological fiction and by way of an (often ideological) aspiration and attempted *Begriffsreinigung* process imagined to be, in actual fact, a "theology- and metaphysics-free zone" of human thought. In reality, such hermetically sealed-off zones do not exist. Hurtado himself professes to sidestep the theological issues in an act of disinterested historical analysis, but it is not evident that this evasion can really be sustained, certainly not by willing away the theological content of the relevant categories he deploys. To correctly capture the confusion of trying to chart, as he does, the Church's ripening doctrinal development, one might recall the revealing remark of R. C. P. Hanson, who said that in the pre-Nicene period, subordinationism *was* orthodoxy.[24] Such a perspective, if accommodating to theological appropriations of Hurtado's reconstruction, dissatisfies in the same way as Walter Bauer's now-ubiquitous thesis on the coequal primitivity of heresy.[25]

---

23 See Segal, *Two Powers in Heaven*; Boyarin, *Jewish Gospels*; Barker, *Great Angel*; and Schäfer, *Zwei Götter im Himmel*.

24 Hanson, *Search for the Christian Doctrine of God*, xix, 64.

25 Bauer, *Rechtglaubigkeit und Ketzerei*. A spirited response to Bauer's legacy can be found in Köstenberger and Kruger, *Heresy of Orthodoxy*. For interesting background to Bauer's work, see Helmut Koester's 2012 SBL address, "Impact of Walter Bauer's *Rechtglaubigkeit und Ketzerei*." See also Walter Völker's devastating "Review of Walter Bauer's *Rechtglaubigkeit und Ketzerei*."

Two things converge here. First, the employment of "proto-orthodoxy" as a heuristic category—a direct theoretical descendent of Bauer's agenda, uncritically accepted today by scholars across the field, Hurtado included—invests one willy-nilly in an uncomfortable, not to say precarious theological position. In effect, the very category of "orthodoxy" has been co-opted and historicized as a post-Constantinian cluster of sociopolitically regnant ideas. It no longer functions as a claim to truth and exegetical measuring rod (*regula fidei*), but only as the more or less arbitrary terminus of a diachronic "trajectory."[26] It would, to this extent, in the collegial spirit of *Begriffsreinigung*, be much preferable when making historical claims to use more specifically historical markers: to describe, for instance, as "proto-*Nicene*" those historically embryonic scriptural patterns of thought and expression that achieved a mature and privileged formulation in AD 325. If the ecclesially ruled reading of Scripture ultimately presents just one of multiple interpretative trajectories, all with equal claims on the scriptural tradition and only retrospectively identifiable as "heretical" or "orthodox," however, the paradigm is theologically inadequate *tout simple*. Quibbling over labels is not the point. Some conceptual, hermeneutical way must be found to preserve a synchronic analysis of Scripture-*cum*-councils—without rejecting the evident historical process that leads from one to the other.

A second, closely related issue also arises at just this point. The emphasis Hurtado himself lays upon the explosive, primitive character of the Christian claim of Christ's divinity makes one wonder why precisely the cautious developmental language of a slowly emerging, politically enabled "orthodoxy" might not simply be abandoned in the same way the developmental model of Christology (from low to high) is boldly shattered. Does not the "early high" claim, if taken with full seriousness, itself force a revised diachronic analysis? Is not the historical originality of "orthodoxy" and a basic surmounting of Bauer's program here being advanced?

What faces New Testament exegesis is a considerable, foundational challenge: the recovery of ecclesially ruled, confessional terms as the rigorously descriptive shape of the most primitive Christianity. In a way, the task is to show that the hermeneutics of conciliar theology are indeed biblically grounded, as they always professed to be.[27] This is naturally an open provocation and not at all easy. But do fully modern analytic abstractions like "God's chief agent" or "dyadic devotion" really have any more profound a claim to

---

[26] See the famous study of Robinson and Koester, *Trajectories through Early Christianity*.

[27] On the biblical nature of Nicene theology, see the treatment of Athanasius's *De decretis* in Anatolios, *Retrieving Nicaea*, 127–32. In this text, Athanasius replies to the (ancient) charge that *homoousios* is not a scriptural term, and "the heart of Athanasius's response is that recourse to non-scriptural language is sometimes necessary precisely to stabilize and fix 'the sense of scripture' in the face of a conflict of interpretations" (127).

be *in the text* than ancient metaphysical abstractions like *ousia* and *hypostasis* (Heb 1:3!)?[28] Is it possible, in other words, to take seriously the claim of patristic theology to be engaged in authentic exegesis of the Scriptures?

In addressing the inevitable objection of succumbing here to a benighted practice of retrogressive ahistorical thinking, it is imperative that the divorce of dogmatic and historical theology be understood and accepted for what it is and principally was: a self-legitimating and "specifically Western prejudice" (Hayden White),[29] tightly bound to the historical decision of German universities (and their intellectual heirs in the academy and culture) to erect and patronize a discipline of biblical science free of socially disruptive confessional commitments.[30] The complex discussion that any "remarriage" of dogma and history must undertake would thus do well to return to Johann Philipp Gabler's famous 1787 address, so often cited as a watershed moment in bringing modern exegesis to birth. His remarks on reconstructing the various theologies of the historically embedded biblical authors are of particular interest, for he evidently presumes the possibility of elaborating the "universal ideas" implicit in their thought.[31] A dependence upon synchronic, philosophical modes of description, in other words, remains integral to the task of historical description and analysis he proposed and had in mind. "Timeless" abstraction is not so easily evaded, nor is analysis of "timebound" ideas destined to hold the mind prisoner in one nominalist moment in time.

Manifestly, the desideratum of somehow yoking biblical and conciliar thought is an ecclesial issue, and non-confessing scholars remain free to adopt the abstractions and models ("universal ideas") they deem most fitting for the task of accurate historical description. If this invites a professional debate complicated by asymmetrical commitments, it nonetheless bears

---

28 In an important contribution to this broad discussion, David Yeago argues "that the ancient theologians were right to hold that Nicene *homoousion* is neither imposed *on* the New testament texts, nor distantly deduced *from* the texts, but rather describes a pattern of judgments present *in* the texts, in the texture of the scriptural discourse concerning Jesus and the God of Israel" ("New Testament and Nicene Dogma," 153).

29 White, *Metahistory*, 2.

30 To put the matter polemically and to quote a recent work, the "death of scripture and the rise of biblical studies" is neither a necessary stage in the enlightenment of our race nor a *sine qua non* for the exercise of academic freedom. See Legaspi, *Death of Scripture*. Such perceptions are simply another variant on the manifold, modern "coming of age" narrative Charles Taylor has so impressively critiqued in his magisterial *Secular Age*.

31 Gabler's model for the sort of historically oriented "biblical theology" of the future was Dietrich Tiedmann's three-volume *System der stoischen Philosophie* (1776); namely, a systematic history of ideas. The difficulty that Gabler signals is that Stoic philosophers thought openly and systematically in "universal ideas," where the biblical authors employ entirely other modes of discourse from which the logic must be extracted.

observing that the distorting pressure exerted on contemporary models of exegesis like Hurtado's to parade "proto-heretical" terms as "proto-orthodox" descriptors is not only a phenomenon of extra-ecclesial-making, as the evangelical subordinationism noted earlier indicates.

Hurtado himself can by no means to be charged with the precise, fundamentalist errors characteristic of this evangelical trend. He is a careful and informed historian of primitive Christian praxis and thought. He seeks, moreover, to ply his trade with an ideal of rigorous objectivity. It is both symptomatic of the problem and an exacerbation, however, that he erects an uncertain conceptual framework in which significant confusions are left unresolved. On the one hand, Hurtado provokes a theologically subordinationist rendering of Christology. On the other hand, he cloaks this impulse in a dubious developmental ("proto-orthodox") paradigm—in some way spiting his own "early high" historical hypothesis. Such moves can only empower those who would assert a congenital opposition between biblical speech and the categories of conciliar theology, to the final detriment of the classical confession. Exactly this sort of opposition, ironically, implicitly undergirds and provokes the Christological project of Richard Bauckham, Hurtado's much more theologically explicit colleague.

RICHARD BAUCKHAM AND TWO-NATURE CHRISTOLOGY

Larry Hurtado's efforts to play the neutral role of a historian must be contrasted with the open theological interests of Richard Bauckham. This doctrinal inclination has led Bauckham to make several significant interventions in the Christological debate. Indeed, at the very outset, Bauckham boldly announces the need to abandon the bifurcation between *function* and *being*. On the face of it, a departure from the classical norms of conciliar Christology such as the new tolerance of a "functional" subordination of the Son represents might make this sound like the voice of doctrinal good order.[32] The situation is more complex and problematic, however.[33]

As an opening move, Bauckham's apparent slicing of the Gordian knot attacks a foundational and classic philosophical axiom (*agere sequitur esse*),

---

32 Bauckham, *Jesus and the God of Israel*, x.

33 For a sharp critique of Bauckham's "Divine Identity" proposal from the perspective formal logic, see Tuggy, "On Bauckham's Bargain." Tuggy's "uncharitable misreading?" exposes both the "crippling ambiguity" and the significant disruptions that Bauckham's apparent idea of the numerical sameness of Jesus and the One Lord of Israel must introduce into ecclesially accepted predications about the Triune God.

which should not be handled as dangerous dichotomy.³⁴ At issue, ultimately, is precisely the principled relationship between the economic and immanent orders, an issue that will come back to haunt Bauckham's theological construction. His replacement proposal, moreover, "divine identity" Christology, embeds a carefully considered perspective and is much more than an apologetic conceit to fend off the neo-Arian charge. It is a sophisticated effort to dethrone metaphysics for a sort of narrative (read "biblical") theology.

Bauckham's diverse contributions to contemporary exegesis are well known and substantial, and it may be gratefully said that his Christology has, much like Hurtado's, profitably focused our attention on the decisive issue of Jewish monotheism and the revelation of Christ's divinity within this frame. Moreover, with a theologian's eye, Bauckham sees that, like the Arian project, which rightly sought to avoid every shade of ditheism, the articulation of a biblical "Christological monotheism" may founder if the reconstruction of a Second Temple Jewish *de Deo uno* is not rigorously accurate, at once sufficiently strict and adequately supple.³⁵

> Some (not all) scholars who seek Jewish precedent for early Christology in allegedly semi-divine or subordinately divine Jewish intermediary figures seem to think that this supports an interpretation of New Testament Christology favorable to later Christological orthodoxy, the confession of the true divinity of Jesus Christ. In fact, such arguments often produce something much more like an Arian Christ, a demi-god who is neither truly divine nor truly human.³⁶

Accordingly, when Bauckham's work conjures up Hurtado's whole cast of Jewish mediating "chief agents," he carefully draws a bright red line, introducing an all-important and purportedly unambiguous distinction between the "personified divine attributes" on the one hand and the created angelic and

---

34 As traditionally understood in the Aristotelian tradition, "action follows being" (*agere sequitur esse*), so the very premise of Bauckham's intervention is already from this perspective inapt. The classic principle, which proclaims that action is derivative of and consequent upon being, preserves the irreducibility of the two terms while holding them in inseparable connection. See De Finance, *Être et Agir*; and Clarke, "Action as the Self-Revelation of Being."

35 "There is first the view that Second Temple Judaism was characterized by a 'strict' monotheism that made it impossible to attribute real divinity to any figure other than God ... Secondly, there are revisionist views of Second Temple Judaism which in one way or another deny its strictly monotheistic character" (Bauckham, *Jesus and the God of Israel*, 3). Bauckham himself tries to find a way between these two, maintaining its strict character but allowing room for a kind of mediating agency.

36 Bauckham, *God Crucified*, 5.

exalted human mediator figures on the other.³⁷ The great difference predicated of these hypostatized "aspects of God" is, then, that they share in God's properly "divine" work of creation, a thing the lower-level mediators never do. An "unmixed" conciliar logic of two natures is evidently implicitly at work here, though this immediately gets rather tangled, as we shall see. The critical strategy and categorical resource used to articulate New Testament Christology against this neat matrix comes by defining "divine identity" (a term borrowed freely from Hans Frei) in essentially narrative terms and then applying this to Jesus.³⁸

The clean distinction into divine and creaturely is important and reacts to the real danger of a neo-Arian style subordinationist Christology, but at least two troubling factors are at silently at work here. First, in bypassing the functional-ontic polarity with an idiom of "identity" focused on the creative agency credited to Jesus, Bauckham has effectively erased Jesus' instrumental *soteriological* mediation from consideration. This behavior is evidently too "low." It was precisely this order of "functional" agency in salvation, however, that led the Fathers to insist upon the ontic categories of the creeds.³⁹ Seen from this soteriological angle, the gap between the scriptural witness and canonical confession is covered not by an act of massive conceptual translation, as if functional Christology (the Jewish, biblical framework) and ontic Christology (the Greek, creedal equivalent) were simply two grand, incommensurate but equivalent, parallel propositional systems.⁴⁰ On the contrary, these two patterns of discourse have a complementary argumentative relation, which epistemically intersects on the question of salvation. This conceptual relation that leads from action to being (Child's internal

---

37 Bauckham, *Jesus and the God of Israel*, 20–22. On the place of these mediator figures in primitive Christology, see further chap. 10 in this volume.

38 Bauckham, *Jesus and the God of Israel*, 7–8. Bauckham acknowledges, "The term identity is mine, not that of ancient literature." In a note he highlights Frei, *Identity of Jesus*, along with a number of other narrative theologians, e.g., Jensen, *The Identity*. The strongly anti-metaphysical trajectory of much of this narrative theology is treated by Murphy, *God Is Not a Story*.

39 See, e.g., Capener, "Being and Acting." Capener argues, "it is clear that the stakes for patristic writers, in working out a Trinitarian theology, were precisely salvation. The lines between heresy and orthodoxy are consistently argued in terms of their relationship to the possibility of salvation—the possibility of a triumph over sin and death."

40 See the influential proposal of Yeago, "New Testament and Nicene Dogma," 152–64. While offering many useful insights, above all focusing on logical judgments, Yeago ultimately seems content with a model of two parallel but equal types of discourse, i.e., scriptural and creedal judgments. The characterization of function (including the action of saving) and ontic as Jewish and Greek, respectively, is Bauckham's own. See his online essay "Orthodoxy in Christology," 5, http://richardbauckham.co.uk/uploads/Accessible/Orthodoxy%20in%20 Christology.pdf.

"pressure" of the Scriptures, as one might take it)[41] is disrupted, however, by Bauckham's attempt somehow to fuse and surmount the whole *actio/esse* issue with the notion of "divine identity." To insist that *Jesus* corresponds rigorously to the pattern of "personified divine attributes," but not to created mediator figures, certainly carries an impressive rhetorical force (Bauckham touts his identity idea as "the highest possible Christology"), and it serves in thinking about the divine hypostasis of the Word.[42] It engenders a worrisome half picture of the "identity" of the Incarnate Eternal Son, however, and excludes the shared soteriological structure of both scriptural and conciliar Christological thought.

Second, however shrewd and useful Bauckham's distinction among mediator agents might appear, it is not difficult to object that Christ's behavior as a co-creator still looks markedly *demiurgic*. Second Temple monotheism, in this connection, was perhaps not so very self-consciously clearminded, nor so uniformly uncompromised as the Early High Christology School insists—and *must* insist, at a certain risk of circular reasoning.[43] With due deference to the picture that certain privileged literary sources preserve, evidence is not lacking that deep tensions characterized Second Temple Jewish views of divinity and, discomfiting as it is, that more than a few Jews of the period in fact tolerated a shocking range of "demi-gods."[44] Here again, Schäfer and the "Two Gods in Heaven" deserves a hearing.[45] This is indeed a vulnerable spot in the whole project, for these scholars tend to reproduce the sharp Jewish-Hellenistic dichotomy of pre-Hengel scholarship—which they themselves criticize in scholars like Bousset—just at the point where it serves their dogmatic interests to reimport it.

If monotheism is clearly the major weight-bearing element in the "Early High" construction, it is not evident that Bauckham's narrative approach sustains the stress or avoids the problems of a reductively "functional" Christology—however actively it seeks to defuse the ontic order. Defining what it means for Jesus to be God is unfortunately not so easily done by suppress-

---

[41] Childs, "Toward Recovering Theological Exegesis." See also Rowe, "Biblical Pressure and Trinitarian Hermeneutics."

[42] Bauckham, *Jesus and the God of Israel*, 19.

[43] Of relevance here is the suggestion that *creatio ex nihilo* was not inherited by Christianity from the Jewish Scriptures the Church received. See May, *Creatio ex Nihilo*.

[44] See, e.g., Stuckenbruck and North, *Early Jewish and Christian Monotheism*. On the deep tensions within Second Temple Jewish "monotheism," see also, e.g., Kister, "Some Early Jewish and Christian Exegetical Problems."

[45] "Was den biblischen Monotheismus betrifft, so lässt sich heute in allen einschlägigen Handbüchern nachlesen, dass dieser eher ein religionsgeschichtlicher Idealtype ist als eine historische überprüfbare Realität" (Schäfer, *Zwei Götter im Himmel*, 8).

ing the question, *Quid est Deus?*, for this alone enables a judgment on the "divine" character of Christ's role, for example, in creation.[46] To sharpen Hurtado's *latreia* argument with the isolation of a Jewish "refusal tradition" (in which angelic figures refuse worship reserved to the Lord) is thus also beside the point.

Bauckham's expansion of Christ's "divine identity" to include a participation in "God's unique sovereignty over all things" through Jesus' sitting upon God's throne ostensibly helps and does look less overtly demiurgic than mere creative agency. But here again, real questions must be raised. The plural "thrones" set up in Daniel 7 raise legitimate concerns about the relevant Son of Man traditions, for instance.[47] So too do Greco-Roman political traditions of throne-sharing (σύνθρονος), since, as D. Clint Burnett explains, unlike σύνναος (temple-sharing), which does not appear in Jewish texts, σύνθρονος was a non-cultic and thus less threatening notion that "did not impinge on the oneness of the Jewish God (Dt 6:4)."[48] The elevation of deceased humans and heroes to a co-enthronement with various divinities is hardly unknown in the ancient world and naturally colors the cultural character of the early Christian data. The question of divine being thus imposes itself willy-nilly once more, for it is not clear why an apotheosis should be any less an apotheosis on account of an uncertain Jewish restrictiveness and understanding about sharing God's divine throne.[49] If it is indeed *theosis*—namely, a divinization soteriology that asserts itself with respect to Jesus (albeit in a manner proper to the Head of the Body)—there is real theological promise in the proposal. To this point, the consistent focus of the scriptural sovereignty motif on Jesus' eschatologically exalted *humanity* must emphatically not be lost from view (e.g., 1 Cor 15:20–28; Phil 2:6–11; Eph 1:21–22; Heb 2:5–9; cf. Pss 8 and 110). If it is lost from view—as it is where exaltation functions as an anti-Arian argument—a major problem will arise in our conception of the deity, since the subjection of all things under Jesus' sovereign feet is fol-

---

46 "In order to know in what sense an activity is a *divine* activity, one must know what is it to be divine, what the essence of divinity is ... Understanding in what sense divine activity, like creating, is divine presupposes a prior understanding of what it is to be divine" (te Velde, *Aquinas on God*, 69).

47 See Schäfer, *Zwei Götter im Himmel*, 29–30.

48 Burnett, *Christ's Enthronement*, 46.

49 Bauckham indicates, "This decisive step of understanding a human being to be participating now in the unique divine sovereignty over the cosmos was unprecedented. This principal angels and exalted patriarchs of Second Temple Jewish literature provide no precedent ... My argument is that the exaltation of Jesus to the heavenly throne of God could only mean, for the early Christians who were Jewish monotheists, his inclusion in the unique identity of God" (*Jesus and the God of Israel*, 28, 31; cf. 29–34).

lowed by (and follows upon) the Son's *subjection* to the Father (1 Cor 15:28). We return here to the new subordinationism.

The underwriting theoretical problem is not far to seek. Talk of "inclusion in the unique identity of God" lacks the necessary sharpness for distinguishing what belongs to God economically in the manhood of Christ and what is proper to him eternally by his divine nature.[50] How is one to speak about those divine perfections and properties of Jesus that manifestly differ? Is the instrumentality of Jesus' manhood operational within this picture? Adequate conceptual resources to address such questions are simply not forthcoming. To attribute this expressive impotence to a naive (narrative) scriptural idiom, foreign to such distinctions, is simply to wish away the problem. It is the scriptural data itself that first confronts us with the tension of subordination and equality in Jesus' relation to God.[51]

It is a familiar move, ultimately, that brings us to this point, when Bauckham abandons the language of *being* in search of more amenable ("biblical") categories. Typically contemporary as a strategy, the result, ironically, has a hauntingly classical precedent.[52] Specifically, the confusing rhetoric of "divine identity" for divine essence/*ousia* causes Cyrillian problems (an overly simple language always aggravated by eager and overly simple disciples). This pattern of scholarship, uncomfortable with the older metaphysical categories, thus runs a certain obvious Monophysite risk in forging what Kavin Rowe calls "the binding of *ho Theos* and *ho Iesus*."[53] It is not accidental or without significance in raising this precise concern that Bauckham's own project is so openly animated by Jürgen Moltmann.

Richard Bauckham's fascination with the thought of Jürgen Moltmann is impressively evident. Over the course of thirty years, Bauckham has engaged the evolving vision of this adventurous, contemporary theologian in a considerable number of books, articles, and reviews. Beginning with what was

---

50 On Bauckham's ambiguity, see Tuggy, "Bauckham's Bargain," 141.

51 See, e.g., Rheaume, *Exegetical and Theological Analysis*. Athanasius identified this point overtly in *Contra Arianos* 3.29, where he identifies the single *skopos* of Scripture as a "double gospel concerning the Savior" (διπλῆν τὴν περὶ τοῦ Σωτῆρος εὐαγγελίαν), i.e., an account entailing both absolute and economic predications.

52 See, e.g., the treatment of Giorgio Agamben in Capener, "Being and Acting," 950–63. The purposes of Agamben and Bauckham are obviously quite different. Agamben sees the "economy" as an argumentative placeholder during the period when metaphysical ideas like "nature" and "person" were being conceived and finds the eventual estrangement of *acting* and *being* as underwriting problematic modern political arrangements.

53 Rowe, *Early Narrative Christology*, 202; cf. 27–29. Rowe himself propagates a variation on the "divine identity" narrative theology (*Verbindungsidentität*), explicitly adopted in turn by his student Leim (*Theological Grammar*, 27).

the first general survey of Moltmann's work in any language, *Moltmann: Messianic Theology in the Making: An Appreciation*, a highly sympathetic treatment, as the title suggests (endorsed in a foreword by Moltmann himself), Bauckham has become a committed observer of the former Tübingen professor's work.[54] In *Theology of Jürgen Moltmann*, Bauckham's earlier "strongly positive" evaluation was extended to embrace the theologian's subsequent publications.[55] Bauckham did here register his "dissent" with certain developments in Moltmann's thought, but always in a context of "considerable sympathy for the nature and direction" of his theological enterprise. In the edited volume *God Will Be All in All: The Eschatology of Jürgen Moltmann*, Bauckham and Moltmann finally collaborated directly in a collection of essays born from personal discussion.[56] To this trilogy of books, a sizable collection of scattered writings may be added.[57]

In light of this corpus—rather formidable as an avocation—it would not be irresponsible to number Bauckham among Moltmann's earliest and most devoted interpreters. Nor would it be wrong to understand Moltmann as a theological muse for Bauckham's work. *Jesus and the God of Israel*, the widely influential and programmatic text outlining the British exegete's Christological proposal, has a subtitle (*God Crucified and Other Studies on the New Testament's Christology of Divine Identity*) that is indeed a transparent homage to the German systematician's celebrated *The Crucified God*. One may wholeheartedly salute this rare energy of engagement with contemporary dogmatic reflection on the part of a truly extraordinary New Testament scholar, but one may also ask—*must* also ask—How should one read Bauckham's open-faced hint at the deeper doctrinal significance of his understanding of Jesus Christ?

The Christology of Jürgen Moltmann is, like so much of his theological work, overtly, defiantly critical of the tradition. Based in the former prisoner of war's intensely personal encounter with wretchedness and suffering, his stubborn dissatisfaction with Chalcedonian Christology (in his autobiography he goes so far as to say, "Because this is my experience of God, I am not open for reasoned criticism")[58] is grounded in his perception of the pressing need to make theology relevant to the contemporary world—and in this case

---

54 Bauckham, *Moltmann*.
55 Bauckham, *Theology of Jürgen Moltmann*.
56 Bauckham, *God Will Be All in All*.
57 See, e.g., Bauckham, "Introduction"; "Jürgen Moltmann"; "Moltmann's Messianic Christology"; "Moltmann's *Theology of Hope* Revisited"; "Evolution and Creation"; "Moltmann's Eschatology of the Cross."
58 Moltmann, *Broad Place*, 195.

to make the impassible God truly sensible to human pain. A staurological kenoticism ("within earshot of the cry of abandonment") thus structures his Christology, which ultimately perceives in the *communicatio idiomatum* a daring warrant to assign suffering to the divine nature of the Triune God.

At work here is a single-subject Christology as provocative as the most unmeasured of Monophysite slogans (albeit pushing in an opposite direction from the classical formulation). The clean lines between the human and divine have been intentionally blurred to gain the advantage of a supposedly more compassionate and biblical deity. To this end, the revised shape of Moltmann's professedly "Alexandrian" Christology appropriates the discourse of the immanent divine life as an incarnational idiom, a conceptual confusion with calculated results. Thus the Trinitarian language of mutual "perichorsesis" regresses into a Christological category to express the mingled indwelling of God and man in Christ, in contradiction to the neat Antiochene accent of Chalcedon (i.e., "without mixture").[59] Even the efforts of Rahner and Barth to identify the immanent and economic Trinity and thus attribute a certain manner of suffering to God are insufficient for Moltmann, who desires to find the cry of derelection eternally sounding within the Trinity.[60]

The other Antiochene pillar of the Chalcedonian formula (i.e., "without change") comes implicitly under fire in another of Moltmann's texts, *The Way of Jesus Christ*, where the relation of divine and human in Christ is plotted in a narrative eschatological process.[61] This represents the author's attempt to break free of both the patristic "cosmological" and contemporary "anthropological" Christologies.[62] Altogether, Moltmann thus forges a self-consciously

---

59 "In Christology, perichoresis describes the mutual penetration of two heterogeneous natures, the divine and the human, in Christ, the God-human being. This is the ontological presupposition for the later so-called *communication idiomatum*" (Moltmann, "God in the World," 373). Here the "one person" (*heni prosōpō*) of Cyril's Third Letter to Nestorius, the classical ground of the exchange of attributes, has been confusingly replaced by a tripersonal designation reapplied to the two natures. Precedent exists, of course, for Moltmann's Christological language of perichoresis. Whether the intervention is attributed to Pseudo-Cyril or John of Damascus, however, the distinct Monophysite risk of this language was identified early on, and the term was reserved for Trinitarian predications. See the classic works of Prestige, "'Perichoreo' and 'Perichoresis,'" and *God in Patristic Thought*; as well as the more recent treatments of Cross, "Perichoresis"; Harrison, "Perichoresis in the Greek Fathers"; and Lawler, "Perichoresis." For a perspective on the role of Moltmann's eschatology in the reshaping of his theology and doctrine of God, see Appendix I in this volume.

60 Bauckham, *Theology of Jürgen Moltmann*, 54. See Moltmann, *Crucified God*, 201–4, and *Future of Creation*, 62–64.

61 Moltmann, *Way of Jesus Christ*.

62 On this terminology, see Bauckham, *Theology of Jürgen Moltmann*, 200–2.

new Christological paradigm, which Bauckham succinctly explains as an effort to replace the metaphysic of substance with a metaphysic of relationship and process.[63]

On the assumption that these Christological innovations are as radical as they mean to be ("a revolution in the concept of God"), the simple question is, How much of Moltmann is to be found in Bauckham? That is a question open to debate, but there are reasons to be concerned—at least for those interested in preserving the traditional, ecclesial role of metaphysics in theology and exegesis. The adoption of Backhaum's "divine identity" rubric in the work of a scholar and disciple like Leim, who hopes explicitly to steer his Trinitarian exegesis by a conciliar hermeneutic, arguably commits him unwittingly to a fundamentally counter-conciliar project.

To be just and perfectly clear, Bauckham is significantly more tolerant of ontology and respectful of the tradition than Moltmann.[64] His frequent apprehension (or dismissal) as essentially a conservative apologist is misleading, however.[65] He is also a progressive and constructive contemporary theologian, and, although no impudent dabbler in heterodoxy, the radical undercurrents of this thought should be better brought to light and understood. To this end the Moltmann connection is revealing. In an article titled "In Defense of *The Crucified God*," Bauckham argues explicitly for divine passibility—though he also happily allows that Moltmann's thought "needs certainly some clarification and perhaps some qualification."[66]

The clarification is to read Chalcedon through the theopaschite controversy of the sixth century, an event neglected in the tale told by the dogmatic handbooks, which normally end with the triumphant Chalcedonian compromise. In this way, Bauckham seeks to legitimate Moltmann's fundamental interest by pointing to the ultimately orthodox claim that "one of the Holy Trinity suffered in the flesh" (Second Council of Constantinople in 553). This is an ecclesial move meant to more generously draw the boundaries of authorized theological discourse. Bauckham's qualification of Moltmann's position is more penetrating, for it seizes upon the formula's all-important concluding phrase "*in the flesh*." Here the exegete rightly sees the need to distinguish between economic and immanent orders of predication, planting himself solidly in the Chalcedonian confessional camp.

---

63 Bauckham, *Theology of Jürgen Moltmann*, 206.
64 See, e.g., Bauckham, *Jesus and the God of Israel*, 8.
65 Tuggy says well of Bauckham's work: "This does not seem to be merely a defensive apologetic or exegesis. He is also doing theology" ("Bauckham's Bargain," 141).
66 Bauckham, "In Defense of *The Crucified God*," 107.

It is a traditional and well-placed correction that Bauckham offers. The sympathy he extends to Moltmann's theopaschism turns more disquieting from a classical perspective, however, when Bauckham promptly entertains the further assertion that God might also suffer immanently *in his divinity* ("God's non-incarnate suffering").[67] Behind this more daring inquiry stands a simple and uncompromising principle: the absolute primacy of revelation. "In *The Crucified God* there is no discovery of the suffering God apart from the cross," Bauckham assures us.[68] Were it otherwise, "it would just be another kind of natural theology."[69] And that, we are to understand, would be a bad thing: indeed, the great deficiency in Chalcedonian thought. "The two-natures Christology was a way of affirming the deity of the Christ who suffered and died without redefining divine nature in the light of the cross."[70]

The Anglican divine has manifestly imported a large dose of the Lutheran *theologia crucis*, finding here a profound resource for the chastening of human reason before the disorienting event of God's revelation.[71] In this line, his mature study of Christology, *Jesus and the God of Israel*, poignantly ends with Jesus' cry of Godforsaken dereliction in Mark's Gospel.[72] Long charged from the Reformed side with a dangerous Monophysite inclination, this staurological, Lutheran brand of Christology ends for Bauckham on a Calvinist, Barthian note: "God's Self-Identification with the Godforsaken."[73]

Bauckham's attempt to use *divine identity* to pass "beyond the fundamentally misleading contrast between 'functional' and 'ontic' Christology"

---

67 Bauckham, "In Defense of *The Crucified God*," 113–15.
68 Bauckham, "In Defense of *The Crucified God*," 97.
69 Bauckham, "In Defense of *The Crucified God*," 97.
70 Bauckham, "In Defense of *The Crucified God*," 94.
71 "In *The Crucified God* Moltmann was developing a theology of the cross in the sense of Luther's *theologia crucis* and explicitly as a modern continuation of the radical direction of Luther's *theologia crucis*. This makes the cross, in all its stark negativity, the basis and criterion of Christian theology ... The cross must be the criterion which distinguishes the Christian understanding of God from all others" (Bauckham, "In Defense of *The Crucified God*," 94). "While the Fathers successfully appropriated, in their own way, in Nicene theology, the New Testament's inclusion of Jesus in the identity of God, they were less successful in appropriating this corollary: the revelation of the divine identity in Jesus' human life and passion. To see justice done to this aspect of New Testament Christology we have to turn to the kind of theology of the cross which Martin Luther adumbrated and which has come to its own in the twentieth century" (Bauckham, *Jesus and the God of Israel*, x).
72 Bauckham, *Jesus and the God of Israel*, 254–68. For Moltmann (*Crucified God*, 153, 151), Jesus died as one "rejected by his God and his Father" and "we must not allow ourselves to overlook this enmity between God and God by failing to take seriously either the rejection of Jesus by God ... or his last cry to God upon the cross."
73 On the controversial Barthian theme of Jesus' reprobation by God and the doctrine of double predestination, see Barth, *Church Dogmatics II/2*.

and thereby enable a starker, more startling identification of God with the manhood of Jesus reduces here to an effort at softening the fathers' *oikonomia/theologia* distinction, the distinction between the economy of revelation and God's own inner being.[74] In risking such a collapse of the eternity of divine life into the economic narrative, Bauckham opens the door to the old Antiochene charges of mythological anthropomorphism (as well as the more recent charge of making "God a story").[75] But, as the Holy Scriptures do not shrink from such anthropomorphic language, Bauckham treads boldly forward. He is admittedly aware of the need for a corrective negative theology "as a permanent qualification of all anthropomorphism."[76] His resulting two-stage theological grammar lacks a final act of hyper-predication, however, for Bauckham has no proper doctrine of analogy.[77] He is seemingly stunted at the level of univocal speech, unable to break beyond the endless, cyclic *sic et non* of metaphoric affirmations and countering negations, self-hindered from making analogical assertions about God that actually stick. "All personal language about God is equally anthropomorphic," he avers—an absolute counsel of despair for theological science.[78] "The deep-rooted prejudice that reference to God's reason and will is more literal than reference to God in emotional and physical terms derives from Platonism, rather than from the Bible."[79] This is *sola scriptura* with a vengeance—not that of the seventeenth-century Reformed and Lutheran scholastics (who, despite Luther's savage dislike of scholastic philosophy, still cherished natural theology) but the newborn, dialectical heritage of twentieth-century neoorthodoxy.

---

74 The shift in early Christian theology from a concentration on the economic activity of God to increasingly ontological explanations of the foundations of this activity was a response the challenges posed by positions the Church did not recognize as her own. See the discussion of Emery, *The Trinity*, 51–82.

75 Bauckham perceives clearly that Moltmann is "open to the charge of speaking mythologically about the divine experience" on account of "his failure to distinguish in his account of the cross as a Trinitarian event, the human suffering of Jesus, which *is* human suffering, from the divine suffering of the Father, which is only analogous to human suffering" ("In Defense of *The Crucified God*," 114). One sees from this and from other passages that although Bauckham appreciates the need for disciplined theological speech, his understanding of "analogous" predication is imprecise. See Murphy, *God Is Not a Story*.

76 Bauckham, "In Defense of *The Crucified God*," 113–14.

77 "To speak adequately of God we need to use both anthropomorphic language and negative language, but not confuse the two. Negative theology should not inhibit the use of anthropomorphism, but stands as a permanent qualification of all anthropomorphism ... We may say that there is something analogous to human suffering in the divine experience, but we may not thereby claim that we know what it is like for Got to suffer" (Bauckham, "In Defense of *The Crucified God*," 118).

78 Bauckham, "In Defense of *The Crucified God*," 117.

79 Bauckham, "In Defense of *The Crucified God*," 117.

In the end, the peculiar posture of Bauckham evidently comes down to this. He wishes his Christology to be constrained by the councils, but not their metaphysics. As such, he is, admirably, a significantly more traditional and ecclesial theologian than Moltmann, though caught in a much more curious and uncomfortable position. Ultimately, though, the two men are not fundamentally divergent thinkers. And where they most profoundly meet is in the urge to forge a truly "biblical" and contemporary Christology—at the expense of the natural theology enshrined in the creeds. This indeed is precisely what ultimately fascinates the exegete in the dogmatician: "The greatest achievement of Moltmann's theology has been to open up hermeneutical structures for relating biblical faith to the modern world."[80] Moltmann helps shatter the ossified idols of our own minds' making, supplying day by day, in his ever-evolving quest to understand, consistently fresh categories capable of returning us, day by day, to the primacy of Holy Scripture.

It is not a vision without forceful appeal. The raw power of God's living Word is magnificently on display. One faces here, nevertheless, the momentous debate regarding the *analogia entis*, these days pitched between the Barthians and the Thomists.[81] When brought to bear on the Chalcedonian two-natures Christology, it is not immediately obvious to what extent this fundamental dispute about the validity of natural theology represents only a theological debate between the schools and to what extent this must touch upon a Church-dividing issue. What can it mean, after all, to confess Christ "consubstantial with the Father in his divinity and consubstantial with us in his humanity" if the theology of natures is (à la Barth) "the invention of the Antichrist"?[82]

---

80 Bauckham, *Moltmann*, 178. Bauckham's own concern to update "orthodoxy" and avoid "fossilized traditionalism" appears in the opening lines of his essay "Orthodoxy in Christology": "An adequate orthodoxy, I should like to suggest, is biblical, credal and contemporary." He then acknowledges, "The third element—that an adequate orthodoxy must be contemporary—may be more controversial" (1).

81 On this debate, see White, *Analogy of Being*. Dahlke, "Invention of the Antichrist," 61–95; Johnson, *Karth Barth and the Analogia Entis*; and Betz, "Translator's Introduction."

82 Hart inverts Barth's famous polemical statement ("the *analogia entis* is the invention of the antichrist and only legitimate reason not to become Catholic") and says that *rejecting* the *analogia entis* might in fact be "the invention of the antichrist and the most compelling reason for not becoming protestant" (*Beauty of the Infinite*, 242).

"Ecclesially Located Theological Reading of Scripture"

Where does Bauckham's anti-metaphysical conciliar exegesis finally lead? Barth himself eventually backed down on his quip about the Antichrist,[83] and in the end, one can be authentically troubled by this aggressively Alexandrian-leaning theology—desirous of clarification and qualification—while remaining respectfully open-minded. Christendom had (and continues to have) terrible trouble swallowing the compromise enshrined in Leo's Tome, and the historic rapprochement between the non-Chalcedonian Syriac and the Roman Catholic Churches (1984) signals a remarkably generous ecclesial readiness to embrace divergent Christological formulae within a unified confession.[84] From an ecumenical perspective, the contemporary, post-denominational Protestant Christology of a Bauckham certainly cannot claim the same tenacious, ethnic and linguistic, liturgico-theological patrimony and tradition as the ancient Miaphysite orthodoxy. Still, a kind of ecclesial heritage stands behind such thought, and "differences in terminology and culture and the various formulae adopted by different theological schools to express the same matter" should not be acrimonious or divisive but mutually enriching.[85]

This significantly cuts both ways, however, for the metaphysical theological tradition is not only a Latin or Roman Catholic predilection. It is the very shape and center of historic, ecclesial confession and represents a truly ecumenical, catholic meeting of East and West. This applies even to the non-Chalcedonian, ancient oriental churches, where philosophical exegesis was cultivated in the Syriac, Coptic, and Armenian contexts.[86] Modern anti-rationalist (i.e., anti-Western) Orthodox theology is demonstrably amnesiac

---

[83] Dahlke describes Barth's curious retraction ("I didn't mean it like that") and determines that "The *analogia entis* is not a doctrine that can divine denominations; it does not present a *punctum stantis et cadentis ecclesiae*" ("Invention of the Antichrist," 61–62).

[84] It is important to see that the resources exist, even within the Cyrillian tradition, to make the necessary distinctions. "The Archbishop of Alexandria certainly distinguishes between divine and human properties, but, because he wants to safeguard the unity of Christ, he uses different language to express it," i.e., ὡς ἄνθρωπος versus ὡς θεός. See Loon, *Dyophysite Theology*, 404.

[85] *Common Declaration of Pope John Paul II and His Holiness Mar Ignatius Zakka I Iwas* 3.

[86] See, e.g., Hovhanessian, *Exegesis and Hermeneutics*. Syrian theology of the post-Ephrem period ultimately felt compelled to adopt a more precise (Greek) theological vocabulary. More inevitable was the Greek influence in Coptic interpretation, which often took catena form. Armenian exegesis ingested huge amounts of John Chrysostom, and with him the language

on this point.[87] The Neo-orthodox effort to evade philosophy is to this extent an anomalous and novel brand of ecclesial exegesis.

In the end one must ask where the results of this new brand of anti-metaphysical Alexandrian exegesis leads. Do efforts like those of Leim to erect a creedal reading of the Scriptures with the tools and arguments afforded by Bauckham and Hurtado imbibe the conceptual shortcoming of these authors? Can the result be considered harmonious with conciliar confession?

On the one hand, Leim's interest in tracking Matthew's Sonship discourse keeps the rudder in the right direction. For all the homage paid to Bauckham's identity language, a Trinitarian grammar structured by paternal-filial difference is bound to give space to relational opposition. On the other hand, Leim's zealous protest against a motif of saving agency (i.e., Mt 14:33) seems to misstep by tilting at a windmill of Bauckham's making. One wonders, as well, where precisely the perceived pattern of dyadic worship leads and whether speaking of two *kyrioi* in the plural does not betray a unhelpful confusion (1 Cor 8:6), following a false route for inscribing the distinction of divine persons within the one Godhead: a route inhibiting a full Chalcedonian extension of this anti-Arian theology.[88]

The Son receives worship because he is God; he is not God because he is worshipped. This obvious logical ordering remains somehow lost in Leim's exposition of Matthean *proskynesis* discourse.[89] It may simply be that modern exegetical practice inevitably stops short at the level of rhetoric, never reaching to the *logic*. It may be that Matthew's soteriologic has not been brought properly into play. Leim's ultimate formulation of his findings falls far short, in any case, of a full Trinitarian profession of faith. "Matthew

---

of Nicene orthodoxy. Cyril's interpretation of the Letter to the Hebrews was also influential, adding an Alexandrian complement to Armenia's geographically Antiochene inclination. See also Edwards, *Aristotle and Early Christian Thought*. Edwards amply illustrates the many creative manners in which Christian thinkers sought to sift and accommodate Aristotelian ideas to their foundational biblical presumptions.

87 The anti-Western, "mystical" posture of much modern Eastern theology (e.g., Russian School of Paris) has forgotten not only Byzantine scholasticism and highly Aristotelian figures like Leontius of Byzantium and John Damascene. It has also invented a distaste for Augustine and Aquinas, which is unfaithful to the frequent enthusiasm with which these Latins were originally greeted in the East. See Plested, *Orthodox Readings of Aquinas*; and Demacopuolos and Papanikolaou, *Orthodox Readings of Augustine*.

88 "There is neither a *Vermischung* of the paternal and filial κύριοι or a relativizing of the worship the Son receives, nor a rivalry between father and Son" (Leim, *Matthew's Theological Grammar*, 241).

89 Following the contours of the Gospel narrative, above all the interaction of Mt 2:1–12 and 4:8–10, Leim's basic syllogism makes Jesus' divinity the logical conclusion: worship is reserved to God alone; Jesus receives worship; therefore Jesus is God.

has reshaped the identity of—and therefore Israel's fundamental confession of and commitment to—'the Lord God' around the Father and the Son."[90] As a *regula fidei*, this would never function to exclude those anathematized by the councils. It is orthodoxy stripped of its hard-won precision, a *proto-Nicene* embryo presented as "ecclesially located" exegesis.

"An adequate orthodoxy must do more than repeat itself," Bauckham tells us, and indeed interest in a contemporary, exegetical reformulation is understandable, right, and good.[91] The drive to capture conciliar theological truth in a "biblical" idiom is not a self-evident procedure, however. It is strange, above all, that a mode of exegesis openly professing to reap "the hermeneutical benefits of the Church's trinitarian and christological Creeds" resists the full conceptual resources at its disposal, resting content with uncertain and susceptible formulae. Why not simply go all the way? Why not demonstrate that the "pressure" of Matthew's logic is fully (not "proto") Trinitarian, however much his rhetoric may lag behind Nicea and Constantinople? Instead of interpreting the Text-in-Tradition as the relevant ecclesial datum, conciliar thought has been rendered a subordinate and finally dispensable hereustic device. *Scripture alone* must provide for this school the language and categories of theological predication. And "Scripture" in this theological application is exposed through biblical categories and historical reasoning alone—not with the aid of philosophical reflection or in twinned tandem with Tradition. "Early High Christology" thus remains *too* early, stunted forever in Nicene-era ambiguity.

Conclusion

The achievements of the Early High Christology School deserve the serious attention of all interested in theological science. The expressed desire to profit more from "the hermeneutical potential of the Christian theological tradition" (Leim) is especially to be warmly welcomed. The deeply Protestant character of the project should not be missed, however. Nor should certain theological shortcomings of its major voices.

The growing popularity of Backhaum-inspired projects, above all, exposes most clearly what is theologically at stake when an attempt is made to affirm Christ's divinity while jettisoning the conceptual apparatus the Church has used since ancient times to hold to and articulate her belief. Caught in a number of tangled commitments, the "divine identity" brand

---

90 Leim, *Matthew's Theological Grammar*, 234.
91 Bauckham, "Orthodoxy in Christology," 1.

of narrative *theologia crucis* pushes New Testament Christology in a distinctly Monophysite direction. It steers us on a verbal course, which, in its stark staurological neo-orthodoxy, answers Arian challenges with an anti-Nestorian rhetoric, thus blurring Trinitarian and Christological (*theologia* vs. *oikonomia*) problems. The narrative dogmatics at work here threaten to strip theology of its traditional range of conceptual resources, which prevent it from veering off into an Apollonarian or Miaphysite cul-de-sac. Adoption of this paradigm leaves exegetical efforts at "orthodoxy in Christology" trapped in univocal and ambiguous predications.

If the integration of creedal categories into historically informed exegesis remains a serious challenge, a first step toward a more satisfying ecclesial Scripture-cum-councils approach may be found in pursuing *a soteriological redirection*. Where does instrumentality figure within "Christological monotheism"? How must we describe Jesus in order to ensure that his biblically chronicled role in saving humanity is truly effective? This question coordinated the biblical and patristic authors' logical concerns and gave substance and direction to the original Athanasian moment (which was unashamed in its philosophical orientation).

The perceived risks in the rising neo-Alexandrian exegesis must not eclipse how wonderfully creative and lively is this contemporary Protestant culture of biblically based theology—unlike anything that the past thirty years of drab Catholic exegesis has produced. Roman Catholics may be deeply grateful for the contribution of scholars of the Early High Christology School. At the same time, our separated brethren are invited, even urged, to rediscover the living resources of the Church's Tradition and conciliar thinking about God's being and the mystery of our Savior.

CHAPTER 8

INTERPRETATIO IUDAICA

The word "monotheism" has become a liability in the view of many contemporary theologians. For some, it implies a kind of cultural intolerance supposedly absent from the more open system of ancient polytheism.[1] For others, this rationalist neologism of pre-Enlightenment English crafting is a simple anachronism, tightly bound up with a fantasy of linear religious evolution, all alien to the biblical world, though the term is now distressingly enmeshed in the lexicon of Western theology.[2] The question therefore arises: "Monotheism—A Misused Word in Jewish Studies?"[3]

For at least thirty years, despite such preoccupations and a number of competing proposals (monolatry, intolerant monolatry, exclusive monolatry, henotheism, and even the open resistance of a binitarian "two gods in heaven" theory, etc.), the response has been to say that the category of *monotheism*, if it is applied with historical rigor and not as a vague and timeless abstraction, is a perfectly legitimate analytical term, even crucial for understanding the Jewish religion in the time of the Second Temple—especially during the Hellenistic and Roman periods.[4] Larry Hurtado's work deserves to be mentioned in a particular way, especially for the care he has taken in describing this form of Jewish religion, not as a belief, but as a monotheistic *praxis*.[5] Hurtado indeed shows the supreme importance of the exclusivity of the worship given to YHWH. According to him, this is the essential mark of ancient Jewish monotheism. The Jews worshiped only one god and vehe-

---

1 See Schwartz, *Curse of Cain*.
2 See, e.g., Schäfer, *Zwei Götter im Himmel*, 8.
3 Hayman, "Monotheism." See also Fredriksen, "Mandatory Retirement."
4 Hurtado, "'Ancient Jewish Monotheism.'"
5 See esp. Hurtado, *Ancient Jewish Monotheism*.

mently opposed any worship offered to other "gods"—even if they believed in their existence.[6]

This coexistence of one God with a multitude of *Mittelwesen* ("intermediate beings") is not inconsistent. Although there were at that time, in the Jewish vision of the world, celestial mediators and powerful demons, they were not prayed to, nor were they offered sacrifice.[7] This is illustrated by the famous "refusal of worship" motif in the Jewish literature of the time, according to which an angel rejects the worship that someone tries to offer to his person.[8] An important rhetoric of the oneness of the Jewish God, especially in his role as creator, also exists, notably in the postexilic sources. Greek documents also have their own proper discourse of a single, unique deity, however.[9] The central difference from Greek religion therefore remains resolutely at the level of cultic behavior. As such, ancient Jewish monotheism appears rather simple to describe—and much less "monistic" than other variations on monotheism, in late antiquity (after the rise of Christianity) and from the Middle Ages (post-Islam).

Without at all denying the great importance of Hurtado's work, the huge weight he places on the strict exclusivity of Jewish worship faces some potential challenges from the messy historical data, though admittedly this often represents behavior on the margins (just where breakoffs like Christianity were likely to form). A methodological objection might additionally be made, however, that similarly questions Hurtado's stark manner of painting the picture. Jonathan Z. Smith, reflecting on the problem of the categories used in the study of ancient Judaism, insists on the importance of avoiding a "monothetic" perspective, that is, the assumption of a single defining difference, *the* differential quality (i.e., the exclusivity of worship), which would define, without remainder, a given *taxon* (i.e., Jewish monotheism).[10]

---

[6] The practical definition of monotheism that H. S. Versnel proposes is suggestive: "The conviction that only one god exists (involving the cultic corollary of exclusive worship), while other gods do not, or, if and as far as they do, must be made inexistent, for instance by relegating them beyond the political or cultic horizon of the community and attributing to them the status of powerless, wicked or demonic forces without any (real) significance" (*Coping with the Gods*, 241). See also Scheid, *Quand faire c'est croire*.

[7] See Hurtado, *Ancient Jewish Monotheism*, 393; Johnson, *Prayer in the Apocyrpha and Pseduepigrapha*; and Enermalm-Ogawa, *Un langage de prière juif en grec*.

[8] On this motif, see Bauckham, "Worship of Jesus in Apocalyptic Christianity"; and Stuckenbruck, *Angel Veneration and Christology*.

[9] See, e.g., Versnel, "One God: Three Greek Experiments in Oneness," chap. 3 in *Coping with the Gods*, 239–307.

[10] Smith, "Fences and Neighbors."

Smith suggests instead a "polythetic" system, where multiple properties and modalities of comparison are simultaneously recognized to be germane.

From this perspective, a major specificity of Second Temple Jewish monotheism, which Hurtado has unfortunately not emphasized enough but is essential to the cult praxis that he highlighted so well, lies, I propose, in its distinctively aniconic character. The prohibition of worshiping foreign gods is found in the Torah alongside the prohibition of idols, which is something closely related but independent and actually different (Ex 20:3–5, 34:17; Lv 19:4, 26:1; Dt 4).[11] It would indeed have be natural enough to imagine the exclusive Jewish cult worshipping its cult image(s) of YHWH in all the places they were scattered. Thus, even if the Jews had a temple, a priesthood, and a system of sacrifices like the other nations, the unheard-of Jewish *manner* of worshipping their god without any images, a practice closely associated with an aggressive polemic against the surrounding nations' idols, set apart the Jewish experience of the one God from all other forms of ancient *latreia*.

Curiously, surprisingly perhaps, a certain resemblance of Jewish anti-idol polemics to analogous Greco-Roman idol critiques has the result that, once account is also taken of the strict moral code (Torah) revealed by the Judeans' guardian God, Jewish monotheism could convincingly appear to be kind of Hellenistic wisdom, indeed a superior philosophy—both in the eyes of the Greeks and in the eyes of Hellenized Jews themselves, such as a Philo. The paradox of this separation from the pagan world and simultaneous rapprochement is explained, in part, because of the distinction at that time between worship (religion) and belief/morality (philosophy). Jewish monotheism does not correspond perfectly to either the one or the other, but it shared important commonalities with each. The restriction of this unique, ethical-and-aniconic cult to one single Temple in Jerusalem—a religious ideal since the time of Deuteronomy that finally became reality under the Hasmoneans and later Herod—reinforced the anomaly of the Jewish religion. A universal God was worshiped, but only in Judea and only in the astonishing way of this proud chosen people.

In the following brief overview of Jewish monotheism at the time of the Second Temple, more suggestive than exhaustive, it is important to keep in mind this complex, dynamic interactivity with the surrounding Greco-Roman world. For frequently this dimension is missing or misrepresented, especially in New Testament studies. It was a mutual Jewish-Greek inter-

---

11 On the relation between these two themes, see Judge, *Other Gods and Idols*. See also Hendel, "Social Origins of the Aniconic Tradition in Early Israel." For a useful cross-cultural reflection on Jewish (and other) constructions of "idolatry" and the use of images, see Janowitz, "Good Jews Don't."

action, however, characterized at once both by an element of reciprocal influence and by an almost cultivated incomprehension. To keep this vital dynamism in proper focus, I adopt the category of "translatability," which Jan Assmann has proposed in order to analyze and, in his case, especially to criticize the phenomenon of Judeo-Christian monotheism.[12] By adopting this angle, but distinguishing between the "emic" (insider) and "etic" (outsider) perspectives, we will see that, in fact, Assmann's sharp (and derogatory) "Mosaic Distinction" obscures a certain kinship and genuine overlap between Jewish and Greek thought—including an "Abrahamic Experience" that is subtle and highly suggestive. Abraham, as a pagan convert to monotheism, symbolized for certain Jews of the Second Temple period an evident *convertability* and indeed powerful continuity between Hellenistic natural theology—expressed in a process of reasoning that led to a confession of the one true Creator—and the revelation of that same Creator God in an apocalypse of worship, beyond any earthly image.

Interpretatio Graeca

The famous parallel between Greek and Roman gods—Zeus with Jupiter, Athena with Minerva, and so on—is the classic example of polytheistic translatability. This so-called *interpretatio romana* was, of course, no novelty of the Romans. It already existed as an Etruscan tradition with respect to the Phoenician gods.[13] The *interpretatio graeca* similarly related the Egyptian gods to their Greek equivalents. Later they were also identified with the gods of Syria and North Africa.[14] But no pantheon monopolized this widespread practice, the globalist ecumenism of another age. Mark Smith has impressively documented the deep roots of such theological translation among the cultures of the ancient Near East, all the way back to the late Bronze Age—including in the early religion of Israel (El = YHWH).[15]

According to researchers like Smith, the birth of a true monotheistic rhetoric in Israel did not begin until the neo-Assyrian period. After the exile, following the successive empires that washed across the Near East,

---

12 Assman, "Mosaic Distinction." Assmann draws attention to the desire of polytheistic traditions to translate their notions of divinity cross-culturally; then he uses this model as a contrast to underline the "mosaic rupture"; namely, the rejection of the irenic principle of equivalence. The effect of this refusal is, for him, the fateful creation of a cultural space divided between two kinds of religion: the good and the bad.
13 See, e.g., Fitzmyer, "Phoenician Inscription from Pyrgi."
14 See Parker, *Greek Gods Abroad*, esp. chap. 2, "*Interpretatio*."
15 Smith, *God in Translation*.

we can observe two major stages in this development toward an increasingly distinctive Jewish monotheism. Both stages are inscribed within acts of *interpretatio* of the cult of YHWH, performed respectively by the Persians and the Greeks.

1. At the very beginning of the Second Temple period, indeed at the precise origin of rebuilding of the Temple that the Babylonians had destroyed, we encounter an important act of theological translatability:

> Thus says Cyrus, king of Persia: YHWH, the God of heaven, gave me all the kingdoms of the earth, it was he who charged me to build him a Temple in Jerusalem, in Judah. (Ezr 1:2)

The divine title "the God of heaven" that the Persian king here uses to designate YHWH, the god of the province of Yehud (Judah), was also used at the time for various other divinities in the Levant: Baalshamim, for example, and especially Ahuramazda, tutelary god of the Achaemenid dynasty.[16]

The official theology of the empire was, according to Thomas Bolin, "an inclusive monotheism (belief in one god in spirit, with regional refractions, centered on *Ahura Mazda*)."[17] To speak of an inclusive Persian monotheism in this way evokes the emergence, prior to the neo-Assyrian period, of a new kind of Babylonian translatability: an imperialist theology of one god, according to which the principal god, Marduk, became the sum and substance of the other gods.[18]

Urash (is) Marduk of the plantations

Lugalidda (is) Marduk of the Abyss

Ninurta (is) Marduk of the Pickaxe

Nergal (is) Marduk of the battle

Enlil (is) Marduk of the seigneury and consultations

Nabu (is) Marduk of accounting, etc.[19]

To describe this form of deism, where a single deity dominates, above every divine name, but where the other gods of the pantheon remain true deities, scholars speak of "summodeism" (Smith) or "monolatry" (Lemaire).[20] More important than the word is the way in which Jewish theology

---

[16] See Beyerle, "'God of Heaven.'"
[17] Bolin, "Temple of יהו," 128.
[18] See Smith, *God in Translation*, 172.
[19] Lambert, "Historical Development of the Mesopotamian Pantheon."
[20] Lemaire ("Review of *God in Translation*," 316) dislikes Smith's word because of its roots in the sphere of ideas, rather than the cult. See Smith, *God in Translation*, 168.

responded, however. When Jeremiah prophesies that all the earth will know God's true name, we see this Babylonian system both presupposed and outflanked. "Therefore I am surely going to teach them, this time I am going to teach them my power and my might, and they shall know that my name is YHWH" (Jer 16:21; cf. 23:27, 33:2). There is only one God, with one name, who will erase all other divine names—and he is not Marduk but YHWH. When Isaiah 40–55 mocks Marduk and YHWH asks, "Who will you compare me to, so that I resemble him?" it is again this Mesopotamian theology that is the target.

Although Persian Achaemenid theology remains close to the Babylonian discourse about Marduk, Persian benevolence toward YHWH and his cult was the reverse of Babylon's violent policies. The response of the Judeans to the Persian theology of the Supreme God was, accordingly, considerably less negative and polemic. They adopted the title of the imperial cult, without any apparent scruples, and applied it with an easy conscience to their own God, YHWH (Neh 1:4–5, 2:4, 2:20; Dn 2:18–19, 2:37, 2:44; Ezr 5:11–12, 6:9, 6:10, 7:12, 7:21, 7:23; Tob 10:11; Jdt 5:8, 6:19, 6:21).[21]

The real possibility exists that the Judeans themselves actually invited this identification of YHWH with Ahuramazda under a single *nomen sacrum*, when they formally petitioned to rebuild their Temple. The famous Elephantine papyri, which preserve the fascinating correspondence between the Persian governor, Bagohi, assigned to Yehud (Judah), and the members of the Jewish community settled in Egypt, who wanted to obtain permission to rebuild their own small temple of YHW like their confreres in Yehud, show that the Judeans were not the only worshipers of YHWH involved in this affair.[22] By naming YHW "God of heaven" on several occasions (AP 27:15, 30:2, 30:27–28, 31:2, 31:26–27), Yedoniah and the Jews of Elephantine aligned themselves with the official imperial theology, but on their own initiative and in a decidedly more polytheistic context. Indeed, it seems that this gesture of translation on the Jewish side was an effort that made it easier for Bagohi to grant an agreement to let the sanctuary be rebuilt.[23] Although the circumstances were different,[24] the fact that those responsible for the cult at

---

21 The title "God of Heaven" has ancient Syro-Palestinian (polytheistic) roots, which of course facilitated its adoption.

22 Porten, *Archives from Elephantine*.

23 See Bolin, "The Temple of יהו," 135–36.

24 Following official practice, Bagohi never names YHWH as such, using only the title "God of Heaven." The possibility exists of a change in Persian policy, however, so that Cyrus (whom YHWH appoints) could have taken the initiative in this identification (recalled later by Yedoniah). See Bolin, "The Temple of יהו," 136–42.

Elephantine were in contact with Johannan, high priest of YHWH in Jerusalem (and also with the officials in Samaria), indicates that the theologies of these two (or rather three) Jewish communities did not develop in complete isolation. The Jews of this early postexilic moment found their theological place in the Persian religious universe. Indeed, it seems that the imperfect monotheism of the Persian state gave them a theological point of reference, insofar as the Persians wisely recognized and even supported the worship of YHWH—at that time still practiced in several temples and in several places.

2. The situation changes dramatically with a change of political regime and policy, when the freedom of Jewish worship was no longer respected. In particular, the crisis provoked by the Seleucids represents a head-on collision with the Greek world and its own theology of the *oikumene*.

> Soon after, the king sent Geronte the Athenian to force the Jews to break the laws of their fathers and no longer rule their lives on the laws of God, to desecrate the Temple of Jerusalem and dedicate it to Olympian Zeus, and that of Mount Garizim to Zeus Hospitaller [Zeus Xenios], as requested by the inhabitants of the place. (2 Mc 6:1-2)

It is no exaggeration to say that this failed effort to dedicate the Temple of Jerusalem to Olympian Zeus is the cornerstone of a new era in Jewish religion. From the moment of the arrival of Seleucid power in the region, we see a hardening of the exclusivity of Jewish theology.[25] But why? What is the real difference between this Greek affront, so vigorously contested, and the official Persian theology that had been so easily adopted?

The question of the specific ritual scandal erected in the Temple still divides scholars. A new altar or some symbol of worship is evidently involved (1 Mc 1:54, 1:59; 2 Mc 6:5), but the character of the innovation remains uncertain. Clearer is the translatability framework. Herodotus (*Hist.* 7.40) and Xenophon (*Cyr.* 8.3.12) inform us that Ahuramazda is the Persian name for Zeus. In Syria, Baalshamim, honored as "God of heaven," just like Ahuramazda and YHWH, was unequivocally equated with this same cult of Olympian Zeus. In Garizim in Samaria, too, where there was an old Yahwist cult similar to the one located in Jerusalem, the identification of YHWH and Zeus had already been made. To all appearances, then, Hellenistic "summodeism" wanted to include Jewish "monotheism," as it was understood on the Greek side, in a broader theological *oikumene*, by bringing together

---

25 Hurtado, "'Ancient Jewish Monotheism,'" 386.

under one name (Zeus) all the cults of the empire offered to God Most High.[26] Far from necessarily being some Seleucid effort to supplant the worship of YHWH as such, a mixed cult under a compounded double title is possible to imagine, like the syncretic devotion to *Iao Sabaoth* and *Iupiter Sabazius* found in Rome at the same period (139 BC). In any case, from an "etic" (outsider = Greek) perspective, the Jewish cult was already a cult of Zeus. And, parallel to the situation at Elephantine, if we follow the classic and still controversial thesis of Elias Bickerman, this identification would even have been anticipated by a Hellenized Jewish party ("emic").[27] Later, Philo would have no qualms about naming the Jewish God in the most open of Greek terms as "the highest father of gods and men," a Homeric epithet for Zeus (*Spec.* 2.164).[28]

It is, in consequence, not at all implausible that in the *Letter of Aristeas* a non-Jew might unambiguously say to the court of Ptolemy (in a double *interpretatio*, betraying a Roman interest):

> These people worship God who watches over all and who is the creator of all, whom all worship, but we, O king, we call him differently after Zeus and Jove. (§16)

Although the one who speaks here is the literary creation of a Jewish author, archeological evidence demonstrates the reality of a real association between Zeus and YHWH and their special cults. One thinks in particular of the worship of *Theos Hypsistos*, "The Most High God," a fascinating cult that emerges from the second century BC and was widespread in the eastern Mediterranean.[29] *Theos Hypsistos* is often identified with Zeus, often with YHWH (but never both together simultaneously, to my knowledge). The title *Theos Hypsistos* itself is probably derived from *El Elyon*, as it was rendered by the Septuagint translators.

There is a certain philosophical aura attached to this cult of *Theos Hypsistos*, and one thing is clear: alongside the identification between Zeus and YHWH, there was also a Greco-Roman perception of Judaism as a kind of philosophical monotheism. The main emphasis here is placed on the startling Jewish ban on images. Hecataeus of Abdera, for example, says that Moses did not allow images διὰ τὸ μὴ νομίζειν ἀνθρωπόμορφον εἶναι τὸν

---

26 See Kenney, "Monotheistic and Polytheistic Elements."
27 Bickerman, *Der Gott der Makkabäer*.
28 For a nuanced considered of Philo's attitude here, see Koskenniemi, "God of the Philosophers."
29 See Mitchell, "Cult of Theos Hypsistos."

θεόν, "since we must not think of the divinity in an anthropomorphic way" (*apud* Diodorus Siculus, *Bib. hist.* 40.4). This is the first use of the word "anthropomorphic" in Greek literature (cf. Herodotus, *Hist.* 1.131). A famous statement by Strabo speaks of Jewish aniconism as an expression of admirable reasoning (*Geo.* 16.2.35–36). Tacitus relates something similar (without being in any way benevolent toward the Jews):

> The Egyptians worship many animals and images of monstrous form; the Jews have purely mental conceptions of Deity, as one in essence (*Iudaei mente sola unumque numen intellegunt*). They call those who make representations of God in human form out of perishable materials as ungodly. They believe that the Being is supreme and eternal, capable of neither representation nor decadence. They therefore do not allow any image to be held in their cities, much less in their temples. (Tacitus, *Hist.* 5.5; cf. *contemnere deos* 5.2, 5.5.3)

Another Roman, Varro, commended the Jews for preserving intact the rational form of imageless worship that he suggested was the original practice of Roman religion in its golden age under Numa (*apud* Augustine, *City of God* 4.31.21–29).[30] And so on. Menachem Stern supplies a complete dossier.[31]

"What else is Plato than Moses speaking Attic Greek?" Numenius of Apamea famously asked in the ultimate assertion of translatability from Hebrew to Greek (*apud* Eusebius, *Praep. ev.* 11.10). Exegetes conventionally take such constructions of the Jews as a rational "nation of philosophers" (an idea already attributed to Theophrastus) as a hyper-Hellenized parody of no real heuristic value. Yet this dismissal flagrantly ignores the enormous effort also made on the Jewish side—an effort not at all restricted to the diaspora—to translate Greek *Sophia* into a properly Jewish idiom. The books of Sirach and the Wisdom of Solomon are the parade examples. The projects of outright concordism, large and small, of a Philo of Alexandria, a pseudo-Aristaeus, or an Aristobulus, are no less revealing. Recent scholarship, in fact, is prepared to take up in earnest the old Plato-read-Moses topos, albeit in the reverse direction: suggesting that the Pentateuch itself relies on Plato's *Timaeus* and *Laws*, rather clearly in the LXX version, and, more controversially, for at least some scholars, based on the uncertain arcana of Pentateuchal text-criticism and dating, even in the earlier (in this case late) Hebrew form.[32] Martin Rösel's

---

30 See Kooten, "Pagan and Jewish Monotheism."
31 Stern, *Greek and Latin Authors*.
32 See, e.g., Rösel, *Übersetzung als Vollendung der Auslegung*; Niesiolowski-Spanò, "Primeval History in the Persian Period?"; and Gmirkin, *Plato and the Creation of the Hebrew Bible*.

landmark study, for instance, forcefully argued for a systematic borrowing of specialized terminology drawn from the cosmogony of the *Timaeus* in the Greek translation of the biblical account of creation in Genesis 1–2. The huge significance of such a thesis is hardly a matter of mere philology. We are facing a monumental philosophical exchange. Whether Moses read Plato, later Jewish readers of Moses unquestionably did—or at least they read later Greek readers of Plato. There is, accordingly, when all the data are gathered, strong reason to agree with the position of Yehoshua Amir, who several decades ago argued that, contrary to its normal presentation, the theological confrontation between the Greek and the Jewish worlds, at least in some real and meaningful sense, took the form of an encounter between two competing forms of *monotheism*.[33]

Assmann thinks that (Jewish) monotheism invented (pagan) polytheism, and this is not wrong. The noun "polytheism" or rather ἡ πολυθεία, is not (as "monotheism" is) a late neologism. It is a slur created already by Philo to describe a dominant worldview to which he did not subscribe.[34] (It was then later a notion recovered by sixteenth-century French thinkers, notably Jean Bodin, and subsequently transposed into English by Samuel Purchas, right around the time "monotheism" was also being coined and put into currency.) In the *De opificio mundi* (61.170–172), Philo places the adjectival πολύθεος alongside the familiar old notion of ἄθεος and contrasts both with a clear doctrine of the existence and oneness of God, discerned on the basis of creation. The same adjectival association of "polytheistic" and "atheistic doctrines" appears with some regularity in other contexts (e.g., *Migr.* 12.69), but in the *De mutatione nominum* (37.205) the nominalized form πολυθεία finally appears. Interestingly, it is here deployed to describe those persons to whom Moses forbids any admittance into the assembly of God; namely, "lovers of a system of polytheism."

Philo's conceptual construction of polytheism as an explicit boundary marker is not an entirely one-sided affair by any means, for Philo's very ability to sneer at error in the way that he does is conditioned by a great many Hellenistic, philosophical presuppositions.[35] To the extent that a hardened "Mosaic Distinction" is thus in truth a product of the Greco-Roman era,

---

33 Amir, "Die Begegnung des biblischen."

34 On the development of this language in Philo and later in Procopius, see Daube, "Contrariness of Speech and Polytheism." On recent scholarly approaches to the study and description of "polytheism," see Pirenne-Delforge and Pironti, "Many vs. One."

35 On this distinctly sociological aspect of the problem, including the Enlightenment appropriation of the ancient discourse and patristic usage in Origen, see the erudite study of Arcari, "'Discorsi monoteistici.'" Arcari's treatment of several little-studied fragments of Xenophanes of Colophon are of particular interest. Xenophanes famously said that if horses could paint,

there is also a reciprocal action on the pagan side—and the point of disagreement is not precisely where Assmann sees it.

The Jewish resistance in Judea did not recognize itself in the brand of Greek monotheism implicated in the ugly Seleucid affair. But why? The answer must be sought not only in a growing reverence for the divine name (a rolling result, as we have seen, reaching back all the way to experiences of monotheism in Mesopotamia). It also derives from the capital fact that the Greeks sought to change much more than just a name. They wanted to transform and re-create the holy city, chosen by YHWH, as a Hellenistic *polis*, by changing the Torah (νόμος) and replacing it with Greek customs and laws. The highly distinctive peculiarity of the special cult of the universal God, YHWH, was now at stake, imperiled by an intolerant inclination of universal liturgical and political organization. The intransigent Jewish particularism, of course, was a type of divine service that included fastidious observance of all the commandments, reaching far beyond sacrificial and liturgical regulations. Jewish monotheism thus emerges in this context as a complete way of life that circumscribes a distinctive social sphere, a mode of existence defining an entire people: "God is one and the Hebrew race is one" (Josephus, *A.J.* 4.200).

Stoic thought, as represented by Varro (*apud* Augustine, *City of God*, 6.5), recognized a revealing threefold division of theology: θεολογία μυθική – πολιτική – φυσική = *theologia mythica – civilis – naturalis*. While the second of these, the political, was for Varro associated explicitly with the public cult, the parallel refraction of philosophy into the three branches of logic, ethics, and physics hints also at the implicit ethical orientation of political theology as such. The final convergence of philosophical and theological perspectives at the level of *natura* also here comes into view; namely, reflection on what the gods actually are: the *natura deorum*. Even if a series of answers to this last order of question was entertained in debate behind the walls of the schools—Varro cites Heraclitus's hypothesis of fire, Pythagoras's theory of number, Epicurus's idea of atoms, and so on—the problem of Jewish-Greek relations was nevertheless not at root a disagreement over *theologia naturalis*. Nor was it a problem on the order of myths, though Jewish polemics might give this misleading impression. Both sides were sufficiently enlightened to view the myths for what they patently were. As Edward Gibbon magisterially said, "The various modes of worship which prevailed in the Roman world were considered by the people as equally true; by the philosopher as

---

they would paint the gods to look like horses. He additionally confessed: "There is one, greatest among gods and men, in no way similar to mortals either in body or in thought" (Frag. 23 *apud* Clement, *Strom.* 5.109.1).

equally false; and by the magistrate as equally useful."[36] The point of tension was, above all, at this level of the magistrates' *theologia civilis*: a matter not of describing divine nature, where agreement could be found, but rather of determining *divina insituta hominum*.

This, it seems, is the major site of misunderstanding and conflict: two forms of monotheism that correspond to two forms of polity with two forms of imperial claim. The limits of translatability strike against the constitution of the chosen people: the "with all your heart, with all your soul, and with all your might" commanded by the one Lord (Dt 6:4–6). Under the Hasmoneans, in a special moment of political expansion, a nationalist theology naturally took shape and was easily united with a destructive "zeal" directed against pagan altars (e.g., 1 Mc 2:25; see Ex 34:13), even against the temple of YHWH-Zeus in Samaria. To Greek eyes, such extremities of "monotheistic" zeal—with its strange observances, such as circumcision, shabbat, and kashrut, and with its open violence against the gods and their shrines (at times including the shrines of the same, one God, YHWH)—was paradoxically guilty both of δεισιδαιμονία (*superstitio*) and of being ἄθεος: of having "too much" and "too little" εὐσέβεια (*pietas*) all at once.[37] Such confusion was perhaps inevitable in the face of this startling Jewish configuration of principles and praxis, which unified worship and ethics in a kind of philosophy-as-religion, all planted solidly within the political sphere: universal yet stubbornly ethnic and local.

If this characterizes, in brief, the knotty point of brutal incomprehension, there is no question of a refusal of translatability altogether, neither on the Jewish side nor on the Greek side. *Theologia naturalis* remained a passable bridge. A statement by Flavius Josephus admirably shows the interesting ambiguity of the situation. He highlights the particularity of the Jews, cast overtly as "the Other" and depicted as the special unique subjects of a "theocracy," yet he does this by using entirely Greek categories and stressing the deep agreement between the philosophers and the Jews on the central question of the *natura deorum* (or rather *Dei*).[38]

> Some peoples have entrusted supreme political power to monarchies, others to oligarchies, still others to the masses. Our legislator was not attracted to any of these forms of politics but gave his constitution the form of what—if forced expression is permitted—can be called theocratic, putting all sovereignty and

---

36 Gibbon, *Decline and Fall of the Roman Empire*, 1:22.
37 See Amir, "Der jüdische Eingottglaube."
38 On the social dynamics here, see Arcarai, "'Discorsi monoteistici,'" 322–23.

authority in the hands of God... Moses represented him as one, uncreated, unchanging to all eternity, with a beauty beyond all mortal thought... That the wisest of the Greeks learned to adopt these conceptions of God from the principles that Moses provided them, I do not want to insist now; but they have testified to the excellence of these doctrines, to their consonance with the nature and majesty of God. In fact Pythagoras, Anaxagoras, Plato, the Stoics who succeeded him, and indeed almost all philosophers seem to have had similar views regarding the nature of God. (*C. Ap.* 2.168–169)

An open theological divergence on the level of social constitutions and custom (*theologia civilis*) yet full theoretical agreement περὶ τῆς τοῦ θεοῦ φύσεως—that is, on the nature of God (*theologia naturalis*)—this is the status. Philo had a similar view of the matter, though he rhetorically blended, somewhat more than Josephus, the philosophical doctrine of God and the range of competing political forms, projecting polytheistic error, for instance, into the metaphysical realm as an acceptance of the mob rule of an "ochlarchy" in heaven (*Opif.* 61.170).[39] Such testimony can be dismissed out of hand as too apologetic, Hellenistic, and ultimately unrepresentative of "genuine" Jewish thinking. The Greek shading is certainly impossible to miss. Hecateus, too, constructed Moses in a similar fashion, at the very dawn of the Greek interpretation of the Jews. Moses was not only the philosopher who correctly knew how not to misunderstand God's divine nature (τὸ μὴ νομίζειν ἀνθρωπόμορφον εἶναι τὸν θεόν). Moses made this rational philosophy known precisely as the legislator who gave specific cultic prescriptions for the Hebrews' *politeia*: τὰ κατὰ τὴν πολιτείαν ἐνομοθέτησέ τε καὶ διέταξε. These overlapping roles of philosopher and statesman and the conjoined overlapping semantics of the Greek word(s) νόμος/νομίζειν need to be particularly observed. The same fateful manner of speaking—νομίζειν τοὺς θεούς—evokes at once both the act of conceptualizing the gods and the act of institutionalizing their presence within the city through religious custom.[40] However we choose to define Second Temple socioreligious normativity or deviance, some Jews in the Greco-Roman era (many Jews, in fact) read and thought and wrote in Greek. These Jews (not limited to Philo and Josephus) represent a manifest locus of translation and reveal an impressive *interpreta-*

---

[39] For a fascinating proposal of how modern neoliberal society is accurately modeled and described by Proclus's committed polytheistic politics/theology, see Vargas, "Conspiracy of the Good."

[40] On this evocative language, see Pirenne-Delforge, *Le polythéisme*.

tio from the interior of Judaism itself: a view that is somehow simultaneously "emic" and "etic."[41]

INTERPRETATIO JUDAICA

For the Hellenistic mind, Jewish monotheism oscillates between a strange δεισιδαιμονία that is ἄθεος on the one hand and rational φιλοσοφία on the other. The irony is that, without denying the fact that the fierce monotheistic zeal that sprang up in the Hasmonean era has real roots in the Persian period, these specific Greek categories expose a revealing link. Namely, the Jewish outlook on the gods of the nations resembles precisely the opinions of Greek "atheists" and philosophers who criticized their own traditions from within.[42] Once again we meet a perspective that is at once both emic and etic, though this time reversed: not insiders looking at themselves like outsiders, but outsiders looking at the others like insiders.

This possibility of Jews thus seeing not only Jewish but also Greek religion through Greek eyes advances the evidence of a significant philosophical/theological rapprochement. The still-classic study of Harold Attridge provides an excellent and accurate survey of the relevant Greco-Roman landscape and critique of religion.[43] Noami Janowitz more compactly summarizes the evocative data. A central point of contact is the reasoned rejection of images in worship.

> As used by writers such as Josephus, arguments against the use of images in worship resonated with existing critiques in the surrounding culture, especially as they were presented to philosophically astute audiences. That is, we find a complex discourse about statues in the Greco-Roman world even as the use of statues was widespread. The practice was criticized from various philosophical stances, beginning, not surprisingly, with the pre-Socratics, who considered traditional worship, including the use of statues, from a number of angles. Xenophanes (sixth century BCE), for example, presented the classic critique that the greatest god is

---

41 See Honigman, "Jews as the Best of All Greeks."

42 The absorption of such viewpoints and redeployment from a Jewish perspective is not surprising. John J. Collins rightly observes that "the most penetrating view in Hengel's great book [*Judaism and Hellenism*] is perhaps that even those forms of Judaism which seem most decidedly anti-Hellenistic are nevertheless often deeply influenced by Hellenistic culture" (*Jewish Cult and Hellenistic Culture*, 43).

43 Attridge, "Philosophical Critique of Religion."

unlike mortals in form and mind. He mocked the use of images of the gods, pointing out that if oxen imagined the form of their gods they would think they looked like oxen. Heraclitus (fl. 500 BCE) rejected offerings prayers to images as part of a philosophical rejection of their efficacy... Antisthenes (mid-fifth to mid-fourth century)... stated that knowledge of the deity cannot come from an image. Zeno of Citium (335–263 BCE), the founder of Stoicism, argued that temples are unnecessary since the work of builders and artisans should not be considered sacred... Plutarch claimed that Numa forbade the Romans to "revere an image of God which has the form of man or beast"... Of particular interest to us, barbarian practices were praised as being aniconic, whether or not they really were. The Persians, according to Herodotus, did not believe that the gods have the same nature as men and therefore rejected building images, altars, and temples... Strabo depicted the rejection of statues as one of the many sensible traits of the Nabateans... Jewish modes of worship received a particularly good advertisement in these discussions.[44]

The good advertising of Jewish worship we have already noted. Here it is question rather of bad press for the alternative Greek option.

The Hellenistic period is, obviously, by no means the start of a Jewish campaign of defamation against the worship practices of the *goyim*. The long-standing and highly polemical manner of the Jews when speaking of the "idolatrous" practices of other nations is indeed a good indication of the vehemence of their exclusive worship of YHWH. The Canaanite gods were already mocked in the period of the monarchy (e.g., Elijah and Baal; 1 Sm 5:3–5), but a new tradition deriding idols as such—dead things made by human hands—begins with Deutero-Isaiah in Persian times.[45] This tradition significantly targets not the Persian gods, but rather the Babylonian deities (Is 37:19, 44:13-20, 45:20, 46:1-2; see Jer 16:20), a point of interest in view of the preceding discussion. Insofar as the very process of making idols becomes the center of the controversy, it seems possible that there is a sort of satirical reversal of the *miš pî* rite, "the washing of the mouth," which was a Mesopotamian ritual way of purifying a statue from the defilements of its manufacture to facilitate the change of the craftsman's product into the persona of the deity.

---

44 Janowitz, "Good Jews Don't," 244–45.
45 See Holer, *Second Isaiah's Idol Fabrication Passages*; Preuss, *Verspottung fremder Religionen*; and Levtow, *Images of Others*, 57–72.

In the oldest traditions, the controversy intertwines with overtly Yahwist/monotheistic rhetoric. Jeremiah 10, for example, alternately joins a satire on idols (vv. 2-5, 8-9) with a confession of the true God (vv. 6-7, 10). Isaiah does something similar (see 40:12–23, 45:16–21, 46:1–7, 48:5). Later anti-idol traditions, on the other hand, lose this framing technique and, oddly enough, become less explicitly monotheistic.

The Epistle of Jeremiah (Bar 6:8–58; LXX EpJer 7–57), a long anti-idol harangue, offers a useful example. The mention of YHWH is almost nonexistent (see 3-5). All interest is now focused on idols.

> They do not notice when their faces have been blackened by the smoke of the temple. Bat, swallows, and birds alight on their bodies and heads; and so do cats. From this you will know that they are not gods; so do not fear them. As for the gold that they wear for beauty—it will not shine unless someone wipes off the tarnish; for even when they were being cast, they did not feel it. They are bought without regard to cost, but there is no breath in them. Having no feet, they are carried on the shoulders, revealing to humankind their worthlessness. And those who serve them are put to shame because, if any of these gods falls to the ground, they themselves must pick it up. If anyone sets it upright, it cannot move itself; and if it is tipped over, it cannot straighten itself. Gifts are placed before them just as before the dead. (21–27)

The Semitic origins of this text date from the fourth or third century, but the Greek version probably dates from the second century BC. In this regard, Michael Wojciechowski observes that the controversy, which is inserted in the Book of Baruch but is little concerned with the God of Israel, strongly resembles a kind of Hellenistic criticism that ridiculed the idea of an idol and that we find in Aesop or Diagoras, for example.[46]

The satirical stories of Bel and the Dragon (LXX Daniel 14) are a more developed example of this motif, still targeting the Babylonian gods and still more solidly anchored in the Hellenistic context.[47] We can see here that the violent iconoclastic impulse, especially evident in the Hasmonean political realm with its periodic bursts of *Beeldenstorm* fury, has been textually sublimated into a more acceptable narrative form. But again, there is nothing in the plot that indicates strict monotheism per se. Isolated from the canonical

---

[46] Wojciechowski, "Ancient Criticism of Religion."
[47] See Bergmann, "Idol Worship."

context (see Dn 14:1–3, 14:24–25, 14:41), we see rather a simple contempt for the gods, which borders on atheism.[48]

Even more interesting is the euhemerist explanation of the origins of pagan cults that enters into the anti-idol tradition, since it unmistakably reveals the affinity of Jewish polemics with the internal criticisms of Greek skeptics regarding their own tradition. The *Letter of Aristeas* (§137–38) and the Book of Wisdom (14:12–21) use this topos, for example, and Wisdom extends the theory beyond the worship of a particular hero as a god to explain the invention of idolatry itself.

> They [the idols] did not exist originally, and they will not always exist; it is through the vanity of men that they made their entry into the world ... It is still on the order of sovereigns that sculpted images receive a cult: those who could not be honored in person, because they lived at a distance, their distant figure was made present by making the venerated king a visible image; thus, thanks to this zeal, one would flatter the absent as if he were present. Even those who did not know him were led by the artist's ambition to expand his cult; for undoubtedly desirous of pleasing the sovereign, he spent all his art making more beautiful than life, and the crowd, carried away by the charm of the work, then made an object of worship of the one who formerly was honored as a man. (Wis 14:13–14, 14:17–20)

A truly exceptional synthesis of Second Temple monotheism and the culmination of this Persian-period-rooted and increasingly Greek-leaning Jewish anti-idol polemic is found in the *Apocalypse of Abraham*.[49] Probably written in Hebrew in Palestine between AD 75 and 150, it is divided into two parts. The first eight chapters tell, in the form of a comic tale, the story of Abraham working in the workshop of his father, Terah, an idol maker in Ur. Young Abraham observes again and again the manifest weakness of the dumb idols, which suffer all manner of indignity—getting soiled and con-

---

[48] Wojciechowski, "Ancient Criticism of Religion," 63. From a theological perspective, aided by the study of comparative religion, it is possible to recognize in many such forms of "atheism" and its various critiques a helpful purification of theism in the shape a *via negativa*. This perspective includes not only the ancient perspectives of Greek and Jewish authors, but also, e.g., forms of Buddhist and Hindu philosophy. For a positive appropriation of this negative theology in the contemporary theological context, see Balathsar, *Die Gottesfrage des heutigen Menschen*. On the importance of the *via negative* in the construction of New Testament Christological monotheism, see chap. 9 in this volume.

[49] See Harlow, "Idolatry and Alterity"; and Ego, "La conversion d'Abraham."

sumed by fire and so on—and whose perishable nature accordingly becomes painfully clear. Abraham thus thinks to himself that it would make more sense to worship his father as the creator of idols than to worship the idols themselves (*Apoc. Ab.* 3.2–4, 8). This topos also exists in Philo (*Dec.*172) and in the *Letter of Aristeas* (§136). Abraham's observations ultimately lead him to a philosophical discovery of the transcendent Creator:[50]

> Father Terah, fire is more venerable than your gods, the gold and silver ones, and the stone and wooden ones, because fire burns your gods. And your gods being burned obey the fire, and the fire mocks them while it is consuming your gods. But neither fire, I will not call it (fire) god, for it is subjugated to the waters. The waters are more venerable than it (fire), because they overcome fire and sweeten the earth with fruits. But I will not call them god either, for the waters subside under the earth and are subject to it. But I will not call it a goddess either, for it is dried by the sun (and) sub-ordinated to man for his work. The sun I call more venerable than the earth, for which its rays it illuminates the whole universe. But I will not call it a god because when the night comes it becomes murky with darkness. Nor again shall I call the moon or the stars gods, because they too at times during the night dim their light. But hear this, Terah my father, let me proclaim to you the God who created all things. But this is the true God who has made the

---

50 With good reason, this text and the striking experience of God's transcendence that it describes grabbed the attention of Eric Voegelin. See, e.g., Voegelin, "What Is History" and "Anxiety and Reason," 4–5, 96–99, 104. "I have selected this text because it demonstrates not only the *via negativa* as the instrument for describing the experience but also the transition from the compact experience of a cosmos full of gods to the experience of transcendence that differentiates being and endows it with the indices *immanent* and *transcendent* ... He [God] is the One beyond all realms of being, which through His revelation cease to be a cosmos full of gods and is transformed into a world whose being carries the index *immanent* in relation to the being of the divine source that carries the index *transcendent* ... [In this text] the realms of being are conceived as elemental or stellar, while in Hellenic philosophy they would be conceived rather as inorganic, vegetative, animal, and human (though this characterization needs serious qualifications), but in either case the realms form a hierarchy leading the searching mind upward to the point of transcendence towards the origin of being, toward the *arche*, or first cause ... The text makes admirably clear the tension of the search—of God seeking man, and man seeking God—the mutuality of seeking and finding one another. Not a space beyond space but the search is the site of the meeting between man and the beyond of his heart ... The divine Beyond thus is at the same time a divine Within the world ... The experience of transcendence, to summarize, is a movement of the soul, culminating in an act of transcendence in which the divine Within reveals itself as the divine Beyond" (5). Cf. Voegelin, *Collected Works*, 395–96.

> heavens crimson and the sun golden, who has given light to the moon and the stars with it, who has dried the earth in the midst of the many waters, who set you yourself among the things and who has sought me out now in the perplexity of my thoughts. If only God will reveal himself by himself to us. (*Apoc. Ab.* 7.1–12)[51]

This extraordinary argument, which, not unlike the reasoning of a Platonic dialogue terminating in a religious myth, ends with an open orientation toward divine revelation, is an argument suggestively grafted onto a familiar Jewish anti-idol narrative. The legend of Abraham as an iconoclast in Ur already appears in the *Book of Jubilees* (12.12–14) in the Hasmonean period.[52] Typically, in this context, Abraham violently destroys the idols by burning a temple—while his brother Haran dies in the fire in a futile effort to save the helpless gods. The originality of the *Apocalypse* is to reorient this narrated iconoclastic violence. In this later version of the tradition, it is now God himself, through his angel, who destroys the workshop of Terah, not Abraham. Abraham, rather, defeats the idols by a process of reasoning, which somehow invites this work of divine destruction. The conversion of an idolater to the true God thus takes the form of a philosophical conversion, supernaturally confirmed by a strike of lightning. The Jewish polemical mockery of the Greek Other surreptitiously transforms into a demonstration of the acumen of the questioning Hellenistic mind.

> And it came to pass as I was thinking things like these … the voice of the Mighty One came down from the heavens in a stream of fire, saying and calling, "Abraham, Abraham." And I said "Here am I." And he said, "You are searching for the God of gods, the Creator, in the understanding of your heart. I am he. God out from Terah, your father, and go out of the house, that you too may not be slain in the sins of your father's house. And I went out. And it came to pass as I went out—I was not yet outside the entrance of the court—that the sound of a great thunder came and burned him and his house and everything in his house. (*Apoc. Ab.* 8.1–6)

After his philosophical rejection of polytheism, Abraham turns toward God in prayer, and immediately YHWH's voice speaks to him from heaven, "Abraham, Abraham." We here exit the imaginative, para-biblical prequel and promptly join the scriptural story at Genesis 12:1 (which will be not less

---

51 Translation here follows the text form attested in Manuscripts A B C K, by R. Rubinkiewicz, in Charlesworth, *Old Testament Pseudepigrapha*, 1:692–93.
52 See Ego, "Abrahams Jugendgeschichte."

imaginative as it develops). The rest of the text from here on recounts a long revelation and a celestial journey, building on Genesis 15. The overall structure of the story is therefore clear. A kind of *praeambula fidei* at the level of human reason prepares, through the reasoned, philosophical discovery of the true God, a theological space newly opened to a (biblical) revelation of that true God, a revelation that is properly personal in form.

The concrete apocalypse offered to Abraham in this highly creative "rewritten Bible" is no less interesting than the interpretation of the pagan experience that precedes it. Briefly, Abraham, accompanied by the angel Jahoel, ascends Mount Horeb, where he offers a sacrifice. He then continues the adoration in a celestial fashion in the presence of God. This figure of the Angel of the Name—the product, it seems, of a Jewish theology developed in Samaria[53]—subtly mingles with God himself, who begins to play the conventional role of the *angelus interpres* during the celestial journey. We accordingly here confront the profound mystery of the "hypostases" or "personified divine attributes": the Name, Shekinah, Wisdom, and so on. One must pause before the immense theological weight invested in this far too casually invoked diagnostic language of *hypostasis*, which was pioneered and defined by Wilhelm Bousset and has entrenched itself in the analytic repertoire of exegetes and scholars of Jewish monotheism ever since. The problems and prospects raised here demand a patient and intelligent investigation that unfortunately cannot presently be pursued.[54] The relevance of the *Logos* will not be missed in this connection.[55]

However precisely the mysterious substance of Jahoel/Angel of the Name is most properly conceived, the disappearance of this mediating angel behind God himself should be read as a monotheistic move that corresponds to the extreme care taken by the author to ensure that the vision of God is not rendered anthropomorphic in any way.[56] This precise concern shows, on another measure, the continuity between the two halves of the text of the *Apocalypse of Abraham*, which move directly from aniconism to apophaticism.[57] No less importantly, however, the extreme worry over anthropomorphism also reveals a polemic against the biblical tradition itself, especially against the traditions of a divine body in Ezekiel and in some pseudepigraphs.

---

53 See Fossum, *Name of God*.
54 Important groundwork has now been done. See the brief but illuminating and learned discussion of this topic in the introduction to Silly, *Les Grands Mystères de la Sagesse*.
55 See chap. 9 in this volume.
56 See Orlov, "'Gods of My Father Terah,'"
57 See Harlow, "Anti-Christian Polemic."

The severity of the *Apocalypse of Abraham* against all forms of idolatrous worship thus begins with the pagans but in the end finally turns against the Jews. *Interpretatio iudaica* becomes self-referential. Jewish monotheism, in other words, has an internal manner of seeing itself as it also sees the pagan other. Abraham's heavenly vision accordingly and strikingly ends with a revelation of idolatry in the Jewish Temple itself, likened to the original idolatry identified and condemned in Ur (§25–27). God smites the Temple in Zion in his blazing anger, just as he had smitten the house of Terah at the beginning.

Who precisely is targeted by this internal Jewish polemic? The abomination committed in the sanctuary recalls the abomination evoked by Daniel in the time of the Maccabees, yet this time the scandal comes forth from the Jewish people, not from the outside: an *emic*, not *etic* problem. Historically, the destruction of the Temple by the Romans in AD 70 is clearly in view, and it seems probable that here we perceive those Jews who adhere to Jesus, who faintly emerge on the radar, dividing the people by worshiping their Messiah as God. Daniel Harlow's analysis of the text urges us to embrace this conclusion.[58] The fact that, ostensibly, at least in certain Jewish circles, blame for the Temple's destruction by fire was passed off on the early Christians would support this reading and fit the situation eminently well.[59] For some in the Second Temple period (or rather at the dawn of the post-Temple age), primitive Christian veneration of Jesus was the height of idolatry: a sin against both exclusivity and aniconism, at once the worship of an alien god and an alien god in the most anthropomorphic form that one might imagine. For others, however, this visible change in the pattern of worship did not introduce any new God alongside YHWH. It did entail, however, both a new manner of worship and thereby a new manner of being God's people. (Erik Petersen's reflections on *ekklesia* as integrally linked to the notion of the *polis* can be usefully inserted right here.[60]) This new Christian manner of being Israel inevitably entailed a new monotheistic "mutation" (to adopt a term preferred and popularized by Hurtado):[61] a reorganization that somehow, at least in its own estimation, superseded the practice of worship of the one God in the one Temple, just as the Jews' own form of "rational" worship itself surpassed an alternative worship of many idols in many temples, a worship

---

58 Harlow, "Anti-Christian Polemic," 167–83.

59 On this complex polemic motif of the burning of the Temple, see Giambrone, "Temple Arsons and Murder of the Prophets."

60 Peterson, *Ekklesia*.

61 For a brief but useful methodological reflection on the use of this term in the study of ancient religion, see Pirenne-Delforge and Scheid, "Qu'est-ce qu'une 'mutation religieuse'?"

like that of Terah and his sons when they "lived beyond the Euphrates and served other gods" (Jos 24:2).

Conclusion

Jewish monotheism in the days of the Second Temple was different from and harshly critical of the forms of worship prevalent in the ancient world, but it was at the same time linked directly to a shared philosophical experience of the divine. If recent scholarship has been characterized by a stance on the relation of Jewish and Greek relations to "monotheistic" perspectives that follows the idea of a dramatic rupture, as is often so vigorously asserted by at least certain Jewish sources, it would be misleading to imagine an absolute "Mosaic Distinction"—not only in the pre- and postexilic periods, but also (and especially) at the time of the great cultural conflict that followed the Maccabean crisis. Ultimately, the deep penetration of Hellenism into Jewish life—both in the Diaspora and in Palestine—resulted in a momentous encounter between natural and revealed religion. The Jewish particularism that this clash provoked clearly aggravated the disagreement, while strongly reemphasizing the integral harmony of worship and doctrine.

For the ancient pagan world, the rigorous practice of an aniconic and exclusive worship, closely linked to a code of moral conduct, was both attractive and disturbing. On the one hand, it suggested a cultic imbalance between atheism and superstition; on the other hand, it was appealing to contemporaries drawn to ethics and metaphysics. The curious and confusing Jewish fusion of religion and philosophy, through the fusion of worship and ethics, of social custom and theological beliefs, prepared and began, if it did not bring to perfection, a unified experience of the God of the Philosophers and the God of Faith.[62] In this way, it is possible to affirm—with confident insistence—that the epic encounter of biblical and metaphysical modes of thought, of the so-called Hebrew and Hellenistic worldviews, usually posed as a later confrontation and a specifically Christian problematic, was in fact already well underway and heading toward its ultimate resolution before the New Testament had even been written.

The study of Jewish monotheism in Hellenistic and Greco-Roman times has often, understandably, been subordinated to an interest in understand-

---

[62] Joseph Ratzinger's inaugural lecture upon taking up the chair for dogmatic theology in Bonn in 1959 remains a programmatic expression of his own theological thought and a wonderful orientation to many of the themes discussed and implicit in this present study. See Ratzinger, "Der Gott des Glaubens."

ing the context of early Christology. It seems judicious, however, to renew and reorient this research through a greater interest in pre-Christian pagan monotheism as well. This will not only lead to a correct understanding of the true character of the pre-Christian Jewish faith and its understanding and worship of God. It will also help to clarify important elements of the philosophical substructure of New Testament Christology, which set in motion subsequent doctrinal developments in patristic thought and the Church's councils.

CHAPTER 9

PRIMITIVE CHRISTOLOGY AS ANCIENT PHILOSOPHY

In several significant recent studies, Charles Stang along with his former professor Fr. Maximos Constas have been advancing the argument that modern scholarly reductions of the *Corpus Aereopagiticum* to supposed Neoplatonic antecedents have dreadfully obscured Dionysius's character as an exegete of St. Paul.[1] Their work demonstrates how categories long taken as conceptual cognates to Neoplatonic doctrine in reality have a firm anchoring in Pauline texts. "Paul animates in fact the entire corpus."[2] The implications are considerable. Martin Luther famously denounced Dionysius as *plus platonisans quam Christianisans*,[3] and while the tenor of Stang and Constas's biblical turn might seem hospitable to a long-standing aversion to Hellenistic influence on Christian theology—a triumph for purified biblical religion—I would like to take this emergent paradigm in precisely the opposite direction. The simple possibility of apprehending an author like Dionysius as an integrally Pauline thinker should challenge not only our image of Dionysius, but also our picture of Paul.

The identical challenge might be extended to embrace any number of similar turns in present-day patristic scholarship. Like the glad recovery of Aquinas as *in sacra pagina magister*, reading Nicene thinkers, from Athanasius to Augustine, first of all as interpreters of the Scriptures is today very

---

[1] See Stang, *Apophasis and Pseudonymity*; and Constas, "Reception of St. Paul and Pauline Theology"; Constas, "Dionysius the Areopagite." See also Golitzin, *Et introibo as altare dei*, 234–42.
[2] Stang, *Apophasis and Pseudonymity*, 3.
[3] WA 6.561.34–562.14; LW 36.109–110.

much in vogue. It seems to me that this seismic shift in the broad practice and character of *Dogmengeschichte*—a kind of exegetical takeover of normative Christian thought—should have real consequences for biblical exegesis at large. But let us remain with Dionysius and Platonism, invoking St. Thomas at the outset to point the way.

Dionysian Themes in St. Thomas's Biblical Christology

It is well established among students of medieval theology that, following the paraphrasing work of Thomas Gallus and Robert Grosseteste's translation of the Dionysian corpus in the first half of the thirteenth century, the influence of the presumed disciple of St. Paul was enormous in the Latin schools.[4] Albert and Aquinas (who employed instead the translation of John Sarrazin) are representative of this broad trend, and both abetted the massive influx of Platonic (and other Greek) sources into the theology of the age.[5] In this sense, all these scholastic innovators come under the facile judgment of leading sacred science ever further astray from its authentic scriptural roots, down the Hellenized road of philosophical speculation.

It is curious in this connection that Aquinas's active instigation of William of Moerbeke's translation of Proclus's *Elements of Theology* led the saint to be the first to discern the inauthenticity of the supposedly Aristotelian *Liber de Causis*, which plainly borrows from Proclus. The same phenomenon of a Proclean debt, of course, today convinces scholars of the inauthenticity of Dionysius's Pauline connection, earning him the sobriquet "Pseudo."[6] Dionysius's affinities with Proclus were interestingly already noted by John of Scythopolis, the first scholiast of the corpus and a scholar noted for skillfully detecting Apollinarian forgeries. John nonetheless accepted the traditional attribution and evidently embraced an alternative explanation for Dionysius's proximity to Proclus (textual corruptions? the reversibility of arguments for dependence?). Whatever might explain Thomas's own failure to draw the same conclusion he drew about the *Liber de Causis* in the case of

---

[4] On the still earlier infusion of Dionysian learning into the Latin tradition, in the translations of Eriugena with their rolling scholia, see the excellent editions and introductions of Harrington, *Thirteenth-Century Textbook*, and Dionysius, *On the Ecclesiastical Hierarchy*.

[5] See Curiello, "'Alia translatio melior est.'"

[6] While the debate over Dionysian authenticity became serious following observations of Lorenzo Valla in the humanistic context and the polemical atmosphere of the Reformation, simultaneous credit for demonstrating the case is usually given to two nineteenth-century scholars: Hugo Koch, "Proklos als Quelle"; and Stiglmayr, "Der Neuplatoniker Proklos."

the Dionysian writings[7]—a conclusion now long granted as the official consensus—it is well worth observing the role played by Dionysius in Thomas's commentaries on St. Paul.

On the one hand, ironically, (Pseudo-)Dionysius's authoritative acceptance of Hebrews as a Pauline letter was used by Thomas to argue for Hebrews' own authenticity (*Super ep. ad Heb.* Proem.). On the other hand, the question of content (*materia*) was for Thomas not less interesting or important than the question of the author (*auctor*).[8] The "Pauline" character of the Dionysian corpus, dogmatically conceived, thus finally helps Thomas, not so much in the arbitration of authenticity, but in the business of recognizing what is genuinely Pauline on the theological order. For Thomas, the Christian Platonist underlines and unlocks several significant motifs in the apostle's thought.

Perhaps the best illustration appears in the commentary on Ephesians, where Thomas engages Paul's potent Christological claim that Christ is enthroned "above every principality and power and virtue and dominion and every name that is named, not only in this world, but also in the one to come" (Eph 1:21). The text is highly suggestive, and two major Dionysian themes converge here, with resonance elsewhere in the Pauline corpus. First, the preeminent status of Christ is articulated in explicit interaction with a hierarchical angelology, eliciting from Thomas an extended discussion of Dionysius's account of the angelic choirs (*Super Eph.* §61–64). Something similar appears in the first chapter of Hebrews, where Christ is said to be as far superior to the angels as his name is superior to theirs, and where Thomas again relies heavily on Dionysian insights (*Super ep. ad Heb.* §58, 86–87). The surpassing excellence of Christ's name in both of these texts represents the second, related motif associated with author of the *Divine Names*: for Thomas sees an apophatic theology of the unnamable God implicit in Paul's Christological thinking. "Lest it be thought that he [Christ] is above the name of God, he [Paul] adds 'that is named.' For the divine majesty can be neither contained nor named by a name (*nullo nomine conclude, vel nominari potest*)" (§64). The influence of Lateran IV can be discerned in Aquinas's apophatic rendition of Paul's Christology of the divine Name—Christ's name entails a greater difference from the angels' names than any difference that can be imagined, since they are infinitely apart (*Super ep. ad Heb.* §47).[9]

---

[7] Thomas was not unattuned to certain of Dionysius's conceptual debts and sources. "Dionysius nearly everywhere follows Aristotle, as will be evident to anyone who diligently examines his books" (*Sent.* 2 D. 14 Q. 1 A. 2).

[8] See Giambrone, "Prologues to Aquinas' Commentaries."

Dionysius's patronage of a negative Pauline theology is also evident, however. This is clear, for instance, from Thomas's commentary on the boldly paradoxical title of Christ in Colossians 1:13 as the "image of the invisible God" (*Super Col.* §1.4).

It is not my intention here to explore these motifs in their specific Thomistic context, desirable and interesting though that would be. Even less do I mean to position these ideas within Dionysian Christology, the contours of which are actually governed by different interests.[10] Instead, in what follows, both of the Christological themes actively seized upon by Thomas—the hierarchy of celestial mediators and a name-based *theologia negativa*—will be pursued not as layered Thomistic or Dionysian motifs, alien Neoplatonic intrusions in the work of biblical exegesis, but rather as valid and even critical perspectives for a historically informed, contemporary New Testament Christology. This effort to valorize distinctively philosophical dimensions of biblical thought will be executed in direct dialogue with a common but, in my view, still too narrow postulate: monotheism as the essential matrix of primitive Christology.[11]

Celestial Hierarchies and Christological Monotheism

One of the touchiest points in the debate over so-called Christological monotheism, at least as the discussion is presently conducted among exegetes, concerns (without ever using the title) the οὐρανίαι ἱεραρχίαι, the celestial hierarchies. Briefly, two perspectives have emerged about just how monotheistic the Jewish worldview really was in its first-century Greco-Roman setting, the worldview in which primitive Christology was born. On the one side, it is claimed that no real ambiguity troubled the bright line

---

9 *Hoc nomen est valde differentius ab illo, quia quantamcumque differentiam ponis, adhuc est maiorem dare, cum distent infinitium.*

10 It is common to plot Dionysius's Christology within post-Chalcedonian sixth-century debates. In this context, he appears to promote a Diphysite viewpoint while carefully chastening his language. See Perczel, "Christology of Pseudo-Dionysius the Areopagite"; and Mainoldi, "Why Dionysius the Areopagite?" But see also Stang, *Apophasis and Pseudonymity*, 92–116.

11 The literature endorsing this view, which focuses specifically on *Jewish* monotheism, is now vast. For a compact, early expression of the paradigm, see Rainbow, "Jewish Monotheism." Rainbow's text is a review article of Larry Hurtado's book *One God, One Lord*, which helped greatly to begin the discussion. For a broader view of Second Temple Jewish monotheism, notably in its relation to *pagan* monotheism, see chap. 8 in this volume.

between the one Creator and his creatures. There was, on this view, no blurring and no mistaking when something was a "personified divine attribute," like hypostasized Wisdom, or when it was by contrast just a powerful angel.[12] On the other side of the debate, as the space between the Most High and his people on earth was so thickly forested with just such heavenly mediators and *Mittelwesen*, it is thought that overly monistic and transcendent constructions of the monotheism of the era are flatly anachronistic and misleading.[13] On this view, first-century Judaism inevitably looked much more like neighboring expressions of ancient Mediterranean religion than some would wish.

It is not difficult to detect behind the conflict of these two positions a much deeper disagreement concerning the relationship between Hellenism and Hebraism. Genuine questions about the very nature of revelation are at stake in getting this relationship right, but, as often, the dichotomy as posed also forces some unnecessary and unhelpful choices. This state of affairs is exposed well by Larry Hurtado, who takes a curious middle position.[14] Situating himself between the two camps more ambiguously than some overeager apologists have understood, Hurtado acknowledges the existence in Second Temple Jewish thought of a messy metaphysical hierarchy of divine beings, yet he apprehends a decisive and distinguishing factor in the Jewish practice of exclusive worship. Only YHWH, or for Christians only YHWH and Christ, is accorded outright worship. Apart from this *latreia*, however, we would be in thick theological darkness, as Hurtado sees it.

Lex Orandi, Lex Credendi?

There is significant promise in this *lex orandi, lex credendi* perspective, if there are also important reasons to qualify and contextualize it. One concern is the praxis-based tendency to sideline conceptual discourse in favor of devotional behavior. Dogmatic development simply falls out. There is an ironic upside to such methodological sidelining, however. Without intending to slice this precise Gordian knot, Hurtado's simple analysis effectively siphons off philosophic from cultic paganism. He neatly (if thus with an artificial analytic clarity) decouples two deeply entangled domains, which indeed stood in a complex opposition to one another but have conventionally been

---

[12] An example of this view would be Bauckham, *Jesus and the God of Israel*.
[13] See, e.g., Newman, *Jewish Roots of Christological Monotheism*; and Fletcher-Louis, *Jesus Monotheism*.
[14] See, e.g., the recent collection of essays in Hurtado, *Ancient Jewish Monotheism*.

bundled up as one polytheistic and hence dangerous non-Jewish lump. This bundling is unfortunate, for it not only stands to the acute disadvantage of philosophical thought. It also impairs our constructions of Judaism.

New clarity on the prestige of philosophy and its multiform links to ancient *latreia* is greatly needed if Christology's interface with ancient monotheism is to be properly understood. For polytheism is hardly the full Greek story, whatever certain Jewish sources would have us believe. Even the allegorizing appropriations of mythological nomenclature by Stoic theoreticians and the rationalized rereadings of pagan ritual adopted by a Plutarch should be viewed as acts of theurgically inclined philosophical annexation, not evidence of rank confusion. Similarly, the oeuvre of Philo, consistently maltreated as an outlier in New Testament discussion, effects a comparable operation on the basis of a different principle of genuine harmony between philosophy and ritual life. Indeed, Philo's project is not an idiosyncratic enterprise of intellectual syncretism, sold out to non-Jewish commitments. It is a recognizable first-century cultural form and a perennial challenge to accept Second Temple Judaism as a genuinely philosophical worldview—indeed the most philosophical of all precisely because it is the most majestically monotheistic.

Philo was not the first or last to think so. The Jewish Aristobulus, surnamed "the Peripatetic," was propounding the same idea in the second century BC, arguing that the Jewish system as found in the Pentateuch was the "true philosophy."[15] The Book of Wisdom and even Ben Sira move in the same direction. Though little is oddly made of the fact, it is no incidental curiosity of ancient ethnographical opinion that, beginning already with Aristotle and his successor Theophrastus, the Jews were openly portrayed as a race of philosophers—and that, above all, by ancient philosophers themselves.[16] The Neoplatonist, Porphyry, was not later innovating when he credited the Hebrews for teaching men happiness by worshipping in a pure manner the "self-produced Ruler as God" (Frag. 323).[17]

The point here is simple. If liturgical praxis is in fact the real criterion of division, separating the pagan from the Jewish and Christian religious worldviews, with some important if implicit consensus at the level of metaphysical doctrine, it suddenly becomes important to think more closely about the whole non-biblical tradition of *pagan* monotheism, including its relation to Jewish worship. This has not been the approach heretofore, and the

---

15 See Arcari, "'Discorsi monoteistici' nell' antichità."
16 See Stern, "Hecataeus of Abdera."
17 Smith, *Porphyrii philsophi fragmenta*. See van der Horst, "Porphyry on Judaism."

exclusively Jewish data generally discussed constitute almost entirely highly polemical material that specifically targets pagan ritual practice.[18] This distorting lens must be more consciously borne in mind; in point of actual fact, in the intellectual climate of the New Testament world, under the governing thesis of the harmony of Aristotle and Plato, there was vast sympathy for the Aristotelian argument in *Metaphysics* book *Lambda* and enormous interest in the Platonic One. If the complex dynamics of New Testament Christology are accordingly to be correctly described, it is thus essential to engage and respect what John Dillon has termed "soft monotheism," the view held by basically all educated Greeks and Romans from the fifth century BC on.[19] It is a rather sobering reflection in this regard, and still more sobering in the face of ancient Jews' and Christians' strident accusations of the pagans' benighted polytheistic error, to recall that Celsus charged the Christians precisely with transgressing proper reverence of the one God (*Cels* 8.12–14).

"Soft Monotheism" and Liturgical Apophasis

Celsus was not alone. There was also the Jewish prosecution. If "Christological monotheism" is somehow cleared of the charge of erecting "two powers in heaven," one must thus also be ready to pause concerning the systems of Greek *gnosis* equally indicted in this Jewish attack.[20] Such a pause before the Greek evidence is salutary—and not only for the evident affinity of Gnosticism and Christianity in rabbinic eyes. The great influence and reach of pagan monotheism are also thereby displayed.

The impressive Orphic fragment cited in Pseudo-Justin (*Cohortatio ad Greacos* 15) is a fine place to start.

> One Zeus, one Hades,
> One Helios, one Dionysius,
> One god in all.[21]

This is a unique, inner-cultural form of so-called *interpretatio*, the famous process by which gods were identified with one another in antiquity (Roman

---

18 See chap. 8 in this volume.
19 Dillon, "Monotheism in the Gnostic Tradition."
20 On this theme, see Segal, *Two Powers in Heaven*; and Schäfer, *Zwei Götter im Himmel*. See also, more recently, the position of Waers, "Monarchianism and Two Powers: Jewish and Christian Monotheism at the Beginning of the Third Century." The hypothesis that Gnosticism ultimately has Jewish roots must not distract from its highly Hellenized character; cf. Fossum, *Name of God*.
21 For the original text, see Pouderon, *Ouvrages apologétiques*.

Jupiter with Greek Zeus, for example).²² Here the Orphic pantheon of divinities has collapsed and merged into one in a kind of pagan Sabellianism, culminating in a cultic exclamation—"One god in all"—similar to the εἷς θεός formula found in many inscriptions. The Christian apologist brings forward this text amid his polemic as a witness to the true doctrine of monotheism preserved by the Greeks despite all their endless errors. If this variety of Greek monotheism is not "Gnostic" in the technical sense, the Orphic mysteries nevertheless had a certain mytho-philosophical color that approximates the Gnostic milieu. Moreover, the hymnic character of the Orphic cult made it a privileged vehicle for "soft" monotheistic sentiment and *latreia*.²³ Liturgical *polyonymia* together with theogonic interest in world generation (e.g., the Derveni Papyrus) make the *Orphica* a prime point of reference, at least on the level of genre, for much of the material that we will see—not least the Christological hymns.

It is possible to go further, however. Dillon is prepared to acknowledge as "softly monotheistic" even genuinely Gnostic systems whose "reckless multiplication of immaterial and quasi-divine entities" and radically dualistic worldview one would have thought should plainly exclude them as candidates for a one-God doctrine.²⁴ He cites, for instance, an extraordinary passage found in the *Apocryphon of John* (2.33ff.) that contains perhaps the most comprehensive expression of Gnostic metaphysics. It is a highly apophatic, negative description of the Monad, Father of all, "existing in uncontaminated light, towards which no vision may gaze."

> We should not think of it as a god or like a god. For it is greater than a god, because it has nothing over it and no lord above it ... illimitable, since there is nothing to limit it, unfathomable, since there is nothing before to fathom it, immeasurable, since there was nothing before it to measure it, invisible, since nothing has seen it ... [and so on and so on for many more lines].²⁵

---

22 On the theme of *interpretatio*, see chap. 8 in this volume.
23 "There is only one common element to Stoics, Pythagoreans, Christians, Neoplatonists, and composers and singers of hymns for different cults (be it the Sun, Mithra, or any other supreme God). They all thought Orphica to be a very suitable vehicle for conveying monotheism while upholding the legitimacy of traditional genres" (Herrero de Jáuregi, "Orphic God(s)," 99).
24 Dillon, "Monotheism in the Gnostic Tradition," 69.
25 Translation by Marvin Meyer in *Nag Hammadi Scriptures*, 108. For a collation and the Coptic text(s), see Waldstein, *Apocryphon of John*, 20–22.

In a word, he is "the ineffable One, since no one can comprehend him, so as to speak about him, the unnamable One, since there is no one prior to him to give him a name."

If this text plainly crawls out of the "Platonic underworld," with traces of the *Parmenides*' negative predications clinging all about it, the same traces of theological negation just as plainly adhere to the lofty deity of 1 Timothy's doxologies: the "eternal, immortal, invisible, the only wise God," he "who alone has immortality and dwells in unapproachable light, whom no one has ever seen or can see" (1:17, 6:16). Romans and the Gospel of John are no less openly committed to this sovereign inaccessibility of God to the bodily senses. Pagans, Jews, and Christians were all of one mind: "No one has ever seen God." John 1:18, in fact, is in word-for-word agreement with the Jewish Aristobulus earlier cited, who notably continues the line (citing an Orphic tradition!): "No one has [ever] seen him ... he is seen only by mind" (Frag. 4).[26]

The way of pure mental apprehension naturally supported a strong apophatic fashion in Greco-Roman theology. This takes root at the latest with the Alexandrian Eudorus, who a generation before the turn of the era taught that the One transcends all attributes whatsoever.[27] Varro, at roughly the same time, imagined an aniconic golden age of Roman religion under Numa, in tune with right reason and resembling Jewish worship.[28] For Philo the aniconism of the Jewish cult was accordingly the uncontroversial, ritual expression of a commonly accepted philosophical truth, an ascetic training of the embodied soul for its rigorous intellectual ascent to the divine realm of the incomprehensible and unseen (Clement of Alexandria, *Strom.* 5.12). For "God is far away from all creation ... and the apprehension of him is removed to a very great distance from all human power of thought" (Philo, *Somn.* 1.66 [Colson/Whitaker, LCL]).

Theos Hypsistos

Even Gnostics knew that there was no lord above the invisible One. This transcendent pinnacle of the pantheon was not a theoretical abstraction, moreover. *Ho Theos* was an object of principled worship. Indeed, the most celebrated and widely attested expression of pagan monotheism takes a litur-

---

26 For Adela Yabro Collins's translation of the full text, see Charlesworth, *Old Testament Pseudepigrapha*, 2:840–41.
27 See Dillon, *Middle Platonism*, 126–29.
28 See Kooten, "Pagan and Jewish Monotheism."

gical form: the cult of *Theos Hypsistos*, "God Most High."²⁹ The profound and tantalizing links of this cult to Jewish synagogue worship pose an ongoing puzzle to scholars in many respects, yet the links are nevertheless certain: archeologically attested by hundreds of inscriptions and by the apparent derivation of the cult title from the Septuagint's rendering of *El Elyon*. With good reason, this phenomenon is frequently associated with the famous "God-fearers," those sympathetic pagans so vital to the narrative progress in Acts, who entertained religious perspectives that would have resonated favorably with Philo. (In this connection, there are more than passing contacts of *Theos Hypsistos* worship with the solar cult of the Therapeutae that Philo so esteemed.) The riveting religious phenomenon—which filled the eastern provinces and can be dated back to the second century BC—is, in any case, a uniquely suggestive hybrid. It is not coincidental that the worship of *Theos Hypsistos* is simultaneously the most Jewish and the most philosophical of the pagan cults, nor is it accidental that it is located in such proximity to the known context of primitive Christian missionary preaching: the Hellenistic synagogue. Luke is appropriately the NT author most attached to the *Hypsistos* title (Lk 1:32, 1:35, 1:76, 6:35, 8:28; Acts 7:48, 16:17).

An exceptional example of the philosophical orientation of this cultic tradition appears in a celebrated inscription discovered in Oenoanda in northern Lydia in 1971. The inscription itself dates from around AD 150 and was found alongside lamps inscribed to *Theos Hypsistos*. It records a widely circulated oracle that resonates perfectly with the pattern of negative predications (and *polyonymia*) already observed.

> Self-born (αὐτοφυὴς), untaught, without a mother, unperturbable, not contained in any name (οὔνομα μὴ χωρῶν), known by many names (πολυώνυμος,) dwelling in fire, this is God (τοῦτο θεός)... you who ask this question about God, what his essential nature is (ὅστις ὑπάρχει), he has pronounced that Aether is god who sees all, on whom you should gaze and pray at dawn, looking towards the sunrise. (SEG XXVII, 933)

This thematization of the unnamable essential nature of God is of special interest in its contact with the title *Theos Hypsistos*, which itself clearly functions as a conceptual cult instrument. A fundamental tension between apophatic philosophical accuracy and liturgical exigency is here plainly

---

29 Substantial research and controversy surround this famous cult. For an orientation, see Mitchell, "Cult of Theos Hypsistos"; idem, "Further Thoughts on the Cult of Theos Hypsistos"; and Lanckau, "*Hypsistos*."

exposed. The need to name a strictly unnamable God in order to worship him rightly is not an insignificant religious conundrum. It is, in fact, the all-important *crux* where the conjoined philosophical and cultic language of any true monotheism, be it Jewish or pagan, refuses to yield before Hurtado's analytical knife.

Divine Naming

The theological penumbra blurring Jewish and pagan enlightenment is evident in the very biblical parentage of the name *El Elyon*, which has deep roots in Israel's long struggle with Canaanite religion. Of course, within Judaism the name does not hold the privileged cultic place of the mysterious Tetragrammaton, uniquely revealed to Moses. It is accordingly not surprising if Philo not only represents the first philosopher to apply to God significant new alpha-privative predicates including "unnamable" (ἀκατονόμαστος) and "unutterable" (ἄρρητος) (*Somn.* 1.67), notions clearly crafted under the influence of Jewish ritual *praxis*. Philo also worries about the implicit theology suggested by "Most High" language. In the end, right philosophy must chasten itself, groping inwardly to come into alignment with the revealed Jewish cult of *HaShem*. For, though biblically sanctioned, the name *Theos Hypsistos* belongs to what Tibor Grüll designates as "Megatheism" and Reinhard Feldmeier calls "Machtpredikaten": a field of agonistic superlatives, divine epithets still trapped within a comparative paradigm with God as one entity among others.[30] Like the *megistos, megistos, megistos* of Hermes Tresmegistos, the taste for superlatives and one-upmanship challenges even those gods at the very top: Juppiter Optimus Maximus, *Dios kratistos megistos* in Greek (*INikaia* 1141), boasts but one *megistos*. The titular inflation, in fact, ultimately grows so bad that, as Robert Parker says, "The world becomes strewn with best and greatest and most manifest gods" (though whether *hypsistos* itself becomes a similarly promiscuous term is disputed).[31] This is the theology of an upward straining, monolatrous, natural religion, locked in an immanent cosmological frame of univocal being. In both theory and praxis, it falls short of the necessary transcendence, philosophically grasped by the *via negativa* and ritually expressed by the Jewish paradox of the Lord's unpronounceable Name.

The *Apocalypse of Abraham* is perhaps the single most revealing and underexploited theological artifact in comprehending the character of first-

30 Grüll, "'Monotheism' or 'Megatheism'?"
31 Parker, *Greek Gods Abroad*, 148.

and early second-century Palestinian monotheism, and notably its vital fusion with Hellenistic perspectives. Probably written in Hebrew sometime after AD 70, the text is neatly divided into two parts. In the first Abraham, the son of Terah, an idol maker in Ur, philosophically reasons his way to a discovery of the one God and Creator of all, reconfiguring a tradition of Jewish anti-idol polemic and Hellenistic religious critique.[32] In the second part, a divine revelation in the form of a voice from YHWH—"Abraham, Abraham"—greets the newly converted, former pagan, and the tale joins the story of the biblical account at Genesis 12:1, culminating in an act of celestial worship. The basic organization of the work is thus clear. Knowledge of the one true God is partitioned between two moments: a sort of philosophical *preambula fidei* and a supernatural apocalypse, leading to true *latreia*.

A great deal should be said here, but suffice it to note that, in the long celestial hymn sung by Abraham and his *angelus interpres*, the two fall prostrate in worship before the Lord. Their liturgy is of immense interest for its near exact echo of *Theos Hypsistos* theology.

> Eternal One, Mighty One, Holy El, God autocrat
> Self-originate, incorruptible, immaculate,
> Unbegotten, spotless, immortal
> Self-perfected, self-devised,
> without mother, without father, ungenerated
> exalted, fiery...
> El, El, El, El, Iaoel. (17.8–13)[33]

This incantatory fourfold repetition of El is rightly reckoned as a substitute for the Tetragrammton, as is the name Iaoel. The wanted liturgical fusion of philosophy and the divinely revealed, unpronounceable Name could not be more wonderfully evident.

Divine Name Theology

The application of all this is in no way hidden, and the Dionysian patronage should by now be clear. I am pushing toward a new context and register of reception for the New Testament's Christology of the divine Name. Rather than appropriating this all-important *topos* exclusively via the Hebrew canon

---

32 See chap. 8 in this volume.
33 Translation by R. Rubinkiewicz in Charlesworth, *Old Testament Pseudepigrapha*, 1:697. The text is only preserved in an Old Slavonic version.

and through an onto-unfriendly narrative theology, constructing "divine identity" like a character emerging in the immanent economy of Scripture, one might instead recognize in the hymnic conferral upon Christ of that "name above every other name" an outstanding biblical effort at hyper-predication. Long before Dionysius, in fact, Plato in the *Parmenides* had already broken this ground. He speaks notably of "a feat of expression ὑπὲρ ἡμᾶς, *beyond our power*," searching some elusive way to name the ultimate principle beyond both its positive designation as "The One" (τὸ ἕν), as well beyond as its negative labeling as the "The Not Many" (το μὴ πολλά) (*Parm.* 128b).[34] When Eudorus much later devised the language of ὁ ὑπεράνω θεός for the supreme Principle beyond Limit (Monad) and Limitlessness (Dyad), we are facing dogmatic Platonism's formulation of the surpassing feat. The Jewish tradition had its own transcendent formulation, of course. For this highest name in Philippians 2, a Name ὑπὲρ πᾶν ὄνομα, excels mere "Mega-theism" precisely by coinciding with Kyrios, the holy Name revealed from God's extra-worldly beyond.

Obviously, the Isaianic resonance of Philippians 2 contributes hugely to its full monotheistic impact, yet such a powerful scriptural orientation must not prevent us from seeing this poem as a variation on the Hellenistic synagogue hymn. This is Christology crafted in the world of God-fearing (*Theos Hypsistos* worshipping?) Gentiles. For Greek ears, τὸ ὄνομα τὸ ὑπὲρ πᾶν ὄνομα is simply hard to divorce from the hymnic philosophy that resonates in sites like Oenoanda, just across the Bosporus from Philippi. Here evangelical exegetes' profound aversion to Bossuet's Hellenistic "Christ cult" theory is a dangerous scholarly tic that risks radically re-inscribing pre-Hengel naiveté about a pure Palestinian (read "biblical") form of Judaism. When "Christological monotheism" serves as a bulwark against supposed Hellenistic infection—as it often does where the influence of Luther and Karl Barth is strong—our modeling of the first-century world has gone all catawampus. The fact is the Hellenistic synagogue was an institution even in first-century Jerusalem itself, as the Greek Theodotus inscription unambiguously proves and the *Apocalypse of Abraham* reflects. Bossuet was incorrect about the character of the Christ cult, yet the new *Religionsgeschichtliche Schule* has no less gravely mis-stepped in trying to drain primitive Christology of its profoundly Greek context.

The open paradox of Christ somehow receiving the name above every name—an evocative apophatic mystery recognized in Thomas' commentaries as we have seen—plots this Christological predication in plain view of

---

34 On transcendental predication in Plato, see Ferber and Damschen, "Is the Idea of the Good beyond Being?"

Hellenistic theorizing on the realm of divine being, which lies beyond all names. Philo's exegesis of Exodus 3:14, for instance, takes "I am He is who Is" as being "equivalent to 'my nature is to be, not to be spoken'" (ἴσον τῷ εἶναι πέφυκα, οὐ λέγεσθαι); for, as the exegete explains, "no personal name can be assigned to the truly existent" (τῷ ὄντι πρὸς ἀλήθειαν, *Mut.* 11). Philo's own handling of the Divine Name, *Kyrios*, ultimately assigns it to God's *Logos*: a scenario to which we must shortly return (e.g., *Conf.* 146). It is already possible, however, to observe the extraordinary theological power of Philippians 2 (no less than Eph 1:21 or Heb 1:3, for that matter), which proceeds one step beyond simply naming Christ with proper transcendental precision. I use the term "proceed" with calculated intent, for Paul's text expresses the divine being of the Son by an act of naming that transpires within *ho Theos*: God names himself.

A provocative gloss on this primordial operation of immanent theology (in the strongest etymological sense of a "Word of God") appears in the second-century Valentinian *Gospel of Truth*. "The Father's Name is not pronounced; it is revealed through a Son, and the Name is great ... Since the Father has no beginning, he alone conceived it for himself as a name before he created the eternal realms, that the Father's Name might be supreme over them."[35] Although the Aeons here, over whom the "invisible" Name reigns supreme, clearly insert us within the Gnostic myth, Valentinus himself, we must recall, was nearly elected pope in Rome, and his theology cannot simply be brushed aside as a homogenous heterodox lump. Paul's own Christological "name that is named" ὑπεράνω πάσης ἀρχῆς καὶ ἐξουσίας καὶ δυνάμεως καὶ κυριότητος in Ephesians carries manifest echoes of the same idea (cf. Aquinas, *Super. Eph.*). In any case, the many links observed between the *Gospel of Truth* and the *Odes of Solomon* attest once again to the site of this brand of theology in the hymnic setting of the synagogue and early Church.[36]

---

35 "The Name of the Father is the Son. In the beginning he gave a name to the one who came from him, while he remained the same, and he conceived him as his Son. He gave him his Name, which belonged to him. All that exists with the Father belongs to him. He has the Name; he has the Son. The Son can be seen, but the name is invisible, for it alone is the mystery of the invisible, which comes to our ears completely filled with it through his agency. Yet, the Father's Name is not pronounced; it is revealed through a Son, and the Name is great ... Since the Father has no beginning, he alone conceived it for himself as a name before he created the eternal realms, that the Father's Name might be supreme over them. This is the true Name, which is confirmed by his authority in perfect power. This Name does not derive from ordinary words or name giving, for it is invisible" (38.6–39.1). Translation by Marvin Meyer in *Nag Hammadi Scriptures*, 45–46. For the text, see Robinson, *Coptic Gnostic Library*. Cf. Smith, *Valentinian Christianity Texts*.

36 It is also important to "normalize" certain Valentinian views by regarding wider theological currents in antiquity to which this material is related. See Strousma, "Nameless God."

It is finally worth underlining in this connection not simply the motif of the Name, but also the special idiom of ὑπέρ/ὑπεράνω + πᾶς in the Philippians and Ephesians hymns, in reference to angelic powers, for it is singular usage within the NT and a type of superlative discourse with a suggestive affinity. The expression finds a remarkably strong parallel, for instance, in the extraordinary hymn preserved in *AposCon* 7.35.1–10.

> There is no god beside you alone,
> There is no Holy One beside you (ἅγιος οὐκ ἔστι πλὴν σοῦ),
> Lord God of knowledge (κύριος θεὸς γνώσεων),
>   God of holy ones,
> *Holy One above all holy ones* (ἅγιος ὑπὲρ πάντας ἁγίους)
> For those who have been made holy are under your hands.
> Honored and exalted exceedingly,
> Invisible by nature (ἀόρατος τῇ φύσει)
> ... unchangeable ... unlimited ... unapproachable ... without
>   beginning ... unending ...
> You are the Father of Wisdom (σὺ γὰρ εἶ ὁ σοφίας πατήρ),
> the Creator, as cause, of the creative workmanship through
>   a Mediator
> (ὁ δημιοργίας τῆς διὰ μεσίτου κτίστης ὡς αἴτιος)
> The God and Father of the Christ.[37]

This powerful monotheistic fusion of Greek philosophical concepts and biblically based liturgical praise (which in this case draws upon the very same chapter in Isaiah 45 as Philippians 2) is too vitally important to neglect in our reconstructions of primitive Christology.

Christ's Creative Agency and "Prepositional Metaphysics"

Divine Name theology in this broad philosophico-liturgical rereading is not the only key index of Christological monotheism that should be rethought and replotted in the habitat of the Hellenistic synagogue. Nor is ὑπέρ the only preposition freighted with philosophical import. Gregory Sterling has identified a phenomenon he labels "prepositional metaphysics"

---

[37] Translation by D. R. Darnell in Charlesworth, *Old Testament Pseudepigrapha*, 2:681–82. For the original text, see Metzger, *Les constitutions apostoliques*.

that is of extremely high relevance to the whole discussion.³⁸ The Colossians hymn is a stellar example, but the prayer formula in Romans 11:36 is more compact and will make the point: "From him and through him and to [or for] him are all things. To him be the glory forever. Amen." The three prepositions here—ἐξ, διά, and εἰς—belong to the standard philosophical lexicon of the era, designating the material, efficient, and final causes, respectively. When Paul employs this discourse as a doxology, he is thus enunciating a simultaneous doctrine of God and of creation (cosmogony) with conceptual tools borrowed from metaphysical speculation, mediated as an expression of praise via Hellenistic synagogue worship. This liturgical line of transmission is confirmed through the corpus of Greek synagogue prayers preserved in the *Apostolic Constitutions* (and Christologically touched up, most frequently with a διὰ Χριστοῦ).³⁹

In the present New Testament discussion, one of the cornerstones of "Christological monotheism" has, of course, been Paul's reconfiguration of the *Shema* around Jesus in 1 Corinthians 8:6. Here I would merely like to highlight that prepositional metaphysics forms the essential substructure of Paul's exegesis and that the distribution of causality is more interesting than generally thought.

> For us there is one God, the Father, *from whom* are all things and *for whom* we exist, and one Lord, Jesus Christ, *through whom* are all things and *through whom* we exist. (1 Cor 8:6)

Jesus Christ is here clearly inserted within a monotheistic frame. It is a reinforced monotheism, moreover, doubly expressed by both Jewish ritual and pagan philosophical language, identical to that seen in Romans 11. Jesus is designated precisely as the bearer of the Name and the instrumental, fashioning cause of all things.

Though it has thus far failed to enter the discussion, Philo, it happens, has a similar exegesis, parsing θεός and κύριος with a somewhat doubtful two-power language: "God (θεός) is the name of the beneficent power, and lord (κύριος) is the title of the royal power" (*Somn.* 1:163; cf. *Her.* 170). The issue that arises here is how this interpretative tradition of dividing in two the divine epithet "Lord God"—an exegesis shared with Paul—ultimately aligns with the instrumental preposition διά, for the provenance of the preposition in Philo is clear. His Middle Platonic *Logos*, who is at once a creature and a "second god" (δεύτερος θεός, *QG* 2.62), is that image of God and archetypal

---

38 Sterling, "Prepositional Metaphysics."
39 See, e.g., Kister, "Prayers of the Seventh Book of the *Apostolic Constitutions.*"

firstborn of creation, the highest intermediary being "through whom" or "by which (δι' οὗ) all the world was made (ἐδημιουργεῖτο!)" literally *demiurged* (*Spec.* 1.81; cf. *Somn.* 1.230). The *Logos* is "the shadow of God which he used like an instrument when he was making the world" (*Leg.* 3.31). The attribution of creative agency to Christ has become a solid peg in the arsenal of those touting his so-called divine identity. Whence an impertinent question: What resonance of Philo's Demiurge should be heard in this Christology, so bound to the ancient metaphysics of fashioning agency designated by διά? The awkward formulation ὁ δημιοργίας τῆς διὰ μεσίτου κτίστης ὡς αἴτιος seen above in the mongrel *Apostolic Constitutions* makes the question very real. Wishing Philo away as a diasporic aberration is the normal response but theologically and historically bad form.

Christ the Demiurge?

The right interpretation of Paul's διά leads to one final and decisive stop on the map of primitive "Christological monotheism." We owe to Philo the neologism "polytheism," which he coined as a slur against the pagans. It is only fair to give him a word in defining the Jewish monotheism around which our Christological variant wills to be built. And here nothing blurs the unmistakable, binary line that first-century Jews supposedly drew between the Creator and his creation like the baffling Philonic *Logos*. The extraordinary passage in Philo's *Quis rerum divinarum heres sit* brings his embrace of ambiguity to perfect expression.

> To his Word (λόγῳ), his chief messenger (ἀρχαγγέλῳ), highest in age and honor, the Father of all has given a special prerogative, to stand on the border and separate the creature from the Creator (τὸ γενόμενον διακρίνῃ τοῦ πεποιηκότος). This same Word both pleads with the immortal as suppliant for afflicted mortality and acts as ambassador of the ruler to the subject. He glories in this prerogative and proudly describes it in these words, "and I stood between the Lord and you" (Dt 5:5), that is neither uncreated as God (ἀγένητος ὡς ὁ θεὸς), nor created as you (γενητὸς ὡς ὑμεῖς), but midway between two extremes (μέσος τῶν ἄκρων), a surety to both sides. (*Her.* 205–206 [Colson/Whitaker, LCL])

An exuberance of additional Philonic descriptions complements this conceptual *metaxy* between the Father God and his world: the *Logos* is sometimes an angel, a high priest, a cutter, a glue, God's image, and, importantly, both the Name of God and the "first born son of God" (cf. *Conf.* 146–147). The infinite space that separates creation from its transcendent Creator poses an insuperable problem for philosophical thought, just as it does for worship: what emerges on both sides thus remains both unnamed and many named, in a kind of diffused *polyonymia*. If Philo accordingly throws a hundred metaphors at the problem and finally waffles with a *Logos* that is somehow both uncreated and created (a confusing successor to Antiochus of Ascalon's *Logos*, which had first fused together Plato's Demiurge and World Soul), this merely shows that even in the regime of a philosophy strengthened by the light of revelation in its firm vision of the Creator Lord, the obscure mystery of mediation was not yet fully disclosed. Like the mysterious "Angel of the Name" in the *Apocalypse of Abraham* and other Jewish traditions, Philo's cosmic pontifex lurks in a stupefying realm of divine darkness.[40] A new doctrine of the *Logos* was needed—and it was given. Philo's Demiurge stepped out of the One God's shadow.

John's Prologue and the still more concise prologue of Hebrews, approached in light of the Platonic Demiurge, opens up, as far as I can see, the great missing discussion in all our contemporary talk of "Christological monotheism."[41] The Demiurge, this monster *Mittelwesen* born of the *Timaeus*, is quite simply the cosmic limit case where everything must be decided[42]—and at Nicea it ultimately was (i.e., "the crisis of Christology").[43]

Hypostatic Being

It is of immense interest for this all-important decision that the author of Hebrews not only (1) conferred on Jesus, as Son, the excellence of a *name* that is immeasurably better than every angel's name and rank of being (τοσούτῳ κρείττων γενόμενος τῶν ἀγγέλων ὅσῳ διαφορώτερον παρ' αὐτοὺς κεκληρονόμηκεν ὄνομα, Heb 1:4; cf. 1:5–14), for which Jesus receives even the angels adoring worship (Heb 1:6), but also that the letter (2) adopted

---

40 On this motif, see Fossum, *Name of God*.

41 A helpful call to widen the religio-historical framework used for understanding John's *Logos* is found in Frey, "Between Torah and Stoa."

42 Mention should be made here of the Tübingen School of Platonic interpretation, with its paradigm-changing insistence on the "Unwritten Doctrines," which has helped prepare new insight into the important place of the Demiurge (and the *Timaeus*) and the doctrine of cosmic Intelligence in Plato's own integral thought. See the fourth part of Reale, *Toward a New Interpretation of Plato*, 305–434.

43 This κρίσις of a "decision about the Demiurge" may be regarded as my own attempt to clarify the somewhat uncertain title of the conference ("Crisis of Christology") for which this essay was prepared.

the cosmological, creative "demiurgical" διά, like Paul and like John in his Prologue (πάντα δι' αὐτοῦ ἐγένετο, Jn 1:3)—identifying Jesus as the divine Son δι' οὗ καὶ ἐποίησεν τοὺς αἰῶνας, "*through whom* he [ὁ θεός] also created the worlds" (Heb 1:2). Hebrews' language continues, calling Jesus the Son ἀπαύγασμα τῆς δόξης καὶ χαρακτὴρ τῆς ὑποστάσεως αὐτοῦ, "the reflection of his glory and imprint of his *hypostasis*" (Heb 1:3).

Ilaria Ramelli, in a groundbreaking study and monumental philological tour de force, has exposed a terminological triangle that tightly links this dense locution in Hebrews with unique hypostasis discourse in both Philo and later in Origen.[44] On the Philonic side (we will come to Origen below) we find in the *De aeternitate mundi* a discussion in which the unusual but fateful philosophical meaning of ὑπόστασις as an "individual substance," a sort of actually existing, self-standing reality, appears.[45] Philo applies this special meaning specifically to the example of an αὐγή—namely, to a "ray" or "beam of light"—in a consideration of whether the derivation of such light from its producer, for example, from a coal or a flame, results in only one hypostasis or two. Philo decides that there is in this case, but one ὑπόστασις: the αὐγή as a luminous flow from the source "has no existence of itself (καθ' ἑαυτὴν γὰρ ὑπόστασιν οὐκ ἔχει; *Aet.* §88)"; "it has no substance of its own" (ὑπόστασιν ἰδίαν οὐκ ἔχει; *Aet.* §92). The language serves a passing point in a larger cosmological discussion; still, the conceptual similarly of Philo's "light from light" language to Hebrews' compact Christological formula is striking. The imprint of the originating ὑπόστασις, like an ἀπαύγασμα = αὐγή radiating from divine glory, is invoked to describe the derivation of the Son from the Father. In view of the widely recognized parallels already binding Philo and Hebrews together—to the point that certain scholars even accept Philo's direct influence upon the letter—Ramelli is prepared to argue for dependence. At a more cautious minimum, it is justified to discern in the weighty appearance of ὑπόστασις in Hebrews 1:3 another prime hint of Greco-Roman philosophy's aboriginal role in the articulation of primitive Christology. In this case, we are handed a precious metaphorical and metaphysical clue elucidating just how the creative (demiurgic?) agent of the cosmos is related to God.

---

44 See Ramelli, "Origen, Greek Philosophy, and the Birth of the Trinitarian Meaning of 'Hypostasis.'"

45 The entire text of the *De aeternitate mundi* is deeply engaged with Plato's *Timaeus*. (See Ruina, *Philo of Alexandria*.) The specific context in *Aet.* §§85–93 is a discussion of this Stoic notion of *ekpyrosis*, the destruction of the world by fire, which helps explains the appearance here of the term ὑπόστασις, which is originally a Stoic concept. It is not impossible that Philo relies here upon some Stoic source.

It must not be overlooked, of course, that Hebrews' same graphic language of God's glory's luminous reflection was already adopted for *Sophia* in the Book of Wisdom.

> For she is a breath of the power of God, and a pure emanation (ἀπόρροια) of the glory (δόξης) of the Almighty, and therefore nothing defiled gains entrance into her. For she is a reflection of eternal light (ἀπαύγασμα γάρ ἐστιν φωτὸς ἀϊδίου), a spotless mirror of the working of God, and an image of his goodness. (Wis 7:25–26)

In Wisdom 7 the specific ontological ὑπόστασις terminology is never employed as it is in Philo and Hebrews. Nevertheless, since the work of Wilhelm Bousset, it has become customary for scholars to describe this sort of presentation of Wisdom and other similar personifications—the divine Name, *Shekina*, *memra*, *Logos*, and so forth—using the explicit language of "hypostasis."

The identification of such "hypostatic" agents within the Jewish sources today explicitly shapes even our interpretation of Philo. Roberto Radice, for instance, leans on this scholarly usage in explaining Philo's doctrine of creation when he asserts that Philo's "use of *logos* as a hypostasis is not paralleled in Middle-Platonic texts," whereas this usage "is consistently present in a Judeo-Hellenistic setting."[46] Radice mentions explicitly John's Gospel and goes so far as to say that the lack of Middle Platonic parallels constitutes, in his judgment, "proof of the biblical origin of *Logos* as a hypostasis, a notion that could not have been shared by thinkers outside the Mosaic tradition."

It is important, I think, not simply to conflate the technical, conceptual resources of an ancient metaphysical lexicon and a purely modern scholarly convention that is in fact open to question. Origen, not Philo and not John either for that matter, appears to be responsible for first describing the *Logos* using the explicit language of ὑπόστασις, with the considered and considerable ontological import that that word implied.[47] Indeed, Philo's understanding of the metaphysics of light, as just reviewed, runs counter to recognizing a "hypostatic" *Sophia* in the imagery of Wisdom 7.

It is therefore not without good reason when Hurtado, as a part of his broader opposition to Bousset's program, openly rejects the hefty language of "hypostases" in the study of Second Temple sources, together with its impli-

---

46 Radice, "Philo's Theology," 137.
47 See Ramelli, "Origen, Greek Philosophy, and the Birth of the Trinitarian Meaning of 'Hypostasis,'" 302–11.

cation of really existing and super-eminent *Zwischenwesen*, that is, "actual quasi-divine entities distinct from God."[48] Hurtado's preference for an alternative analytic terminology of "personified divine attributes" transposes the phenomenon to the rhetorical order and thus erases these characters as really existing mediating agent(s). This position abruptly cuts off Schäfer's suspect "Two Gods in Heaven" school but also construes the critical background of the Johannine Prologue as essentially being a form of Jewish "mythology," an imaginative manner of ancient Jewish discourse developed to describe the transcendent God's interactions with the world.[49]

Myth and Metaphysics

The distinctly mythical register of the *Timaeus*, with its talking Demiurge (41 A-B) and personified cosmic principles, is not irrelevant to Hurtado's concern and to the necessary analysis of person-like Jewish descriptions of divine agents/agency in the world. Particularly in consideration of the vast and creative body of speculative Hellenistic literature that Plato's cosmogonic presentation directly spawned, this point becomes all the clearer. By various routes the *Timaeus* itself had seeped into the Hellenistic Jewish bloodstream, not only in authors like Philo, whose highly metaphorical, personified doctrine of the *Logos* has been described, but even into the text of the Septuagint itself, notably in its version of the creation of the cosmos in Genesis.[50] Personified *Sophia* in the Book of Wisdom must surely take this into account. That John's own discourse about the creative *Logos* might also register as a form of mythic cosmogony is not at all simply to be discounted.

The extraordinary paraphrase of the Johannine Prologue preserved in Eusebius's *Praeparatio evangelica* (11.19) and attributed to Amelius, a third-century Platonist, avid reader of Numenius, and student of Plotinus in Rome, in fact helpfully exposes exactly how an ancient philosopher was likely to hear the Fourth Gospel's solemn opening words.[51] Amelius's literary lens leads him to perceive in John 1 precisely a *Timaeus*-inspired fusion of metaphysics and myth. Samuel Vollenweider offers the following assessment.

---

48 Hurtado, *One God, One Lord* (1998), 37.

49 Hurtado's perspective at this point swings in the direction of a Sabellian/modalist theology of the Jewish sources, as opposed to the contrasting Arian/subordinationist character of his more metaphysically realist Christology. See chap. 7.

50 See the important demonstration of the use of the *Timaeus* in the Greek version of Genesis 1–2, in Rösel, *Übersetzung als Vollendung*, 25–55.

51 For a useful survey of the frequent reception of John's Logos in a philosophical way, see Frey, "Between Torah and Stoa," 197–201.

> Es hat den Anschein, dass Amelios den johanneischen Logos mit dem Demiurgen, also dem Nūs, identifiziert, der seinerseits triadisch ausdifferenziert wird. Der Abstieg des Logos wäre dann genauer auf den zweiten oder dritten Demiurgen zu beziehen, der mit der Verteilung des Oberen im materiellen Kosmos beschäftigt ist, dabei selber aber in die Zerteilung emaniert. Der Brückenschlag vom demiurgischen Nūs zum Logos lag für den Plotinschüler nahe, hatte der Lehrer doch selber diesen der zweiten Hypostase zugeordnet. Zu diesem Schluss könnte auch die allegorische Exegese einer Passage aus dem Timaios geführt haben, nämlich der Rede des Demiurgen (λέγει) an die jüngeren Götter (41a). Die Wiederherstellung des Uranfänglichen schließlich, zu der Amelois am Schluss seiner Paraphrase die johanneische Ostergeschichte komprimiert, gewinnt von seiner neuplatonischen Metaphysik her klares Profil: Es handelt sich um die Rückwendung des demiurgisch tätigen Geistes zu seinem eigen Ursprung (ἐπιστροφή).[52]

Identification of John's *Logos* as the Demiurge, Numenius's Second God, and the detection of a grand *exitus-reditus* movement make the Gospel message appear to Amelius like any other religious myth worthy of reverent attention for a third-century Middle Neoplatonist's reflection. Specifically, the Prologue is an allegorical code for cosmogonic speculation. As a kind of variation on the Genesis story, John's account evidently held some discursive status similar to a text like the *Hypostasis of the Archons*, but much more sublime and succinct in diction.[53]

An orthodox rectification of this Gnostic-tending, demiurgical reading of John's assertions about the creative-Logos-made-man requires at least two critical adjustments. Both concern the evangelist's reality discourse.

---

52 "It looks as though Amelius identifies the Johannine *Logos* with the Demiurge, thus with the *Nous*, which for its part is distinguished in a triadic fashion. The descent of the *Logos* would then correspond more precisely to the second or third Demiurge, which is concerned with the repartition of the superior realm in the material cosmos, but itself thereby emanates into this partition. The bridge built from the demiurgic *Nous* to the *Logos* was not far for the disciple of Plotinus to find; indeed the teacher himself had assigned this to the second hypostasis. The allegorical exegesis of a passage out of the *Timaeus* could have also led to this conclusion: namely, the speech of the Demiurge (λέγει) to the younger gods (41a). The restoration of the primitive origin finally, to which Amelius compresses the Johannine Easter account at the end of his paraphrase, attains a clear profile from its neoplatonic metaphysics: it concerns the return of the demiurgically active spirit to its origin (ἐπιστροφή)" (Vollenweider, "Der Logos," 388).

53 On this text, see Bullard, "Introduction."

First, while the mythological shape of the Prologue's movement from eternal presence with God, to creation of the world, to *homo factus est* may be freely acknowledged, at least in the original sense of *mythos* as plotline and also in the stronger sense of *mythos* as specifically a story about the gods (Northrup Frye), the account must nevertheless also be understood—at least in pretension—as "a true myth ... a myth ... with this tremendous difference, that it really happened" (C. S. Lewis).[54] John's emphatic rhetoric of eyewitness at the climax of the same Prologue's incarnational movement alone compels this vital adjustment (Jn 1:14; cf. 19:35; 1 Jn 1–4). That an ancient philosopher and Platonist like Justin was so conscious of the issue and careful to disentangle his *Logos* theology and its particular claims, notably concerning the Incarnation, from the not entirely dissimilar world of Greco-Roman myth testifies to the concrete historical dimension that here somehow becomes a component of primitive Christian metaphysical reflection (cf. 1 *Apol.* 21–22, 33, 54, 67; *Dial.* 67).[55] The Gospel's historical claim thickens the ontic force of God's personified Word, over against all mythical renditions, even at the risk of metaphysical scandal of the mutable ἐγένετο of John 1:14. (Πῶς δ' ἂν ἔπειτα πέλοιτὸ ἐόν; πῶς δ' ἄν κε γένοιτο; Parmenides, *On Nature* 19.) This *Logos* really does become man.

The second adjustment is more delicate and difficult and entails a rethinking of the character of the second hypostasis. In good Platonic tradition, it was already perfectly clear for figures like Amelius and Numenius that absolute being, divine *esse*, stands apart from all Heraclitan mutability in this world of becoming and perishing. The transcendent oneness of divine *ousia* was accordingly also perfectly clear.[56] Based on the clarity of this *opinio communis*, Eusebius thus easily links the *Shema* of Deuteronomy 6:4 with Plato's monotheistic doctrine in the *Timaeus* and concludes that, in regard to the First Cause of all things, the agreement of Scripture and philosophy, Moses and Plato, admits no dispute (*Praep. ev.* 11.13–14).[57] With respect to the Second Cause, however, which, as Eusebius says, the Hebrew Scriptures call

---

54 Frye, *Great Code*, 31–52; Lewis, "Letter to Arthur Greeves." See also Lewis, "Myth Became Fact."

55 On Justin, myth, and the stories of the Incarnation, see chap. 3 in this volume.

56 "We ought to say of God, he is, and is in relation to no time, but in relation to eternity the motionless, and timeless, and changeless ... the sole self-dependent real 'Being,' having neither past nor future, without beginning and without end. Thus then ought we in worship to salute and address Him, or even indeed as some of the ancients did, *Thou Art One*, For the Deity is not many, as each of us is, a promiscuous assemblage of all kinds compounded of numberless differences arising in its conditions: but 'being' must be One, just as One must be 'being': for otherness, as a differentia of 'being,' inclines towards a becoming of 'not-being'" (*apud* Eusebius, *Praep. ev.* 11.11); translation by Edwin Hamilton Gifford, *Preparatio evangelica*, 529a.

57 On this point of Jewish-Greek monotheistic accord, see chap. 8 in this volume.

the Word of God, the alignment of thinking is a bit less clear and a great deal more problematic. Indeed, in the end, the Semi-Arian Eusebius cannot get beyond the *homoiousios* of his own ecclesial party any more than Numenius himself was able to imagine an immanent procession within the One God (*Praep. ev.* 11.15-19). Amelius was stalled in the same intellectual place.

The Gospel's decisive discursive shift out of the mythical mode and into a historical order of predication appears to me critical once more, for it works to loosen this conceptual logjam and enable the necessary speculative breakthrough to a Trinitarian form of monotheism. That breakthrough entails, as Aquinas would later formulate the matter, a sharp theoretical precision at once distinguishing and uniting the *ad extra* and the *ad intra* divine processions.[58] Moreover, this entails two related things: (1) surmounting the paired but contrasting *ad extra* explanations—namely (in the language of classical orthodoxy), the temptations of modalism (Sabellianism) and subordinationism (Arianism)—and (2) conceiving a clear notion of *ad intra* divine powers, a key insight already approached in distinct but converging ways by two Alexandrian thinkers, namely, Philo[59] and, before him, Eudorus, with his idea of τρόποι.[60]

---

58 In *ST* I, q. 27, a. 1, Thomas observes that both Arius and Sabellius make a similar error in imagining the *processio* of the Son *secundum quod est ad extra*; namely, as an *exterior effect* either resulting in (Arius) or imprinting itself upon some creature (Sabellius). The procession of divine Word, however, must instead be conceived of as *interior* to the simple act of divine *esse* (*ad intra*).

59 Philo's two powers—the beneficent and royal—remain *ad extra* principles of creation and providence. Philo interestingly claims to have this doctrine of the two powers through some mysterious religious experience. "But there is a higher thought than these. It comes from a voice in my own soul, which oftentimes is god-possessed and divines where it does not know. This thought I will record in words if I can. The voice told me that while God is indeed one, His highest and chiefest powers are two, even goodness and sovereignty. Through His goodness He begat all that is, through His sovereignty He rules what He has begotten. And in the midst between the two there is a third which unites them, Reason, for it is through reason that God is both ruler and good" (*Cher.* 27 [Colson/Whitaker, LCL]; cf. *Spec.* 3.1-6; *Som.* 2.252).

60 "Eudore entend rendre compte des données complexes du *Timée* de Platon. Il distingue deux modes (τρόποι) pour l'Un d'être principe: au sens absolu, où il se suffit à lui-même et ne tolère aucune prédication; d'une manière relative, par rapport aux êtres de l'univers. La distinction des *modes* de la principialité de l'Un permet de situer une certaine dualité dans le principe, en lui-même et en tant qu'il se distingue de la nature. Cette dualité préfigure les puissances qui instaurent une médiation entre la transcendance divine et l'immanence. Le principe est ainsi purement transcendant, il n'a dans son absolu aucun engagement dans le multiple. Puisque la génération est éternelle, l'Un doit en être le principe mais *selon un autre mode* qui n'est pas celui en vertu duquel il est l'Un absolument. Par conséquent, l'élément intermédiaire ne l'est que par rapport à nous, non par rapport au principe auquel il s'identifie et ne se distingue que par le mode. C'est toujours l'Un qui est principe, mais selon la diversité de ses modes. Il s'agit d'une pensée rigoureusement monothéiste, qui a laissé des traces profondes chez Philon" (Silly, *Les Grands Mystères*, 12).

Lumen de Lumine: The Metaphysics of a Metaphor (and the Mysteries)

It is highly significant in accomplishing the philosophical reconceptualization that I have described that the *Logos* in human (thus scandalously Heraclitan) flesh attracted to itself not only a clear historiographical claim but also a corresponding philosophical predicate. The same thick ontological term that Hebrews applied to the Father's own being was explicitly extended also to the Son: ὑπόστασις. Origen (as Ramelli has shown) was the first to take this momentous but carefully measured interpretative step. Following Philo's usage, Origen adopted a clear technical deployment of ὑπόστασις to mean an "individual substance," and this served him both to deny the reality of mythical pagan deities like Athena (*Cels.* 3.23, 8.67) and especially to assert, against Valentinian speculation, the full reality of the Son, as something substantially more than a mere (modalist) conception or appearance of the Father (e.g., *Comm. Jo.* 10.37.246).[61] Hebrews' construction ἀπαύγασμα τῆς δόξης καὶ χαρακτὴρ τῆς ὑποστάσεως [θεοῦ] was accordingly understood (1) to bear this same Philonic sense of ὑπόστασις and (2) to imply that the χαρακτὴρ/ἀπαύγασμα of the hypostatic being of the Father was more than an insubstantial projection or unstable luminous shadow. The Son-*Logos*-Christ, "made for a while lower than the angels" (Heb 2:7), is a truly existing, individual center of reality over against the Father.

In making this assertion, Origen clear-sightedly maintained, now in contrast to Philo, that in the case of the derivation of the Son from the Father as *Lumen de Lumine*, there were in fact two distinct ὑποστάσεις at play. The "character/imprint" of a divine hypostasis is a second divine hypostasis.

The Father's ὑπόστασις was clear on the surface. The author of Hebrews 1:3 already affirmed this philosophically in offering his metaphysical rephrasing of the Hellenistic Jewish rhetoric of Wisdom 7:25–26. The concrete reality of personified *Sophia* (is she hypostatic or not?) may remain a blurry question in the Hellenistic Jewish context. The Son's ὑπόστασις, by contrast, was clear. It is manifest from reading Hebrew's formula through the *Heilsgeschichte*, that is, by inference from John 1:14; namely, from the *Logos*'s self-revelation as a really existing, subsisting individual, manifest in an observable show of refulgent divine *doxa*. Hebrews' ἀπαύγασμα of the Father's ὑπόστασις (like the corresponding idiom of Johannine "glory") was thus recognized through the economy to be ontologically coequal with its source. Origen is firm on the point and directly opposes those who would deny it (δύο εἶναι

---

61 See Ramelli, "Origen, Greek Philosophy, and the Birth of the Trinitarian Meaning of 'Hypostasis,'" 303–6.

ὑποστάσεις, *Cels.* 8.12). For this reason, he was specifically accused of introducing in his (now lost) commentary on Hebrews "two principles of light," as Pamphilius records in his *Apology* for Origen (§50).⁶² In a revolutionary way, yet simply following the New Testament data, Origen establishes the divine agents of *Heilsgeschichte* as the substantial individual ἀρχαί of classical philosophical reason: Father and Son (and the Holy Spirit as well) are the really real personifications of the principles that underlie the cosmos.⁶³

In passing beyond Philo's earlier metaphysics of light, which was based on created analogies like candles and coals, Origen runs an obvious risk in maintaining the integrity of his strict montheism (at least inasmuch as he worships the Word). Specifically, the conceptual constellation of a hypostatic dyad posited between light and its reflection easily suits a demiurgic construction, for the metaphysics of light can literally be like playing with fire. A Gnostic reading of John's Prologue, in fact, takes the *Logos*'s birth as *Lumen de Lumine* to be an individual and substantial, thus implicitly hypostatic, but therefore derivative, created, subordinate and unequal *piece* of light: a divine "spark" (σπινθήρ).

In the *Apocryphon of John* 6:10–20, the birth of the Father's μονογενής from out of the light is described.

> This is the androgynous pentad, which is the decad of aeons of the Father. And Barbelon gazed intently into the pure light. And turned to him and gave birth to a spark (σπινθήρ) of light, resembling the blessed light, but he is not equal in greatness. The is the only-begotten One (μονογενής), who came forth from the Father, the divine self-Generated (αὐτογέντος), the first-born Son of all the Father's (sons), the pure light.⁶⁴

Unambiguously, this first-born Son of the "self-Generated" Father is Arian-type Demiurge, unmistakably unequal to his engendering principle. It is beside the point to seek to avoid the relevance of such a text and insist upon the later dependence of the *Apocryphon* upon John's Gospel. Exactly this permits us to see how the New Testament language was understood by ancient

---

62 Ramelli, "Origen, Greek Philosophy, and the Birth of the Trinitarian Meaning of 'Hypostasis,'" 343–44.
63 The *principles* referred to in the title of the Περὶ Ἀρχῶν are not the classic Platonic cosmogonic triad of the One, the Ideas, and Matter, but rather the Father, Son, and Holy Spirit. "Die Tatsachen der Heilsgesichte sind für ihn [Origenes] Mittel des Weltverstehens geworden, der *Siens*rang der Wesen wird als Funktion ihres *Gnaden*standes aufgefaßt" (Ivánka, *Plato Christianus*, 113).
64 Waldstein, *Apocryphon of John*, 40–41.

readers. And yet the critical adjustment in the *Apocryphon* from ἀπαύγασμα to σπινθήρ must above all be stressed, for the shifting metaphor represents a correlative shift in metaphysics. The "spark" breaks off and fragilely holds itself in being in radical independent distance from the self-begotten and spark-begetting fire. This Son-Spark, who is named as Christ, is unmistakably an inferior and subordinate creature. The New Testament's Father-Light with his *Logos*-radiance, by contrast, reveals an entirely different interrelation.

The implicit spring to a transcendent and immutable order of divine being is expressed in perhaps the most important of the many attestations of Hebrews 1:3 in Origen's entire corpus: a fragment of the Περὶ Ἀρχῶν (Frag. 33) so gloriously anti-Arian *avant le lettre* that in the height of the crisis Athanasius cited it verbatim (*Decret*. 27.1–2).

> If he is "the image of the invisible God" (εἰκὼν τοῦ θεοῦ τοῦ ἀοράτου), he is an invisible image (ἀόρατος εἰκών). I would even dare add that, being also similar (ὁμοιότης) to the Father, there is no time when he did not exist (οὐκ ἔστιν ὅτε οὐκ ἦν). For, when is it that God, who according to John is called Light ("For God is Light" [ὁ θεὸς γὰρ φῶς ἐστιν]), did not have an effulgence (ἀπαύγασμα) of his own glory, so that someone would dare posit a beginning (ἀρχὴν) of the Son, while he did not exist before (πρότερον οὐκ ὄντος)? When is it that the image and impression of the ineffable and inexpressible substance of the Father (ἀφθέγκτου ὑποστάσεως τοῦ Πατρὸς), the imprint (ὁ χαρακτὴρ), the Logos who knows the Father, did not exist? The person who dares say, "There was a time when the Son did not exist" (Ἦν ποτε ὅτε οὐκ ἦν ὁ Υἱός) should consider that he will also affirm, "Once upon a time Wisdom did not exist, the Logos did not exist, Life did not exist." (Cf. PG 25, 183)[65]

A dense concentration of closely related New Testament metaphors—image, reflection, imprint, light—converges here and is viewed by Origen through the lens of God's divine *ousia*, which is implicitly evoked by the locution in Colossians 1:15, "the invisible God." God is invisible: the alpha-privative ἀόρατος in Colossians intones the same negative theology of the divine nature by now familiar from other Hellenistic hymns and so many sources. Aquinas, in his comment on the verse, still understood this metaphysical message with perfect precision: *Deus dicitur invisibilis, quia excedit capacita-*

---

[65] Following the translation cited by Ramelli ("Origen, Greek Philosophy, and the Birth of the Trinitarian Meaning of 'Hypostasis,'" 310), but adjusted to conform more closely to the Greek.

tem visionis cuiuscumque intellectus creati, ita quod nullus intellectus creates naturali cognitione potest pertingere ad euis essentiam (*Super Col.* §1.4). We must thus recognize here the habitual shorthand for an affirmation of God's divine being beyond created being. Embracing this same register of language and perceiving the provocatively paradoxical Pauline hyper-predication of an ἀόρατος εἰκών, Origen recognizes that the Son as God's effulgence must inevitably co-eternally share the Father's nature as mysterious invisible light.[66]

An orderly ontological balancing out of the hypostatic and essential planes of divine being was obviously not the work of a day. (Here Ramelli seems a bit optimistic about Origen's achievement.) Above all, time was required to articulate the elegant entanglement on the hypostatic order of the distinct immanent and economic modes of divine action, together with the clean separation of created and uncreated essence in this special locos of divine-cosmic union, an intersection that mysteriously cuts across God's *ad extra* and *ad intra* modes of being in the very person of the eternal Son.[67] Still, the Trinitarian coordinates of a full Christological monotheism are all exegetically and doctrinally in place.

The topos of light, which so decisively controls Origen's thought and ultimately entered the canonical formula of the creed, and which thus reveals itself as a locus *éminentissme* of Christological reflection, is in no way less important than the hymnic theology, with its philosophical negations and prepositional metaphysics—at least if the Demiurge question is to find a convincing monotheistic resolution on clear New Testament terms. "God is light and in him there is no darkness at all" (1 Jn 1:5; cf. Jn 1:5; Heb 1:3). "He alone has immortality and dwells in unapproachable light (φῶς οἰκῶν ἀπρόσιτον)" (1 Tm 6:6). Conceiving the *Logos* as the Father's reflected Light is not simply a pretty metaphor (although it is that), as our exegesis too often

---

[66] Thomas's refutation of Arianism on the basis of Col 1:15 retrieves Heb 1:3 as a key intertext and explicates a similar reasoning to that of Origen: *Quantum ad secundum sciendum est quod Arriani hoc verbum male intellexerunt, iudicantes de Dei imagine secundum imagines quae fiebant ab antiquis, ut viderent in eis charos suos subtractos sibi, sicut et nos facimus imagines sanctorum, ut quos non videmus in substantia, videamus in imagine. Et ideo dicunt quod invisible est proprium patri, filius autem est primum visibile, in quo manifestatur bonitas patris, quasi pater sit vere invisibilis, filius vero visibilis, et sic alterius essent naturae. Hoc autem excludit apostolus ad Hebr. I, 3 dicens: qui cum sit splendor gloriae, et figura substantiae eius, et cetera. Et sic est imago non solum Dei invisiblis, sed etiam ipse est invisiblis sicut pater. Qui est imago invisiblis Dei* (*Super Col.* §1.4).

[67] See Ramelli ("Origen, Greek Philosophy, and the Birth of the Trinitarian Meaning of 'Hypostasis,'" 334) for an interesting text in Porphyry's Κατὰ Χριστιανῶν, in which Porphyry openly "criticizes the Johannine presentation of Christ as God's Logos by reading it through the lenses of Origen's understanding of the Son having the same οὐσία as the Father but a different ὑπόστασις."

lazily takes it. Primitive Christology is here once again in direct contact with the cosmological discourse of ancient philosophy.[68] And, as always, Greco-Roman *latreia* is not far behind.

The explicit naming of *Theos Hypsisos* as Aether, already cited, a divinity who sees all and who "dwells in fire," reveals Greek worship of the One God in the form of a solar cult. It is a connection at least as old as the pagan monotheism of Ahkenaten, and it reached at least as far as Julian's extraordinary, philosophical "Hymn to King Helios" (*Oration* IV).[69] What explains this liturgical tradition? It is much more interesting and more sophisticated than a crude vestige of ignorant, servile worship of stars. It hides, mystery-like, a Platonic philosophical topos. The "hyper-cosmic sun" evidently animates this solar cult, and perhaps others as well, like the Mithraic mysteries of *Sol Invictus*. Hans Yohanan Levy and others have shown in this connection that in the theurgic Middle Platonic milieu a distinction was made "between two fiery bodies: one possessed of a noetic nature and the visible sun" and that Plato's explicit image of the sun to depict the ideal form of the Highest Good stands behind this usage (*Rep.* 508A).[70] A pair of twinned lights, one seen and one unseen, one belonging to the cosmos and one transcendent beyond, thus stood in some intimate relation of hyper-predication.

> Of light [Moses] says that it is beautiful pre-eminently (ὑπερβαλλόντως καλόν): for the intelligible (τὸ νοητὸν) as far surpasses the visible in the brilliancy of its radiance (λαμπρότερον

---

68 See Corey, *Light from Light*. Beginning with the pre-Socratics, continuing through the Hellenistic period, and down to the Greco-Roman age, light and the fiery *aether* were central to the speculations of philosophers about the character of the absolute *arche* and the realm of the divine. See also, for a related approach to patristic Christology, Lyman, *Christology and Cosmology*.

69 The opening period of Julian's encomium sufficiently captures the mood: "This divine and wholly beautiful universe, from the highest vault of heaven to the lowest limit of the earth, is held together by the continuous providence of the god, has existed from eternity ungenerated (ἀγέννητος), is imperishable for all time to come, and is guarded immediately by nothing else than the Fifth Substance [i.e., aether] whose culmination is the beams of the sun; and in the second and higher degree, so to speak, by the intelligible world; but in a still loftier sense it is guarded by the King of the whole universe, who is the centre of all things that exist. He, therefore, whether it is right to call him the Supra-Intelligible (τὸ ἐπέκεινα τοῦ νοῦ), or the Idea of Being, and by Being I mean the whole intelligible region, or the One (τὸ ἕν), since the One seems somehow to be prior to all the rest, or, to use Plato's name for him, the Good; at any rate this uncompounded cause of the whole reveals to all existence beauty, and perfection, and oneness, and irresistible power; and in virtue of the primal creative substance that abides in it, produced, as middle among the middle and intellectual, creative causes, Helios the most mighty god (Ἥλιον θεὸν μέγιστον), proceeding from itself and in all things like unto itself" (§132D [Henderson, LCL]).

70 Levy, *Chaldean Oracles and Theurgy*, 151–52.

τε καὶ αὐγοειδέστερον), as sunlight assuredly surpasses darkness and day night, and mind (νοῦς), the ruler of the entire soul, the bodily eyes. Now that invisible light perceptible only by mind (τὸ δὲ ἀόρατον καὶ νοητὸν φῶς ἐκεῖνο) has come into being as an image of the Divine Word (θείου λόγου γέγονεν εἰκὼν) Who brought it within our ken (διερμηνεύσαντος τὴν γένεσιν αὐτοῦ): it is a supercelestial constellation (ὑπερουράνιος ἀστήρ), fount of the constellations obvious to sense. It would not be amiss to term it "all-brightness" (παναύγειαν), to signify that from which sun and moon, as well as fixed stars and planets draw, in proportion to their several capacity, the light befitting each of them: for that pure and undiluted radiance (αὐγῆς) is bedimmed so soon as it begins to undergo the change that is entailed by the passage from the intelligible to the sensibly discerned, for no object of sense is free from dimness. (*Opif.* 8.31 [Colson/Whittaker, LCL])

The heavenly bodies, of course, are angelic minds, and a "font of the perceptible stars" (πηγὴ τῶν αἰσθητῶν ἀστέρων), a cascade of light, *a celestial hierarchy* pours down from the pure divine mind; it spills into and brightens the dim cosmos, as created natures are able to receive the light of the Nous, reflecting the radiance that comes down from the one whom Philo calls elsewhere simply "the intelligible sun" (τὸν νοητὸν ἥλιον): the "Father and creator, the uncreated God ... the truly existent One," he who alone is possessed of "unchanging being" (*QG* 4.1). The visible sun is itself but the image of this invisible, rational light: the divine *Logos*.

What might primitive Christology, with its characteristic Johannine discourse of light, know of this "supercelestial star" and cosmic image of the invisible *Logos*? When the early Christians met on "the first day of the week, which is called the day of the Sun" (Justin, 1 *Apol.* 67), convening *ante lucem* and singing hymns to Christ *quasi deo* (Pliny, *Ep.* 96), hymns like Philippians 2, Colossians 1, and the Φῶς Ἱλαρόν—the earliest Christian hymn outside the New Testament (cf. *AposCon* 8.34), a graceful song in praise of the divine light sung at the setting of the sun—to whom and what did they understand themselves to be offering their cult and worship?[71] In Asia Minor, Pliny decided that whatever their creed might be (*qualecumque essent quod faterentur*), if they would not call upon and adore the gods, offer incense to Caesar, and worship the images and statues, they deserved death. Some complied; others courageously embraced their mortal fate. They chose

---

71 The Φῶς Ἱλαρόν already considered an ancient hymn when Basil invoked it in support of the divinity of the Spirit on the basis of the song's second strophe (*On the Holy Spirit* §§27, 73).

to die rather than betray the "gladsome light" who was the reflection of the *immortal* Father's glory (φῶς ἱλαρὸν ἁγίας δόξης / ἀθανάτου Πατρός): Jesus Christ, who rose again like the dying and rising sun.

As for Pliny and judges like him, his theological discernment was not optimally shrewd. "The man is not worthy of the name of philosopher who publicly bears witness against us in matters which he does not understand, saying that Christians are atheists and impious," Justin says in his *Second Apology* (2 *Apol.* 3 [ANF]).[72] Who is worthy of that noble name *philosopher*, and who truly understands the divine? The one whose life and death is ordered toward right worship of the one true God. More revealing than any literary, angelic "refusal of worship motif" is thus the real, life-and-death decision of those followers of the "divine philosophy" (φιλοσοφιάν θείαν) of Christ, who refused to offer false worship and so embraced the fate of the archetype of the philosophical life. For "Socrates ... was accused of the very same crimes as ourselves. For they said that he was introducing new divinities and did not consider those to be gods whom the state recognized" (2 *Apol.* 10 [ANF]). And yet, although Socrates "exhorted them to become acquainted with the God who was to them unknown, by means of the investigation of reason," his teaching remained the possession of an elite, and no one was bold to die for Socrates' doctrine of the Father and Maker/Demiurge of all (πατέρα καὶ δημιουργὸν παντῶν). The eternal Son's same doctrine of the one Creator and Father was more powerful, however, and was made publicly known, so that "not only philosophers and scholars believed, but also artisans and people entirely uneducated" (2 *Apol.* 10 [ANF]). Like a new nation of philosophers, these simple and wise believers boldly held suffering and death in lofty contempt, choosing to die in the manner of their "wise king" (cf. Mara bar Serapion) in order to participate and imitate (ἡ μετουσία καὶ μίμησις) bodily in the grace of the *Logos*'s own passion. The Christological monotheism of the martyrs' sacrificial worship of God's Wisdom made flesh, their self-offering to that divine Reason that is wiser than men, stood at the center of the new cult and mystical form of true spiritual *latreia* (ἡ λογική λατρεία; cf. Rom 12:1).[73]

---

[72] On the bewildering issues surrounding the authorship of the *Second Apology*, see Ehrhardt, "Justin's Martyrs Two Apologies."

[73] "I confess that I both boast and with all my strength strive to be found a Christian; not because the teachings of Plato are different from those of Christ, but because they are not in all respects similar, as neither are those of the others, Stoics, and poets, and historians. For each man spoke well in proportion to the share he had of the spermatic word, seeing what was related to it ... Whatever things were rightly said among all men, are the property of us Christians. For next to God, we worship and love the Word who is from the unbegotten and ineffable God, since also He became man for our sakes, that becoming a partaker of our

Conclusion:
Neoplatonism *avant le lettre*?

What has Athens to do with Jerusalem? Reimagining the Areopagite as a genuine biblical thinker rather than a raw Neoplatonic plant signals a momentous paradigm shift, I have contended. The Bible and philosophy are not so fundamentally opposed. In this line, the salvation historical turn that an Origen ultimately took in naming Father, Son, and Holy Spirit as the three ἀρχαί from which, through which, and for which the whole of the cosmos exists might even signal a reason to rethink the old trope of Plato reading Moses. Indeed, Porphyry it seems later liked Origen's Christian cosmology enough to mock-up a hypostatic trinity in Neoplatonic flavors and retroject it into Plotinus.[74] So much for Hebrews despoiling Egyptians and Christian plundering the Greeks.[75] A pagan Phoenician (i.e., syncretistic Syrian) is now pilfering ideas from an Alexandrian Christian, to the profit of a philosopher from a Roman city (Lycopolis) that was the center of Mani's Gnostic missionary work on the Nile. It becomes hard to say which is the direction to Athens.

---

sufferings, He might also bring us healing. For the seed and imitation impacted according to capacity is one thing, and quite another is the thing itself, of which there is the participation and imitation according to the grace which is from him" (Justin, 2 *Apol.* 13 [ANF]).

[74] Ramelli has provocatively shown that the celebrated passage in Plotinus's *Enn.* 5.1— *locus classicus* of the "Neo-Platonic Trinity," a text that Porphyry titled Περὶ τῶν ἀρχικῶν ὑποστάσεων and that speaks of the three principal ἀρχικαί, the One, the Intellect, and the Soul—far from being a testimony to Plotinus's articulation of a conceptual system later aped by Christian theologians, in fact never employs the ("orthodox") language of ὑπόστασις in a technical sense to designate his three principles. This suggests, as Ramelli sees, that Porphyry "inspired by Origen, whose work he knew quite well . . . may have had in mind Origen's Trinitarian technical terminology of ὑπόστασις and his philosophical masterpiece the Περὶ ἀρχῶν" (Ramelli, "Origen, Greek Philosophy, and the Birth of the Trinitarian Meaning of 'Hypostasis,'" 331–34). Porphyry even tried unconvincingly in his *History of Philosophy* to cover his traces and attribute Origen's hypostatic doctrine to Plato directly. The separation of Origen the Platonist from the Christian doctor is a problematic interpretation of the evidence from Porphyry and symptomatic of the tortured views of Hellenism's relation to Christian thought. See Ramelli, "Origen, Patristic Philosophy, and Christian Platonism." Taking Origen, the student of Ammonius Saccas, to be head of the catechetical school at Alexandria and not a pagan of the same name, it is interesting to note that the only view attributed to him by pagan authors is to have considered the first principle not as the One beyond both intellect and being, but rather as itself the supreme intellect and first being. Accordingly, he would be more in line with traditional "Middle" Platonic (and Christian) conceptions than with the ideas of Plotinus. Cf. Proclus, *In Platonis Theologiam* 2.4.

[75] Eusebius ironically adopted Porphyry's exact title of *Enn.* 5.1 as his own title for Book 11 of the *Praeparatio evangelica*, where he attempts to demonstrate that the Platonic triad depends on "Jewish oracles." On the motif of despoiling the Egyptians, pioneered by Origen (*Epistula ad Gregorium*) and taken up by Augustine, see Allen, "Despoliation of Egypt."

More important for my purpose than deciding who is stealing from whom is simply insisting upon the irreducible and omnipresent philosophical and cosmological, speculative interests of the Greco-Roman / New Testament world. That Athanasius adopted a prepositional theology reminiscent of Paul (later taken up and developed by Basil) should convince us of his bona fides as a biblical thinker. Origen's view of John's ἐγώ εἰμι as a Hellenistic Jewish exegesis of the divine name in Ex 3:14 is also not eisegesis in my estimation. One need read only a few pages of Philo.

If in this Hellenistic philosophical milieu the Demiurge represents the key point of decision, Christology faces a real challenge, as Church history proves. For the ecclesially minded exegete the basic conciliar lines are nevertheless clear. No amount of creative agency or even *latreia* accorded by Christians to Christ can successfully assert his divinity without some idea of divine homo-*ousia*. And that requires some proto-Dionysian, hymnic grammar of transcendent being or Thomistic-like notion of *ipsum esse subsistens*. Otherwise, the *Logos* will remain an Arian Artisan and worshipful superangel: a divine spark and heavenly sun, above all of creation, but merely atop and not entirely beyond the cosmos.

In truth, Jesus Christ is the *ad extra* refulgence of an *ad intra* imprint of eternal intelligible light. He thereby shines a mysterious light of eternal glory into the created cosmos. Amelius discerned in John's Gospel's motif of Jesus' return to the Father a mythical image of the great cosmic return: the return of all things back into the *arche*. "When I am lifted up from earth, I will draw all men to myself" (Jn 12:32). The pagan philosopher was not entirely off the mark. God's creative Word is also God's agent of redemption: the One *from whom* and also *for whom* all things are.

Pagan philosophy knew this without knowing it knew, like its worship of the *Agnostos Theos* in Acts 17:23.[76] Scant notice is given, even in the new "Pauline Dionysius" paradigm, but the architectonic *exitus-reditus* dynamic in the opening sentence of the *Celestial Hierarchy* is articulated by a citation of Romans 11:36 (minus the διά).[77] "From him and for him all things are." In other words, Paul's biblical metaphysics, or better, Paul's classical

---

[76] The negative theology implicit in this divine title reveals Acts' scene at the Areopagus as suggesting Dionysius's specific program of apophatic theology, not just providing a persona for the pseudepigraphal ploy. The still classic, if somewhat dated, study on this title remains Norden, *Agnostos Theos*.

[77] Stang (*Apophasis and Pseudonymity*, 140) is alert to the issue, though *exitus-reditus* as such is not one of the major "Neoplatonic" categories that he concentrates upon. As he perceptively sees, however, the process of divinization through participation in the Body of Christ represents a native Christian idiom, at once Pauline and Dionysian, for the back end of this return movement to God.

metaphysics (which through Paul appear in the Bible) help animate this supposed sixth-century motif (which later becomes a thirteenth-century motif in Thomas's *Summa*), no less than the philosophical preacher of Acts 17 also activates other major movements in the Dionysian corpus identified by Constas and Stang. The cosmic return to the One Cause from whom all creatures came is not an unbiblical way of thinking.

If this is Neoplatonism *avant la lettre*, or rather "Middle Platonism," to employ the misleading pedagogical term,[78] Romans 11 remains an essential control on our designs of Christological mediation. On the one hand, the διά in 11:36 makes no mention of Christ but only the supreme God: first and final and also instrumental cause. On the other hand, it is just this perspective that clarifies Paul's innovation in 1 Corinthians 8:6. For Paul's *de Deo Uno* of the cosmic wellspring and telos is not yet the full Christian solution. The New Testament collectively communicates an experience of Israel's Lord and his *Logos* that at once explodes the doxographical frame of Greco-Roman philosophy yet already begins reassembling the conceptual pieces in a momentous doxological act of creative destruction. In Christ a new structure of mediation between the One God and the world is established, surpassing the gift of the Name made to Moses. And just as that true religion of Moses was radically reconfigured yet not damaged but rather fulfilled, so the landmarks of true philosophical doctrine, coordinate with that true religious worship (even a new *Shema*), remain unmoved yet interiorly transformed in the alternative Christian vision: suffused with new clarity, content, and force, and recalibrated to a new ritual system based on Christ's cross.

The final fate of Philo's ambiguous *Logos* was that it quietly disappeared, rightly finding no doctrinal disciples, yet the Middle Platonic double-mindedness of this Jewish contemporary of Jesus forever marks the essential theological fork in the road. On the one hand, Neoplatonic thought went enthusiastically down the path of successive emanations, first distinguishing the Demiurge from the Highest God as a buffer from the stain of matter (Numenius) before finally interring this Artisan as an obsolete cosmogonic relic (Porphyry).[79] The Christian confession, by contrast, boldly resisted this turn—with its ultimate dead end and inert transcendent Monad—as it also

---

[78] It should stand as a scholarly caution in regard to this artificial schema of periodization, drawn from courses on the history of Western Philosophy, that no less an expert than A. H. Armstrong eventually came to see that, regarding the *Logos*, "the doctrine he had attributed to Plotinus was in fact Philo's," as Michel René Barnes observes ("Rereading Augustine's Theology of the Trinity"). Barnes himself is determined to limit excessive constructions of Augustine's Neoplatonic cast of mind.

[79] On this history of the Demiurge concept, see the helpful study of O'Brien, *Demiurge in Ancient Thought*.

defied the Arian temptation, instead planting divine mediation firmly in the *manhood* of a divine *Logos* through the theurgic mechanism of a hypostatic grace: a deifying solution never even faintly dreamed of before.[80] For as the Gospels reveal and as Paul learned at Athens, there are more things in heaven and on earth (such as heaven come down to earth) than the philosophers (even Jewish ones) ever dared to imagine.

---

80 See the fine discussion of Pauline and Platonic theurgy in Stang, *Apophasis and Pseudonymity*, 105–16.

CHAPTER 10

Two Loci of Greco-Roman Jewish Monotheism

Over the past decades, a now senior generation of scholars has devoted immense energy to providing an improved reconstruction of Second Temple Jewish monotheism. The project is of obvious interest not only for understanding the theology of early Christian texts, but also for understanding Jesus' own ideas about himself and Israel's God. While a loose federation of exegetes working on these problems has often been lumped together as the so-called Early High Christology School—a group broadly upholding the sudden appearance of Christological claims to divinity, audaciously articulated within the parameters of a strict Jewish monotheistic ethos—these scholars have met resistance precisely on the all-important characterization of this "monotheistic" context. Accurately understanding and describing the role played in Greco-Roman Judaism by principal agents and heavenly mediator figures has been a key point of contention, and for the moment it is not clear that a new generation of scholars has yet found a compelling way forward.

In this essay I pursue a slightly new line of approach, highlighting the Temple in Jerusalem as a decisive locus of Jewish monotheism, in both its clarity and complex nuance, while tracing its momentous metaphoric transference onto Jesus. In various ways the Temple bears the functional marks of the controversial mediator figures while also embodying with unusual force the highly exclusive devotional praxis of first-century Jewish religion. In assimilating both the immanent and transcendent dimensions of YHWH's presence in the Temple, a model of primitive Christological monotheism was thus enabled that gave powerful articulation to Christian belief in YHWH's divine incarnation, respecting and asserting both the divinity and the mediating humanity of Jesus.

The argument unfolds in three stages. First, I will expose the state of the Christological debate, noting the central problem of satisfactorily situating *Mittelwesen* on a Greco-Roman Judaic grid. Next, I will reorient the discussion around the Temple in two complementary ways: as a locus of monotheistic Jewish identity and as a locus of divine-human mediation. Finally, I will briefly suggest how this multivalent Temple logic is reapplied in the Gospel of John to give expression to finely nuanced Christological convictions.

From Polytheism to Monotheism and Back Again?

The present state of Christological debate owes much to a foundational disagreement between Wilhelm Bousset and Larry Hurtado. Bousset's classic text, *Kyrios Christos: A History of the Belief in Christ from the Beginnings of Christianity to Irenaeus*, first published in 1913, in fact represents the determined target of Hurtado's substantial oeuvre.[1] One of his earliest publications was a direct critique of Bousset's influence on New Testament Christology (1979), and in an agenda-setting 1981 paper, Hurtado honed in again expressly on "the mistakes of the scholars of the *religionsgeschichtliche Schule*," clearly taking Bousset as a leader of the pack.[2] From Hurtado's vigorous reaction to Bousset's *Schule* emerged a so-called New *religionsgeschichtliche* School, which takes aim at a number of problematic assumptions and positions.[3] At the heart of these contested perspectives stands a complete remodeling of the emergence of primitive Christology. Two salient features of the new paradigm are immediately clear. It is now imagined as an eruption, not a slow corruption. It is also now reconceived within a starkly Jewish, monotheistic context, rather than a promiscuously pagan, polytheistic frame.

The programmatic *One God, One Lord* (1988) was a kind of breakthrough book for Hurtado, which, alongside his later *Lord Jesus Christ* (2003), stands as his settled answer to Bousset's *Kyrios Christos*.[4] Hurtado

---

1 Bousset's work was recently republished as part of Baylor University's new *Library of Early Christology*, alongside a significant collection of thirty-two of Hurtado's essays: Hurtado, *Ancient Jewish Monotheism*.

2 Hurtado, "New Testament Christology"; and idem, "Study of New Testament Christology," 188–90.

3 The popular "New History of Religions School" designation can be traced to Martin Hengel's dust-jacket blurb for Hurtado, *One God, One Lord*, whence it was taken up by Jarl Fossum, "New *Religionsgeschichtliche Schule*," 638.

4 Hurtado, *Lord Jesus Christ*.

urges two points specifically about Second Temple Jewish monotheism: it held together, namely, "(1) a remarkable ability to combine a genuine concern for God's uniqueness with an interest in other figures with transcendent attributes which are described in the most exalted terms and which we may call 'principal agent' figures who are even likened to God in some cases; and (2) an exhibition of monotheistic scruples, particularly and most distinctively in public cultic/liturgical behavior."[5] The accommodation of Jesus as such a "principal agent" figure *together with* the public, corporate worship offered to him alongside YHWH is the striking reconfiguration that one finds among the early Christians. Hurtado likes to call this novel pattern of worship "binitarian" or (in his later work) "dyadic" in form, a "Christological mutation" in the shape of Second Temple Judaism.

In leaving space in his vision for these "principal agent" figures, Hurtado retains something of Bousset's emphasis on *Mittelwesen*, and Hurtado is even ready to describe "this ancient Jewish outlook as constituting a distinctive version of the commonly attested belief structure ... involving a 'high god' who presides over other deities."[6] The decisive difference for Hurtado is the Jewish reservation of worship exclusively to this "high god," identified as YHWH, to the cultic neglect of all other divine and heavenly beings. It is, correspondingly, also the exclusive "dyadic" worship accorded to Jesus and YHWH together that represents the critical datum on the Christological end. Hurtado's taxonomy has accordingly evolved so that he now finds it best to speak of "pagan monotheism," "ancient Jewish monotheism," and "early Christian monotheism."[7]

This triple distinction is useful and names distinctive patterns, though the interpenetration of ideas and behavior should not be underestimated. Certainly, the fact that in the pagan context certain types of monotheistic (or minimally, "henotheistic") rhetoric and praxis can also be found should not be left out of account in thinking of early Christology's formative setting.[8] An overt philosophical resonance here comes to the fore, too often underplayed in the current analysis. The reorganization of an ancient "prepositional metaphysics" around the person of Jesus in texts like Colossians 1:16 is an eminent illustration of this dynamic (cf. Jn 1:3, 1:10; Heb 1:2; also Rom 11:36; 1 Cor 8:6;

---

5 Hurtado, *Ancient Jewish Monotheism*, 115.
6 Hurtado, *Ancient Jewish Monotheism*, 132.
7 Hurtado, "Observations on the 'Monotheism' Affirmed in the New Testament," 52n9.
8 See, recently, Gers-Uphaus, "Paganer Monotheismus." Gers-Uphaus contends that "henotheism" is a more accurate label than monotheism in the context of these two famous inscriptions.

Heb 2:10): "For in him (ἐν αὐτῷ) all things in heaven and earth were created ... all things were created through him and for him (δι' αὐτοῦ καὶ εἰς αὐτόν)."

Behind this language, borrowed directly from the lexicon of classical philosophy, we can detect the efficient (δι' αὐτοῦ) and final (εἰς αὐτόν) causes of creation. They have here converged on Jesus and been cast into a doxological mode, turned to the universal praise of Christ. We might name this a kind of *metaphysical Christ devotion* and with Gregory Sterling trace its liturgical shaping through sapiential currents at work in the synagogue context.[9] While Greco-Roman, especially Stoic, philosophy knows many similar formulae applied to the "high God" in one way or another, we must also note the manifest demiurgic connotations that equally hang around such language. Philo's Middle Platonic *Logos*, for instance, who is at once a creature and a "second god" (δεύτερος θεός, *QG* 2.62), is that image of God and archetypal firstborn of creation, the highest intermediary being, "by which (δι' οὗ) all the world was made (ἐδημιουργεῖτο)" (*Spec.* 1.81; cf. *Somn.* 1.230): "the shadow of God which he used like an instrument when he was making the world" (*Leg.* 3.31).

If the great push at the moment is thus insistence on "Jewish Monotheism as the Matrix for New Testament Christology," many scholars would prefer to take Philo here as a Greek rather than a Jew.[10] For others, however, such a move is special pleading and would represent a return to the naive pre-Hengel era, when two hermetically sealed, contrasting Jewish and Greek worlds were still the operative analytical model. Moreover, even if Philo himself is not a Jew of the Palestinian sort, can he be credibly cast a theological pagan? Philo, it should be recalled, is the very man who invented the word "polytheism" in the first place as a term of abuse for the absurdity of non-Jewish doctrines of the divine. His own (exegetical) speculation on the demiurge is not likely to be a sudden *lapsus* within his broader system, but by all appearances it is integral to his insistence upon Jewish belief in one God.

The stakes are high in our handling of this matter, and *Logos* theology undoubtedly deserves greater specific focus in contouring the entire Christological discussion, for recent trends have naturally also pushed to read Johannine Christology from within a strictly inner Jewish context. In the absence of decisive parallels from the Dead Sea Scrolls, a hypostatized Targumic *memra* is thus adopted as the proper point of reference, while the enormously suggestive (and often frankly proto-Arian) Hellenistic material is conveniently set aside.[11] Jörg Frey is undoubtedly right that we must "reopen the window" and widen the history of religions perspective.[12]

---

9 Sterling, "Prepositional Metaphysics."
10 See, e.g., Rainbow, "Jewish Monotheism."

Ultimately, not all are prepared to make generous concessions to the religious environment of the ancient Mediterranean world, however. Richard Bauckham might in particular be mentioned.[13] Glad to acknowledge early Christian worship of Jesus, these scholars are disinclined to attribute a prominent Christological role to mediator figures. Instead, in harmony with the hoary Protestant preference for a pure "biblical" (i.e., non-Greek) theology, emphasis is laid on Paul's Christological manipulations of soaring monotheistic Old Testament texts, such as the reworking of the *Shema* in 1 Corinthians 8:6 around the "one Lord Jesus Christ" and the insertion of Jesus into the unequivocal rhetoric of Isaiah 45 in Philippians 2.[14] The result is a conceptually transparent Creator-creature monotheism, which for some is an almost evident axiom and for others, by contrast, is historically problematic. In this tidy two-tiered universe, all demiurgic characters of any Christological relevance become unambiguous "personified attributes of God," securely on the Creator side of the theological bright line. Here Bauckham's firm assertion that this ontological frontier is clearly drawn by YHWH's exclusive agency in creating the cosmos stands in rather open disregard of the demiurgic data from Philo. As far as Christological thinking is concerned, one has the impression that, while a "gradient" universe may be nominally admitted (but only as a subordinate element in a more fundamental "binary" scheme), the congested ancient cosmos of *Mittelwesen* effectively vanishes from view: neither divinized heroes nor subordinate creative agents have much specifically to add in the early Christian modeling of God's action in Christ.

The stark divinity claims in many New Testament texts are compelling and should not be disputed. The reach of ambient polytheism must not be underestimated, however, for it inevitably touches everything, once we read our texts as Greco-Roman artifacts (as we must and should). Even Paul's hyper-Jewish parsing of the divine oneness of the *Shema* mixes in some ambiguous metaphysics, after all, attributing to the εἷς θεός the dignity of being the first source and final cause (ἐξ οὗ τὰ πάντα καὶ ἡμεῖς εἰς αὐτόν), while making the εἷς κύριος Ἰησοῦς Χριστός sound like a Philonic instrument (δι' οὗ τὰ πάντα καὶ ἡμεῖς δι' αὐτοῦ) (cf. 1 Cor 8:5). Read against

---

11 See, e.g., the commentaries of Theobald, *Das Evangelium nach*, 117–19; Beutler, *Das Johannesevangelium*, 86–87; Keener, *Gospel of John*, 339–63, esp. 61–62; and Wengst, *Das Johannesevangelium*, 44.
12 Frey, "Between Torah and Stoa."
13 See the important essays in Richard Bauckham, *Jesus and the God of Israel*.
14 Alongside the works of Hurtado and Bauckham, see Juel, *Messianic Exegesis*; and Capes, *Old Testament Yahweh Texts*. See also Newman, *Paul's Glory-Christology*.

Philo's own parsing of θεός and κύριος with a murky two-power language, Paul's interpretative move takes on a rather different color: "God (θεός) is the name of the beneficent power, and Lord (κύριος) is the title of the royal power" (*Somn.* 1:163).[15] The prepositional doxology in Romans 11:36 provides a critical control on Paul's language in 1 Corinthians, of course, and "Christological monotheism" is not a misleading name for whatever is happening in this remarkable passage, but questions remain about just what is actually transpiring. Perhaps, in the end, it is thus better to think in terms of "Christological *monotheizing*" and see primitive Christology as a particular stage in Israel's perennial wrangling with its surrounding polytheistic culture(s):[16] a decisive new phase that engaged the world of the Greeks with unheard of openness, energy, and boldness. There is thus real merit in Peter Schäfer's suggestion of "ein dynamisches, auf Werturteile verzichtendes Modell mit dem beiden Polen 'Monotheismus' und 'Polytheismus,' zwischen denen sich zahlreiche Konfiguration und Kombinationen zu unterschiedlichen Zeiten und in unterschiedlichen geographischen Räumen herausbilden."[17] If the specific Pauline evidence is thus indeed foundational in construing the shape of the primitive "Christological mutation" in all its sudden eruptive force, one ought certainly not ignore Paul's specific Gentile-oriented version of monotheism. His confession of the one God emphasizes this same God's relation to the *goyim* specifically as *goyim* (Rom 3:28–30), not as strangers who must come over to him by Judaizing. The apostle's missionary zeal nevertheless urged him to turn the nations "from idols, to serve a living and true God" — while waiting for "his son from heaven," Jesus, who appears as a prophylactic agent in the looming drama of eschatological wrath (1 Thes 1:9–10), not at all unlike Michael "the majestic angel of the authority" in 1QM 17.6–7. "Jewish monotheism" is indeed the matrix, but it is a Jewish monotheism preached to non-Jews that often leaves ample play for angelic Christologies.[18]

Part of the problem is certainly that, like the polytheism around it, "Jewish monotheism" is itself a moving target, and this makes "mutations" hard to capture. To this extent, it is important to take account of not only of

---

15 In *Somn.* 1:163, these two powers are evidently immanent to the one "Lord God" of Abraham. In QE 2.64–66, however, the two powers, described now as royal and creative powers, seem to be at once creatures, striving upward toward the Father and something somehow internal to God: all symbolized in the two winged cherubim facing each other on the mercy seat, while in QE 2.83 the demiurgic logos may be directly called the "overseer and guardian and curator" of God's creative power (τὸν ἔφορον καὶ ἐπίτροπον καὶ ἐπιμελητὴν αὐτοῦ δυναμέως).

16 This language is borrowed in allusion to Sanders, *Canon and Community*, 51–52.

17 Schäfer, *Zwei Götter im Himmel*, 8.

18 See, e.g., Hannah, *Michael and Christ*.

Israel's long theological passage from Canaanite days down to the Roman period (which, as Bauckham insists, was not necessarily an evolutionary process),[19] but also the movement after the turn of the era "from a more flexible and monarchical monotheism toward a more stringently 'monistic' stance."[20] Rabbinic policing of the "Two Powers in Heaven" heresy, for instance, seems to signal exactly such a reconfiguration in the permissible forms of Jewish monotheism, made in response to perceived threats on both the Christian and Gnostic fronts (although Schäfer would also recontextualize this motif).[21] An exaggerated and anachronistic marginalization of mediator figures must accordingly be avoided in modeling the generative context of primitive Christology. Reconstructions of YHWH's divine transcendence too categorically inhospitable to a world of celestial hierarchies are dangerous retrojections that are also, ultimately, inhospitable to the theophanic mystery primitive Christology sought to express.

From an ancient perspective, the penetration of the divine into this sublunary sphere was not the essential novum of the Christ-event. Nor was the ambiguous mingling of mediators with the Most High an unthinkable thought. Even from an Old Testament perspective this is true. The biblical theophanies of the Angel of the Lord, which routinely become theophanies of the Lord himself, indicate that, as James Kugel remarks, this divine realm is "not something tidy and distinct, another order of being."[22] That such a conventional, canonical blurring of the line between the Creator and his mediating creature, between the gradient and binary cosmological schemes, might actually serve a concrete theological need of the biblical authors—to prevent YHWH from losing contact with the human world—perhaps helps to put the matter in a more amiable light. For a basic problem of divine-human mediation must be confronted. No creature can ever reach up all the way to God, in which case he must somehow reach down.

Hurtado's ultimate path is to acknowledge openly the subordinationist character of the New Testament's dyadic monotheism and to throw attention instead upon the *homotimia*, the equal honor of worship paid to Jesus Christ yet refused to angels. The effect, of course—and it is a calculated methodological move—is to redirect Christological inquiry from notional beliefs to

---

[19] The bibliography of relevant texts here is long. Bauckham ("Biblical Theology and the Problems of Monotheism" in *Jesus and the God of Israel*) offers an incisive challenge to much of the available scholarship, including a problematization of the heuristic dogma of the evolutionary character of Israel's theological development. See chap. 8 in this volume.

[20] Hurtado, *Ancient Jewish Monotheism*, 134.

[21] See Segal, *Two Powers in Heaven*. See also the recent reappraisal of Stephen Waers, "Monarchianism and Two Powers."

[22] Kugel, *God of Old*, 36.

the realm of religious experience. This correctly takes distance from overly intellectualized Enlightenment models of "monotheism," though it also risks occluding the New Testament's "triadic shaped *discourse*" by "dyadic shaped *worship*."[23] It also means that in a more Bauckhamian mood and mode the heavenly mediators so curiously tolerated by the Jewish monotheism of the period can accordingly fall by the wayside, uninteresting except insofar as they receive no cult. Here even Hurtado demurs, and the displaced theme, so central to Bousset and his school, is straining to reassert its importance in certain streams of scholarship, for this broad disengagement of *Mittelwesen* has not gone unremarked or unchallenged.[24] Theories of adoptionism (Ehrman) and Adam Christology (Dunn) are accordingly on offer, along with a whole range of angelomorphic approaches.[25] In this connection, a protest has also been raised in the face of much excitement about the "divine identity" of Jesus to recall the New Testament's specific interest in Jesus "the man chosen by God."[26]

The special position of Crispin Fletcher-Louis may provide the most helpful intuition of where, after a generation of much focused study, the debate over New Testament Christology presently stands.[27] Fletcher-Louis enthusiastically accepts the thesis that divine Christology was a sudden appearance and no evolutionary process. He is unready, however, to concede the basic irrelevance of Jewish mediator figures. A number of idiosyncrasies complicate his ideas, but he may have his finger on a critical point. Perhaps instead of forcing a choice between either an evolution from low (human) to high (divine) or alternately a simple "early high" Christology model, it would be better to uphold an "early simultaneously low and high" perspective—or perhaps, better, an early "high and higher" vision, for being a heavenly mediator is not a trivial employment. It may be that, as later conciliar theology proclaimed, properly analyzing the early high New Testament claims of Christ's *divinity* becomes problematic when it forgets his created *humanity* as an integral part of the picture.

---

[23] Nathan MacDonald has worked to free scholars of major anachronisms derived from the Enlightenment, arguing that the identification of religion with a set of theoretical propositions misconstrues the character of ancient religion (*One God or One Lord?*).

[24] See Hurtado, *Ancient Jewish Monotheism*, 104–6.

[25] See Ehrman, *How Jesus Became God*; and Dunn, *Christology in the Making*. See also Fossum, *Name of God*; Stuckenbruck, *Angel Veneration and Christology*; Gieschen, *Angelomorphic Christology*; and more recently Garrett, *No Ordinary Angel*.

[26] See Kirk, *Man Attested by God*.

[27] Fletcher-Louis, *Jesus Monotheism*.

Recovering the Multivalent Logic of "The Place"

In the current rendering of New Testament Christology, a model of *Lex orandi, lex credendi* has widely sidelined interest in conceptual development. While this move away from the theoretical and discursive is not always positive or without problems, the logic of devotional behavior can nevertheless be profitably pushed still further, though in a slightly different way than heretofore. A reorientation toward the Temple as the cultic center of early Jewish devotion may help to reimagine the complicated conjunction of monotheism and mediation in the Greco-Roman Jewish context and thereby provide a helpful Christological base.

The Jerusalem Temple as a Locus of Monotheism

The case might easily be made that nothing within "Second Temple Judaism" defines the whole socioreligious phenomenon designated by that phrase so much as the Second Temple itself. Majestically rebuilt and adorned by Herod to radiate throughout the empire as a tangible source of Jewish identity and pride, it was the visible and symbolic center, whose presence was felt deep into the diaspora and pagan world. If a monotheism characterized by the exclusive worship of YHWH thus represents one of the most distinctive marks of the Jewish *ethnos*, this was easily associated specifically with their national Temple: "The Temple of the Most High God" (Philo, *Flacc.* 46; *Legat.* 278). The pouring into Jerusalem of pilgrims who came from distant parts to pay their worship (together with the gathering of the Temple tax from non-Judean Jews) strengthened a perception of the universal significance of this cult. As "The Place" where YHWH's exclusive worship might alone be truly and adequately offered, the Temple in Ἱεροσόλυμα, that re-etymologized temple polis of the Judeans, was an inevitable physical metonym for first-century Jewish monotheism.[28]

The *locus classicus* of this understanding is the formula found in Josephus's *Contra Apionem*: "The one Temple of the one God (Εἷς ναὸς ἑνὸς θεοῦ) ... [a temple] common to all as God is common to all" (2.193). The tight connection Josephus makes here is not a passing link. In *A.J.* 4.200, for instance, in recounting Moses's injunction to build one single temple, we

---

28 This form of the name was connected directly with the Temple. Eupolemus (Frag. 2) recounts: "The shrine was first called the 'Temple of Solomon' (Ἱερὸν Σολομῶνος). Later, corruptly the city was named from the Temple 'Jerusalem' (ἀπὸ τοῦ ἱρεοῦ Ἱερουσαλήμ); and by the Greeks it is correspondingly called Ἱεροσόλυμα.'" Cf. Josephus, *B.J.* 6.10.3 (§438); *A.J.* 7.3.2 (§67); *C. Ap.* 1.22 (§174).

read again: "Let there be one holy city in that place ... and let there be one temple therein, and one altar of stones ... for God is one and the Hebrew race is one." More severe than the biblical tradition, Josephus goes so far as to reproach Solomon himself for having introduced images into the Temple, soiling its integrity as a pure cult to the one true God. No confusion with nations' idols could be allowed. Clearly, for Josephus, the Jerusalem Temple held special status as a kind of philosophical theology writ in stone.

Philo is of precisely the same opinion. A single citation will suffice here to make the point. Moses spoke "concerning the proper idea to be entertained of the one, real, and true, and living God" and thus explained "in what manner one ought to pay the honors that are his due." Accordingly, he "foresaw that there could not be any great number of temples built either in many different places, or in the same place, thinking it fitting that as God is one, his temple also should be one" (*Spec.* 65, 67).

Other authors and types of literature found alternative ways to make the same connection. In the *Apocalypse of Abraham*, for instance, an amazingly sharp monotheistic document, an absolute intolerance for idols and their temples is shown (§1–8). "The handsome temple" that bears the beauty of God's own glory is somehow different in essence, however, and the moment it is revealed as polluted by idolatrous worship, becoming like these other temples, it is put to destruction (§25–27). What Bauckham has called "eschatological monotheism"—the expectation of a universal recognition of YHWH—also gives expression to the monotheistic import of the Temple, for the sanctuary stands at the center of the liturgical *mise-en-scène*. An excellent example is the final hymn in Tobit 13.

The biblical roots of this whole manner of thinking are not difficult to find. The recent monograph of Matthew Lynch has ably demonstrated how in Chronicles, for instance, the unique "categorical supremacy" of YHWH is powerfully tied to Judea's focal institutions, that is, the Temple, its cult, and the king.[29] The Holy Place thus organizes an embodied manifestation of God's divine uniqueness: functionally through its cult, qualitatively through its greatness, and materially through its status as a divine creation.

If, during the days of Herod, a surge of royal propaganda reinvigorated the Temple institution with this traditional monotheistic meaning, pagan contempt for Jewish cultic exclusivity also served to highlight the Temple's role as a focal point of monotheistic fervor.[30] We might thus speak of an "enacted monotheism" that surrounds the sanctuary in the intense resistance

---

29 Lynch, *Monotheism and Institutions*.
30 On the complexity of "monotheism" as a commitment in Herod's own political program of temple construction, see Giambrone, "Herod's Temple."

to idolatrous encroachments, like the placement of Pilate's eagle standards or the drama around Caligula's statue. This latter attack on the monotheistic integrity of the Temple excited Jewish protests well beyond Judea.

As always, one must take proper account of the difficulty of capturing a "Jewish monotheism" in motion, for (as Josephus's censure of Solomon hints) in earlier periods a different praxis was often tolerated. The existence of rival sanctuaries is the most obvious reminder that the story is more complicated. To just this point, however, John Hyrcanus's violent destruction of Gerizim is a clear statement in favor of the Jerusalem sanctuary's exclusive monotheistic rights. Whatever the ongoing competition to its claims may have been, the unequaled prestige of Herod's structure during the first century is not in doubt. The following may thus be affirmed. In the first century the Temple was one of the most important, if not *the* central expression of Jewish monotheism, and monotheism was one of the most important and wide-reaching associations of the Temple. Whatever "monotheism" meant for Jews at this moment, it cannot be separated from the complex signification of the Jerusalem Temple.

The Jerusalem Temple as a Locus of Mediation

Charles Taylor has noted the challenge that we as moderns face in grasping ancient thoughts about God because of what he calls our "excarnational" Enlightenment paradigm, in which certain persons, places, times, and things are no longer reverenced as somehow holier and more divine than others. Accordingly, however transcendent YHWH was, the universal God of Heaven had a terrestrial street address. He lived on a hill in Judea. This immanent pole of meaning was obviously shared with other temples in the Greco-Roman world, even if the exclusive nature and worldwide reach of Judea's YHWH cult heightened the experience of the Jerusalem Temple's localized power.

Within this ancient framework, a major part of the pragmatic signification of the Temple was invested in its role in a vast hierarchical structure of cosmic mediation. Populated by elaborate crowds of priests and liturgical ministers, this site was animated as a living point, *the point* of divine-human contact and communion. The precise mediatorial functions performed by this vast *Temple-cult-priest* apparatus correspond, moreover, with central functions of intermediary figures in the Judaism of the period. Comparison with a few representative examples illustrates the sorts of Temple-oriented and priestly roles routinely played by these mediating agents.

- Philo explicitly identifies God's unique, demiurgic *logos*, the immanent, divine mediator of the created universe, as God's chief angel and the high priest (*Somn.* 1.228–239; *Cher.* 1–3; *Mos.* 2.134), while the earthly priest is also the personification of the *logos* (*Fug.* 108; *Migr.* 102; *Somn.* 1.125). The *logos* is thus the expiator of sins and the intercessor (ἱκέτης) and the advocate (παράκλητος) of mankind (*Her.* 42; *Mos.* 3.14). In *QE*, the *logos* is an agent of sacred actions within the Holy of Holies in the Jerusalem Temple.
- Personified Wisdom in Sirach 24, who tells of her own glory in the angelic assembly of the Most High and is created before the ages, "ministers in the holy Tent before him" and is established on Zion (24:10).
- The mysterious first-person voice behind the *Self-Glorification Hymn* (4Q491 11 I) claims to be incomparable in glory and seated upon a "throne of power" among the "gods" (אלים) (l. 12), reckoned with the divine beings (l. 14). Whether or not he is identified as the archangel Michael, this figure bears the clear profile of a "liturgical-eschatological priest" whose "portion lies in glory of the holy Dwelling" (ll. 14–15).[31] He both teaches and exercises a liturgical role, calling on the righteous ones to sing and give "praise in the holy Dwelling" (ll. 8–9, 20–23).
- Melchizedek in 11Q13 is identified by scholars as an angelic figure, perhaps Michael, or else a kind of messianic cipher, bearing distinct divine attributes, seemingly even called *Elohim* who is enthroned in the divine assembly and executes judgment (ll. 10–13). His unique high priesthood is exercised through the proclamation of an eschatological Jubilee ("Year of Grace for Melchizedek") that culminates in a great Day of Atonement, through which the sons of light find forgiveness of "the debt of all their iniquities" (l. 6).
- Yahoel, the *angelus interpres* in the *Apocalypse of Abraham*, has the specific role of enabling Abraham to somehow enter and withstand YHWH's divine presence. Abraham cannot himself directly look upon God (§16.4), but the angel's strength is somehow communicated to him, and he sees God's glory in the form of Ezekiel's Temple/Throne-Room vision (§18.1–14). To prepare and brace him for this revelation, Yahoel leads the father of Jewish mono-

---

31 See Angel, "Liturgical-Eschatological Priest."

theism in singing a long liturgical hymn addressed to the "Eternal One, Mighty One, Holy El, God autocrat" (§17.1–21).

- In the *Testament of Levi*, Levi ascends in vision up to heaven, where he sees the Lord seated upon his throne (5.1) and is granted the priestly dignity. He is then brought back down to earth by the "Angel of Intercession" and entrusted with a sword to execute vengeance on Israel's enemies in Shechem.

- In the *Testament of Moses*, both Moses and his mysterious messianic successor, the Levite Taxo, are depicted as priestly mediators. The sinlessness of Taxo and his innocent death is understood in parallel to the destruction of the holy Temple (cf. Mk 15:38) as an event that somehow triggers the eschaton.[32]

The list might easily be extended, and it should be noted that mediator agents from the highest "hypostatic" sort, like God's Word and Wisdom, through the graded angelic ranks down to exalted human leaders, all evidence the same priestly/cultic/temple associations. Heavenly mediators naturally did the same work that priests accomplished in and by means of the Temple—or at least the work these priests were supposed to accomplish—were the Temple (or priesthood) for one reason or another not properly functioning.[33]

As the privileged locus of cosmic mediation, the Temple was the precise point not only of divine-human, but also of divine-*angelic* contact. In union with its mysterious doppelgänger, the heavenly Temple, it was the majestic footstool and throne room. The celestial court of the "high god" was held on this spot. It is no accident, then, that the Temple is the regular site of angelic visions. Angels were in the very walls. Texts like the *Songs of Sabbath Sacrifice* reveal how powerful this vision could be. The seventh of the *Songs* (4Q103) strikingly gives voice even to the very Temple stones: to "the foundations of the holy of holies," to all the pillars and corners of the holy Abode, that the building itself might also sing praise. The Temple's own voice is then merged with the teeming angelic choirs, "the spirits of the Holy of Holies, living god-like beings, spirits of eternal holiness above all the holy ones," who praise in their turn ... *the heavenly beams and walls!* "The divinized temple not only offers praise, but itself becomes the object

---

[32] See Atkinson, "Taxo's Martyrdom."
[33] It is interesting to observe that Enoch's heavenly adventures begin as an intercessory *Ersatz* for the fallen Watchers, who are themselves depicted as fallen priests. See Suter, "Fallen Angel, Fallen Priest."

of praise," Gary Anderson marvels.[34] Carol Newsome comments that these "spirits of the Holy of Holies" are somehow the "animate spiritual substance of the Temple itself."[35] The Temple is reckoned as one great, living angelic agent, itself worthy of the highest and holiest angelic praise. Hurtado may be correct that heavenly mediators received no worship in the Second Temple period, but it is striking how free worshipers at Qumran evidently felt to worship *God* by venerating and praising the glory of his *Temple*—and not merely as a mere literary trope, but in hymnic texts used for real worship.[36]

Anderson has forcefully used such traditions to demonstrate that in the biblical mindset the entire Temple complex, the very building right down to the sacred vessels, is so thoroughly suffused with YHWH's divine presence that to praise the Temple *is* to praise its resident God. God becomes so identified with his dwelling, that, as with the shape-shifting Angel of the Lord, to see The Place is somehow to see the unseeable God. Such liturgical transparency of the Temple to YHWH himself ultimately means that the mechanics of bridging the transcendent abyss that separates Israel from her Creator God were somehow mysteriously worked out precisely here. We might speak of a paradoxical "unmediated mediation."[37]

Whatever distance the strict practice of cultic monolatry put between Israel and the surrounding nations, the Temple in Jerusalem still functioned much like others nations' temples. Dangerous as the idea may seem, the Temple, as the Lord's true Dwelling, carried in Israel's aniconic cult something close to the same weight of numinous presence that the cult statues of the nations also bore, enabling concrete, incarnate contact with the divine. And yet, as in these cults (despite Israel's polemics), it was not a case of simple fetishism. The Temple was not mistaken for God. Nor, evidently, did the intimate linkage of the Jewish Temple system with a huge range of intermediary functions and figures compromise its emblematic monotheistic meaning. On the contrary, the double identification both with the Lord's exclusive oneness and a vast cosmic priesthood of exalted creatures rendered the Temple a unique kind of two-natured locus of divine encounter.

---

34 Anderson, *Christian Doctrine*, 111.

35 Newsome, *Songs of Sabbath Sacrifice*, 233.

36 Hurtado (*Ancient Jewish Monotheism*, 128–29) rejects the angels' worship of Adam in *Life of Adam and Eve* (§12–16), seeing here perhaps a text "laden with theological meaning" but not evidence of actual, organized Jewish devotion to a non-YHWH figure.

37 On the biblical notion of revelation as an "immediate mediation," see Giambrone, "Revelation in Christian Scripture."

Jesus as the New Temple in John

Temple Christology, in view of the foregoing exposition, appears in a newly clarified and suggestive light. A few remarks on John's striking application of Temple themes to Jesus will indicate the potential of this perspective as an integrally expressive Christological idiom.[38]

John's Prologue reaches an internal climax in a reference to the Temple. "And the Word was made flesh and dwelt among us (ἐσκήνωσεν ἐν ἡμῖν) and we have seen his glory (δόξαν), glory as from the Only One (μονογενής) of the Father, full of grace and truth" (Jn 1:14). As Raymond Brown remarks on this text, "What we are primarily interested in is the constant connection [in the Old Testament tradition] of the glory of God with his presence in the Tabernacle and the Temple ... Thus it is quite appropriate that, after the description of how the Word set up a Tabernacle among men in the flesh of Jesus, the Prologue should mention that his *glory* became visible."[39] The point here is simple. The evangelist has appealed to Temple traditions in order to describe the character of the Word's incarnation precisely as a kind of "immediate mediation" of YHWH's divine glory. To see Jesus in the flesh is to see the invisible God (Jn 1:18, 14:9). The glory, which the one God shares with no other, as he poignantly says in Isaiah 42:8, is resplendent in the humanity of Jesus. From John's perspective, this mystery is best understood through the evocative analogy of the Temple.[40]

John's Temple logic was still entirely apparent to an interpreter like Athanasius.

> [The Jews] did not, when they saw the temple of stones, suppose that the Lord who spoke in the Temple was a creature; nor did they set the temple at naught and retire far off to worship. But they came according to the Law, and worshipped God who uttered his oracles form the Temple. Since this was so, how can it be other than right to worship the body of the Lord, all-holy and all-reverend as it is, announced by the Holy Spirit and made the

---

[38] John's Temple Christology is a well-established motif and object of study. Recent full-length studies include Coloe, *God Dwells with Us*; Kerr, *Temple of Jesus' Body*; Hoskins, *Jesus as the Fulfillment of the Temple in the Gospel of John*; and Troost-Cramer, *Jesus as Means and Locus of Worship*. An additional, shorter treatment, worthy of note is Grappe, "Du sanctuaire au jardin." The destruction of the Jerusalem Temple in 70 AD is commonly seen as a significant element in the historical context of John's Temple replacement theology.

[39] Brown, *Gospel According to John I-XII*, 34.

[40] See the highly suggestive analysis of Anderson, *Christian Doctrine and the Old Testament*, 95–120.

> vestment of the Logos ... Therefore, he that dishonors the Temple dishonors the Lord in the Temple; and he that separates the Logos from the body sets at naught the grace given us in him.[41]

Jesus' *sarx*, which for the Jewish mind means his whole created humanity, mediates the divine, just as YHWH was present to Israel by means of the Temple. One cannot pull these two apart, the humanity and divinity of the Logos, any more than one can honor the one Lord without honoring his one Temple.

But just here we have the crucial "mutation," for in John's Christological appropriation of the Temple's transparency to God's glory, there is no longer a need for any sacred structure. Not even Philo, with all his allegorizing and universalizing inclinations, was ready to do away with the concrete Jerusalem Temple and simply "retire far off to worship" (cf. *Spec.* 66–70). John, however, sees in the Temple-Body of the Logos a manifest replacement of the earlier order: "grace in place of grace" (χάριν ἀντὶ χάριτος). "Believe me woman that the hour is coming when neither on this mountain nor in Jerusalem will you worship the Father ... The hour is coming and now is, when true worshipers will worship the Father in spirit and truth" (Jn 4:21, 4:23). As Hyrcanus earlier crushed Samaria's rival claims in order to exalt the one cult of the one God, now Jesus himself asserts that his own body (Jn 2:19) is the one true Place where God's glory is manifested and worshipped, leveling both Jerusalem and Gerizim.

The concept of "true worshipers" (ἀληθινοὶ προσκυνηταί) and a worship "in spirit and truth" evokes language characteristic of the anti-idol polemics of Second Temple monotheism—now, remarkably, if gently and obliquely turned against the Temple itself. This is to make way, of course, for the one who is himself ἀληθινός (cf. Jn 1:9, 6:32, 6:55, 15:1), precisely as the one sent by τὸν μόνον ἀληθινὸν θεόν (17:3).[42] The series of Jewish feasts fulfilled by Jesus as the "true bread" and "true light" and so on all belong to this same motif of replacing the former with the final, true Temple worship.[43] The "hour" of the obsolescence of Jerusalem's ancient cult is, of course, the eschatological

---

[41] Letter 60.8 (PG 26: 1082); translation following Anderson.

[42] Rainbow ("Jewish Monotheism," 81–83) helpfully identifies ten explicit forms of monotheistic speech in Greco-Roman Jewish texts, the third of which is a divine title linked with "living" and/or "true." John's characteristic Christological rhetoric ("true light," etc.) is thus recognizable as a sort of monotheistic claim. The extension of the "true" descriptor to "worshippers" in Jn 4 is connected with the Son's mediation of the Father's glory to believers in the Spirit: an important variation on Rainbow's sixth point: God's glory defined as nontransferable (cf. Is 42:8 and see below).

[43] See Hoskins, *Jesus as the Fulfillment of the Temple*, 160–80.

hour of Jesus' own glorification, when the *eschatological monotheism* that traditionally saw in the Temple the great end-time magnet drawing in all the nations is transferred onto the person of Jesus: "When I am lifted up, I will draw all men to myself" (Jn 12:32). The gathering of "one flock" around Jesus (10:16) also belongs to this monotheistic ethos in an eschatological key: one people, one God, one Temple. All the Fourth Gospel's striking talk of oneness, in fact, together with the conjoined mutual inherence discourse, should be heard in this profoundly monotheistic register. Jesus himself has become the absolute locus of oneness, for he is the μονογενής, the "Unique One" of God, so much so that he may say, "The Father and I are one" (Jn 10:30). No bolder statement of "Christological monotheism" could be demanded.

"Destroy this Temple and in three days I will raise it up" (Jn 2:19). The divine Word speaks of his own Temple-Body in the very midst of the Jerusalem Temple, and he challenges his hearers to tear down that Temple that he might renew it. In fulfillment of the prophecies, the humanity (*sarx*) of Jesus has become YHWH's unique Dwelling Place and presence in the midst of men: ἐσκήνωσεν ἐν ἡμῖν. Yet in the resurrected Jesus the sense of this ἐν ἡμῖν takes on a meaning not anticipated by the prophets. For the Tabernacle of the glorified Logos is not a geographical *hic* like the former Temple. He dwells "within us" through the sending of the Spirit, which pours out like water gushing from the eschatological Temple (cf. Ezek 47:1-12; Jn 7:37-39). A new spatiality of indwelling union is communicated from the one God to humankind.

It is important, from this perspective, that Jesus *mediates* to creatures the divine oneness that he shares with the Father, by communicating the incommunicable glory he has as the Father's μονογενής. "The glory that you have given me I have given them, so that they may be one, as we are one" (Jn 17:22). The scandal, again, is Isaiah 42:8—"I am the Lord, that is my Name, *my glory I give to no other*, nor my praise to idols." God's divine *doxa*, his divine oneness, and even his divine Name are all shared by the Father and the Son, and in the Son this all passes to the sons of men (cf. Jn 17:26), who now also become Temples. In this light, the most open and interesting confrontation in John's Gospel between the alternatives of Jewish and Christological monotheism is revealing. To defend his claim to be one with the Father against the charge that he a man has made himself equal to God, Jesus quotes Psalm 82—"I said, you are gods"—the most famous "polytheistic" text in the Hebrew Bible (Jn 10:30-36). Divinization appears to be integral to the divinity claims in John's Gospel.

Jesus' mediating function, like his claims to God's divine oneness, is again linked to the Temple replacement motif. Specifically, he presents himself as the new Bethel—the old and now superseded sanctuary site—so that as *Son of Man* he becomes the new ladder of Jacob, where the angels of God ascend and descend (Jn 1:51). Like the former Temple(s), Jesus himself is thus the concentrated locus of angelic ministry and mediation. And the angels' movement, ascending and descending, first up and then back down, parallels his own upward movement on the cross—which is importantly different than the reversed directionality in the incarnation: the living Word coming down from heaven. The Logos descends that the Son of Man may be exalted that the Spirit might then through him come back down. The *sarx* of the Word works as the middle term of this double divine condescension. It is in this context of Jesus' angelic heavenward movement, from below, that he can thus speak a subordinationist word, which seems directly to contradict his earlier claim: "You heard me say to you, 'I am going away, and I am coming to you.' If you loved me, you would rejoice that I am going to the Father, because *the Father is greater than I*" (14:28).

Contemporary Christological discussion remains torn between mediation and monotheism, while scholars of John have long puzzled how Jesus is both the revealer and the content of revelation. Patristic interpretation adopted a strategy that John Behr has named "partitive exegesis," distributing texts like John 10:30 and 14:28 across Christ's two unconfused divine and human natures. Perhaps a new approach to this venerable problem is to read John's Christology through the twin monotheistic and mediating poles of the first-century Second Temple.

PART III

JESUS AND THE SCRIPTURES

CHAPTER 11

SCIENTIA CHRISTI
Three Theses

Greeks once upon a time looked for wisdom, not only debt relief. They sought it in the gymnasium, in the Stoa, and in a special way in Homer, whom Plato calls *protos didaskalos* and *hegemon paideias*, "the first teacher and leader of all learning."[1] What Homer (however dubiously) was for history, for law, medicine, mathematics, and philosophy—indeed for every branch of knowledge cultivated in ancient Greece—the holy Scriptures were, and much more, for the Jews. Ben Sira's overt identification of Hellenistic Wisdom with the Torah only gave poetic expression to this established fact. For the sage, Israel's Scripture pours forth with instruction, runs over like the world's great rivers, floods its banks with knowledge like the Nile (Sir 24:25–27). *Everything*, all knowledge, natural science (uncomfortable as that makes us), ethics, and logic, and not least what was once styled the study of divinity, was for the Jews of Jesus' age focused in a single source: the holy Scriptures.[2] "We do not have countless books," Josephus said, "discordant and disarrayed, but only twenty-two, containing the history of every age."[3] If we wish to ask about the human knowledge of

---

1 *Republic* 595c, 606a,e.
2 "To the Torah was attributed an unlimited richness of content: everything was to be found in it. It was considered that there was not a single element in the lives of the society or of the individual which had no message from the Torah: it applied to every part of life" (Gerhardsson, *Memory and Manuscript*, 19). The well-known saying of Hillel in *m. Aboth* 5.22—"Turn it [i.e., Torah] this way and turn it that way, for all is contained therein"—articulates a widely attested sentiment, e.g., CD 16:2; cf. also Jerome, *Prologue to Isaiah*.
3 *C. Ap.* 1:8.

the Incarnate Word, the Son of Mary, it is exactly in this tiny little library, large enough to hold the world, where we must begin.

Jerome's famous dictum is a precious theological patrimony: *ignorantia scripturae, ignorantia Christi est*. The converse, I propose, is also true: *scientia Christi*, the knowledge of Christ (subjective genitive now, "his knowledge"), *scientia scripturae est*. It is precisely in Jesus' own knowledge of the Scriptures that we confront what most deeply informed his human mind. Jesus read the Scriptures. He knew and cherished every yod and serif (Mt 5:18). He drank deeply as the prophets and doctors drank and as saints still drink from this overflowing fountain.

I take this all to be perfectly concrete and, in itself, also perfectly uncontroversial. Nevertheless, I find this highly productive and indeed provocative principle to be curiously and consistently overlooked. We do not, at any rate, reckon adequately with the scholarly yet almost magical reverence for books characteristic of the ancient mind—uniquely so in Judaism, in Jesus' day a still ripening religion of the book. Misled perhaps by the prominent aspects of orality and illiteracy in antique society, we must understand that the status of written texts in such cultures is simply all the more marked and central.[4] The problem of Christ's knowledge certainly has its upper speculative reaches, where philosophy and theology are bound to soar.[5] But like the Word's own taking on of human flesh, our search for Christ's knowledge must plant its feet solidly on the ground, seeking his wisdom humbly in a definite time and place. "My Creator chose the place for my tent. He said make your dwelling in Jacob" (Sir 24:8). It is in the tent of the text Israel's Torah that we find the privileged instrument mediating Christ's human knowledge.

In what follows, I propose three interlocking and, in a way, cumulative theses, which all in some way push against the tide. These are offered from the perspective of an exegete and center upon what I take to be a series of neuralgic points in contemporary New Testament Christology. In a variety of ways, however, all come into contact with this single potent and overarching idea. We concretely encounter the mind of Christ in and through Israel's Scriptures.

---

[4] On this issue, see Witherington, "*In Principio Erat Verbum*."

[5] See, e.g., *ST* III, q. 9–12. On the question of Christ's knowledge in its original medieval scholastic context, see Ernst, *Die Lehre*. Twentieth-century theology has challenged many of the conclusions of earlier centuries on this theme, e.g., Balthasar, *Theologie der Drei Tage*. See also the response of Gaine, *Did the Savior See the Father?*

Thesis One: Recovering the "Messianic Consciousness" of Jesus Should Not Be Abandoned by Contemporary Exegesis

The impertinent fantasy of psychologically probing the mind of Jesus was, by popular consent, laid to rest when Albert Schweitzer dismantled the nineteenth-century project of the Liberal Lives.[6] If, at least for the (problematic) "Three Quest" historiography of the matter now regnant, Schweitzer's landmark work thus signaled a hiatus in the "Quest" for the Historical Jesus, this was not his direct intention but the effect of other factors, above all the later influence of Rudolph Bultmann. Schweitzer himself, in fact, was engaged in exposing precisely how Jesus' messianic thinking developed and reckoned it as a function of the eschatology in fashion in the Judaism of Jesus' day. The skepticism of William Wrede, for whom Jesus' own personal messianic pretentions were at best no longer historically retrievable and at worst to be discounted altogether, was for Schweitzer an absolute error in the historical understanding of the Gospels: a grave theological misstep to be openly resisted. As a founding father of the modern study of Jesus, Schweitzer is on this point at least, if not in the specific solution and construction of Christ's consciousness that he offers, an important voice to respect. The necessity of insisting upon the messianic claims of Jesus is a more important and more penetrating insight than Schweitzer's personal proposal of a radical "thoroughgoing eschatology," which he saw as the only viable alternative to an equally thorough skepticism (*tertium non datur*).[7] If there is a Schweitzerstraße, as N. T. Wright would have it, it is at the intersection with Jesus' "messianic consciousness" that we should make our turn off the skeptical road.[8]

Conceived rather differently than Wrede's earlier proposal, Rudolph Bultmann's own skeptical resignation to the irrelevance of Jesus is a debated topic.[9] As a literary solution, however, form criticism represents a clear swing in the direction of Wrede.[10] Of most immediate bearing here, however, is

---

6 Schweitzer, *Quest*. See chap. 2 in this volume.

7 The effective dissolution of "thoroughgoing eschatology" into an equally "thoroughgoing skepticism" is frequently on display, exposing the basic failure of Schweitzer's purported project. See Fredriksen, *When Christians Were Jews*, note 28 below.

8 Wright, *Jesus and the Victory of God*, 21.

9 See, e.g., Painter, "Bultmann, Archeology, and the Historical Jesus"; and Waldstein, "Foundations of Bultmann's Work." On Bultmann's effort to outflank all skeptical challenges through a full embrace of the skeptical position, see chap. 6 in this volume.

10 Paul Meyer correctly observed that "Since both he [Schweitzer] and Wrede appeared to pay their ultimate respects to the Jesus of history over against all the orthodoxies around

Bultmann's negative verdict on the supposedly biographical nature of the Gospels. The recent reversal of this long-entrenched position is also implicated, oddly enough. In Richard Burridge's argument specifically, which overturns Bultmann's classic thesis, strong emphasis is laid upon the form critic's anachronistic misconception of (hence rejection of) biography as a kind of psychological study.[11] By signaling this as a false objection, the moratorium on knowledge of "Christ according to the flesh" enforced by Bultmann's theologically committed skepticism ironically lingers on in a continued discomfort or disinterest in speculating about the human consciousness of Jesus. Jesus' psychology remains off limits. Craig Keener's recent *Christobiography*, boasting the impressive dimensions of documentation typical of all Keener's work, is a good instance of the way Burridge's *bios* paradigm, even when coupled with an evangelical apologetic orientation (thus temperamentally susceptible to Ben Meyer's classic *The Aims of Jesus*), still leaves little room for interest in Jesus' own thinking.[12]

Such discomfort, of course, is to a real degree salubrious. It is not only properly chastened before the mystery of the Incarnate Lord and rightly suspicious of Schleiermacher's long shadow. It is also (and here's the point) sensitive to the salient literary and historical facts. In particular, assessing the Gospels no longer according to modern canons of biographical writing, but as *bioi* on the Greco-Roman model, has freed scholars from a great many futile preoccupations, not excluding the fool's errand of hunting for a sustained story of Jesus' internal development.[13]

In ancient biographical literature, characterization is fully exteriorized. It is expressed through words and deeds, not pursued through authorial conjectures about the genesis of the protagonist's motives or evolving inner life. Lucian's *Demonax* is no study of a developing cynic philosopher or his

---

them—the one to a Jesus devoid of Messianic pretensions, the other to a Jesus consumed by his Messianic passion—the vast difference which separated them [i.e., Schweitzer and Wrede] and which has been correctly divined in Schweitzer's disjunctive proposition, was for the time being not apparent." Meyer accordingly propounded "the thesis that it was form-criticism which made this difference clear and which confronted New Testament scholarship with the kind of critical choice which has divided the heirs of Wrede from the heirs of Schweitzer ever since" ("Problem of the Messianic Self-Consciousness of Jesus," 125). Swayed by the power of Schweitzer's own rhetoric, scholars' wide failure to appreciate this essential role played by Bultmann and the form critical moment has not contributed to a clear understanding of the field and state of the question. See chap. 2 in this volume.

11 Burridge, *What Are the Gospels?*
12 Keener, *Christobiography*; Meyer, *Aims of Jesus*.
13 On this broad perspective, see Keener, *Christobiography*, Part I-II.

doctrine, as Eric Foner's *Lincoln* explores the president's continually deepening thought on slavery.[14]

A vital but neglected distinction should be highlighted here. We have forfeited offering a narrative of the Lord's *development* as a human personality; we have not forsaken all hope of gaining exegetical insight into his self-understanding. The Lord in the Gospels confronts us, in other words, like all the figures in ancient *bioi*: as an *established* rather than as an *emerging* character. This simple and far-reaching point has unfortunately been missing in the exegetical discussion.

Certainly, classical verses like Luke 2:52 allow for the waxing expansion of Jesus' humanity, but—while not as outrageous as apocryphal infancy Gospels, which depict only the implausible mock-up of a real child—the precocious Christ child in Luke is simply, already from the first time he opens his mouth, in perfectly secure possession of his identity. Thus, even if we are uncomfortable with the formulation, Raymond Brown's declaration is basically right. In the infancy narratives, "the revelation of Jesus as God's Son has been moved back from the baptism."[15] Wherever they commence, at Jesus' birth or baptism, the Gospels permit no peeking behind the Lord's mature identity—no more than Plutarch allows us to see in the child Alexander, wisely questioning the Persian ambassadors to their astonishment, anything other than the heroic man who will grow and conquer the world.[16] The characters of ancient *bioi* are born like Athena, fully formed.

If we wish to attune ourselves to the historical shape of the reveled data, we must consequently seek in the Gospels an essentially stable and well-configured persona. An emerging event of self-discovery is thus in Jesus' case formally excluded. There is, if you will, despite much anxiety about Greek metaphysics, an ontic, indeed static quality to the biblical data. Dutiful modern attunement to historical dynamism here uncovers, perhaps to our chagrin, outmoded essentialism. Small wonder. We can hardly acknowledge Gospel revelation to be generically Greco-Roman, without permitting it thereby to be stamped at the same time with some hint of the abstracting Hellenistic spirit.

A subtle but substantial difference must nevertheless be registered. The highly stylized depictions of Greco-Roman biographical literature flatten their subjects and subordinate them to various pedagogical programs: most commonly as stereotyped exemplars of vice or virtue. Like the Kings of Israel, the Caesars of Suetonius are always object lessons. The Gospels, by

---

[14] Foner, *Fiery Trial*.
[15] Brown, *Birth of the Messiah*, 137.
[16] *Life of Alexander* 5.1–3.

contrast, while advancing an undisguised kerygmatic program, nevertheless accommodate a proper space for the irreducible untidiness of history, with an artless realism unknown to the *bioi*. The Gospels thus somehow successfully portray with prodigious verisimilitude the unclassifiable figure of Jesus. I have in mind here Auerbach's famous analysis in *Mimesis* of the momentous literary disruption launched by the Gospels.[17] The classical separation of styles, the Jewish critic saw, simply breaks down before Christian belief in the Incarnation and the evangelists' effort to give this faith a literary form. To gesture only at what is most tremendous, depicting the base abuse and crucifixion of any figure other than a lowborn slave, let alone a noble leader, not to say the purported Son of God, is simply unimaginable to the aristocratically conditioned conventions of ancient society, religion, and literature—as Celsus clearly sensed and said.[18]

The collapse of categories, social and otherwise, by which we might capture Jesus is thoroughgoing. It is not simply that Jesus' relation to Josephus's three great parties of first-century Judaism leaves the Lord in a striking no-man's-land. Efforts such as that of Schweitzer, who despite his decisive critique of the theology of the Liberal Lives still confidently located "The Problem" facing any historically credible reading of the Gospels in determining the messianic consciousness of Jesus, and whose paradigmatic attempt to identify Jesus' aims with a specific Second Temple apocalyptic outlook, fail.

In Schweitzer's case, of course, the undertaking was doomed from the outset by a naively narrow construal of Jewish eschatology (and by extension an equally narrow estimate of Jesus' mind): the feverish and ultimately deluded expectation of the imminent end of space and time.[19] The bewildering diversity of Second Temple messianic figures and perspectives—in fairness still largely unknown to that generation of scholars—a chaos that still struggles to find a neatly ordered taxonomy, makes it now simply impossible to adopt this simplistic rendering.[20] Just as "consciousness" must be taken in some ontic and not evolutionary sense, the "messianic" in "messianic consciousness" must also be reconfigured—and in such a way that allows for the fully variegated character of first-century Jewish belief.

---

17 Auerbach, *Mimesis*. See also the excellent and suggestive study of Taylor, *Treatment of Reality in the Gospels*.

18 The (representative) aristocratic perspectives and prejudices of Celsus are nicely described by Wilken, *Christians as the Romans Saw Them*, 94–125.

19 For a frontal assault on modern exegesis's assumptions on this score, see Wright, "Hope Deferred?"

20 See Alexander, "Towards a Taxonomy of Jewish Messianisms." Alexander catalogues various messianisms according to Time, Scene, Agency, and Scope.

The extreme messianic multiformity of the first century so strains the project, however, that it is no longer plausible to aggressively align Jesus' self-perception with this or that antecedent Jewish expectation: the Davidic or Aaronic Anointed One, Deuteronomy's prophet like Moses, the fascinating and forgotten Joshua ben Joseph of 1Q175, or any other Second Temple "christ" whom you might fancy.[21] The very diversity of messianic expectations is itself the relevant phenomenon, and ultimately—enter now our metathesis—this plurality is simply the historical outgrowth of a diversity of personified hopes, aroused through the reading of Israel's Scriptures. This unusually energized reading, moreover, is characterized by a profoundly typological and participationist lens.[22] Messianism, in other words, might be advantageously understood simply as a mode of scriptural interpretation.[23] This understanding hedges against the minimalistic perspective of, say, a Joseph Fitzmyer, who strains to bind messianism as a category to the (relatively infrequent) appearance of the word "messiah."[24] Admittedly, viewing messianic expectation as a broad typological mode of thought invites all manner of imprecisions. Nevertheless, I consider the methodological challenge of refining this approach more adequate to the phenomenon than a simplistic attempt to control the problem. The Jews of Jesus' day found prophetic hints of "King Messiah" in all manner of texts that we might consider non-messianic. And with due respect to our own diachronic methods, these source-critically naive first-century Jews were right by definition, by the very rules of the game that they themselves invented.

To this extent, measuring the mind of Jesus entails, I submit, reposing the question of messianic consciousness in specifically exegetical terms. John reports of Jesus his remarkable, indeed stunning sense that the Scriptures spoke about him (Jn 5:39).[25] Clear hints of this are not lacking in the synoptic

---

21 On this broader issue, see Collins, *The Scepter and the Star*; and Porter, *Messiah in the Old and New Testaments*. See also Novenson, *Christ among the Messiahs*. Novenson argues from a socio-linguistic perspective that "Christ" in Paul's usage is neither a name nor a title but an honorific, grounded in specific scriptural source texts. In this, it resembles the wider phenomenon of early Jewish messianism.

22 The typological character of exegesis at Qumran has long been noted. See, e.g., Betz, "Past Events and Last Events." For a treatment of the metaphysical presuppositions of such exegesis, see Levering, *Participatory Biblical Exegesis*.

23 Alexander ("Towards a Taxonomy," 55–56) locates a series of four propositions about the divine purposiveness of history at the heart of Jewish messianism. These are helpful and figure within what I take to be the broad "typological" pattern of thought. In attempting to accommodate modern phenomena such as secular Zionism, however, Alexander's propositions fail to appreciate the personified and scripturally anchored character of messianic expectation in the NT context.

24 See Fitzmyer, *The One Who Is to Come*.

25 On Jesus and Jn 5, see chap. 12 in this volume.

tradition, and I take it as a fundamental datum. If we bracket for the moment the beatific knowledge of Christ, I believe we draw most near to Jesus' complex human self-understanding, natural and infused (if there is a "still a place for it in Catholic Theology and Exegesis"),[26] by pursuing, in a historically informed fashion, what was traditionally sought through the so-called Christological reading of the Old Testament. Jesus' "messianic consciousness" is born of his entirely unique self-identification with Israel's Scriptures.

Thesis Two: The Regnant Portrayal of Jesus as a Thoroughly Apocalyptic Figure Must Be Abandoned or Revised

When Jesus in Luke 7 quotes Isaiah 61 to reveal to John's messengers his identity as the "One who is coming," he recalls, with no mistaking, the use of this same prophetic passage in 4Q521, the so-called Signs of the Messiah text.[27] Such connections to the amazing cache of materials found at Qumran have lured scholarship ever farther down the road of Schweitzer's kamikaze *konsequente Eschatologie*. It has honestly become a bit wearisome to read.[28] If John Dominic Crossan and his cohort are excepted as the roguish anomalies they are, one struggles to find any scholar who does not present the historical Jesus as some variation on an apocalyptic prophet.

Today it is not generally the case that Jesus is imagined in the freakishly stark colors painted by a Reimarus or Johannes Weiss, who perceived a radically immanent eschatology in Jesus' preaching. Since the 1960s, Norman Perrin's "tensive symbol" settlement has effectively canonized an *already-but-not-yet* perspective on the "Kingdom of God"—a reprise really of exactly the old "mediating theology" toward which Schweitzer was so religiously intolerant.[29] Even so, the prophetic identity of Jesus, which at present controls the field, remains systematically uncomfortable with the rabbinic sources that still informed that older nineteenth-century exegesis. A bookish Christ given to apolitical and intricate exegetical truths has no real place here. "No mouse of the scrolls was the Goodly Fere," Ezra Pound's Simon Zelotes, a

---

26 See Gaine, "Is There Still a Place?" Gaine asserts that there is, but on different grounds than those given in Aquinas's classical account.

27 For a distinctive reading of the messianic construct presented in this important text, see Giambrone, "Meaning of חק חסד in 4Q521." See also chap. 12 in this volume.

28 See, e.g., Fredriksen, *When Christians Were Jews*, and my review included here as Appendix II.

29 Perrin, *Kingdom of God*.

kind of Johann Baptist Metz and spokesmen for all apocalyptic zealots, says of the Lord.

The principled exclusion of Jewish scribal culture from our image of Jesus' persona I deem to be a serious misstep.[30] The title *rabbi*, which is applied to the Lord in both the earliest (and latest) Gospel strata and used as an address for him by seven different groups (both insiders and outsiders), cannot, of course, be identified with the ordained rabbinate or the self-conscious formative Judaism of Judah Hanasi and the Tannaim. But neither can it be wished away *tout court*. Rabbinic Judaism, however much a creation of later centuries, already represents a staggering bulk of tradition at its first written appearance in the Mishnah, and this substance did not materialize out of thin air. A common scholarly overinflation of the catastrophic trauma of the First Roman War must here be carefully avoided, as Jonathan Klawans rightly argues, as though first-century Judaism did not possess the real religious resources to survive (yet another) destruction of the Temple.[31]

The upshot for our purposes is that the Lord's activity specifically as a *teacher*, a recognizable first-century doctor of the sacred page, whose authority astonished the crowds, whose regular preaching was based upon his reading of the Law, and whose halahkic interpretations aroused a deadly resistance, this teacher whose *mathetai* were the students of a school in some real Second Temple sense is not to be so lightly displaced by the sociological models of either a "leadership" or "charismatic" prophet.[32] Jesus remains elusive but is proto-rabbinic in many ways, just as much as his Pharisee counterparts, and I submit that the same streams of anti-Semitism (a sublimated anti-Catholicism) that poisoned so much Protestant NT scholarship, especially German, well into the mid-twentieth century also stands behind this stubborn image of a non-institutional and certainly non-rabbinic Jesus.

---

30 Typical of the policy in most historical Jesus research is John P. Meier's clear methodological decision to exclude rabbinical material from his study: *Marginal Jew*, 94–98. Meier's critique of Joseph Klausner may be correct in arguing that Jesus is nowhere directly mentioned in the rabbinic corpus, at least independent of Christian writings, but this has almost no bearing on the question of offering a plausible historical reconstruction of Christ in the context of the Judaism of his day.

31 Klawans, *Purity, Sacrifice, and the Temple*. Klawans stands opposed to the extreme position espoused by Schwarz, *Imperialism and Jewish Society*. For an effort to find the right balance, see Giambrone, *Rethinking the Jewish War*.

32 On these categories, see, e.g., Wright, *Jesus and the Victory of God*, 162–70. Linked with a new emphasis on Jesus as "rabbi" must be a rehabilitation of Christ as Teacher: a theme dear to the tradition from Clement (*Paedagogus*) to the Scholastics and closely connected with the developed medieval doctrine of revelation. See, e.g., Sherwin, "Christ as Teacher." See also the narrower elaboration of the theme "Jesus was a Teacher" as an element of memory studies (à la Gerhardsson) in Keener, *Christobiography*, chap. 15.

If a rabbinic model wins for us a culture of cultivated memory among the Lord's disciples and hence a more stable link of tradition penetrating back to his earthly life, and pulls Christ from marginal Judaism into the center, this scribal orientation does not entail the simple surrender of eschatology. Martin Hengel is thus right to challenge the image of a rabbi Jesus in drawing attention to the sovereignly self-focused call of the "charismatic leader."[33] But this only means that Jesus stands apart from other teachers, as does his teaching (διδαχὴ καινὴ κατ' ἐξουσίαν; Mk 1:27), and that the later, radical sanitizing of study from an often militant eschatological expectation had not yet transpired (indeed was not yet imagined). It is enough to recall the eight hundred armed *talmidim* (disciples) of Hillel—or for that matter the violently blustering Pharisee Saul of Tarsus—to appreciate that Torah study in this period was easily coupled with ferocious zeal. (Even Metz could be happy if these are rabbis.) The opposite might also be said, of course. Apocalyptic theology is increasingly recognized as heavily hybridized with sapiential/scribal currents. Crossan and company are thus not entirely misguided in seeking a wisdom setting for Jesus, even if the balance here has been lost in the opposite direction. In this vein, and on the note of praxis, the intensely scholastic, literary character of the Essene enterprise is representative of the heavily scribal mood of the age, every bit as much as it embodies any extremism. As an icon we might take the revered "Teacher of Righteousness" and the "scriptorium" excavated at Qumran—a great library hall littered with inkhorns and desks—where "mice of the scrolls" studiously busied themselves with copies and calendric calculations, preparing themselves for Armageddon with *Pesherim*.

The Lord himself, who clearly knew how to read, belonged thereby to a certain social elite. Nevertheless, he did not study, at least not in the secondary system of the day. So, at least, say the Jews in John 7:15. The romance that during the hidden years Jesus trained at Qumran belongs with the Arthurian legends that place him during the same time in Great Britain. Whatever period the Lord may have spent in the circle of the Baptist—not a period without high interest—Jesus was never the apprentice of a master or a school, as Paul was, for instance, at the feet of Gamaliel. "Where, then, did he get all this?" we must ask with the crowds.

There is, as I see it, one obvious and immediate (though certainly not complete) answer. We must allow regular, if also ad hoc, channels of learning through normal exposure to the Scriptures, above all in the weekly synagogue and festal cycle—opportunities optimized by Jesus' singular love of

---

33 Hengel, *Charismatic Leader*.

wisdom. The twelve-year-old child who precociously depicts *teaching* in the Temple is, in fact, said by Luke to be "listening" and asking the doctors questions. His own astonishing "answers" and "understanding" do not make him less the student, but rather reveal the give-and-take of a scholastic exercise plotted somewhere between Ben Sira's and the later rabbinic *Bet Midrash*. We meet here the mysterious collision of the Lord's experiential, dialectical, human knowledge with the scriptural deposit that objectively reveals him.

Jesus in this scene stands in the posture of the archetypal wise son, fervently eager for Torah instruction, the Son of God Israel was meant to be: "Hear my son your father's teaching and the instruction (Torah) of your mother" (Prv 3:1). With childlike simplicity, the twelve-year-old child understands this command more deeply than his own law-observant Nazarene mother and father, literally fulfilling it in the House of his Father in the holy city that Scripture calls Mother.

If native intelligence and disarming insight are revealed in the Christ child's rare understanding, his eager attachment to the Law of the Lord is grounded in a secure self-knowledge of being the "Son" of the God who must be Father. This is perfectly clear from Jesus' response to Mary. I take this uniquely strong perception of filial identity, first of all, in a rigorously Israelogical sense, in line with Exodus 4:22—"Israel is my firstborn son." This verse captures, I believe, with great profundity, a vital dimension of Jesus' human experience of divine paternity.[34] Christ so identified with his people, so loved belonging to those chosen according to the flesh, that he instinctively felt himself implicated and involved wherever he found Israel in the Scriptures either depicted or addressed—which is to say everywhere.

"Shema Yisrael! Hear O Israel," the wise Son, indeed the Son who is Wisdom, prayed daily upon rising. In Hebrew, *Shema* has the sense of both of hear and obey, which is why this docile listening posture the Lord perfectly assumes in praying Deuteronomy 6, a Scripture he may like others have even carried on his person, identifies Jesus with Isaiah's Servant, at once both Israel and Christ. "Morning after morning he awakens me, to listen as those who are taught" (Is 50:4).

As God, Jesus is *auctor scripturae*. Rather than seeking an event of *anamnesis* in his confrontation with the Scriptures, however—as when I reread a paper I myself wrote in the fourth grade—we should seek, I suggest, at least in his humanity, *anagnorisis*: recognition, even in the strong Aristotelian sense

---

[34] The "dyadic personality" of ancient persons, tilted toward a collective rather than an individual identity, is of obvious sociological relevance here. See Malina and Neyrey, *New Testament World*, 67.

of discovery.³⁵ In the NT, of course, this word also simply means "reading," which is exactly the appropriate connotation for the event of recognition we have in mind. Jesus found himself in Scripture because he experienced himself with an unequaled, focused intensity as the proper object and audience of Israel's revelation. As the Lord's Servant, he lived in a state of obedient alacrity and heard God's Word addressed to him with perfect directness, an almost unimaginable immediacy: as if every word of the sacred text had that singular power that gripped St. Anthony when he walked into church and heard the reading of Matthew's Gospel. And as Anthony later had no need to keep a written Gospel, since it had been written on his heart, no word had dropped sterile to the ground, so the grace to absorb and indeed be fused as one with the Word must reach its acme in the human soul of Christ.

So unmediated and indeed uninterrupted is the address of God's Word to Jesus that it becomes identified with his own "I." Here we touch the all-important "Son of Man" title, a central plank in the conscious of Jesus and undoubtedly the most significant casualty of the trend to make him too apocalyptic. A long-standing debate, unlikely to end before this figure's coming on the clouds, has obscured the precise meaning of the locution.³⁶ A connection to Daniel 7:13 nevertheless dominates the scholarship, and Jesus' preferred self-designation is overwhelmingly heard as an apocalyptic reference to a heavenly, often preexistent, messianic figure, with echoes in *1 Enoch* and *4 Ezra*.

This exclusively apocalyptic, titular meaning I hold to be problematic and misleading. Daniel's *bar enasha* is not an absolute red herring, of course. Jesus certainly finds himself figured in this massively important text, as he makes triumphantly plain in his trial before Caiaphas (Mk 14:60–63). This bedrock principle of self-identification, however, I am maintaining applies in a plenary way to *all* the Scriptures.³⁷ To this extent, it is useful to note that the value of Daniel in determining the concrete "Son of Man" expression,

---

35 Aristotle, *Poetics* 10–11. On this concept, see especially the work of Northrop Frye: "Much of my critical thinking has turned on the double meaning of Aristotle's term anagnorisis, which can mean 'discovery' or 'recognition', depending on whether the emphasis falls on the newness of the experience or its recurrence" (*Words with Power*, 26). See chap. 14 in this volume.

36 The scholarship on "The Son of Man" title is overwhelming. For an overview, see Burkett, *Son of Man Debate*; Vermes, "Son of Man Debate Revisited"; and Hurtado and Owen, *"Who Is This Son of Man?"*

37 At issue here is the need, addressed in Thesis One, to expand Jesus'"messianic consciousness" beyond a narrow identification with some discrete apocalyptic title. The "Son of Man" circumlocution for Jesus' own "I" is of major significance in this connection, for its breadth must somehow embrace Christ's full subjectivity.

which Jesus also uses in *dozens* of other contexts (pointing in entirely different scriptural directions), is weaker than supposed. The confident titular force of the phrase collapses considerably when *1 Enoch* and *4 Ezra* are recognized to be in many ways false parallels, and it does not seem that Daniel's "one like a human being" was in fact circulating and on everybody's mind.[38] Maurice Casey, whose cranky scholarship hits closer to the mark, detects a common idiom that means "someone in my position," but this also ultimately leads us astray.[39] We have, rather, in "the son of man" what must be reckoned an idiolect, the characteristic speech pattern of an individual, in this case the raw *vox Christi*.[40] Nor is the sense of the queer expression inevitably so mystifying—"*the* (definite article!) descendant of the human race"; "the human being"—a peculiarly emphatic and suggestive self-description.[41]

Ezekiel's anarthrous usage is the closest parallel to at least this valence of the usage, and there is a distinct biblical ring to Jesus' language, which was seemingly inspired by the memorable way the Word of God addressed this prophet-priest nearly one hundred times. Just as Ezekiel's human frailty was vulnerably exposed to the sudden speech of God's Word from heaven and radically seized by the Spirit, who yanked him around violently by the hair, addressing him almost derisively as *ben Adam*, so Jesus' strangely forceful sense of his own humanity—expressed in his altogether idiosyncratic *self-referential* use of heaven's address to mankind—hints silently at a similar rapture from above, a vigorous and absolute appropriation of his humanity by God's Word and Spirit. In calling himself "*The* Son of Man," Jesus made himself that frail human being to whom God's Word from heaven was

---

38 See Hannah, "Elect Son of Man."

39 Casey, who develops the position of Vermes, has written a great deal on this topic. See most recently Casey, *Solution to the Son of Man Problem*. Casey's handling of the definite articles is uncertain. Moreover, even if texts like the Sefire inscription illustrate the philological prehistory of the idiom, the syntagm in Jesus' usage, as a *consistent* circumlocution for his "I," is more peculiar than anything found in these sources.

40 See Larry Hurtado, *Lord Jesus Christ*, 290–306. See also chap. 12 in this volume.

41 There are important connections here with the theory of Joel Marcus ("Son of Man as Son of Adam," 38–61 and 370–86), who highlights the double definite article and sees in "The Son of (the) Man" a reference to the figure of the first man, Adam, in Genesis. See also Hooker, *Son of Man in Mark*. The rejection of the patristic and medieval human "Son of Man" in the nineteenth and early twentieth centuries was largely based on scholars' inability to imagine why Jesus should speak so strangely. "Jesus could not possibly have felt any need of again and again assuring his contemporaries of his true human nature, which none of them could doubt" (Beyschlag, *New Testament Theology I*, 61). See Burkett, *Son of Man Debate*, 20–21. This is a failure in both historical and theological imagination. The overwhelming impression caused by the Lord's mighty deeds (cf. Acts 14:15) and his distinct pedagogy of revelation come directly into play here.

uniquely addressed. The Eternal Word, robed in flesh, did not then wander around repeating that he was the star of some Jewish apocalypse, but rather delighted to voice his personal "I" with the unambiguous affirmation that he was a full-blooded, thus mortal, son of Adam. But who speaks like this except a mad man, or else a man who is also the Lord?

Thesis Three: Contemporary Exegesis Must Recover a Chalcedonian Hermeneutic

The full mystery of the Incarnation is hidden in the Eternal Son naming his own subjective I "the Son of Man" and voicing this in a human throat. The pedagogical aspect of this circumlocution should not be lost from view, however. With Fr. Dreyfus, we do well to contemplate the considerable difficulty Jesus faced in initiating stridently monotheistic Jews into the mystery of his divine identity and the restrained strategy of esoteric teaching he consequently adopted.[42] A recent funny and frustrating experience trying to explain (not establish) the doctrine of the Trinity to a family of orthodox Jews has impressed me with the rather comical magnitude of the challenge and the Lord's wisdom in mysteriously intoning his humanity. One does not simply introduce oneself as the second divine hypostasis.

Even after his glorious resurrection, Jesus appears preoccupied with insisting that he is really human (Lk 24:36–43); the revelation of his Godhead passes resolutely by way of his fleshly nature (Jn 20:26–29). While Jesus' self-designation as the "Son of Man" at times obviously evokes the enthroned heavenly figure in Daniel, whose special relation to the "Ancient of Days" invites important speculation about his identity, the distinctively human manifestation of this mysterious personage is incontestably intoned.

There is accordingly something odd in straining too hard to sidestep or spring over this primal data point, as much apologetic literature appears preoccupied to do. The human (not angelic) figure startlingly enthroned above the angels in the so-called *Self-Glorification Hymn* at Qumran (4Q171b, 4Q491, 4Q427, 1QH^a XXV-XXVI) provides an extraordinarily useful point of reference for considering the theological space in which a Danielic-type figure might be plotted in the Second Temple context, particularly if Eric Miller is correct to draw a line here to the enthroned Enochic "son of man."[43]

---

42 Dreyfus, *Jésus savait-il qu'il était Dieu?*, 41–55.
43 On this text, see Miller, "*Self-Glorification Hymn* Reexamined." This potential link to Enoch need not necessarily take the strong and specific form of "an earlier Hymn of Enoch," independent from the community and practices at Qumran, as suggested by Miller.

At the same time, as Enoch himself was understood to have been a priestly figure through his own heavenly ascent (2 *Enoch* 22:8–9), the editor Esther Eshel is not at all off-base when she detects the voice of the eschatological High Priest behind this hymn.[44] The alignment of Isaiah's Suffering Servant with the protagonist of the hymn, finally, fills out an extremely bracing picture, and Israel Knohl is prepared to see in the *Self-Glorification Hymn* nothing less than a direct precursor to and influence upon the messianic conception of Jesus.[45] In my estimation this entire line of reflection—not least the priestly resonance—is of crucial importance in correctly calibrating the Christological character of Jesus' own self-presentation.

But here the impolite question finally imposes itself: How far or under what circumstances would Jesus' own human understanding, let me specify as *viator*, of his identity as the Eternal Son have been possible or even remotely comprehensible given his own historical circumscription within Second Temple messianism and monotheism? Is the pattern of mediating agent figures enough to accommodate an incarnate divine Person as a viable conceptual possibility?[46]

A pronouncement here on the radical notion of a robust pre-Christian binitarianism, such as is envisioned by a Daniel Boyarin or Peter Schäfer, will obviously be of decisive importance in declaring what is imagined as a thinkable thought. Was the mental space available to the Jewish contemporaries of Jesus (thus also to Jesus himself) in fact disposed for the easy recognition of a "junior god" ("Kleiner oder Junger Gott"), as Schäfer, for instance, suggests? Was Jesus simply able to slip into the slot of *YHWH ha-qatan*, held by Metatron in *3 Enoch*? Even apart from the difficult chronology of the traditions here envisioned, metaphysically considered, it seems to me that we have a problem. Distinctions of immanent and economic theology are being blurred, which the process of conciliar debate worked hard and quite rightly to distinguish. Does *die Wissenschaft* thus really understand whatever exactly it thinks it is helpfully saying when it announces, "Die Wissenschaft hat für dieses Nebeneinander von zwei Mächte oder Göttern analog zu dem christlich-dogmatischen Begriff 'trinitarisch' den Begriff 'binitarisch' entwickelt"?[47] *Two Gods in Heaven* is certainly no award-winning description of anything truly analogous to the Christian dogmatic conception of the Trinity. If our present question concerns the conceptions of Jesus and not

---

44 Eshel, "4Q471b," 426.
45 See Knohl, *Messiah before Jesus*.
46 Hurtado, *Lord Jesus Christ*, 27–78; idem, *How on Earth Did Jesus Become God?*
47 Schäfer, *Zwei Götter im Himmel*, 12. See chap. 7 in this volume.

of the later Christian councils, crude caricatures of the latter are unlikely to clarify the former, I am afraid.

An alternative approach to this conceptual muddle is thus to turn for help to the developing strains of Jewish mysticism that historically fueled texts like those just invoked, the *Self-Glorification Hymn* and the Hekalot/Merkabah speculations of *3 Enoch*. Hurtado's own model ultimately requires an explosive religious experience to explain the appearance of what he also (not without introducing the same problems) calls Christian binitarianism. In the Gospels, Peter's confession of Christ as "Son of the living God" comes, we are told, not from flesh and blood but from a revelation on high (Mt 16:16–19). Is it accordingly reasonable or right to imagine some such experience in the case of Christ? Did his human nature in some way even require it?

In approaching this difficult and embarrassing issue, an apologetic anxiety inclining toward Monophysitism must first be flagged. At least since the time of Lessing, an ongoing, low-grade iteration of the Nicene crisis has been plaguing NT exegesis, as the divinity of Jesus is alternately attacked and defended. At present, the Early High Christology School represents a kind of modest Athanasian moment, and, along with Hurtado, Richard Bauckham's Christological reflection has profitably focused our attention on the decisive issue of Jewish monotheism and ultimately on the revelation of Christ's divine nature within this framework.[48] Bauckham's language of "divine identity" for divine essence causes certain Cyrillian problems, however, and this pattern of scholarship runs a risk in forging what Kavin Rowe calls "the binding of *ho Theos* and *ho Iesus*."[49] It is not accidental or without significance that Bauckham's own project is so strongly animated by the no-nature, all-person Christology of Jürgen Moltmann.[50]

Historically, in response to conciliar Christology, a programmatic, "partititve" division of texts between Jesus' human and divine natures was adopted in Gospel exegesis. This was honestly a utilitarian protocol, serviceable for a time in sidelining problem texts like the Son's *nescience* in Mark 13:32, but in its decadence often a bizarre proof of the Lord's own conciliar orthodoxy when he went off script and seemed to forget his divinity (e.g., Jn 14:28).[51] As a doctrinal expedient, this reading strategy is perfectly sound,

---

48 See esp. Bauckham, *Jesus and the God of Israel*.

49 Rowe, *Early Narrative Christology*, 202.

50 See Bauckham, *Theology of Jürgen Moltmann*. Moltmann's avowed intention to revise the classical doctrine of God drives toward an explicit rejection of Chalcedonian Christology and the *communicatio idiomatum*, predicating suffering directly to Christ's person. The echo of Moltmann's *The Crucified God* in Bauckham's *God Crucified* is obvious. See chap. 7 in this volume.

51 On the patristic response to this text, see Madigan, "*Christus Nesciens*?" See also chap. 15 in this volume.

but the alternating identification of Jesus' "I" with one nature rather than the other is admittedly strange: an unlikely pattern, seemingly, when the authorial intention of the evangelists' is sought through the historical and literary context. The program of historical-critical exegesis has accordingly found the procedure anachronistic, arbitrary, and unconvincing and allotted no place in its methodology for this neat Chalcedonian sifting of passages. Faced with a now long defunct tradition, we must thus struggle anew to find a proper hermeneutic of the two natures, plausible within the framework of modern interpretation—otherwise, NT study will remain stalled at a single-subject Christology, vulnerable to what in the present climate manifests as the distortions of extreme kenotic theology.

As a first step in moving neo-Nicene exegesis in a fuller Chalcedonian direction, it is necessary perhaps simply to give special attention, more than is customary among the small and nervous guild of orthodox exegetes, to Christ's created, mediating, instrumental human nature. A good place to start is in braving the adoptionist waters of the Baptism. At the Jordan, the Father's voice from heaven, refracted through the synoptic prism, says both (in Matthew) "this is" and (in Mark and Luke) "*you are* my beloved Son." The later version is closer to the scriptural text of Psalms 2:7, which is linked in all versions with an allusion to the Servant of Isaiah 42:1. Granting that Luke permits us no room for imagining that Christ experienced a breaking newsflash in this moment, what could such an extraordinary experience of this *genui te* mean?

I will not attempt to describe what I said lies forever hidden within the ontic quality of Jesus' persona in the Gospels, but I would like, nevertheless, to suggest two things. First, the inevitable boundaries of Jesus' natural knowledge were broken open by an experience something like (but only something like) a private revelation—albeit in this case at the Jordan, with an onlooking, eavesdropping audience, as at the conversion of St. Paul. At the Baptism, Christ was thus given, in who knows how much infinitely greater intensity, an experience with an analogy to the vision of the Trinity that Ignatius had in the Dominican church at Manresa. As an event, however, the personal involvement of Jesus in this vision reaches an entirely new order, for it does not remain an object over against him, however gripping to the seer's depths. Jesus' own subject is implicated in the words, "You are my Son." The Spirit's unction thus radiates through all Jesus' senses and his soul and somehow involves Christ within the Trinitarian processions in a way entirely unique. Moreover, this epiphanic event comes precisely in the form of a word of Scripture, with exactly the literary character of *anagnorisis*. Indeed, we should allow the Baptism this decisive character: structurally similar to (however materially different from) the paradigmatic dramatic moment when Oedipus discovers that it is he who (being adopted) stands spoken of in the prophecy.[52] At the Jordan, the Son "discovers," let us say rather *recognizes*, himself precisely in discerning the voice of the Father speaking in the scriptural text, and he perceives himself in this *speculum* of the Word at once as *Son* and *Servant*: the one uniquely beloved by the Father and he who is uniquely obedient, even to the bearing our infirmities unto death (Is 53:4). This all comes mediated through Jesus' Jewish flesh and kin, for it as "son of David" *kata sarka* (Rom 1:3; cf. Mt 1:1–16) that these verses, directed to David's heir, are activated and speak so personally to Christ. This leads me to the second point.

Scripture somehow circumscribes the center of Jesus' *revealed* identity (what abysses lie hidden!), and in his case and his alone, private and public revelation somehow perfectly coincide. For Christ, who subsists perfectly as God's firstborn Son incarnate, Israel's shared body of normative revelation *is* his own singular grace of private teaching from on high. Christ experiences the Scriptures as a private and personal revelation: a religious experience, if you will, in the sense perhaps that Hurtado requires; the archetypal faith of Jesus (i.e., the *Christform*) to use von Balthasar's language; another view on the *pistis Christou*.[53]

This convergence of the intensely personal and the public in Jesus' experience of Scripture refracts his consciousness and magnifies what I have said about Scripture's unmediated address to Christ's humanity. It also clarifies the evangelists' vacillating reports of the Baptism, signaling the objective, normative revelation of Jesus' person. What is spoken in a fully personal, I-Thou form to Christ, "You are my son," is somehow one with what the deictic sense renders before the world as a pointer: "This is he." The Son's own second person, his first personal "I," merges with the proclamation of both Testaments. The "prophets and apostles," John the Baptist and Paul, both announce of Christ what the Father also says to the Son: "*houtos estin*! *This* is the one!" heard by Christ as, "You are he!"

---

52 Aristotle, *Poetics* 10. For Aristotle, the recognition (*anagnorisis*) most intimately connected with plot and action is recognition of persons. The integral movement from recognition to *catastrophe*, moreover, is central to the tragic force of a plot. In the Gospel, the decisive orientation of the Baptism to the cross undergirds the entire dramatic "eucatastrophe" (Tolkien).

53 See Hadley, "Archetypal Faith of Christ." It is noteworthy that Balthasar's attention to "Christ consciousness" (a point of clear, present interest in view of Thesis One above) puts his theology in close contact with that of Rahner, often viewed as Balthasar's rival. Hadley's effort to engage exegesis on the dogmatic order is admirable, though I would take a different line toward what he calls Jesus' "biblically attested growth in awareness of being loved and sent by the Father."

The scene of the Lord's Temptation provides an immediate annotation to the extraordinary revelation at the Jordan, as the tempter promptly sows his doubts: "If you are the son of God." Dare we say that Jesus' human intellect is assailed here to the point of crisis? I see no reason why, in principle, this should be more scandalous than the assailing of his human will in Gethsemane and in the *timor gehennalis*. Perhaps monothelitism has a counterpart in *mononousitism* (what is not assumed, after all, is not redeemed). Should we then concoct some intellective equivalent of Maximus's *gnomic will* to preserve Christ's unshakable self-understanding in midst of the horrible battle?[54]

What really is the temptation, however? To be God's Son in the wrong way, it would seem.[55] And how? By mishearing the Scriptures. The Lord in the wilderness again stands solidly in the place of Israel and victoriously resists a series of false messianic personae.[56] This victory takes the form, significantly, of an interpretative debate, structured around the decisive text of Deuteronomy 6:1–16, quoted three separate times. (Soloviev's devil as an exegete from Tübingen may be more than entertaining fiction, it seems.[57]) Against an alluring misapprehension of the Word, the Christ of God overcomes in his flesh every false Christological reading and, as faithful Israel, fulfills the call of the *Shema*. For in order truly to be God's Son and to be God's Son in truth, Jesus must find himself figured in not only the text but also "in the same Spirit in which it was written."[58] And he must in exactly this *Spirit* obediently embody all that is there contained, down to the *letter*, so that the prophetic Word to Israel becomes the Son's internal script, ensuring all that he accomplishes "in order to fulfill" is perfectly "according to the scriptures" (cf. Mt 1:22, 2:6, 2:15, 2:17–18, 4:14, 8:17, 12:17–21, 13:14, 13:35; 21:4, 27:9–10; 1 Cor 15:3–4).[59]

---

54 Not all are pleased with Maximus's solution to the problem, of course. See, e.g., Blowers, "Maximus the Confessor."

55 "The three scenes have a common subject in that they correct a false understanding of Jesus' mission as Son ... The unifying link in the three is the series of quotations from Deuteronomy, derived from passages that recall three events of the Exodus in which the Israelites in the desert were put to the test and failed" (Fitzmyer, *Gospel According to Luke I-IX*, 509–10).

56 On this dimension of the text, see Reisenfeld, "Le caractère messianique."

57 Soloviev, *Story of Anti-Christ*.

58 "Cum sacra scriptura eodem Spiritu quo scripta est etiam legenda et interpretanda sit" (*Dei Verbum* 12). The continuity of this principle with all ecclesial interpretation is vital. It underscores the archetypal character of Christ's consciousness; see note 53 above.

59 The stress that Vanhoozer (*Drama of Doctrine*) lays upon "ecclesial performance" of the "script" of Scripture is helpful and creative, but such ecclesiology must have a Christological prologue. Attention to the theandric nature of Christ's fulfillment of the Scriptures could,

The Temptation discloses some terrible but victorious struggle to preserve the grace that suffuses the Messiah's flesh after the Spirit's descent upon him at the Jordan. This grace not only expands Jesus' experiential knowledge humanly to perceive in some fuller way his substantial relations within the Trinity at the level of his person, but it also equips him to undertake his temporal mission.

On Tabor, the veil is once more pulled back on Christ's divine filiation, but here we observe a new accent laid upon overcoming the *scandalon* of the Cross, in fulfillment of the Son's priestly mission.[60] In some fashion, it is here that the man Jesus is fortified in thinking not as men do (e.g., his companion Peter) but like God—a grace that appears in the form of a kind of terrestrial celestial journey. Jesus' experience on Mount Tabor is thus an exaltation in the Johannine sense—a simultaneous revelation of cross and heavenly glorification—for it is precisely as the glorified heavenly high priest that Christ must perfect his sacrificial journey to Jerusalem to die (Heb 7–9).

Again the event is scripted explicitly through the word of Scripture. The voice of the Father, content to quote Deuteronomy 18:15, reveals the fulfillment of the prophecy in glorifying the flesh of his Son. The appearance of Moses and Elijah is the enacted "performance" of Malachi 3. Both the voice and the vision are together at work illumining Jesus' embodied human mind—not merely his clothes. The living word of Scripture that thus envelopes Jesus and his disciples is not only a condescension to the three chosen witnesses who accompanied him up the mountain. It is also the revelation of a *capital* grace given to the chosen humanity of the Son. It is an initiation into the "mysteries" of the execution of his mediating, messianic, cultic service on the cross.

In his flesh—extending up through all those ranged powers of his soul to the very place where he abides serenely as *comprehensor*—Jesus had to live through the selfsame lesson he later explained to the two confused disciples on the road, when he teaches them everything written about him in the Law and Prophets. As Gabriel helped Daniel unlock the riddle of Jeremiah's seventy years (Dn 9:1–26), so Jesus' understanding of the scribes' teaching and of his own mission was illumined by a grace of experiential exegesis

---

in fact, substantially help to address the breakdown in Protestant-Catholic debate over the relationship of the Church (i.e., as Mystical Body) to the Word. Specifically, a sharp and typically Protestant opposition of the *divine authorship* of Scripture over against Church authority (as the enacted locus of fulfillment/interpretation) cannot function in Christ, where the Word is not only passively received, but is also in some sense waiting upon an authoritative, performative exegesis from the subjective *auctor scripturae*.

60 See chap. 13 in this volume.

from on high. So quickened was the Lord's knowledge of Scripture that this personal script of his unique destiny spoke to him with the living voices of the historical subjects and the divine *auctor* of the Word.

Jesus' experiential understanding of his identity and mission came through a spectrum of historical encounters with the Scriptures. Each had an *event* quality, extending from humble hearing (or reading) of the Word in its liturgical proclamation to, at the far end, extraordinary infusions of supernatural grace and light—actual graces always configured to the normative shape of the Scriptures. For the Son who lived perfectly by every word that falls from the mouth of God, however, the immediacy of his hearing was *unbroken*.[61] Despite the punctuated historical quality of his encounters, Jesus is, by his enduring internal identification with the Word, most perfectly the man sung of in Psalm 1, the aspiration of every Law-loving Jew: he who mediates on the Torah "unceasingly day and night." The *blessedness* of this man is the *beatific* vector of all Christ's human knowledge and the point at which Christ the Teacher's *sacra doctrina* is grounded in the *speculum* of the sacred page.[62] The answer to our query, "Where did he get all this?" now at last is clear. The human nature of Christ was washed unceasingly and to its utmost depths in the surging stream of God's revealing Word.

"What does the Lord think about in heaven?" The wonderful answer the rabbis gave to this wonderfully impertinent question applies, I offer, also to the man who now sits at the Lord's right hand. What does he think about? "He reads Torah."

---

[61] A permanent, habitual character to Christ's prophetic, Spirit-endowed knowledge appears to be essential in explaining his enduring capacity to rightly interpret the sacred text. The punctiliar confirmations and intensifications of Jesus' self-knowledge and understanding of his mission, coordinated with a narrative of his contact with the scriptures, must thus find their justification on a different order.

[62] Organizing the integral knowledge of Christ (experiential, prophetic, and blessed) around scriptural revelation helps secure the continuity of all *sacra doctrina*, which binds theological science on earth with the science of God and the Blessed (*ST* I, q. 1).

CHAPTER 12

Another Johannine Thunderbolt?
The Legatio Baptistae *and "The Poetic Christ"*

In one of the most beautiful and revealing lines that he ever wrote, Johann Adam Möhler confessed the following: "Without the scriptures the characteristic form of the speech of Jesus would be withheld from us; we would not know how the God-man spoke; and I think, that I would no longer wish to live, if I should no longer hear him speaking."[1] This statement comes to mind as I read through the remarkable book of my confrere: Olivier-Thomas Venard's *The Poetic Christ*, now wonderfully translated, reedited, and arranged by Francesca Murphy and Kenneth Oakes.[2] In his acknowledgments to the work, Fr. Olivier-Thomas mentions the brothers of St. Étienne in Jerusalem, who "in the midst of a biblical monoculture" have patiently endured his presence as our "resident French intellectual."[3] Being the only American at the École, I am keenly aware just how alien French intellectual solar systems can sometimes be. I am also curious what this particular self-description makes of all the other Frenchmen with whom we reside. Eschewing the pursuit of such imprudent speculation, however,

---

1 "Ohne Schrift wäre uns die eigentümliche Form der Reden Jesu vorenthalten; wir wüssten nicht, wie der Gott-mensch sprach, und ich meine, leben möchte ich nicht mehr, wenn ich ihn nicht mehr reden hörte" (Möhler, *Die Einheit in der Kirche*, 54).
2 Venard, *Poetic Christ*. The original French text of Venard's work appears in three separate volumes: *Thomas d'Aquin poète théologien: Littérature et théologie*; *Thomas d'Aquin poète théologien: La langue de l'ineffable*; and *Thomas d'Aquin poète théologien: Pagina sacra*.
3 Venard, *Poetic Christ*, ix.

I will here simply consider Fr. Olivier-Thomas to be our resident German Romantic, expressing my admiration for the audacious brio of his stupendous work. I offer him this small reflection with fraternal affection. While to the regnant biblical monoculture my own course may appear more theologically adventuresome than customary *Bibelwissenschaft* permits, it may seem tame by other measures. I have withstood the literary siren song of lyrical adumbrations and steered clear of daring maneuvers on the radically orthodox, ontotheological high seas. Whether or not I have rightly caught the spirit of the *poète théologien*, I leave for others to decide. My study has a directly exegetical aim and is structured in two large movements.

The Poetic Gospel

In the first two chapters of his newly reordered magnum opus, *A Poetic Christ*, Fr. Olivier-Thomas Venard makes an opening move of what was once, in the earlier French version, a climatic application and conclusion. He spreads out with all his creative, synthetic, and aphoristic power the vista of a poetic Gospel and a poetic Christology. Reducing his wide-ranging trilogy down to a single volume is perhaps no more ambitious or foolhardy than boiling these rich chapters down to one leading idea, yet I would like to identify as something like an evocative core insight the following redolent suggestion from page 68: "It may well be that the canonical text reaps the perlocutionary effects of a strategy inaugurated by Jesus himself."

The import of this idea, although expressed here less imposingly than in some denser and more teasing formulations, rests shrouded beneath a jargon-heavy carapace of theoretical linguistics. The thrust is nevertheless clear. A unified experience of language carries us from Jesus' speech to the discourse of the Gospel authors; the sacred texts thus give us access to the Word made man. "Christian speech continues Christic speech," to capture it in a slogan.[4] At one level, the phenomenon here is not unlike Plato's textualization of Socrates, whom we somehow vitally encounter through the interpretative memory of his brilliant student. Just as the unique force of the master's inquiring personality gave birth to and even demanded the new literary form of the dialogue, so does the personality of Christ compel and engender a new form of language as he passes immortal into the *euaggelion*.

The Gospels themselves are thus more mysterious than Richard Burridge has led us to believe in reducing them to Greco-Roman *bioi*.[5] If indeed

---

4 Venard, *Poetic Christ*, 99.
5 Burridge, *What Are the Gospels?* See also Keener, *Christobiography*.

in evangelic poetics "signification, significance, and 'significativity' are mixed together"[6]—which is to say, if in the genre of the Gospels the narrated historical referent and the existence of both relator and reader are profoundly blended to some acute degree—then Bultmann's kerygmatic analysis is not entirely misguided. The point is not idle, since I would note here a strong Bultmannian character to radical theological theses on the primacy of language and the "la domination de la parole sur l'histoire."[7] God, as we know, is not a story; nor is Jesus a text.[8]

Venard nevertheless presents us with something quite different than an exegete like Francis Watson, whose recent tome *Gospel Writing: A Canonical Perspective* I would classify as a landmark of post-Bultmannian Bultmannian scholarship.[9] ("Quite different" is mildly stated; the world knows as yet but one French German Romantic practitioner of "Thomistic Kabbala." Still the comparison has some warrant.) Where Watson's project creatively envisions an exegetical "life without Q" nevertheless still bound to disembodied logia and piecemeal sayings sources—clearly a Christ of the word, rather than the deed—his wholesale rejection of the historical Jesus enterprise leads him to throw all his weight into what he designates "interpretation," a literary placeholder for Bultmann's more theologically potent *kerygma*. Gospel speech is in consequence for Watson a communicative medium that "somehow mediates Jesus directly and simultaneously renders him historically inaccessible"—and even uninteresting. Venard, by contrast, while approvingly citing Marcel Gauchet's statement that "the religion of the Incarnation is fundamentally a religion of the interpretation," wields this reduction to hermeneutics in another manner.[10] Tempted perhaps to demonize the "intentionalist fallacy" with excessive structuralist zeal, Venard nevertheless outflanks Watson's terminally redaction-critical paradigm. He leaves space; namely, in his theo-linguistic vision for the memory of the eyewitnesses and the historical, narrative agency of Christ. So he sneaks in an Ur-intentionality of the highest order.

Quidquid recipitur ad modum repientis recipitur. A physical, memorial continuum binds the words spoken by Jesus and the words written about him. The performative, symbolic matter of Jesus' gestures, being baptized or breaking bread, for instance, likewise belongs to this discursive continuum, finding enacted echoes in the liturgical praxis of the Church. A Christo-

---

6 Venard, *Poetic Christ*, 79.
7 Venard, *Littérature et théologie*, 25.
8 See Murphy, *God Is Not a Story*.
9 Watson, *Gospel Writing*. See my "Review of Francis Watson, *Gospel Writing*."
10 Venard, *Littérature et théologie*, 173.

logical-ecclesial nexus of *illocution-perlocution* thus emerges, an embodied nexus of revelatory intention and inspired reception, which preserves two distinct poles in the single event of divine communication: Incarnation and *Scripture-cum-Tradition*. When Jesus preaches the Kingdom, this is not simply reducible to or convertible with the apostolic kerygma. Nevertheless, the one is the complement and imprint of the other. The "memoires of the apostles," to use Justin's name for the Gospels, are inaugurated and shaped by patterns traceable to the speech and behavior, the signifying of the incarnate Word.

This historic blending of Christic speech into Christian speech forms part of a larger fusion, moreover, for in a poetic Christology, catalyzed by the revealing Word, the canonical whole coalesces into a unified poetic artifact, as the biblical voices converge symphonically around a single tone. The resulting scriptural unit may be envisioned as a complex literary object on a vast scale like Northrup Frye's *Great Code*.[11] Frye's striking characterization of the entire Bible as *kerygma*, moreover, a term classically reserved for the evangelical proclamation, perfectly suits Venard's broad biblical poetics, for the unity of the Christian Bible is again resolutely hermeneutic. As often in Venard's thought, François Martin provides the essential premise. The "interpretative competence" exercised by the New Testament over the Old depends upon recognizing in Jesus "the perfect hearer and authentic interpreter of the Law and the Prophets ... *le sujet énonciataire* par excellence."[12] Jesus is the addressee, the target of the sacred page. I would add—and the point is major—that Christ is also the perfect *sujet énonciateur* as well as the *referent* itself. The Scriptures are all spoken to, by, or about him.

Is it possible to give any historical traction to this supercessionist Christological claim upon Israel's Scriptures? Theologically and linguistically, how should ecclesial exegesis and its plenary, poetic appropriation of the Old Testament be justified? As kerygmatic discourse par excellence, the Gospels hold the key to answering such questions.

Being the principal witness to the Incarnate Word, *Dei Verbum* 18 identifies the Gospels as holding a special preeminence among all the Scriptures, even the writings of the New Testament. Rightly discerning the unity of the four Gospels is accordingly somehow the kernel of the whole canonical problem. New Testament scholars have not been insensitive to the issue. For instance, in an important set of essays, Martin Hengel gave attention to the early adoption of a singular kerygmatic title, εὐαγγέλιον, for the whole fourfold collection, interiorly differentiated by the preposition κατά and

---

11 Frye, *Great Code*.
12 Venard, *Littérature et théologie*, 176.

an underwriting *auctor/auctoritas*: ΚΑΤΑ ΛΟΥΚΑΝ, ΙΩΑΝΝΗΝ, and the like.¹³ The "canonical perspective" promoted by Watson departs entirely from this model of authoritative and unified proclamation. The inherent indistinguishability of canonical and noncanonical texts is for him an axiomatic theorem, as Jesus is textualized in a busy, performative overgrowth of variant interpretations, well into the second century. The late construction of a new hermeneutical object in the fourfold Gospel is accordingly an arbitrary juridical intervention of the Church, an act of authorship not on the literary but on the strictly ecclesial order. While Watson is not unaware of the primitive historical line leading from "datum" through "recollection" to "inscription" (the terms are his, but this maps to a memory-mediated *illocution-perlocution* axis), and while he acknowledges the theoretical possibility of misinterpretation, tracing the Church's approbated Jesus literature back to some postulated apostolic experience of Christ—what Balthasar wonderfully called "the impact of the meteor"—is a program that holds absolutely no interest. Irreducible variety is the watchword. Watson has no ear and no patience for the harmony of the four Gospels.

The harmonious unity and final authority of the Gospels, of course, lies ultimately in the unity and authority of the person of the Word. In line with this, Venard, for his part, thus also offers a variety of reflections on the unity of the fourfold canon, predictably keen not to fall prey to the *oublie du langage*. Of special interest in this connection, as least to me, is the reference he makes to an idea evoked by various exegetes from Joachim Jeremias to Raymond Brown, the so-called *ipsissima vox*. Drawn up in intentional contrast to the irrecoverable *ipsissima verba*, the elusive exact words spoken by Jesus himself, the interest of registering instead his discernible voice, which somehow remained operative and accessible in the transmission of Jesus' memory, has more than a fugitive apologetic interest.

In the case of Jeremias, whose 1954 article remains the most significant treatment of the issue, two "Kennzeichen der *ipsissima vox Jesu*" can be confidently named: Jesus' habitually bold address of "Abba" for God and his curious use of the word "Amen" to introduce his own statements, rather than to answer and affirm the words of another.¹⁴ This is suggestive matter beyond any doubt, despite Jeremias's overstatements about the singularity of such usage and erroneous infantilization of "Abba" as "Daddy."¹⁵ Jesus' *vox* here is nevertheless reduced to two diamond-like *verba*—contextualized in some minimal way but ultimately painfully constrained. Venard takes a

---

13 See Hengel, "Titles of the Gospels."
14 See Jeremias, "Kennzeichen der ipsissima vox Jesu."
15 See famously Barr, "Abba Isn't Daddy."

more expansive approach, by contrast, in reaching for the whole dexterous élan that electrifies Jesus of Nazareth's thought.[16] By endorsing attention to the *vox* of the incarnate *Verbum* in this way, moreover, Venard means not to salvage a historical nugget from the kerygmatic rough of the early Church, but quite the contrary: he works to raze the iron curtain raised between John and the other Gospels; in short, to make the kerygma resonate with a pitch and timbre that is more than human. Accordingly, features generally considered to be Johannine techniques are not absent from Jesus' speech in the Synoptics, the famous (supposedly) Johannine irony, for instance. Certain "loftier traditions" also resisted the standardization of the oral traditioning process, Venard asserts. We are meant to think here, I am quite sure, of the famous Johannine Thunderbolt preserved in Matthew 11:27 and Luke 10:22. "No one knows the Son except the Father and no one knows the Father except the Son and anyone to whom the Son chooses to reveal him."

The Johannine ring of this language is unmistakable. We are encouraged, however, to hear instead a Jesuanic note. Such a striking interpenetration of normally distinct modes of discourse, this transgression of the neat separation of independent Johannine and Synoptic styles, thus reveals not merely the mingled prehistories and permeable literary boundaries of the Gospels. It congeals these documents for an exhilarating moment in a unified and heightened transparency to the Word. The one Gospel of Jesus Christ still vibrates with the enunciative authority of the Logos, which cuts across the warp and woof of the human authors' crafted words. The deep importance of discerning Jesus' unique *vox* remains only a passing hint in Venard's vast study, and a quest for the Linguistic Jesus is far from free of methodological snares. Hunting for the historical Jesus is not a less treacherous (or an unrelated) enterprise, however, and the study of Christic speech is integral to Venard's wider vision. One might thus push the exercise with considerably more vigor.

The *Vox Jesu*

The concentrated tangle of themes intertwined in John 5 offers but one of multiple threads that might be pulled to let loose the *ipsissima vox*. It is a key text, nevertheless, since in the Fourth Gospel it initiates Jesus' explicit thematization of his own voice. After declaring that he shall accomplish greater works than simply healing the lame—as he has just done—he proclaims in verses 25–29 that the hour is coming when the dead and those in

---

16 See Venard, *Poetic Christ*, 13.

the grave will hear the voice of the Son of God and that all who hear it will live. Chapter 10 will develop the theme of this voice at length, before Jesus dramatically calls Lazarus out of the tomb in chapter 11, in illustration of his statement in chapter 5. The voice of Jesus is thus intimately tied to the great work given him by the Father to accomplish: bringing into the world a life stronger than death. In chapter 12, the voice of the Father sounds from the sky like thunder: a heavenly echo, ratifying Jesus' own voice in raising Lazarus (12:28)—or, rather, manifesting the eternal voice of which Jesus himself is the perfect echo. "What I speak, I speak just as the Father has told me" (12:50). The voice of Jesus calling forth life from the grave makes audible for the sake of the crowds the unending inner dialogue, which also has no beginning, by which the Eternal Son calls out to his Father and is himself in turn called forth to life: "Father glorify your name"; "I have glorified it and I will glorify it again" (12:28); "Father I thank you for having heard me. I knew that you always hear me" (11:41–42).

The *vox* of Jesus also has another dialogue partner. In John, as in the Synoptics, it is John the Baptist at the very outset of the Gospel who is openly named the *vox clamantis*. But in John, the Baptist not only applies Isaiah 40 to himself, but he also rejoices to hear a different voice: that of the bridegroom (Jn 3:29). John's language alludes to an important scriptural topos. In the first place, it describes the devastation of exile: "I will bring to an end the sound of mirth and gladness, the voice of the bride and bridegroom in the cities of Judah and in the streets of Jerusalem, for the land shall become a waste" (Jer 7:34, 16:9, 25:10). Then it becomes the very sound of Jeremiah's new covenant: "In this place ... in the towns of Judah and streets of Jerusalem that are desolate ... there shall once more be heard the voice of the bridegroom and the voice of the bride and the voices of those who sing, as they bring thank offerings to the House of the Lord" (Jer 33:11). The blending of the bride's voice with the liturgical music of the Temple already prepares the symbolic Israelogical reading of the Song of Songs, which makes the voice of the Bride the voice of Israel at worship and the Bridegroom's voice the voice of YHWH himself. "My companions are listening for your voice; let me hear it" (8:13); "The voice of my beloved, look he comes" (2:8). Heard in this way, the voice discerned by John carries a distinct undertone of divine thunder—it is the sound of the New Covenant/Testament itself: a joyous clap announcing the rain that ends a famine. It is again the sound of Israel rising from the dead. "As a bridegroom rejoices over his bride, so will your God rejoice over you" (Is 62:5).

The *vox sponsi* trope echoed by John (echoed by John) is more than just a scriptural description for the joyful event of God's long-desired reversal of Israel's misfortunes, however. It also reflects Jesus' own synoptic self-deflecting self-description. "A king made a wedding feast for his son." This is the first hint of a massively important pattern, to which I will return: the fusion of the biblical idiom with Jesus' own elusive speech about himself. Jesus not only adopts and applies the bridegroom motif to his own person; he also uses it to contrast himself with John—as John also does in the Fourth Gospel. "Can the wedding guests fast while the bridegroom is with them?" It is impossible to say whether John the evangelist has transposed a synoptic theme and placed it in the Baptist's mouth or whether inversely the synoptic Jesus is echoing the historical John. Exegetes are likely to presume the former, though it is worth noting that for the synoptics themselves, Jesus becomes John's successor and perfect echo. Luke 3:18, for instance, says that John "with many exhortations, *preached the Gospel* to the people (εὐηγγελίζετο)." Matthew, similarly, is careful to place the identical formula in the mouth of each man: "Repent for the Kingdom of God is at hand" (Mt 3:1, 4:17). For the First Gospel, there is a perfect relay of the clarion *vox*. When the same tradition also records the dissonance between the sound of these two preachers, it should be read in the light of the bridegroom saying on fasting. "Why do John's disciples fast and your disciples do not fast?"

> We played the flute for you and you did not dance; we wailed and you did not mourn. John came neither eating nor drinking...the Son of Man came eating and drinking. (Mt 11:18)

In the Matthean context (and Luke's as well), this logion that distinguishes John and Jesus as the sound of mourning and the sound of feasting, respectively, is part of Jesus' extended response to the question posed by John's disciples: "Are you the one who is to come or are to wait for another?" (Mt 11:3; Lk 7:19). After the Baptism, this is the second so-called Baptist block in the Double Tradition. Fr. Meier observes in favor of the authenticity of this material that it is "surprisingly free of the christologies of the post-Easter Church."[17]

In line with the assumption of a low Christological profile, theologically anemic commentaries and the dubious homilies they sire have habituated us to hear in this question—"Are you the who is to come?"—the Baptist's bewildered personal crisis. John's query "in its Matthean context must reflect waning faith," W. D. Davies and Dale Allison calmly assure.[18] As John sits in prison, the shadows of doubt flicker across his sullen heart as he hears reports of τὰ ἔργα τοῦ Χριστοῦ, the works of the Messiah. Instead of breath-

---

[17] Meier, *Marginal Jew*, 2:131.
[18] Davies and Allison, *Gospel According Matthew*, 2:39.

ing apocalyptic fire, Jesus, it seems, is going about announcing pardon and doing good.

> Go and tell John what you hear and see: the blind receive their sight, the lame walk, the lepers are cleansed, the deaf hear, the dead are raised, and the poor have good news brought to them. (Mt 11:4–5; cf. Lk 7:22)

The response of Jesus to John's question is essentially a catena of quotations from Isaiah (26:19, 29:18–19, 35:5–6, 61:1). Impressively, the scriptural bouquet gathered here resembles a florilegium already gathered in a celebrated text from Qumran, 4Q521, where a similar list of signs of the Messiah are serially recounted.[19] The response of Jesus is likewise an instruction to these disciples to offer witness, however: witness specifically to the fulfillment of the Scripture in what they apprehend with their own senses. Now it is certainly impossible to do more than observe that Luke's mention of John's delegation of two anonymous disciples recalls the two anonymous disciples similarly sent to Christ by John at the beginning of the fourth Gospel. And it can further merely be observed that this commission of Jesus to these disciples to report what they see and hear corresponds strikingly with the Johannine language of witness. "What we have heard, what we seen with our eyes, what we have looked at and touched with our hands" (1 Jn 1:1). And, finally, one cannot do anything more than observe here as well that the miracles spoken of by Jesus and Isaiah and witnessed to by these two disciples—healing the blind, making the lame walk, raising the dead—nicely sketch of the core contents of the Book of Signs.

The Synoptic Gospels are more fastidious than John in accounting for all the species of enumerated wonders, of course, if they are also more summary and less reflective. John is content to select his themes, simply adding that Jesus also did many other things. The climatic, summative phrase καὶ πτωχοὶ εὐαγγελίζονται "the poor are evangelized," nevertheless captures something essential to the unified structure of the Fourfold Gospel, both in its Johannine and synoptic inflections. Rather than resolutely finding the roots of the Christian *euaggelion* in the staurological Pauline kerygma, as New Testament scholars are accustomed to do, perhaps more attention should thus be paid to this decisive moment when Jesus, using Old Testament "Gospel" language, commissions the first witnesses to his person through his revealing deeds.

For indeed Jesus' illocution is not an innocent enunciation. "Tell John what you hear and see" exacts a perlocutionary act with a double *sujet énon-*

---

19 On this text, see Giambrone, "Meaning of חסד קץ in 4Q521."

ciataire. On the one hand, the delegation of two disciples is the recipient of this utterance. At the same time, John himself is addressed by Jesus' word. We have here a mediated dialogue between Jesus and John. The net effect of Jesus' response is thus ultimately to initiate a pre-paschal evangel, a narration of the Messiah's revelatory actions: not an account of his words, we note, but rather a verbalization of his deeds. This pre-resurrection kerygma is not lacking the divine work of resurrection, moreover, for the prophetic list of wonders strikingly terminates with "the dead are raised"—a marvel missing from the base texts in Isaiah 35 and 61. It is accordingly no narrative accident that Luke records the raising of the widow's son immediately before this exchange, for this stands at the very center. "God's visitation of his people" should enter the eyes and ears of the two disciples. The voice that resounds from Christ's dialogue with John thus carries once more the message of resurrection: a prophetic, proleptic orientation to Jesus' greater, as yet unaccomplished work. Unlike sending his own disciples out by twos in order to preach the Kingdom, which was the prolongation and extension of his own echo of John's word, this pre-paschal message, which again has John at its inception, with Jesus' identity at its very heart and his own victory over death as its transcendent aspiration. This is the referent and content of the kerygmatic *énoncé*. The Lord here speaks the Gospel into being.

In just this respect, Jesus' illocution is not an innocent enunciation for another capital reason: he refuses to testify directly about himself. Accustomed as he is to mysteriously say ἦλθον, "I have come"—and here Jeremais might have also heard the *vox*—Jesus refuses simply to answer: "Yes, I am indeed ὁ ἐρχόμενος, the one who is coming."[20] Instead, Jesus redirects his hearers to the Scriptures and through the Scriptures to his works. Thus Christ consciously effaces his own status as *énonciateur* on a double front: declining to produce his own self-attesting utterance, he instead allows and compels other witnesses to come to speech. He defers to the Scriptures on the one hand, then commissions evangelists on the other. So, he places the word of testimony in their mouths. And both of these interpenetrating modes of speech—the prophetic and kerygmatic—testify with one voice to Jesus' works.

With this form of vanishing Christic speech underlying and enabling the Christian proclamation, we rejoin the discourse of John 5.

> If I testify about myself, my testimony is not true. There is another who testifies on my behalf, and I know that his testimony to me is true. You sent messengers to John, and he testified to the truth.

---

[20] On the Christology implicit in the ἦλθον motif, see Gathercole, *Preexistent Son*.

> Not that I accept such human testimony, but I say these things so that you may be saved. He was a burning and shining lamp, and you were willing to rejoice for a while in his light. But I have a testimony greater than John's. The works that the Father has given me to complete, the very works that I am doing, testify on my behalf that the Father has sent me. And the Father who sent me has himself testified on my behalf. You have never heard his voice or seen his form, and you do not have his word abiding in you, because you do not believe him whom he has sent. You search the scriptures because you think that in them you have eternal life; and it is they that testify on my behalf. Yet you refuse to come to me to have life. (Jn 5:31–40)

Let us unfold some key themes from this dense discourse. First, Jesus refuses to be a witness on his own behalf. "If I testify about myself, my testimony is not true." This motif is implicit in the enonciative structure of the *Legatio Baptistae*, as we have just seen. The elusive silence of Jesus to pronounce with respect to himself is not an incidental element in the wider Gospel tradition, moreover. It is a consistent pattern of his speech. "How long will you keep us in suspense? If you are the Messiah tell us plainly" (Jn 10:24). Jesus' highly expressive self-effacement concerns not only his third-person circumlocutions like "Son of Man" or the so-called Messianic Secret. The refusal specifically to *testify* on his own behalf evokes above all the remarkable memory of Jesus' deliberate silence in his Passion.

> Then Pilate said to him, "Do you not hear how many accusations they make against you?" But he gave him no answer, not even to a single charge, so that the governor was greatly amazed. (Mt 27:13–14; cf. Mk 15:4; Jn 10:10)

Mirabile dictu: "Like a lamb led to the slaughter, like a sheep that before its shearers is silent, so he opened not his mouth" (Is 53:7). "Here is my servant who I have chosen … he will not wrangle or cry aloud, nor will anyone hear his voice in the streets" (Is 42:1–2; Mt 12:18–20). Jesus is not only the heir of Isaiah's *vox clamantis*; despite the commentaries, he is also as capable as John of apocalyptic fire: "Woe to you scribes and Pharisees, you hypocrites! Woe to you Chorazin! Woe to you Bethsaida!" The *vox Jesu* is also modeled strictly upon Isaiah's servant. His voice is not taken from him; he lays it down of his own accord. "Why did you not arrest him?" they ask. "Never has a man spoken like this" (Jn 7:45–46). The Word cannot be seized or apprehended until the moment he chooses to fall utterly silent.

Jesus does not defend himself, nor does he accept John's witness. "You sent messengers to John, and he testified to the truth. Not that I accept such human testimony." The Son only accepts the testimony of the Father. At the Baptism, John had access to the Father's witness—thence derives the truth of his word. Yet Jesus' hearers have never heard the voice of nor seen the invisible Father. What they *can* see and hear, however, is the testimony of Jesus' own works along with the testimony of the Scriptures. Here we confront again precisely the same configuration encountered in the synoptic episode. In place of auto-proclamations, Jesus allows the Scriptures and his works—and the witnesses of those works—to speak for him and become the very voice that he withholds. This is proof by Spirit (prophecy) and power.

The Johannine Jesus' refusal of the Baptist's witness accords with a subtle aspect of the apothegmatic rhetoric of the synoptics. The Baptist never supplies a response to Jesus' answer to his question; he simply fades into silence, as Jesus goes on singing John's praise. The muting of John's voice has not escaped exegetes' notice. "The silent John of this Q pericope," says Meier, "stands out starkly against the background of the Lucan babe leaping in Elisabeth's womb, the Matthean 'I should be baptized by you,' and the Fourth Gospel's 'Behold the lamb of God.' Whatever the silence of John is, it is not Christian apologetics."[21]

"Are you the one who is to come?" We are not forced to hear a waning faith behind this question. The Gospels, at least, show a positive disinterest in the question of John's act of assent. Did he ratify Jesus' messianic insinuation or not? It does not matter. Read through a poetic canonical and even simply a Matthean or Lukan lens, the question in the end becomes: Who can properly testify to Jesus? In the pragmatics of the mediated dialogue between Jesus and John, a stage is reached beyond Jesus' baptism when John directs his disciples toward a higher testimony than his own earlier witness. He disappears behind a first-person plural, decreasing to let the others increase, giving them a word to speak with their proper voice: "Should *we* wait for another?" Positioned midway between the Baptist and the stronger one coming after him, John's disciples are thus invited by Christ to resolve John's question for themselves. "Go tell John" should finally work like "Go show yourself to the priests": it should return the converted witnesses to the feet of Christ.

"You search the scriptures ... it is they that testify on my behalf." Jesus' parting words at the end of John 5 reiterate this point. "If you believed Moses, you would believe me, for he wrote about me. But if you do not believe what he wrote, how will you believe what I say?" (5:45–46). The force of this

---

21 Meier, *Marginal Jew*, 136.

claim should not be facilely dismissed. Here we have the critical presupposition implicit in Jesus' reply to John's disciples. The Scriptures speak about him. This is the consistent, startling claim, the principle underwriting an all-pervasive feature of Jesus' voice: *the* feature of his sacred voice we might even risk to say. *Jesus speaks as though the Bible speaks uniquely to, about, and for him*. I assert this as an Archimedean Christological point, but also as a firm historical datum. I have treated various aspects of this elsewhere, and here I must be brief, but Jesus' proper idiolect—his specific, distinctive way of speaking—emerges through the same sort of big-picture, memory-based argumentation that Allison and others have erected to supplant a program of criteriology in collapse. And on this measure, "if the memory of him presented in the Gospels is any reliable guide, the pre-Paschal Jesus... read his personal history explicitly through a scriptural lens."[22] Theologically this is the Christological axiom that grounds the New Testament's hermeneutical claim upon the Old.

Historically we may say that, like many other Jews of his day, Jesus' mouth and mind were filled with Israel's Scriptures. These writings provide the lexicon and themes, the texture and patterns of his thought and speech. In absorbing these elements of style, however, the instinctive resonance of his speech with the language of Israel's sacred poetics is something different than the archaizing idiom found in certain Dead Sea Scrolls or Luke's channeling of Septuagint Greek. The phenomenon resembles instead John's startlingly direct self-perception in Isaiah's *vox clamantis*: as if the "Teacher of Righteousness" had composed those *pesherim* that read Habakkuk's text as a prophecy specifically about him. More than this, however, John presents himself as not only the realization but also the individualization of an interpretation of Isaiah 40:3 applied to the whole community at Qumran in the text of 1QS. With an extraordinary sense of self, somehow far distant from egoism, John finds concentrated in his own person the destiny of the entire eschatological people. The constitution of this *voice* thus assumes a highly Christological posture. This must be qualified in at least two directions. With these two points I will conclude.

First, the unchecked scale of Jesus' self-projection into the Scriptures surpasses all we know or can reconstruct of John. The Lord confronted in the Gospels presents himself not as a cameo figure but as the universal protagonist. He speaks himself into the roles of the anointed of Isaiah 61 and the Suffering Servant. He is the Bridegroom and desire of Israel. He is David's Lord, the cornerstone, and the innocent sufferer of the psalms. He is the prophet like Moses, Daniel's "son of man," Isaiah's "messenger of good tidings," the

---

22 Allison, *Constructing Jesus*.

agent of Jeremiah's new covenant, and the shepherd of Zechariah 13. All of these dramatic roles Jesus appropriates for himself, and the list might easily go on. Together, the reciprocal mirroring of the Scriptures and Christ's self-perception offers a plenary account of his great work in rising from the dead. "Was it not necessary that the Messiah should suffer these things and so enter into his glory? Then beginning with Moses and all the prophets, the things said about himself in *all* the scriptures" (Lk 24:26–27). In the Scriptures Jesus finds his script, and through the Scriptures he gives voice to his speechless works—above his surpassing work of entering into his glory.

Second, the identification of the Baptist with the קוֹל קוֹרֵא of Isaiah 40 is spoken by the omniscient narrator in all three synoptic Gospels. Only John's Gospel places this statement on the Baptist's lips. Jesus, by contrast, is multiply attested in whatever imaginable source theory as the *énonciateur*, who through revealing self-deflections speaks of being himself the prophesied content of the Scriptures. It is Jesus' own speech, moreover, that also, after John's messengers depart, confers on John his assigned scriptural role.

> This is the one about whom it is written,
> "See, I am sending my messenger
> ahead of you, who will prepare your way before you."

What Mark speaks in his own voice as a prophetic citation at the beginning of his Gospel the Double Tradition channels instead through Jesus. A clearer case of the melding of Christic and Christian speech could hardly be found. And Christic speech in some much more enigmatic way prepares John's own distinctive *vox* by emplotting him in the Scriptures precisely as the precursor. "After me comes a man who ranks ahead of me because he was before me" (Jn 1:15, 1:30). It is impossible to disentangle the hermeneutical and historical circle, but the speech of John and the speech of Jesus are poetically linked through the words of Malachi and Isaiah and a great prophetic *gezerah shawa* about preparing and paving the way.

In this citation of Malachi, finally, Scripture speaks not only *for* Jesus *about* John; it also speaks *to* Jesus *about* himself in his own Trinitarian relations. For Jesus has become the second-person singular "you" addressed by the first-person voice who sends his messenger to prepare the way. This mysterious voice, of course, is the voice of the Lord of Hosts. And where in the Hebrew text the Lord speaks, "Ahead of me to prepare my way," in Jesus' mouth the word sounds differently: "Your way before you." Spoken once to Israel by the one God and now refracted through the human nature of the Word, the divinity of the Son comes to expression in the accent of personal distinction. Here postmodernity bends back to touch premodern perspectives. The linguistic turn and its theological fruit lead us to the very same questions posed by the literary critics of the ancient world, the Homeric scholars of Alexandria who anticipated the whole tradition of patristic prosopological exegesis: Τίς λέγει, πρὸς τίνα, καὶ περὶ τίνος—"Who is speaking, to whom, and about whom?" The voice of Jesus, human and divine, is subtly heard in his own silent listening to the Scriptures. And in his listening, through the opening of his ear, we discern the revelation of the eternal dialogue between Father and Son. When several verses on the thunder of Jesus' *vox* thus rings out—"No one knows the Father except the Son and anyone to whom the Son wishes to reveal him"—perhaps this *Jubelruf* should not come as such a bolt from the blue. Perhaps the discursive Jesus of Q and the Fourth Gospel is after all one and the same divine revealer, the Eternal Word.

CHAPTER 13

"Why Do the Scribes Say?"
Scribal Expectations of an Eschatological High Priest and the Interpretation of Jesus' Transfiguration

Immediately after his Transfiguration, in both Mark and Matthew but not in Luke, Jesus informs Peter, James, and John that "Elijah has indeed come" (Mk 9:2–13; Mt 17:1–13; cf. Lk 9:28–43). Matthew's version clarifies Jesus' reply as referring to John the Baptist (Mt 17:13). This comes in response to their question, "Why do the scribes say that Elijah must come first?" They ask, of course, in the wake of the extraordinary event that they have just witnessed: Jesus atop a high mountain, transformed and brilliant in radiant white clothing, speaking with Moses and Elijah, covered in clouds, and attested by a thundering voice from heaven.

The pivotal place of the Transfiguration scene in the narrative structure of all the synoptic Gospels underscores the special importance of this particular exchange after the event between Jesus and his disciples. While Luke has obviously gone his own way in addressing the relationship of John to Elijah and of Jesus to John, with the result that Jesus' Transfiguration functions somewhat differently in Luke's account, Mark and Matthew together present us with a concerted perspective. And in this Markan-Matthean view, the importance of Elijah's eschatological return stands front and center.

In this study, I mean to work backward from this central heuristic hint. Such a strategy will help provide traction for handling a rather slippery miracle story that for classical historical-critical canons has often proven difficult to understand on its own terms. How does one tackle a text largely comprised of imagery and symbols? While it has been common to view the Transfiguration scene as either a displaced Resurrection account or a doublet of the Baptism, I mean to argue that, while the pericope has obvious connections in both of these directions, it belongs to a different, self-standing context: a context adequately indicated by Matthew and Mark. The key to their conjoint presentation of the scene is the Second Temple expectation of a coming eschatological priest.

My argument for this position moves methodically in five steps. While the conclusion will be new, the reasoning essentially requires ordering a sequence of data points, the main building blocks of which have mostly already been defended by other scholars. Although the data have not previously been assembled in this precise way and to this precise end, a couple creative insights and some fresh materials will make the ensemble gel. First, I will evoke the broad Second Temple expectation of an eschatological high priest, highlighting two pertinent examples (§1). Next, I will expose important evidence that the famous rabbinic identification of Elijah as a high priest was already in place at the time the Gospels were composed (§2). With these two interlocking planks secure, I will next propose viewing the John-Jesus relation through the lens of a variant on Second Temple diarchic messianism (§3). Next, I will consider Moses, Elijah's colleague in conversation with Jesus, noting some revealing priestly traditions about the Prophet that illuminate Jesus' identification as a priest-prophet "raised up" after Moses' model (§4). Finally, engaging the phenomenon of Jesus' transfiguration in glory itself, I will concentrate briefly on the scene's resonance with Second Temple interest in the high priestly garments (§5). My cumulative conclusion will see Jesus as endowed atop the mountain with the transfigured glory of a heavenly priesthood: a kind of reception of the cloak of the eschatological high priest and heavenly recognition as Malachi's Messenger of the Covenant—an aggregated identity of multiple scriptural chief agents. This interpretation of the scene will help to plant the Transfiguration account more firmly within the Gospel narratives themselves and also within the wider Second Temple eschatological milieu in which they were written and in which Jesus appeared.

The Eschatological High Priest

Eschatological expectation in Second Temple Judaism is a famously variegated affair. It is nevertheless possible to observe certain fundamental trends that hold wide significance and that clearly shaped the context in which Jesus lived and the Gospels were written. The expectation of an eschatological high priest is one of these socioreligious points of reference, diversified as its internal expressions may be. Indeed, the expectation of a heavenly empowered, end-time priest figure presents a model for primitive Christology of very real but also curiously neglected importance.[1] Two illustrations, certainly not exhaustive but having important contacts with relevant material for our study, will serve to evoke this sacerdotal variety of Jewish, chief-agent eschatology. Many additional examples that disclose similar eschatological expectations and perspectives might have also easily been offered (e.g., 1 En. 10:10–21, 12:1–6, 15:2–3; *Jub.* 4:25, 6:18, 30:18, 31:13–17; *Aramaic Levi Document*; 4Q543–558; Sirach 50; 4QInstruction[d]; 4QApocryphon of Levi[b]; *Songs of Sabbath Sacrifice*; 1QSb 3:22–4:21; 4QSongs of the Sage; *The Self Glorification Hymn*; 11QMelchizedek; 1QSa; etc.). It is important to stress already here at the outset the attunement of these expectations to an associated cosmology, which envisioned an angelic priesthood ministering in a heavenly cult.[2]

Malachi's Messenger / Ideal Levite

Given the chronological framework generally accepted in Pentateuch studies, the Persian-period Book of Malachi represents the earliest written source concerning Levi that has been preserved. The text exercised a measurable influence on later, extracanonical Levi traditions, and the prophecy's impact is clearly felt at Qumran.[3] Malachi is also the clear scriptural reference point for the disciples' question after Jesus' Transfiguration. From the kernel of some historical dialogue with Jesus about the coming of Elijah, whatever form it originally took, the text of Malachi 3 also arguably assumed a larger defining significance, expressive of John the Baptist's entire role within the

---

[1] Secondary literature on primitive Christology and so-called chief agent figures is obviously immense. For a broad historical background of messianic expectation, including expectation of priestly figures, see the classic study of Collins, *Scepter and the Star*, esp. 74–135. For a collection of foundational perspectives that still shape the present Christological discussion, see Davila and Newman, *Jewish Roots of Christological Monotheism*. The attempts of Margaret Barker of Crispin Fletcher-Louis to engage a priestly Christology, both in their contributions to the St. Andrew's collection and in other contexts, differ in some rather basic ways from the perspective engaged in the present study. The recent work of Nicolas Perrin, *Jesus the Priest*, also follows a different course than my proposal here.

[2] For an overview, attentive to the dense concentration of priestly cosmology/eschatology in both nonsectarian and sectarian texts and traditions, see the useful survey of Angel, *Otherworldly and Eschatological Priesthood*.

[3] The snowballing significance of Malachi in Second Temple Levi traditions is explored by Kugel, "Levi's Elevation."

Gospel tradition. This is most prominently expressed in the scriptural epigraph hung over Mark's Gospel in the citation of Malachi 3:1 in Mark 1:2 (though in a prophetic *Mischform* credited to Isaiah).

The prophecy of Malachi probably stems from a Levitical scribal circle that identified in some way with the chief protagonist depicted at the book's opening and end.[4] For modern scholars, the prophetic personage identified as "Malachi" and named as author of the book in Malachi 1:1 is retroactively drawn from the mysterious figure called "My Messenger" in 3:1.[5] The account of the sending of the Messenger is a celebrated, foundational text.

> [1] See, I am sending my messenger (מלאכי) to prepare the way before me, and the Lord whom you seek will suddenly come to his temple. The messenger of the covenant (ומלאך הברית) in whom you delight—indeed, he is coming, says the Lord of hosts. [2] But who can endure the day of his coming, and who can stand when he appears?
>
> For he is like a refiner's fire and like fullers' soap (וכברית מכבסים); [3] he will sit as a refiner and purifier of silver, and he will purify the descendants of Levi and refine them like gold and silver, until they present offerings to the Lord in righteousness. [4] Then the offering of Judah and Jerusalem will be pleasing to the Lord as in the days of old and as in former years.

Considerable interest naturally arises concerning the identity of this מלאכי figure, and modern exegetes are hardly the first to wonder just who and what exactly is here in view.[6] Second Temple interpreters, like their contemporary heirs, instinctively looked for clues in the context. In this connection, it is of high significance that an additional "Messenger" appears within the book, in the description of the ideal Levite/priest in Malachi 2:4–7.

> [4] Know, then, that I have sent this command to you,

---

4 See Lear, *Scribal Composition*.

5 See O'Brien, *Priest and Levite in Malachi*, 143–48. See also Malchow, "Messenger of the Covenant"; and Mason, "Prophets of Restoration." The Targum fancifully identifies the "Malachi" in the book's superscription by the clause "whose name was Ezra the scribe," a suggestion that fits well with certain concerns shared by both the prophet and the priest/scribe, e.g., endogamy (Ezr 9:1–2, 10:10–24).

6 The echo in Mal 3:1 of Ex 23:20 is strong (especially in the Greek), as all commentators note: "Behold, I send an angel/messenger (מלאך MT; τὸν ἄγγελόν μου LXX) before you to guard your way." For some, the confusion blurring the lines between "my Messenger" in Mal 3:1a and the Lord himself in 3:1b, named again "Messenger of the Covenant" in 3:1c, indicates a redactional seam. Exactly this confusion is typical of Angel of the Lord in the Bible, however.

> that my covenant with Levi (ברית את לוי) may hold,
> says the Lord of hosts.
> [5] My covenant (בריתי) with him
> was a covenant of life and well-being (והשלום), which I gave him;
> this called for reverence, and he revered me and stood in awe of my name.
> [6] True instruction (תורת אמת) was in his mouth,
> and no wrong was found on his lips.
> He walked with me in integrity and uprightness,
> and he turned many from iniquity.
> [7] For the lips of a priest should guard knowledge,
> and people should seek instruction (ותורה) from his mouth,
> for he is the messenger of the Lord of hosts (מלאך יהוה צבאות).

In James Kugel's view, the text of Malachi 2:4–7 suggested to later Second Temple readers the existence of a special priestly covenant with Levi, with the key line at the end of 2:5—"he stood in awe of my name"—suggesting a cosmic voyage in the Lord's celestial court.[7] While this priestly voyage motif will be encountered repeatedly below (§4–5), Malachi's mysterious "covenant with him/Levi" is not less important. It is somehow different than the much more prominent covenants made with Noah, Abraham, and David, and the like. The heavy emphasis that is laid in Malachi 2:4–7 both upon the word "covenant" and upon the ideal of priestly instruction is, in any event, striking. It contrasts directly with the actual state of affairs promptly revealed in the following verse.

> [8] But you have turned aside from the way; you have caused many to stumble by your instruction; you have corrupted the covenant of Levi (ברית הלוי), says the Lord of hosts.

The "corruption" of the covenant made with Levi, on account of the priests' bad example and bad instruction, makes all the more compelling the coming of "The Messenger of the Covenant" in Malachi 3:1. An eschatological rescue operation is underway to ensure that the priestly covenant with Levi might endure (Mal 2:4; cf. Ex 40:15; Num 25:13; Jer 33:17–18, 33:20–22). A fabulous wordplay in Malachi 3:2 underscores this interest. The Messenger of the Covenant will wash the sons of Levi with *bōrît*, "soap"—an evident pun in the unpointed Hebrew on the "covenant" (*bĕrît*) motif. It occasions little

---

7 Kugel, "Levi's Elevation," 30–31.

surprise that in the Second Temple context, where such intense criticisms of the Temple's priestly establishment are to be observed, Malachi's rudimentary framework of a degenerate priesthood and an end-time priestly agent, who comes with right teaching and a cleansing reaffirmation of the covenant, should have raised interest and expectation and found a potent subsequent echo. Qumran alone is adequate to show the immense interest of Malachi's vision.

The "New Priest" (*Test. Lev.* 18:1–14)

The long description of the "new priest" in *Testament of Levi* 18:1–14 is a particularly impressive witness to the developed Jewish expectation of a priestly chief agent. The *Testaments of the Twelve Patriarchs*, which represent a tradition broader than the sectarian perspectives unique to Qumran, admittedly also represent a highly controverted corpus.[8] The most recent scholarship has strongly defended this material's importance as a witness to pre-Christian and notably Hasmonean Judaism, however, despite the later Christian editing of the texts, which now appears more restrained and isolable than has often been imagined.[9] A reassessment of the shorter Armenian version contributes to this new perspective.[10] More fundamentally, however, this revised position belongs to a larger, foundational discussion that concerns how to distinguish methodologically between Jewish and Christian elements in the scribal transmission of mixed materials.[11]

The different sections of the *Testaments* have clearly been reworked to varying degrees. While the *Test. Ben.* seems to represent the most Christianized of the tracts, the *Test. Levi*, though clearly edited and not transmitted in a pristine form, nevertheless stands secure as preserving a substantial and fundamentally Jewish core. This is clear, for instance, from the enduring, positive value placed upon the Temple cult (e.g., *Test. Levi* 9:5–7),[12] but above all from *Test. Levi*'s open relation to a range of parallel Levi traditions,

---

[8] For an introduction, critical text, translation, and commentary, see Jonge, *Testaments of the Twelve Patriarchs*; and Hollander and Jonge, *Testaments of the Twelve Patriarchs*, 129–83.

[9] See, e.g., Kugler, *Testaments of the Twelve Patriarchs*, esp. 11–40; idem, "*Testaments of the Twelve Patriarchs*"; and deSilva, "*Testaments of the Twelve Patriarchs*." See also the nuanced, alternative approach taken by Jonge, *Jewish Eschatology*, 145–313.

[10] See, e.g., deSilva, "*Testaments of the Twelve Patriarchs*," 25–27, *pace* Jonge.

[11] See Davila, *Provenance of the Pseudepigrapha*, 10–119. The earlier reflections of Robert Kraft mark an important starting point to this debate. See Kraft, "Christian Transmission of Greek Jewish Scriptures"; and idem, "Pseudepigraph and Christianity Revisited."

[12] So deSilva, "*Testaments of the Twelve Patriarchs*," 34.

attested in the unambiguously pre-Christian literature of the Second Temple period, especially in the so-called *Aramaic Levi Document* (cf. *Test. Levi* 8–9, 11–14; also *Jub.* 30:1–32:9).[13] Against extreme positions that acknowledge only a Christian interpretative lens, an original, integral Jewish composition should, accordingly, not be doubted. And at the very heart of this integral composition—and here not only the *Test. Levi* but also the entirety of the *Testaments* should be understood—stands an unmistakable elevation of Levi: a valorization that is difficult to gut and explain away as a Christian theologoumenon.[14] In short, we confront in the *Testaments*' broad Levi motifs the eschatological framework of genuine Jewish expectation.

The *Testaments* are not prophetic or apocalyptic literature in the generic or classical sense, but they are filled with eschatological and messianic prognostications. In this connection, central as he is to the document's integral project, the "new priest" in *Test. Levi* 18 is not the only chief agent in the *Testaments*' eschatology. He also appears, rather, within some sort of "two-messiahs" framework. Although Marinus de Jonge would cautiously distinguish between a Jewish two-tribe (Levi-Judah) expectation and a Christian single-savior (Jesus Christ) perspective, James deSilva has exposed problems in de Jonge's reconstruction and is more assertive about the presence of Jewish-style chief agents.[15] DeSilva may be excessively optimistic in various elements of his overall approach, but his confidence here does not appear ill considered, and he is far from alone in his conclusion. Thus, while the tangled witness of the *Testaments* must be plainly acknowledged, it seems safe to affirm that "some of the *Testaments* articulate an expectation of two messianic figures, a priestly one emerging from the line of Levi and a kingly one coming from the line of Judah, a messianic view also well attested among the Dead Sea Scrolls."[16] Multiple indications suggest that the priestly Levitical

---

13 On the interrelation of these diverse Second Temple Levi traditions, see Kugel, "Levi's Elevation," 1–64; and Kugler, *From Patriarch to Priest*.

14 "Given early Christian discourse about the priesthood of Jesus and the ways in which it is legitimated, it seems to me impossible to conceive of a Christian composing a collection of texts that would work so hard to redeem Levi (who, together with Simeon, stood under Jacob's curse and was passed over in favor of Judah; see Gen. 49.5–12), when other Christian leaders had already found perfectly sufficient grounds upon which to legitimate Jesus' high priesthood other than the invention of a genetic link between Levi and Jesus (alongside the generally acknowledged link between Judah and Jesus)" (deSilva, "Testaments of the Twelve Patriarchs," 50).

15 See deSilva, "*Testaments of the Twelve Patriarchs*," 27–29. Speaking of the prehistory of the document, Jonge concludes: "There are no clear traces of 'two agents of divine deliverance,' one from Levi and one from Judah. Every time a 'messianic' figure appears, there is one, clearly Jesus Christ, who is connected with Judah, or with Judah and Levi" (*Jewish Eschatology*, 203).

16 deSilva, "*Testaments of the Twelve Patriarchs*," 36. See Jonge, *Jewish Eschatology*, 193–203.

agent stands over the Judean royal agent, moreover (e.g., *Test. Jud.* 21:1–4). Nevertheless, the duties of the two agents stand in an apparently complementary relation, even if certain confusions and tensions are also apparent, which at times seem to fuse the two figures as one (e.g., *Test. Levi* 2:11; *Test. Dan* 5:4; *Test. Gad* 8:1; *Test. Jos.* 19:7).[17] Most remarkable in this regard is the elevation of Levi as "king" (e.g., *Test. Reub.* 6.11–12). That a distinctively Christian tendency is discernable at this point is not to be discounted out of hand, and here the issue is rightly flagged by Jonge. Indeed, the present study will argue that the Gospels themselves, not least the Transfiguration tradition, already stand at the head of this primitive Christological trajectory of fusing together priestly and royal figures in Jesus. Yet this perspective also inserts the phenomenon in a considerably more Jewish context for understanding Christian messianism than Jonge has in mind.

The eschatological manifestation of the *Testaments*' "new priest" not only fits within a recognized Second Temple two-messiahs pattern (see §3 below); it is also set within a recognizable narrative framework. Namely, building on Daniel's seventy weeks prophecy (*Test. Levi* 17.1–11), a degenerative series of Jubilees is described. After seven ages of increasingly debased priestly service, culminating in priests who are "adulterers, money lovers, arrogant, lawless, voluptuaries, pederasts, those who practice bestiality" (*Test. Levi* 17:11), the saving figure of this "new priest" arrives.[18]

> [18:1] And after vengeance on them will have come upon them from the Lord, the priesthood will fail. [2] Then *the Lord will raise up a new priest* (ἐγερεῖ κύριος ἱρέα καινόν), to whom all the words of the Lord will be revealed; and he will execute a judgment of truth upon the earth in course of time. [3] And his star will arise in heaven, as a king, lighting up the light of knowledge as by the sun of the day; and he will be magnified in the world until his assumption. [4] He will shine as the sun on the earth and will remove all darkness from under heaven, and there will be peace on the earth. [5] The heavens will exult in his days and the earth will be glad and the clouds will rejoice, and the knowledge of the Lord will be poured out on the earth like the waters of the sea and the angels of the glory of the presence of the Lord will rejoice in him.[19]

---

17 deSilva, "*Testaments of the Twelve Patriarchs*," 37.

18 "Original *Testament of Levi* 18 is intended as Levi's ancient pledge that a new priesthood— one in keeping with the glorious beginning the office had in him—will commence after the office's long decline" (Kugler, *From Patriarch to Priest*, 216).

19 Translation by Hollander and Jonge, *Testaments of the Twelve Patriarchs*, 177.

In the view of Robert Kugler, "key elements of its present form make certain that it [*Test. Levi* 18] can be read only as a predication of Jesus as the ideal high priest."[20] That Jesus should be in view is an obvious function of the text's Christian reception/transmission (cf. *Test. Levi* 18:6–7 and §3.3 below). The similar prophecy in *Test. Levi* 8:14, moreover, that "a king will arise from Judah and will establish a new priesthood after the fashion of the Gentiles for all the Gentiles," rightly raises questions.[21] Nevertheless, as Kugler himself also immediately adds concerning the text at hand in *Test. Levi* 18, the "Christian authors almost certainly relied on a Jewish source that anticipated a priestly (and royal?) messiah."[22] One is moved to say not "Christian authors" but rather "meddling tradents"; the critical point about Jewish expectation is made, however.

It is necessary to push back still more in asserting the thoroughly pre-Christian character and extent of this priestly expectation, however. In the first place, at the level of the deep narrative grammar, it must be observed that a manifest logic binds together the Danielic/Jubilee scenario laid out in *Test. Levi* 17 and the resolution that comes with the arrival of the priestly agent in the denouement of *Test. Levi* 18. The essential resemblance of this plotline, not only to the rudimentary pattern of priestly degeneration and an end-time priestly agent noted in Malachi above but also to the specific vision of 11QMelchizedek, in which an eschatological priest again appears at the critical culmination of a downward spiral of Jubilees, is obvious on its face. In this light, it is not an incidental detail when *Test. Lev* 18:12 says of the "new priest" that "Beliar will be bound by him." This is precisely what Melchizedek was also expected to do in 11QMelchizedek: "He will deliver all the captives from the power of Belial" (II,13 25; cf. CD 4:17–18 and *Test. Levi* 14.5–8). The essential block of *Test. Levi* 17–18 can thus hardly be construed as anything other than this same attested Jewish pattern.

Within this shared Second Temple eschatological-priest framework, more focused details in *Test. Levi* 18 are likewise traceable to a Jewish milieu. Most importantly, the phrase "raise up" applied to the "new priest" casts him in the recognizable guise of the much awaited "prophet like Moses" whom the Lord promised to "raise up" in Deuteronomy 18:15. The same language

---

20 Kugler, *Testaments of the Twelve Patriarchs*, 52. See also Jonge, *Jewish Eschatology*, 199–201.

21 See the comments on this passage of Hollander and Jonge, *Testaments of the Twelve Patriarchs*, 154. See also the Christian interpolation discussed in note 41 below.

22 Kugler, *Testaments of the Twelve Patriarchs*, 52. Kugler acknowledges John Collin's suggestion of the possible influence here of 4Q541. For my purposes, I find it useful to highlight certain other materials, i.e., 11Q13 and 1 Sm 2:35, as seen below.

is repeated in *Test. Sim.* 7:2, and it is hardly necessary (or even helpful) to appeal to a doctrine of Jesus' priesthood to explain this figure—though as we shall see it is not unconnected to Gospel traditions.[23] The language and expectation, however, are ultimately accessed through the anonymous *man of God*'s prophecy of the "faithful priest" whom the Lord will "raise up" in 1 Samuel 2:35.[24]

> I will raise up for myself a faithful priest (והקימתי לי כהן נאמן), who shall do according to what is in my heart and in my mind. I will build him a sure house, and he shall go in and out before my anointed one forever (לפני משיחי כל הימים).

In its original Deuteronomistic context, this passage foretells the appearance in Solomon's court of a new, non-Elide dynasty—namely, Zadok and his high priestly line—but this striking prophecy of an idealized priestly agent clearly also fueled later speculations and expectations. What Jonge takes to be a smoking-gun indication of Christian theology—the eternity of the reign of Jesus as the "new priest" modeled on Psalm 110—is in fact a feature lifted directly from this prophecy in 1 Samuel.[25] "He shall go in and out before my anointed one *forever*." Further, this idealized Deuteronomistic "faithful priest" bears a special, mysterious relation to the Lord's Messiah: a pattern optimally susceptible to the double-chief-agent eschatology that touches the *Testaments* and will be explored further below (§3). The full *Nachleben* of this original Deuteronomistic priestly spin on Deuteronomy 18:15 is of keen interest and is not exhausted by the *Testaments*, as we shall see.

The biblical profile of the "new priest" of *Test. Levi* 18 also taps other prophetic traditions. Most importantly, in harmony with Malachi 2, the *Testaments*' priest is amply depicted as a literal fountain of instruction (cf. *Test. Levi* 18:9).

The unique "We-passage" that appears in *Test. Levi* 19:2–3 betrays the document's authors as being (or at least wishing to be seen as) sons of Levi. In this, the text follows a similar pattern to the scribal circle behind Malachi. That they imagined a future for themselves alongside the eternally active

---

23 The frequent, transparent Christian scribal gloss "Savior of the world" never intrudes here, as in other passages, where, incidentally, the mishandling and suffering of this "Savior" are intoned (*Test. Levi* 10:2–4; 14:2–3): themes that play no role in *Test. Levi* 18:1–14.

24 The importance of Dt 18:15, read through 1 Sm 2:35, must be stressed as the controlling allusion in *Test. Levi* 18:2, without denying the allusion to Balaam's oracle (Nm 24:17) in the following line. The suggestion of Kugler (*Testaments of the Twelve Patriarchs*, 52) that the entire passage should be read as "resting squarely on Balaam's oracle" unfortunately misses this critical intertextual dynamic.

25 Jonge, *Jewish Eschatology*, 202.

"new priest," for whom "there shall be no successor for him from generation to generation forever," is not to be doubted (cf. *Test. Levi* 18:7). The possibility that this represents a Christian scribal voice need not be settled for our purposes.[26] It is sufficient to insist upon the original Jewish content of the prophetic expectation as such. A much more primitive Christological appropriation of this "new priest" content than that of the *Testaments* is precisely what we intend to demonstrate in what follows.

THE RETURN OF ELIJAH-PHINEAS

The reality of a diverse but demonstrable Second Temple expectation of the coming of an end-time priestly agent can be accepted as axiomatic, however difficult it may be to measure this idea's extension. Particularly in light of Malachi's importance both in the history of this expectation and in the specific interpretation of Jesus' Transfiguration, it is vital now to make an additional point. Through the close reading and creative reasoning of Jewish scribal culture, Elijah the prophet was himself, at least in certain contexts, awaited as the great High Priest of the messianic era.[27] In this role he was often even identified with Phineas, the grandson of Aaron.

This well-attested identification is well known from the targums and rabbinic texts (e.g., Tg. Ps-J Ex 4:13, 6:18, 40:9–10; Nm 25:10–13; Dt 30:4–6, 33:11; *Pirqe R. El.* 29, etc.). Significantly, it is not a late creation of the rabbinic era, however, as it has generally been treated. Recent research, above all a fine study by Lotta Valve, has shown that the notion has a prehistory reaching deep into the Second Temple period, owing much to the merging of Malachi's two Messenger figures.[28] The outlines of this process can be quickly sketched. It is a simple function of successive, transitive equations: a sort of aggregation of scriptural identities.

By sheer proximity and similarity of description, the "Messenger of the Lord of Hosts" in Malachi 2 was easily identified with the "Messenger of the Covenant" in Malachi 3. For a number of reasons, moreover, not least proximity once again, the latter figure was understood from the context to be equal to Elijah.[29] Once Elijah was thereby finally linked through Malachi

---

26 See Jonge, *Jewish Eschatology*, 262.
27 On this tradition, see Hayward, "Phineas"; and Zeron, "Martyrdom of Phineas-Elijah."
28 Valve, *Early Modes of Exegesis*. A broader, also useful study is that of Vallençon, *Le développement des traditions*.
29 In addition to the shared language of "sending," several things point to the link between Elijah and the Messenger in Mal 3:1–4. Valve (*Early Modes of Exegesis*, 97–99) points to the following. The first is the association of the refiner's fire and the burning oven, which links

3 to the Ideal Levite in Malachi 2, a dynamic interior to that earlier chapter equated him with the priestly personage of Phineas in the following manner.

First, the description of the "Covenant with Levi" in Malachi 2:5 as a covenant of life and שלום suggestively echoes the formulation of Phineas's covenant in Numbers 25:12: "I hereby grant him [Phineas] my covenant of peace (בריתי שלום)." (We see that, typical of scribal argumentation, the "interior" dynamic of Malachi 2 quickly exits the prophetic text itself to become a wide-ranging inner-biblical tour.) The echo is not empty. Hints of a deeper interaction with the Phineas tradition are not wanting, as Valve has ably shown.[30] Levi's turning many away from sin in Malachi 2:6 invites the first step. What can this behavior refer to?, early exegetes asked themselves. If the Levi figure in Malachi 2 is read in the light of the patriarch Levi's story—as ancient readers seem to have done—the Shechem episode in Genesis 34 presents itself as the only obvious narrative referent, for this violent episode was viewed as preventing the sin of intermarriage between the Israelites and their pagan neighbors, a misdeed closely connected to cultic "adultery" (cf. 1 Kgs 11:1–4). In this line of thought, the continuation of Malachi's oracle in Malachi 2:8–16 reveals a keen contextual interest in exactly this issue and pursues an open polemic against intermarriage.[31] The connection to the covenant made with Phineas is thereby easily seen. Like his forefather Levi, Phineas, who skewered the Israelite coupling with Midianite woman, was seen as a zealot not simply against idolatry, but specifically against intermarriage. More positively stated, Phineas's zeal acts in favor of absolute fidelity to the Lord. To maintain his covenant uncorrupted means observing proper sexual purity and absolute fidelity to YHWH.

---

the Messenger's purifying work in 3:2 and the arrival of the day in 4:1 (3:19 MT): "See the day is coming, burning like an oven." The description of Elijah in Sir 48:1 (Heb) already made this connection: "A prophet arose like a fire / and his words were like a burning oven." A subtle hint that reinforces this link and might have influenced early readers of Mal 3:1–4 is a play on the Hebrew phrase "like a refiners fire" (kĕʾēš mĕṣārēp), which, with different vowel pointing, might also be understood as "like a fire from Zareph(ath)" or even "like a man from Zareph(ath)." Zarephath is, of course, the village where Elijah stays before dramatically appearing to Ahab in 2 Kgs 18.

30 For what follows, see Valve, *Early Modes of Exegesis*, 63–89.

31 The corrupting of the "Covenant of Levi" in Mal 2:8 evidently concerns the same issue addressed in Neh 13:29, which similarly speaks of the "defilement of the priesthood and the covenant of the priesthood and the Levites." Nehemiah spoke of such defilement because of the sin of intermarriage, and he found guilty even one of the sons of Jehoida, son of the high priest Eliashib and Joshua's great grandson (Neh 13:28; cf. 13:23–29; Ezr 9:1–2, 10:10–24). Ezra knows of seventeen priest violators (Ezr 10:18–22). On this tricky passage in Malachi, see Zehnder, "Fresh Look at Malachi."

Returning to the Elijah connection, inner-biblical hints of murderous zeal for the Lord, especially the slaying of idolaters (Nm 25:11, 25:13; 1 Kgs 19:10, 19:14), were independently at work in forging a priestly Elijah-Phineas hybrid, which would have only reinforced this concerted reading of Malachi's texts. Elijah's contest with the false prophets of Baal in 1 Kings 18 further presents him in a priestly guise, moreover, and he exercises the distinctly priestly duties of offering sacrifice and of anointing kings (cf. Sir 46:13, 46:16, 48:3, 48:8).

One of the additional and most prominent priestly duties of Elijah-Phineas's return in the rabbinic traditions is his resolution of halakhic debates. This can be directly connected to the characterization of the Messenger of Malachi 2:7, whose lips guard knowledge and from whom "the people should seek instruction." This idea clearly found traction. In the view of John Poirier, the "Interpreter of the Law" awaited at Qumran (e.g., CD 7:18–19) is already a reference to this view of Elijah as the messianic priest (cf. 4Q558, 4Q521).[32] The implicit but transparent identification of Phineas with Elijah is complete, in any case, at the latest by Pseudo-Philo's *Liber Antiquitatem Biblicarum* (48:1), a first-century AD repository of creative Second Temple exegetical traditions.[33] The passage is striking.

> And in that time Phineas laid himself down to die, and the Lord said unto him, "Behold you have now passed the 120 years that have been established for every man. And now rise and go from here and dwell in Danaben on the mountain and dwell there many years. And *I will command* my eagle, and *he will nourish you there*, and you will not come down to mankind until the time arrives and you be tested in that time; and you will shut up the heaven then, and by your mouth it will be opened up. And afterward you will be lifted up into the place where those who were before you were lifted up, and you will be there until I remember the world. Then I will make you all come and you shall taste what is death (*gustabitis quod est mortis*)."[34]

While the identification remains embedded in a narrative fabric of intertexts and suggestions, it is impossible to be more explicit on this order. The allu-

---

32 Poirier, "Endtime Return."

33 For a slightly dated but still useful statement on this still understudied text, see Harrington, "Decade of Research." The text is preserved in Latin via a Greek translation of a Hebrew original.

34 Translation by Daniel Harrington in Charlesworth, *Old Testament Pseudepigrapha*, 2:362.

sions to 1 Kings 17 are unmistakable. Worthy of special notice, however, is the final line, in which the direct expectation is expressed that Elijah-Phineas's eschatological return at the time of God's good pleasure will result in this priestly figure's death. His death seems plotted in some hinted-at great distress, moreover. It is hardly possible to draw closer to Jesus' contention that John-Elijah died "just as it is written about him" (Mk 9:13), and it is to Jesus' exchange with his disciples that we now turn.

Diarchic Messianism

The moment that, historically considered, Elijah's return as eschatological high priest becomes a viably thinkable thought for Jesus in the Gospels, the invitation is open to read his brief dialogue with the disciples in this highly illuminating light. Arguably, in the absence of compelling alternatives and especially in view of Pseudo-Philo's striking Return-of-Elijah-to-die motif, we should presume that this attested idea is implicitly at play in the Gospel dialogue.

The idea of Elijah as the eschatological priest destined to return and (in at least some variations) to die is hovering in the cultural background, in any event. This cultural background has a specifically scribal character, moreover, and this scribal milieu is openly foregrounded in Matthew and Mark. The disciples' evocation of a scribal thesis in trying to make sense of Elijah's coming in fact subtly highlights the elaborate distance that Second Temple exegetical/eschatological doctrine had taken from the plain sense of Malachi and the Scriptures. It would have been easy enough to inquire more simply, "Why must Elijah come first?" with no mention of any scribes, but this is not what the disciples ask. Their interest to understand what is not immediately obvious plots the pericope squarely in the tangled web of Second Temple exegetical culture, with its bold tradition of creative, but also carefully thought-out, inner-biblical connections. Whether or not the disciples' own independent familiarity with Malachi's prophecy as it stands in the text can or should be presumed, the prophecy stood under a kind of scribal custody, and its transmission was wrapped up in an envelope of scribal explanations and tradition.

In Mark 9:12–13, in response to the disciples' question, Jesus himself enters this same scribal arena, averting twice to the Scriptures to evoke the suffering fate of two named and central figures: the Son of Man and Elijah. It is all succinctly expressed, but there is reason to suppose that Jesus works here with some variety of diarchic expectation, such as we have already encountered in the *Testaments*. The intriguing possibility mentioned in passing above that

Elijah, understood as messianic priest and halakhic "Interpreter of the Law," might have already concretely occupied a place in one form of this diarchic expectation found at Qumran (i.e., 4Q558 and 4Q521), creates the clear conditions for finding something similar within the Gospel setting.

The Two Messiahs in Scripture and at Qumran

The Essenes' celebrated dual expectation of a priestly Messiah of Aaron and a royal Davidic Messiah was not invented at Qumran.[35] This is important, as it normalizes and expands the idea, which is actually anchored in the Scriptures. For this reason one need not suppose a derivative relation between the viewpoints in the *Testaments* and Qumran, for instance. The "faithful priest" and Davidic messiah (in context, Solomon) already appear as distinct but interrelated agents in 1 Samuel 2:35, as already noted. Of special importance for the development of this diarchic tradition is plainly the prophecy of Zechariah, however.

The two "sons of oil" (בני היצהר) in Zechariah 4:6–14 certainly contributed to the typology of two anointed eschatological figures (cf. 4Q254). In the original Persian setting of Zechariah's oracle, these two concrete figures, Joshua and Zerubbabel, represent the royal and priestly powers, who together share a conjoint mission to restore Israel's fortunes after the humiliation of Exile. The "Joshua" immediately in view is thus the first of Israel's high priests after the Babylonian captivity, the Aaronide son of Jehozadak, who is mentioned several times (Hg 1:1, 1:12, 1:14, 2:2, 2:4; Ezr 2:2, 3:2; Neh 12:10–11), while Zerubbabel is the Davidic scion.

As the self-described "Son of Man," Jesus' own David ancestry (through Zerubbabel) is prominently thematized in Matthew's genealogy, but Mark also knows of Jesus as the "son of David" (Mk 10:47–48, 12:35). "Son of Man" itself is, of course, a much-debated title, but at the very least one may note that the key allusion to Daniel 7:13 in Jesus' words before the high priest in answer to the question, "Are you the Messiah?" directly recalls a scene of the conferral of eternal kingship and is bound directly to the Davidic heir envisioned in Psalm 110 (cf. Mk 14:62). A strong Davidic/royal valence underwriting Jesus' understanding of himself as the "Son of Man" thus ought not be lightly dismissed. The hint in Mark 9:1 that the Transfiguration perhaps

---

35 Actually, the group at Qumran expected (at least) three end-time redeemer figures: a Prophet, a Priest, and a Prince/King, with both of the latter (but only the latter), for obvious reasons, being explicitly described as "anointed" messiah figures (cf. 1QS 9:9–11; cf. CD 12:23–13:1, 14:19, 19:10–11, 20:11). On these complicated and not always well-understood views, see Collins, *The Scepter and the Star*, 74–135.

provides some sort of vision of the Kingdom come in power associates Jesus as Son of Man in the cloud on the mountain both with the royal Davidic motif and Daniel's figure coming on the clouds.

The case for the Aaronic agent looks rather different. Luke alone of the synoptic Gospels mentions John the Baptist's impeccable priestly pedigree (Lk 1:5). Joel Marcus argues that this is no Lukan invention but comes from preexisting sources, while John's likely association with Qumran also points in a priestly direction.[36] With due caution regarding the questions that such data naturally raises, it is nevertheless not reckless reasoning to imagine that a tradition of John's priestly identity informs Mark 9:2–13 / Matthew 17:1–13. In fact, identification of John as the coming Elijah—which is not confined to the dialogue after the Transfiguration and is also a Lukan idea (Lk 1:17, 7:27; cf. Mt 11:7), as well as (at least for Marcus) also John's own idea, points rather persuasively in this direction.[37] In the end, of course, no mathematical demonstration can be offered that Jesus in Matthew and Mark took John to be the prophesied eschatological priest. Jesus says no more (and no less) than just what he says. A two-pronged pincer argument nevertheless makes this historical assumption a compelling explanation. In the first place, Jesus' appeal to a double chief-agent pattern—i.e., Son of Man and Elijah—evokes the familiar diarchic pattern of expectation so strongly associated with a priestly/Aaronic and royal/Judean pairing, and Jesus clearly assumes the role of the latter. At the same time, a scenario featuring the death of Elijah after his coming positions Jesus' perspective in open contact with the Elijah-as-eschatological-priest tradition, precisely as it is attested in Pseudo-Philo. It should not be overlooked, moreover, that John died specifically preaching against an illicit marital union, which plants him firmly within the tradition of Phineas's priestly zeal, even while reversing the equation and putting John on the receiving end of the bloody violence.[38] Whatever Jesus may have accepted as his own messianic narrative and frame, with the death of John, the Son of Man / Son of David clearly saw it as his own role specifically to continue John's mission—and ultimately to share John's same fate.

---

36 On the question of John's priestly background, see Marcus, *John the Baptist*, Appendix 4, 133–34. For a different but also important set of historical questions relating to John and his movement, see the methodical analysis of Backhaus, *Die Jüngerskreis des Täufers Johannes*.

37 Marcus devotes a chapter to "John's association of himself with Elijah" and accepts this association as another piece of evidence for a priestly lineage/identity. Marcus goes on to say: "If the equation of Elijah with Phineas was already existent in the first century [!], Phineas' strong objection to an illicit union is an interesting and perhaps significant parallel to John's repudiation of Herod Antipas' marriage to Herodias (Mark 6:17–18; see chap. 6). John's action may have reflected his sense of himself as Elijah = Phineas returned from the dead" (*John the Baptist*, 134).

38 Marcus, *John the Baptist*, 134.

"Just as It Is Written about Him"

The close identification of Jesus with John through their shared fate of passive suffering helps clarify Jesus' remark about his precursor: "They did to him whatever they pleased, *just as it is written about him*" (Mk 9:13). It has proven puzzling for modern scholars to determine what Scripture could possibly be in view in Jesus' comment. The most revealing text is Sirach 48:10, which comes at the end of the praise of Elijah in 48:1–11.

> At the appointed time, it is written (הכתוב, ὁ καταγραφείς), you are destined
> > to calm the wrath of God before it breaks out in fury,
> > to turn (להשיב) the hearts of parents to their children,
> > and to restore *the tribes of Jacob*.

This dense verse, which begins with the only use of "it is written" in Sirach, includes a loose citation of Malachi 4:6 (MT 3:24; LXX 3:23), combined with a recognized allusion to Isaiah 49:6, the second of the so-called Servant Songs.[39]

> It is too light a thing that you should be my servant
> > to raise up (להקים) *the tribes of Jacob*
> > and to restore (להשיב) the survivors of Israel;
> > I will give you as a light to the nations,
> > that my salvation may reach to the end of the earth.

The links between Deutero-Isaiah and Malachi are not unique to this text in Ben Sira. In Malachi 3:1 there is already a citation of Isaiah 40:3—"See I am sending my Messenger to prepare the way before me"—a key point of reference in John the Baptist tradition (cf. Mk 1:2–3; Jn 1:23). If, as certainly seems to be the case, the *sending* of Elijah in Malachi 4:5 (3:23–24 MT) was already identified with this *sending* of the Messenger in 3:1, Elijah would thereby linked directly to Isaiah's vision. As Isaiah 42:19 speaks alternately of "my servant" and "my messenger whom I send," all the conditions are in place for Second Temple interpreters to draw the easy conclusion that eschatologi-

---

[39] "Elijah's future role was to reconcile parents and children: 'to bring back the heart of fathers towards sons.' This phrase echoes part of the description of Elijah's task in Mal 3:24: 'And he will bring back (והשיב // ἀποκαταστήσει, 'restore') the heart of fathers towards sons and the heart of sons to their fathers.' Elijah's forthcoming mission was also 'to reestablish the tribes of Israel,' echoing the task of God's servant (perhaps originally Cyrus) in Is 49:6: 'to raise up (להקים = στῆσαι) the tribes of Jacob and to bring back (להשיב = ἐπιστρέψαι) the survivors of Israel.'" Jeremy Corley, "Elijah among the Former Prophets," 215. Ultimately, according to Corley, "In Ben Sira's thinking, the returning Elijah would revive the nation, just as on an individual level he had resuscitated the widow's son (Sir 48:5; 1 Kgs 17:22)" (216).

cal Elijah was Isaiah's Servant.[40] From here Elijah's eschatological suffering would be easily inferred.

As can be seen, once started, the irrepressible associative logic of scriptural aggregation is hard to hold down. This entrance of Isaiah's Servant into the picture is a crucial development by any measure, moreover, for it becomes the intersection point where royal and priestly—that is, Jesus' and John's identities—meet. Jesus clearly accepts as his own John's legacy of servant-like suffering in both Mark 9 and Matthew 17. As such the Son of Man blends with the eschatological Elijah-Phineas-Servant. At one level, this dynamic of melding resembles the fusion between the "new priest" and the Judean king witnessed in the *Testaments of the Twelve Patriarchs*, which Jonge would situate at the Christian layer of the tradition. Similar blending of personae is not only already present in the Gospels, however, but also already at work long before. The diffusion of Isaiah's Servant into the biblical bloodstream naturally also reached Zechariah, for instance, where the title came into contact with the foundations of diarchic expectation. In this context, the Davidic heir, not Elijah-Phineas, is clearly identified as the Servant or, more specifically, "My Servant, the Branch" (Zec 4:2–3), for Jeremiah's messianic play on Isaiah's sprout of Jesse (Jer 33:15) is now also fused and identified with Deutero-Isaianic *Ebed*-YHWH.

In Zechariah 4:9, God's purpose in restoring Israel is ultimately realized by the Davidic Branch-Servant. In Zechariah's vision, moreover, the manner in which this plan is accomplished is "Not by might, nor by power, but by my Spirit, says the Lord of hosts" (Zec 4:6), for this is manner by which the prophesied Servant pleases God.

> Here is my servant, whom I have chosen,
> My beloved, with whom my soul is well pleased.
> I will put my Spirit upon him,
> and he will proclaim justice to the nations.
> He will not wrangle or cry aloud,
> Nor will anyone hear his voice in the streets.
> He will not break a bruised reed
> Or quench a smoldering wick. (Is 42:1–3; cf. Mt 12:17–21)

With this text we are brought to Jesus' all-important, direct encounter with John.

"Here is my servant, whom I have chosen, my beloved, with whom my soul is well pleased" (Is 42:1). "You are my son, the beloved, with whom I am

---

[40] See Valve, *Early Modes of Exegesis*, 109–11.

well pleased" (Mk 1:11). The foundational identification of Jesus as Isaiah's Servant spreads out its roots throughout the Gospel tradition, but it has its deepest anchor in Jesus' Baptism in the Jordan by John.[41] It is here that the Father's voice clarifies that this one, Jesus, is the Servant. Here God's Spirit comes upon the Servant, just as Isaiah prophesied (Mk 1:10; Is 42:1b). In some sense, the emphatic deictic clarification from heaven—"*this* one"—radically resolves the confusing scribal web of eschatological constructions, by the power of a supernatural multimedia event. After the Baptism, Second Temple "diarchic messianism" is radically simplified, at least as far as the Gospels are concerned. One no longer risks misapprehending the essential roles of Jesus and John.

A Prophet Like Moses, the (Priestly) Messenger

The Father's voice from heaven is the most obvious link binding the Baptism and the Transfiguration. At the Jordan the Father expresses his good pleasure in Jesus, his Son and Servant (Mk 1:11). At the Transfiguration the message is different, however. By instructing the disciples specifically to "listen" to the Father's beloved Son (Mk 9:7), Jesus is being identified as "the prophet like Moses," whom the Lord promises to "raise up" (יקים) and to whom the people must "listen" (תשמעון) in Deuteronomy 18:15. It is revealing that in Deuteronomy 18, the prophet-like Moses figure is given specifically as an answer to the people's fear of the theophany at Horeb, when they shuddered before the voice of God and the sight of the great fire (cf. Dt 5:23–31). The fit with the Transfiguration is perfect. The disciples "were terrified" at what they saw and heard (Mk 9:6). The theophany then vanishes and leaves Jesus alone, authorized to speak in the Lord's own name (cf. Dt 18:18). Viewed

---

41 One must acknowledge that the description of the heavenly attestation of the "new priest" in *Test. Levi* 18:6–7 *too* perfectly recalls the Gospel reports.
  The heavens will be opened,
  and from the temple of glory sanctification will come upon him
  with a fatherly voice, as from Abraham to Isaac.
  And the glory of the Most High shall burst forth upon him.
  And the spirit of understanding and sanctification
  shall rest upon him [in the water].
As the editors Hollander and Jonge indicate, the phrase "in the water" is easily recognized to be a later Christian interpolation alluding to Jesus' Baptism. The rest of the scene, nevertheless, strong as its New Testament resonance is, also resonates with purely Jewish motifs used in the *Testaments* and elsewhere (cf. *Test. Levi* 2:6; *Test. Jud.* 24:2). The opening of the heavens motif (cf. *Test. Levi* 2:6, 5:1), specifically, belongs to a much wider usage. See Walton, "'The Heavens Opened.'"

as a narrated version of Deuteronomy 18:15, the Transfiguration is not a clumsy rehearsal or reworking of the Baptism scene but an integral and coherent unit, merely sharing common motif of the *bat kōl*.

As seen in §1.2 above, the allusion to Deuteronomy 18:15 has a prehistory in Jewish texts, and this prehistory points in a distinctly sacerdotal direction. The verse appears in application to the *raising up* of the "faithful priest" in 1 Samuel 2:35, and this collocation is reechoed in the "new priest" in *Test. Levi* 18:2. This priestly interpretation of Deuteronomy 18:15 might at first seem strange. It is not a superficial or isolated appropriation, however.[42] The Deuteronomist in depicting Samuel played in a variety of ways with a "*priest* like Moses" twist on Deuteronomy 18:15, for instance.[43] The same spin found purchase in other contexts as well. Although in 1 Maccabees 4:46, for example, the defiled altar is stored away until a prophet should "appear" and give instructions, clearly with Deuteronomy 18:15 in mind, we find a notable contrast in Ezra and Nehemiah. In Ezra 2:63 and Nehemiah 7:65, it is determined instead to leave unresolved halakhic disputes to stand until *a priest* bearing the *urim* and *thummim* should "arise" (עד עמד כהן). Ezra's own overt casting as a priestly neo-Moses also fits within this broader scheme. That the Hasmoneans, for their part, preferred to stress a neatly prophetic rather than a priestly reading of Deuteronomy 18:15 stands to reason, as they had already laid a (dubious) claim to the sacerdotal (and regal) role for themselves.[44] In view of all this, Ben Sira's language about Elijah takes on a suggestive new resonance. Elijah majestically "arises" (ἀνέστη, Sir 48:1): yet another identification with the Mosaic prophet and another fusion of typological end-time agents. Given what we have already seen of Elijah the priest, there is reason to wonder whether Ben Sira's presentation of Elijah the Moses-like prophet carrying out the priestly duties of offering sacrifice and of anointing kings might not point back the earliest scribal hints of the whole tradition (cf. Sir 46:13, 46:16, 48:3, 48:8).

Against this background, the open signaling of Jesus as the priest-prophet "raised up" like Moses takes on a particular character, transpiring

---

[42] In the Book of Deuteronomy, the law of the prophets (18:9–22) and the law of the king (17:14–20) frame the law of Levitical priests in 18:1–8, which stands structurally at the center of the whole book. This conjunction evidently invited reflection. "In large measure one can argue that the so-called Deuteronomic History (Joshua through 2 Kings) is a midrash on Deut 17:14–18:22" (Christensen, *Deuteronomy*, 394).

[43] See Leuchter, "Samuel."

[44] The arising of the *prophet*-like Moses is set as the only limit on the Hasmonean power grab. According to 1 Mc 14:41, Simon is established in office as "leader" and high priest "until a faithful prophet shall arise" (ἕως τοῦ ἀναστῆναι προφήτην πιστόν).

as it so ostentatiously does in the personal presence of both Moses and Elijah. Through the collocation of these two particular persons, the Gospel plots us squarely in the final verses of Malachi, where both of these figures appear. The pairing had further acquired a fused priestly color, as was just glimpsed in Ben Sira. Of course, as commentators also correctly note, the appearance of Moses and Elijah beside Jesus is ultimately most certainly indebted to the related traditions about their mysterious ends. In particular, the tradition of Elijah's assumption into heaven (2 Kgs 2:1–9) was complemented by a similar tale that arose surrounding Moses. On the basis of the notice at the end of Deuteronomy that no one knows where Moses was buried (Dt 34:6), the story easily developed that he had also been carried into heaven.[45] "Arising" or being "raised up" like Moses assumes a suggestive sense in this connection: it now evokes the thought of going up into heaven. The appropriation of Zechariah 4 in the "two olive trees/two witnesses" of Revelation 11:3–13 offers a revealing, primitive Christian twist on this theme in its binding together of these two "sons of oil" with the pair Moses and Elijah *redivivi*.[46] Elijah's priestly credentials can easily explain his position as one of Zechariah's two anointed; Moses's position in the pair, by contrast, appears forged through his heavenly assumption, which binds him to Elijah. In Revelation, both are finally linked, through their heavenly journeys and through the convention of a *bat qōl*, to the Resurrection of Jesus: "After three and a half days the breath of life entered them ... they heard a loud voice form heaven saying to them, 'Come up here!' and they went up to heaven in a cloud" (Rv 11:12–13).

Moses's assumption contains critical evidence for understanding the whole constellation of Jesus' Transfiguration. The *Assumption of Moses*, an apocryphal text preserved in the first-century Latin translation of a Semitic original, dating from the first or second century BC, has unfortunately not preserved intact the final, crucial narration of Moses's assumption itself.[47] One extant verse does refer to Moses's heavenly existence, however. This is spoken of in a deeply significant way.

> Then will be filled the hands of the messenger (*implebuntur manus nuntii*)
> who is in the highest place appointed (*in summo constitutus*).
> (*As. Mos.* 10:2)

---

[45] On the origins of this tradition, see Stokes, "Not over Moses' Dead Body."
[46] See Aune, *Revelation 6–16*, 622–30.
[47] See Tromp, *Assumption of Moses*.

The phrase "filling the hands" should be recognized as the technical Hebrew idiom for the ordination of a priest. That this priestly *nuntius* is Moses himself has been cogently shown on the basis of another passage in which he is called *magnus nuntius* and depicted as interceding day and night and placating the Lord on Israel's behalf (*As. Mos.* 11:7; cf. 12:6).[48] The language of a *nuntius* is itself also worthy of note, and it points in a suggestive direction. Arguably, the Latin here covers a reference to the Levitical *Messenger* of Malachi. Indeed, as the preeminent agent of covenant making, who better than Moses to be the mysterious "Messenger of the Covenant" (Mal 3:1)? Moses's appearance alongside Elijah at the end of Malachi's prophecy also puts Moses—who was an actual Levite after all—in a contextually advantageous position to be exegetically identified as the priestly *nuntius*. This identification becomes all the more compelling given the Messenger's explicit task of instruction in Malachi 2. "True teaching (תורת אמת) was in his mouth ... The people should seek teaching (תורה) from his mouth, for he is the messenger of the Lord of hosts" (Mal 2:6, 2:7); "Remember the teaching (תורת משה) of my servant Moses" (Mal 4:4, 3:22 MT).

Whatever part Malachi's prophecy may play, if the ascended Elijah's *descent* from heaven carries a priestly connotation in Second Temple sources, Moses's *ascent* on high carries the same association. This is captured in the locative phrase *in summo* in *As. Mos.* 10:2. The idea of Moses's entering heaven and there becoming a priest appears to have been modeled upon Moses's ascent up the holy mountain of Sinai and his entrance into the cloud and YHWH's living presence. In the pointed phrasing of Exodus 19:3, "Moses went up to God (ומשה עלה אל האלהים)." At Qumran, in fact, in the text of Apocryphal Pentateuch B, we find a closely related (typically fragmentary) tradition where Moses is called "God's anointed one," literally "his messiah" (משיחו, 4Q377 ii 5). The title is nowhere else conferred upon Moses, but here it is explicitly suggestive of priesthood, as his entrance into the cloud is described as a "sanctification" or "consecration," seemingly envisioned as a sort of ordination (cf. Ex 28:41, 29:33).

> Moses the man of God, was with God in the cloud. And the cloud covered him because ... when he was sanctified (בהקדשו), and like a messenger (וכמלאך) he would speak from his mouth. (4Q377 ii 10–11)[49]

Here alongside that messianic discourse that brings him into contact with the two messiahs of Zechariah 4, we again find an allusion to the Messenger.

---

[48] See van Henten, "Moses as Heavenly Messenger."
[49] Translation by VanderKam and Brady, *Dead Sea Scrolls Reader*, 599.

The allusion "from his mouth" buttresses the suggestion that we are dealing with a Mosaic reading of Malachi's figure, moreover, for "from his mouth" (מפיהו) comes instruction in Malachi 2:7.

Similar to the text of 4Q377, Psalms 99:6–7, the most prominent (but not only) biblical tradition of Moses's priesthood, links this idea closely with Moses speech to God in the cloud. Paul, too, arguably knows the notion of Moses being mystically *sanctified* by his entrance into the cloud (cf. 1 Cor 10:2). The cloud of incense that enveloped the high priest when he entered into the Holy of Holies, guarding his life against the deadly vision of God (Lv 16:13), would have been easily linked to the cloud that descended upon Sinai, which portrayed in the manner of the Tabernacle—or rather, vice versa, the Tabernacle was cast as a mini-Sinai.[50]

It seems unlikely that the cloud that appears at Jesus' Transfiguration upon the mountain could have failed to evoke Moses's ascension into the mysteries of God (Ex 24:15). It happens in Moses's own presence, in order to designate his successor. Read in the light of Moses's parallel terrestrial and otherworldly ascensions into the sanctifying mysteries of God's presence, Jesus' own entrance into the cloud atop the high mountain accordingly takes on the striking shape of a priestly consecration via a celestial journey: the foretaste of a more definitive heavenly initiation in his coming assumption/resurrection/exaltation. Jesus is the Prophet-Priest like Moses, from whose mouth comes authoritative divine instruction, to which the disciples must *listen*. Like Moses's "ascension" up Sinai, Jesus' ascent up the mountain into the divine presence is an earthbound heavenly journey—and an image of that more perfect priestly entrance into the Holy of Holies that the Letter to the Hebrews will locate after his death.

The Priestly Garments

The central image that reveals Jesus' glory on the mountain, the sudden change of the appearance of his clothes, has rarely been analyzed in any depth. In Matthew and Luke, of course, Jesus' face is also said to be somehow transfigured. Matthew says it shone like the sun (Mt 17:2); Luke is more sober and says simply, "the appearance of his face was different" (τὸ εἶδος τοῦ προσώπου αὐτοῦ ἕτερον), perhaps hinting at the immanent setting of his face like flint to march on to Jerusalem (Lk 9:29; cf. 9:51). What little

---

50 "The equivalence of the Tabernacle to Sinai is an essential, indeed indispensable, axiom of P. The Tabernacle, in effect, becomes a portable Sinai, an assurance of the permanent presence of the deity in Israel's midst" (Milgrom, *Leviticus 1–16*, 574).

attention has been paid to the actual description of Jesus' transfiguration has, in a Matthean line, focused implicitly on Jesus' face and pursued an allusion to Moses's veil. This is not incorrect inasmuch as Jesus' glowing countenance can certainly be reckoned as pointing to Moses on Sinai. Such an identification of Jesus with Moses is undergirded by the open allusions to Deuteronomy 18:15 just explored, whence it is also filled out with a ready priestly interpretation. What this line of reflection fails to engage, however, is the more original, unusual, and prominent detail about the *clothes* themselves. Nothing is said of Moses's clothes on Sinai, and unlike Moses's veil, Jesus' clothes do not dampen but rather augment and radiate his glory.

Brilliant garments are not unknown in the New Testament context. Everyone from angels to kings, as well as gods themselves, might be described in this fashion (e.g., Mt 28:3; Lk 24:1; Acts 12:21–23; cf. Josephus, *A.J.* 19.343–354; also, e.g., Apuleius, *Metam.* 11.3–5; Suetonius, *Nero* 25.1; etc.).[51] As Crispin Fletcher-Louis has worked to show, however, the shining garments of Jesus find their strongest parallel in traditions connected with the radiant *doxa*, the glory of the high priestly vestments.[52] While it is not necessary to follow Fletcher-Louis's larger argumentative interest in his article, his insight here is extremely helpful. The high priestly vestments are far and away the most amply developed tradition of radiant clothing in the Judaism of the period, and this particular link is of obvious and enormous interest in the context of all that has preceded our analysis to this point.

The attention paid to the high priestly vestments by authors such as Ben Sira, Philo, and Josephus is well known (cf. Sir 50:5–11; Philo, *Leg.* 1.95; Josephus, *B.J.* 5.236; *A.J.* 3.151–187). The close symbolic attunement of the vestments to a Jewish cosmology of the cult indicates that these special garments somehow evoke a celestial theophany.[53] Josephus explains, for instance, that the bells jingling on the hem of the high priest's tunic sound like "thunder" and the pomegranates resemble "lightning"; the golden ephod shines like the sun, as does the golden weave of the cloth, which is also an image of "sunlight" (αὐγῆς); and so on (*A.J.* 3.184). The extraordinary, indeed supernatural and epiphanic, character attributed to these garments can hardly be overstated. After describing the "great amazement" (μεγάλην ἔκπληξιν) of those who saw the high priest Eleazar wearing his priestly vestments, the *Letter of Aristeas* compares the effect of such an apparition upon the witnesses to a sort of ecstatic, otherworldly vision.

---

51 On the cosmic apparel of the gods in the Greco-Roman context, see Pena, "Wearing the Cosmos."
52 Fletcher-Louis, "Revelation of the Sacral Son of Man."
53 See Pena, "Wearing the Cosmos," 1–29.

The wearer is considered worthy of such vestments at the services. Their appearance makes one awestruck and dumbfounded (φόβον καὶ ταραχήν): A man would think he had come out of this world into another one (εἰς ἕτερον ἐληλυθέναι ἐλτὸς τοῦ κόσμου). I emphatically assert that every man who comes near the spectacle of what I have described will experience astonishment (εἰς ἔκπληξιν) and amazement (θαυμασμὸν ἀδιήγητον) beyond words, his very being transformed by the hallowed arrangement of every single detail. (§99)[54]

Is the experience of Jesus' three disciplines before the transfigured Jesus a parallel sort of epiphanic ecstasy? The Dead Sea Scrolls and other Second Temple traditions were also captivated by the luminous power of the priestly clothes (e.g., *LAB* 26:9; 4QpIsa[d]). In the thirteenth of the *Songs of the Sabbath Sacrifice*, the high priest possesses, through his gleaming vestments, "the appearance of splendor and the likeness of the spirit of glory" (4Q405 23 ii 9), an allusion to the theophany in Ezekiel 1:28 ("an appearance of the likeness of the Glory of the Lord"). The origins of this tradition of the vibrant theophanic character of the priestly clothing reach back to Exodus 28:2, which commands, "You shall make sacred vestments for the glorious (לכבוד) adornment of your brother Aaron." The ostentatious wearing of the glorious divine name upon the high priest's brow obviously fueled this whole tradition (cf. 1QSb 4:28). At the same time, the various close associations that Exodus forges between the high priestly vestments (בגדי הקדש) and the *Miškan* itself—which are both made of the same sorts of precious textiles and multicolored weaves—result in the former, like the latter, holding status as a sort of dwelling of the divine כבוד (Ex 39:1–31).

The later traditions of Adam's "garments of light/glory" (e.g., *Gen. Rab.* 12.6, 20:12; *Pirqe R. El.* 14; Tg. Gen 3:21)—a prelapsarian vesture of light in punning contrast with the "garments of skin" (כתנת עור, Gn 3:21)—sometimes brought into discussion of the Transfiguration should be seen, one could argue, as at origin an anachronistic retrojection of this older tradition of luminous priestly vesture.[55] The primal man in Ezekiel 28:13–14 is notably adorned with an elaborate garment studded with precious jewels, reminiscent of the ephod, and set upon "the holy mountain of God," where an "anointed" cherub is with him. This is all suggestive of Adam's primal priesthood, which became a major motif in Second Temple sources. The "garments of glory" motif, in fact, seems to be derived from exactly this anachronistic

---

54 Translation by R. J. H. Shutt in Charlesworth, *Old Testament Pseudepigrapha*, 2:19.
55 On this connection, see the discussion in Marcus, *Mark 8–16*, 1112–15.

fantasy. Specifically, it was offered as a solution to the problem created by conceiving of Eden as a sanctuary with Adam as its priestly minister, since priests were specifically prohibited from exposing their nakedness (Ex 20:26, 28:41–42).[56] The concern is evident in *Jub.* 3:27–31, for instance, where Adam's covering his shame is interpreted as a special privilege not granted to any of the animals but part of the careful observance of his priestly dignity as one who offers a pleasing sacrifice.[57]

As an addendum to and further confirmation of this perspective on the Edenic garments of light, it is worth noting the proposal of Robin Darling Young concerning the "garments of light" and "red robe" motifs that structure the (second-century? Gnostic?) *Hymn of the Pearl*.[58] Namely, distancing herself from Sebastian Brock's suggestion of an Adam theology directly informing the image, she concludes that we have here instead a Jewish high priestly symbol.[59] The hymn's "land of the East," as the region of light, where one must don these special robes, would represent the image of the heavenly Temple as the true Holy of Holies.

The *Hymn of the Pearl*'s simultaneously priestly and cosmic journey is not an isolated topos unconnected with the wearing of garments that are somehow proper to the celestial realm. As Fletcher-Louis observes, one of the most impressive and helpful parallels to the specific event of Jesus' sudden transfiguration and donning of new radiant clothes is an unambiguously priestly scene: the redressing/ordination of Enoch in 2 *Enoch* 22:8–9.

> The Lord said to Michael, "Take Enoch and extract him from the earthly clothing. And anoint him with the delightful oil, and put him into the clothes of glory. And Michael extracted me from my clothes. He anointed me with the delightful oil; and the appearance of that oil is greater than the greatest light, its ointment is like sweet dew, and its fragrance like myrrh; and its shining like the sun.[60]

---

56 On the traditions of Adam's priesthood, see Anderson, *Genesis of Perfection*.
57 See Orpana, "Awareness of Nudity."
58 Young, "Notes on Divesting and Vesting."
59 "As numerous recent studies have demonstrated, the first centuries B.C.E. and C.E. saw the production, among Jewish authors, of an extensive literature concerned with the Temple, its liturgy, and its priesthood, including the garments of the high priest. Perhaps to the list of possible contexts of, and allusions in, the Hymn of the Pearl should be added the robe of the high priest, transferred to an Edessan context and adding meaning to a quest story related as well to the parable of the prodigal son and the pearl of great price" (Young, "Notes on Divesting and Vesting," 214).
60 Translation by F. I. Andersen in Charlesworth, *Old Testament Pseudepigrapha*, 1:138–39.

With his celestial "clothes of glory" and the delightful anointing oil, Enoch is ostensibly raised to a priestly dignity.[61] While the text and tradition are difficult to date precisely, it is of special interest that Enoch's priestly "ordination" transpires in the form of a journey into the heavenly sanctuary, such as we saw in the *Apocalypse of Moses*. The pedigree for such an otherworldly elevation to priestly status evokes one prominent strain of what James Kugel describes as typical Second Temple exegetical "overkill": namely, the tradition that the patriarch Levi himself was ordained by means of a celestial vision/voyage, where he was initiated into the angelic cult of heaven (cf. *ALD*; *Jub.* 31:2; *Test. Levi* 2–5, 8).[62]

The Levi ordination-vision/voyage traditions share the special interest in the priestly vestments.

> And I saw seven men in white clothing, saying to me:
>> Arise, put on the robe of the priesthood
>>> and the crown of righteousness
>>> and the breastplate of understanding
>>> and the garment of truth
>>> and the plate of faith
>>> and the turban of (giving) a sign
>>> and the ephod of prophecy
>
> And each of them carried these things and put them on me, and said:
>> From now on become a priest of the Lord, you and your seed, forever.
>
> And the first anointed with holy oil ...
> The third clothed me with a linen vestment like an ephod.
> The fourth put round me a girdle like (a) purple (robe) ...
> The sixth put a crown on my head.
> The seventh put on me a diadem of the priesthood. And they filled my hands with incense that I might serve as priest to the Lord.
> (*Test. Levi* 8.1–10)[63]

Light imagery is likewise prominently employed to describe Levi's transformation into the glory of a priest: "You will light up a bright light of knowledge in Jacob, and you will be as the sun to all the seed of Israel" (*Test. Levi* 4:2); "He will shine as the sun on the earth and will remove all darkness

---

61 Stokes ("Not over Moses' Dead Body," 204) observes several connections that link this passage in 2 *Enoch* to the prophecy of Joshua the high priest in Zechariah 3.
62 Kugel, "Levi's Elevation," 7–13, 27–30.
63 Translation by Hollander and Jonge, *Testaments of the Twelve Patriarchs*, 149.

from under heaven" (*Test. Levi* 18:4). From the Gospel perspective, this entire priestly metamorphosis of Levi transpires in a suggestive place and manner. Levi sees a high mountain, and then "behold the heavens were opened" (*Test. Levi* 2:5–6; see also *Test. Levi* 5.1, 18:6; cf. 4QTestLevi[a] II 13–17).[64]

Whether or not it represents another case of "overkill," Levi's vestments are not the only symbol of his new status. Like Moses the *nuntius* in *As. Mos.* 10.2, Levi's hands are *filled* in expression of consecration, and like the use of משיח for Moses in 4Q377, Levi (like Enoch) is anointed as priest with a holy unction (cf. *ALD* 6). Whether a less fragmentary witness to the Second Temple Moses traditions might produce attention to his own vesture is impossible to say. What is worthy of note, however, is that some notion of a metamorphosis/glorification/apotheosis that outfits the mortal flesh of Moses for his sojourn in the heavenly courts already bears close contacts with the Enochian vestment tradition and exposes an underlying symbolic dimension of this entire mode of expression (cf. Philo, *Mos.* 2.288).[65] For eschatological eyes, vestments are more than vestments: they are a mysterious bodily bearing of the Lord's own כבוד. Heavenly priesthood from the Second Temple perspective obliged some such manner of quasi-angelomorphic transfiguration in glory. How else might one worthily enter the Holy of Holies in heaven? This pattern is confirmed repeatedly. The *Apocalypse of Abraham* provides yet another example, as Andrei Orlav observes in an important chapter of his book on heavenly priesthood titled "The Transformation of the Celebrants."

> In the *Apocalypse of Abraham*, as in many Jewish pseudepigraphical narratives, the hero's access to the sacred realm coincides with his metamorphosis as a celebrant of the heavenly liturgy. This translation, hinted at symbolically via the change in Abraham's garments, was often taken to mark the transition from the earthly to the celestial. Here, as in the Yom Kippur ordinance, the changes affecting the celebrant's wardrobe are the climax of the transformation.[66]

Zechariah's prophecy of Joshua the high priest's re-clothing, changing out of his old and soiled priestly vestments into new "clean garments," a transformation and purification of the priestly establishment mysteriously carried out by the Angel of the Lord and seemingly playing on the Day of Atonement,

---

64 See note 41 above.
65 See Stokes, "Not over Moses' Dead Body," 196.
66 Orlav, *Heavenly Priesthood*, 119.

offers scriptural precedent for this developing view of the eschatologically renewed, newly glorified priestly order, symbolized and defined by its new order of priestly vesture (Zec 3:1–10).

An additional observation on the diverse marks of the priesthood can help to put the specific importance of the glorious vestments in their proper light. The Dead Sea Scrolls' curiously reserved employment of the term משיח for the eschatological high priest (restricted to 1QS IX 11) indicates a certain reticence to appeal to priestly anointing and may perhaps, according to an intriguing suggestion of Jonge, owe something to the rabbinic tradition that during the reign of Josiah the oil of unction was hidden away and by the Second Temple period lost altogether.[67] The corresponding Mishnaic (*m. Hor.* 2.4) distinction between the "anointed priest" (כהן המשיח) and "he that has a larger number of garments" (המרובה בבגדים) may thus also reflect an earlier perspective. That a group such as the Yahad could not accept the official high priest, unsmeared by the missing holy oil and parading himself in a cultic costume held in custody by a corrupt institution, reveals an atmosphere in which both a unique unction by the Holy Spirit and unique investiture in garments of heavenly light might emerge as fitting eschatological expedients to remedy a fundamental cultic dysfunction. It is not impossible to imagine some dynamic like this at play in the twinned stories of Jesus' heavenly attestation at the Jordan and upon the mountain.

In considering not only the celestial clothes of Jesus but also the particular company he enjoys when he dons his bright white vestments, it is useful to mention another model of ordination that, alongside the heavenly journey motif, also shapes the Levi tradition. Kugel calls this the "chain of priests" motif; namely, Levi's elevation to sacerdotal dignity through personal contact with a hoary line of priestly agents that reach through Abraham and Noah all the way back to Adam.[68] Notably, it was not only instructions about sacrificial and cultic matters that were passed on through these intergenerational meetings—the priestly garments were also handed down. "And his [Levi's] father put priestly clothes on him and filled his hands" (*Jub.* 32:4; cf. *ALD* 9).[69] This hand-to-hand transmission of the high priestly garments has its biblical base in Numbers 20:26–28, where the cultic vestments are ceremonially removed from Aaron transferred to his son Eleazar (cf. Ex 29:29).

---

67 Jonge, *Jewish Eschatology*, 32–34.
68 Kugel, "Levi's Elevation," 17–24.
69 See Kugel, "Levi's Elevation," 49. The case of Jacob is special, as he was not himself considered a priest; Levi thus (also) received the priestly dignity from his grandfather, Isaac, who was imagined as a priest. The text in *Jub.* 32:4 binds the handing over of the garments specifically with the "Jacob Counts Backwards" motif.

In Numbers, the stripping of Aaron and clothing of his heir is suggestively carried out by Moses. This highlights Moses's prominent place in the Pentateuch as the Lord's designated *high priest maker* (cf. Ex 29; Lv 8–9). Given the attested sacerdotal character of Moses, Elijah, and John, Jesus' proximity to all three figures and clear status as a designated successor puts the Elijah-like motif of transmitting priestly garments well within imaginative reach of the Transfiguration's symbolic universe. We do not see Jesus wearing John's rugged clothing—a recognized allusion to Elijah (2 Kgs 1:8)—yet their startling contrast in apparel corresponds to the shift from the "filthy" to the angelically "clean" clothes in Zechariah 3 as well as to the relative greatness of "the mightier one," whose sandal strap the Baptist will not dare to touch the dressing of the one who is announced as coming with fire.

Mark's manner of describing Jesus' garments may appear at first mundane, with its allusion to the lowly trade of a cloth-carder.[70] Jesus' clothes became "dazzling white, such as no fuller on earth could bleach them" (ἐγένετο στίλβοντα λευκὰ λίαν, οἷα γναφεὺς ἐπὶ τῆς γῆς οὐ δύναται οὕτως λευκᾶναι, Mk 9:3). Rhetorically, Mark obviously evokes the otherworldly through an absolute contrast with the worldly and the well known. It is permitted to ask, however, whether in this precise language we are not perhaps permitted to hear an allusion to the כברית מכבסים of Malachi 3:2, the strange "fuller's soap" that is like a refiner's fire (כאש מצרף) for purifying the corrupted covenant priesthood. Although hues of crimson and blue were threaded into the earthly vestments of Aaron and his sons when they appeared "in their splendor" (Sir 50:13), pure linen garments were the priestly garb in Ezekiel's vision of the eschatological Temple (Ezek 44:15–18).

One final clue, interior to the Gospels, represents a last bit of data. The reference to the Feast of Sukkoth, implicit in Peter's offer to build booths, reinforces a priestly reading. On the one hand, the feast is closely calendrically hinged to the celebration of Yom Kippur—when the priest is ritually reclothed. Sukkoth comes five days after the Day of Atonement, making the otherwise free-floating chronological allusion in Mark 9:2, "after six days," quite suggestive and rather compelling. The inherent linkage of Booths to this highest of priestly and cultic rites becomes evident in the strong priestly and cultic associations of the latter feast, moreover. As the immediate answer to an annual renewal imaging an eschatological newness, Sukkoth embodied the inauguration of the newly purified cult. In Ezra 3:4, Joshua and his fellow priests among the returned exiles inaugurate the altar, laying its foundation and offering the first sacrifices since their deportation on the Feast of Booths

---

70 On this menial trade, see Jeremias, *Jerusalem in the Time of Jesus*, 5, 20.

(cf. Neh 8:14–17). In the same spirit, after the Maccabean crisis, the purification/rededication of the Temple was closely associated the feast, which took on special importance for the new Hasmonean order (e.g., 2 Mc 1:18, 10:6). Especially in the Hasmonean and Herodian periods, the festival accordingly became the day on which the acclamations of kings were made and, importantly, high priests formally assumed their office (e.g., Josephus, *A.J.* 15:50–52; *B.J.* 1:437). In 1 Maccabees 10:21, we thus read that "Jonathan *put on the sacred vestments* in the seventh month of the one hundred sixtieth year, *at the festival of booths*." Both the technical expression here for a high priestly ordination—putting on the sacred vestments—and the festal time of its occurrence at the festival of booths are a perfect fit for the Gospels' key graphic symbols.

Jesus' solemn announcement in Caesarea Philippi, precisely six (inclusive) days before his metamorphosis, that he was laying a new foundation stone—acting arguably as the "Davidic Temple Builder," with Eliakim's priestly vesture in the background—closely followed by Jesus' own clothing in glorious vesture at the Feast of Booths, is thus a conjunction that implies a portentous statement.[71] This one, the Priest-Prophet like Moses, the Messenger of the Covenant like Elijah, he is the true High Priest, *Joshua*, whose garments are cleansed with otherworldly power, who will enter Jerusalem to purify the cult and rebuild the Temple.

Conclusion

At the end of this study, which has covered considerable ground yet maintained its essential focus, it should be perfectly clear how deeply implicated Jesus' Transfiguration is in the diverse Second Temple expectations that surround an eschatological high priest. It should thus be unnecessary to rehearse all the results for review. It is revealing, nevertheless, to note in closing that we are not the first to discern this connection. In nearly the earliest preserved Christian reflection on Jesus' Transfiguration, Origen's commentary on Matthew's Gospel, basing itself on a variant in one of the earliest papyri of Mark 9:2 (εν τω προσευχεσθαι, P[45]), an explicitly high priestly light illumines the whole event.

> Since it will be necessary to explain Mark's phrasing, "and in the act of praying he was transfigured before them," we should say

---

[71] See Barber, "Jesus as the Living Temple Builder," esp. 944–45. On the living Temple motifs at work in Matthew 16, see Holmén, "Caught in the Act."

> that perhaps it is above all possible to see the Word transfigured before us, if we do what we have mentioned before and ascend the mountain and see the one who is the Word himself, conversing with the Father and praying to him for those for whom a true high priest would pray to the true and only God. And that he might thus converse with God and pray to the Father, he ascends the mountain. And then according to Mark "his garments became white and radiant as the light."[72]

Jesus ascends the mountain in order to be able to converse with the true God as a true high priest. Origen's worldview naturally differs from both the Gospels' and our own. It is not impossible, however, to construct some conceptual bridges. I would accordingly like to offer a modest interpretative proposal in the form of a short synthetic statement, followed by two brief suggestions.

Jesus' answer to the disciples' question can perhaps be best understood against a Second Temple grid as follows. Jesus, and perhaps not Jesus alone, recognized John as a priestly/Aaronic Elijah figure. Jesus read John's martyr's fate, moreover, to have taken an unexpected but prophesied turn: John *tasted death*, as was fitting for God's Messenger and Servant. At this point, as the Davidic Servant-Son-of-Man-Messiah, Jesus' role was to take up John's mantle to share his fate and complete the priestly mission, and this is what transpires at the Transfiguration. Jesus is clothed in radiant vestments in such a way and in such company as to be identified with the priestly role otherwise, earlier accorded to John. It is a passing of the baton already evident in Jesus and John's common announcement of the Kingdom, but which here turns dramatically from the Message to the *Messenger* as such.

The narrative orientation of the Transfiguration scene around Jesus' person and his coming Passion and Resurrection cannot be rightly understood without attention to the pronounced priestly dimension inherent in the ample contextual clues considered in this study. Other valid dimensions at work in the passage are in no way here excluded: on the contrary, the agglutinative scribal approach to Jesus' eschatological identity assimilates these alternative/complementary perspectives with unusual ease. Still, the prominence of the priestly aspect deserves considerable, hitherto lacking attention.

As a first suggestion, on the basis of this, I would propose a new line of access to broader New Testament traditions of Jesus' priesthood. In historical context, the scenario presented in this study resembles an attested Jewish model of ordination by immersion into the realm of God. This applies to

---

[72] Daley, *Light on the Mountain*, 82.

figures like Moses, Enoch, and Levi himself, and it permits new insight into the priestly discourse of the Letter to the Hebrews, as already mentioned. It also opens up a more theologically robust reflection on the apotheosis character of Jesus' Transfiguration, which can no longer be reduced to an exaltation tradition void of all cultic cosmology and interest.[73] The priestly-clad "Son of Man" who appears in Revelation 1:13, glorious in the midst of the celestial cult and radiant in his long robe and golden sash, provides an important link to the Gospel accounts both via his vestments and via his title.[74] Gospel studies may likewise find in the notion of Jesus' heavenly initiation a needed bridge to a developed body of scholarship on mysticism in the early Jewish context.[75] The "chain of priests" model, associated with Levi, additionally illuminates how notions of transmission and succession might contour Jesus' assumption of a priestly role. Jesus' continuation of John's (priestly) work of purification might be richly expanded from this perspective. At the same time, finally, Levi's deed of Phineas-like "zeal" was also invoked to explain the patriarch's special election for priestly service. In this light, an alluring new lens is revealed for interpreting Jesus' own action in cleansing the Temple (cf. ζῆλος, Jn 2:17), which has an obvious echo in Malachi 3, which might even be thought of as a kind of prophetic script and resulting from Jesus' new identification with Phineas-Elijah in the wake of John's demise.[76] Plotting the Passion events in this priestly direction may deliver important clues for contextualizing the cultic elements evident at the Last Supper. In sum, Christologically speaking, the Gospels present us with a formidable paradigm for exploring Jesus' priestly consecration in engagement with diverse scholarly agendas, open to new paths of historical-contextual reasoning and attuned to the unavoidable, perennial bugbear of Christ's own consciousness as Messiah.

One additional, final corollary of more than passing hermeneutical interest. Jesus' apparent engagement with and adjustment to the diarchic messianism of the scribal culture of his day indicates an understanding of Scripture open to multiple prophetic fulfillments. In his mind, John is Elijah the High Priest and the suffering Servant, yet so is Jesus himself, and more definitively so. Fluid Second Temple exegesis, which was inclined to multiply its mediators, resulting in a pluriform eschatology with scripturally based

---

73 See Burkett, "Transfiguration of Jesus."
74 On the clothing of this figure, see Pena, "Wearing the Cosmos," 8.
75 See, e.g., Hamdović et al., *La 'sacerdotalisation.'*
76 The controverted meaning of Jesus' action in the Temple represents a strategic point of leverage in historical Jesus scholarship. See, e.g., Sanders, *Jesus and Judaism*, 61–76; and Evans, "Jesus' Action in the Temple."

chief agents aplenty, was also marked by an unmistakable scribal trajectory prone to fuse these agents and generate a conglomerate messianic colossus: precisely such as we triumphantly confront in Jesus in the Gospels. This essential interplay of a primordial multiplicity and a totalizing Christological impulse is not simply resolved in full favor of the latter, however. Even the "Christology of Jesus" entertains notes of striking ambiguity, it seems. The harmony of this polyvalent view of prophecies and scriptural types with patristic perspectives on Old Testament exegesis presents contemporary theology with a healthy goad to reconsider its own hermeneutical assumptions.

CHAPTER 14

Prosopological Exegesis and Christological *Anagnorisis*

In a recent book ambitiously titled *The Birth of the Trinity*, Matthew Bates has helpfully called attention to the significance of prosopological exegesis in the early history of Trinitarian thought.[1] Observation of this connection is not new. More than half a century ago, Carl Andresen rigorously traced the portentous appearance of the language of "person" (*prosopon*) in theological speech to the second- and early third-century practice of what he called *prosopographische Exegese*.[2] Marie-Josèphe Rondeau subsequently gave the issue still more sustained attention, expanding the investigation to demonstrate the continuation and increasing theological sophistication of this early exegetical trend in later patristic witnesses.[3] Moving in the opposite direction, Bates has similarly advanced Andresen's original claim by demonstrating that this mode of proto-Trinitarian scriptural interpretation (if not the explicit language of "persons") can be solidly anchored in the text of the New Testament itself. More than this, Bates also means to attribute prosopological exegesis to "the historically plausible" Jesus himself.[4]

Historically, the emergence of the Trinitarian vision of God is more complex than any one single explanation.[5] A profound Christian engagement

---

1 Bates, *Birth of the Trinity*.
2 Andresen, "Zur Entstehung und Geschichte." See also the discussion in Ratzinger, "Zum Personverständnis in der Theologie," esp. 55–58.
3 Rondeau, *Les commentaires patristiques*.
4 Bates, *Birth of the Trinity*, 40–44.
5 For a good, recent presentation of this complex process, see Anatolios, *Retrieving Nicea*.

with the philosophical traditions of antiquity has long been appreciated in this regard (or observed with dismay, as the case may be).[6] The ongoing role of biblically based exegetical argument is nevertheless increasingly recognized to be a factor of central importance. These scriptural modes of thinking were not only of importance for developing patristic theology, moreover. They were also of central importance in what may be called the "Christology of Jesus." Thus, while I suggest in the following study that a much more ample and variegated range of exegetical operations must be envisioned than Bates's presentation of prosopological reasoning indicates, I emphatically agree in plotting an important source of Trinitarian thought in Jesus' own acts of biblical interpretation. This exegesis, I further suggest, invites precisely the same sorts of theological tension that were ultimately resolved ecclesially through the Arian crisis: namely, a high mediator Christology coupled with claims of being the one true God.

In order to illustrate these aspects of Jesus' personal understanding of the Scriptures—above all the way in which he finds himself spoken of in the sacred text—I focus upon what Martin Hengel called "the most important Old Testament proof passage for the development of Christology": Psalm 110.[7] Bates is hardly the first to see here a text of major significance, and Jesus' direct quotation of the text in Mark 12:36 makes it an obvious cornerstone in any Christology that takes seriously the history of exegesis. Rather than seeking to draw from this psalm the preexistence theology that Bates has suggested, however, I prefer to propose another route.[8] I will speak of "plenary *anagnorisis*" to designate a certain extension of the prosopological mindset that I see at work: a wider, less logocentric, and dialogical slant on Jesus' exegesis. I will also intone a priestly/messianic self-application on the part of Jesus as providing a more historically solid Christological foothold than Bates's eager spring to the divine subsistent relations.

The essay has four parts. After offering an introduction to prosopological exegesis and its recent appearance in New Testament studies through Bates's work, I will proceed to suggest certain limitations of this perspective as a foundation for Trinitarian exegesis, appealing to the so-called iconic turn. I will then propose *anagnorisis* as a more promising approach for histori-

---

6 See, e.g., Harnack, *History of Dogma*, 1:43–50; and Kelly, *Early Christian Doctrines*, 83–135.

7 Hengel, *Son of God*, 80. See also idem, *Studies in Early Christology*, 119–226.

8 Mention should also be made here of the monograph of Lee, *From Messiah to Preexistent Son*. Lee's analysis helpfully seeks to build a bridge between Jesus' own self-understanding and early Christian exegesis. It is typical of the Early High Christology school, however, in Lee's narrow desire to explain Jesus' claims to divinity, not his soteriological mediation, with a corresponding resistance to adopting mediator figures as a constitutive component of the conceptual field of primitive Christology. See chap. 7 in this volume.

cally imagining and theologically exploiting the personal exegesis of Jesus. Finally, I will offer two examples of this wider perspective in application to Psalm 110, which will point to Jesus' priestly identity as a cosmic mediator.

Contextualizing Prosopological Exegesis

Τίς λέγει, πρὸς τίνα, καὶ περὶ τίνος: "Who is speaking, to whom, and about whom?"[9] Ancient interpreters routinely asked this battery of questions in their efforts to make sense of the texts they set about to study. Made more urgent by the difficult, unmarked character of ancient manuscripts, "solution-by-person" (*lusis ek tou prosopou*) or prosopological exegesis addresses the problem of determining the voice of the speakers by positing the adequate *prospopa*: so-and-so is speaking to such another. Ultimately rooted in the work of Alexandrian Homeric scholars and the rhetorical exercises of the Greco-Roman age (i.e., *prosopopeia/ethopoeia*), this interpretative method is perhaps best known today to readers of the roman rhetor Augustine through the studies of Michael Fiedrowicz and others.[10]

The concrete procedure is easily grasped. Confronted with a line such as *Illiad* 16.22-23—"With a wrenching groan you answered your friend, O my rider"—the exegete (both ancient and modern) must identify and reflect upon this startling Homeric use of apostrophe, that is, the poet's own direct address (τίς λέγει) to the character of Patroclus (πρὸς τίνα), speaking about his friend, Achilles (περὶ τίνος). The result is a clarified understanding not only of the referential functioning of the phrase, but also ultimately of the whole complex fabric of the poem (in this case, the unique poetic handling and significance of Patroclus). Such secular exegetical techniques naturally and easily penetrated early Christian culture.[11] Applied to biblical texts, this or that enigmatic verse was accordingly set in the mouth, say, of the Father and thus said to be spoken ἐκ προσώπου πατρός, "from the Father's person." The textbook case is Genesis 1:26—"Let us make man in our image." Here, of course, the voice of the speaker (τίς λέγει) is not the only pressing question but also the mysterious πρὸς τίνα. Theophilus of Antioch provides the

---

9 Hippolytus, *Contra Noetum* 4.

10 See Fiedrowicz, "Introduction"; and idem, *Psalmus vox totius Christi*. See also, e.g., Fischer, *Die Psalmen als Stimme der Kirche*, 15-35; and Lienhard, "Reading the Bible and Learning to Read."

11 The same methods, of course, had also earlier penetrated Jewish exegetical culture, which in many cases thus became a mediator of ideas and methods adopted by early Christian thinkers. See Niehof, *Jewish Exegesis*.

acceptable answer, posing the rhetorical question in *Ad. Aut.* 2.18: Οὐκ ἄλλῳ δέ τινι εἴρηκεν Ποιήσωμεν, ἀλλ᾽ ἢ τῷ ἑαυτοῦ λόγῳ καὶ τῇ ἑαυτοῦ σοφίᾳ?

Far flung as the fathers' prosopological reading of Genesis 1:26 may seem to modern minds, it is hardly a technique limited to the divine conversation about the creation of mankind—or limited to patristic authors, for that matter. Bates convincingly shows that the same sort of thinking can be solidly anchored in the text of the New Testament itself. Peter's application of Psalm 16 to Jesus is a perfect example. "You will not abandon my soul to death, nor let your Holy One see corruption." How could David be the speaker, Peter asks, when that king's tomb is here among us (Acts 2:29–31)?[12] The words must be heard coming from the mouth of Christ, that is, from his *prosopon*. The same applies to Psalm 110 and the exaltation to God's right hand. "For David did not ascend into heaven," Peter argues; David cannot therefore be the one who is both spoken to and spoken of (Acts 2:34).

Bates's introduction of prosopological reading into the contemporary New Testament conversation is welcome. It is important, moreover, to see what he intends his new datum to contribute. His work belongs within a broader current in New Testament study, at once strongly attracted by the basic claims of the Early High Christology school, yet also in various ways dissatisfied. The effort, broadly, is to explain better both the origins and the precise character of the primitive Christian reconfiguration of Jewish monotheism.[13] Crispin Fletcher-Louis is perhaps the most significant voice of the school's dissatisfied adherents, but others could be mentioned.[14] For his part, Fletcher-Louis means to give more place to those chief agent and divine mediator figures that scholars like Richard Bauckham have severely marginalized. Bates, without entirely knowing what to do with Bauckham, nevertheless has concerns with his "divine identity" language and prefers what, on the basis of this prosopological model, he promisingly calls a "Christology of divine persons."[15] The design is to equip the discussion with more adequate historical categories for articulating an orthodox and systematically accurate doctrine of God.

Focus upon solution-by-person exegesis undoubtedly permits an alluring dialogical articulation of divine relations, in contrast to the unity intoned in Bauckham's notion of "divine identity."[16] To the extent that a diversity of

---

12 See Holladay, "What David Saw."

13 On the present state of the question, particularly the debate over the role of mediator figures, see chap. 10 in this volume. See also Hurtado, "Observations."

14 Fletcher-Louis, *Jesus Monotheism*.

15 Bates, *Birth of the Trinity*, 2, 22–26.

16 Above all, see Bauckham, *Jesus and the God of Israel*. For a Catholic perspective on this influential "divine identity" proposal, see chap. 7 in this volume.

dramatis personae thus finds a place within Bates's project, it is implicitly hospitable to the work of Fletcher-Louis. Bates even invokes Melchizedek in 11Q13 as a divine figure constructed through a prosopological reading of Psalm 110, in precise parallel to Christ.[17] While there are good reasons to be open in this direction and prosopological thinking should take its place in our reconstructions, there are nevertheless also reasons to be concerned about placing too much weight upon the discovery of this manner of reading Scripture.

Trinitarian Exegesis and the Iconic Turn

In his enthusiasm to establish his model's importance in the scriptural shape of Trinitarian meaning (a significant, promising insight), Bates at times adopts a needlessly dismissive posture toward other forms of theological thought. Here the wider history of prosopological exegesis might itself serve as a ready warning. The easy adoption by Sabellian authors of *prosopon*/mask language and a development of the associated biblical interpretation was shown by Andresen. This highlights the need for clear philosophical underpinnings, if a doctrinally adequate approach to the Tri-une God is ultimately desired. Plainly, the history of Trinitarian theology cannot be imagined apart from a great deal of ancient philosophy—even if central categories like "person" have stronger exegetical roots than many have heretofore appreciated. A raw historical approach will therefore in the end not be enough to fully equip an orthodox exegesis.

In addition to this ancillary metaphysical reasoning, however, one must likewise be sensitive to the key contributions of alternative biblical modes of thought. Historically, this factor is also clear. Noting the much greater role that typological and allegorical perspectives have classically played in the development of doctrine, as well as the ways prosopological interpretation risks discarding the *sensus literalis*, Christopher Seitz thus wonders in his review why Bates seems unwilling to "share the terrain" with a fuller range of exegetical techniques.[18] The point is well made. For the depth and nuance of Trinitarian doctrine is not served by narrowing its biblical base or exaggerating the problems posed and answered with solutions by person.

It is revealing to observe in just this connection the manifest inadequacies of prosopological exegesis taken alone. The case of Genesis 1:26 again

---

[17] Bates, *Birth of the Trinity*, 59–60; and Bates, "Beyond *Stichwort*."
[18] Seitz, "Review of *The Birth of the Trinity*," 765. Bates's tacit dissatisfaction with *Stichwort* exegesis might be added to the list of ancient techniques worthy of more attention and esteem.

serves as a prime example. Neither *Barnabas* (6:12) nor Justin (*Dial.* 62) in their prosopological readings ever detected a Trinity of characters in the plural forms of the verse, envisioning simply the two-way converse of Father and Son. Together with his contemporary Theophilus of Antioch, Irenaeus is the first to perceive a three-sided conversation between Father, Son, and Spirit; though even Irenaeus himself also settles for a two-member dialogue (cf. *Ad Haer.* 5.15.4; *Epideixis* 55.15), except in the celebrated image of the Son and Spirit as God's two hands. The connection of the full Trinitarian vision with this anthropomorphic idea is crucial, for it also appears explicitly in Theophilus (*Ad Aut.* 2.5–6, 9, 18, 25, 35). Robert Grant suggested that Irenaeus knew Theophilus's work, without ever mentioning him by name, and with other evidence the shared two-hands trope makes some form of contact entirely likely.[19] Unfortunately, Theophilus's commentary on Genesis has not been preserved. Still, Irenaeus provides all that is necessary to recreate his Trinitarian reading of Genesis 1:26.

The famous image of God's two hands is far too rarely contextualized, even within Irenaeus's own work. It appears several times, but the foundational text comes in *Adversus Haereses* Book 4, just after an affirmation that "it is impossible that the Father can be measured." His unattainable height of love has nevertheless been revealed in his Word and Wisdom (4.20.1). This comment refers back to a highly evocative statement several chapters before, where Irenaeus describes the Son as the μέτρον, the measure of the immeasurable Father (4.4.2). Continuing in the present passage, Irenaeus then offers a monotheistic exegesis of Genesis's creation account—or the two creation accounts, to be more exact.

> "*And God formed man, taking dust of the earth, and breathed into his face the breath of life*" (Gn 2:7). Therefore, angels did not make us, nor did they form us, nor, indeed, could angels make an image of God, nor [could] any other besides the true God, nor [could] a Power far removed from the Father of all things (*virtus longe absistens a Patre universorum*). For God did not need these [beings] to make what he had himself beforehand determined to make, as if he himself did not have his hands (*quasi ipse suas non haberet manus*). For always present with him are the Word and Wisdom, the Son and Spirit, by whom and in whom he made all things freely and of his own will, to whom he also speaks, when he says, "*Let us make man after our image and likeness*" (Gn 1:26). (*Ad. Haer.* 4.20.1; cf. 5.1.3, 5:15.4, 5.28.4)[20]

---

19 Grant, *Greek Apologists*, 146–73.
20 Translation from *Ante-Nicene Fathers*, vol. 1.

It is well known that Genesis 1:26 was by an early date already a problem text for Jewish monotheism. Against his Gnostic interlocutors, Irenaeus here obviously means to attribute all creative agency to God, to the exclusion of any outside demiurgic helpers. The a priori oddity of reconfiguring a defense of monotheism around a kind of two powers conception—albeit two powers "not far removed from the Father"—is a bold strategy to say the least.[21] Yet the Lord God's modeling the clay in Genesis 2:7 has suggested the theme.[22] God's creative Word and his Wisdom first clearly appear as two distinct "powers" when they map onto the visual logic of his two hands.

The twinned cosmogonies in Genesis 1 and 2 accordingly supply Irenaeus's parallel rhetoric of *verbum* and *manus*. In the majestic discourse of Genesis 1 the Lord creates by his sovereign Word, while in the anthropomorphic account of Genesis 2 his *hands* become the agents of creation: thus his Word and Wisdom (not just the Logos alone), like two hands, do the creating. It is true that the word יד or ימין never appears—just as דבר is also wanting. Later exegesis supplied what was implicit, however.[23] The graphic imagery of Genesis 2:7, with its anthropomorphically imagined pair of hands, thus seems to provide an essential Trinitarian key, reversing for a moment the invisibility of the *Sophia*-Spirit. Accordingly, by the time Tertullian in *Adversus Praxeam* (12.3) first explicitly names the Spirit as a *tertia persona* in the celestial conversation at the creation, the tripersonal reading had been grounded through an innovative fusion of allegorical and prosopological interpretations.

Such theologically fruitful blending of an image- and speech-based exegetical logic is highly suggestive in grasping something of the very structure of revelation itself. A pattern of visualizing in duplicate what is elsewhere merely spoken is integral to the incarnational telos of prophetically ordered divine discourse. Without endorsing some post-rational bogeyman of "logocentrism," exegetes and theologians would accordingly do well to reflect on the so-called iconic turn announced by Gottfried Boehm and others.[24] Whether or not Boehm's *Bildwissenschaft* points exactly the right way forward, at a historical level it is perfectly clear that a much more associative and graphically minded exegetical logic must be highlighted and recovered.

---

21 On the "two powers" conception, see Segal, *Two Powers in Heaven*.

22 The hint of an embodied God and a physical *imago* should not be overlooked—*quasi ipse suas non haberet manus*—though the idea must naturally also be properly contextualized (cf. Ad. Haer. 5.7.1, 5.16.2). See Gottsein, "Body as Image of God."

23 4 *Ezra*, for instance, has no hesitation in adding *dextera tua* to the creation narrative: "You brought him [Adam] to that paradise which your right hand planted before the earth came to be" (4 *Ezra* 3:6). 2 *Enoch* says, "The Lord with his own two hands created mankind, in the facsimile of his own face both small and great he created them" (2 *Enoch* 44:1).

24 See, e.g., Boehm, "Jenseits der Sprache?"

The Trinitarian theophany at Jesus' Baptism underscores the point through the visible presence of the Spirit in the likeness of a dove. In Bates's rendering this silent dove vanishes completely before the disembodied words of Psalm 2, spoken to Christ *ex persona Patri*: "You are my Son, today I have begotten you." The dialogical, person-based exegesis remains essentially binitarian in form. When Sergei Bulgakov, by contrast, says that "The Holy Spirit was revealed as a dove because this image most resembled both the Holy Spirit and Christ the Lord," his own dyadic perspective is playing on a robustly Trinitarian patristic trope.[25] The magisterial commentary of Cyril of Alexandria on this scene, for instance, perceives the identity of divine nature shared between both Son and Spirit precisely in the fact that Jesus like a dove is "gentle and humble of heart." However tenuous modern minds may be inclined to judge it, unity of essence and trinity of persons were once grasped through the fruitful conjunction of image and word. Besides the famous *oublie du langage*, we must guard against the *oublie de l'icône* in reimagining the shape of Trinitarian scriptural thought.

Περὶ τίνος: Christological Anagnorisis

If ancient habits of exegesis carry us far from what might be considered professionally sanctioned modern practice, such interpretative instincts are not inevitably so foreign. Hans Joachim Kraus thus begins his classic commentary on Psalm 110 with the perennial question: *Wer redet*? "Who is speaking?"[26] Jesus, for his part, takes David to be speaking "by the Holy Spirit" (Mk 12:36). If solution-by-person logic is accordingly a key piece of the puzzle, it is best not to land exclusively on the query τίς λέγει, but to pose the much broader question περὶ τίνος: "*About whom* is the prophet speaking (περὶ τίνος ὁ προφήτης λέγει)?" (Acts 8:34). This too invites a person-centered exegesis, yet without the same limiting orientation to dialogue. For while Jesus did evidently identify himself as a participant within various "divine dialogues" (as Bates calls them), including importantly the enthronement Psalms 2 and 110, Christ's interpretive self-detection inside the sacred text did not stop at the exegesis of biblical conversations but extends to every shape and manner of prophecy.

I have found useful the language of *anagnorisis*, which in Greek means both reading and recognition, to describe Jesus' plenary self-perception within every jot and tittle of the Scriptures, alternately as object, audience,

---

25 Bulgakov, "Holy Theophany."
26 Kraus, *Psalms 60–150*, 346.

and speaker.²⁷ I take this as a foundational principle, in fact. Christ reading the Scriptures is the incarnate Word regarding his own image in a mirror inspired by the Holy Spirit; it is the Son knowing himself through the *speculum scripturae*.

If I call plenary Jesus' intelligence of the Scriptures in order to secure theologically his status as revealer, there is certainly nothing wrong (or new) in singling out Psalm 110, the most quoted Old Testament Scripture in the New Testament. Scholars like Bauckham and Hengel, for instance, have leaned heavily upon this psalm to help explain the origins of "Christological monotheism."²⁸ Bauckham is rather less venturesome than Bates, however, and perhaps rightly so, for, congenial as is the latter's effort to detect here Jesus' robust self-awareness of his preexistence, the strong dependence of Bates's argument on the divergent LXX tradition (an issue, in fact, throughout the book) severely cripples the plausibility of his "historically plausible Jesus."²⁹

Bates's effort to support his case by appeal to 11Q13, which he cites as precedent to Jesus' prosopological manner of reading, requires a number of uncertain and questionable assumptions.³⁰ With its disappearance we also lose a firm Palestinian hold. Thus, without overdrawing an outmoded and useless dichotomy, greater caution about the Hellenistic pedigree and context of the *lusis ek tou prosopou* is in order. It is no accident that Acts and the Letter to the Hebrews are the two main New Testament loci where the practice is found. Bauckham saw the matter with clarity twenty years ago, laying stress precisely on the contrast between the huge importance Psalm 110 holds in early Christian reception and its near complete neglect within the

---

27 See chap. 11 in this volume: "Jesus found himself in Scripture because he experienced himself with an unequaled, focused intensity as the proper object and audience of Israel's revelation. As the Lord's servant, he lived in a state of obedient alacrity and heard God's Word addressed to him with perfect directness, an almost unimaginable immediacy: as if every word of the sacred text had that singular power that gripped St. Anthony when he walked into church and heard the reading of Matthew's Gospel."

28 Bauckham, *Jesus and the God of Israel*, 22, 173–75; Hengel, *Studies in Early Christology*, 119–26.

29 Bates (*Birth of the Trinity*, 54n25) is aware of the basic problem, but judgments will differ whether his effort to address it is sufficiently thorough.

30 Bates ("Beyond *Stichwort*," 390–403) usefully appeals to a narrative logic in his reconstruction and sensibly tries to hold together the various biblical traditions about Melchizedek. His attempt to move from how Psalm 110 *can* be read prosopologically (e.g., taking nouns as vocatives), to how it *was* in fact read at Qumran *in persona Melchizedek*, requires some significant jumps, however, which are not clearly articulated in (or always demanded by) his larger argument. The highly associative nature of the exegesis in 11Q13 nevertheless offers a good instance of the wider interpretative matrix against which I mean to position Jesus' behavior.

Jewish milieu.[31] This discrepancy potentially owes something significant to the simple linguistic factor, for in Hebrew the psalm is frankly less impressive.

The double Greek *kyrios* mystifies two perfectly distinct Hebrew characters, YHWH and Adonai, who share neither a single name nor unambiguously sit upon a single throne.[32] Admittedly, it is difficult to determine precisely when the fusion of the two figures witnessed in the Greek historically arises. On the one hand, while the later LXX codices agree in reading εἶπεν ὁ κύριος τῷ κυρίῳ μου, the extant evidence of all our known *pre-Christian* Greek manuscripts indicates a consistent scribal tendency to render the Tetragrammaton either in Hebrew (or Paleo-Hebrew) characters or else with the distinctive Greek vocalization ΙΑΩ.[33] This evidence naturally inclines many to image that the *kyrios*-for-Tetragrammaton convention was not yet actually in place in the time of Jesus and the evangelists. Whether in Hebrew or Greek, David Hay thus not unreasonably contends that the psalm was originally perceived as useful for early Christians precisely as a way of keeping Jesus and YHWH close but distinct.[34] Conversely, as Albert Pietersma has stressed, Second Temple texts composed in Greek, like the Wisdom of Solomon or the works of Philo, do employ *kyrios* for the divine name, while John Williams Wevers, for his part, points to the suggestive anarthrous use of *kyrios* within the Greek Psalter.[35] In other words, we are not facing some subsequent (Christian) invention in the use of the *kyrios* convention for the *nomen sacrum*. If the New Testament accordingly knows the double *kyrios* form of Psalms 110:1, it is not necessary to follow Bultmann in seeing here a creation of the Greek-speaking Church. Fitzmyer, in fact, proposes that Jesus himself might have spoken the text in Aramaic as מָרֵא לְמָרְאִי; namely, with a double use of מָרֵא, Lord.[36] This is pure speculation, however, and one

---

[31] "There is no convincing case of allusion to Psalms 110:1 (or any other part of the psalm) in Second Temple Jewish literature, apart from *Testament of Job* 33:3 where it used [sic] quite differently ... Psalms 110:1, perhaps the most foundational text for the whole configuration [of key messianic texts applied to Jesus], was a novel choice, evidence of the exegetical and theological (the two are inextricable) novelty of the earliest Christian movement" (Bauckham, *Jesus and the God of Israel*, 174–75).

[32] Fletcher-Louis (*Jesus Monotheism*, 138–41) is keen to underscore this point in his treatment of the psalm: "In various ways the psalm stresses the subordination of the 'messianic' *kyrios* to the divine '*Kyrios*'" (139).

[33] See Skehan, "Divine Name at Qumran." Skehan holds for a linear four-stage development of the scribal convention for writing the divine name: from (1) ΙΑΩ, to (2) Aramaic square script, to (3) Paleo-Hebrew script, to (4) *kyrios*. See also Fitzmyer, "Semitic Background."

[34] Hay, *Glory at the Right Hand*, 21.

[35] See Pietersma, "Kyrios or Tetragram"; and Wevers, "Rendering of the Tetragram."

[36] Fitzmyer, "Semitic Background," 90.

must in the end confess the limits of our knowledge. The safest conclusion is thus simply to be cautious, not historically presuming an inevitable textual identification between David's messianic master and his God, at least in the earliest stratum of the tradition. The double *kyrios* form, however, though perhaps not present in the original Old Greek translation, nevertheless soon advanced the interests of Christian theological speculation.

Another of Bates's exegetical footholds begins to vanish on closer inspection: YHWH's begetting of Adonai the before the morning star, which in the Masoretic Text (MT) vanishes like the morning dew. Adrien Schenker, carefully examining the infamous textual issues affecting this verse, makes the intriguing suggestion that the underlying Hebrew *Vorlage* of the LXX betrays the influence of a polytheistic Mesopotamian royal ideology, later sanitized by the (proto?) rabbinic monotheism of the MT recension.[37] This perspective would privilege the LXX as the earlier text form but also strengthen the differentiation of the two *kyrioi* elided in the Greek, pushing in the opposite direction from a *homoousios* understanding of πρὸ ἑωσφόρου ἐξεγέννησά σε.

Who knows ultimately what form of the text was in circulation in Jesus' time and place? And who knows exactly how mediator figures (*Mittelwesen*) were assimilated into the Jewish monotheism of the period, including that emergent variant form that is today conventionally called "Christological monotheism"? The debate is far from settled.[38] I have no fetish about the MT and do not exclude the possibility of some text-critical resolution, but the ground around Psalms 110:3 will always be uncomfortably shaky.

If Jews of the period saw little in the text of Psalm 110, as Bauckham emphatically insists, then what drew Jesus to it? It is a question of underestimated importance. In the final section of this essay I would like to propose two ways to come at the text of the psalm, both representing a kind of archeology of Christological *anagnorisis*: contextualized by the exegesis of the epoch and suitable, I submit, for any historically plausible Jesus.

JESUS AND PSALM 110

Jesus' self-identification with Psalm 110 was presumably not attracted in the first place by the Greek riddle of the psalm's identical dialogue partners. Instead, stepping within the hermeneutical circle, one might propose as a

---

37 See Schenker, "Textkritik und Textgeschichte."
38 See chap. 10 in this volume: "Perhaps, in the end, it is thus better to think in terms of 'Christological *monotheizing*' and see primitive Christology as a particular stage in Israel's perennial wrangling with its surrounding polytheistic culture(s): a decisive new phase that engaged the world of the Greeks with unheard of openness, energy, and boldness."

kind of exegetical first principle Jesus' provocative self-understanding as eschatological priest and living Temple.[39] With this approach to the psalm we confront a type of associative logic that admirably coheres with the pervasively iconic character of ancient biblical interpretation. This perspective opens the doors to the plenary intelligence just invoked, situating the psalm within a much larger web of interwoven biblical readings.

The Priesthood of Melchizedek

Bates's appeal to 11Q13 points in a helpful direction, though the question of prosopological exegesis at Qumran obscures the more important exegetical dynamic. *Jesus, like other Jews of the period, was evidently attracted to the pattern of priesthood embodied in the mysterious figure of Melchizedek.*[40] This, it seems, has something important to do with his special interest in Psalm 110. It is true that Jesus never mentions Melchizedek's name, just as 11Q13 for its part never cites Psalm 110. Both nevertheless play with a shared, interlocking series of Scriptures that point to an eschatological Jubilee.

It is not difficult to see how the figure of Melchizedek was pulled into a discussion of Jubilee regulations and speculation. In Genesis 14, Abraham pays a tithe to Melchizedek, the first mention of tithing in the Bible. Sadly, a lacuna interrupts the text of the *Book of Jubilees* just at this point in the story, but it is clear enough that, for those who believed that Abraham overserved Torah *avant la lettre*, Melchizedek stands in here for the priestly attendants in Deuteronomy 14:22–26, appearing as a kind of protological version of the Jerusalem priesthood (cf. *Jub.* 13.25–27). Through its citation of Deuteronomy 15:2, it is clear that 11Q13 has made a similar interpretative connection, now stressing a specific link between Melchizedek and the sabbath year of release (II.3). From here a rich cluster of intertextual connections crystallizes, as Deuteronomy's year of release easily leads the author to the Jubilee legislation in Leviticus 25:9, 25:13 and ultimately to the "Year of the Lord's Favor" in Isaiah 61:1–3. In fact, the passage from Isaiah—which already represented a theologized reapplication of the financial arrangements proscribed in Leviticus 25[41]—becomes the controlling text in 11Q13, supplying Melchizedek's

---

39 See chap. 13 in this volume.
40 For an orientation to Second Temple Melchizedek traditions, see Stuckenbruck, "Melchizedek."
41 See Gregory, "Post-Exilic Exile."

apparent characterization as the Anointed One, who liberates captives from the "debt" of sin in an eschatological Jubilee (II.6).[42]

If 11Q13 never actually cites Psalm 110 in shaping its picture of Melchizedek as the anointed figure of Isaiah 61:1, it is critical to recall that we possess only damaged and partial fragments of the complete scroll. The possibility of some exegetical interaction with the psalm should not therefore simply be excluded.[43] Loren Stuckenbruck is even prepared to argue that Psalm 110, in conjunction with Genesis 14, functions as a silent but critical dialogue partner in the development of a whole range of Second Temple Melchizedek traditions, not least in 11Q13, where he discerns no less than five lines of indirect influence.[44] At a minimum, then, one must readily allow that a Second Temple Jew might have easily moved exegetically between Isaiah 61 and Psalm 110, with Melchizedek as the mediator interpretatively holding the texts together.

This brings us, then, to Jesus. When he cites Psalm 110 and introduces himself as the *addressee* spoken to by YHWH, he thereby invites an implicit and potent reading of the entire psalm. Bates pushes directly to the thorny expressions in verse 3b: a defensible but rather risky move, as noted. An alternative, more historically secure approach would be to move to the steadier footing in verse 4. Indeed, whatever mysterious attributes we consign to the silent character created by the second-person statements of the psalm, there is no mistaking the significance of this figure's priestly status: "The Lord has sworn an oath he will not change, 'You are a priest forever according to the order of Melchizedek,'" or perhaps, by another possible reading of דברתי, "You are a priest forever according to my order, O Melchizedek." The suggestion is thus very simple. Jesus' interest in Psalm 110 can be explained, at least in part, by a concomitant interest in the figure of Melchizedek, with whose priesthood and priestly identity Jesus somehow identified.

The argument here is obviously circumstantial, but it goes deeper than simply the general Second Temple interest in Melchizedek. It is based, first of all, upon a prominently shared scriptural middle term. Through Isaiah 61, the Lukan tradition has unmistakably presented Jesus as the proclaimer of a Jubilee of forgiveness, in striking parallel to the role assigned to the eschato-

---

[42] "As acknowledged by many scholars, Is 61:1-2 stands in the background of the entire sectarian text of 11QMelch. Melchizedek is identified as the one who has to perform the liberation of the captives (II:4-6) ... It seems probable therefore that the title 'Anointed of the Spirit' [in II.18] was borrowed from this same prophetic passage" (Bertalotto, "Qumran Messianism," 335).

[43] *Pace* Bauckham, *Jesus and the God of Israel*, 174n50.

[44] Stuckenbruck, "Melchizedek," 128-35.

logical High Priest Melchizedek in 11Q13.[45] The Sermon at Nazareth is Luke's most ostentatious illustration of this conception, yet the Jubilee motif has a variety of other echoes, while the identity centered on Isaiah 61:1–3 is more deeply embedded in the synoptic tradition than this Lukan passage might suggest. It certainly cannot be dismissed wholesale as a fabrication of the Third Gospel. The Double Tradition (Q) citation of Isaiah 61:1 in Matthew 11:2–6 and Luke 7:18–23—widely accepted as going back to the historical Jesus—indicates that Luke 4's dramatic presentation of Jesus as the Anointed One of Isaiah 61 is anything but pure Lukan fantasy.[46] It evidently owes something to a primitive tradition of Jesus' own messianic self-identification with the figure who proclaims Isaiah's prophecy of the arrival of the Lord's Year of Favor. Coupled with his self-perception as the addressee of Psalm 110 and the exegetical traditions known from 11Q13, it is accordingly hard not to suspect some concern with the eschatological priesthood of Melchizedek.

Additional indices of this typological role might be adduced to fill out the picture. Most immediately and significantly, the strong priestly resonance that colors the Gospels' Transfiguration traditions reinforces this suspicion, prominently planting Jesus' role as eschatological priest as a central datum within the synoptic tradition. I have exposed this conceptual matrix in another context, and those reflections can figure as a firm peg around which to weave a growing web of messianic coherence.[47] Here I would merely highlight that Melchizedek in 11Q13 is specifically charged with a proclamation and is to a high degree cast explicitly as a *messenger* figure, thickly intertwined and identified with the מבשר character of Isaiah 61 (cf. ll. 17, 19). Melchizedek is thus within easy reach of the eschatological priest similarly called "my Messenger" (מלאכי) in Malachi 3, who stands at the base of the Transfiguration's priestly perspectives on both Elijah/John and Jesus. Jesus' own foundational role as the proclaimer of the Kingdom of God—an unmistakable enacted exegesis of Isaiah 61—here stands in perfect alignment with the priestly protagonist of 11Q13: both announce comfort, peace, and the good news that "your God reigns." (How beautiful upon Mount Tabor are the radiant feet of this Messenger-Melchizedek!)

The use of bread and wine at the Last Supper should, finally, not be too summarily dismissed in this whole connection. The pattern of Melchizedek's sacrificial offering in Genesis 14 is naturally not necessary as an explanation of Jesus' use of these elements at the meal; nevertheless, his behavior fits a

---

45 See Giambrone, *Sacramental Charity*, 127–39.
46 See chap. 12 in this volume.
47 See chap. 13 in this volume.

broader pattern inspired by an eschatological high priestly order. One way or another, the extraordinary iconic force of the eucharistic bread and wine must not be bypassed or negated.[48] Its hearty reception in early Christian homiletics and art insists upon the connection with Melchizedek, which in some ways even holds priority over Christ's own actions. It is striking that Cyprian, for instance, in Letter 62 to Caecilius on the Chalice of the Lord, defends the use of wine at the Eucharist (against sects who simply used water), not by appeal to Jesus' own clear example in the institution narratives but by invoking Genesis 14 and the high priesthood of Psalm 110. From the perspective of Boehm's *Bildwissenschaft*, this widespread mode of referential logic is both comprehensible and compelling.

To conclude, a Second Temple hermeneutical circle tightly binds Genesis 14, Psalm 110, and Isaiah 61. The missing link in both 11Q13 and the Gospels is a citation of Psalms 110:4. Buttressed by his self-recognition in Isaiah 61:1–3, however, and through graphic typological hints such as his offering of bread and wine, Jesus' certain self-recognition in Psalms 110:1 grounds an assumption that concerns his identification with the priestly character in verse 4.

The "novelty" of Jesus' exegesis in this hypothetical reconstruction would thus be essentially twofold. He would exploit the latent Melchizedek potential of the psalm, otherwise unattested in the pre-Christian literature of the period (not so daring), and he would apply this priestly messianism to himself (much more audacious). As such, Jesus' own exegesis would contextualize the claims developed at length in the Letter to the Hebrews. That letter's focused combat against angel Christology would further add to this mediator theology an important anti-Arian reading of Psalm 110, pointing presciently ahead to later theological controversies.

The Son-Stone Temple

Another hermeneutical epicycle similarly links up with Psalm 110. Again the exegetical texture reveals a pattern of Jesus' self-recognition in the Scriptures, much wider than prosopological thinking. We may take as two fixed points of departure two broadly accepted interpretative acts. (1) First, Jesus cites Psalm 110 not only in the question about David's son (where the question is indeed explicitly πρὸς τίνα), but a second time in answering the high priest before his passion, now in conjunction with Daniel 7:13 and

---

[48] The call to reconsider the eucharistic potentialities of Genesis 14, so evident in the early Christian tradition, is not an exclusively Catholic preoccupation but is now explicitly made in Protestant circles. See Vandergriff, "Melchizedek and the Eucharist?"

the coming Son of Man. It is the shared image of enthronement—not any speaker or *Stichwort*—that brings these two passages into relation. Iconic logic is thus already at work assembling a biblical base, with the enthronement of Psalm 110 in a prominent position. (2) Second, Jesus also identifies himself as the stone rejected by the builders in Psalms 118:22, just after the parable of the vineyard (cf. Mk 12:10; Mt 21:42).

These two seemingly distant scriptural self-descriptions, Daniel's enthroned "son man" and the rejected stone of Psalm 118, together point forcibly to one common yet concealed messianic text: the stone not hewn by hand in Daniel 2. In perfect parallel to "the one like a son of man" in Daniel 7, the mysterious stone in chapter 2 enters the visionary drama to mark the finality of the sequence of four world empires. For any ancient reader, the linkage of the two visions with their parallel characters would have been automatic. Hippolytus in Fragment 4 on Daniel makes explicit that ancient readers indeed saw the two visions and two figures as one. Josephus records a popular Hebrew play on words between "son" and "stone," *ben* and *eben*, which would only have reinforced the connection (*B.J.* 5.6.3). As for Psalm 118, the link here is not only the stone image itself, but also above all the odd fact of its not being quarried. Luke 20:18 confirms the logic holding these two particular texts together by adding to Mark's parable of the vineyard an open allusion to Daniel 2. *4 Ezra* and Josephus, finally, both confirm the messianic character of this Danielic stone. When Jesus thus circles this text in a kind exegetical enthymeme, it is hard not to find him making the same connections as other ancient readers.

Where, then, does this bring us? To an *aniconic iconic* turn, if the expression be permitted. For the action of the unhewn stone in crushing the colossus is not merely triumphalist David-and-Goliath messianism, although it is that. "He will shatter kings on the day of his great wrath" (Ps 110:5). The statue seen by Nebuchadnezzar and crushed by the stone is cast precisely as an idol, a false image—and not a typical Babylonian bearded bull, but a simulacrum of the *imago dei*—a human form. When the stone that demolishes this image is described in Daniel 2:45 as being cut לא בידין, "without two hands" (dual in the Aramaic), we have stumbled on the backside of a monotheistic polemic topos. The Stone-Son is being consciously contrasted with those false images of wood and stone, the mere works of *human hands*. But like the unhewn sacred steles of the ancient Near East or the altar in the Temple, which likewise could not be hewn (Ex 20:25), it is the *hands of God* that have directly shaped this *eben*.

The sacred stone that brings down the statue replaces the idolatrous image as the God-made locus of true worship, and the mountain that grows out of the stone is widely recognized to be the image of a temple, a Babylonian ziggurat that recalls the world dominance of Mount Zion. "In days to come, the mountain of the Lord's house shall be greatly exalted" (Is 2:2). The Temple was seen in Tannaitic tradition to be the work of *God's hands* to a still greater degree than the creation.

> When the Holy One, blessed be he, created his world he created it with but one hand, as it is said, "Yea, my hand has laid the foundation of the earth" (Is 48:13). But when he came to build the Temple, he did it, as it were, with both his hands, as it is said: "Thy sanctuary O Lord which your hands have established" (Ex 15).[49]

We have here something greater than Genesis's *imago*. A cultic and not merely a military dominion is being depicted in the stone's victorious elevation over the collapsed (may we say fallen?) image of man. On cue, in Daniel 2:46, Nebuchadnezzar drops in worship, confessing the one true God.

In identifying himself with Daniel's iconoclastic and imageless work of God's hands, Jesus makes a mysterious messianic claim about his more than human origin and about his mission. He who was reported to say that he would build a sanctuary ἀχειροποίητον, "not made by hands" (Mk 14:57), identifies himself through Daniel 2 and Psalm 118 as being the very cornerstone of that eschatological Temple. This identification transpires, moreover, within as a strident a Second Temple monotheistic discourse as we might wish to find. Daniel 2 is determined to say that no mere human should be worshipped. In this context, Jesus' graphic self-depiction as a divinely fashioned image and as the living foundation of a postexilic Temple is not so dissimilar to Paul's operation with the divine name in Philippians 2 and 1 Corinthians 8. But on several counts, it is a new way of envisioning Jesus' own "Christological monotheism."

Were we to pursue this agglutinative process of visual logic, it could take us quite far and quite fast: Isaiah's cornerstone and stone of stumbling (Is 8:14, 28:16), Zechariah's stone of seven facets (Zec 3:9, 4:7, 12:3), even the itinerant stone gushing water in the desert (cf. 1 Cor 10:4). One picture leads to another as the Christological portrait accumulates ever new dimensions, accenting both divine essence and personal distinction—and, importantly, also the human nature of Christ. Yet we can leave this work to the authors of the New Testament and the Church fathers, who admirably perceived and advanced the scriptural "pressure" (to borrow an important idea of Brevard Childs). It suffices to say that Jesus approached the Scriptures in a similar

---

[49] *Mekilta de-Rabbi Ishmael*, Shirata 10. Translation from the Lauterbach edition (vol 2., 79), lightly modernized.

way to other ancient readers, generating vast webs of interpenetrating associations—with the great difference that, unlike other readers, he ever placed himself in the center of the *mis-en-scène*.

Conclusion

Prosopological reading highlights a massively significant Christological datum. Yet Jesus' self-projection into the Scriptures is not limited to his assuming roles in Scripture's divine dialogues. It extends to a startlingly comprehensive range of prophetic images and tropes and embraces highly revealing but "inarticulate" pragmatic, enacted aspects of his life and ministry. To this degree, insofar as the origin of Trinitarian exegesis is bound up with Jesus' own reading of Psalm 110, it seemingly has its roots in a prior, Scripture-oriented awareness of himself as at once a cosmic priestly mediator and the unique temple-like locus of worship of the one true God: both the Anointed One and the Father's Son, God's true Image not made by human hands.

By expanding the scope and nature of Jesus' self-identification with key biblical characters, we move away from an overly logocentric, puzzle-based model of his self-discovery in the Scriptures toward a "recognition" on the swift order of intuition. Dialogical self-definition between Father and Son clearly plays a hugely important revelatory role, but in his humanity the Logos has no need to apprehend his divine *ousia* by exegetical calculations.[50] He spoke from the fullness of his two natures and found both spoken of in the word prophetically revealed by the Spirit.[51] In the creative tension of Jesus' scripturally/pneumatically expressed identity as the uncreated mediator of the created cosmos we can anticipate the controversies in which the Church later parsed its orthodox understanding of God. In Jesus' reading of texts like Psalm 110, we discern the primitive Christological ferment in which this Trinitarian exegesis was born.

---

50 For the sake of illustration, Bates reconstructs a syllogistic act of Jesus' exegesis of Psalm 2, in which he reasons his way to the prosopological conclusion that "this *me* was begotten before the time of the speech" (*Birth of the Trinity*, 65). Whatever such ratiocination might correspond to in the psychology of Christ's human nature (he was certainly capable of exegetical argumentation about what pertained to him), I prefer to intone a more mysterious and instinctive, even experiential mode of *anagnorisis* (reading/recognition) in the delicate matter of Christ's self-knowledge. On adoptionism and Jesus' self-perception in Psalm 2 (not only as Son but also as Servant), see chap. 11 in this volume.

51 I would add here a significant fact noted by neither by Andresen nor by Bates. *Lusis ek tes physeos*, solution-by-*nature*—that is, attributing logia to the human or divine nature of Christ—was the inevitable Christian development of prosopological reading.

Two Brief Dogmatic Afterthoughts

1. A fascinating recent study on the celebrated Aristotelian concepts of *logos* and *nous* has challenged the traditional perception of this classical pair.[52] No longer are they viewed as mutually exclusive powers of reason, where the *nous* is seen as a purely alogical capacity of insight, tasked with delivering universal principles to the discursive *logos* for its apodictic demonstrations. In fact, a much more complex interrelationship obtains between these two centers and powers of mind, by which the *nous* appears in various ways as a logical and the *logos* as a noetic faculty. It is not necessary to repeat the technicalities of the discussion except to observe that the interpenetration of these distinctive intellective powers is most admirably and visibly at work in alliance with the capacity of perception (αἴσθησις) and the mind's gathering into a unity a multiplicity of singulars and sensations.[53] For our purposes, this helps characterize as *optimally rational* the highly sensate and otherwise perhaps dubious exegetical operations that I have collectively described as an "agglutinative process."[54] The forging of a Christological unity—namely, from the multiple images singularly present in the diverse scriptural data—appears somehow naive. Yet in truth it is simple in the high sense of that word: at once a highly intuitive act and a rigorously logical prosecution, universal in application and in abstract extension.

The specific Christological unity that emerges from this integral, contemplative, and discursive process of intellection, apprehended in a sensual mode and resolutely focused upon the identity of Jesus, recalls what Balthasar describes as the perception of the *Christform*. The exegetical perspectives exposed in the study above may thus be usefully brought into dialogue with Balthasar's theological aesthetics. Apprehension of the *Gestalt*, as Balthasar conceives it, plots us in some manner beyond the propositional realm and supplies a new analysis of the ground of faith through what is, in effect, a reconceived form of transcendental cognition, in fact, a calculated inversion of the Kantian epistemological order.[55] This ground of belief, while

---

52 See Lee and Long, "Nous and Logos in Aristotle."

53 "Such a gathering requires that *logos* must already have an insight into a certain commonality. Here the stark contrast between *nous* and *logos* dissolves: there is a *logos* that is noetic but *nous* itself also becomes logical" (Lee and Long, "Nous and Logos in Aristotle," 354).

54 Pieper (*Muße und Kult*, 23–30) has some classic and concise remarks about the medieval *ratio* and *intellectus* that move in the same direction and helpfully position these concepts relative to Kant and Aquinas.

55 In contrast to Kant's successive critiques of pure (1781) and practical (1788) reason and the aesthetic power of judgment (1790), Balthasar's trilogy consciously proceeds from aesthetics, to dramatic action, to logic.

retaining its logical character, has an emphatically (analogously) sensual aspect, naturally configured to the manifestation of God's glory in the incarnate flesh of the *Logos*.[56]

As a historical approach to the human *nous* of the *Logos*, reflection upon Christ's *anagnorisis* stands as near to the radiant and living intersection of time and eternity as theological study seems likely to come. Resoundingly anti-Apollinarian would nonetheless be a fair description of this attention to the *apex animae* and "gnomic intelligence" of Jesus: a calculated corrective of Alexandrian excess, yet with an Alexandrian instinct for the optimally *high minded*.[57] As a cognitive basis for the pursuit of dogmatic reflection, moreover, recovery of some such mode of exegesis methodologically open to the wholistic *Gesamtschau* of the radiant form of divine glory in Christ holds special promise for advancing a renewed, more contemplatively attuned theological culture. It would be a great mistake, in any event, to dismiss an iconic/noetic moment from our theological method and access to the sources of revelation as some relic of feeble-minded *poiesis*.

2. The phenomenologist, mystic, and god-mother of Edith Stein, Hedwig Conrad-Martius, spoke of a dialectic between *Transzendenz und Retroszendenz*.[58] In careful contrast to Heidegger's description of the salient relation of an individual to his or her own existence as simple *Dasein*, a kind of existential experience of being thrown, Conrad-Martius perceived that, different from material being, the spiritual subject—that is, the *person* (or "*archonal*" being)—casts itself beyond itself and in this act of self-transcendence meets itself in a heightened awareness as somehow already *there*. This reflexive moment of so-called *Retroszendenz* results in a mysterious kind of double *Dasein*—a layering and fusion of two existences. It signifies that the person not only nakedly *is* but most properly stands *to be* itself in the conscious act of meeting the other. Joseph Ratzinger has formulated this dense but important observation about the existential structure of the person with characteristic clarity and precision: *Das Beim-Andern-Sein ist seine Form, bei sich selbst zu sein*.[59]

---

56 "No metaphysics of Being as such and its transcendental qualities can be separated from concrete experience, which is always of the senses" (Balthasar, "Transcendentality and *Gestalt*"). See also two important essays on the spiritual senses: "Seeing, Hearing, and Reading within the Church" and "Seeing, Believing, Eating" in Balthasar, *Explorations in Theology II*, 379–404.

57 See chaps. 7 and 11 in this volume.

58 See Conrad-Martius, *Das Sein*. See also Behler, *Realität und Ek-sistenz*.

59 Ratzinger, "Zum Personverständnis in der Theologie," 68.

This insight of being oneself precisely in meeting the other leads to another point that Ratzinger also helpfully makes. Beyond the "I-Thou" relation, the category of *person* ought ultimately to lead our theological reflection on to the fused existence of the corporate "We." This comment may help to the break open in a truly Trinitarian way the narrow binitarian, dialogical structure that is so prominent in prosopological exegesis. In Genesis 1:26, the divine "We" is enunciated clearly, but, as indicated, it is not immediately obvious precisely what voices lurk within this perspective of a shared personal union. An analysis of Psalm 110, however, permits the Holy Spirit to emerge from its invisible position behind the Father and the Son, assuming the distinct form of "doubling" or layering in the dialogical word.

Tertullian in his *Adversus Praxeam*, already alert to discern the Third Person and in that awareness pursuing a fully prosopological interpretation, specifically lists three Scriptures where the Holy Spirit speaks out loud and in his proper *persona* (noting in parenthesis that there are plenty more). The first instance Tertullian lists is, interestingly, Psalm 110: "The Lord said to my Lord, 'Sit at my right hand until I put your enemies under your feet.'" While Jesus plainly attributes this psalm to David "by/in the Holy Spirit" (Mk 12:36), the key feature betraying the Spirit's voice is in fact the subtle presence of a third-party observer, who here reports the speech of two others from outside their dialogical frame: namely, "the Lord" and "My Lord." Syntactic and Trinitarian grammar thus intersect precisely in what is spoken *ex tertia persona* (rather than simply in my first person "I" to your second person "Thou").

The otherwise self-concealing character of the Spirit is remarkably revealed if we follow Tertullian's insight, for what the Spirit says for himself is simply and precisely the word that the Father addresses to the Son: "Sit at my right hand." The Spirit is hence a kind of resonance, an exact external echo of the dialogue between Father and Son. In this sense, the Spirit ecstatically confirms their Father-Son, *I-Thou* relation. Indeed, the Spirit strengthens the unshakable character of the Father's word, conferring on it the quality of an oath. "*The Lord has sworn an oath he will not change*," the Spirit prefaces before repeating the Father's words addressed to the Son: "*You are a priest forever.*" If the form of this pneumatic gemination of the Father's voice to the Son has the character of an inaudible but actual "We," a unified first-person voice in which more than one speaker is present, it is in harmony with this that, though hidden behind the drama passing between Father and Son, in self-effacing service to the amplification of their exchange, the Spirit nevertheless also somehow comes to direct and unique expression, offering his own word. In this case it is addressed to the Father as a word that seals and accomplishes the message that he himself, the Father, first sent forth, in the Spirit, to the Son: "Sit at my right hand, O Son," speaks the Father in verse 1, through the Spirit; "The Lord is at your right hand, O Father," the Spirit replies in verse 5, perfecting in his own *persona* the enacted answer of the Son and the perichoretic circle of *Retroszendenz*. The Spirit's "I" (τίς λέγει) that addresses the Father as "Thou" (πρὸς τίνα) occupies here the dialogical spot of the Son, now sitting at the Father's right hand (forming their personal *Dasein* doubling as a "We"), spirated thus precisely in the space shared between Father and Son, just as the Son himself appears in the (Spirit's) Third Person (περὶ τίνος).

CHAPTER 15

Jesus' Prophetic Knowledge and the Gospels

In 1965, at that adventitious moment when a classical dogmatic formation of the Church's critically trained exegetes could still simply be assumed, a young Raymond Brown addressed the twentieth annual convention of the Catholic Theological Society on the broad topic of Jesus' knowledge in a way and in a context that is today difficult to imagine. The survey he offered is honestly rather boring. Its interest is above all that it was in many ways the first and last study of its kind. Importantly, though he could not at the time guess that his contribution would find no echo, Brown did note that "dogmatic theologians, not exegetes, have led the way in the modern discussion of Jesus' human knowledge. If exegetes had begun the discussion," he said, "the orientation might have been different."[1]

The lassitude of Catholic exegetical investigations into this theme certainly owes something to magisterial interventions. Pius X's condemnations in *Lamentabili* are only one of several factors that might be mentioned.[2] The neo-Modernist panic of the early 1960s also made Brown's effort a manifestly delicate exercise.[3] More than half a century later, the air has cleared, but the knowledge of Christ, for all its importance in the scholastic tradition, is still not a concern that shapes contemporary exegesis. One may lament the fact, but before promptly construing this as yet another index of the theological insensitivity of modern Scripture scholars (such indices are not wanting), it is only fair also to reverse the charge. Systematic theologians investigating

---

1 See Brown, "How Much Did Jesus Know?"
2 See especially Pius X, *Lamentabili sane exitu* §§ 32–34.
3 On this crisis, see chap. 1 in this volume.

this theme have shown themselves remarkably disinterested in probing its scriptural foundations. A thin film of parenthetical proof texts still marks the general depth of the engagement.[4] At its worst—and I wish I were only thinking of manuals from the 1920s—biblical revelation is flagrantly overruled.[5]

Traditionally, in addition to his divine knowledge, Christ was reckoned to possess three types of human knowledge:[6] acquired,[7] infused or prophetic (which are overlapping but not coextensive categories),[8] and beatific.[9] As a rule, the arguments formulated in favor of Christ's possession of infused science follow formal logical lines—for example, appeal to the necessary perfection of his knowledge,[10] its regulative role in his meritorious deeds,[11] or the necessary fullness of his charismatic endowments, and so on[12]—ignoring the fundamental testimony of the Gospels. It is appropriate, however, and indeed imperative to ask: Do the Scriptures reveal Jesus as possessed of infused, prophetic species, and if so, in what way and in what specific connections? It is to be held *de fide*, as Vatican I teaches, that Christ both performed

---

4 Earlier stages of the discussion were much more preoccupied with the scriptural witness, however different many hermeneutical presuppositions may have been. See Kevin Madigan, "Christus Nesciens?"

5 The precise danger is that abstract principles simply steamroll revelation. A recent and baffling example is the egregious *non sequitur* at the end the following argument: "La nescience est intrinsèquement liée à la condition humaine, condition finie et limitée. A ce titre l'ignorance, comme la tristesse ou la crainte, sont le signe de la présence de l'âme dans le Christ, car elles sont le signe caractéristique de l'homme de la possession d'une âme humaine. Il est vrai que l'homme ne peut pas tout savoir, c'est pourquoi il ignore bien des choses; c'est une imperfection, mais non un mal. En revanche, l'ignorance est un mal moral quand on ignore ce que l'on devrait savoir. Or, dans le domaine moral et religieux, il ne peut y avoir dans le Christ aucune imperfection, aucune ignorance en ce concerne la fin dont il est, comme Fils et Juge, l'instrument et le principe. *L'ignorance du jour du jugement (connaissance religieuse et eschatologique du dessein de Dieu) est donc incompatible avec l'impeccabilité du Christ*" (Margelidon, "La science," 411, emphasis added). This ostentatious disregard of Mk 13:32 is ultimately bound up with a version of the "apparent ignorance" argument. On the difficulty with this position, see below.

6 On this theological tradition, see Johannes Ernst, *Die Lehre*.

7 Remarkably, it seems that Aquinas was the first thirteenth-century theologian to posit experiential human knowledge in Christ. See Torrell, "Le savoir acquis du Christ."

8 A significant modern discussion of Jesus' infused knowledge appears in Maritain, *On the Grace and Humanity of Jesus*.

9 See most recently Gaine, *Did the Savior See the Father?*

10 See, e.g., *ST* III, q. 11.

11 John of St. Thomas crafted this argument. See Joannis a S. Thoma, *Cursus Theologicus*, vol. 8, q. 9, d. 11, a. 2, nn. 3–5.

12 Other arguments, or variations of these arguments, also appear. For instance, the necessary expressability of Jesus' knowledge has also been emphasized by, e.g., Durand, "La science du Christ."

miracles and uttered prophecies (DS 3009). Is there anything more, or more interesting, left for the Gospels to say? The question is plainly rhetorical. If *sacra doctrina* is indeed a single science, the contributions of positive and speculative theology must here (as elsewhere) be better synthesized.

So, if exegetes had begun the discussion—or if even now we have the liberty to intervene—in which direction might the investigation go? In what follows, I would like to suggest that upon inspection the evangelists attribute prophetic knowledge to Jesus less often and less fantastically, but in far more provocative and diverse ways than is often assumed or understood in dogmatic discussion. Let me say that, although I will attempt to thread the needle and avoid some extremes as I see them, I do not discount the possibility of a maximalist construction of the Lord's hidden knowledge. His words in John 16:12 certainly leave open a tempting crack in the speculative door: "I still have many things to say to you, but you cannot bear them now." Nevertheless, I stick to the positive evidence revealed in the scriptures—which seems to me little preoccupied with demonstrating a plenary endowment.

Let me start with a curious irony. Leaving aside Augustine's *scientia vespertina*, the infused angelic knowledge that he detected lurking behind Genesis 1,[13] the category of so-called infused science, while it appears at first blush to be improbably medieval and abstract—hardly the way a hard-nosed exegete would choose to get the conversation rolling—it is not, in fact, an unbiblical idea. From the earliest strands of biblical prophecy right down to its final transition into apocalyptic, in the biblical tradition, prophets routinely behold visionary portents, infused species, if you will. The book of Zechariah provides one of multiple examples:

> Zechariah, What do you see? A lampstand all of gold with a bowl on top ... What do you see? A flying scroll. (Zec 4:2, 5:2)

This form of imaginary apparition, mysterious as it is, while hardly exhausting the range of possible prophetic experience in Israel or the ancient Near East, nevertheless occupies an important place in both the literary construction and wider representation of prophecy for the biblical mind.

A quick glance at Jewish apocalyptic writings of the Second Temple period confirms the endurance and even expansion of this construction. The characters of this literature are consistently *seers*, men who penetrate hidden mysteries and peer far into the future. To take just one example, the *Book of Enoch* is, from start to finish, "a holy vision from the heavens" (1.2), punctuated by phrases like "he showed me" and "I saw" (cf. 14:8, 18:1, 21:1,

---

[13] *City of God* 11.29.

22:1, 23:2, 24:1, 26:1, 28:1, 29:2, 30:2, 31:1, 32:1, 33:1, 34:2, 36:2, 37:1, 40:1, 41:1, 41:3, 43:1, 43:2, 44:1, 46:1, 48:1, 52:1, 53:1, 54:1, 56:1, 57:1, 59:1, 60:1, 61:1, 64:1, 66:1, 72:1, 73:1, 74:1, 76:1, 80:1, 81:1, 83:1, 85:1, 86:1, 87:1, 88:1, 89:2, 89:28, 89:51, 90:1, 90:13, 90:20, 90:30, 90:37, 90:40, 93:2, 103:2, 107:1, 108:4). Other examples could easily be cited.

As a rule, prophets see visions. Nevertheless (and here is the irony toward which I am driving), despite being a legitimate biblical possibility, the reception of infused species does not provide the best lens for understanding the scriptural account of Jesus' prophetic behavior.[14] Jesus does, of course, report a vision of Satan's fall (Lk 10:18), and one could perhaps imagine Jesus' repeated language of "seeing" and "hearing" the Father in John (e.g., 3:11, 3:32, 5:19) concretely on the order of ecstasy and locutions. That is hardly certain, however, and beatific knowledge is the better way to understand this broad motif in my view. In any case, John breaks the mold, and Jesus is not presented as a seer according to the classic recipe. As much as texts like Enoch and Daniel do marvelously illuminate Jesus' historical context, a great gap separates the Lord from the protagonists of these books.

This does not simply throw us back upon sociological categories, however, though historical Jesus scholars have favored such an approach. Distinguishing oracular and leadership prophets is certainly a helpful move, and there is no doubt that Jesus corresponded to real social patterns and expectations set by previous prophets. The Lord was certainly judged in this light by his contemporaries in different ways. None of this is quite the analysis we are seeking, however.

The Hellenistic figure of the so-called *theios aner* is perhaps more immediately helpful (if also perhaps a complete scholarly fiction). Apollonius of Tyana, whose *bios* is so often (and so tenuously) compared to the Gospels, profiles the persona. In Philostratus's report, Apollonius's boundless, superhuman knowledge is a constant theme.

> "I know every one of the barbarian languages [said Apollonius] ... I know them all, and have learned none." The man from Ninos was amazed, but Apollonius said, "Do not be surprised if I know all human languages: I also know (οἶδα) all that humans keep unspoken." (1.19, [Henderson, LCL])

If texts like the *Infancy Gospel of Thomas* (not unlike the *Tertia Pars*) transmit a Christ figure endowed with hypertrophic gifts of infused knowledge on

---

14 Aquinas addresses the question whether Christ's prophetic knowledge came though the (transient, therefore imperfect) gift of prophecy or directly through his infused science, ultimately arguing that Jesus indeed had the charismatic gift, though in a stable manner. See *De Veritate* q. 20 a. 6; and *ST* II-II, q. 174, a. 5, ad 3, and III, q. 7, a. 8.

this same order—the child Jesus knows the Greek letters (and their mystic meaning) without being taught, to the befuddlement of his would-be tutor (§6.1–4)—we are distant here from the presentation of the canonical Jesus.[15] This para-biblical Christ has nevertheless enjoyed quite a career in dogmatic theology. Conversely, there are and theologians hasten to highlight repeated cases where the canonical Lord displays some penetrating insight into the thoughts of others: "Jesus knew what they were thinking" (εἰδὼς δὲ τὰς ἐνθυμήσεις αὐτῶν, Mt 12:25).

This does, admittedly, look a bit more like what so amazed the man from Ninos, and the verb *to know* lands us precisely where we wish to be. We must, all the same, be careful in evaluating such knowledge. First of all, although the gift of reading hearts is a form of prophecy of *present* realities, as both St. Paul and St. Thomas aver (1 Cor 14:24–25; *ST* II-II q. 171, a. 3), and while it is a real charism attested in ecclesial life, it is not always obvious that the Gospel scenes in question unambiguously reveal more than Jesus' keen attunement to the psychology of those around him, as commentators have often observed.[16] This is not simply a rationalistic lack of piety, but often sound critical judgment.[17] Indeed, in some cases, taken within the narrative context (or read in synoptic parallel), Jesus knows what his opponents are thinking after they speak their thoughts aloud (as in Mt 12:24).[18] An itemized inventory is not my objective here, but generally, if a careful exegesis of the

---

15 "Pour nombreux interprètes modernes, saint Thomas surdéterminé la plénitude de la science du Christ. Certes, la perfection de sa connaissance surnaturelle des mystères révélés répond à la fin de l'Incarnation rédemptrice, mais l'entendue et le mode infus du savoir du Christ apparaissent toujours comme le résultat audacieux d'une construction complexe éloignée des évangiles" (Margelidon, "La science," 404).

16 See, e.g., Fitzmyer, *Gospel According to Luke X-XXIV*, 584. Taylor, *Gospel According to St. Mark*, 196. See also Brown, "How Much Did Jesus Know?," 16.

17 One may ask, for instance, whether Jesus' perfectly apt response to the "amazement" (ἐθαύμασεν) of his Pharisee host at the fact that the Lord did not wash his hands before eating inevitably implies some sort of supernatural mindreading, or whether the host's amazement was simply not well hidden (Lk 11:38–39; cf. Mt 15:2).

18 Lk 5:21 seems to advance this explanation in interpreting Mk 2:6 (cf. Mt 9:3), for example, since Luke drops Mark's ἐν ταῖς καρδίαις αὐτῶν from the description of scribes' questioning and omits the Markan phrase τῷ πνεύματι to qualify Jesus' knowledge. At the same time, curiously, Lk 6:8 adds ᾔδει τοὺς διαλογισμοὺς αὐτῶν to Mk 3:3. Yet even when the text says explicitly that Jesus "knew their inner thoughts" (εἰδὼς τὸν διαλογισμὸν τῆς καρδίας αὐτῶν) in Lk 9:47, the triggering event can hardly be imagined as Jesus eavesdropping on a telepathic argument among the disciples about who was the greatest (Lk 9:46), and the force here *may* indeed simply be that Jesus saw through their words the disciples' deeper dispositions. However, Luke does not have Jesus openly ask his disciples what they were discussing, as Matthew and Mark both do (Mt 18:1–2; Mk 9:33–34), a data point that could be taken in two different directions.

relevant texts is undertaken, we must chasten too widespread and transparent an accounting of this phenomenon.[19]

That being said and despite some curious counterindications, the motif of reading thoughts is indeed there in the tradition and particularly present and amplified in Luke. The characteristic Lukan syntagm of οἶδα + διαλογισμός is suggestive (e.g., Lk 5:22, 6:8, 9:47; cf. Lk 11:17 εἰδὼς αὐτῶν διανοήματα), and it may well play upon Simeon's oracle in 2:34–35 about Jesus revealing the thoughts (διαλογισμοί) of many hearts.[20] If some extraordinary form of knowledge beyond mere keen awareness is indeed at play, as it seems to be, major questions nevertheless remain. In a recent dissertation, Collin Blake Bullard has in fact argued that, when read against its closest parallels, we should see not *prophetic* but *divine* knowledge in this Lukan motif. Jesus is depicted as "the knower of hearts" in a way that is proper to God alone (ὁ καρδιογνώστης θεός, Acts 15:8), as the Lord often appears for instance in the Psalms, Isaiah, and indeed in much Second Temple literature (e.g., Ps 138 [139]; 4Q185 1–3 III, 10–14; Jos., *B.J.* 5.413; Philo, *Cher.* 16–18; 2 Bar 83.1–3; Sir 42:18–21).[21]

To this I would just add as a point of form critical interest that in the Gospels' mind-reading narratives, which are nearly always controversy stories, the reactions of others never manifest any special astonishment at Jesus revealing the secrets of their hearts. Astonishment is reserved, rather, for the unexpected ways the Lord speaks and acts despite what he knows (in whatever way) that others are thinking, for example, provocatively healing a man on the Sabbath or audaciously absolving a woman's sins (e.g., Mk 2:1–12; Lk 7:50). "My thoughts are not your thoughts" (Is 55:8) seems to be the general provocation of these *chriae*.

The Fourth Gospel's story of Jesus' dialogue with the Samaritan woman at the well is one obvious case where controversy is not in play and a different perspective may be gained. Here the Lord inexplicably reveals the secrets of his interlocutor's past life, and she responds directly, "Sir I see that you are a prophet" (Jn 4:19) and to the people of her village, "Come and see a man who told me everything I have done. He cannot be the Messiah, can he?" (Jn 4:29).

---

[19] It is a healthy warning in gauging the significance of the evangelists' "mind-reading" language that Codex Bezae (D5) records at Lk 3:15 that *John the Baptist* "knowing their thoughts" (επιγνους τα διανοηματα αυτων)—i.e., that the people were wondering "in their hearts" if he were the Christ—responded in answer to their misapprehension. Is John here depicted as a being moved by some special mystic knowledge, or is this simply a compact Lukan variant of the rather straightforward dialogue paralleled in Jn 1:19–28?

[20] Cf. Mt 12:25 εἰδὼς δὲ τὰς ἐνθυμήσεις; Mt 9:4 ἰδὼν τὰς ἐνθυμήσεις αὐτῶν; cf. also Mk 12:15, εἰδὼς αὐτῶν τὴν ὑπόκρισιν; and *GEger* 2r, II. 9–10, ὁ δὲ Ἰη εἰδὼς [τὴν δι]άνοιαν [αὐτ]ῶν).

[21] Bullard, *Jesus and the Thoughts of Many Hearts*.

As the Fourth Gospel reveals it, Jesus' gift of present prophecy thus functions like a miraculous sign and is ordered toward his own messianic self-revelation. Read through a Johannine lens, ambiguity accordingly clings to prophetic portents like other *semeia*; just as for all the evangelists the title "prophet" is finally inadequate as a full confession of faith in Christ. Openly reading hearts is a risky game that Jesus rarely played. Were the Lord to have acted too frequently as a mere mind reader, the profound depth of his true identity would have inevitably been obscured.

Jesus' knowledge of *past* and *present* realities to which he had no normal or natural access obviously operated with convicting power upon those to whom it was revealed. The Samaritan woman does not hesitate to recognize Jesus as a figure of God-ordained authority, however inadequate her lofty estimate of his person remains. It is a different matter with the revelation of *future* realities, however. These cannot be immediately confirmed (or invalidated). Who is to judge whether the prophecy will come to pass, while it still remains in the future?

In point of fact, Jesus' revelation of future knowledge has an entirely different effect than his other acts of prophetic insight. It reconfigures the invited act of faith in his person around entirely different epistemological dynamics. Rather than prompting confessions or confounding opponents by a manifest show of power, future prophecy works as an opaque revelation that leaves Jesus' hearers in a state of bewildered miscomprehension. "'Let these words sink into your ears: The Son of Man is going to be betrayed into human hands.' But they did not understand this saying; its meaning was concealed from them, so that they could not perceive it. And they were afraid to ask him about this saying" (Lk 9:44–45; cf. 18:31–34).

In the Gospels, Jesus' prophetic knowledge of *future* contingents is strikingly concentrated around two great events: the destruction of the Temple and the Paschal Mystery. The Lord does not dabble in incidental prognostications. Even Jesus' odd and seemingly superfluous foreknowledge of the coin in the fish's mouth in Matthew 17—an almost isolated case of such minute clairvoyance in the Gospels—is closely bound to Jesus' anticipation of the Temple's end and his own coming Passion. The former prophecy belongs, of course, within a familiar line of Second Temple prophetic discourse, including the famous case of Jesus ben Ananias recorded by Josephus (*B.J.* §6.5.3). Craig Evans has exhaustively catalogued the parallels.[22]

A few examples, more or less contemporaneous with Jesus, will give the flavor: one from the Dead Sea Scrolls; one from a first-century text called *The Lives of the Prophets*; one attributed by a later rabbinic source (however uncer-

---

22 Evans, "Predictions."

tainly) to an important tannaitic leader, Johannan ben Zakkai (ca. 30–90 AD). All three prophecies, interestingly, are forms of scriptural interpretation—a point to bear in mind in thinking about Jesus as a first-century Jew.

> *Whither the lion, the lioness went, the lion cub and none to terrify* (Na 2.12). Its interpretation concerns Demetrius, king of Greece, who sought to enter Jerusalem by the counsel of the Seekers-after-Smooth-Things. But he did not enter, for from Antiochus until the appearance of the rulers of the Kittim God did not deliver it into the hands of the kings of Greece. But afterwards it will be trampled underfoot by the Kittim. (4QpNah 1.1–3)

> And concerning the end of the Temple he [Habbakuk] predicted, By a western national it will happen. At that time, he said, the curtain of the Dabeir will be torn into small pieces, and the capitals of the two pillars will be taken away and no one will know where they are; and they will be carried away by angels into the wilderness, where the Tent of Witness was set up in the beginning. (*Lives of the Prophets* 12.11 [Torrey, JBLMS])

> [When Vespasian objected to Yohannan ben Zakkai's greeting, Vive domine Imperator, Yohannan explained,] If you are not the king, you will be eventually, because the temple will only be destroyed by a king's hand, as it says, *And Lebanon shall fall by a mighty one* (Is 10:34). (*Lam Rab* 1.5 §31 [Socino])

In light of such material, the basic historical plausibility of Jesus' prophecy, at least in some form, is thus difficult to impugn, as most scholars agree. Exaggerated insistence that the Gospels record a *vaticinium ex eventu* is accordingly misplaced, however much later redactional touches may be freely recognized in the evangelists' reports, whether to clarify or develop some motif. At the same time, this same wide presence during the Second Temple period of an aggressive anti-Temple-establishment sentiment (which is different than being anti-Temple) and the ample premonitions of coming judgment considerably reduce the singular impression of Jesus' warning. Far from revealing his unparalleled powers of augury, Jesus' bold certainty that "not one stone will be left here upon another" (Mk 13:2) inserts him within a recognizable tradition.

What the Jewish parallels conceal, however—and this is the all-important difference—is the profound inner relation of Jesus' Temple prophecy to the foreseen drama of *his own fate*. In John, the merging of these two events is made explicit. The Synoptics are less clear about the identification, but the confused presence of the saying as a charge in Jesus' trial before the Sanhedrin indicates that his condemnation and death were bound up with reports of this prediction. In my estimation, John is plausibly responding to Mark, who confusingly tells of discordant "false" witnesses who testify: "We heard him saying, 'I will destroy this Temple made by hands and in three days I will build another not made by hands'" (Mk 14:58; cf. 14:56–59; cf. Mt 26:55–61). With his different version, John evidently means to clarify and reinterpret this "false witness," which attributes to Jesus a statement that comes entirely out of the blue for readers of Mark, who have never previously heard any such saying. (The prediction of the Temple's destruction in Mk 13 was not spoken publicly and made no mention of three days or a new building.) Jesus, John assures, did indeed previously say *something* of this sort as he was cleansing the Temple. "He was speaking about the Temple of his body" (Jn 2:21).

Luke, by contrast, famously drops the confusing Markan charge altogether. It must not be imagined that Luke is unaware of Jesus' prophecy about the Temple, however (cf. Acts 6:14). Nonetheless—and the point is important—Luke's emphasis has shifted from the destruction of the *sanctuary* to wasting of the *whole city*. The Third Evangelist thus preserves two unique lament oracles that refer to Jerusalem's fall, plotted as mile markers along Jesus' journey to the holy place. In both cases, the prophecies about Jerusalem are intertwined with prophecies about Jesus himself. Thus, in Luke 13:35, the evangelist reproduces the minatory saying, "Jerusalem, Jerusalem, city that murders the prophets ... behold, your house is abandoned" (cf. Mt 23:38; also Jer 22:5), appending this logion after another fateful saying about the city, referring to Jesus' coming death: "It is impossible that a prophet perish outside of Jerusalem" (Lk 13:33). In so doing, Luke at once ties the destiny of the Temple to Jesus' own coming Passion and situates this future within the long and tragic history of the rebellious nation. Jesus must suffer the fate of all the prophets, and Jerusalem must suffer the consequence of its murderous deeds. In the oracle of Luke 19:41–44, Jesus again weeps over the city, saying that Jerusalem's enemies "will not leave a stone upon a stone (λίθον ἐπὶ λίθον) within you, since you did not know the time of your visitation (ἐπισκοπῆς)" (Lk 19:44). The moment of visitation is, of course, a reference to Jesus himself and the Lord's visitation of Israel in and through his person (cf. Lk 1:78; 7:16). Jesus has thus once more oriented his prophecy about the nation's doom directly around the rejection of his own mission.

Jesus' prophetic woe oracles against Chorazin and the fishing villages of Bethsaida and Capharnum should also be mentioned here. They represent a fragment of Galilean provenance, formulaic but likely preserved in something close to the original form, and they offer a convincing sign that

Jesus comported himself in the guise of an oracular prophet at least to some degree. While almost embarrassingly provincial, these stereotyped forecasts of doom extend the scope of Israel's devastation to the northern reaches of the land and fit the same self-oriented pattern already seen (Mt 11:20–24; Lk 10:13–15; cf. Is 14:13–15). Failure to recognize and respond to Jesus' ministry invites judgment and apocalyptic cataclysm.

At the canonical level, the confusing Markan memory thus radiates out in two different directions, taking on a clarified shape along distinct Lukan and Johannine axes. These two axes furthermore represent the two sides of Jesus' self-identification, revealed in this remarkable fusion of the Temple and Passion prophecies. In a vertical direction, Jesus identifies himself as the Temple—namely, the living presence of YHWH in the midst of his people—a provocation and high theological claim in the Johannine mode. Simultaneously, on the horizontal Lukan plane, Jesus melds his personal history with the history of the people, the city, a sort of deep solidarity that makes Israel's national story both a prequel and a sequel to his own. A Chalcedonian, two-natured harmony thus contours the Christology of Jesus' Temple prophecy in its canonical form.

Of course, Jesus' prophecy of his own Passion also has a self-standing expression. Two contrary tendencies are observable, moreover, in the interpretation of the thrice-repeated prediction. On the one hand, these texts are conventionally dismissed as post-Paschal fictions manufactured by some pre-Markan tradition. On the other hand, the miraculous element in Jesus' supposed foreknowledge of his Passion is frequently minimized, with the argument that any sensible person might have seen a violent death coming. Certainly, the murder of John would already suggest, at the very start of Jesus' ministry, the danger of taking up the Baptist's ministerial torch. Growing conflict with the religious leaders, whatever historical form this took, could have then only added to the impression.

There is no doubt something reasonable in this minimalistic line. Aquinas speaks of a kind of natural prophecy, based on experience and a person's powers of imagination and understanding (*ST* II-II, q. 172, a. 1). If something more is still required to secure and elevate the character of this premonition, the old dogmatic manuals speak of a science infused *per accidens*— namely, an extraordinary comprehension of things that might be learned in an ordinary way—similar to the knowledge granted to Adam and Eve (cf. *ST* III, q. 1, a. 2; qq. 8–12; q. 15, a. 2). Abraham Lincoln reportedly knew that he was in danger and dreamed of warnings of his death (which he did not believe). It is certainly possible to think of Jesus' prophetic knowledge of his suffering along such lines. At its outer limit, however, knowledge of future contingents is not merely a miracle *praeter naturam*—that is, a supernatural path to natural effects—like knowing things a good detective could know, but without employing the detective's methods. It is *super naturam*, that is, a supernatural *effect*, not obtainable by any natural means.

One may thus go a step further. A huge number of Gospel traditions remember Jesus as anticipating and freely accepting his own execution (Mt 10:38 || Lk 14:27; Mk 8:34; Mt 10:39 || Lk 17:33; Mk 8:35; Jn 12:25; Mk 8:31–33, 9:31, 10:33–34; Mk 10:45, 14:17–65, 15:1–15; Mt 26:51–54; Lk 13:31–33, 23:6–12; Jn 10:11–18, 12:23–27, 15:12–13, 16:5–10, 18:10–12)—too many to simply be ignored.[23] What stands behind this massive impression made on the tradition of Jesus' extraordinary confidence in the face of death? If account is taken of Jesus' own experience of divine power in his working of miracles, notably in raising the dead (Mk 5:22–43; Lk 7:11–17; Jn 11:1–44), one must inevitably extend the scope of his natural prophetic insight to include not only certainty of his death, but also the anticipation of his own resurrection. "I lay down my life, that I may take it up again ... I have power to lay it down of my own accord, and I have power to take it up again" (Jn 10:17–18). The intervention here of God's supernatural activity obviously reconfigures the entire calculation in a substantial way. It must not be ignored in this regard, however, that Jesus had access not only to his own circumscribed human experience of divine intervention—and the inferences that might be drawn from that. He also had human access to the deposit of religious experience of all Israel, including all the prior prophecies about the Messiah that were revealed and handed down in the Scriptures. I would gesture here to the deep grammar of the death-and-resurrection of the beloved son that the Jewish scholar Jon Levenson has detected as underwriting the length and breadth of the Old Testament tradition.[24]

A more theologically satisfying path than mere "natural prophecy" thus opens up for analyzing Jesus' certain foreknowledge of his Paschal Mystery, precisely at the moment when we acknowledge miraculous activity and the revelatory role of Israel's Scriptures. Indeed, it bears saying that to foresee one's death is one thing; to foresee one's resurrection after three days is quite another. The apologetic appeal of a low-bar modesty must thus yield before more telling factors. Foretelling a miracle *super naturam* is itself *super naturam*, and the minimalistic approach simply breaks down at this point.[25]

---

[23] Brown rightly remarks, "Modern criticism would cast doubt on a foreknowledge of the details, but we should not undervalue the general agreement of the Gospel tradition that Jesus was convinced beforehand that, while his life would be taken from him, God would ultimately vindicate him" ("How Much Did Jesus Know?," 17).

[24] Levenson, *Death and Resurrection*.

[25] This is stronger than position of Brown, who says: "Such a prediction should have come from his interpretation of the OT (e.g., of Is, and perhaps of Dn) and would not presuppose

How, then, shall we proceed? Following Aquinas, who allows that prophecy might be split between the representation and the judgment of things (*ST* II-II, q. 173, a. 2), we might, I suggest, conjecture that the modality of Jesus' prophetic knowledge—at least as it is presented in the Gospels—excelled principally on the (more excellent) judgmental, interpretative order (cf. *ST* II-II, q. 174, aa. 2–3). This need not exclude the divine presentation of interior sensible forms, of course, or experiences of mystical rapture (*abstractio a sensibus*). One should note, moreover, that both *nubes* and *vox exterius formata* are forms of prophecy according to Thomas (*ST* II-II, q. 174, a. 1, ad. 3), so that the Baptism and Transfiguration must be collocated among the varieties of Jesus' prophetic experience (Mk 1:9–11, 9:2–8). Still, we might prefer to think generally of a more mundane external apperception through the senses (*mediante sensu exterius*), as when Daniel saw the writing on the wall (Dn 5:25). Daniel, it should be recalled, perceived not the miraculous act of inscription itself (Dn 5:5–9), but simply the words already publicly revealed by God. In the same way, the revelation of which Christ was the prophetic interpreter and judge was that word communicated already by God through the prophets and contained in Israel's sacred text (cf. Ex 31:18). In other words, Jesus possessed an extraordinary comprehension of what might theoretically be learned in an "ordinary" way *on the order of revelation/redemption*. Like Joseph, who could penetrate the meaning of prophetic dreams obscure to all the wise men of Egypt, Jesus' prophetic knowledge was eminently at work precisely in his penetrating comprehension of the Law and Prophets. Through his own singular human experience of Israel's election as God's Son (e.g., Mk 1:9–11, 9:2–8), Christ enjoyed an interpretative light that could lay open the otherwise sealed book of revelation. This special light of prophetic understanding in Jesus' human soul thus represents a seal, comprehending and completing God's prior acts of revelation through Israel's prophets (cf. Heb 1:1). It is the absolute apex of religious insight possible among the Jews.

This perspective is no speculative fantasy. Following the hint offered by Luke, who records Jesus aligning his fate with the fate of all the prophets—"It is impossible that a prophet perish outside of Jerusalem"—it is possible to view the *passion predictions as exegetical acts*.[26] The Gospels, in other words, give us ample hints that Jesus foresaw his inevitable fate with calm clarity, not as a shrewd conclusion gathered from political analysis, but as a divinely ordained inevitability discernable from scriptural prophecy.

---

a superhuman knowledge. It could represent the unshakable conviction of a man who was sure that he knew God's plan" (How Much Did Jesus Know?," 17).

26 See chap. 11 in this volume.

The plain starting point for this interpretation of Jesus' *scriptural* foreknowledge of his Passion is his own post-Paschal explanation in Luke 24:25–27.

> "Oh, how foolish you are, and how slow of heart to believe all that the prophets have declared! Was it not necessary (δεῖ) that the Messiah should suffer these things and then enter into his glory?" Then beginning with Moses and all the prophets, he interpreted to them the things about himself in all the scriptures.

This portentous, famous δεῖ is not simply a construct of Luke's private theological lexicon and fancy. It has its roots in Jesus' first passion prediction in Mark 8:31.

> Then he began to teach them that the Son of Man must (δεῖ) undergo great suffering, and be rejected by the elders, the chief priests, and the scribes, and be killed, and after three days rise again.

The precise force of this *necessity*, moreover, is its anchoring in the divine *mystery* or *raz*, made accessible in the last days through the writings of the prophets to those able to unlock their deepest secrets. "This plan is revealed in scripture," Adela Yabro Collins says, "for those with the proper principles of interpretation, and is now being revealed by the Markan Jesus to his disciples." Following Jesus' word in Mark 14:49 ("let the scriptures be fulfilled"), Matthew, still more clearly, attests Jesus' specifically scriptural apprehension of the *necessity* of his death, when he resigns himself to arrest in the garden (Mt 26:53–54).

> Do you think that I cannot appeal to my Father, and he will at once send me more than twelve legions of angels? But how then would the scriptures be fulfilled, which say it must happen in this way (ὅτι οὕτως δεῖ γενέσθαι)?

John, too, employs the same δεῖ language as a scriptural foreordination, when Jesus predicts his Passion in John 3:14 on the typological logic of Numbers 21:8–9.

If the memory of him presented in the Gospels is any reliable guide, the pre-Paschal Jesus thus read his personal history explicitly through a scriptural lens.[27] Indeed, on at least four unique occasions just before his death, Jesus himself speaks of the specific need for the *Scriptures to be fulfilled* in

---

27 See chap. 11 in this volume. I sympathize with Dale Allison's basic perspective on the "Christology of Jesus." See Allison, *Constructing Jesus*, 221–304.

the events of his Passion, that is, in his betrayal by Judas (Jn 13:18; cf. Ps 41:9; also Jn 6:70–71), in his being "counted among the lawless" like the suffering servant ("this scripture must [δεῖ] be fulfilled in me," Lk 22:37; cf. Is 53:12), in his arrest (Mt 26:54, 26:56; Mk 14:49), and in the scattering of the disciples, including Peter (Mk 14:27; Mt 26:31–35; cf. Zec 13:7). Of the central fact of the crucifixion, John's Gospel depicts Jesus clearly embracing in advance the scriptural antitypes of his fate: his exaltation upon the cross will be like the raising up of Jacob's ladder and like Moses's lifting up of the serpent in the desert (Jn 1:51, 3:14–15; see also Jn 19:28; cf. Ps 69:3, 69:21 [?]).

Such prophetic insight into the details and significance of his Passion contributes to the unmistakable impression that the entire coming drama lies within Jesus' perfectly free control. Additional hints of prophetic knowledge move in the same direction. Thus in advance of his triumphal entry into Jerusalem, for instance, Jesus mysteriously directs his disciples to find a certain colt, upon which no one has ever ridden (Mk 11:1–3): a sign that Matthew 21:1–11 understands as fulfilling Isaiah 62:11 and Zechariah 9:9.

The impressive role of scriptural imagination in contouring and concretizing Jesus' predictions of his Passion must be fitted within a larger framework. On the one hand, I think it is absolutely correct to arrange the "Christology of Jesus" around his pronounced conviction that the Scriptures spoke about him (Jn 5:39) and his expansive identification with a full panoply of biblical agents, for example, the anointed one of Isaiah 61, the star of the Psalms, and Daniel's son of man, to name a few. This self-identification—which some will reckon as form of psychosis or religious delusion[28]—must at the same time be plotted within a much larger world-historical scenario within which Jesus understood himself to be moving. It is here that apocalyptic Judaism is of service.

In the concise statement of Joel Marcus the scenario runs thus: "The Temple will be destroyed and the cosmos will be drawn into its downfall."[29] Two major scriptural points of reference, moreover, structure this apocalyptic storm, which the synoptic Gospels record Jesus as painting (Mk 13:1–37): (1) the abomination of desolation, described in Daniel (9:27, 11:31, 12:11), and

---

28 See, e.g., Murray et al.: "The New Testament (NT) recalls Jesus as having experienced and shown behavior closely resembling the DSM-IV-TR–defined phenomena of AHs, VHs, delusions, referential thinking (see Figure 3), paranoid-type (PS subtype) thought content, and hyperreligiosity... Jesus' experiences can be potentially conceptualized within the framework of PS or psychosis NOS. Other reasonable possibilities might include bipolar and schizoaffective disorders... There is a potential parallel of Jesus' beliefs and behavior leading up to his death to that of one who premeditates a form of suicide-by proxy" ("Role of Psychotic Disorders," 414–15).

29 Marcus, *Mark 8–16*, 874.

(2) the coming on the clouds of the one like a son of man, prophesied in the same book (7:13–14). That the desecration of the Temple and the fate of the "Son of Man" should be linked in Jesus' view causes no surprise by this point. This is fully consistent with the pattern that has been seen. What is new is the reversal of the ordering, so that the Temple's destruction now triggers an end-time drama surrounding Jesus as eschatological judge. The millenarian mood that enters into the picture at this point charges Jesus' views of prophetic/scriptural actualization with an uncomfortably, at times seemingly incoherent, fanatical character. Efforts to sort through the evidence have not proven universally convincing, to say the least.

Here we confront the true scandal of Jesus' prophetic "knowledge" and an all-important point of decision. Dale Allison, that brilliant and eclectic Pyrrhonian heir of Albert Schweitzer, is crushingly clear:

> He does not come to us as one unknown. We know him well enough. Jesus is the millenarian prophet ... Jesus' generation, however, passed away. They all tasted death. And it is not the kingdom of God that has come but the scoffers who ask, Where is the promise of his coming? For all things continue as they were from the beginning of creation. Jesus the millenarian prophet, like all millenarian prophets, was wrong: reality has taken no notice of his imagination.[30]

The best model for Jesus in Allison's comparative religions perspective is the long line of failed messiahs, from Bar Kochba to David Alroy to Rabbi Schneerson and David Koresh.

Aside from Gamaliel's counsel in Acts 5:39, it is not obvious how best to engage this perspective, whether on historical-critical or theological grounds. Is Jesus' prediction of the end in fact the true *scandalon* of foolishness, the invitation to a purified faith? "Once, long ago, Christ crucified was foolishness, the great rock of offense," Allison preaches: "Today it is Jesus' status as a millenarian prophet that causes those who believe to stumble." Aquinas remarks that "since the prophet's mind is a defective instrument ... even true prophets know not all that the Holy Ghost means by the things they see, speak or even do" (*ST* II-II, q. 173, a. 4). Is it possible to imagine within the bounds of orthodox belief that the Holy Spirit also withheld secrets from the Word in his human condition? Could Christ's nescience extend so far as to allow some positive misapprehension? Or have we not yet rightly understood what the Lord was saying? "In a little while you will see

---

30 Allison, *Jesus of Nazareth*, 218.

me no more, then after a little while you will see me" (Jn 16:16). What is this "little while"? Jesus did, after all, promptly return in glory in his resurrection. Did he understand a sequence of successive fulfillments? Did time simply collapse in the vision he had of his entry out of time and into eternal life? Did Jesus distinguish a near catastrophe from a more distant expectation, as conservative commentators like to contend in the case of Mark 13 and Matthew 24?[31] Was his cataclysmic imagery of universal judgment only a way of speaking about the historical destruction of Jerusalem, not a literal end of time at all?[32] Or was all the talk of the imminent end perhaps only prophetic "denunciation," contingent doom rhetoric ordered to a repentant change in behavior: *prophetia comminationis* rather than *prophetia praedestinationis* to take a distinction from Aquinas (*ST* II-II, q. 174, a. 1)?

Without averting to this classical language, the recent argument of Christopher Hays and his fellows in the Oxford Post-Doctoral Colloquium in their interesting collaborative volume *When the Son of Man Did Not Come* plays with Aquinas's precise distinction.[33] Specifically, they mount an argument that Jesus' prophecies of the eschaton should be read in the light of a conditional, "Jeremianic," hortatory tradition of prophecy, which must be contrasted with the "Mosaic" tradition of predestinary prediction. While the truth of the latter is judged by whether a prophecy comes to pass, the former is subject to revision and postponement. There is indeed a broad ancient Near East conception that a god had the right to change his mind, without undermining the essential truth of prophecies, and the Scriptures, too, are replete with the record of such seeming divine indecision. Accordingly, the delay of the Parousia fits within a long history of the Lord's mysterious rever-

---

[31] See, e.g., Lane, *Gospel of Mark*, 474; France, *Gospel of Mark*, 541–43.

[32] See Wright, "Hope Deferred?" Wright is correct, it seems to me, that the apocalyptic language of Mk 13:24–27, with its darkening of the sun and falling of the stars and, above all, the Son of Man's coming on the clouds with great power and glory, is not all so obviously about the end of the world—at least as we typically imagine that phrase. Rather, when taken in view of a wide base of New Testament data, "everything ... insists that we should read this language in terms of the death, resurrection and ascension of Jesus on the one hand and the fall of the Temple (the heaven-and-earth place) on the other" (77). "Everything" might be a bit strong, and I am not certain that Wright has disentangled all that is wound up in these dense lines. Potentially the sending (ἀποστελεῖ) of the "angels" to gather the elect from the four winds (Mk 13:27) could be construed as referring to the Gentile mission, though this is not the most obvious reading. The *Gleichnis* that comes in 13:33–37, however—"It is like a man going on a journey"—is harder to hold in an anything but the Parousia interpretation of the passage. Nevertheless, the mingled thematic conjunction of Jesus' personal fate and the Jewish-Roman war—which did, in fact, all happen on the timescale foreseen—lands us again by my earlier observation of the dynamic prevailing between the dossier of Jewish Temple destruction traditions and Jesus' striking self-insertion into this drama.

[33] See Hayes et al., *When the Son of Man Didn't Come*. See also Gaine, "Veracity of Prophecy."

sals and redirections of his prophesied plans, which Hays et al. contend is ultimately a repentance motif.

Clever and welcome as the work of these openly confessing scholars is, applying this paradigm to Jesus' end-time oracles faces certain difficulties. I see at least two significant issues that incline me in a slightly different direction.

1. First, this approach plays directly into the hands of the comparative religion critique. I will not belabor the point but simply observe that appealing to a "deferred" prophecy was already mocked in the Greco-Roman period and is hardly an unproblematic way to defend a prophecy as true. Reinterpretation and recalculation, in fact, are precisely the documented characteristics of failed millenarian sects. How, then, shall the New Testament data be distinguished from this embarrassing corpus of parallel material?

2. The second difficulty with the view is on the rhetorical order, for there is a gap that separates the prophetic discourse of the Gospels from the "Jeremianic" tradition to which it is compared. The *conditional* character of the parallel prophetic material and its ordering toward repentance is explicit. Jeremiah 18 is an excellent example:

> At one moment I may declare concerning a nation or a kingdom, that I will pluck up and break down and destroy it, but if that nation, concerning which I have spoken, turns from its evil, I will change my mind about the disaster that I intended to bring on it. And at another moment I may declare concerning a nation or a kingdom that I will build and plant it, but if it does evil in my sight, not listening to my voice, then I will change my mind about the good that I had intended to do to it. (Jer 18:7–10)

Nothing so obvious as this condition and prophetic escape hatch appears in the future (or alternatively "apocalyptic") Son of Man sayings.[34] Conventional repentance tropes are likewise ostentatiously missing.

If there is thus little to suggest contingent oracles of denunciation, there is nevertheless a certain hortatory character to Jesus' apocalyptic discourse in the appeal to be watchful. One suggestive remark also exists, which hints that a ray of mercy (if only a ray) might intervene to adjust the timescale: "Pray that it might not happen in winter" (Mk 13:18; cf. μηδὲ σαββάτῳ, Mt 24:20). This distressingly concrete counsel—which can hardly be the creation of the early Church—sounds like the word of a man who is thinking

---

[34] See, e.g., Collins, "Apocalyptic Son of Man Sayings."

not in millennia but in months. Even so, and small as it is, it represents an all-important wedge in the door. The hour is not foreordained. It is subject to adjustment through prayer.

The implication is far-reaching. If it is indeed the case that not even the Son knows the day or hour, as he explicitly insists (Mk 13:32), he may well entertain his own suspicions yet still leave the moment to be decided by the Father in his just mercy—and in response to the prayers of his elect. Perhaps I am simplistic, but Jesus' openly professed nescience on this point, which is again no imaginable ecclesial fabrication, coupled with the cluster of sayings insisting that the disciples too cannot know the time, which will come like a thief (cf. Mt 24:42–44 || Lk 12:39–40; Mt 24:50 || Lk 12:46; Mt 25:13), appears to me to be a solid revealed datum of monumental import that has somehow failed to register as it should. *Naherwartung* is only *Erwartung*. What Jesus prophetically *knew* did not extend to the time of his return. We may be uncomfortable or scandalized with the thought of this sudden blank in Jesus' knowledge, and calling his thoughts on the matter private opinion may put too fine a point upon it. Yet, according to the Gospels, it is undeniably here that we must draw a line. *Jesus never predicted when he would return*, however much he implied his own expectant readiness (seemingly tying his return to a Temple catastrophe, confidently predicted to be seen by "this generation"; cf. Mk 13:14–37). And you cannot be wrong about what you admit you do not know.[35]

If I must risk drawing an analogy from the Church's long experience of prophetic *charismata*, St. Vincent Ferrer's remarkable letter to Benedict XIII concerning the end of the world I find to be enormously instructive in thinking about Jesus' situation.[36] Here is a man with charismatic gifts of extraordinary magnitude, including prophecy, who found his preaching confirmed by miracles and the receptive response of a culture apocalyptically predisposed, a man who somehow identified himself with a mysterious figure foretold in the Scriptures and who is commonly presumed to have falsely predicted the end of the world—but who did not in fact commit himself to such a claim and who in the most sober way exposed his text-based, exegetical reasoning for preaching what? "The coming of Antichrist and the end of the world are near." That's all. Vincent clearly further personally believed, on the basis of supposed revelations made to acquaintances that

---

[35] One thus evades Pius X, *Lamentabili sane exitu* 33, condemning the following proposition: "Everyone who is not led by preconceived opinions can readily see that either Jesus professed an error concerning the immediate Messianic coming or the greater part of His doctrine as contained in the Gospels is destitute of authenticity."

[36] For the text of the letter, see the appendix to Fages, *Histoire de Saint Vincent Ferrier*.

he trusted, that the Antichrist had in fact already been born in his day—yet he carefully added that this was *"not sufficiently proven"* that he felt free to preach it. Publicly, he was bold to say no more than that "in an exceedingly short time" the end of the world will come. Then he subjected even this message to the Holy Father's correction. The saint's threshold of hesitation, in the midst of near certain conviction and manifest kerygmatic boldness, I find to be tremendously suggestive.

At an important level, the "Angel of the Judgment" fits Jesus' circumstance rather well, I submit: fervent persuasion and deep personal investment with a self-chastening admission of final ignorance on a critical point. Obviously, only a great deal of close exegesis can ultimately secure this model as the right one, and I recognize the divergence of any number of my assumptions from the norm. Still, in part precisely on account of such divergence, I believe that as a paradigm this lens correctly reorients our research and shows the right theological and exegetical direction to pursue. At the very least, it parries the thrust of Allison, boldly owning Christ's nescience and in return supplanting the figure of the failed millenarian with a more appropriate and nuanced analogue.

The upstanding Oxford Post-Doctoral Colloquium confesses that "good exegesis and responsible history" must recognize that Jesus possessed "a prophetic and immediate eschatological expectation." Perhaps I am simply too impressed by Plato's divided line, but I wonder whether I would express the matter in just this way. Jesus did not stand in double ignorance about the eschaton; he knew a great deal about the end, but he also knew distinctly where his prophetic knowledge stopped. This is not the privative, error-ridden, and groping ignorance that results from sin. I thus ask myself if, in discussing *the knowledge of Christ*, we must not "concoct some intellective equivalent of Maximus's *gnomic will*" to speak with more confidence about the precise mode of his *nescience* and about Christ's two intellects (human and divine).[37] Here the "apparent" or "pedagogic" ignorance, which gained momentum in anti-Arian writings and for centuries dominated commentary on Mark 13:32, though not derisible and obviously built upon a sound theological foundation, has hardly covered orthodox interpreters in glory.[38] It is an evasive maneuver and simply not a solution that privileges "good exegesis and responsible history"—far from the balance of speculative and historical reason we seek. Gregory's *in ipsa, non ex ipsa* in his letter against

---

[37] See chap. 11 in this volume. Extending the logic of Maximus's dyothelite thought in this direction is an unfinished job. See *Opuscules theoloqiues et polemiques*, 234, 245.

[38] On this theme, see Margelidon, "La science infuse," 412–13; and Madigan, "*Christus Nesciens?*," 259–74.

the Agnoetes is indeed *subtilius*, "more subtle," and the risk of Nestorianism that he detects is real (DS 474–476). One may nevertheless dwell historically on this *non ex natura humanitatis* without automatically confessing two sons.

At our own peril, however, we might make bold to imagine or explain the interplay the divine *scientia* of the Eternal Word with the human nescience of the incarnate Son—perhaps like a language one knows but choses for whatever reason not to speak (*scientia* vs. *operatio*)—we should be cautious of a lurking Docetism. Some genuine human ignorance of that day ultimately left Jesus ample room to negotiate an orientation to the situation as he both knew and did not know it. This implies no imperfection whatsoever in his integral humanity, and I personally would above all stress two things. First, the Lord's attitude of almost fanatic vigilance, his obsessive alacrity in the face of the pending judgment, responds to and fills in the space opened up by a divinely willed—and humanly co-willed—amoral void of knowledge and it is a correlative watchfulness to what Jesus also urged upon his disciples. Second, this vital posture of readiness bears no essential noetic likeness to the Lord's burning prophetic certainty concerning one supreme, future fact: his Paschal fate as bearing the corporate fate of all God's elect.

Jesus knew in advance what was required that he might steadfastly accomplish his mission and engender supernatural faith in his disciples.[39] "I have told you this before it occurs, so that when it does occur, you may believe" (Jn 14:29; cf. 13:19, 16:4). That through his exaltation the risen Son of Man would also send the Spirit and one day sit enthroned to judge the world did not remain hidden from him—or through him, from us. This all belonged to his messianic mission and was salutary for others to learn. But knowledge of the times and seasons established by the Father was evidently no more needful or benefic for the pilgrimage of the earthly Jesus than it was or is for any of the sons of men.[40] On the contrary, with absolutely noth-

---

39 Thomas allows the super-angelic and super-Adamic perfection of Christ's knowledge to trump its subordination to his redemptive mission, while simultaneously offering a soteriological argument for such perfection. See *De Veritate* q. 20, a. 4, obj. 11–12; cf. a. 4, ad 11–12. Nuanced as it is, the ability to accommodate comfortably the nescience of nonmoral ignorance is a direct and significant causality of this view; cf. *De Veritate*, a. 5, ad 6.

40 Ambrose, *De Fide* 5.16.209-11. Here I would plead for reversing Ambrose's "for you—not for me" argument: "Vnde alibi quoque ipse dominus interrogatus, ab apostolis inquam, qui utique non sicut Arrius intellegebant, sed filium dei futura scire credebant—nam nisi hoc credidissent, numquam interrogassent—interrogatus ergo, quando restitueret regnum Istrahel, non se nescire dixit, sed ait: Non est uestrum scire tempora et annos, quae pater posuit in sua potestate. Adtende, quid dixerit: Non est uestrum scire! Lege iterum: Non est uestrum dixit, non 'meum'" (*De Fide* 5.17.212). I would add that the text in Acts 1:7 reveals the knowledge of the risen and ascending Christ, which cannot simply be equated with the knowledge he

ing to dread for himself from the coming Day of Wrath, Jesus' impeccable ignorance of the hour was his economic entrance, his accommodation to and vicarious taste of that saving fear he was sent to communicate to others. Jesus could and did acutely fear *for* sinners. Even in his nescience the Lord reveals the way (CCC §474).[41]

Raymond Brown at the end of his discussion of Jesus' knowledge, which predictably does not finally move in my direction, nevertheless laid down a trump card that I will happily pick up to close:

> When all is said and done, the great objection that will be hurled again and again against any exegete (or theologian) who finds evidence that Jesus' knowledge was limited is the objection that in Jesus Christ there is only one person, a divine person... Perhaps the best answer to this objection is to call upon Cyril of Alexandria, that Doctor of the Church to whom, more than to any other, we are indebted for the great truth of the oneness of the person of Christ. It was that ultra-orthodox archfoe of Nestorianism (two persons or powers in Christ) who said of Christ, "We have admired his goodness in that for love of us he has not refused to descend to such a low position as to bear all that belongs to our nature, *included in which is ignorance*" [PG 75.369].

---

held in his freely chosen mortal state. This sort of pre- vs. post-Paschal distinction is different than the evacuation of supernatural phenomenon characteristic of certain "Jesus of history" vs. "Christ of faith" models.

41 CCC §474 is a well-balanced statement that allows for two possible interpretations: either Jesus humanly knew and withheld what he was not sent to reveal, or Jesus humanly did not know and thus did not reveal what he was not sent to reveal. I prefer the less obtuse, latter position, adding that in not revealing the Day of Judgment, Jesus *did reveal* the constant need to be on guard. Even in "concealing" Jesus is always the redemptive revealer.

APPENDIX I

Anti-Hegelian Postlude on the Religion of the Future

Schweitzer's "critical Jesus of the future" is the evident archetype of that prophesied "religious thinking of the future" whose thoroughgoing eschatology will somehow be its defining mark.[1] Given Jesus' profound eschatological delusion, the ethical-religious challenge here is considerable but nevertheless clear.

> We must take the ethical religion of Jesus out of the setting of his worldview and put it in our own. Whereas he expected the Kingdom of God to come at the end of the world, we must endeavor, under the influence of the spirit of his ethical religion, to make the Kingdom of God a reality in this world by works of love.[2]

How far have we progressed, we might ask with interest, in the direction of this vision of a new form of Christian faith?

The early decision of Bultmann to turn from Schweitzer and adopt the Wrede-like solution of living by literary fiction seemed for a moment to hold the future.[3] Despite openly rejecting a "messianic consciousness" for Jesus, the half-Schweitzerian parentage of Bultmann's project is nonetheless

---

[1] "The historical Jesus of whom the criticism of the future ... will draw the portrait ... will be a Jesus, who was Messiah, and lived as such, either on the ground of a literary fiction of the earliest Evangelist, or on the ground of a purely eschatological Messianic conception." Schweitzer, *Quest*, 398. See also chap. 2 in this volume.
[2] Schweitzer, "Religion in Modern Civilization," 77.
[3] See Bowman, "From Schweitzer to Bultmann." On the reception of Bultmann among systematic theologians, see Landmesser, *Bultmann Handbuch*, 441–52.

clear.⁴ Demythologization responded directly to the historical problem of a delusional *Naherwartung* and carried a contemporary seriousness about the *krisis* of Jesus' message. On the need to react against the earlier liberal theology, Bultmann and Schweitzer were thus on the same page. Still, the truth of Bultmann's Gnostic decoding of the secret meaning of apocalyptic Jewish myths was conspicuously floating on air. Coupled with the fading appeal of a fideistic neo-Kantian subjectivity and a disengaged religion of words not of deeds (which in Lutheran fashion must be rejected as "works"), Bultmann's religious hegemony evaporated in sudden and surprising fashion. Growing disenchantment with his ethically thin, existential "decision" led more than a few theologians to make a dramatic "U-Turn."⁵ The sense of a "rapid decline" and collapse of Bultmann's newfound *sens du christianisme* is widely attested, and all eyes instinctively turned in the direction of "a new movement towards the re-eschatologizing of theology."⁶

"From first to last, and not merely in the epilogue, Christianity is eschatology," Jürgen Moltmann, a recognized leader of the new movement, says in his landmark work *Theology of Hope*, which credits Schweitzer for this foundational discovery. "The eschatological is not one element of Christianity, but it is the medium of Christian faith as such, the key in which everything in it is set."⁷ The vigorous entrance of eschatology into the center of twentieth-century theological discussion here plainly betrays its immense debt to Schweitzer's proposals.⁸ Ernst Käsemann's famous claim about apoca-

---

4 Bultmann's alliance with Wrede's "messianic secret" idea and rejection of a "messianic conscious" for Jesus is laid out at the beginning of the first volume of *Theology of the New Testament*, 3–32.

5 Bultmann's ethics never gets far beyond the basic category of "obedience." See *Radical Obedience*, the published version of Thomas Oden's dissertation, written under H. Richard Niebuhr at Yale. See also Oden's personal account of his own theological drift and ultimate "U-Turn" from an early enthusiastic embrace of Bultmann and the existentialist project of demythologization to any entirely different point of view in *Change of Heart*, 69–178.

6 "Just when it seemed that the Bultmannian existentialist translation of New Testament eschatology was to rule the day, a new movement towards the re-eschatologizing of theology was launched a few years ago in Germany. The leading bearers of this movement are Wolfhart Pannenberg and Jürgen Moltmann. They are grafting on to the rediscovery of eschatology at the turn of the century through the research of Weiss and Schweitzer" (Braaten, "Towards a Theology of Hope"). On this sense of "rapid decline" and turn in the eschatological direction, see further Park, "Christian Hope."

7 Moltmann, *Theology of Hope*, 16. The original (German) publication of this work in 1964, along with the English translation in 1967, was itself also of crucial importance for bringing eschatology into the center of theological discussion. "With this work [Moltmann's *Theology of Hope*], Jesus apocalyptic eschatology was taken seriously by mainstream systematic theology for the first time since Irenaeus" (Viviano, "Eschatology and the Quest for the Historical Jesus," 82).

8 Acknowledgment of Schweitzer's direct role in pulling eschatology into the center of contemporary theological conversation appears, e.g., in Joseph Ratzinger, "Eschatologie," 39:

lyptic as the "mother of all Christian theology" was, for instance, already a similarly confident stride in Schweitzer's determined direction (and away from Bultmann's preference for Gnosticism), even if the Bultmann *Schüler* Käsemann's Jesus departs in important ways from Schweitzer's version.[9]

Fortified by such robust affirmations of eschatology as the deepest DNA of Christian thought, the Christian faith of the future, at least in its stark and systematic Moltmannian mode, attains such a thoroughgoing *future* fixation that the realized, static (Bultmannian) "now" is erased as a dangerous miscarriage of theological reflection and Christian praxis. The ethics proper to this forward leaning perspective (which, reminiscent of Schweitzer's *Ehrfurcht vor dem Leben*, announces itself explicitly as "An Ethics of Life") spring from a so-called Transformative Eschatology, in which evil is named as evil but the imperative call is not simply to endure, submit, escape, or defer, but rather to transform and change the world.[10]

In Moltmann's *Trinity and the Kingdom*, this theology of hope at last becomes a full-blown doctrine of God. Here, "in the tradition of left-wing critiques of Hegel, the future is the category that displaces God, rather than simply qualifying him, as Bloch provisionally suggests when he follows Buber in translating Exodus 3.14 *'eh'je asher eh'je* as 'I will be who I will be.'"[11] The effective dissolution of God into an utopian historical process of world-transforming ethical progress obviously ambles on the outer edge of where the "Radical Reformation" tradition is likely to wander.[12] To this degree Moltmann's bold dialogue with Marxism, particularly in the figure of Bloch (his colleague in Tübingen), was admittedly also obviously a major

---

"Als äußeres Datum für den Umbruch [i.e., the arrival of eschatology as a central theological theme] kann man die Werke von Johannes Weiß und Albert Schweitzers frühe exegetische Untersuchungen angeben. Hier bricht mit der Deckung des modernen wissenschaftlichen Denkens eine Einsicht durch, die vorher in der Aufklärung nur von Außenseitern geäußert und von den übrigen kaum ernst genommen worden war: Die ganze Botschaft Jesu sei eschatologisch gewesen; sie habe ihre Stoßkraft davon empfangen, dass Jesus mit Vollmacht das nahe Ende der Welt, den Einbruch Gottes Reich verkündet habe. In der Wucht dieser Erwartung sei das Explosive, das Neue, das Große Jesu gelegen, und alle seine Worte müssten einzig von dieser Mitte her verstanden werden." The continued attraction of eschatological themes for dogmatic theology is immense and evident from a survey of recent publications.

9 "Die Apokalyptik ist—da man die Predigt Jesu nicht eigentlich als Theologie bezeichnen kann—die Mutter aller christlichen Theologie gewesen" (Käsemann, "Über die Anfänge christlicher Theologie," 180). For Käsemann, Jesus' preaching was essentially a message of the nearness of God; apocalyptic entered the tradition in force only as a post-Paschal factor.

10 Moltmann, *Ethics of Hope*.

11 O'Regan, *Theology and the Spaces of Apocalyptic*, 38. "Despite his intentions, Moltmann has hardly done enough to escape the gravitation pull of a Hegelian-style theodicy" (110).

12 It is important to recognize other Protestant and also Catholic voices who have articulated related but alternative eschatological visions in Moltmann's wake, e.g., Pannenberg, Meeks, Metz, Gutierrez, Sobrino, Boff, and the like.

ingredient in the recipe for his neo-millenarian vision.[13] Yet Moltmann's special genius remains precisely to have recognized just how easily adapted Schweitzer's exegetical stance was to secular eschatology in the line of Hegel. Amidst much buzz about choosing the "Schweitzerstraße," Moltmann thus remains diagnostically useful for judging where Schweitzer's version of the *via negativa*, with its instinct for a thoroughgoing, immanent eschatological solution, easily ultimately leads.[14] We might well end with precious little *Theos* for our theology.

Schweitzer's personal distaste for Hegel's dogmatic rationalism does not stand in question.[15] Nevertheless, an unambiguous interest in the secular eschatology of world transformation confirms the correctness of Moltmann's theological instinct in appropriating Schweitzer as a partner and ally in his sympathetic dialogue with Marx. Schweitzer's status as the exegetical/theological grandfather of liberation theology (with its spawn of more recent eco-theologies) must be accordingly acknowledged, whatever estimate one makes of this whole family of ideas.[16] It is not without interest, in view of this, that a recent dissertation proclaims Schweitzer's entire project to be a form of "secular soteriology."[17] "Secular," moreover, corresponds here—the phrase is pointedly well chosen—to a work of "*thoroughgoing de-eschatologization.*" It occasions no surprise, then, when another writer further discerns that "a radical severing of ethics and eschatology" is, in fact, ironically at work in the thought of that very scholar who, with his proposal of an *Interims-*

---

13 After reading *Theology of Hope* with enthusiasm but real hesitations, Karl Barth wrote to Moltmann and asked him, "To put it somewhat brutally: isn't your *Theology of Hope* just a baptized version of Herr Bloch's Principle of Hope?" (Moltmann, *A Broad Place*, 109).

14 "Those who are fond of talking about negative theology can find their account here. There is nothing more negative than the result of the critical study of the Life of Jesus" (Schweitzer, *Quest*, 398).

15 "In the nineteenth century the spirit of realism rose against this spirit of idealism. The first personality in which it was realized was Napoleon I. The first thinker in whom it announced itself was the German philosopher Hegel. Men, Hegel maintained, do not have to transform reality in order to bring it into accord with ideals devised by thinking. Progress takes place automatically in the natural course of events. The passions of ruling personalities and of peoples in some way or other are in the service of progress—even war is. The view that ethical idealism is a form of sentimentality of which no use can be made in the world of reality began with Hegel. He was the first to formulate the theory of rationalism. He wrote: 'What is reasonable is real, and what is real is reasonable.' On the night of June 25, 1820, when the sentence was written, our age began, the age that moved on to world war—and which perhaps some day will end civilization!" (Schweitzer, "Religion in Modern Civilization," 77).

16 For an important evaluation of these trends, see Ratzinger, "Eschatologie," 489–641.

17 Obikonu Igbokwe, *Albert Schweitzer's Thoroughgoing De-eschatologization Project*, esp. 245–311.

ethik, supposedly tried to hold these two together.[18] Severing is only half the story, however, for more specifically what we find is simply an old fashioned switcheroo: "Schweitzer's replacement of Jesus' eschatology with his own."[19]

It takes little reflection to understand that such a shift was inevitable. For Schweitzer, Jesus' disappointed end on the cross puts the final lie to his historically bound apocalyptic vision: "Instead of bringing in the eschatological conditions, He has destroyed them."[20] Yet not destroyed them to no higher purpose! *Negation, Aufbewahrung, Erhöhung* may not be the automatic operations of inevitable historical progress; here Schweitzer's estimation of Hegel's error is clear. Still, in some magical, synthetic act of what looks hauntingly like a Hegelian *Aufhebung*, Jesus' cross becomes the annihilating historicizing of an otherworldly eschaton. The *Naherwartung* goes (*tollere*), while the Kingdom message remains (*conservare*), as Jesus' "interim ethics" is transvaluated into a "super-moral" mystical meaning of life affirmation (*elevare*).[21] In the alchemy of the cross, through Schweitzer's *theologia crucis*, an idealist this-worldly eschatology is forged.

For Schweitzer, the disappointment of Jesus' eschatological expectation, as naively expressed in Matthew 10:23, ultimately drives him to force history's hand, setting off by his vicarious sufferings one final, epoch-making "revolution" of history's wheel.[22] "Jesus' purpose is to set in motion the eschatological development of history"; indeed, Jesus himself sets "the times in motion by creating eschatological facts." Something important is being expressed here, for "it is this mighty creative force," we are told, "that constitutes the difficulty in grasping historically the eschatology of Jesus."[23] Acute end-of-

---

18 See Witmer, "Pastoral Pensées." The enduring appeal of Schweitzer's "interim ethics" proposal is clear and on display, e.g., in its rehearsal with almost catechetical precision in Ehrman, *Jesus*, 165; cf. 177.

19 Witmer, "Pastoral Pensées," 498.

20 Schweitzer, *Quest*, 371.

21 In Schweitzer's view, Jesus' ethics of the Kingdom transcend good and evil: "All moral criteria are to be abolished. The Kingdom of God is super-moral" (Schweitzer, *Mystery of the Kingdom of God*, 58). For Schweitzer's critical appreciation of Nietzsche's life-affirmation and elementary, pre-social ethics, see Schweitzer, "Schopenhauer and Nietzsche's Quest," 123–34.

22 "Soon after that comes Jesus, and in the knowledge that He is the coming Son of Man lays hold of the wheel of the world to set it moving on that last revolution which is to bring all ordinary history to a close. It refuses to turn, and He throws Himself upon it. Then it does turn; and crushes Him. Instead of bringing in the eschatological conditions, He has destroyed them. The wheel rolls onward, and the mangled body of the one immeasurably great Man, who was strong enough to think of Himself as the spiritual ruler of mankind and to bend history to His purpose, is hanging upon it still. That is His victory and His reign" (Schweitzer, *Quest*, 370–71).

23 Schweitzer, *Quest*, 370–71.

the-world expectation evidently leads (like *Fire in the Minds of Men*) to revolutionary efforts to immanentize the eschaton.[24] This rendition of the Kingdom is far indeed from an otherworldly Ritchl'sches Reich. Its gigantic titanism is frankly more reminiscent of the Napoleonic *Weltseele zu Pferd*.

Jesus' promethean eruption of vital heroism in his death-struggle on the cross is somehow functional as the necessary, purely immanent Kingdom of God horizon against which Schweitzer's ethic of "Reverence for Life" acquires its evangelical force. The eschatological life principle for Schweitzer is not Christ's resurrection! Built instead upon a sharp and often gloomy *Kulturkritik*, which resembles Jesus' own *Weltuntergang* prognostications,[25] *Ehrfurcht vor dem Leben* is theological praxis articulated in a complex philosophical mish-mash and grand vision of *Verfall und Wiederaufbau*.[26] Nevertheless, in many ways, it remains a simple code for putting the intra-historical ethics of humanitarian justice at the center of the Gospel—hardly a marginal movement, globally considered, but also not an operation without a devilish risk, as Dostoyevsky perceived: "Can justice become the banner of the Antichrist?"[27]

God's glorious triumph is not an event for which he himself, in himself, is somehow eternally impatiently waiting, though the theological heirs of Hegelian thought might entertain this proposition.[28] God abides in and as the *Eschaton* and the *Arche*, always both Alpha and Omega; he is not, as we are, in a temporal passage from one to the other. It is critically important, in consequence, that the character of the Kingdom of God be accurately and rightly perceived. Fidelity to Jesus' own message—not simply interest in "eschatology" as such, whatever we may take or make that to mean—must serve as a vital safeguard against going astray and following after those ψευδόχριστοι καὶ ψευδοπροφῆται (Mk 13:22) who will arrive with their own enticing proclamations of the *telos*: proclamations sure to be full of good

---

24 Billington, *Fire in the Minds of Men*. On "immanentizing the eschaton," see the famous work of Voegelin, *New Science of Politics*.

25 One sees clearly here that Schweitzer's presentation of Jesus awaiting the end of the world was not independent of the *Untergangsbewusstsein* afflicting Europe in Schweitzer's own day. The direction of influence from exegesis to contemporary critique is not unambiguous. On this point, see Ratzinger, "Eschatologie," 40; also Wright, "Hope Deferred?"

26 See Schweitzer, *Kulturphilosophie*.

27 In the Grand Inquisitor scene, but also elsewhere, Dostoyevsky "worries about the hunger for justice replacing the word and work of Christ rather than expressing it ... [posing] a question that will have to asked again and again: can justice become the banner of the Antichrist?" (O'Regan, *Theology and the Spaces of Apocalyptic*, 53).

28 See O'Regan, *Heterodox Hegel*. For an attempt to trace Hegel's theology to highly problematic propositions in Luther, see Stockhausen, *Der Geist im Widerspruch*.

things like justice and freedom.[29] In response to this lot of false messiahs with their utopian temptations (among which many would include Jesus himself), the instruction of the Lord directly and simply puts us on guard in advance: "Be alert; I have already told you everything" (Mk 13:23).

---

[29] On this alluring measure, the *Jetztzeit* Marxist messianism of a Walter Benjamin is not so different from the yearly legends of liberation on Bar Kochba's coins, which so eloquently testify to their own tragic doom. In other words, there is good reason to understand even cloaked, contemporary variations of the "Son of the Lie" under Jesus' warnings issued in Mk 13.

APPENDIX II

Review of Paula Fredriksen, *When Christians Were Jews: The First Generation*
(New Haven, CT: Yale University Press, 2018)

By natural disposition, I am normally inclined to follow the (now not so) New Criticism. But Paula Fredriksen has written a book that begs for a good old-fashioned Freudian reading: *When Christians Were Jews: The First Generation*. The title hides an autobiographical interest, for Paula Fredriksen is herself a *Jew who was a Christian*. Still more, she is a formerly Catholic, now Jewish historian of early Jewish Christians, who on her last page rejects her own catchy title as a distorting anachronism. "Christians" did not yet exist in that faraway first generation, she confesses (*pace* Acts 11:26), only misguided Jews who thought that they would be history's last. In the meantime, of course, when the world did not end, these misguided Jews somehow turned into misguided Christians, and the book ends as an ethical thrust aimed at "one of the West's most sustained fonts of anti-Judaism" (183); namely, a Christian faith built up on layer upon layer of illusion. Lamentable as Christian anti-Judaism surely is, one wonders if a moralizing font of ex-Christian Jewish anti-Christianism, dispensing speculative historical reconstructions seductively packaged as vulgarization, is what better Christian-Jewish relations really needed.

At the base of the study stands a sharp variant on a perfectly benign first principle of historical reason: Jesus was a Jew. From here, with characteristic verve, the book—which is a kind of smashed-together summary of positions developed in her previous works (e.g., *Jesus of Nazareth, King of* Jews [1999] and *Paul, the Pagan's Apostle* [2017])—launches Fredriksen's long-standing enterprise of rethinking and rewriting the entirety of Christian origins as a fully Jewish story. Such a project is obviously, perfectly unobjectionable as far as it goes, though this particular realization of that abstract project takes many turns and pronounces many judgments that can and really should be disputed and resisted. A few select issues will be evoked below. In essence, for Fredriksen, Jesus was a doubly duped victim, bilked by the failure of history to end and swindled by a mismanaged political game: a religious enthusiast who, by a bungled act of Roman plotting, unwittingly founded a new Jewish lunatic fringe, a crowd of mentally "marginal Jews" made in his image, a first-century prophetic sect of blundering and impervious dullness. Such a formulation freely sounds unfair and overstated. It is unfortunately rather accurate, however, and at least serves to signal the problem of genre at the outset. Professionally responsible as it strives to be and personal as it inevitably is, the text is in every way a typical trade book: meant for mass consumption (and mass sales) and thereby prone to (well-selling) sensationalistic views. In this connection it is merely the latest, well-paced, and well-written iteration of the "Jesus the Failed Millenarian Prophet" series—which, like *Star Wars* books, at some point all start to look the same, with some minimal rearrangement of Wookiees and Death Stars.

The genus is well known. Atop the turn to apocalyptic Judaism and a misled Jesus—now classic with its Schweitzerian pedigree—comes the accustomed citation of Leon Festinger & Co.'s *When Prophecy Fails: A Social and Psychological Study of a Modern Group that Predicted the Destruction of the World*. This combination of historical and sociological modeling then spins out the whole paradigm. Jesus was gravely mistaken in his expectation of the imminent end of the world, and on this point, his followers proved to be good disciples—indeed, even better than the master. For again and again, they retried the same prophecy, repeatedly getting it wrong in their turn, reinterpreting and reviving the discredited view with a dense ingenuity born of complete and excitable delusion. In Fredriksen's reconstruction, we thus trace the arc through four specific eschatological let-downs: Jesus at his final Passover; then again when the Resurrection appearances stopped; once more during the tense showdown with Caligula; and, finally, during the Great Revolt against Rome. This chronicle of an unrelieved string of the first generation's end-time errors marks the way in which Schweitzer's original Jesus-centered vision has been expanded into a full, integral history of early Christianity's incorrigible eschatological madness.

There is a fundamental and commendable honesty in binding the story of Christ so closely to the story of Christian origins. Père Lagrange saw this with clarity long ago in his response to the old German historical Jesus project. Fredriksen's fused tale of Jesus-and-Paul thus wonderfully confirms Lagrange's prescient critique of that Schweitzerian school of scholarship that engendered her own. Her work serves as an excellent example—namely, of a self-annihilating analysis—an explanation that explains away the very phenomenon that it exhausts itself explaining. Fredriksen's discardable Jesus oddly reminds one of Turgenev's *Superfluous Man*.

Fredriksen's text mounts its argument through five chapters. The first is foundational in placing Jerusalem front and center and contending that Jesus, like most Jews of the period (Paul included and the Essenes at Qumran excluded), actually had nothing against the Temple. That this position further proves Jesus' blithe contentment in general with the way things were in the Second Temple world *va de soi* for Fredriksen, it seems. All signs of halakhic friction and other tensions and challenges to the system from within fall out of view as irrelevant data. This is at root an E. P. Sanders-type move, privileging deeds over words and plotting the hero in serene relations to his Jewish surroundings.

The second chapter takes up the thread and works toward an interpretation of Jesus' turning over of the money changer's tables (Sanders again), which on the basis of chapter 1 can now signal no antagonism toward the religious establishment. Here Fredriksen makes a significant option for John's chronology, with the result that a giant hole is left in the (synoptic) account of the reason for Jesus' crucifixion. As she hunts for the cause, she observes that Jesus was arrested and killed, but not his disciples. Thus, she concludes, Pilate knew that Jesus and his followers posed no real practical political threat. This leads her to the provocative assertion that he was accordingly crucified as "King of the Jews" in order to disabuse, silence, and scatter the overexcited crowds who at this feast were suddenly claiming him as Messiah—an opinion of himself that Jesus never shared or entertained. Jesus was thus the direct victim of his own uncontrolled popularity, which fed on his own overexcited expectation of the end.

The conceit that Jesus had no messianic pretensions has a long (and dubious) history, of course. What is interesting to observe here is that what Albert Schweitzer understood to be the forced *either-or* choice between his view and that of William Wrede—namely, between an apocalyptically minded Jesus and one who never thought he was the Messiah—is a *both-and* in Fredriksen's portrayal. Jesus oddly stumbles into his postmortem messianic identity precisely because of his contagious eschatological fixation—yet not as the literary invention of Mark, as Wrede supposed, and still less to "turn the wheel of history," as Schweitzer preferred, but rather through a Roman prefect's miscalculated gambit. Pilate's mocking *titulus*, pure political invention for policing the crowds, is the true proto-evangelium: the historical rock on which the Christian faith stands in Fredriksen's alternative vision.

One must admire the bravado of this anti-Gospel. Jesus had no enemies, only too much success, and he was never rejected on any side. He occupied no personal place within his kingdom proclamation, which had no place, in fact, for anything other than the end of the world. This alone sufficed, it seems, to make him madly popular. Reading against the grain of the sources is too weak to describe this clever revisionist strategy. Fredriksen has somehow lifted Renan's "Galilean Spring" and managed to make it the background for Jesus' Judean Passion. That all fault falls upon squarely Pilate's head and Roman hands will, of course, be reckoned as a well-measured corrective of the pernicious blood libel.

Chapter 3 must naturally confront the failure of Pilate's deadly *reductio ad absurdum* to disband the excited throng (which was curiously not excited enough to pose any real or imminent threat, but just excited enough to need immediate disbanding by drastic and deadly measures). This means addressing the disciples' experience of the Resurrection and working to explain how this Jesus, whose (unwanted) messianic credentials had just been rather rudely undermined, nevertheless became "Christ." As Fredriksen recounts it, this process is essentially a double cycle of eschatological disappointment churned out to glorious Christological profit, by the raising of Jesus and by the creation of the Parousia expectation. In a word, the Resurrection appearances—the disciples' first efforts to hold on to Jesus' immanent Kingdom dream, after it was forcibly blunted by his crucifixion—worked nicely for a while, but then these experiences curiously stopped, and the world went unobligingly on. The resourceful believers accordingly re-prophesied their way out of this new jolt of "cognitive dissonance" by creating the coming Son of Man.

At least theologically considered, the reduction of the Resurrection to an *idée fixe* is certainly the most pivotal move that Fredriksen must make. Apart from the momentous assumption that the New Testament makes no claims upon this score that merit any serious historical interest whatsoever, and also bracketing for the moment a nagging puzzlement over how exactly "cognitive dissonance" successively explains the unique experience of Saul (a Jew who was anything other than a Christian and for whom Jesus' staying dead would seem to be "cognitive consonance" of the most self-satisfied kind), Fredriksen's notion that for the early believers the Resurrection exclusively concerned a way to sustain hope in the *very* immanent end of the cosmos, neither revealing nor confirming anything special about Jesus' personal divinity, requires a comprehensive jettisoning of primitive traditions. The postulate of a monomaniacal fixation on the end of the world also exposes a staggering insensitivity to early Christian experiences and expressions of realized eschatology (again a spot where Pauline as well as Johannine data are clumsily handled or not handled at all). This is a major point and a major blind spot in Fredriksen's whole narrow construction. Subsequently functionalizing the "Son of Man" sayings as concocted props for the maintenance of the happy eschatological illusion further fails to account for the variegated character of this tricky material in the Gospels, which is more complex than Fredriksen's opportunistic "coming on the clouds" motif would admit. That scholars (and nonscholars) should be permitted not to believe in the Resurrection may be generously granted. Still, one begins to wonder whether it is not perhaps Paula Fredriksen who is tenaciously clinging to one stubborn idea.

The following two chapters continue the experience of déjà vu, and it is not critical to trudge through every detail. We encounter additional Christological metamorphoses, like the scripturally resourced "Davidization" of Jesus (who by the *titulum* was made a king in spite of himself). The phenomenon of mission becomes an apostolic "improvisation" that co-opted Greeks who had a preexisting attachment to Judaism, entering them into the prophetic expectation of an end-time ingathering of the nations. Ultimately, two Roman showdowns close the show with fitting fireworks ... but not the sort sufficient to pull down history's final curtain.

At the conclusion of the book, it is hard to know where precisely to engage. There are, in fact, surprising as it may seem, great swaths of common ground and even useful formulations and insights along the way. Still, one wishes to jump off so often than it is probably best not to board this train of thought at all. At the level of historical Jesus methodology, I might gesture only to one major opening move, for instance: a plain vote for Dale Allison over E. P. Sanders. Discounting the huge bulk of sayings materials and ignoring the whole shape and role of memory in the Jesus tradition, as Fredriksen à la Sanders does, is not the most likely approach to plant us on historical terra firma. Allison's "gist" arguments also result in the familiar failed millenarian prophet, of course. Here I can only say that I have worked to respond to this issue elsewhere. For me, without draining any apocalyptic, eschatological sap, Jesus' Judaism is much broader and more nuanced than the overblown picture we conventionally get. His Jewish context has (among other things) much more scribal cultural and hence rabbinism in its blood than these scholars of the radical Schweitzer school seem ready to see.

The deep heritage of Schweitzer's specific brand of "Jewish Jesus" in an express Protestant loathing for rabbinic religion should not be simply bypassed in this connection. Christian (and ex-Christian) constructions of Judaism are not uncomplicated creations. If a clarification of Jewish-Christian relations is accordingly at stake in these questions about Jesus and his first believers—and it is hard to avoid such ecumenical implications—it seems to me that Fredriksen has above all worked one monumental disservice to Jewish identity. In rejecting Jesus for herself, as she has every right in the world to do, she refuses to allow a historical "No" be spoken by first-century Jews. In fact, she has not even allowed those first Christians who were Jews to speak their own robust "Yes." Like Jesus himself, all they can do is cling to an illusion, for which he himself is ultimately superfluous dressing. Is it not, however, precisely the initial and prime duty in a genuine dialogue in these delicate matters first to acknowledge and respect the intellectual and spiritual space both to make and to refuse a real messianic claim about this particular Jew? Must the traumas of a messy, often inexcusable past so trouble and deflect us that we cannot let the texts say what they clearly wish to say and force the choice that they so clearly wish us to confront?

In the last analysis, Fredriksen's project invites reflection on religious epistemology and specifically the relation between historical intelligence and confessional conviction. In a word: Are the reasons elaborated in this book the ultimate reasons that the author no longer accepts Christ as Lord? Or is this instead historical cover for a decision already made in conscience on different intellectual and personal (i.e., illative) grounds?

A penetrating paragraph early in Ratzinger's *Eschatology* clarifies a crucial interdynamic of existence and understanding that undergirds Fredriksen's whole project. He asks why two hundred years ago the claim that Christian expectation was a deception found no resonance and was even a claim somehow without meaning (*eine ganz sinnlose Behauptung*). The answer, he says, is a simple factor of what we understand reality (*Wirklichkeit*) itself to be. Once upon a time, Christian truth bore up reality and was the ground upon which a whole society could confidently live and die, building vast works like a brilliant Baroque culture entirely upon its assumption and basis. "Today we see exactly the opposite phenomenon." To claim today that Christian truth itself is the ground that somehow carries the world has for most now become the empty, unintelligible claim. In this atmosphere, Fredriksen's views are almost blasé.

Blasé perhaps, but not banal, in the sense that much stands in the balance. For whether Christian faith can coexist in any meaningful sense should the essential view of this book be true is an earnest question. At least since Schweitzer, both liberal Protestants and Modernist Catholics have made strenuous efforts to assimilate Fredriksen-like visions into the Christian creed. For my part, I vigorously doubt that such theological acrobatics really convince, and Fredriksen's Judaism should be taken as her own earnest agreement and answer to the question.

The fundamental incompatibility of this book with the Christian account of Jesus is obviously not in itself a rebuttal for nonbelievers. Yet the annihilation of the Christian faith itself should at least appear to interested outsiders as an obstacle in their understanding of this derisible faith. In the *City of God*, Augustine reports an oracle of Apollo recorded by Porphyry. It is the answer to a man inquiring how to dissuade his wife from her Christian belief. "Let her continue as she pleases, persisting in her vain delusions (*inanibus fallaciis*), and lamenting in song a god who died in delusions (*fallaciis*)" (*City of God* 19.23). That a modern Jewish scholar might heartily agree with an ancient pagan author concerning Christianity and Jesus is permissible enough and interesting in its own right. This is seemingly a form of (Delphic) prophecy more to Fredriksen's liking (though Porphyry also goes on to say that the *Jews* did well to condemn Jesus to a shameful death). Augustine, for his part, responded by asking who was so foolish not to recognize that such words were "composed by a clever man with a strong animus against Christians." In the same line, it is also permitted if a modern Christian scholar still sees matters rather like Augustine and wonders whether Fredriksen's latest installment in the *Deluded Prophet* series, superannuated already for a good long time, might not fit well under the title of another article composed by the same clever woman: "Mandatory Retirement: Ideas in the Study of Christian Origins Whose Time to Go Has Come."

Bibliography

Adams, Sean A. "Luke's Preface and Its Relationship to Greek Historiography: A Response to Loveday Alexander." *JGRChJ* 3 (2006): 177–91.

Alexander, Loveday. *Acts in Its Ancient Literary Context*. London: T&T Clark, 2005.

———. "Fact, Fiction, and the Genre of Acts." *NTS* 44, no. 3 (1998): 380–99.

———. *The Preface to Luke's Gospel: Literary Convention and Social Context in Luke 1:1-4 and Acts 1:1*. SNTSMS 78. Cambridge: Cambridge University Press, 1993.

Alexander, Philip. "Towards a Taxonomy of Jewish Messianisms." In *Revealed Wisdom: Studies in Apocalyptic in Honor of Christopher Rowland*, edited by John Ashton, 52–72. Ancient Judaism and Early Christianity 88. Boston: Brill, 2014.

Allen, Joel. "The Despoliation of Egypt: Origen and Augustine—From Stolen Treasures to Saved Texts." In *Israel's Exodus in Transdisciplinary Perspective*, edited by T. E. Levy et al., 347–55. Cham: Springer International, 2015.

Allison, Dale C. *Constructing Jesus: Memory, Imagination, and History*. Grand Rapids, MI: Baker Academic, 2010.

———. "It Don't Come Easy: A History of Disillusionment." In *Jesus and the Demise of Authenticity*, edited by Chris Keith and Anthony Le Donne, 186–99. New York: T&T Clark, 2012.

———. *Jesus of Nazareth: Millenarian Prophet*. Minneapolis: Fortress, 1998.

———. *Resurrecting Jesus: The Earliest Christian Tradition and Its Interpreters*. New York: T&T Clark, 2005.

———. *The Historical Christ and the Theological Jesus*. Grand Rapids, MI: Eerdmans, 2009.

Amir, Yehoshua. "Der jüdische Eingottglaube als Stein des Anstoßes in der hellenistisch-römischen Welt." *JBTh* 2 (1987): 58–75.

———. "Die Begegnung des biblischen und des philosophischen Monotheismus als Grundthema des jüdischen Hellenismus." *EvTh* 38 (1978): 2–19.

Anatolios, Khaled. *Retrieving Nicaea: The Development and Meaning of Trinitarian Doctrine*. Grand Rapids, MI: Baker, 2011.

Andersen, Marvin. "Erasmus the Exegete." *Concordia Theological Monthly* 40, no. 11 (1969): 722–33.

Anderson, Gary. *Christian Doctrine and the Old Testament: Theology in the Service of Biblical Exegesis*. Grand Rapids, MI: Baker Academic, 2017.

———. *Genesis of Perfection: Adam and Eve in Jewish and Christian Imagination*. Louisville, KY: Westminster John Knox, 2001.

Andresen, Carl. "Zur Entstehung und Geschichte des Trinitarischen Personbegriffes." *ZNW* 52, no. 1–2 (1961): 1–38.

Angel, Joseph. "The Liturgical-Eschatological Priest of the Self-Glorification Hymn." *RdQ* 96, no. 4 (2010): 585–605.

———. *Otherworldly and Eschatological Priesthood in the Dead Sea Scrolls*. STDJ 86. Leiden: Brill, 2010.

Arcari, Luca. "'Discorsi monoteistici' nell' antichità: L'unicità divina come strumento di auto-definizione." *Mediterraneo antico* 13, no. 1–2 (2010): 311–52.

Assman, Jan. "The Mosaic Distinction: Israel, Egypt, and the Invention of Paganism." *Representations* 56 (1996): 48–67.

Atkinson, Kenneth. "Taxo's Martyrdom and the Role of the *Nuntius* in the *Testament of Moses*: Implications for Understanding Other Intermediary Figures." *JBL* 125, no. 3 (2006): 453–76.

Attridge, Harold. "The Philosophical Critique of Religion in the Early Empire." In *Religion (Heidentum: Römische Religion, Allgemeines)*, edited by Wolfgang Haase, 45–78. ANRW II 16.1. Berlin: Walter de Gruyter, 1978.

Auerbach, Eric. *Mimesis: The Representation of Reality in Western Literature*. Princeton, NJ: Princeton University, 2007.

Aune, David. "Luke 1:1-4: Historical or Scientific *Prooimion*?" In *Paul, Luke, and the Greco-Roman World: Essays in Honour of Alexander J. M. Wedderburn*, edited by A. Christopherson et al., 138–48. JSNTSup 217. Sheffield: Sheffield Academic, 2002.

———. *Prophecy in Early Christianity and the Ancient Mediterranean World*. Eugene, OR: Wipf and Stock, 2003.

———. *Revelation 6-16*. WBC 52B. Nashville, TN: Thomas Nelson, 1998.

Baasland, Ernst. "Fourth Quest? What Did Jesus Really Want?" In *Handbook for the Study of the Historical Jesus*. Vol. 1, *How to Study the Historical Jesus*, edited by Tom Holmén and Stanley Porter, 31–56. Leiden: Brill, 2011.

Backhaus, Knut. "Asphaleia: Lukanische Geschichtsschreibung im Rahmen des antiken Wahrheitsdiskurses." In *Wahrheit und Geschichte: Exegetische und hermeneutische Studien zu einer dialektischen Konstellation*, edited by Eva Ebel and Samuel Vollenweider, 79–108. AThANT 102. Zurich: TVZ, 2012.

———. *Die Jüngerskreis des Täufers Johannes: Eine Studie zu den religionsgeschichtlichen Ursprüngen des Christentums*. Paderborn: Schöningh, 1991.

Backhaus, Knut, and G. Häffner, eds. *Historiographie und fiktionales Erzählen: Zur Konstruktivität in Geschichtstheorie und Exegese*. BThSt 86. Neukirchen-Vluyn: Neukrichener, 2007.

Bale, Alan. *Genre and Narrative Coherence in the Acts of the Apostles*. LNTS 514. London: T&T Clark, 2015.

Balthasar, Hans Urs von. *Die Gottesfrage des heutigen Menschen*. Freiburg: Johannes, 2009.

———. *Explorations in Theology II: Spouse of the Word*. San Francisco: Ignatius, 1991.

———. *Origen: Spirit and Fire. A Thematic Anthology of His Writings*. Washington, DC: The Catholic University of America Press, 1984.

———. *Presence and Thought: Essays on the Religious Philosophy of Gregory of Nyssa*. San Francisco: Ignatius/Communio Books, 1995.

———. *Theologie der Drei Tage*. Einsiedeln: Johannes, 2011

———. "Transcendentality and *Gestalt*." *Communio: International Catholic Review* 11, no. 1 (1984): 4–12.

Bainton, Roland. "The Left-Wing of the Reformation." *Journal of Religion* 21, no. 2 (1941): 124–34.

Barber, Michael. "Jesus as the Living Temple Builder and Peter's Priestly Role in Matt 16:16-19." *JBL* 132 (2013): 935–53.

Barker, Margaret. *The Great Angel: A Study of Israel's Second God*. Louisville, KY: Westminster John Knox, 1992.

Barnes, Michel René. "Rereading Augustine's Theology of the Trinity." In *The Trinity: An Interdisciplinary Symposium on the Trinity*, edited by Stephen T. David, Daniel Kendell, and Gerard O'Collins, 145–76. Oxford: Oxford University Press, 2002.

Barnes, T. D. "The Fragments of Tacitus' Histories." *CPh* 72, no. 3 (1977): 224–31.

Barr, James. "Abba Isn't Daddy." *JTS* 39, no. 1 (1988): 28–47.

Barth, Karl. *Church Dogmatics II/2: The Doctrine of Election*. Translated by G. W. Bromiley. London: T&T Clark, 2010.

———. *Protestant Theology in the Nineteenth Century*. Edited by Colin Gunton. Grand Rapids, MI: Eerdmans, 2002.

Bates, Matthew W. "Beyond *Stichwort*: A Narrative Approach to Isa 52,7 in Romans 10,15 and 11QMelchizedek (11Q13)." *RB* 116 (2010): 387–414.

———. *The Birth of the Trinity: Jesus, God, and Spirit in the New Testament and Early Christian Interpretations of the Old Testament*. Oxford: Oxford University Press, 2015.

Bauckham, Richard. "Evolution and Creation: (9) in Moltmann's Doctrine of Creation." *Epworth Review* 15 (1988): 74–81.

———. "Eyewitnesses and Critical History: A Response to Jens Schröder and Craig Evans." *JSNT* 31, no. 2 (2008): 221–35.

———. ed. *God Will Be All in All: The Eschatology of Jürgen Moltmann*. New York: T&T Clark, 1999.

———. "Historiographical Aspects of the Gospel of John." *NTS* 53, no. 1 (2007): 17–36.

———. "In Defense of *The Crucified God*." In *The Power and Weakness of God: Impassibility and Orthodoxy*, edited by N. M. de S. Cameron, 93–118. Edinburgh: Rutherford House, 1990.

———. "Introduction." In *Jürgen Moltmann: Collected Readings*. Minneapolis: Fortress, 2014.

———. *Jesus and the Eyewitnesses: The Gospels as Eyewitness Testimony*. Grand Rapids, MI: Eerdmans, 2006. [2nd ed., Grand Rapids, MI: Eerdmans, 2017.]

———. *Jesus and the God of Israel: God Crucified and Other Studies on the New Testament's Christology of Divine Identity*. Grand Rapids, MI: Eerdmans, 2008.

———. *Jude and the Relatives of Jesus in the Early Church*. Edinburgh: T&T Clark, 1990.

_____. "Jürgen Moltmann." In *The Modern Theologians: An Introduction to Christian Theology since 1918*, edited by David Ford, 147–62. Malden, MA: Blackwell, 2013.

_____. *Moltmann: Messianic Theology in the Making: An Appreciation*. London: Marshall Pickering, 1987.

_____. "Moltmann's Eschatology of the Cross." *Scottish Journal of Theology* 30, no. 4 (1977): 301–11.

_____. "Moltmann's Messianic Christology." *Scottish Journal of Theology* 44, no. 4 (1991): 519–32.

_____. "Moltmann's *Theology of Hope* Revisited." *Scottish Journal of Theology* 42, no. 2 (1989): 199–214.

_____. "Orthodoxy in Christology: Lecture Given at Oxford University," June 9, 2002. https://web.archive.org/web/20150915123543/http://richardbauckham.co.uk/uploads/Accessible/Orthodoxy%20in%20Christology.pdf.

_____, ed. *The Gospels for All Christians: Rethinking the Gospel Audiences*. Grand Rapids, MI: Eerdmans, 1998.

_____. *The Theology of Jürgen Moltmann*. New York: T&T Clark, 1995.

_____. "The Worship of Jesus in Apocalyptic Christianity." *NTS* 27, no. 3 (1981): 322–41.

Bauer, Bruno. *Christus und die Cäsaren: Der Ursprung des Christentums aus dem römischen Griechentum*. Berlin, 1877.

Bauer, Walter. *Rechtglaubigkeit und Ketzerei im ältesten Christentum*. Tübingen: Mohr, 1934.

Baum, Armin. "The Anonymity of the New Testament History Books: A Stylistic Device in the Context of Greco-Roman and Ancient near Eastern Literature." *NovT* 50, no. 2 (2008): 120–42.

Bea, Augustine. *The Study of the Synoptic Gospels: New Approaches and Outlooks*. New York: Harper & Row, 1965.

_____. *The Word of God and Mankind*. London: Geoffrey Chapman, 1967.

Bechard, Dean Philip. "Review of *Jesus and the Eyewitnesses: The Gospels as Eyewitness Testimony*." *Bib* 90 (2009): 126–29.

Becker, Eve-Marie, ed. *Die antike Historiographie und die Anfänge der christlichen Geschichtsschreibung*. BZNW 129. Berlin: De Gruyter, 2005.

Behler, Wolgang. *Realität und Ek-sistenz: Auseinandersetzung mit der Konzeption Martin Heideggers in Konfrontation mit den ontologischen Schriften von Hedwig Conrad-Martius*. Munich, 1956.

Beiser, Frederick C. *David Friedrich Strauss, Father of Unbelief: An Intellectual Biography*. Oxford: Oxford University Press, 2020.

Benedict XVI. "Address to the Roman Curia Offering Them His Christmas Greetings," December 22, 2005.

_____. *Jesus of Nazareth: Holy Week. From the Entrance into Jerusalem to the Resurrection*. San Francisco: Ignatius, 2011.

_____. *Jesus of Nazareth: The Infancy Narratives*. New York: Image, 2012.

Benoit, Pierre. "Refléxions sur la 'formgeschichtliche Méthode.'" *RB* (1946): 481–512.

Berger, Adolf. *Encyclopedic Dictionary of Roman Law*. Philadelphia: American Philosophical Society, 1953.

Bergmann, Claudia. "Idol Worship in Bel and the Dragon and Other Jewish Literature from the Second Temple Period." In *Septuagint Research: Issues and Challenges in the Study of the Greek Jewish Scriptures*, edited by Wolfgang Kraus and R. Glenn Wooden, 207–23. SBLSCS 53. Atlanta: SBL, 2006.

Bermejo-Rubio, Fernando. "The Fiction of the 'Three Quests': An Argument for Dismantling a Dubious Historiographical Paradigm." *JSHJ* 7, no. 3 (2009): 211–53.

Bertalotto, Pierpaolo. "Qumran Messianism, Melchizedek, and the Son of Man." In *The Dead Sea Scrolls in Context: Integrating the Dead Sea Scrolls in the Study of Ancient Texts, Languages, and Cultures*, edited by Armin Lange, Emanuel Tov, and Matthias Weigold, 325–39. VTS 140/1. Leiden: Brill, 2011.

Bettini, Maurizio. "Looking at Ourselves Backwards: Modern Recourses to the Ancient World." *History of Religions* 41, no. 3 (2002): 197–212.

Betz, John. "Glory(ing) in the Humility of the Word: The Kenotic Form of Revelation in J. G. Hamann." *Letter and Spirit* 6 (2010): 141–80.

———. "Translator's Introduction." In Erich Pryzwara, *Analogia Entis: Metaphysics. Original Structure and Universal Rhythm*, edited by John Betz and David Bentley Hart, 1–118. Grand Rapids, MI: Eerdmans, 2014.

Betz, O. "Past Events and Last Events in the Qumran Interpretation of History." *WCJS* 6 (1977): 27–34.

Beutler, Johannes. *Das Johannesevangelium*. Freiburg: Herder, 2013.

Beyerle, Stefan. "'The God of Heaven' in Persian and Hellenistic Times." In *Other Worlds and Their Relation to This World: Early Jewish and Ancient Christian Traditions*, edited by Tobias Niklas et al., 17–36. JSJSup 143. Leiden: Brill, 2010.

Beyschlag, Willibald. *New Testament Theology I*. Edinburgh: Clark, 1894.

Bickerman, Elias. *Der Gott der Makkabäer: Untersuchungen über Sinn und Ursprung der makkabäischen Erhebung*. Berlin: Schocken/Jüdischer Verlag, 1937.

Billington, James. *Fire in the Minds of Men: Origins of Revolutionary Faith*. London: Routledge, 1999.

Bird, Michael, ed. *How God Became Jesus: The Real Origins of Belief in Jesus' Divine Nature—A Response to Bart Ehrman*. Grand Rapids, MI: Zondervan, 2014.

Blanton, Ward, James G. Crossley, and Halvor Moxnes, eds. *Jesus beyond Nationalism: Construction the Historical Jesus in a Period of Cultural Complexity*. London: Equinox, 2009.

Blomberg, Craig L. *The Historical Reliability of John's Gospel: Issues and Commentary*. Downers Grove, IL: IVP Academic, 2001.

Blough, Neal. *Jésus-Christ aux marges de la Réforme*. Paris: Desclée, 1992.

Blowers, Paul. "Maximus the Confessor and John of Damascus on Gnomic Will (γνώμη) in Christ: Clarity and Ambiguity." *Union Seminary Quarterly Review* 63, no. 3/4 (2012): 44–50.

Blumenthal, Christian. "'Augustus' Erlass und Gottes Macht: Überlegungen zur Charakterisierung der Augustusfigur und ihrer erzählstrategischen Funktion in der lukanischen Erzählung." *NTS* 57, no. 1 (2011): 1–30.

Boehart, William. *Politik und Religion: Studien zum Fragmentenstreit (Reimarus, Goeze, Lessing)*. Schwarzenbek: Martienss, 1988.

Boehm, Gottfried. "Jenseits der Sprache? Anmerkungen zur Logik der Bilder." In *Iconic Turn: Die neue Macht der Bilder*, edited by Christa Maar and Hubert Burda, 28–43. Cologne: DuMont, 2004.

Bolin, Thomas. "The Temple of יהו at Elephantine and Persian Religious Policy." In *The Triumph of Elohim: From Yahwisms to Judaisms*, edited by Diana Edelman, 127–42. Kampen: Kok Pharos, 1995.

Bousset, Wilhelm. *Kyrios Christos: A History of the Belief in Christ from the Beginnings of Christianity to Ireneaus*. Translated by John Steeley. Waco, TX: Baylor University Press, 2013. [Originally published as *Kyrios Christos: Geschichte des Christusglaubens von den Anfängen des Christentums bis Irenaeus*. FRLANT 4. Göttingen: Vandenhoeck & Ruprecht, 1913.]

Bovon, François. *Das Evangelium nach Lukas III/4*. EKKNT. Neukirchener Verlag, 2009.

———. *Luke 1: A Commentary on the Gospel of Luke 1:1–9:50*. Hermeneia. Minneapolis: Fortress, 2002

Bowen, A. J. *Plutarch: The Malice of Herodotus*. Warminster, UK: Aris & Phillips, 1992.

Bowersock, Glen. *Fiction as History: Nero to Julian*. Berkeley: University of California Press, 1994.

Bowman, John Wick. "From Schweitzer to Bultmann." *Theology Today* 11, no. 2 (1954): 161–78.

Boyarin, Daniel. *The Jewish Gospels: The Story of the Jewish Christ*. New York: New Press, 2012.

Braaten, Carl. "Towards a Theology of Hope." *Theology Today* 24, no. 2 (1967): 208–26.

Brandt, Wilhelm. *Die evangelische Geschichte und der Ursprung des Christentums auf Grund einer Kritik der Berichte über das Leiden und die Auferstehung Jesu*. Leipzig, 1893.

Brown, Raymond. "How Much Did Jesus Know? A Survey of the Biblical Evidence." *CBQ* 29, no. 3 (1967): 9–39.

———. *The Birth of the Messiah: A Commentary on the Infancy Narratives in the Gospels of Matthew and Luke*. ABRL. New Haven, CT: Yale University Press, 1999. [Originally published in New York: Doubleday, 1977.]

———. *The Community of the Beloved Disciple: The Life, Loves, and Hates of an Individual Church in New Testament Times*. New York: Paulist, 1979.

———. *The Gospel According to John I-XII*. AB 29. Garden City, NY: Doubleday, 1966.

Bulgakov, Sergei. "The Holy Theophany of Our Lord Jesus Christ." In *Handbook for Church Servers*, 2nd ed., 16–19. Kharkov, 1900. [Translated by Archpriest Eugene D. Tarris, December 31, 2004. https://web.archive.org/web/20181025080430/http://modeoflife.org/the-holy-theophany-of-our-lord-jesus-christ.]

Bullard, Collin Blake. *Jesus and the Thoughts of Many Hearts: Implicit Christology and Jesus' Knowledge in the Gospel of Luke*. LNTS [JSNTS] 530. London: Bloomsbury, 2015.

Bullard, Roger A. "Introduction." In *Nag Hammadi Codex II,2-7*, edited by Bentley Layton, 220–26. Coptic Gnostic Library 1, Nag Hammadi Studies XX. Leiden: Brill, 1989.

Bultmann, Rudolf. *New Testament and Mythology and Other Basic Writings*. Translated by Schubert M. Ogden. Minneapolis: Fortress, 1989.

———. "Review of Landräumig: Sebastian Franck, ein Wanderer an Donau, Rhein und Keckar." *Mennonite Quarterly Review* 32 (1958): 314.

_____. *The History of the Synoptic Tradition*. Oxford: Blackwell, 1963.

_____. *Theology of the New Testament*. Translated by Kendrick Grobel. Waco, TX: Baylor University, 2007.

_____. *Theology of the New Testament II*. New York: Charles Scribner's Sons, 1955.

Burkett, Delbert. *The Son of Man Debate: A History and Evaluation*. SNTSMS 107. Cambridge: Cambridge University Press, 1999.

_____. "The Transfiguration of Jesus (Mark 9:2-8): Epiphany or Apotheosis." *JBL* 138 (2019): 413–32.

Burnett, D. Clint. *Christ's Enthronement at God's Right Hand and Its Greco-Roman Cultural Context*. BZNW 232. Berlin: De Gruyter, 2021.

Burns, R. M. *The Great Debate on Miracles: From Joseph Glanvill to David Hume*. Lewisburg, PA: Bucknell University Press, 1981.

Burridge, Richard. *What Are the Gospels? A Comparison with Graeco-Roman Biography*. 2nd ed. Biblical Resource Series. Grand Rapids, MI: Eerdmans, 2004.

Butler, B. C. *The Originality of St. Matthew: A Critique of the Two Document Hypothesis*. Cambridge: Cambridge University Press, 2011. [Originally published 1951.]

Byrskog, Samuel. *Story as History—History as Story: The Gospel Tradition in the Context of Ancient Oral History*. WUNT 123. Tübingen: Mohr Siebeck, 2000.

Byrskog, Samuel, Raimo Hakola, and Jutta Maria Jokiranta, eds. *Social Memory and Social Identity in the Study of Early Judaism and Early Christianity*. NTOA 116. Göttingen: Vandenhoeck & Ruprecht, 2016.

Caba, José. "Historicity of the Gospels (*Dei Verbum* 19): Genesis and Fruits of the Conciliar Text." In *Vatican II: Assessments and Perspectives*, vol. 1, edited by Rene Latourelle, 299–320. New York: Paulist, 1988.

Campbell, William Sanger. *The "We" Passages in the Acts of the Apostles: The Narrator as a Narrative Character*. Studies in Biblical Literature 14. Atlanta: SBL, 2007.

Capener, Sean. "Being and Acting: Agamben, Athanasius, and the Trinitarian Economy." *Heythrop Journal* 57, no. 6 (2016): 950–63.

Capes, David. *Old Testament Yahweh Texts in Paul's Christology*. WUNT II 47. Tübingen: Mohr Siebeck, 1992.

Carlyle, Thomas. "The Hero as Divinity." In *On Heroes, Hero Worship, and the Heroic in History*, 21–51. New Haven, CT: Yale University Press, 2013. [Carlyle's original lectures delivered in 1840.]

Carroll, Lewis. *Through the Looking Glass and What Alice Found There*. London: Macmillan, 2009.

Cary, Philip. "The New Evangelical Subordinationism: Reading Inequality into the Trinity." In *The New Evangelical Subordinationism: Perspectives on the Equality of God the Father and God the Son*, edited by Dennis Jowers and H. Wayne House, 1–12. Eugene, OR: Wipf and Stock, 2012.

Casey, Maurice. *Jesus of Nazareth: An Independent Historian's Account of His Life and Teaching*. New York: T&T Clark, 2010.

_____. *The Solution to the Son of Man Problem*. New York: T&T Clark, 2009.

Charlesworth, James. "The Historical Jesus in the Fourth Gospel: A Paradigm Shift?" *JSHJ* 8 (2010): 3–46.

_____, ed. *The Old Testament Pseudepigrapha*. Vol. 1, *Apocalyptic Literature and Testaments*. Peabody, MA: Hendrickson, 2011.

_____, ed. *The Old Testament Pseudepigrapha*. Vol. 2, *Expansions of the Old Testament and Legends, Wisdom and Philosophical Literature, Prayers, Psalms, Odes, Fragments of Lost Judeo-Hellenistic Works*. Peabody, MA: Hendrickson, 2011.

Childs, Brevard. "Toward Recovering Theological Exegesis." *Pro Ecclesia* 6, no. 1 (1997): 16–26.

Christensen, Duane L. *Deuteronomy 1:1–21:9*. Word Biblical Commentary 6a. Nashville: Thomas Nelson, 2001.

Clarke, William Norris. "Action as the Self-Revelation of Being: A Central Theme in the Thought of Saint Thomas." In *Explorations in Metaphysics: Being—God—Person*, 45–64. Notre Dame, IN: University of Notre Dame Press, 1994.Colazilli, Alessandra. "Reproducing Human Limbs: Prosthesis, Amulets, and Votives Objects in Ancient Egypt." *Res Antiquitatis* 3 (2012): 147–74.

Collins, Adela Yabro. "The Apocalyptic Son of Man Sayings." In *The Future of Early Christianity: Essays in Honor of Helmut Koester*, edited by B. A. Pearson, 220–28. Minneapolis: Fortress, 1991.

Collins, John J. *Jewish Cult and Hellenistic Culture: Essays on the Jewish Encounter with Hellenism and Roman Rule*. JSJSup 100. Leiden: Brill, 2005.

_____. *The Scepter and the Star: The Messiahs of the Dead Sea Scrolls and Other Ancient Literature*. ABRL. New York: Doubleday, 1995.

Coloe, Mary L. *God Dwells with Us: Temple Symbolism in the Fourth Gospel*. Collegeville, MN: Liturgical Press, 2001.

Comella, Annamaria. *Il deposito votivo presso l'Ara della Regina*. Materiali del Museo Archeologico Nazionale di Tarquinia 4. Rome: Giorgio Bretschneider, 1982.

Conrad-Martius, Hedwig. *Das Sein*. Munich: Kosel, 1957.

Constas, Maximos. "Dionysius the Areopagite and the New Testament." In *The Oxford Handbook to Dionysius the Areopagite*. Oxford: Oxford University, forthcoming.

_____. "The Reception of St. Paul and Pauline Theology in the Byzantine Period." In *The New Testament in Byzantium*, edited by Derek Krueger and Robert Nelson, 147–76. Washington, DC: Dumbarton Oaks, 2016.

Conzelmann, Hans. *The Theology of St. Luke*. Philadelphia: Fortress, 1961.

Corey, Judith L. *Light from Light: Cosmology and the Theology of the Logos*. Minneapolis: Fortress, 2016.

Corley, Jeremy. "Elijah among the Former Prophets in Heb Ben Sira 48:1-12." *Studia Biblica Slovaca* 12 (2020): 198–226.

Cotter, Wendy. "Greco-Roman Apotheosis Traditions and the Resurrection Appearances in Matthew." In *The Gospel of Matthew in Current Study: Studies in Memory of William G. Thompson, S.J.*, edited by David Aune, 127–53. Grand Rapids, MI: Eerdmans, 2001.

Craig, William Lane. "*Noli Me Tangere*: Why John Meier Won't Touch the Risen Lord." *Heythrop Journal* 50, no. 1 (2009): 91–97.

Cross, Richard. "Perichoresis, Deification, and Christological Predication in John of Damascus." *Medieval Studies* 62 (2000): 69–124.

Crystall, Andreas. *Gustav Frenssen: Sein Weg vom Kulturprotestantismus zum Nationalsozialismus*. Gütersloh: Kaiser, 2002.

Cullmann, Oscar. *Vatican II: The New Direction*. New York: Harper and Row, 1968.

Curiello, Gioacchino. "'Alia translation melior est': Albert the Great and the Latin Translations of the Corpus Dionysiacum." *Documenti e studi sulla tradizione filosofica medieval* 24 (2013): 121–51.

Dahlke, Benjamin. "The Invention of the Antichrist: Catholic Reactions to Barth's Condemnation of the *Analogia Entis*." In *Karl Barth: Catholic Renewal and Vatican II*, 61–95. New York: T&T Clark, 2012.

Daley, Brian. *Light on the Mountain: Greek Patristic and Byzantine Homilies on the Transfiguration of the Lord*. Popular Patristics Series 48. Yonkers, NY: St. Vladimir's Seminary Press, 2013.

Daube, David. "The Contrariness of Speech and Polytheism." *Journal of Law and Religion* 11, no. 1 (1994): 317–21.

Davies, W. D., and Dale C. Allison, *The Gospel According Matthew*. Vol. 2. Edinburgh: T&T Clark, 1991.

Davila, James. *The Provenance of the Pseudepigrapha: Jewish, Christian, or Other?* JSJSup 105. Leiden: Brill, 2005.

Davila, James, and Carey Newman, eds. *The Jewish Roots of Christological Monotheism: Papers from the St. Andrew's Conference on the Historical Worship of Jesus*. JSJSup 62. Leiden: Brill, 1999.

De Finance, Joseph. *Être et Agir dans la Philosophie de Saint Thomas*. Paris: Beauchense, 1945.

del Olmo Lete, Gregorio. "Les inscriptions puniques votives: Suggestions d'intepétation." In *Studies in Ugaritic Linguistics: Selected Papers*, 451–56. Münster: Ugarit-Verlag, 2017.

de Lubac, Henri. *Le Mystère du surnaturel*. Paris: Aubier, 1965.

———. *Medieval Exegesis: The Four Senses of Scripture*. Vol. 2. Grand Rapids, MI: Eerdmans, 2000.

———. *Surnaturel: Etudes historique*. Paris: Aubier, 1946.

Demacopuolos, George, and Aristotle Papanikolaou, eds. *Orthodox Readings of Augustine*. Crestwood, NY: St. Vladimir's Seminary Press, 2008.

DeSilva, David A. "The *Testaments of the Twelve Patriarchs* as Witnesses to Pre-Christian Judaism: A Re-Assessment." *JSP* 22 (2013): 21–68.

Destrée, Pierre, and Fritz-Gregor Herrmann, eds. *Plato and the Poets*. Mnemosyne Supplements. Leiden: Brill, 2011.

Destro, Adriana, and Mauro Pesce. *Encounters with Jesus: The Man in His Place and Time*. Minneapolis: Fortress, 2011.

———. *From Jesus to His First Followers: Continuity and Discontinuity: Anthropological and Historical Perspectives*. Biblical Interpretation Series 152. Leiden: Brill, 2017.

Diehl, Judith. "What Is a Gospel? Recent Studies in the Gospel Genre." *Currents in Biblical Research* 9, no. 2 (2011): 171–99.

Dillon, John. *Middle Platonism, 80 B.C. to A.D. 220*. Ithaca, NY: Cornell University, 1977.

———. "Monotheism in the Gnostic Tradition." In *Pagan Monotheism in Late Antiquity*, edited by Polymnia Athanassiadi and Michael Frede, 69–79. Oxford: Clarendon, 2008.

Dillon, M. P. J. "The Didactic Nature of the Epidaurian Iamata." *ZPE* 101 (1994): 239–60.

Dillon, Richard. *From Eye-Witnesses to Ministers of the Word*. AnBib 82. Rome: Biblical Institute, 1978.

———. *The Hymans of Saint Luke: Lyricism and Narrative Strategy in Luke 1-2*. CBQMS 50. Washington, DC: CBA, 2013.

Dionysius. *On the Ecclesiastical Hierarchy: The Thirteenth-Century Paris Textbook Edition*. Translated by L. Michael Harrington. Dallas Medieval Texts and Translations 12. Leuven: Peeters, 2011.

Dormeyer, Detlev. "Wundergeschichten in der hellenistischen Medizin und Geschichtsschreibung: Eine religionsgeschichtliche Annäherung." In *Hermeneutik der frühchristlichen Wundererzählungen*, edited by Bernd Kollmann and Ruben Zimmermann, 127–51. WUNT 339. Tübingen: Mohr Siebeck, 2014.

Douglas, Anglican Bishop John. *The Criterion or Rules by Which the True Miracles Recorded in the New Testament Are Distinguished from the Spurious Miracles of Pagans and Papists*. 1774.

Dreyfus, François. *Jésus savait-il qu'il était Dieu?* Paris: Cerf, 1984.

Duchatelez, K. "La 'condescendance' divine et l'histoire du salut." *NRTh* 95, no. 10 (1973): 594–98.

Duncker, Peter. "Biblical Criticism (Instructions of the Church and Excesses of Form Criticism)." *CBQ* 25, no. 1 (1963): 22–33.

Dunn, James D. G. *Christianity in the Making*. Vol. 1, *Jesus Remembered*. Grand Rapids, MI: Eerdmans, 2003.

———. *Christology in the Making: A New Testament Inquiry into the Origins of the Doctrine of the Incarnation*. London: SCM, 1980.

———. *Did the First Christians Worship Jesus? The New Testament Evidence*. London: SPCK, 2010

———. *Jesus Remembered*. Grand Rapids, MI: Eerdmans, 2003.

———. "Q¹ as Oral Tradition." In *The Written Gospel*, edited by Marcus Bockmuehl and Donald Hagner, 45–69. Cambridge: Cambridge University Press, 2005.

Duprez, André. *Jésus et les dieux guérisseurs a propos de Jean, v*. CRB 12. Paris: Gabalda, 1970.

Durand, Alexandre. "La science du Christ." *Nouvelle Revue Théologique* 71, no. 5 (1949): 497–503.

Dzielska, Maria. *Apollonius of Tyana in History and Legend*. Rome: L'erma di Bretschneider, 1986.

Edelstein, Emma J., and Ludwig Edelstein. *Asclepius: Collection and Interpretation of the Testimonies*. Baltimore: Johns Hopkins University Press, 1998.

Edwards, Mark. *Aristotle and Early Christian Thought*. London: Routledge, 2019.

Ego, Beate. "Abrahams Jugendgeschichte in der Literatur des frühen Judentums: Ein Paradigma theologischer Rezeptionskonzepte in der Antike." In *Beyond Biblical*

Theologies, edited by Heinrich von Assel, Stefan Beyerle, and Christfried Böttrich, 431–544. Tübingen: Mohr Siebeck, 2012.

———. "La conversion d'Abraham au monothéisme: Le portrait du patriarche dans l'Apocalypse d'Abraham." In *Le monothéisme biblique: Evolution, contexts et perspectives*, edited by Eberhard Bons and Thierry Legrand, 299–311. Paris: Cerf, 2011.

Ehrhardt, Arnold. "Justin's Martyrs Two Apologies." *Journal of Ecclesiastical History* 4, no. 1 (1953): 1–12.

Ehrman, Bart. *Did Jesus Exist? The Historical Argument for Jesus of Nazareth*. New York: HarperCollins, 2012.

———. *How Jesus Became God: The Exaltation of a Jewish Preacher from Galilee*. New York: HarperOne, 2014.

———. *Jesus: Apocalyptic Prophet of the New Millennium*. New York: Oxford University, 1999.

———. *Jesus, Interrupted: Revealing the Hidden Contradictions in the Bible (and Why We Don't Know about Them)*. New York: HarperOne, 2009.

Eire, Carlos. *Reformations: The Early Modern World, 1450–1650*. New Haven, CT: Yale, 2016.

Emery, Gilles. *The Trinity: An Introduction to Catholic Doctrine on the Triune God*. Translated by Matthew Levering. Washington, DC: The Catholic University of America Press, 2011.

Emmenegger, Gregor. *Wie die Jungfrau zum Kind kam: Zum Einfluss antiker medizinischer und naturphilosopher Theorien auf die Entwicklung des christlichen Dogmas*. Paradosis 56. Münster: Aschendorff, 2017.

Enermalm-Ogawa, A. *Un langage de prière juif en grec: Le témoignage des deux premiers livres des Maccabées*. ConBNT 17. Uppsala: Almquist and Wiksell, 1987.

Erasmus, Desiderius. *Praise of Folly, and Letter to Martin Dorp, 1515*. Edited by A. H. T Levi. Translated by Betty Radice. Hardmondsworth: Penguin, 1971.

Ernst, Johannes Theodorus. *Die Lehre der hochmittelalterlichen Theologen von der vollkommenen Erkenntnis Christi: Ein Versuch zur Auslegung der klassischen Dreiteilung. Visio beata, scientia infusa und scientia acquisita*. Freiberg: Herder, 1971.

Eshel, Esther. "4Q471b: 4QSelf-Glorification Hymn (=4QHe frg. 1?)." In *Discoveries in the Judean Desert XXIX, Qumran Cave 4 XX: Poetical and Liturgical Texts, Part 2*, edited by Bilhah Nitzan et al., 421–32. Oxford: Clarendon, 1999.

Evans, Craig A. "Jesus' Action in the Temple: Cleansing or Portent of Destruction." *CBQ* 51, no. 2 (1989): 237–70.

———. "Predictions of the Destruction of the Herodian Temple in the Pseudepigrapha, Qumran Scrolls, and Related Texts." *JSP* 10, no. 10 (1992): 89–147.

———. "The Implications of Eyewitness Tradition." *JSNT* 31, no. 2 (2008): 211–19.

Eve, Eric. "Meier, Miracle, and Multiple Attestation." *JSHJ* 3, no. 1 (2005): 23–45.

Fages, Père. *Histoire de Saint Vincent Ferrier*. Paris, 1894.

Fant, Clyde, and Mitchell Reddish. *Lost Treasures of the Bible: Understanding the Bible through Archeological Artifacts in World Museums*. Grand Rapids, MI: Eerdmans, 2008.

Farkasfalvy, Denis. *Inspiration and Interpretation*. Washington, DC: The Catholic University of America Press, 2010.

Farmer, William. *The Synoptic Problem*. 2nd ed. Dillsboro: Western North Carolina Press, 1974.

Fast, Heinold. *Der linke Flügel der Reformation: Glaubenszeugnisse der Täufer, Spiritualisten, Schwärmer und Antitrinitarier*. Bremen: Schünemann, 1962.

Feldmeier, Reinhard. "'Der Höchste': Das Gottesprädikat Hypsistos in der paganen Religiosität, in der Septuaginta und im lukanischen Doppelwerk." In *Die Septuaginta—Text, Wirkung, Rezeption*, edited by Wolfgang Kraus and Siegfried Kreuzer, 544–58. Tübingen: Mohr Siebeck, 2014.

Ferber, Rafael, and Gregor Damschen. "Is the Idea of the Good beyond Being? Plato's *epekeina tēs ousias* Revisted (Republic 6,509b8–10)." In *Second Sailing: Alternative Perspectives on Plato*, edited by Debra Nails and Harold Tarrant, 197–204. Commentationes Humanarum Litterarum 132. Helsinki: Societas Scientiarum Fennica, 2015.

Fiedrowicz, Michael. "Introduction." In *Exposition of the Psalms 1–32*, translated by Maria Boulding, 19–49. Works of St. Augustine III/15. New York: New City Press, 2000.

———. *Psalmus vox totius Christi: Studien zu Augustins "Ennarrationes in Psalmos."* Freiberg: Herder, 1997.

Fischer, Balthasar. *Die Psalmen als Stimme der Kirche: Gesammelte Studien zur christlichen Psalmenfrömmigkeit*. Edited by Andreas Heinz. Trier: Paulinus Verlag, 1982.

Fitzmyer, Joseph A. "A Recent Roman Scriptural Controversy." *TS* 22, no. 3 (1961): 426–44.

———. "The Biblical Commission's Instruction on the Historical Truth of the Gospels." *TS* 25, no. 3 (1964): 386–408.

———. *The Gospel According to Luke I–IX*. AB 28. New York: Doubleday, 1979.

———. *The Gospel According to Luke X–XXIV*. AB 28A. Garden City, NY: Doubleday, 1985.

———. *The One Who Is to Come*. Grand Rapids, MI: Eerdmans, 2007.

———. "The Phoenician Inscription from Pyrgi." *JAOS* 86, no. 3 (1966): 285–97.

———. "The Semitic Background of the New Testament Kyrios-Title." In *A Wandering Aramean: Collected Aramaic Essays*. Missoula: Scholars Press, 1979.

Fletcher-Louis, Crispin. *Jesus Monotheism*. Eugene, OR: Cascade, 2015.

———. "The Revelation of the Sacral Son of Man: The Genre, History of Religions Context and the Meaning of the Transfiguration." In *Auferstehung—Resurrection*, edited by Friedrich Avemarie, 247–98. Tübingen: Mohr Siebeck, 2001.

Foner, Eric. *The Fiery Trial: Abraham Lincoln and American Slavery*. New York: W. W. Norton, 2010.

Fossum, Jarl. *The Name of God and the Angel of the Lord: Samaritan and Jewish Concepts of Intermediation and the Origin of Gnosticism*. WUNT 36. Tübingen: Mohr Siebeck, 1985. [Repr., Waco, TX: Baylor University, 2017.]

———. "The New *Religionsgeschichtliche Schule*: The Quest for Jewish Christology." In *Society of Biblical Literature 1991 Seminar Papers*, edited by E. Lovering, 638–46. SBL Seminar Paper Series 30. Atlanta: Scholars Press, 1991.

France, R. T. *The Gospel of Mark*. NIGTC. Grand Rapids, MI: Eerdmans, 2002.

Francis, James A. "Truthful Fiction: New Questions to Old Answers on Philostratus' Life of Apollonius." *American Journal of Philology* 119, no. 3 (1998): 419–41.

Fredriksen, Paula. "Mandatory Retirement: Ideas in the Study of Christians Origins Whose Time Has Come to Go." *SR* 35, no. 2 (2006): 231–46.

———. *When Christians Were Jews: The First Generation.* New Haven, CT: Yale University Press, 2018.

Frei, Hans. *The Identity of Jesus.* Philadelphia: Fortress, 1975.

Frey, Jörg. "Between Torah and Stoa: How Could Readers Have Understood the Johannine Logos?" In *The Prologue of the Gospel of John: Its Literary, Theological, and Philosophical Contexts*, edited by Jan G. van de Watt, Alan Culpepper, and Udo Schnelle, 189–234. WUNT 359. Tübingen: Mohr-Siebeck, 2016.

Frye, Northrup. *Anatomy of Criticism: Four Essays.* Princeton, NJ: Princeton University Press, 1990.

———. *The Great Code: The Bible and Literature.* New York: Harcourt, 1982.

———. *Words with Power: Being a Second Study of "The Bible and Literature."* Toronto: University of Toronto Press, 2008.

Funk, Robert F. *The Acts of Jesus: What Did Jesus Really Do?* New York: HarperCollins, 1998.

Gabba, Emilio. "True History and False History in Classical Antiquity." *JRS* 70-71 (1980–81): 50–62.

Gaine, Simon Francis. *Did the Savior See the Father? Christ, Salvation, and the Vision of God.* London: Bloomsbury T&T Clark, 2015.

———. "Is There Still a Place for Infused Knowledge in Catholic Theology and Exegesis?" *NV* 16, no. 2 (2018): 601–15.

———. "The Veracity of Prophecy and Christ's Knowledge." *New Blackfriars* 98, no. 1073 (2017): 44–62.

Garrett, Susan. *No Ordinary Angel: Celestial Spirits and Christian Claims about Jesus.* AYBRL. New Haven, CT: Yale University Press, 2008.

Garrigou-Lagrange, Reginald. "La nouvelle théologie, où va-t-elle?" *Angelicum* 23, no. 3/4 (1946): 126–45.

Gasque, W. Ward. *A History of the Criticism of the Acts of the Apostles.* Grand Rapids, MI: Eerdmans, 1975.

Gathercole, Simon. "The Critical and Dogmatic Agenda of Albert Schweitzer's *The Quest of the Historical Jesus*." *TynB* 51, no. 2 (2000): 261–83.

———. *The Preexistent Son: Recovering the Christologies of Matthew, Mark, and Luke.* Grand Rapids, MI: Eerdmans, 2006.

———. "The Titles of the Gospels in the Earliest Manuscripts." *ZNW* 104, no. 1 (2013): 33–76.

Gatier, Pierre-Louis. "Inscriptions du 1er siècle a Gérasa." *Syria* 79 (2002): 271–83.

Gatier, Pierre-Louis, et al. "Greek Inscriptions in the Jordan Museum." *ADAJ* 58 (2017): 341–50.

Gehrke, Hans-Joachim. "Die Bedeutung der (antiken) Historiographie für die Entwicklung des Geschichtsbewußtseins." In *Die antike Historiographie und die Anfänge der christlichen Geschichtsschreibung*, edited by Eve-Marie Becker, 29–52. BZNW 129. Berlin: De Gruyter, 2005.

Geldhof, Joris. *Revelation, Reason and Reality: Theological Encounters with Jaspers, Schelling, and Baader.* Leuven: Peeters, 2007.

Genette, Gerard. *Paratexts: Thresholds of Interpretation.* Cambridge: Cambridge University Press, 1997.

Georgiadou, Aristoula, and David Larmour. "Lucian and Historiography: 'De Historia Conscribenda' and 'Verae Historiae.'" In *Sprache und Literatur (einzelne Autoren seit der hadrianischen Zeit und Allgemeines zur Literatur des 2. und 3. Jahrhunderts [Forts.])*, edited by Wolfgang Haase, 1448–509. ANRW II 34.2. Berlin: Walter de Gruyter, 1993.

Gerhardsson, Birger. *Memory and Manuscript.* ASNU 22. Uppsala: Almqvist and Wikselis, 1961.

_____. *Memory and Manuscript: Oral Tradition and Written Transmission in Rabbinic Judaism and Early Christianity.* Grand Rapids, MI: Eerdmans, 1998.

_____. *The Origins of the Gospel Traditions.* Philadelphia: Fortress, 1979.

_____. *The Reliability of the Gospel Tradition.* Peabody, MA: Hendrickson, 2001.

Gers-Uphaus, Christian. "Paganer Monotheismus anhand der θεὸς ὕψιστος- und εἷς θεός-Inschriften." *Jahrbuch für Antike und Christentum* 60 (2017): 5–83.

Giambrone, Anthony. "A Note on Luke's Parable of the Minas and the Ancient Practice of Burying Coin Hoards." *NTS* 65, no. 4 (2019): 589–97.

_____. "Augustus as Censor and Luke's Worldwide Enrollment: Roman Propaganda and Lukan Theology from the Margins." *Revista Bíblica* 83, no. 3–4 (2021): 337–62.

_____. "Comments on a New Fragment of Julius Africanus: Pre-, Para-, and Post-Lukan Perspectives on the Genealogy of Jesus." In *Mélanges Étienne Nodet.* Leuven: Peeters, forthcoming.

_____. "Herod's Temple of the 'Most High God' in Jerusalem: The Sacral Architecture of Judea's Client King." In *Tempel, Synagogen, Kirchen und Moscheen: Sakralarchitektur in Palästina von der Bronzezeitbs zum Mittelalter*, edited by Jens Kamlah and Markus Witte. Abhandlungen des Deutschen Palästina-Vereins. Wiesbaden: Harrassowitz, forthcoming.

_____. "In der Exegese wie im Krieg. Bibelstudium am Ende Einer Welt: Lagrange und Denifle zu Luther." In *Bibelstudium und Predigt im Dominikanerorden: Geschichte, Ideal, Praxis*, edited by Viliam Štefan Dóci, OP, and Thomas Prügl, 307–23. Dissertationes Historicae 36. Rome: Angelicum University Press, 2019.

_____, ed. *Rethinking the Jewish War: Archeology, Society, Traditions.* EB 84. Leuven: Peeters, 2021.

_____. "Revelation in Christian Scripture." In *Oxford Handbook of Divine Revelation*, edited by Balázs Mezei, Francesca Murphy, and Kenneth Oakes, 68–84. Oxford: Oxford University, 2021.

_____. "Review of *Gospel Writing: A Canonical Perspective* by Francis Watson." *The Thomist* 82, no. 1 (2018): 133–39.

_____. "Review of John Barclay's *Paul and Gift*." *The Thomist* 82, no. 2 (2018): 287–92.

_____. *Sacramental Charity, Creditor Christology, and the Economy of Salvation in Luke's Gospel.* WUNT 439. Tübingen: Mohr Siebeck, 2017.

———. "Temple Arsons and Murder of the Prophets: Early Christian Responses to Jews and the Jewish Revolt(s)." In *Rethinking the Jewish War: Archeology, Society, Traditions*, edited by Anthony Giambrone, 249–76. ÉB 84. Leuven: Peeters, 2021.

———. "The Coins of Philip the Tetrarch and the Imperial Cult: A View from Paneas on the Fall of Sejanus." *JSJ* 52 (2021): 1–31.

———. "The Meaning of חסד חק in 4Q521: A Neglected Element in Apocalyptic Messianism." In *Mélanges Émile Puech*, edited by Jean-Sébastian Rey and Martin Staszak, 82–99. ÉB 88. Leuven: Peeters, 2021.

———. "The Prologues to Aquinas' Commentaries on the Letters of St. Paul." In *Towards a Biblical Thomism: Thomas Aquinas and the Renewal of Biblical Theology*, edited by Piotr Roszak and Jörgen Vijgen, 23–38. Pamplona: EUNSA, 2018.

Gibbon, Edward. *The Decline and Fall of the Roman Empire*. New York: Modern Library, 1995.

Gibson, Shimon. "The Pool of Bethesda in Jerusalem and Jewish Purification Practices of the Second Temple Period." *Proche-Orient Chrétien* 55, no. 3/4 (2005): 270–93.

Gieschen, Charles. *Angelomorphic Christology: Antecedents and Early Evidence*. AJEC 42. Leiden: Brill, 1998.

Gifford, Edwin Hamilton, trans. *Preparatio evangelica*. Oxford: Typographeo Academico,Giles, Kevin. *Modern Evangelicals Reinvent the Doctrine of the Trinity*. Grand Rapids, MI: Zondervan, 2006.

Gmirkin, Russel. *Plato and the Creation of the Hebrew Bible*. London: Routledge, 2017.

Godly, A. D. *Herodotus: The Persian Wars*. LCL 120. Cambridge, MA: Harvard University Press, 1920.

Golitzin, Alexander. *Et introibo as altare dei: The Mystagogy of Dionysius Areopagita with Special Reference to Its Predecessors in the Eastern Christian Tradition*. Thessalonike: George Dedousis, 1994.

Goodacre, Mark. "Scripturalization in Mark's Crucifixion Narrative." In *The Trial and Death of Jesus: Essays on the Passion Narrative in Mark*, edited by Geert Van Oyen and Tom Shepherd, 33–47. CBET 45. Leuven: Peeters, 2006.

———. *The Case against Q: Studies in Markan Priority and the Synoptic Problem*. Harrisburg, PA: Trinity, 2002.

Gottsein, Alon Goshen. "The Body as Image of God in Rabbinic Literature." *HTR* 87, no. 2 (1994): 171–95.

Goulder, Michael. *Midrash and Lection in Matthew*. London: SPCK, 1974.

Graf, F. W. *Kritik und Pseudo-Spekulation: David Friedrich Strauss als Dogmatiker im Kontext der positionellen Theologie seiner Zeit*. Münchener Monographien zur historischen und systematischen Theologie 7. Munich: Kaiser, 1982.

Graf-Reventlow, Hennig. *History of Biblical Interpretation*. Vol. 3, *Renaissance, Reformation Humanism*. Resources for Biblical Study 62. Atlanta: SBL, 2010.

Graham, Emma-Jayne. "Mobility Impairment in the Sanctuaries of Early Roman Italy." In *Disability in Antiquity*, edited by Christian Laes, 248–66. London: Routledge, 2017.

Grappe, Christian. "Du sanctuaire au jardin: Jésus, nouveau et véritable Temple dans le quatrième évangile." In *Études sur Matthieu et Jean: Mélanges offerts à Jean Zumstein pour son 65e anniversaire*, edited by Andreas Dettwiler and Uta Poplutz, 285–96. Zurich: Theologischer Verlag, 2009.

Grappin, P. "La theologie Naturelle de Reimarus." *Études Germaniques* 6 (1951): 161–81.

Grant, Robert. *Greek Apologists of the Second Century*. Philadelphia: Westminster, 1988.

Gräßer, Erich. "Die ethische Denk-Religion: Albert Schweitzers Ablehnung einer doppelten Wahrheit." In *Geschichte—Tradition—Reflexion: Frühes Christentum, Festschrift Martin Hengel*, edited by Hubert Cancik, Hermann Lichtenberger, and Peter Schäfer, 677–94. Tübingen: Mohr-Siebeck, 1996.

Graverini, Luca. "The Ass's Ears and the Novel's Voice: Orality and the Involvement of the Reader in Apulius' *Metamorphoses*." In *Seeing Tongues, Hearing Scripts: Orality and Representation in the Ancient Novel*, edited by Victoria Rimeli, 138–67. Groningen: Barhuis and Groningen University Press, 2007.

Green, Peter. *Alexander to Actium: The Historical Evolution of the Hellenistic Age*. Berkeley: University of California Press, 1990.

Gregory, Brad S. "No Room for God? History, Science, Metaphysics, and the Study of Religion." *History and Theory* 47, no. 4 (2008): 495–519.

———. *The Unintended Reformation: How a Religious Revolution Secularized Society*. Cambridge, MA: Belknap Press of Harvard University Press, 2012.

Gregory, Bradley. "Postexilic Exile in Third-Isaiah: Isaiah 61:1–3 in Light of Second Temple Hermeneutics." *JBL* 126, no. 3 (2007): 475–96.

Grube, Dirk-Martin. "The Lessing/Schumann Controversy: Lessing's Stance on Contingency Compared to Kant's Stance." In *Religions Challenged by Contingency: Theological and Philosophical Approaches to the Problem of Contingency*, edited by Dirk-Martin Grube and Peter Jonkers, 89–115. Studies in Theology and Religion 12. Leiden: Brill, 2008.

Grüll, Tibor. "'Monotheism' or 'Megatheism'? Religious Competition in Late Antiquity as Mirrored in the Inscriptions Dedicated to Theos Hypsistos." Hahn 100 konferencia. ELTE BTK. March 22, 2013. https://pte.academia.edu/TiborGrull.

Grundem, Wayne. "Biblical Evidence for the Eternal Submission of the Son to the Father." In *The New Evangelical Subordinationism: Perspectives on the Equality of God the Father and God the Son*, edited by Dennis Jowers and H. Wayne House, 223–61. Eugene, OR: Wipf and Stock, 2012.

Guardini, Romano. *Christliches Bewußtsein: Versuche über Pascal*. Mainz: Grünewald, 1991.

Haake, Gerhard. *Hans Denk, ein Vorläufer der neueren Theologie: 1495–1527*. Soltau: Norden, 1897.

Hadley, Christopher. "The Archetypal Faith of Christ." *TS* 81, no. 3 (2020): 671–92.

Haecker, Theodor. *Christentum und Kultur*. Munich: Josef Kösel, 1946.

Hamdović, David, Simon Claude Mimouni, and Louis Painchaud, eds. *La "sacerdotalisation" dans les premiers écrits mystiques juifs et chrétiens: Actes du colloque international tenu à l'Université de Lausanne du 26 au 28 octobre 2015*. Judaïsme antique et origines du christianisme 22. Turnhout: Brepols, 2021.

Hamm, Dennis. "Paul's Blindness and Its Healing: Clues to Symbolic Intent." *Bib* 71, no. 1 (1990): 63–72.

Hannah, Darrell D. *Michael and Christ: Michael Traditions and Angel Christology in Early Christianity*. WUNT II 109. Tübingen: Mohr Siebeck, 1999.

———. "The Elect Son of Man in the Parables of Enoch." In *"Who Is This Son of Man": The Latest Scholarship on a Puzzling Expression of the Historical Jesus*, edited by Larry

Hurtado and Paul Owen, 130–58. Library of New Testament Studies. New York: T&T Clark, 2011.

Hanson, R. C. P. *The Search for the Christian Doctrine of God: The Arian Controversy 318-81.* Edinburgh: T&T Clark, 1988.

Harlow, Daniel C. "Anti-Christian Polemic in the Apocalypse of Abraham: Jesus as Pseudo-Messiah in *Apoc. Ab.* 29.3–14." *JSP* 22, no. 3 (2013): 167–83.

———. "Idolatry and Alterity: Israel and the Nations in the Apocalypse of Abraham." In *The "Other" in Second Temple Judaism: Essays in Honor of John J. Collins,* edited by Daniel C. Harlow et al., 302–30. Grand Rapids, MI: Eerdmans, 2011.

Harnack, Adolf von. *History of Dogma.* 7 vols. Translated by Neil Buchanan. London: Wiliams & Norgate, 1894–99.

———. "Kritik des Neuen Testaments von einem griechischen Philosophen des. 3. Jahrhunderts." In TU 37/III.7. Leipzig: J. C. Hinrichs, 1911.

Harrington, Daniel. "A Decade of Research on Pseudo-Philo's Biblical Antiquities." *Journal for the Study of the Pseudepigrapha* 2 (1988): 3–12.

Harrington, L. Michael. *A Thirteenth-Century Textbook of Mystical Theology at the University of Paris.* Dallas Medieval Texts and Translations 4. Leuven: Peeters, 2004.

Harrison, Brian. *The Teaching of Pope Paul VI on Sacred Scripture.* Rome: Pontificium Athenaeum Sanctae Crucis, 1997.

Harrison, Peter. "'I Believe Because It Is Absurd': The Enlightenment Invention of Tertullian's *Credo. Church History* 86, no. 2 (2017): 339–64.

Harrison, Verna. "Perichoresis in the Greek Fathers." *St. Vladimir's Theological Quarterly* 35, no. 1 (1991): 53–65.

Hart, David Bentley. *Beauty of the Infinite.* Grand Rapids, MI: Eerdmans, 2003.

Hartmann, Eduard von. *Das Christentum des Neuen Testaments.* Sachsa-in-the-Harz: H. Haacke, 1905.

Hartsock, Chad. "The Call-Stories in Luke: The Use of Type Scene for Lucan Meaning." *RevExp* 112, no. 4 (2015): 573–90.

Havukainen, Tuomas. *The Quest for the Memory of Jesus: A Viable Path or a Dead End?* Contributions to Biblical Exegesis and Theology 99. Leuven: Peeters, 2020.

Hay, David. *Glory at the Right Hand: Psalm 110 in Early Christianity.* Nashville, TN: Abingdon, 1973.

Hayes, Christopher M., in collaboration with Brandon Gallagher, Julia S. Konstantinovsky, Richard J. Ounsworth, OP, and C. A. Strine, *When the Son of Man Didn't Come: A Constructive Proposal on the Delay of the Parousia.* Minneapolis: Fortress, 2016.

Hayman, Peter. "Monotheism—A Misused Word in Jewish Studies?" *JJS* 42, no. 1 (1991): 1–15.

Hays, Richard. "Review of *Jesus of Nazareth: From the Baptism in the Jordan to the Transfiguration.*" *First Things* 175 (August 2007): 49–53.

Hayward, Robert. "Phineas—The Same Is Elijah: The Origins of a Rabbinic Tradition." *JJS* 29 (1978): 22–34.

Hebblethwaite, Peter. *John XXIII: Pope of the Century.* New York: Continuum, 2000.

Hellín, Francisco Gil. *Concilii Vaticani II Synopsis in Ordinem Redigens Schemata cum Relationibus necnon Patrum Orations atque Animadversions Constitutio Dogmatica De Divina Revelatione Dei Verbum.* Rome: Libreria Editrice Vaticana, 1993.

Hendel, Ron. "The Social Origins of the Aniconic Tradition in Early Israel." *CBQ* 50, no. 3 (1988): 365–82.

Hengel, Martin. "Der Lukasprolog und seine Augenzeugen: Die Apostel, Petrus, und die Frauen." In *Studium zum Urchristentum: Kleine Schriften VI*, 242–97. WUNT 234. Tübingen: Mohr Siebeck, 2008.

———. "Die Evangelienüberschriften." In *Kleine Schriften. V. Jesus und die Evangelien*, 526–67. WUNT 211. Tübingen: Mohr Siebeck, 2007.

———. *Die johanneische Frage.* WUNT 67. Tübingen: Mohr Siebeck, 1993.

———. *Studies in Early Christology.* London: T&T Clark, 2004.

———. *The Charismatic Leader and His Followers.* Eugene, OR: Wipf and Stock, 2005.

———. *The Four Gospels and the One Gospel of Jesus Christ.* London: SCM, 2000.

———. *The Son of God: The Origin of Christology and the History of Jewish Hellenistic Religion.* Philadelphia: Fortress, 1976. [Repr., Eugene, OR: Wipf and Stock, 2017.]

———. "The Sources of Earliest Christianity." In *Acts and the History of Early Christianity.* Philadelphia: Fortress, 1979.

———. "The Titles of the Gospels and the Gospel of Mark." In *Studies in the Gospel of Mark.* Eugene, OR: Wipf and Stock, 1985.

Hennell, Charles Christian. *An Inquiry Concerning the Origin of Christianity.* London, 1838.

Herrero de Jáuregi, Miguel. "Orphic God(s): Theogonies and Hymns as Vehicles of Monotheism." In *Monotheism between Pagans and Christians in Late Antiquity*, edited by Stephen Mitchell and Peter van Nuffelen, 77–99. Leuven: Peeters, 2010.

Hock, Ronald F. *The Infancy Gospels of James and Thomas.* Scholars Bible 2. Santa Rosa, CA: Polebridge, 1995.

Holer, K. *Second Isaiah's Idol Fabrication Passages.* BET 28. Frankfurt: Peter Lang, 1995.

Holladay, Carl. "What David Saw: Messianic Exegesis in Acts 2." *Stone-Campbell Journal* 19, no. 1 (2016): 95–108.

Hollander, Harm, and Marinus de Jonge, eds. *The Testaments of the Twelve Patriarchs: A Commentary.* Studia in Veteris Testamenti pseudepigrapha 8. Leiden: Brill, 1985.

Holmén, Tom. "Caught in the Act: Jesus Starts the New Temple—A Continuum Study of Jesus as the Founder of the *Ecclesia*." In *The Identity of Jesus: Nordic Voices*, edited by Samuel Byrskog, Tom Holmén, and Matti Kankaanniemi, 181–231. WUNT II 373. Tübingen: Mohr Siebeck, 2014.

Holms, Jeremy. "Aquinas' *Lectura in Matthaeum*." In *Aquinas on Scripture: An Introduction to His Biblical Commentaries*, edited by Thomas Weinandy and Daniel Keating, 73–98. London: T&T Clark, 2005.

Holzberg, Niklas. *The Ancient Novel: An Introduction.* New York: Routledge, 1995.

Honigman, Sylvie. "Jews as the Best of All Greeks: Cultural Competition in the Literary Works of Alexandrian Judeans of the Hellenistic Period." In *Shifting Social Imaginaries in the Hellenistic Period: Narrations, Practices, and Images*, edited by Eftychia Stravrianopoulou, 207–32. Leiden: Brill, 2013.

Hooker, Morna. "On Using the Wrong Tool." *Theology* 75, no. 629 (1972): 570–81.

———. *The Son of Man in Mark: A Study of the Background of the Term "Son of Man" and Its Use in St. Mark's Gospel.* London: SPCK, 1967.

Horst, Ulrich. *The Dominicans and the Pope: Papal Teaching Authority in the Medieval and Early Modern Thomist Tradition.* ND Conway Lectures in Medieval Studies. Notre Dame, IN: University of Notre Dame Press, 2006.

Hoskins, Paul. *Jesus as the Fulfillment of the Temple in the Gospel of John.* Paternoster Biblical Monographs. Eugene, OR: Wipf and Stock, 2006.

Hovhanessian, Vahan, ed. *Exegesis and Hermeneutics in the Churches of the East.* Atlanta: SBL 2009.

Hubbard, Robert L. *The Book of Ruth.* NICOT. Grand Rapids, MI: Eerdmans, 1988.

Hurtado, Larry. *Ancient Jewish Monotheism and Early Christian Jesus-Devotion: The Context and Character of Christological Faith.* Waco, TX: Baylor University, 2017.

———. "'Ancient Jewish Monotheism' in the Hellenistic and Roman Periods." *JAJ* 4, no. 3 (2013): 379–400.

———. *At the Origins of Christian Worship: The Context and Character of Earliest Christian Devotion.* Grand Rapids, MI: Eerdmans, 1999.

———. *God in New Testament Theology.* Library of Biblical Theology. Nashville, TN: Abingdon, 2010.

———. *How on Earth Did Jesus Become God? Historical Questions about Earliest Devotion to Jesus.* Grand Rapids, MI: Eerdmans, 2005.

———. *Lord Jesus Christ: Devotion to Jesus in Earliest Christianity.* Grand Rapids, MI: Eerdmans, 2003.

———. "New Testament Christology: A Critique of Bousset's Influence." *TS* 40, no. 2 (1979): 306–17.

———. "Observations on the 'Monotheism' Affirmed in the New Testament." In *The Bible and Early Trinitarian Theology,* edited by Christopher A. Beeley and Mark Weedman, 50–70. CUA Studies in Early Christianity. Washington, DC: The Catholic University of America Press, 2018.

———. *One God, One Lord: Early Christian Devotion and Ancient Jewish Monotheism.* Philadelphia: Fortress, 1988. [Rev. 3rd ed., London: T&T Clark, 2015.]

———. "The Study of New Testament Christology: Notes for the Agenda." In *Society of Biblical Literature 1981 Seminar Papers,* 185–97. SBL Seminar Paper Series 20. Chico, CA: Scholars Press, 1981.

Hurtado, Larry, and Paul Owen, eds. *"Who Is This Son of Man?" The Latest Scholarship on a Puzzling Expression of the Historical Jesus.* Library of New Testament Studies. New York: T&T Clark, 2011.

Ivánka, Endre V. *Plato Christianus: Übernahme und Umgestaltung des Platonismus durch die Väter.* Einsiedeln: Johannes, 1990.

Jacoby, Felix, Guido Schepens, and Jan Radike, eds. *Die Fragmente der griechischen Historiker: Continued, Biography and Antiquarian Literature.* Leiden: Brill, 1999.

Jahn, Gustav. *Über die Person Jesu und über die Entstehung des Christentums.* Leiden: Brill, 1911.

James, John. "An Examination of Homotimia in St. Basil the Great's *On the Holy Spirit,* and Contemporary Implications." *Westminster Theological Journal* 74, no. 2 (2012): 257–77.

Janowitz, Naomi. "Good Jews Don't: Historical and Philosophical Constructions of Idolatry." *History of Religions* 47, no. 2 (2007): 239–52.

Jensen, Robert. *The Triune Identity*. Philadelphia: Fortress, 1982.

Jeremias, Joachim. *Jerusalem in the Time of Jesus*. Minneapolis: Fortress, 1969.

_____. "Kennzeichen der ipsissima vox Jesu." In *Abba: Studien zur neutestamentlichen Theologie und Zeitgeschichte*, 142–52. Göttingen: Vandenhoeck & Ruprecht, 1966.

Jervell, Jacob. *The Unknown Paul: Essays on Luke-Acts and Early Christian History*. Minneapolis: Fortress, 1984.

Johnson, Keith. *Karl Barth and the Analogia Entis*. New York: T&T Clark, 2010.

Johnson, Luke Timothy. "Review of *Jesus of Nazareth: From the Baptism in the Jordan to the Transfiguration*." *Modern Theology* 24, no. 2 (2008): 318–20.

Johnson, Norman B. *Prayer in the Apocrypha and Pseduepigrapha: A Study of the Concept of God*. SBLMS 2. Philadelphia: SBL, 1948.

Jones, Christopher. *Philostratus: Apollonius of Tyana, Books I–IV*. LCL 16. Cambridge, MA: Harvard University Press, 2005.

Jonge, Marinus de. *Jewish Eschatology, Early Christian Christology, and the Testaments of the Twelve Patriarchs: Collected Essays*. NovTSup 63. Leiden: Brill, 1991.

_____. *The Testaments of the Twelve Patriarchs: A Critical Edition of the Greek Text*. Pseudepigrapha Veteris Testamenti Graece 1/2. Leiden: Brill, 1978.

Judge, Thomas A. *Other Gods and Idols: The Relationship between the Worship of Other Gods and the Worship of Idols within the Old Testament*. LHBOTS 674. London: Bloomsbury T&T Clark, 2019.

Juel, Donald. *Messianic Exegesis: Christological Interpretation of the Old Testament in Early Christianity*. Philadelphia: Fortress, 1988.

Jung, Chang-Wook. *The Original Language of the Lukan Infancy Narrative*. LNTS 267. London: T&T Clark, 2004.

Kaiser, Robert Blair. *Clerical Error: A True Story*. New York: Continuum, 2002.

Käsemann, Ernst. "Über die Anfänge christlicher Theologie." *ZThK* 57, no. 2 (1960): 162–85.

Kautsky, Karl. *Der Ursprung des Christentums*. Stuttgart, 1908.

Keener, Craig S. *Christobiography: Memory, History, and the Reliability of the Gospels*. Grand Rapids, MI: Eerdmans, 2019.

_____. *The Gospel of John: A Commentary*. Hendrickson: Peabody, 2003.

Keith, Chris. "Memory and Authenticity: Jesus Tradition and What Really Happened." *ZNW* 102, no. 2 (2011): 155–77.

Keith, Chris, and Anthony Le Donne, eds. *Jesus and the Demise of Authenticity*. New York: T&T Clark, 2012.

Kelley, Nicole. "The Cosmopolitan Expression of Josephus' Prophetic Perspective in the *Jewish War*." *HTR* 97, no. 3 (2004): 257–74.

Kelly, J. N. D. *Early Christian Doctrines*. New York: Harper & Row, 1958.

Kemezis, Adam. "Lucian, Fronto, and the Absence of Contemporary Historiography under the Antonines." *American Journal of Philology* 131, no. 2 (2010): 285–325.

Kennedy, George. *New Testament Interpretation through Rhetorical Criticism*. Chapel Hill: University of North Carolina Press, 1984.

Kenney, J. P. "Monotheistic and Polytheistic Elements in Classical Mediterranean Spirituality." In *Classical Mediterranean Spirituality*, edited by A. H. Armstrong, 269-92. New York: Crossroad, 1986.

Kerr, Alan. *The Temple of Jesus' Body: The Temple Theme in the Gospel of John*. JSNTSup 220. London: Sheffield Academic, 2002.

Kierkegaard, Soren. *Post-Scriptum définitif et non scientifique aux miettes philosophiques*. Vol. 1. Œuvres complètes de Soren Kierkegaard 10. Paris: Éditions de l'Orante, 1977.

Kirk, Alan. *Memory and the Jesus Tradition*. London: Bloomsbury T&T Clark, 2018.

Kirk, Daniel. *A Man Attested by God: The Human Jesus of the Synoptic Gospels*. Grand Rapids, MI: Eerdmans, 2016.

Kister, Menahem. "Some Early Jewish and Christian Exegetical Problems and the Dynamics of Monotheism." *Journal for the Study of Judaism in the Persian, Hellenistic and Roman Period* 37, no. 4 (2006): 548-93.

―――. "The Prayers of the Seventh Book of the *Apostolic Constitutions* and Their Implications for the Formulation of Synagogue Prayers." *Tarbiz* 77, no. 2 (2008): 205-38.

Klawans, Jonathan. *Purity, Sacrifice, and the Temple: Symbolism and Supercessionism in the Study of Ancient Judaism*. Oxford: Oxford University, 2006.

Klink, Edward, III, ed. *The Audience of the Gospels: The Origin and Function of the Gospels in Earliest Christianity*. Library of New Testament Studies 353. London: T&T Clark, 2010.

Knohl, Israel. *The Messiah before Jesus: The Suffering Servant of the Dead Sea Scrolls*. Berkeley: University of California Press, 2000.

Koch, Hugo. "Proklos als Quelle des Pseudo-Dionysius Areopagita in der Lehre von Bösen." *Philologus* 54 (1895): 438-54.

Koester, Helmut. *Ancient Christian Gospels: Their History and Development*. Philadelphia: Trinity, 1990.

―――. "The Impact of Walter Bauer's *Rechtglaubigkeit und Ketzerei im ältesten Christentum*." Address to the SBL Conference, November 15-17, 2012. http://ccat.sas.upenn.edu/psco/year50/text/koester-bauer.pdf.

Kollmann, Bernd, and Ruben Zimmermann, eds. *Hermeneutik der frühchristlichen Wundererzählungen*. WUNT 339. Tübingen: Mohr Siebeck, 2014.

Kooten, George H. van. "Pagan and Jewish Monotheism According to Varro, Plutarch, and St. Paul: The Aniconic, Monotheistic Beginnings of Rome's Pagan Cult—Romans 1:19-25 in a Roman Context." In *Flores Florentino: Dead Sea Scrolls and Other Early Jewish Studies in Honour of Florentino García Martínez*, edited by Anthony Hillhorst, 633-51. JSJSup 122. Leiden: Brill, 2007.

Koskenniemi, Erkki. "The God of the Philosophers, and the God of Israel." In *Philo of Alexandria and Greek Myth*, edited by Francesca Allese and Ludovica De Luca, 129-52. Studies in Philo of Alexandria 10. Leiden: Brill, 2019.

Köstenberger, Andreas, and Michael Kruger. *The Heresy of Orthodoxy: How Contemporary's Culture's Fascination with Diversity Has Reshaped Our Understanding of Early Christianity*. Wheaton, IL: Crossway, 2010.

Kraft, Robert. "Christian Transmission of Greek Jewish Scriptures: A Methodological Probe." In *Paganisme, Judaïsme, Christianisme: Influences et affrontements dans le monde antique*, edited by A. Benoit, M. Philonenko, and C. Vogel, 207–26. Paris: Éditions E. de Boccard, 1978.

———. "The Pseudepigraph and Christianity Revisited: Setting the Stage and Framing Some Central Questions." *JSJ* 32 (2001): 371–95Kraus, Hans-Joachim. *Psalms 60–150*. Continental Commentary. Minneapolis: Fortress, 1993.

Kugel, James. "Levi's Elevation to the Priesthood in Second Temple Writings." *HTR* 86, no. 1 (1993): 1–64.

———. *The God of Old: Inside the Lost World of the Bible*. New York: Free Press, 2003.

Kugler, Robert. *From Patriarch to Priest: The Levi-Priestly Tradition from Aramaic Levi to Testament of Levi*. Early Judaism and Its Literature 9. Atlanta: Scholars Press, 1996.

———. *The Testaments of the Twelve Patriarchs*. Sheffield: Sheffield Academic, 2001.

———. "The *Testaments of the Twelve Patriarchs*: A Not-So-Ambiguous Witness to Early Jewish Interpretative Practices." In *A Companion to Biblical Interpretation in Early Judaism*, edited by Matthias Henze, 337–60. Grand Rapids, MI: Eerdmans, 2012.

Lachmann, Karl, and Franz Muncker, eds. *Gotthold Ephraim Lessings Sämtliche Schriften*. Vol. 13. Stuttgart: Göschen'sche, 1964.

———. *Gotthold Ephraim Lessings Sämtliche Schriften*. Vol. 18. Leipzig: G. J. Göschen'sche 1904.

Lagrange, Marie-Joseph. *La méthod historique*. Paris: Lecoffre, 1903.

———. *L'Évangile de Jesus Christ*. Paris: Gabalda, 1928.

———. *Le messianisme chez les Juifs*. Paris: Gabalda, 1909.

———. *Le sens du christianisme d'après l'exégèse allemande*. Études bibliques 5. Paris: Gabalda, 1918.

———. "Melanges: La Vie de Jésus de Renan." *RB* 27 (1918): 433–506.

Lambert, Wilfred. "The Historical Development of the Mesopotamian Pantheon: A Study in Sophisticated Polytheism." In *Unity and Diversity*, edited by Hans Goedidcke and J. J. M. Roberts, 191–200. Baltimore: Johns Hopkins University Press, 1975.

Lanckau, Jörg. "*Hypsistos*: Cultural Translation of Jewish Monotheism in the Hellenistic Period." *Asiastische Studien/Etudes asiatiques* 65, no. 4 (2011): 861–82.

Landmesser, Christof, ed. *Bultmann Handbuch*. Tübingen: Mohr Siebeck, 2017.

Lane, W. L. *The Gospel of Mark*. NICNT. Grand Rapids, MI: Eerdmans, 1974.

Lang, Mabel. *Cure and Cult in Ancient Corinth: A Guide to the Asclepieion*. Princeton, NJ: American School of Classical Studies at Athens, 1977.

Latourelle, René. *Theology of Revelation*. New York: Alba House, 1987.

Lawler, Michael. "Perichoresis: New Theological Wine in an Old Theological Wineskin." *Horizons* 22, no. 1 (1995): 49–66.

Lear, Sheree. *Scribal Composition: Malachi as a Test Case*. FRLANT 270. Göttingen: Vandenhoeck & Ruprecht, 2018.

Le Donne, Anthony. *The Historiographical Jesus: Memory, Typology, and the Son of David*. Waco, TX: Baylor University Press, 2009.

Lee, Aquila H. I. *From Messiah to Preexistent Son: Jesus' Self-Consciousness and Early Christian Exegesis of Messianic Psalms*. WUNT II 192. Tübingen: Mohr Siebeck, 2005.

Lee, Richard A., Jr., and Christopher Long. "Nous and Logos in Aristotle." *Freiburger Zeitschrift für Philosophie und Theologie* 54, no. 3 (2007): 348–67.
Legaspi, Michael C. *The Death of Scripture and the Rise of Biblical Studies*. Oxford Studies in Historical Theology. Oxford: Oxford University Press, 2010.
Lehtipuu, Outi. *Debates over the Resurrection of the Dead: Constructing Early Christian Identity*. Oxford Early Christian Studies. Oxford: Oxford University Press, 2015.
Lehner, Ulrich. *The Catholic Enlightenment: The Forgotten History of a Global Movement*. Oxford: Oxford University Press, 2016.
Leim, Joshua. *Matthew's Theological Grammar: The Father and the Son*. WUNT II 402. Tübingen: Mohr Siebeck, 2015.
Lemaire, André. "Review of *God in Translation: Deities in Cross-Cultural Discourse in the Biblical World* by Mark Smith." *Bib* 93, no. 2 (2012): 316.
Lessing, G. E. *Die Erziehung des Menschengeschlechts und andere Schriften*. Stuttgart: Reclam, 1965.
———. *Gotthold Ephraim Lessings Sämtliche Schriften*. Vol. 13. Edited by Karl Lachmann and Franz Muncker. Stuttgart: Göschen'sche, 1964.
———. *Gotthold Ephraim Lessings Sämtliche Schriften*. Vol. 18. Edited by Karl Lachmann and Franz Muncker. Leipzig: G. J. Göschen'sche 1904.
———. "Über den Beweis des Geistes und der Kraft." In *Gesammelte Werke VIII*, ed. Paul Rilla. Berlin: Aufbau, 1956.
Leuchter, Mark. "Samuel: A Prophet or a Priest Like Moses?" In *Israelite Prophecy and the Deuteronomistic History: Portrait, Reality, and the Formation of a History*, edited by Mignon R. Jacobs and Raymond F. Person Jr., 147–68. Ancient Israel and Its Literature 14. Atlanta: SBL, 2013.
Levenson, Jon. *Death and Resurrection of the Beloved Son: The Transformation of Child Sacrifice in Judaism and Christianity*. New Haven, CT: Yale University Press, 1993.
Levering, Matthew. *Participatory Biblical Exegesis: A Theology of Biblical Interpretation*. Reading the Scriptures. Notre Dame, IN: University of Notre Dame Press, 2008.
Levtow, Nathaniel B. *Images of Others: Iconic Politics in Ancient Israel*. BJSUCSD 11. Winona Lake: Eisenbrauns, 2008.
Levy, Hans Yohanan. *Chaldean Oracles and Theurgy: Mysticism, Magic, and Platonism in the Later Roman Empire*. Paris: Institut d'Études augustiniennes, 2001.
Lewis, C. S. "Letter to Arthur Greeves, Oct. 18, 1931." In *The Collected Letters of C. S. Lewis*. Vol. 1, *Family Letter 1905–1931*. San Francisco: HarperCollins, 2004.
———. "Myth Became Fact." In *God in the Dock: Essays on Theology and Ethics*. Grand Rapids, MI: Eerdmans, 1970.
Licona, Michael. *The Resurrection of Jesus: A New Historiographical Approach*. Downers Grove, IL: IVP Academic, 2010.
LiDonnici, Lynn R. *The Epidaurian Miracle Inscriptions: Text, Translation and Commentary*. Texts and Translations Greco-Roman Religion Series 11. Atlanta: Scholars Press, 1995.
Lienhard, Joseph T. "Reading the Bible and Learning to Read: The Influence of Education on St. Augustine's Exegesis." *Augustinian Studies* 27, no. 1 (1996): 7–25.

Lincoln, Andrew. *Born of a Virgin? Reconceiving Jesus in the Bible, Tradition, and Theology.* Grand Rapids, MI: Eerdmans, 2013.

Lohse, Eduard. "Jesu Worte über den Sabbat." In *Judentum, Urchristentum, Kirche*, edited by Walther Eltester, 79–89. BZNW 26. Berlin: Töpelmann, 1960.

Lowrie, Walter. "Translator's Introduction." In *The Mystery of the Kingdom of God: The Secret of Jesus' Messiahship and Passion.* London: A. & C. Black, 1914.

Lüdemann, Gerd. *Virgin Birth? The Real Story of Mary and Her Son Jesus.* London: Bloomsbury, 1998

Lundsteen, A. C. *Hermann Samuel Reimarus und die Anfänge der Leben-Jesu-Forschung.* Copenhagen: O. C. Olsen, 1939.

Lyman, J. Rebecca. *Christology and Cosmology: Models of Divine Activity in Origen, Eusebius, and Athanasius.* Oxford: Clarendon, 1993.

Lynch, Matthew. *Monotheism and Institutions in the Book of Chronicles: Temple, Priesthood, and Kingship in Post-Exilic Perspective.* FAT II 64. Tübingen: Mohr Siebeck, 2014.

MacDonald, Dennis R. *Does the New Testament Imitate Homer? Four Cases from the Acts of the Apostles.* New Haven, CT: Yale University Press, 2003.

_____. *The Homeric Epics and the Gospel of Mark.* New Haven, CT: Yale University Press, 2000.

MacDonald, Nathan. *One God or One Lord? Deuteronomy and the Meaning of "Monotheism."* FAT II 1. Tübingen: Mohr Siebeck, 2012.

MacMullen, Ramsay. "The Epigraphic Habit in the Roman Empire." *American Journal of Philology* 103, no. 3 (1982): 233–46.

Madigan, Kevin. "*Christus Nesciens*? Was Christ Ignorant of the Day of Judgment? Arian and Orthodox Interpretations of Mark 13:32 in the Ancient Latin West." *HTR* 96, no. 3 (2003): 255–78.

Magness, Jodi. "Sweet Memory: Archeological Evidence of Jesus in Jerusalem." In *Memory in Ancient Rome and Early Christianity*, edited by Karl Galinsky, 324–43. Oxford: Oxford University Press, 2016.

Mainoldi, Ernesto Sergio. "Why Dionysius the Areopagite? The Invention of the First Father." In *Studia Patristica*, vol. XCVI, edited by Markus Vinzent, 425–40. Leuven: Peeters, 2017.

Malchow, B. "The Messenger of the Covenant in Mal. 3:1." *JBL* 103 (1984): 252–55.

Malina, Bruce, and Jerome Neyrey. *The New Testament World: Insights from Cultural Anthropology.* Louisville, KY: Westminster, 1993.

Marchetto, Agostino. *Il Concilio Ecumenico Vaticano II: Contrapunto per la sua storia.* Vatican City: Libreria Editrice Vaticana, 2005.

_____. *Il Concilio Ecumenico Vaticano II: Per la sua corretta ermeneutica.* Vatican City: Libreria Editrice Vaticana, 2012.

Marcus, Joel. *John the Baptist in History and Theology.* Columbia: University of South Carolina, 2018.

_____. *Mark 8–16.* AB 27A. New Haven, CT: Yale University Press, 2009.

_____. "Son of Man as Son of Adam." *RB* 110, nos. 1 and 3 (2003): 38–61 and 370–86.

Margelidon, Philippe-Marie. "La science infuse du Christ selon saint Thomas." *Revue Thomiste* 114, no. 3 (2014): 379–416.

Marguerat, Daniel. *The First Christian Historian: Writing the "Acts of the Apostles."* SNTS 121. New York: Cambridge University Press, 2002.

Marincola, John. *Authority and Tradition in Ancient Historiography.* Cambridge: Cambridge University Press, 1997.

Maritain, Jacques. *On the Grace and Humanity of Jesus.* New York: Herder, 1969.

Martin, Francis. "Some Aspects of Biblical Studies since Vatican II: The Contribution and Challenge of *Dei Verbum*." In *Sacred Scripture: Disclosure of the Word,* 227–48. Ave Maria, FL: Sapientia Press, 2006.

Mason, Rex A. "The Prophets of Restoration." In *Israel's Prophetic Tradition: Essays in Honour of Peter R. Ackroyd,* edited by Richard Coggins, Anthony Philips, and Michael Knibb, 155–80. Cambridge: Cambridge University Press, 1982.

Massaux, Édouard. *Influence de l'Évangile de Saint Matthieu sur la littérature chrétienne avant saint Irénée.* Louvain: Presses universitaires de Louvain, 1950.

Maximus. *Opuscules théologiques et polemiques.* Traduction par Emmanuel Ponsoye. Paris: Cerf, 1998.

May, Gerhard. *Creatio ex Nihilo: The Doctrine of "Creation Out of Nothing" in Early Christian Thought.* New York: T&T Clark, 2004.

McCullough, Ross. "God and the Gaps." *First Things* 232 (April 2013): 19–20.

McIver, Robert. *Memory, Jesus, and the Synoptic Gospels.* SBLRBS 59. Atlanta: SBL, 2011.

McKim, Donald, ed. *Dictionary of Major Biblical Interpreters.* Downers Grove, IL: InterVarsity, 2007.

Meier, John P. *A Marginal Jew: Rethinking the Historical Jesus.* 5 vols. ABRL. New York/New Haven, CT: Doubleday/Yale University Press, 1991–2016.

Menzies, Robert. *The Development of Early Christian Pneumatology with Special Reference to Luke-Acts.* JSNTSup 54. Sheffield: Sheffield Academic, 1991.

Metzger, Marcel, ed. *Les constitutions apostoliques: Tome III: Livres VII et VIII.* SC 336. Paris: Cerf, 1987.

Meyer, Ben F. *The Aims of Jesus.* Princeton Theological Monograph Series 48. Eugene, OR: Pickwick, 2002.

Meyer, Marvin, ed. *The Nag Hammadi Scriptures.* New York: HarperCollins, 2008.

Meyer, Paul. "The Problem of the Messianic Self-Consciousness of Jesus." *NovT* 4, no. 2 (1960): 122–38.

Michalson, G. E., Jr. "Lessing, Kierkegaard, and the 'Ugly Ditch': A Reexamination." *Journal of Religion* 59, no. 3 (1979): 324–34.

Milgrom, Jacob. *Leviticus 1-16.* AB 3. New York: Doubleday, 1991.

Miller, Athanaius. "Das neue biblische Handbuch." *Benediktinische Monatschrift* 31 (1955): 49–50.

Miller, Eric. "The *Self-Glorification Hymn* Reexamined." *Henoch* 31, no. 2 (2009): 307–24.

Miller, Richard. "Mark's Empty Tomb and Other Translation Fables in Classical Antiquity." *JBL* 129, no. 4 (2010): 759–76.

Mirhady, David. "Athens' Democratic Witnesses." *Phoenix* 56, no. 3/4 (2002): 255–74.

Mitchell, Stephen. "Further Thoughts on the Cult of Theos Hypsistos." In *One God: Pagan Monotheism in the Roman Empire,* edited by Stephen Mitchell and Peter van Nuffelen, 167–208. Cambridge: Cambridge University Press, 2010.

———. "The Cult of Theos Hypsistos between Pagans, Jews, and Christians." In *Pagan Monotheism in Late Antiquity*, edited by Polymnia Athanassiadi and Michael Frede, 81–148. Oxford: Clarendon, 2008.

Moessner, David. "'Eyewitnesses,' 'Informed Contemporaries,' and 'Unknowing Inquirers': Josephus' Criteria for Authentic Historiography and the Meaning of ΠΑΡΑΚΟΛΟΥΘΕΩ." *NovT* 38, no. 2 (1996): 105–22.

Möhler, Johann Adam. *Die Einheit in der Kirche, oder das Prinzip des Katholizismus*. Köln: Hegner, 1956.

Moltmann, Jürgen. *A Broad Place: An Autobiography*. Minneapolis: Fortress, 2008.

———. *Ethics of Hope*. Translated by Margaret Kohl. Minneapolis: Fortress, 2012.

———. "God in the World—The World in God: Perichoresis in Trinity and Eschatology." In *John's Gospel and Christian Theology*, edited by Richard Bauckham and Carl Mosser, 369–81. Grand Rapids, MI: Eerdmans, 2008.

———. *The Future of Creation*. London: SCM, 1979.

———. *Theology of Hope: On the Ground and Implications of a Christian Eschatology*. Translated by James W. Leitch. Minneapolis: Fortress, 1993. [Original German publication of this work in 1964; original English translation in 1967.]

———. *The Way of Jesus Christ: Christology in Messianic Dimensions*. Minneapolis: Fortress, 1993.

———. *The Crucified God*. 40th anniversary ed. Minneapolis: Fortress, 2015.

Momigliano, Arnaldo. *The Development of Greek Biography*. Cambridge, MA: Harvard University Press, 1971.

Morgenthaler, Robert. *Die lukanische Geschichtsschreibung als Zeugnis: Gestalt und Gehalt der Kunst des Lukas*. Zürich: Zwingli Verlag, 1948.

Moxnes, Halvor. *Jesus and the Rise of Nationalism: A New Quest for the Nineteenth-Century Historical Jesus*. London: I. B. Tauris, 2012.

Muller, Richard. *Post-Reformation Reformed Dogmatics: The Rise and Development of Reformed Orthodoxy, ca. 1520–1725*. Grand Rapids, MI: Baker Academic, 2003.

Murdock, D. M. *Christ in Egypt: The Jesus-Horus Connection*. Stellar House, 2008.

Murgatroyd, Paul. "Tacitus on the Death of Octavia." *Greece & Rome* 55 (2008): 263–73.

Murphy, Dennis J. *The Church and the Bible: Official Documents of the Catholic Church*. New Delhi: St. Paul's/Alba House, 2007.

Murphy, Francesca Aran. *God Is Not a Story: Realism Revisited*. Oxford: Oxford University Press, 2007.

Murray, Evan D., Miles G. Cunningham, and Bruce H. Price. "The Role of Psychotic Disorders in Religious History Considered." *Journal of Neuropsychiatry Clinical Neurosceinces* 24, no. 4 (2012): 410–26.

Nagel, Thomas. *Mind and Cosmos: Why the Materialist, Neo-Darwinian Conception of Nature Is Almost Certainly False*. Oxford: Oxford University Press, 2012.

Nenci, Giuseppe. "Il motivo dell'autopsia nella storagraphia greca." *Studi Classici e Orientali* 3 (1955): 14–29.

Newman, Carey. *Paul's Glory-Christology: Tradition and Rhetoric*. NovTSup 69. Leiden: Brill, 1992.

———, ed. *The Jewish Roots of Christological Monotheism*. JSJSup 63. Leiden: Brill, 1999.

Newman, John Henry. *An Essay in Aid of a Grammar of Assent.* London: Longmans, Green, 1947.

———. *Apologia Pro Vita Sua.* New York: Norton, 1968.

———. *Letters and Diaries.* Vol 24. Edited by C. S. Dessain. Oxford: Clarendon, 1973.

———. "Text of Scripture Not a Sufficient Protection to the Revealed Dogma." In *Arians of the Fourth Century*, edited by Rowan Williams, 143–50. Notre Dame, IN: University of Notre Dame Press, 2001.

———. *Two Essays on Biblical and on Ecclesiastical Miracles.* Works of Cardinal John Henry Newman VIII. Notre Dame, IN: Notre Dame University Press, 2010.

Newsome, Carol. *Songs of Sabbath Sacrifice: A Critical Edition.* HHS 27. Atlanta: Scholars Press, 1985.

Nicklas, Tobias, and Janet E. Spittler, eds. *Credible, Incredible.* WUNT 321. Tübingen: Mohr Siebeck, 2013.

Niehof, Maran. *Jewish Exegesis and Homeric Scholarship in Alexandria.* Cambridge: Cambridge University, 2014.

Niesiolowski-Spanò, Lukasz. "Primeval History in the Persian Period?" *SJOT* 21, no. 8 (2007): 106–26.

Nineham, Dennis. "Foreword." In Albert Schweitzer, *Quest of the Historical Jesus*, edited by John Bowden, xiii–xxxii. Minneapolis: Fortress, 2001.

Nisbit, Hugh Bar. *Gotthold Ephraim Lessing: His Life, Works, and Thought.* Oxford: Oxford University Press, 2008.

Norden, Eduard. *Agnostos Theos: Untersuchung zur Formgeschichte religiöser Rede.* Helsingfors: B.G. Teubner, 1913.

Novenson, Matthew. *Christ among the Messiahs: Christ Language in Paul and Messiah Language in Ancient Judaism.* Oxford: Oxford University, 2012.

Obikonu Igbokwe, Anthony. *Albert Schweitzer's Thoroughgoing De-eschatologization Project as a Secular Soteriology.* Münster: Aschendorff, 2019.

O'Brien, Carl Séan. *The Demiurge in Ancient Thought: Secondary God and Divine Mediators.* Cambridge: Cambridge University Press, 2015.

O'Brien, Julia M. *Priest and Levite in Malachi.* Atlanta: Scholars Press, 1990.

O'Connor, Flannery. *Wise Blood: A Novel.* New York: Farrer, Straus, and Giroux, 1949. [Repr., 2007.]

O'Connor, Michael. *Cajetan's Biblical Commentaries: Motive and Method.* St. Andrew's Studies in Reformation History. Leiden: Brill, 2017.

Oden, Thomas. *Change of Heart: A Personal and Theological Memoir.* Downers Grove, IL: IVP Academic, 2014.

———. *Radical Obedience: The Ethics of Rudolph Bultmann, with a Personal Response from Rudolph Bultmann.* Philadelphia: Westminster, 1964.

Oermann, Nils Ole. *Albert Schweitzer: A Biography.* Oxford: Oxford University Press, 2017.

Orchard, Bernard. "*Dei Verbum* and the Synoptic Gospels." *This Rock* 7, no. 5 (May 1996).

O'Regan, Cyril. *The Heterodox Hegel.* Albany: State University of New York, 1994.

———. *Theology and the Spaces of Apocalyptic.* Père Marquette Lecture in Theology. Milwaukee: Marquette University, 2009.

Orlav, Andrei A. *Heavenly Priesthood in the Apocalypse of Abraham.* Cambridge: Cambridge University Press, 2013.

Orlin, Eric. "Augustan Reconstruction and Roman Memory." In *Memory in Ancient Rome and Early Christianity*, edited by Karl Galinsky, 115–44. Oxford: Oxford University Press, 2016.

Orlov, Andrei A. *Heavenly Priesthood in the Apocalypse of Abraham.* Cambridge: Cambridge University, 2013.

──────. "'The Gods of My Father Terah': Abraham the Iconoclast and the Polemics with the Divine Body Traditions in the Apocalypse of Abraham." *JSP* 18, no. 1 (2008): 33–53.

Orpana, Jessi. "Awareness of Nudity in Jubilees 3: Adam Portrayed as a Priest in the Garden." In *Crossing Imaginary Boundaries: The Dead Sea Scrolls in the Context of Second Temple Judaism*, edited by Mika S. Pajunen and Hanna Tervanotko, 241–58. Publications of the Finnish Exegetical Society 108. Helsinki: Finnish Exegetical Society, 2015.

Padget, James Carleton. "Schweitzer and Harnack: An Unlikely Alliance." *Zeitschrift für Kirchengeschichte* 122, no. 2/3 (2011): 257–87.

Painter, John. "Bultmann, Archaeology, and the Historical Jesus." In *Jesus and Archeology*, edited by James Charlesworth, 619–38. Grand Rapids, MI: Eerdmans, 2006.

Paley, William. *On the Evidence of Christianity: A New Edition.* London: W. Clowes & Sons, 1851.

Park, Aaron Pyungchoon. "The Christian Hope According to Bultmann, Pannenberg, and Moltmann." *Westminster Theological Journal* 22, no. 2 (1971): 153–74.

Parker, Robert. *Greek Gods Abroad: Names, Natures, and Transformations.* Sather Classical Lectures. Berkeley: University of California Press, 2017.

Paterson, Lee. "Geographers as Mythographers: The Case of Strabo." In *Writing Myth: Mythography in the Ancient World*, edited by Stephen Trzaskoma and R. Scott Smith, 201–22. Leuven: Peeters, 2013.

Peabody, David, Lamar Colpe, and Allan McNicol, eds. *One Gospel from Two: Mark's Use of Matthew and Luke.* Harrisburg, PA: Trinity, 2002.

Pearson, Lionel. *The Lost Histories of Alexander the Great.* New York: American Philological Association, 1960.

Pelling, Christopher. *Literary Texts and the Greek Historian.* New York: Routledge, 2000.

Pena, Joabson Xavier. "Wearing the Cosmos: The High Priestly Attire in Josephus' *Judean Antiquities*." *JSJ* 52 (2021): 21–24.

Perczel, István. "The Christology of Pseudo-Dionysius the Areopagite: The Fourth Letter in Its Indirect and Direct Traditions." *Le Muséon* 117 (2004): 409–46.

Perrin, Nicolas. *Jesus the Priest.* Grand Rapids, MI: Baker Academic, 2018.

Perrin, Norman. *The Kingdom of God in the Teaching of Jesus.* Philadelphia: Westminster, 1963.

Pervo, Richard. *Profit with Delight: The Literary Genre of the Acts of the Apostles.* Philadelphia: Fortress, 1987.

Pesce, Mauro. "Per una ricerca storica su Gesù nei secoli XVI–XVIII: Prima di H.S. Reimarus." *ASE* 28, no. 1 (2011): 433–64.

Peterson, Erik. *Ekklesia: Studien zum altchristlichen Kirchenbegriff*. Edited by Barbara Nichtweiß and Hans-Ulrich Weidemann. Ausgewählte Schriften, Sonderband. Würzburg: Echter Verlag, 201Pfleiderer, Otto. *Das Urchristentum, seine Schriften und Lehren in geschichtlichem Zusammenhang beschreiben*. Berlin, 1902.

Pieper, Joseph. *Muße und Kult*. Munich: Hegner, 1948.

Pietersma, Albert. "Kyrios or Tetragram: A New Quest for the Original Septuagint." In *A Question of Methodology: Albert Pietersma Collected Essays on the Septuagint*, edited by Cameron Body-Taylor, 25–40. Leuven: Peeters, 2013.

Pirenne-Delforge, Vinciane. *Le polythéisme comme objet d'histoire: Leçons inaugurales du Collège de France*. Paris: Fayard, 2019.

Pirenne-Delforge, Vinciane, and Gabriella Pironti. "Many vs. One." In *The Oxford Handbook of Ancient Greek Religion*, edited by Esther Eidinow and Julia Kindt, 39–50. Oxford: Oxford University Press, 2015.

Pirenne-Delforge, Vinciane, and John Scheid. "Qu'est-ce qu'une 'mutation religieuse'?" In *Panthée: Religious Transformations in the Graeco-Roman Empire*, edited by Laurent Bricault and Corinne Bonnet, 309–14. Leiden: Brill, 2013.

Pitre, Brant. "The Mystery of God's Word: Inspiration, Inerrancy, and the Interpretation of Scripture." *Letter and Spirit* 6 (2010): 47–66.

Pius X. *Lamentabili sane exitu*. Decree of the Holy Office against Modernism, July 3, 1907.

Plested, Marcus. *Orthodox Readings of Aquinas*. Oxford: Oxford University Press, 2012.

Plisch, Uwe-Karsten. *The Gospel of Thomas: Original Text with Commentary*. Stuttgart: Deutsche Bibelgesellschaft, 2008.

Poirier, John C. "The Endtime Return of Elijah and Moses at Qumran." *DSD* 10, no. 2 (2003): 221–42.

Porten, Bezalel. *Archives from Elephantine: The Life of an Ancient Jewish Military Colony*. Berkeley: University of California Press, 1968.

Porter, Stanley. *The Criteria for Authenticity in Historical-Jesus Research: Previous Discussion and New Proposals*. Sheffield: Sheffield Academic Press, 2000.

———, ed. *The Messiah in the Old and New Testaments*. Grand Rapids, MI: Eerdmans, 2007.

Pouderon, Bernard. *Ouvrages apologétiques: Pseudo-Justin. Introduction, texte grec, traduction et notes*. SC 528. Paris: Cerf, 2009.

Pouliot, François. *La doctrine du miracle chez Thomas d'Aquin: Deus in omnibus intime operator*. Bibliotheque thomiste 56. Paris: Librairie Philosophique J. Vrin, 2005.

Prestige, G. L. *God in Patristic Thought*. London: SPCK, 1952.

———. "'Perichoreo' and 'Perichoresis' in the Fathers." *Journal of Theological Studies* 29 (1928): 242–52.

Preuss, H. D. *Verspottung fremder Religionen im Alten Testament*. BWANT 92. Stuttgart: Kohlhammer, 1971.

Price, H. H. *Belief*. Gifford Lectures. New York: George Allen & Unwin, 1969.

Prince, Deborah Thompson. "'The Ghost of Jesus': Luke 24 in Light of Ancient Narratives of Post-Mortem Apparitions." *JSNT* 29, no. 3 (2007): 287–301.

Radice, Roberto. "Philo's Theology and Theory of Creation." In *The Cambridge Companion to Philo*, edited by Adam Kamesar, 124–45. Cambridge: Cambridge University Press, 2009.

Rainbow, Paul. "Jewish Monotheism as the Matrix for New Testament Christology: A Review Article." *NovT* 33, no. 1 (1991): 78-91.

Ramelli, Illaria. "Origen, Greek Philosophy, and the Birth of the Trinitarian Meaning of 'Hypostasis.'" *HTR* 105, no. 3 (2012): 302-50.

———. "Origen, Patristic Philosophy, and Christian Platonism: Re-Thinking the Christianisation of Hellenism." *VC* 63, no. 3 (2009): 217-63.

Ratzinger, Joseph. "Der Gott des Glaubens und der Gott der Philosophen." In *Der Gott des Glaubens und der Gott der Philosophen*, 189-210. Gesammelte Schriften 3/1. Freiburg: Herder, 2020.

———. "Eschatologie—Tod und Ewiges Leben." In *Auferstehung und Ewiges Leben*. Gesammelte Schriften 10. Freiburg: Herder, 2011.

———. "Heilsgeschichte, Metaphysik und Eschatologie." In *Der Gott des Glaubens und der Gott der Philosophen*, 73-97. Gesammelte Schriften 3/1. Freiburg: Herder, 2020.

———. *Jesus of Nazareth: From the Baptism in the Jordan to the Transfiguration*. New York: Doubleday, 2007.

———. *Jesus of Nazareth: Holy Week. From the Entrance into Jerusalem to the Resurrection*. San Francisco: Ignatius, 2011.

———. *Jesus of Nazareth: The Infancy Narratives*. New York: Image, 2012.

———. "Zum Personverständnis in der Theologie." In *Der Gott des Glaubens und der Gott der Philosophen*. Gesammelte Schriften 3/1. [Originally published in *Dogma und Verkündigung*. Munich: Erich Wewel, 1973.]

Reale, Giovanni. *Toward a New Interpretation of Plato*. Washington, DC: The Catholic University of America Press, 1997.

Reardon, B. P. *Collected Ancient Greek Novels*. Berkeley: University of California Press, 2008.

Redman, Judith. "How Accurate Are Eyewitnesses? Bauckham and the Eyewitnesses in the Light of Psychological Research." *JBL* 129, no. 1 (2010): 177-97.

Reisenfeld, H. "Le caractère messianique de la tentation au desert." In *La venue du Messie*. RechBib 6. Bruges: Desclée de Brouwer, 1962.

Renberg, Gil H. "Public and Private Places of Worship in the Cult of Asclepius at Rome." *MAAR* 51/52 (2006): 87-172.

Rheaume, Randy. *An Exegetical and Theological Analysis of the Son's Relationship to the Father in John's Gospel: Equal Yet Subordinate*. Lewiston, NY: Mellen, 2015.

Rhys, Joceyln. *Shaken Creeds: The Virgin Birth Doctrine*. London: Watts, 1922.

Rigaux, Béda. "Commentary on Chapter V of *Dei Verbum*." In *Commentary on the Documents of Vatican II*, vol. 3, edited by Herbert Vorgrimler, 258-60. New York: Herder and Herder, 1969.

Roberts, Arthur. *Selected Lives from Cornelius Nepos*. Boston: Ginn, 1895.

Robinson, James M. *A New Quest of the Historical Jesus*. Studies in Biblical Theology 25. London: SCM Press, 1959.

———, ed. *The Coptic Gnostic Library*. Vol. 1. Leiden: Brill, 2000.

Robinson, James M., and Helmut Koester. *Trajectories through Early Christianity*. Library of Early Christology. Grand Rapids, MI: Baker Academic, 2018.

Rodgers, Peter. "Review of *Jesus and the Eyewitnesses: The Gospels as Eyewitnesses Testimony*." *NovT* 52, no. 1 (2010): 88–100.

Rodríguez, Raphael. "Review of *Remembrance of Things Past? Albert Schweitzer, the Anxiety of Influence, and the Untidy Jesus of Markan Memory* by Michael Thate." *Theological Studies* 66, no. 2 (2015): 769–72.

———. *Structuring Early Christian Memory*. JSNTSup 407. London: T&T Clark, 2010.

Romeo, Antonino. "L'Enciclica *Divino afflante Spiritu* e le *opiniones novae*." *Divinitas* 4 (1960): 387–456.

Rondeau, Marie-Josephe. *Les commentaires patristiques du Psautier (IIIe-Ve siècles)*. Vol. 2, *Exégèse prosopologique et théologique*. Orientalia Christiana Analecta 220. Rome: Institutum Studiorum Orentalium, 1985.

Root, Michael. "The Achievement of Wolfhart Pannenberg." *First Things* (March 2012): 37–42.

Rösel, Martin. *Übersetzung als Vollendung der Auslegung: Studien zu Genesis-Septuaginta*. BZAW 223. Berlin: De Gruyter, 1994.

Roth, Dieter. "The Link between Luke and Marcion's Gospel: Prolegomena and Initial Considerations." In *Luke on Jesus, Paul and Christianity*, edited by Joseph Verheyden and John Kloppenborg, 59–80. Biblical Studies and Tools 29. Leuven: Peeters, 2017.

Rothschild, Clare K. *Luke-Acts and the Rhetoric of History*. WUNT 175. Tübingen: Mohr Siebeck, 2004.

Rowe, C. Kavin. "Biblical Pressure and Trinitarian Hermeneutics." *Pro Ecclesia* 11, no. 3 (2002): 295–312.

———. *Early Narrative Christology: The Lord in the Gospel of Luke*. BZNW 139. Berlin: De Gruyter, 2006.

Ruina, David. *Philo of Alexandria and the Timaeus of Plato*. Philosophia antiqua 44. Leiden: Brill, 1986.

Sanday, William. *The Life of Christ in Recent Research*. Oxford: Clarendon, 1907.

Sanders, E. P. *Jesus and Judaism*. Philadelphia: Fortress, 1985.

———. *Paul and Palestinian Judaism*. Minneapolis: Fortress, 1977.

Sanders, James A. *Canon and Community: A Guide to Canonical Criticism*. Philadelphia: Fortress, 1984.

Schäfer, Peter. *Zwei Götter im Himmel: Gottesvorstellungen in der jüdischen Antike*. Munich: C. H. Beck, 2017.

Scheid, John. *Quand faire c'est croire: Les rites sacrificiels des Romains*. Paris: Aubier, 2005.

Schelkens, Karim. *Catholic Theology of Revelation on the Eve of Vatican II: A Redaction History of the Schema* De fontibus revelationis *(1960-1962)*. Leiden: Brill, 2011.

———. "From *Providentissimus Deus* to *Dei Verbum*: The Catholic Biblical Movement and the Council Reconsidered." In *La Théologie catholique entre intransigeance et renouveau: La réception des mouvements préconciliaires à Vatican II*, edited by G. Routhier, P. J. Roy, and K. Schelkens, 49–68. Leuven: Leuven Universiteitsbibliotheek, 2011.

Schenker, Adrian. "Textkritik und Textgeschichte von Ps 110(109),3: Initiativen der Septuaginta und der protomasoretische Edition." In *La Septante en Allemagne et en France: Textes de la Septante à traduction double ou à traduction très littérale; Septuaginta Deutsch und Bible d'Alexandrie. Texte der Septuaginta in*

Doppelüberlieferung oder in wörtlicher Übersetzung, edited by Wolfgang Kraus and Olivier Munnich, 172–90. Fribourg: Vandenhoeck & Ruprecht, 2009.

Schepens, Guido. *L'"autopsie" dans la méthod des historiens grec du Ve siècle avant J.-C.* Brussels: Palais der Academiën, 1980.

Schmidt, K. L. *Der Rahmen der Geschichte Jesu*. Berlin: Trowitzch, 1919.

———. "Die Stellung der Evangelien in der allgemeinen Literaturgeschichte." In *Eucharisterion: Studien zur Religion und Literatur des Altes und Neues Testaments. Hermann Gunkel 60. Geburtstag, Teil 2*, 50–134. Göttingen: Vandenhoeck & Ruprecht, 1923.

Schmiedel, Otto. *Die Hauptprobleme der Leben-Jesu-Forschung*. Tübingen: J. C. B. Mohr, 1902.

Schökel, Louis Alonso. "Dove va l'esegesi cattolica?" *La Civiltà Cattolica* 111, no. 2645 (September 3, 1960): 449–60.

Schröter, Jens. "The Gospels as Eyewitness Testimony? A Critical Examination of Bauckham's Jesus and the Eyewitnesses." *JSNT* 31, no. 2 (2008): 195–209.

Schumann, Johann Daniel. *Ueber die Evidenz der Beweise für die Wahrheit der christlichen Religion*. Hannover: Schmidt, 1778.

Schurmann, Heinz. *Das Lukasevangelium*. HTKNT 3. Freiburg im Breisgau: Herder, 1982.

Schwartz, Regina. *The Curse of Cain: The Violent Legacy of Monotheism*. Chicago: University of Chicago Press, 1997.

Schwarz, Sandra. "Clitophon the *Moichos*: Achilles Tatius and the Trial Scene in the Greek Novel." *Ancient Narrative* 1 (2000/2001): 93–113.

Schwarz, Seth. *Imperialism and Jewish Society: 200 B.C.E. to 640 C.E.* Princeton, NJ: Princeton University Press, 2001.

Schweitzer, Albert. *A Treasury of Albert Schweitzer*. Edited by Thomas Kierman. New York: Citadel, 1965.

———. *Aus meinem Leben und Denken*. In *Ausgewählte Werke: Band 1*. Berlin: Union Verlag, 1971.

———. *Das Messianitäts- und Leidensgeheimnis: Eine Skizze des Lebens Jesu*. Tübingen: J. C. B. Mohr, 1901.

———. *Geschichte der Leben-Jesu-Forschung*. Tübingen: Mohr, 1913.

———. *Kulturphilosophie: Verfall und Wiederaufbau der Kultur, Kultur und Ethik*. Munich: C. H. Beck, 2007.

———. "Religion in Modern Civilization." In *Albert Schweitzer's Ethical Vision: A Sourcebook*, edited by Predrag Cicovacki, 75–84. Oxford: Oxford University, 2009.

———. "Schopenhauer and Nietzsche's Quest for Elementary Ethics." In *Albert Schweitzer's Ethical Vision: A Sourcebook*, edited by Predrag Cicovacki, 123–34. Oxford: Oxford University Press, 2009.

———. *The Mystery of the Kingdom of God*. Buffalo: Prometheus, 1985.

———. *The Quest of the Historical Jesus*. Edited by John Bowden. Minneapolis: Fortress, 2001. [Originally translated by W. Montgomery. London: A. & C. Black, 1910.]

———. *Von Reimarus zu Wrede: Eine Geschichte der Leben-Jesu-Forschung*. Tübingen: Mohr, 1906.

Segal, Alan. *Two Powers in Heaven: Early Rabbinic Reports and Christianity and Gnosticism.* SJLA 25. Leiden: Brill, 1977. [Repr., Waco, TX: Baylor University, 2012.]

Seitz, Christopher. "Review of *The Birth of the Trinity: Jesus, God, and Spirit in the New Testament and Early Christian Interpretations of the Old Testament* by Matthew W. Bates." *CBQ* 78, no. 4 (2016): 765.

Sheeley, S. M. *Narrative Asides in Luke-Acts.* JSNTSup 72. Sheffield: Sheffield Academic, 1992.

Sherwin, Michael. "Christ as Teacher in St. Thomas' Commentary on the Gospel of John." In *Reading John with St. Thomas Aquinas*, edited by Matthew Levering and Michael Dauphinais, 175–93. Washington, DC: The Catholic University of America Press, 2005.

Sider, Robert D., ed. *Collected Works of Erasmus.* Vol. 41, *The New Testament Scholarship of Erasmus.* Toronto: University of Toronto Press, 2019.

Silly, Renaud. *Les Grands Mystères de la Sagesse: Proverbes de Salomon 8 & 9 dans la version des Septante.* Paris: Les Belles Lettres, 2020.

Simpson, Benjamin. "Current Trends in Third-Quest Research." *Bibliotheca Sacra* 171 (2014): 189–209.

Skehan, Patrick W. "The Divine Name at Qumran, in the Masada Scroll, and in the Septuagint." *BIOCSC* 13 (1980): 14–44.

Skuckburgh, Evelyn. *Histories.* Bloomington: Indiana University Press, 1962.

Smith, Andrew. *Porphyrii philsophi fragmenta.* Stuttgart: Teubner, 1993.

Smith, Geoffrey S. *Valentinian Christianity Texts and Translations.* Berkeley: University of California Press, 2020.

Smith, Jonathan Z. "Fences and Neighbors: Some Contours of Early Judaism." In *Imagining Religion: From Babylon to Jonestown.* Chicago: University of Chicago Press, 1982.

Smith, Mark. *God in Translation: Deities in Cross-Cultural Discourse in the Biblical World.* Grand Rapids, MI: Eerdmans, 2010.

Smith, William. *A New Classical Dictionary of Greek and Roman Biography, Mythology, and Geography.* New York: Harper & Brothers, 1851.

Soden, Hermann Freiherr von. *Die wichtigsten Fragen im Leben Jesu.* Berlin: Alexander Duncker, 1904.

Soloviev, Vladimir. *A Story of Anti-Christ.* Kassock Bros., 2012.

Spadafora, Francesco. "Un document notevole per l'esegesi cattolica." *Palestra del clero* 40 (1961): 969–81.

Stabile, F. Michele. "Il cardinal Ruffini e il Vaticano II: Le lettere di un intransigente." *Cristianismo nella Storia* 11 (1990): 83-176.

Stang, Charles. *Apophasis and Pseudonymity in Dionysius the Areopagite: "No Longer I."* Oxford: Oxford University Press, 2012.

Stanley, David Michael. "New Understanding of the Gospels." In *The Bible in Current Catholic Thought*, edited by John L. McKenzie, 169–83. New York: Herder and Herder, 1962.

Stein, Robert. "The Ending of Mark." *BBR* 18, no. 1 (2008): 79–98.

Steinmann, Jean. *La Vie de Jésus.* Paris: Éditions de Noël, 1959.

———. *Une foi chretienne pour aujourd'hui.* Paris: B. Grasset, 1967.

Steinmueller, J. E. *Sword of the Spirit*. Waco, TX: Stella Maris, 1982.

Sterling, Gregory. *Historiography and Self-Definition: Josephos, Luke-Acts, and Apologetic Historiography,* NovTSup 64. Leiden: Brill, 1992.

———. "Prepositional Metaphysics in Jewish Wisdom Speculation and Early Christian Liturgical Texts." In *The Studia Philonica Annual*, vol. 9, edited by David T. Runia, 219–38. Atlanta: Scholars Press, 1997.

Stern, Jacob. *Palaephatus: On Unbelievable Tales*. Wauconda, IL: Bolchazy-Carducci, 1996.

Stern, Menahem. *Greek and Latin Authors on Jews and Judaism*. Jerusalem: Israel Academy of Sciences and Humanities, 1974.

———. "Hecataeus of Abdera and Theophrastus on Jews and Egyptians." *Journal of Egyptian Archeology* 59 (1973): 159–68.

Stiglmayr, Joseph. "Der Neuplatoniker Proklos als Vorlage des sog. Dionysius Areopagita in der Lehre vom Übel." *Historisches Jahrbuch* 16 (1895): 253–73, 721–48.

Stockhausen, Alma von. *Der Geist im Widerspruch: Von Luther zu Hegel*. Schriftenreihe der Gustav-Siewerth-Akademie 3. Weilheim-Bierbronnen: Gustav-Siewerth-Akademie, 2003.

Stokes, Ryan. "Not over Moses' Dead Body: Jude 9, 22-24 and the Assumption of Moses in their Early Jewish Context." *JSNT* 40 (2017): 195–98.

Strauss, D. F. *Das Leben Jesu für das deutsche Volk bearbeitet*. Leipzig: Brockhaus, 1864.

———. *Der alte und der neue Glaube: Ein Bekenntnis*. Bonn: Emil Strauss, 1875.

———. *Der Christus des Glaubens und der Jesus der Geschichte: Eine Kritik des Schleiermacher'schen Leben Jesu*. Berlin: Franz Duncker, 1865.

———. *Hermann Samuel Reimarus und seine Schutzschrift für die vernünftigen Verehrer Gottes*. Leipzig: Brockhaus, 1862.

Strecker, Georg. "Walter Bauer's *Rechtglaubigkeit und Ketzerei im ältesten Christentum*." *JECS* 14, no. 4 (2006): 399–405.

Strousma, Guy. "A Nameless God: Judeo-Christian and Gnostic 'Theologies of the Name.'" In *The Image of Judeo-Christians in Ancient Jewish and Christian Literature*, edited by Peter-Jan Tomson and Doris Lambers-Petry, 230–43. WUNT 158. Tübingen: Mohr Siebeck, 2003.

Stuckenbruck, Loren T. *Angel Veneration and Christology: A Study in Early Judaism in the Christology of the Apocalypse of John*. WUNT II 70. Tübingen: Mohr Siebeck, 1995.

———. "Melchizedek in Jewish Apocalyptic Literature." *JSNT* 41, no. 1 (2018): 124–38.

Stuckenbruck, Loren T., and Wendy North, eds. *Early Jewish and Christian Monotheism*. JSNTSup 263. New York: T&T Clark, 2004.

Suter, David. "Fallen Angel, Fallen Priest: The Problem of Family Purity in 1 Enoch 6–16." *HUCA* 50 (1979): 115–35.

Swafford, Andrew Dean. *Nature and Grace: A New Approach to Thomistic Ressourcement*. Eugene, OR: Pickwick, 2014.

Sweeney, James P. "Modern and Ancient Controversies over the Virgin Birth of Jesus." *BSac* 160, no. 638 (2003): 142–58.

Tatum, Gregory. "The Limits of Reliability." *NV* 6, no. 3 (2008): 523–28.

Tatum, W. Barnes. *In Quest of Jesus*. Atlanta: John Knox, 1982.

Taylor, Charles. *A Secular Age*. Cambridge, MA: Belknap Press of Harvard University Press, 2007.

Taylor, Justin. *The Treatment of Reality in the Gospels: Five Studies*. CRB 78. Paris: Gabalda, 2011.

Taylor, Vincent. *The Gospel According to St. Mark: The Greek Text with Introduction, Notes, and Indexes*. London: Macmillan, 1959.

te Velde, Rudi. *Aquinas on God: The "Divine Science" of the Summa Theologiae*. Burlington, VT: Ashgate, 2006.

Thackery, H. St. J. *Josephus: The Jewish War*. LCL 203. Cambridge, MA: Harvard University Press, 1927.

Thate, Michael. *Remembrance of Things Past? Albert Schweitzer, the Anxiety of Influence, and the Untidy Jesus of Markan Memory*. WUNT II, 351. Tübingen: Mohr Siebeck, 2013.

Theobald, Michael. *Das Evangelium nach Johannes, Kapitel 1–12*. RNT. Regensburg: Pustet, 2009.

Thiessen, Gerd, and Annette Merz. *The Historical Jesus: A Comprehensive Guide*. Minneapolis: Fortress, 1998.

Thompson, Robin. "Healing at the Pool of Bethesda: A Challenge to Asclepius?" *BBR* 27, no. 1 (2017): 65–84.

Thornton, Claus-Jürgen. *Der Zeuge des Zeugen: Lukas als Historiker der Paulusreisen*. WUNT 56. Tübingen: Mohr Siebeck, 1991.

Tiedemann, Dietrich. *System der stoischen Philosophie*. 3 vols. Leipzig: Weidmann, 1776.

Toews, John. *Becoming Historical: Cultural Reformation and Public Memory in Early Nineteenth-Century Berlin*. Cambridge: Cambridge University Press, 2004.

Torrell, Jean-Pierre. "Le savoir acquis du Christ selon les théologiens médiévaux." *Revue Thomiste* 101 (2001): 355–408.

Tromp, Johannes. *The Assumption of Moses: A Critical Edition with Commentary*. Studia in Veteris Testamenta Pseudepigrapha 10. Leiden: Brill, 1993.

Troost-Cramer, Kathleen. *Jesus as Means and Locus of Worship in the Fourth Gospel: Sacrifice and Worship Space in John*. Eugene, OR: Wipf and Stock, 2017.

Tuggy, Dale. "On Bauckham's Bargain." *Theology Today* 70, no. 2 (2013): 128–43.

Tyrrell, George. *Christianity at the Cross-Roads*. London: Longmans, Green, 1909.

Vallençon, Henri. *Le développement des traditions sur Élie et l'histoire de la formation de la Bible*. ÉB 80. Leuven: Peeters, 2019.

Valve, Lotta. *Early Modes of Exegesis: Ideal Figures in Malachi as a Test Case*. Åbo: Åbo Akademis, 2014.

Vandergriff, Kenneth. "Melchizedek and the Eucharist? Rediscovering Eucharistic Interpretations of the Bread and Wine in Genesis 14." *Review & Expositor* 117, no. 4 (2020): 549–54.

van der Horst, Pieter. "Porphyry on Judaism: Some Observations." In *Studies in Ancient Judaism and Early Christianity*. AJEC 67. Leiden: Brill, 2014.

VanderKam, J., and M. Brady. *Dead Sea Scrolls Reader, Part 3: Parabiblical Texts*. Leiden: Brill, 2005.

van Henten, Jan Willem. "Moses as Heavenly Messenger in Assumptio Mosis 10:2 and Qumran Passages." *JJS* 54 (2003): 216–27.

Vanhoozer, Kevin. *The Drama of Doctrine: A Canonical Linguistic Approach to Christian Theology*. Louisville, KY: Westminster/John Knox, 2005.

van Loon, Hans. *The Dyophysite Theology of Cyril of Alexandria*. Leiden: Brill, 2009.Vargas, Antonio. "The Conspiracy of the Good: Proclus Theodicy qua Political Theological Paradigm." *Political Theology* 21, no. 8 (2020): 1–15.

Vattuone, Riccardo. "Looking for the Invisible: Theopompus and the Roots of Historiography." In *Between Thucydides and Polybius: The Golden Age of Greek Historiography*, edited by Giovanni Parmeggiani. Hellenic Studies Center 64. Washington, DC: Center for Hellenic Studies, 2014.

Venard, Olivier-Thomas. *Poetic Christ: Thomistic Reflections on Scripture, Language and Reality*. Translated by Kenneth Oakes and Francesca Aran Murphy. London: T&T Clark, 2019.

———. *Thomas d'Aquin poète théologien: La langue de l'ineffable. Essai sur le fondement théologique de la métaphysique*. Geneva: Ad Solem, 2004.

———. *Thomas d'Aquin poète théologien: Littérature et théologie. Une saison en enfer*. Geneva: Ad Solem, 2002.

———. *Thomas d'Aquin poète théologien: Pagina sacra. Le passage de l'Écriture sainte a l'écriture théologique*. Geneva: Ad Solem, 2009.

Verbin, John Kloppenborg. *Excavating Q*. Minneapolis: Fortress, 2000.

Vermes, Géza. "The Son of Man Debate Revisited (1960-2010)." *JJS* 61, no. 2 (2010): 193–206.

Versnel, Henk S. *Coping with the Gods: Wayward Readings in Greek Theology*. Leiden: Brill, 2011.

Viviano, Benedict. "Eschatology and the Quest for the Historical Jesus." In *The Oxford Handbook of Eschatology*, edited by Jerry L. Walls, 73–90. Oxford: Oxford University, 2008.

———. "Who Wrote Q? The Sayings Document (Q) as the Apostle Matthew's Private Notebook as a Bilingual Village Scribe (Mark 2:13–17; Matt 9:9–13)." In *Mark and Matthew II*, edited by A. Runnesson and E.-M. Becker, 75–91. WUNT 271. Tübingen: Mohr Siebeck, 2013.

Voegelin, Eric. *The Collected Works of Eric Voegelin*. Vol. 17, *Order and History*. Vol. 4, *The Ecumenic Age*. Edited by Michael Franz. Baton Rouge: Louisiana State University Press, 2000.

———. *The New Science of Politics: An Introduction*. Chicago: University of Chicago, 1987.

———. "What Is History" and "Anxiety and Reason." In *The Collected Works of Eric Voegelin*, vol. 28, edited by Thomas A. Hollweck and Paul Caringella, 1–111. Baton Rouge: Louisiana State University Press, 1990.

Völker, Walter. "Review of *Rechtglaubigkeit und Ketzerei im ältesten Christentum* by Walter Bauer." *Zeitschrift für Kirchengeschichte* 54 (1935): 628–31. [Recently reprinted as "Walter Bauer's *Rechtglaubigkeit und Ketzerei im ältesten Christentum*," *JECS* 14 (2006): 399–405.]

Vollenweider, Samuel. "Der Logos als Brücke vom Evangelium zur Philosophie: Der Johannesprolog in der Relektüre des Neuplatonikers Amelios." In *Studien zu*

Matthäus und Johannes/Études sur Matthieu et Jean, edited by Andreas Dettwiler and Uta Poplutz, 377-98. Zurich: TVY Theologischer Verlag, 2009.

Vollhart, Friedrich. *Gotthold Ephraim Lessing*. Munich: C. H. Beck, 2016.

Vorgrimler, Herbert, ed. *Commentary on the Documents of Vatican II*. Vol. 3. New York: Herder and Herder, 1969.

Waers, Stephen. "Monarchianism and Two Powers: Jewish and Christian Monotheism at the Beginning of the Third Century." *VC* 70, no. 4 (2016): 401-29.

Waldstein, Michael. "The Foundations of Bultmann's Work." *Communio: International Catholic Review* 14, no. 2 (1987): 115-45.

_____, ed. *The Apocryphon of John: Synopsis of Nag Hammadi Codices II,1, III,1, and IV,1 with BG 8502,2*. Leiden: Brill, 1995.

Walton, Steve. "'The Heavens Opened': Cosmological and Theological Transformation in Luke and Acts." In *Cosmology and New Testament Theology*, edited by Jonathan T. Pennington, 60-73. London: T&T Clark, 2008.

Wassén, Cecilia, and Tobias Hägerland. *Jesus the Apocalyptic Prophet*. London: T&T Clark, 2021.

Watson, Duane, ed. *Miracle Discourse in the New Testament*. Atlanta: SBL, 2012.

Watson, Francis. "Eschatology and the Twentieth Century: On the Reception of Schweitzer in English." In *Eschatologie—Eschatology*, edited by Christof Landmesser, Hermann Lichtenberg, and Hans-Joseph Eckstein, 339-44. WUNT 272. Tübingen: Mohr Siebeck, 2011.

_____. *Gospel Writing: A Canonical Perspective*. Grand Rapids, MI: Eerdmans, 2013.

Weaver, Walter P. "In Quest of the Quest: Finding Jesus." In *Jesus Research: New Methodologies and Perceptions*, edited by James Charlesworth, 28-57. Grand Rapids, MI: Eerdmans, 2014.

_____. *The Historical Jesus in the Twentieth Century, 1900-1950*. Harrisburg, PA: Trinity International, 1999.

Weinel, Heinrich. "Review of *Das Messianitäts- und Leidensgeheimnis* by Albert Schweitzer." *Theologische Rundschau* 15, no. 6 (1902): 242-45.

Wengst, Klaus. *Das Johannesevangelium*. TKNT 4/1. Stuttgart: Kohlhammer, 2000.

Wernle, Paul. *Die Anfänge unserer Religion*. Tübingen, 1902.

_____. "Review of *Das Messianitäts- und Leidensgeheimnis* by Albert Schweitzer." *TLZ* 18 (1906): 501-6.

Wevers, John Williams. "The Rendering of the Tetragram in the Psalter and Pentateuch: A Comparative Study." In *The Old Greek Psalter: Studies in Honor of Albert Pietersma*, edited by Robert Hiebert, Claude Cox, and Peter Gentry, 21-35. JSOTSup 332. Sheffield: Sheffield Academic, 2001.

White, Hayden. *Metahistory: The Historical Imagination in Nineteenth-Century Europe*. Baltimore: Johns Hopkins University Press, 2014.

White, Thomas Joseph. *The Incarnate Lord: A Thomistic Study in Christology*. Thomistic Ressourcement Series. Washington, DC: The Catholic University of America Press, 2017.

_____, ed. *The Analogy of Being: Invention of the Antichrist or the Wisdom of God?* Grand Rapids, MI: Eerdmans, 2010.

Wilken, Robert L. *The Christians as the Romans Saw Them*. New Haven, CT: Yale University Press, 1984.

Williams, George Hunston. *The Radical Reformation*. Cambridge: Cambridge University Press, 1991.

Wiseman, T. P. "Lying Historians: Seven Types of Mendacity." In *Lies and Fiction in the Ancient World*, edited by Christopher Gill and T. P. Wiseman, 122–46. Exeter: University of Exeter Press, 1993.

Witherington, Ben, III. "*In Principio Erat Verbum*: Sacred Texts in an Oral Culture." SBL Lecture for the Paul and Scripture Seminar. Atlanta, 2010.

Witmer, Stephen. "Pastoral Pensées: Keeping Ethics and Eschatology Together: The Teaching of Jesus, the Work of Albert Schweitzer, and the Task of Evangelical Pastor-Theologians." *Themelios* 39, no. 3 (2014): 484–500.

Wojciechowski, Michael. "Ancient Criticism of Religion in Dan 14 (Bel and the Dragon), Bar 6 (Epistle of Jeremiah), and Wisdom 14." In *Deuterocanonical Additions of the Old Testament Books: Selected Studies*, edited by Géza G. Xeravitis and József Zsengellér, 60–76. DCLS 5. Berlin: De Gruyter, 2010.

Wood, Allen, et al., eds. *Kant: Religion within the Bounds of Bare Reason and Other Writings*. Cambridge Texts in the History of Philosophy. Cambridge: Cambridge University Press, 1998.

Wright, N. T. "Hope Deferred? Against the Dogma of Delay." *EC* 9, no. 1 (2018): 37–82.

———. *Jesus and the Victory of God*. Christian Origins and the Question of God. London: SPCK, 1994. [Repr., Minneapolis: Fortress, 1996.]

———. *The New Testament and the People of God*. Christian Origins and the Question of God. Minneapolis: Fortress, 1992.

———. *The Resurrection of the Son of God*. Christian Origins and the Question of God. Minneapolis: Fortress, 2003.

———. *Times Literary Supplement*. December 14, 2011.

Yeago, David. "The New Testament and Nicene Dogma: A Contribution to the Recovery of Theological Exegesis." *ProE* 3, no. 2 (1994): 152–64.

Young, Robin Darling. "Notes on Divesting and Vesting in *The Hymn of the Pearl*." In *Reading Religions in the Ancient World: Essays Presented to Robert McQueen Grant on His 90th Birthday*, edited by Robert Grant, David Aune, and Robin Darling Young, 201–14. NovTSup 125. Leiden: Brill, 2007.

Zarafa, Peter Paul. "The Limits of Biblical Inerrancy." *Angelicum* 39, no. 1/2 (1962): 92–119.

Zehnder, Markus. "A Fresh Look at Malachi II 13-16." *VT* 53, no. 2 (2003): 224–59.

Zeron, Alexander. "The Martyrdom of Phineas-Elijah." *JBL* 98, no. 1 (1979): 99–100.

Ziegler, Theobald. *David Friedrich Strauß*. Strassburg: Karl Trübner, 1908.

Ziolkowski, Theodore. *Clio, the Romantic Muse: Historicizing the Faculties in Germany*. Cornell, NY: Cornell University Press, 2004.

Scriptural Index

OLD TESTAMENT

Genesis
1: 359
1–2: 196, 230, 341
1.26: 337–41, 355
2.7: 340–41
3.21: 325
12.1: 205, 221
14: 346–49
15: 206
34: 312
49.5–12: 307

Exodus
3.14: 223, 242, 381
4.22: 275
15: 351
19.3: 322
20.3–5: 189
20.25: 350
20.26: 326
23.20: 304n6
24.15: 323
28.2: 325
28.41–42: 322, 326
29: 330
29.29: 329
29.33: 322
31.18: 368
34.13: 198
34.17: 189
40.15: 305

Leviticus
8–9: 330
16.13: 323
19.4: 189
25: 346
25.9: 346
25.13: 346
26.1: 189

Numbers
20.26–28: 329
21.8–9: 369
24.17: 310n24
25.10–13: 311
25.11: 313
25.12: 312
25.13: 313
35.30: 132n81

Deuteronomy
4: 189
5.5: 226
5.23–31: 319
6: 275

6.1–16: 283
6.4: 175, 232
6.4–6: 198
14.22–26: 346
15.2: 346
17.6: 132n81
18: 319
18.15: 284, 309–10, 319–20, 324
18.18: 319
33.11: 311
30.4–6: 311
34.6: 321

Joshua
320n42

Ruth
84

1 Samuel
2.35: 309n22, 310n24, 315, 320
5.3–5: 201

1 Kings
11.1–4: 312
17: 314
17.22: 317n39
18: 313

19.10: 313
19.14: 313

2 Kings
320
1.8: 330
2.1–9: 321
18: 312n29

1 & 2 Chronicles
254

Ezra
1.2: 191
2.2: 315
2.63: 320
3.2: 315
3.4: 330
5.11–12: 192
6.9: 192
6.10: 192
7.12: 192
7.21: 192
7.23: 192
9.1–2: 304n5
10.18–22: 313

Nehemiah
1.4–5: 192
2.4: 192
2.20: 192
7.65: 320
8.14–17: 331
12.10–11: 315
13.9: 312n31
13.23–29: 312n31
13.28: 312n31
13.29: 312n31

Tobit
10.11: 192
13: 254

Judith
5.8: 192

Job
28

Psalms
1: 285
2: 342, 352n50
2.7: 281
16: 338
41.9: 370
69.3: 370
69.21: 370
82: 261
99.6–7: 323
110: 310, 315, 336–39, 342–50, 352, 355
110.1: 344, 349
110.3: 345
110.4: 349
110.5: 350
118: 350–51
118.22: 350
138: 362

Proverbs
3.1: 275

Song of Songs
292

Wisdom
195, 215, 230
7: 229
7.25–26: 229, 234
14.12–21: 203

Sirach
195, 215
24: 256
24.25–27: 265
24.8: 266
42.18–21: 362
46.13: 313, 320
46.16: 313, 320
48.1: 312n29, 320

48.3: 313, 320
48.5: 317n39
48.8: 313, 320
48.10: 317
50: 303
50.5–11: 324
50.13: 330

Isaiah
138n94, 201, 304, 362, 367n25
2.2: 351
6.9–10: 137
8.14: 351
10.34: 364
14.13–15: 366
26.19: 294
28.16: 351
29.18–19: 294
35: 295
35.5–6: 294
37.19: 201
40: 292, 299
40–55: 192
40.3: 298, 317
40.12–23: 202
42.1: 281, 318, 319
42.1–3: 318
42.8: 259, 260n42
42.19: 317
44.13–20: 201
45: 249
45.16–21: 202
45.20: 201
46.1–2: 201
46.1–7: 202
48.5: 202
48.13: 351
49.6: 317
50.4: 275
53.4: 282
53.7: 296

53.12: 370
55.8: 362
61: 272, 295, 298, 347–49, 370
61.1: 294, 347
61.1–2: 347n42
61.1–3: 346, 348–49
62.5: 292
62.11: 370

Jeremiah
7.34: 292
10: 202
10.2–5, 8–9: 202
10.6–7, 10: 202
16.9: 292
16.20: 201
16.21: 192
18.7–10: 373
22.5: 365
23.27: 192
25.10: 292
33.2: 192
33.11: 292
33.15: 318
33.17–18: 305
33.20–22: 305

Baruch
6.8–58: 202

Ezekiel
1.28: 325
28.13–14: 325
44.15–18: 330
47.1–12: 261

Daniel
360
2: 350–51
2.18–19: 192
2.37: 192
2.44: 192
2.45: 350
2.46: 351
5.5–9: 368
5.25: 368
7: 175, 350
7.13: 276, 315, 349
7.13–14: 371
9.1–26: 284
9.27: 371
11.31: 371
12.11: 371
14: 202
14.1–3: 203
14.24–25: 203
14.41: 203

Jonah
28

Nahum
2.12: 364

Habakkuk
1.5: 113n27, 137

Haggai
1.1: 315
1.12: 315
1.14: 315
2.2: 315
2.4: 315

Zechariah
315
3: 327n61, 328, 330
3.1–10: 329
3.9: 351
4: 321, 322
4.2: 359
4.2–3: 318
4.6: 318
4.6–14: 315
4.7: 351
4.9: 318
5.2: 359
9.9: 370
12.3: 351
13: 299
13.7: 370

Malachi
299, 314, 321
1.1: 304
2: 310–12, 322
2.4: 305
2.4–7: 304–5
2.5: 312
2.6: 312, 322
2.7: 313, 322–23
2.8: 312
2.8–16: 312
3: 284, 303, 311–12, 333, 348
3.1: 304–5, 317, 322
3.1–4: 311n29, 312n29
3.2: 305, 330
3.24: 317n39
4.4 [3.22 MT]: 322
4.5 [3.23–24 MT]: 317
4.6 [3.24 MT]: 317

1 Maccabees
1.54: 193
1.59: 193
4.46: 320
10.21: 331
14.41: 320n44

2 Maccabees
1.18: 331
2.13: 83
2.19–32: 90
2.25: 198
2.28: 90
6.1–2: 193
6.5: 193
10.6: 331

NEW TESTAMENT

Matthew
1–2: 35n70
1.1–16: 282
1.22: 283
2.1–12: 184
2.6: 283
2.15: 283
2.17–18: 283
2.22–23: 87
2.39: 293n18
3.1: 293
4.8–10: 184
4.14: 283
4.17: 293
5.18: 266
8.17: 283
9.3: 361n18
9.4: 362n20
9.9: 75
10.20: 133
10.23: 383
10.38: 367
10.39: 367
11.2–6: 348
11.3: 293
11.4–5: 294
11.7: 316
11.18: 293
11.20–24: 366
11.27: 291
12.17–21: 283, 318
12.18–20: 296
12.24: 361
12.25: 361, 362n20
12.38–40: 157
13.14: 283
13.35: 283
14.33: 184
15.2: 361n17
16: 23n14, 331n71
16.16–19: 280
17: 318, 363
17.1–13: 301, 316
17.2: 323
17.13: 301
18.1–2: 361n18
21.1–11: 370
21.4: 283
21.42: 350
23: 87
23.38: 365
24: 372
24.20: 373
24.42–44: 374
24.50: 374
25.13: 374
26.31–35: 159, 370
26.51–54: 367
26.53–54: 159, 369
26.54: 370
26.55–61: 365
26.56: 159, 370
27.9–10: 283
27.13–14: 296
28.1–7: 130
28.3: 324
28.11–15: 124
28.19: 162

Mark
1–2: 103, 104
1.2: 304
1.2–3: 317
1.9–11: 368
1.10: 319
1.11: 319
1.27: 274
1.29: 102
1.29–31: 102
1.32–34: 102
2: 102, 103
2.1: 102
2.1–12: 362
2.6: 361n18
2.11: 103
3.1–6: 101
3.3: 361n18
5.22–43: 367
6.17–18: 316n37
8.31: 159, 369
8.31–33: 367
8.34: 367
8.35: 367
9: 318
9.1: 316
9.2: 330, 331
9.2–8: 368
9.2–13: 301, 316
9.3: 330
9.6: 319
9.7: 319
9.11: xi
9.12–13: 314
9.13: 314, 317
9.31: 367
9.33–34: 361n18
10.33–34: 367
10.45: 367
10.47–48: 315
11.1–3: 370
12.10: 350
12.15: 362n20

SCRIPTURAL INDEX

12.35: 315
12.36: 336, 342, 355
13: 365, 372, 385n29
13.1–37: 370
13.2: 364
13.11: 133
13.14–37: 374
13.18: 373
13.22: 384
13.23: 385
13.24–27: 372n32
13.27: 372n32
13.32: 280, 358n5, 374, 375
13.33–37: 372n32
14.17–65: 367
14.27: 159, 370
14.49: 159, 369, 370
14.56–59: 365
14.57: 351
14.58: 365
14.60–63: 276
14.62: 315
15.1–15: 367
15.4: 296
15.38: 257
16.8: 126n59
16.9–20: 126n59
16.12–13: 126

Luke
1–2: x, 72–91 (Ch 4)
1.1: 40n93, 43, 47, 84, 113
1.1–4: 40–41, 112–14, 119
1.2: 43, 82, 114, 114n29
1.2–4: 20
1.3: 43
1.4: x
1.5: 316
1.17: 316
1.32: 219
1.35: 219
1.37: 91
1.65: 83
1.76: 219
1.78: 365
2: 87
2.1–4: 33n56
2.7: 82
2.19: 130n77
2.34–35: 362
2.51: 42, 130n77
2.52: 269
3.15: 362n19
3.18: 293
4.14–15: 120
4.37: 120
4.42: 120
5.1–10: 130
5.15: 120
5.15–16: 120
5.19: 120
5.21: 361n18
5.22: 362
5.29: 120
6.8: 361n18, 362
6.17: 120
6.35: 219
7: 272
7.11: 120
7.11–17: 367
7.16: 365
7.17: 120
7.18–23: 348
7.16: 365
7.19: 293
7.22: 294
7.27: 316
7.50: 362
8.1–3: 130, 130n77
8.4: 120
8.28: 219

8.40: 120
9.28–43: 301
9.29: 323
9.37: 120
9.44–45: 363
9.46: 361n18
9.47: 361n18, 362
9.51: 323
10.13–15: 366
10.18: 360
10.22: 291
11.17: 362
11.38–39: 361n17
12.1: 120
12.39–40: 374
12.46: 374
13.17: 120
13.31–33: 367
13.33: 365
13.35: 365
14.27: 367
17.33: 367
18.31–34: 363
19.37: 120
19.41–44: 365
19.44: 365
20.18: 350
21.12–13: 131
22.37: 159, 370
22.47: 120
22.53: 120
23.1: 120
23.6–12: 367
23.8: 120
23.13: 120
23.27: 120
23.48: 120
24: 130, 131n80
24.1: 324
24.1–10: 130

24.10: 130, 130n77
24.11: 137, 158
24.12: 128
24.12–35: 126
24.13–35: 128
24.16: 138
24.18: 120
24.24: 131, 137
24.25–27: 159, 369
24.26: 158
24.26–27: 299
24.28: 129
24.31: 138, 158
24.32: 128, 138
24.33: 121
24.34: 130, 131n80
24.35: 127
24.36–43: 278
24.37: 128, 135, 158
24.39: 136, 136n92, 158
24.41: 128, 137
24.41–43: 136
24.45: 138

John
1: 230
1.3: 228, 247
1.5: 237
1.9: 260
1.10: 247
1.14: 35, 232, 234, 259
1.15: 299
1.18: 218, 259
1.19–28: 362n19
1.23: 317
1.30: 299
1.51: 159, 262, 370
2.11: 102
2.17: 333
2.19: 260, 261
2.21: 365

3.11: 360
3.14: 369
3.14–15: 159, 370
3.29: 292
3.32: 360
4: 260n42
4.19: 362
4.21: 105, 260
4.23: 260
4.29: 362
5: 98–105, 291, 295, 297
5.1–15: 99
5.2: 99n20
5.3: 99
5.7: 99
5.8–12: 101
5.14: 99
5.19: 360
5.23: 102
5.31–40: 296
5.39: 271, 370
6.32: 260
6.55: 260
6.70–71: 370
7.15: 274
7.37–39: 261
7.45–46: 296
10.10: 296
10.11–18: 367
10.17–18: 367
10.24: 296
10.30: 261, 262
10.30–36: 261
11.1–44: 367
12.23–27: 367
12.25: 367
12.32: 242, 261
13.18: 159, 370
13.19: 376
14.9: 31, 259

14.28: 262, 280
14.29: 376
15.1: 260
15.12–13: 367
15.26–27: 130, 133
16.4: 376
16.5–10: 367
16.12: 359
16.16: 372
17.3: 260
17.22: 261
17.26: 261
18.10–12: 367
18.20–21: 120
19.25: 126n58
19.28: 370
19.35: 35n69, 117n45, 127n66, 232
20.26–29: 278

Acts
1.1: 43
1.1–2: 20, 27
1.4: 133
1.7: 377
1.8: 107, 133
1.13–15: 121
1.22: 114n29, 130, 130n77, 134
2.22: 120
2.22–36: 132
2.29–31: 338
2.29–35: 131
2.34: 338
3.12–16: 132
3.37: 137
4.10: 132
4.13: 133
4.20: 132
4.13: 133
5: 132

5.29–32: 132, 133
5.32: 133
5.39: 371
5.40: 132
6.14: 365
7.48: 219
8.34: 342
9.1–9: 121
10–11: 127
10.39–42: 121
11.26: 386
12.21–23: 324
13.41: 113n27, 137
14.15: 277
15.8: 362
15.9: 137
16.9: 134
16.14: 137
16.17: 219
17: 243
17.23: 242
17.32: 137
22.1–21: 127
22.4–16: 121
22.17: 134
22.14–15: 134
22.20: 134
24.34: 129
26: 138n94
26.1–29: 127
26.6–7: 113n27
26.8: 113n27
26.9–17: 121
26.26: 120
28.26–27: 137

Romans
1.3: 282
3.28–30: 250
11: 225, 243
11.36: 225, 242, 247, 250
12.1: 240

27.8: 137

1 Corinthians
2.4: 148
8: 351
8.2–3: 14
8.5: 250
8.6: 184, 225, 243, 247, 249
10.2: 323
10.4: 351
14.24–25: 361
15.3–4: 283
15.4–5: 130
15.6: 120, 121
15.20–28: 175
15.28: 176

Galatians
1.13–24: 127

Ephesians
1.21: 212, 223
1.21–22: 175
3.19: 15

Philippians
2: 222–24, 239, 249, 351
2.6–11: 175
3.4–11: 127
3.8: 15

Colossians
1: 239
1.13: 213
1.15: 165n16, 225, 236, 237n66
1.16: 247

1 Thessalonians
1.5: 134
1.9–10: 250

1 Timothy
1.4: 77
1.13–14: 127
1.17: 218

2.5: 168
4.7: 77
6.6: 218, 237

2 Timothy
4.4: 77

Titus
1.14: 77

Hebrews
333, 343, 349
1: 212
1.1: 368
1.2: 228, 247
1.3: 170, 223, 228, 234, 236, 237, 237n66
1.4: 227
1.5–14: 227
1.6: 227
2.5–9: 175
2.7: 234
2.10: 248
7–9: 284

2 Peter
1.16: 77

1 John
1–4: 232
1.1: 294
1.5: 237

Revelation
1.13: 333
11.3–13: 321
11.12–13: 321

Ancient Sources Index

Qumram Texts
CD: 265, 309, 313, 315n35
1Q175: 271
1QH^a: 278
1QM: 250
1QS: 296, 315n35, 329
1QSa: 303
1QSb: 303, 325
3Q15: 99
4Q103: 257
4Q171b: 278
4Q185: 362
4Q254: 315
4Q377: 322, 323, 328
4Q405: 325
4Q427: 278
4Q471b: 278n44
4Q491: 256, 278
4Q521: 272, 294, 313, 315
4Q541: 309n22
4Q543–548: 303
4Q558: 313, 315
4QApocryphon of Levi^b: 303
4QInstruction^d: 303
4QpIsa^d: 325
4QSongs of the Sage: 303
11Q13: 256, 303, 309n22, 339, 343, 346–49

Other Sources
A.J. = *Antiquitates judaicae* (Josephus): 131n78, 197, 253, 324, 331
Ad Haer. = *Adversus Haereses* (Irenaeus): 340, 341n22
Adversus Praxeam (Tertullian): 314, 355
Ad. Aut. = *Apology to Autolycus* (Theophilus of Antioch): 338, 340
Aet. = *De aeternitate mundi* (Philo): 228
ALD = *Aramaic Levi Document*: 303, 327–28, 329
Alexander Romance: 81, 116n40
AP = *Aramaic Papyri of Elephantine*, 192
Apoc. Ab. = *Apocalypse of Abraham*: 203–7, 220, 222, 227, 254, 256–57, 328
Apocalypse of Moses: 327
1 *Apol.* = *First Apology* (Justin): 42, 77, 101, 122, 232, 239
2 *Apol.* = *Second Apology* (Justin): 240–41
Apollonius of Tyana (Philostratus): 82, 116-17, 123, 360
AposCon = *Apostolic Constitutions*: 224–25, 239
As. Mos. = *Assumption of Moses*: 321–22, 328

B.J. = *Bellum judaicum* (Josephus): 41n95, 73, 99n20, 112n19, 119, 127, 128n68, 131, 253n28, 324, 331, 350, 362–63

ANCIENT SOURCES INDEX

bib. hist. = *Bibliotheca historica* (Diodorus Siculus): 73, 122, 195

C. Ap. = *Contra Apionem* (Josephus): 73, 83, 118n46, 130, 199, 253, 265n3
Cels. = *Contra Celsum* (Origen): 74, 79, 82, 144, 216, 234–35, 270
Cher. = *De cherubim* (Philo): 233n59, 256, 362
Comm. Jo. = *Commentary on John* (Origen): 33, 234
Commentary on Matthew (Jerome): 75
Conf. = *De confusione linguarum*: 223, 226
Cyr. = *Cyropaedia* (Xenohon): 116n40, 193, 215

Dec. = *De decalogo* (Philo): 204
Decret. = *de Decretis Nicaenae Synodi* (Athanasius): 161, 236
De Fide (Ambrose): 376n40
De Veritate (Thomas Aquinas): 360n14, 376n39
Dial. = *Dialogue* (Justin): 77, 82, 122, 232, 340

1 *Enoch*: 276–77, 359-60
2 *Enoch*: 279, 326, 327n61, 341n23
3 *Enoch*: 279, 280
Enn. = *Enneads* (Plotinus): 241n74
Ep. Serap. = *Letter to Serapion* (Athanasius): 166n17
4 *Ezra*: 276, 277, 341n23, 350

Flacc. = *In Flaccum* (Philo): 253
Fug. = *De fuga* (Philo): 256

Geger = *Egerton Gospel* (British Library Egerton Papyrus 2): 362n20
Gen. Rab. = *Genesis Rabbah*: 325
Geo. = *Geographica* (Strabo): 96, 195
Gospel of Thomas: 33

H. E. = *Historica Ecclesiastica* (Eusebius): 42n102, 126n58
Her. = *Quis rerum divinarum heres sit* (Philo): 225–26, 256
Hist. =
  History (Herodian): 118–19
  The Histories (Herodotus): 110–11, 113, 125, 129, 193, 195
  The Histories (Polybius): 74, 114n30, 118n47
  The Histories (Tacitus): 195
  History of the Peloponnesian War (Thucydides): 118
Hist. Conscr. = *De Historia Conscribenda* (Lucian): 73n4, 115n34, 118

Infancy Gospel of James: 85
Infancy Gospel of Thomas: 85n33, 360

Jub. = *Jubilees*: 205, 303, 307–9, 326–27, 329, 346

LAB = *Book of Biblical Antiquities* (Pseudo-Philo): 313, 325
Leg. = *Legum allegoriae* (Philo): 226, 248, 324
Legat. = *Legatio ad Gaium* (Philo): 253

Metam. = *Metamorphoses* (Apuleius): 324
Migr. = *De migratione Abrahami* (Philo): 196, 256
Mos. = *De vita Mosis* (Philo): 256, 328
Mut. = *De mutatione nominum* (Philo): 196, 223

Opif. = *De opificio mundi* (Philo): 196, 199, 239

Pan. = *Panarion* (Epiphanius): 75, 161n3, 165n15
Parm. = *Parmenides* (Plato): 218, 222 (cf. 232)
Poet. = *Poetics* (Aristotle): 76, 276, 282

Praep. ev. = *Praeparatio evangelica* (Eusebius): 195, 230, 232–33, 241

Prot. Jas. = *Protoevangelium of James*: 82

QE = *Quaestiones et solutiones in Exodum*: 250n15

QG = *Quaestiones et solutiones in Genesin* (Philo): 225, 239, 248

Rep. = *Republic* (Plato): 238

Romulus (Plutarch): 78–79, 122–24, 131, 137

Sel. In Ez = *In Ezekielem* (Origen): 29n37

Sent. = *Commentary on the Sentences* (Thomas Aquinas): 212n7

Sib. Or. = *Sibylline Oracles*: 87

Somn. = *De somniis* (Philo): 218, 220, 225–26, 248, 250, 256

Spec. = *De specialibus legibus* (Philo): 194, 226, 233, 248, 254, 260

ST = *Summa Theologiae* (Thomas Aquinas): 28n32, 29n36, 29n37, 30n42, 155, 233n58, 266n5, 285n62, 358n10, 360n14, 361, 366, 368, 371–72

Strom. = *Stromata* (Clement of Alexandria): 197, 218

Super Col. = *Commentary on Colossians* (Thomas Aquinas): 213, 237

Super ep. ad Heb. = *Commentary on Hebrews* (Thomas Aquinas): 212–13

Super Eph. = *Commentary on Ephesians* (Thomas Aquinas): 212, 223

Super Galatians = *Commentary on Galatians* (Thomas Aquinas): 33n57

Sym. = *Symposiacs* (Plutarch): 116n39

Test. Ben. = *Testament of Bejamin*: 306

Test. Dan = *Testament of Dan*: 308

Test. Gad = *Testament of Gad*: 308

Testament of Job: 344n31

Test Jos. = *Testament of Joseph*: 308

Test. Jud. = *Testament of Judah*: 308, 319n41

Test. Levi = *Testament of Levi*: 257, 306–11, 319n41, 320, 327–28

Testament of Moses: 257

Test. Reub. = *Testament of Reuben*: 308

Test. Sim. = *Testament of Simeon*: 310

Ver. Hist. = *Verae Historiae* (Lucian): 73n4, 115

Subject Index

adoptionism, 252, 352n50
Alexander, Loveday, 75n10, 85–86, 109n8, 111, 112n24
Alexander, Philip, 270n20, 271n23
Alexandrian: Christology, 178, 354; exegesis, 160–86; thinkers, 218, 233, 241, 337
Allison, Dale, 10–11, 32n50, 34, 36, 38n82, 57n35, 58, 85n35, 92n1, 154n49, 293, 298, 369n27, 371, 375, 390
anagnorisis (recognition), xi, 11, 275, 276n35, 281, 282n52, 335–36, 342–45, 352n50, 354
Andresen, Carl, 335, 339, 352n51
apocalyptic. *See* historical Jesus; prophecy
apologetics/apologetic, x, 5, 40, 56, 112n23, 143, 153, 162n8, 164, 172, 179n69, 268, 278, 280, 290, 297, 367; exegetes' disdain of, 5; Jewish, 199; value of Paul's witness, 121, 134; and the virgin birth, 91n48
apotheosis. *See* resurrection
Arianism, 160, 161, 166, 172, 186, 230n49, 233n58, 235, 242, 244, 336; anti-Arian, 175, 176n51, 184, 236, 237n66, 349, 375; neo-Arian, 161, 172–73; proto-Arian, 167, 248; semi-Arian, 165, 233
Asclepius, cult of, 94n10, 95–97, 100–1, 103, 105, 122; in Jerusalem, 98–99
asphaleia, 20, 41, 47, 49, 72n1, 78, 91, 128. *See also* credibility

autoptai/ αὐτόπται. *See* eyewitness/eyewitnesses
autopsy, 40, 89n46, 107–11, 114n28, 114n32, 118, 124, 136

Balthasar, Hans Urs von, 7n4, 29n38, 31n47, 266n5, 282, 290, 353–54
baptism. *See* John the Baptist
Barth, Karl, 27, 59, 163, 178, 180, 182, 183, 222, 382n13
Bates, Matthew, 335–36, 338–39, 342–43, 345–47, 352n50
Battle of the Biblicum. *See* Steinmann, Jean
Bauckham, Richard, x, 40n91, 47–48, 108, 126, 130, 155, 162–63, 171–85, 249, 251, 252, 254, 280, 338, 343, 344n1, 345; *Jesus and the Eyewitnesses*, 38n82, 47n128, 92n1, 108n3, 109n6, 126n58, 127n63, 128n69, 130n77, 156. *See also* divine identity Christology
Bauer, Bruno, 52, 67n74
Bauer, Walter, 168–69
Benedict XVI, Pope/Joseph Ratzinger, 1, 7n4, 8, 21n7, 29n34, 45n117, 151, 208n62, 335n2, 354–55, 380n8, 382n16, 382n25, 391; *Jesus of Nazareth*, 35–38, 42n104, 49n131
"big picture" theory/"gist" arguments, 32–38, 42, 298, 390

biography, ancient, 40, 81–83, 90, 105; examples of, 115–17, 122, 124, 268–70, 287, 360
biography, modern, 3, 56, 154
bioi. *See* biography, ancient
Boehm, Gottfried: *Bildwissenschaft*, 341
Bousset, Wilhelm, 164, 174, 206; disagreement with Larry Hurtado, 229, 246–47, 252
Brown, Raymond, 47n125, 85–86, 259, 269, 290, 357, 361n16, 367n23, 367n25, 377; *Birth of the Messiah*, 42n103, 86n37, 269n15
Bultmann, Rudolph, 6, 8, 10, 25, 27, 28n31, 29, 30, 40–41, 58, 60, 64, 65n67, 66, 70, 79, 84n30, 147, 148, 150, 267–68, 288, 344, 379–81
Burridge, Richard, 40, 81n24, 115n35, 268, 287. *See also* biography, ancient

Caba, José, 19–21, 33, 43
Cary, Philip, 161
Chalcedon/Chalcedonian, 10–11, 105, 163, 177–80, 184, 213, 278, 280n50, 281, 366; non-Chalcedonian Churches, 183
chief agent figures, 163, 166, 168–69, 303, 306–7, 310, 316, 338. *See also* divine agents, subordinationism
Christology:
• Adam, 252, 277n41, 278, 325–26
• angelic, 250, 349
• conciliar (Nicene), 3, 6, 9–10, 161n3, 162–63, 166n16, 168–71, 173–74, 177, 179–80, 182, 183–85, 242, 252, 280–81, 366
• contrast with Demiurge, 226–27, 230–31, 235, 237, 240, 242–43, 248
• crisis of (Nicene), x, 12, 160, 227, 236, 280
• "of divine persons," 338
• dyadic devotional pattern, 165–66, 169
• Early High Christology, 10, 71, 162–64, 169, 174, 185–86, 245, 252, 280, 336n8, 338
• "Ebionite," 161n3

• functional versus ontic, 173–74, 180
• "of Jesus," 279, 298, 334, 336, 369n27, 370
• Johannine, 239, 248, 259n38, 260, 262
• "low," 13, 169, 173, 252, 293
• and metaphysics, 7n4
• Miaphysite, 183
• New Testament, 7, 8, 10, 12, 28, 42, 66n71, 160, 163, 172, 173, 177, 180n71, 186, 203n48, 209, 211–13, 216, 221, 222, 225, 228, 235–37, 239, 243, 246, 248–49, 251–53, 266, 295, 298, 303, 344, 351
• and the Old Testament, 272, 283, 289, 390
• patristic, 238n68
• Pauline/Pseudo-Dionysian, 12, 212–13, 223
• poetic, 287, 289
• priestly/mediator, 12, 13, 243, 249, 262, 303n1, 333, 336
• primitive/early, 12, 168, 173n47, 209, 213, 222, 224, 228, 238, 245–47, 250, 251, 303n1, 308, 311, 336n8, 345n38, 352
• (Suffering) Servant, 275–76, 279, 281–82, 296, 298, 317–19, 333, 352, 370
• Studite, 166n16
• *See also* adoptionism; Alexandrian; *anagnorisis* (recognition); Arianism; Chalcedon/Chalcedonian; chief agent figures; divine agents; divine identity Christology; infancy narrative; Jesus, knowledge; Lessing, Gotthold Ephraim; *Logos*; Lutheranism; messianic consciousness of Jesus; Moltmann, Jürgen; Monophysite Christology; monotheism/monotheistic; Nestorianism; Nicene/Nicea; priestly figures; prophets; Sabellius/Sabellianism; Schleiermacher, Friedrich; *scientia Christi*; subordinationism; Temple; Thomas Aquinas; Venard, Olivier-Thomas
Congar, Yves, 24, 45
credibility: of Asclepius cult, 125; of Bultmann, 40; in cases of anonymous writings, 89; of faith, 6, 36; of gospel of Luke, 36n73, 42, 88, 109, 129–30,

133, 137, 155; of Herodotus, 125; of prophets, 133; of Resurrection stories, 129. *See also asphaleia;* eyewitness/ eyewitnesses

criteriology (method), 9, 19, 34, 49, 151, 155, 298

de Lubac, Henri, 30n42, 31n48, 147–48

Dei Verbum (DV), 19–20, 24–28, 29n34, 30, 39n85, 43, 44n113, 49, 154n47, 156, 283n58, 289. *See also* historicity

divine agents, 166, 230, 235

divine identity Christology, 162–64, 171n33, 172–77, 179–80, 185, 222, 226, 280, 338

divine revelation, 11, 30, 32, 35, 38, 152, 155, 157n58, 190, 204n50, 205–6, 221, 276, 277n41, 343n27, 358, 363, 368; denial of, 25n21; and Gospels, 11, 31, 40, 262, 269; in Jesus, 278, 280–84, 300; and the *Logos*, 227, 234; primacy of, 180; sources of, 48, 354; theology of, 28–30, 214, 258n37, 273n32, 341; transmission of, 44

Ehrman, Bart D., 32n55, 85n35, 161n4, 252n25, 383n18

Elijah, 201, 284, 301–3, 311–18, 320–22, 330–33, 348. *See also* priestly figures; prophets

Enlightenment, 4, 34, 60, 62, 65, 70, 151, 160, 252, 255; appropriation of Origen, 196n35; Catholic, 68, 142, 160n1; and miracles, 145, 148; pre-Enlightenment, 49, 187

Erasmus, 5, 141–42, 144, 147

eschatological expectation. *See* historical Jesus; messianism, first-century/Second Temple

exegesis: allegorical, 231n52, 341; Armenian, 183; boring, 5; Bultmannian, 25; Catholic, 3, 6, 21, 23, 25, 45n115, 46, 48–49, 186, 357; "common sense," 69; ecclesial, 36, 162–64, 169, 184–85, 242, 289; ecumenical, 3, 68; German, 48, 64–66, 272, 339n18; historical, 9, 28, 156, 186, 281; inspired, 133; of Jesus, 284, 336–37, 345, 348–49, 352, 368; Jewish, 11, 242, 271n22, 313–14, 327, 333; modern, 3, 4, 11, 25, 32, 72, 79, 147, 155, 167, 170–72, 184, 270n19, 304, 337, 357; magisterial, 20 (*Dei Verbum*); participatory, 34n62, 167; patristic, 169–70, 262, 280, 300, 334, 336, 340; of Philo, 223, 225; Protestant, 69, 222; and question of truth, 5, 169; and theology, 2–3, 7, 11, 160, 162–63, 174n61, 179, 211, 272, 282, 341, 354, 375; Thomistic, 213. *See also* historical-critical method; literal sense of scripture; prosopological exegesis

eyewitness/eyewitnesses; accreditation of, 129–34; ancient, 109–12, 115–19, 123–28, 136, 158; apostolic, 48, 108n4, 117n45; in gospel of John, 35n69, 42, 108, 232; in Luke, 107–9, 114, 117, 119–21, 125–29, 136, 158; in Matthew, 45; and Newman, 155–56; reliance on, 19, 43, 111; revival of interest in, 9, 47, 107–8, 126, 156, 288. *See also* autopsy; historiography; Thucydides

Fitzmyer, Joseph, 22, 25n21, 25n22, 26–27, 33n55, 40, 47, 84, 109n6, 190n13, 271, 283n55, 344, 361n16

Fletcher-Louis, Crispin, 214n13, 252, 303n1, 324, 326, 338–39, 344n32

form criticism/*Formgeschichte*, 20, 25, 27, 32, 33, 39, 42, 43, 46, 48, 107–8, 267–68, 362

Grube, Dirk-Martin, 143n11, 150n30, 151, 152n36, 153n41

Harnack, Adolf von, 60, 61, 74n6, 336n6

healing: narratives of, 96–97; as prophetic act of Jesus, 291, 294, 362; shrines of, 94–96; sites in the Gospel, 98–106. *See also* Asclepius, cult of; memory

Hegel, Georg, 59, 60n51, 61, 64, 381–84

Hengel, Martin, 37n78, 39n86, 47n125, 88, 107–8, 129–30, 162, 167, 200n42, 246n3, 274, 289–90, 336, 343; post-Hengel consensus, 167; pre-Hengel era, 174, 222, 248; "Sources of Earliest Christianity," 40n91, 42n99

Herodotus, 73, 76, 89, 110, 111, 124, 125n54, 126–29, 193, 195, 201; and eyewitness reports, 125

historical Jesus: as apocalyptic/eschatological (failed) prophet, 11–13, 52n4, 270, 272–76, 294, 296, 366, 370–71, 373, 379n1, 380, 387, 390; concept of, 2, 9, 30n44, 53n10, 71; German roots of, 51–71, 387; and nationality, 59; opposed to theological inquiry, 61; Radical Reformation roots of, 64–65, 70, 149, 381; research, 38n82, 51, 63, 67n75, 92, 143, 146, 151, 161n3, 273n30, 333n76; rejection of, 288; scholars of, 3, 37n78, 51, 56, 62, 360; versus the "real Jesus," 154, 159. *See also* criteriology (method); memory; quest(s) for the historical Jesus; Schweitzer, Albert

historical-critical method, 11, 22, 37, 48, 66n71, 68, 151, 156, 281, 301–2, 371. *See also* exegesis

historicity: of Gospels, 19–21, 23, 24, 26–27, 34–36, 40, 48, 154, 156; of Jesus, 63; of the virgin birth, 86. *See also Dei Verbum (DV)*

historiography, 9; applied to historical Jesus research itself, 51, 54, 63n59, 64, 70, 267; current standpoint, 19, 86, 91; "gaps in," 38n79; Greco-Roman, 40, 41n95, 72–75, 90, 108, 110–12, 115–16, 122–23, 125, 130, 158; Humean, 68n85; Judaean, 84, 89–90; Lucan, 40–43, 72, 80–84, 87, 89–91, 107–21, 123–32, 134–37; modern, 57–60; and mythography, 75–80; and narration of wonders (θαύματα), 122–24; 19th century, 55–56, 59, 149; and witnesses, 129–34. *See also* eyewitness/eyewitnesses

Humani Generis, and new exegesis, 21–22, 24–25

Hume, David, 68n85, 143–44, 156

Hurtado, Larry, 162–63, 172, 175, 184, 187–89, 193n25, 207, 213n11, 214, 220, 229–30, 246–47, 249n14, 251–52, 258, 276n36, 277n40, 279–80, 282, 338n13; and primitive "proto-orthodoxy," 164–71. *See also* Bousset, Wilhelm

iconic turn, 10, 336, 339, 341, 346, 349–50, 354

infancy narrative: absence from "proto-Luke," 77; Christology in, 42, 269; of Luke, 5, 82, 83–84, 90; of Matthew compared to Luke, 87; omission from a work of scholarship, 21n6; in Pope Benedict's *Jesus of Nazareth*, 35, 36n73

Irenaeus, 340–41, 380n7

Jesus, knowledge, 3; divine, 362; experiential, 284, 358n7; human consciousness of, 268, 283n58, 285, 357; ignorance/nescience of, 358n5, 374–77; mind of Christ, 14; natural, 281; prophetic knowledge, 13, 159, 266, 285n61, 352n50, 358–63, 366, 368, 370–71; question of beatific vision bracketed, 13, 272, 285, 358, 360; of risen Christ, 376n40; scholastic *quaestio*, 11, 266n5, 285n62, 357–58; of Scripture, 265–66, 285, 368; subjective human self-knowledge, 11, 14, 275; of thoughts of others, 361. *See also anagnorisis* (recognition); messianic consciousness of Jesus

John Chrysostom, 36n72, 183n86

John of Damascus/Damascene, 178n59, 184n87

John the Baptist, 11, 87, 274, 292–99, 362n19, 366; baptism of Jesus by, 75, 130, 281–82, 293, 297, 302, 319–20, 342, 368; as Elijah, 301–2, 314, 316, 333, 348; questioning whether Jesus was messiah, 272, 293–95, 298–99; role in Gospel tradition, 303–4; shared fate with Jesus, 317–18, 332. *See also* priestly figures; prophets

Josephus, 41n95, 83–84, 99n20, 114, 130, 131, 134, 200, 265, 270, 350, 363; criticism of "lying historians" and second-hand accounts, 73–74, 87, 111–12, 117–19; and oneness of God, 197–99, 253–55; Titus as source, 127–28; and vestments, 324, 331

Judaism, Second Temple, 10–11, 190–91, 199, 253, 262, 311, 328–29, 332, 334, 364, 388; exegesis, 304–5, 313, 314, 317, 327, 333, 347, 349; literature/sources/traditions/writings, 175n49, 229, 303n3, 307, 322, 325, 328, 344, 347, 359, 362–63; relationship to primitive Christianity, 10, 165, 207, 247, 273. *See also* Christology; messianism, first-century/Second Temple; monotheism/monotheistic; Philo; prophecy

Kant, Immanuel, 142, 353; neo-Kantian thought: 2, 66n72, 380
Keener, Craig, 249n11, 268, 273n32, 287n5
Kenoticism/kenotic, 29, 178, 281
Kierkegaard, Søren, 9, 150–53, 159

Lagrange, Marie-Joseph, OP, 4, 12, 20n5, 46, 49n131, 52, 62–70, 387–88
Lessing, Gotthold Ephraim, 2, 8, 9, 12, 54, 56, 143–45, 147, 149–57, 159, 160–62, 164, 280
literal sense of scripture, 28–31, 34; in connection with spiritual sense, 32; in Origen, 31
Logos, 13, 206, 223, 225–27, 229–32, 234–37, 239–40, 242–44, 248, 256, 260–62, 291, 341, 352, 354
Lutheranism, 63, 65, 142, 181, 380; *theologia crucis*, 180, 186

Meier, John, 3, 33–34, 36, 37n76, 103, 104, 147n18, 151, 154–55, 273n30, 293, 297; "unpapal conclave" idea of, 3, 33, 67
Melchizedek. *See* priestly figures
memory: cultivated, 274, 322; within the Gospels, 11, 104, 289–90, 296, 366–67, 369; in historical Jesus research, 38–39, 92, 159, 288, 298, 390; *memoria*, 38; memorialization associated with objects, 92–94, 96–98, 101–2; memorialization associated with places, 61, 96, 98, 100–5; Plato's of Aristotle, 287; in relation to the Eucharist and preaching, 9, 39–42; Mary's, 42, 130n77; of strange circumstances, 104, 296

messianic consciousness of Jesus, 10, 57n27, 61, 267, 270–72, 276n37, 279, 333, 336, 348–49, 351, 363, 376, 379, 388

messianism, first-century/Second Temple, 57, 67, 270–71, 276, 278–79, 302–5, 308–11, 331, 350; diarchic, 11, 302, 314–19, 333

miracles: context in Gospels, 98, 104, 125n57, 143, 155; contrasting Gospel accounts with pagan stories, 96, 98, 100–3, 104n31; of Paul, 148; as proof of Jesus' authority, 143–44, 294, 359, 367, 374; skepticism about, 64, 65n69, 68, 91n48, 145, 147–48, 151, 155; relationship to history: 34, 79, 142, 149, 151–52, 154, 156–57

modalism. *See* Sabellius/Sabellianism
Modernism/Modernist, 4–5, 22–23, 24, 28, 44, 66, 68, 391; anti-Modernist, 21, 30; neo-Modernism, 357
Moltmann, Jürgen, 79n19, 382n13; influence on Early High Christology, 163–64, 177–80, 181n75, 182, 280n50; theology of hope, 380–81
Monophysite Christology, 163, 164, 176, 178, 180, 186, 280, 281
monotheism/monotheistic, x; Christian, 165n12, 207, 233, 249–51, 262, 338, 340; Christological, 10, 172, 186, 203n48, 213–18, 222, 224–27, 237, 240, 245, 247, 250, 261, 343, 351; Jewish, 99, 164–65, 175n49, 193–94, 196–98, 200, 206, 220, 225–26, 248, 258, 341, 345; Jewish, Second Temple, 172–74, 187–91, 202–3, 207–8, 213–15, 245–47, 250–55, 260, 262, 278–80, 350–51; pagan, 10, 196–97, 209, 215, 217–18, 220, 225, 232, 238, 247, 253; Persian, 193; "soft," 216–17; zeal for,

198, 200, 202, 312–13. *See also* Philo; Temple; Trinity/Trinitarian

Moses, 67, 85n35, 146, 166, 253–54, 257, 271, 297–99, 301–2, 309, 319–24, 327–28, 330–31, 333, 369–70; and Plato, 194–96, 199, 220, 232, 238, 241, 243. *See also* priestly figures, prophets

mythography, 75–76, 78, 80, 122–23

nativity stories, 77–83

Nestorianism, 186, 376, 377

Newman, John Henry, 9, 21n7, 152–57, 161n7

Neoplatonism, 10, 12, 77, 205, 210, 211, 213, 216, 218, 222, 225, 227, 229, 231n52, 232, 235n63, 238, 241, 242n77, 243, 248. *See also* Moses; Philo

Nicene/Nicea, 160–61, 163, 166–70, 173n40, 180n71, 184n86, 185, 210, 227, 280, 316. *See also* Christology

Origen, 31, 82, 83, 144–45, 228–29, 234–37, 241–42, 331–32

Paul the apostle, 12, 14, 65, 144, 168, 274, 281, 323, 361, 387–88; blinding of, 127, 135, 138n94; companion of Luke, 44, 47, 88, 108n1, 109n6, 113n27, 134; as reader of the Old Testament, 225, 244, 249–50, 351; reception of, 210–12, 223, 225–26, 228, 242–43; as witness, 120–21, 127, 130, 134, 148, 282

Philo, 13, 189; beneficent and royal powers in God, 225, 233n59, 250; concordism between Judaism and Greek philosophy against "polytheism," 194–96, 199, 204, 215, 218–19, 226, 248–49; and divine *hypostatis*, 228–29, 234–35; and divine naming, 220, 223, 242, 250, 344; and the *Logos*, 225, 227, 230, 239, 243, 256; and Moses, 115n36; and the Temple, 253–54, 260; and priestly vestments, 324, 328. *See also* Christology; *Logos*; Neoplatonism

Platonism. *See* Neoplatonism

Plutarch, 72–73, 117n43, 122–24, 131, 137, 201, 215, 269

positivism, 69, 71, 72, 86, 151; rejection of, 49, 62, 150

postmodern, 5, 6, 33, 49, 90, 156; versus premodern, 3, 10, 38, 72, 86, 299

priesthood: chief priests, 120, 133, 369; cosmic, 12–13, 256, 258, 284, 336–37, 352; eschatological high, 11, 256, 279, 284, 302–3, 309, 311, 314, 316, 329, 331, 346, 348–49; garments of, 323–31; Greco-Roman, 80–83, 94–95; high, 193, 226, 256, 302, 315, 320n44, 323, 324–25, 330–31, 333, 349; Jewish, 189, 255, 297

priestly figures: Adam, 325–26, 329; Elijah and Phineas, 311–19, 332–33; Enoch, 326–27; Ezekiel, 277; Jesus, 11–13, 168, 279, 284, 302–3, 307n14, 308–10, 320, 331–34, 336–37, 347–49, 352, 355; John the Baptist, 84, 316, 330, 332–33, 348; in Malachi, 304–6, 309; Melchizedek, 256, 309, 339, 343n30, 346–49, 355; Moses and Elijah, 302, 319–23, 331; in *Testament of Levi*, 306–12, 319n41, 320, 327–28. *See also* Elijah; Jesus, knowledge; Moses

prophecy: Christian prophets as purported source of Jesus sayings, 42n100; denunciation, 372; fulfillment in Gospels and Acts of, 85n35, 87, 113n27, 131, 133, 137, 261, 283–84, 295, 297–99, 316, 332, 342, 352, 371; Jesus about his suffering and death, 366–70; messianic, 271–72; natural, 366–67; in *Oedipus Rex*, 282; open to many fulfillments, 333–34; postponement of fulfillment, 372–74; as proof of Jesus' authority, 143–45, 152, 157–59; about the Temple, 363–66, 370. *See also* historical Jesus; Jesus, knowledge; priestly figures; prophets

prophets, 266; Daniel, 308; Elijah, 311, 313, 318, 320; Ezekiel, 277; Isaiah, 304, 318–19, 348; Jeremiah, 192; Jesus, 272–73, 295, 298, 359–60, 365; John the Baptist, 282; Josephus, 134; "law and," 284, 289, 368; Malachi, 303–4, 312, 314, 322, 333;

Moses, 166, 271, 298, 302, 309, 319–20, 323, 331; Paul, 134, 282; Samuel, 310, 320; Zechariah, 315, 318, 328, 359

prosopological exegesis, xi, 300, 335–41, 343, 346, 349, 352, 355

prosopon (person/mask), 335, 338, 339

Protestantism: contrast with the author's Catholic approach, 3–4, 6, 63; and Early High Christology, 183, 185, 249; German, 25, 46n118, 52, 56, 60, 69–70, 273, 390; "left-wing," 64–65, 70; and miracles, 142; searching for "a new social order," 146; theology of revelation, 29. See also Lutheranism

Q (*Quelle*), 12, 41, 46, 297, 300, 348; "life without Q," 288

quest(s) for the historical Jesus, 20; as eschewing John, 43; proposal for a "Fourth Quest," 39n82; rejecting term, 1, 9, 49; Romantic obfuscation of the real goal of finding the primitive meaning of Christianity, 66; Second, 58; Third, 57–58, 67n78; "Three Quests," 51, 54, 56, 57–60, 63n59, 64n64, 68, 70, 267; as treacherous pursuit, 291. See also historical Jesus; Schweitzer, Albert

Ranke, Leopold von, 61; *wie es eigentlich gewesen ist*, 86

rationalism, 25n21, 48–49, 63, 65, 151, 160, 183, 187, 361; Hegel's, 382; Protestant, 21n6, 65; versus supernatural, 37, 59, 90, 149. See also Enlightenment

rationality: areligious, 70, 160; Catholic, 69; human, 152; which/whose?, 59, 67

Ratzinger, Joseph. See Benedict XVI, Pope

redaction criticism, 19–20, 26, 49, 89, 104, 288, 304n6, 364

Reimarus, Hermann Samuel, 51n1, 54–57, 62–63, 143, 150, 157, 160, 272

reliability. See *asphaleia*

Renan, Ernst, 22, 59, 62, 63n63, 67n74, 389

resurrection, 11, 21n6, 35, 37n76, 77, 100, 109, 113n27, 114n29, 157, 159, 278, 295, 321, 332, 367, 372, 384, 387, 389–90; and apotheosis tradition, 123; Emmaus account/tradition of the, 125–29; and ghost stories, 135–37; as historiographical problem, 109, 120, 121n49, 122, 124–25, 129, 132, 134, 135, 154. See also credibility

revelation. See divine revelation

rumor rhetoric, 79, 123–24

Sabellius/Sabellianism, 217, 230n49, 233–34, 339

Sanders, E. P., 34n64, 148, 250n16, 333n76, 388, 390

Schleiermacher, Friedrich, 2n1, 43n107, 61–62, 268

Schökel, Louis Alonso, 21, 22

Schweitzer, Albert, 1, 4, 8, 11, 49, 51–71; and apocalypticism, 379, 388; and German nationalism, 59–61, 68, and immanent eschatology, 10, 380n7, 381n8, 382, 387; and messianic consciousness of Jesus, 267; and *Quest of the Historical Jesus*, 1, 9, 30n44, 37n74, 43n107, 49, 51–62, 64n63, 66, 68, 143n9, 150n31, 267n6, 379n1, 382n14, 383; and Radical Reformation, 52, 65, 70. See also historical Jesus; Protestantism; quest(s) for the historical Jesus

scientia Christi, 8, 13, 265, 376. See also Jesus, knowledge

scribes/scribal, 11, 12–13, 284, 296, 301, 304, 306, 310–12, 314, 319, 320, 344, 361n18, 390; orientation of Jesus, 273–74, 332–34

single-subject Christology. See Monophysitism

subordinationism, 166–71, 344n32; and role of women, 161

Steinmann, Jean, 20–24, 123n53

Strauss, D. F., 33n55, 36, 52, 56n27, 61, 64, 149n28; *Das Leben Jesu für das deutsche Volk* (first), 59; *Das Leben Jesu* (second), 60, 67n74; *Der Christus des Glaubens*, 2n1; and Schweitzer, 37n74, 43n107, 54, 56–59, 62

Synoptic: congruence of gospels, 41, 281; gospels as historical sources, 37n74, 55, 74, 271–72, 293, 294, 297, 301, 316, 348, 370, 388; gospels in contrast with John's Gospel, 291–92, 299, 364; parables, 33; problem, 46, 47n125; studies, 11

Taylor, Charles, 63, 147, 255; *Secular Age*, 63n61, 141, 147n20, 170n30

Temple: anti-establishment sentiment, 306, 364; destruction of, 128n68, 207, 259n38, 273, 363–66, 370–71, 372n32, 374; eschatological, 330, 351; exclusivity and monotheism, 175, 189, 193, 195, 198, 207, 253–55; heavenly, 326; Jesus' body as New Temple, 10, 11, 253, 259–62, 346, 350–52; and John's Gospel, 98–100, 259–62; as locus of mediation, 245–46, 255–58; music of, 292; rebuilding of, 191–92, 331; Second, 253, 258; setting of Luke 1–2, 83; site of Jesus' activity, 120, 134, 275, 333. *See also* Judaism, Second Temple

temples: to Apollo, 81; for Jews in exile, 193, 195; polemics against, 201–2, 205, 207, 254; Roman, 94; shrines of healing, 93, 95–99

Tertullian, 88, 158, 341, 355

Thate, Michael, 51n3, 52, 54, 55n22, 56, 61n54, 61n55, 63

Thomas Aquinas, 33n57, 49n131, 147, 159, 184n87, 210, 222–23, 233, 236, 237n66, 272n26, 353n54, 366, 368, 371, 372, 376n39; Dionysian themes in Christology of, 211–13; *Summa Theologiae*, 28n32, 29n36, 29n37, 30n42, 155, 233n58, 243, 266n5, 285n62, 358n10, 360n14, 361, 366, 368, 371, 372

Thucydides, 73, 110–14, 118, 122n60, 127

Transfiguration, 11, 301–3, 308, 311, 315–16, 319–21, 323–26, 328, 331–33, 348, 368

Trinity/Trinitarian: anti-, 65; creeds/doctrine/dogma, 162, 185, 278–79, 281, 339; exegesis, 179, 335–36, 340–42, 352; grammar, 162, 184, 186, 241n74, 355; immanent and economic, 178; Jesus' experience of, 284, 299, 336; monotheism, 233, 237; patristic theology, 173n39, 342; processions, 281; "proto-," 14; suffering of, 179, 181n75. *See* prosopological exegesis

two natures Christology. *See* Chalcedon/Chalcedonian

Vaganay, Léon, 46

Vatican I (council), 27, 152, 358

Vatican II (council), 9, 19–21, 27–28, 29n34, 30n41, 34, 43, 44, 47–50. *See also Dei Verbum (DV)*

Venard, Olivier-Thomas, 286–91; quest for the Linguistic Jesus, 291

virgin birth/virginal conception, 77–80, 84n30, 85–86, 90n48

Watson, Francis, 51, 54–56, 57n32, 60n49, 61n52, 61n54, 66n73, 147n19, 288, 290

Weiss, Bernhard, 52, 54

Weiss, Johannes, 57, 272, 380n6

White, Hayden, 5, 86–87, 91

White, Thomas Joseph, OP, 7n4, 182n81

Wookiees, 13n6, 387

Wrede, William, 53n7, 54, 55, 57–58, 63, 267, 268n10, 379, 388

Wright, N. T., 32n54, 37n76, 38n81, 57–58, 67n75, 136n92, 154, 267, 270n19, 273n32, 372n32, 384n25

www.ingramcontent.com/pod-product-compliance
Lightning Source LLC
Chambersburg PA
CBHW030250010526
44107CB00053B/1648